D-Day Documents

Paul Winter

BLOOMSBURY
LONDON · NEW DELHI · NEW YORK · SYDNEY

First published in Great Britain 2014

Bloomsbury Publishing Plc
50 Bedford Square
London
WC1B 3DP

www.bloomsbury.com
Bloomsbury is a trade mark of Bloomsbury Publishing Plc

Bloomsbury Publishing, London, New Delhi, New York and Sydney

A CIP catalogue record for this book is available from the British Library

ISBN 978 1 4081 9400 3 (hardback edition)

10 9 8 7 6 5 4 3 2 1

Typeset by Saxon Graphics Ltd, Derby
Printed and bound by CPI Group (UK) Ltd, Croydon, CR0 4YY

D-Day Documents

Dedication

D-Day Documents is dedicated to the memory of Professor M.R.D. Foot (1919–2012), who as SAS Brigade Intelligence Officer in June 1944 made his own vital contribution to the success of Operation *Overlord*.

The documents contained in this book have been accurately transcribed but may contain errors and omissions (indicated by a ?) carried through from the original documents due to their age and nature.

CONTENTS

ACKNOWLEDGEMENTS

First of all I would like to pay special tribute to Laura Simpson and Ed Field of the National Archives, Kew. They are the embodiment of what public service should be: professional, dedicated and incredibly helpful. Their assistance in finding documents, answering queries and supplying endless photocopies has been immense and without their tireless work and belief in the project, *D-Day Documents* would never have left the drawing board. Further thanks must go to Major Mark Bentinck RM, Corps historian, and to the 47 Royal Marine Commando Association for the trouble they took in attempting to track down the Commando's war diary entries for May, June and July 1944, which are sadly missing from the archives, and consequently from this book.

I must also thank Professor Lord Peter Hennessy who, for over twenty years, has acted as something of a mentor to me. His love for and profound understanding of history have inspired and motivated me during periods when words would not flow, and even the dazzling spectacle of history receded into the gloom. In recent years, Professor Sir Hew Strachan, Chichele Professor of the History of War at Oxford University, has also become a source of great encouragement to me. Unstinting in his support and advice, I owe him a great debt for allowing me to become a visiting fellow on the 'Changing Character of War' programme at Oxford. His generosity in supplying the foreword to this book is much appreciated by the author.

Thanks also goes to my late grandfather, Lionel Watson, whose wartime experiences in Normandy helped inspire the publication of this book, and to my parents-in-law, Michael and Susan Moberly, whose generosity, support and belief in what I do have enabled me to carve out a niche as an independent historian.

Last but not least I must thank my wife, Fe, for all her love, support and understanding over the last few years. They have been far from easy but without her in my corner I could not have completed this book. Words cannot describe my love and gratitude.

FOREWORD

For the liberal democracies fighting Hitler, the Normandy landings of 6 June 1944 were the most complete manifestation of modern war. Few operations conducted since then by Britain, Canada and the United States (an alliance which, seventy years on, is still in place) can match its purity of purpose. Its aim was liberation – a word devoid of rhetorical excess when western Europe was subject to occupation by a totalitarian and brutal regime. And the country to which it brought freedom, France, had itself, through the revolution of 1789, cradled European ideals of democratic government. If war is the continuation of policy by other means (and in practice the connection is frequently unclear), then D-Day was.

It was not just in their objectives that the landings matched aspiration to execution. Operation *Overlord* required its participating states to apply the resources and methods of sophisticated and industrialised economies to war. If strategy finds its most obvious application in planning, then *Overlord* is its epitome. The accumulation of intelligence, the covert surveying of the beaches, the technological sophistication of the Pluto pipeline and the Mulberry harbours, the complex deception operation to draw the Germans' attention to the Pas de Calais, and – crucially – the meteorological reports, all harnessed science to war, making it seemingly a matter of management more than leadership. And yet, for Dwight D. Eisenhower, the allies' chain-smoking supreme commander, the final decision was still a matter of personal judgement. The weather forecast was not clear enough in either direction, for good or ill, to relieve him of the obligation to exercise command in a real and personal sense.

His call, to go ahead, proved the right one. His generalship has provided a template for coalition command. D-Day was a combined effort: indeed the French suffered greater losses on 6 June, and many of those to allied bombing, than did those of the armed forces of the nationalities sent to free them. In this respect too the operation was modern: coalition warfare, even if our understanding of its mechanics is still imperfect, and although our newspapers still tell war stories in national – even nationalistic – terms, has been the norm ever since.

The collection of documents which Paul Winter presents in this volume is confined to Britain and Canada. Many of those who contributed to the success on 6 June are not represented in the pages that follow, not least many of those who fought at sea and in the air. Indeed the roll call of the latter would not only widen the book's compass geographically and nationally, it would also do so temporally. The preparation for the invasion of northern Europe began two years before, and its most important preliminary was victory in the war at sea, specifically in the romantically but ill-named Battle of the Atlantic. Without first overcoming the threat from German submarines, the allies could not concentrate the manpower, ships and resources necessary for a successful amphibious operation. The latter depended on the expertise acquired through the allied landings in North Africa, Sicily and Italy.

Rather than the *longue durée*, Paul Winter gives us 'the longest day'. Erwin Rommel's own anticipatory phrase was to capture the reality of 6 June itself, and so does Paul Winter's choice of documents. He shifts the focus from the strategic to the tactical, from the managerial to the physically courageous. This book presents all the surviving war diaries of those British Commonwealth units that went ashore on D-Day. These are, in Winter's own memorable phrase, 'the Cinderella of historical sources'. Written close to the battlefield, in the immediacy of the moment, and amidst the uncertainty of what was to come, they endeavoured to capture tactical events almost as they happened. We can never fully recapture the moment of combat, since those who fight have other, more urgent matters to preoccupy them than writing for posterity. But this is as close as we are likely get.

Professor Sir Hew Strachan
Chichele Professor of the History of War, All Souls, Oxford

AUTHOR'S NOTE

Despite being an instantly recognisable term which, over the last seventy years, has entered the modern lexicon, few people know exactly what 'D-Day' stands for. A common refrain from those who accompany me on tours of the Normandy landing beaches is: what does the 'D' in D-Day actually stand for? Some think it means 'deliverance' while others believe it to be 'decision' or 'decisive'. All are incorrect. In fact, the term is meaningless for D-Day was simply an esoteric Anglo-American staff term employed to denote the day on which a specific military operation was to be launched. As much is attested to by the Oxford English Dictionary (OED), which defines 'D-Day' as 'The military code-name for a particular day fixed for the beginning of an operation; *spec* the day (6 June 1944) of the invasion of the Atlantic coast of German-occupied France by Allied forces'.[1] Yet despite its historic resonance, the term 'D-Day' was only admitted into the OED in 1972, twenty-eight years after it first gained common currency in the western world.[2]

NOTES

[1]   *The Oxford English Dictionary*, Second Edition, Volume IV: Creel-Duzepere, prepared by J.A. Simpson and E.S.C. Weiner, (Oxford: Clarendon Press, 1989), p. 279. Etymologically speaking, the first use of the term 'D-Day', as recorded by the Oxford English Dictionary, occurred on 7 September 1918 when the American Expeditionary Force (AEF) issued Field Order No. 8 ordering the US First Army to 'attack at H-Hour on D-Day with the object of forcing the evacuation of St-Mihiel salient'. Notably, a young Tank Corps officer named Lieutenant-Colonel George S. Patton took part in this offensive. Later rising to the rank of Lieutenant-General, Patton would go on to take a leading role in the Normandy campaign, firstly as an integral part of Operation *Fortitude South*, the strategic deception plan to deceive the Germans into thinking the Allies would launch their 'Second Front' at the Pas de Calais (as part of this *ruse de guerre*, Patton was portrayed as the commander of the notional First United States Army Group (FUSAG) threatening to lead the Cross-Channel assault; and later as the highly-successful commander of the US 3rd Army in Normandy. See Carlo D'Este, *A Genius For War: A Life of General George S. Patton*, (London: Harper Collins, 1995), pp. 226-247 and p. 566.

[2]   I am grateful to Mr Simon Thomas of the Oxford English Dictionary for supplying me with this information. Correspondence with Mr Simon Thomas, 18 February 2013.

INTRODUCTION

Remember we shall never stop, never weary and never give in, and that our whole people and Empire have vowed themselves to the task of cleansing Europe from the Nazi pestilence and saving the world from the new dark ages... Good night then; sleep to gather strength for the morning. For the morning will come.

WINSTON S. CHURCHILL, BBC radio broadcast to occupied France, 21 October 1940.[3]

For the people of occupied France dawn broke finally on Tuesday 6 June 1944, a date that will forever go down in the annals of military history as 'D-Day'. On this day the Allied powers of Britain, the United States and Canada finally launched their long-anticipated cross-Channel attack against Hitler's 'Atlantic Wall'. Codenamed *Overlord,* this offensive along fifty-five miles of the Normandy coastline was, and still is, the 'greatest assault that has ever been made on a fortified and strongly defended coast by combined sea, land and air forces'.[4] The scale of this operation was colossal involving as it did 7,000 naval vessels, 11,000 aircraft and over 1,750,000 men.[5] As the largest amphibious invasion in the history of warfare it has, unsurprisingly, become an iconic moment in the story of the Second World War. Measuring eight or nine on the Richter scale of historic global events, D-Day has registered itself in the collective historical consciences of numerous participating countries. For the British, in particular, it has entered the Pantheon of military heroics alongside other symbolic feats of arms such as Dunkirk, the Battle of Britain, El Alamein and the Battle of the Atlantic. Yet largely forgotten is the fact that D-Day was a truly international undertaking.

Aside from British, American and Canadian forces, New Zealanders, Free French, Danes, Norwegians, Dutchmen, Poles and Greeks all took part. Moreover, it has been estimated that one in every hundred men who participated in *Overlord* was Australian serving in a multitude of roles such as crew members of RAF fighter and bomber squadrons, landing craft personnel or as junior officers attached to the British Army.[6]

The multi-national dimension to the operation was captured in the directive issued to General Dwight D. Eisenhower, Supreme Commander Allied Expeditionary Force, by the Anglo-American Combined Chiefs of Staff on 12 February 1944. It read, 'You will enter the continent of Europe and, in conjunction with other United Nations, undertake operations aimed at the heart of Germany and the destruction of her armed forces'.[7] In order to achieve this end, on 6 June over 156,000 Allied troops were landed on five separate assault beaches on the Normandy coastline. Running from the Cotentin Peninsula in the west to the mouth of the River Orne in the east, each of the five beaches was designated a code name. The two American landing zones in the west were 'Utah' and 'Omaha'. By midnight on D-Day the US 4th Infantry Division and its supporting units had landed 23,000 men on the open beaches of 'Utah', while at 'Omaha' the US 1st and 29th Infantry Divisions, after heavy fighting, had landed 34,250 troops.[8]

To the east lay the three Anglo-Canadian beaches, 'Gold', 'Juno' and 'Sword'. On 'Gold' beach the British 50th Infantry Division, in conjunction with various attached units, landed 24,970 men, while at 'Juno' the Canadian 3rd Infantry Division, aided by a host of British units, disembarked 21,400 troops. Having undertaken an assault landing on 'Sword' beach, the British 3rd Infantry Division, plus supporting units, succeeded in depositing 28,845 personnel ashore. In order to help facilitate the landings and protect the vulnerable flanks of these beachheads, the Allies also employed 23,000 airborne troops. In the west the Americans dropped or landed by glider 15,500 troops from the 82nd 'All American' and 101st 'Screaming Eagles' divisions, while in the east the British executed parachute drops and glider landings involving 7,900 men of the elite 6th Airborne Division.[9] It is perhaps not surprising, therefore, that Britain's wartime Prime Minister, Winston Churchill, called D-Day, 'The most difficult and complicated operation that has ever taken place'.[10]

Writing in 2004 on the 60th anniversary of the Normandy landings, one author commented wearily that, '…we probably know almost all there is to know about the planning and execution of Operation OVERLORD, the sequence of events, the parts played by individual units, the facts and figures and so on'.[11] This is indeed true. Since the end of the Second World War countless books have been published on the subject of D-Day. These range from the various post-war official histories published by Britain, Canada and the United States (*Victory in the West: Volume I: The Battle of Normandy; Official History of the Canadian Army in The Second World War: The Victory Campaign: The Operations in North-west Europe, 1944-1945*; and the *US Army in World War II: European Theater of Operations: Cross-Channel Attack*),[12] through the personal memoirs of leading participants, such as Eisenhower, Bradley, and Montgomery, to first-hand accounts, pictorial histories and monographs addressing notable episodes such as the British glider-borne attack on 'Pegasus Bridge', the cliff-face assault on Pointe-du-Hoc by the US 2nd Rangers and the near disaster on 'bloody Omaha' beach.

Aside from the multitude of divisional and regimental histories commissioned by Anglo-Canadian units who undertook the Normandy landings, there has, in recent years, been a literary explosion on the subject producing oral histories, battlefield guides, volumes dedicated to individual beaches and publications containing facsimile documents from the planning stages of the D-Day offensive. If one then takes account the numerous single volumes published by well-known writers and historians such as Max Hastings (*Overlord*), John Keegan (*Six Armies in Normandy*), Carlo D'Este (*Decision in Normandy*), Antony Beevor, (*D-Day*), Cornelius Ryan (*The Longest Day*), and Stephen E. Ambrose (*D-Day: June 6, 1944*), and it becomes evident that Operation *Overlord* is one of the most written about military actions in modern history. Consequently, *D-Day Documents* does not profess to be a definitive account of the launch of the Allies' Second Front. Rather, it aims to commemorate the 70th anniversary of this remarkable feat of arms by means of carefully selected documents from the shelves of the National Archives, Kew, repository of the nation's history. The first batch of ten historical sources address various aspects of the invasion such as intelligence reporting, strategic deception, individual heroism and the role of the Navy, Army and Air Force. The main bulk of the book, however, is unprecedented containing, as it does, all of the available divisional, brigade and battalion war diary entries for the main Anglo-Canadian formations who spearheaded the invasion on 5/6 June 1944.

REGIMENTAL WAR DIARIES

When John Wilson Croker, Tory MP, scholar and friend of Sir Arthur Wellesley, the first Duke of Wellington, proposed in August 1815 to write a 'full history of [the Battle of] Waterloo', His Grace thought it prudent to warn his fellow Irishman that,

> The history of a battle is not unlike the history of a ball. Some individuals may recollect all the little events of which the great result is the battle won or lost, but no individual can recollect the exact order in which, or the exact moment at which, they occurred, which makes all the difference as to their value or importance.[13]

The lack of consensus as to the exact sequence of events on Sunday 18 June 1815, on a muddy battlefield twelve miles south of Brussels, would in fact characterise the record keeping of the British Army for virtually the next one hundred years. Not until the Boer farmers of South Africa had, in the immortal words of Rudyard Kipling, bard of Empire, taught the British Army 'no end of a lesson' during the Anglo-Boer War of 1899-1902, was a standardised form for chronicling the activities of individual units instituted by the War Office. This came about through the efforts of the Liberal Secretary of State for War, Lord Haldane, who in 1906 set in train a series of reforms aimed at modernising the British Army in the wake of its poor performance in the Transvaal and Orange Free State.[14] Consequently, by 1909 a new doctrinal and bureaucratic framework had emerged inside the War Office with one of the most important by-products being a fresh set of guidelines governing the organisation of the Army in the field.

Entitled 'Field Service Regulations', these new rules were broken down into two parts neatly separated into two volumes. Part I dealt with 'Operations' while Part II focused on 'Organisation and Administration'.[15] As laid down in Part II, from April 1909 onwards each unit of the British Army, be it at battalion, brigade, division or Army level was instructed to keep a war diary in which significant daily events were to be recorded. The object of this exercise, the War Office reasoned, was twofold: (i) 'To furnish an accurate record of the operations from which the history of the war can subsequently be prepared'; and (ii) 'To collect information for future reference with a view to effecting improvements in the organization, education, training, equipment and administration of the army for war'.[16] In other words, the avowed aim of war diaries was not only to reduce confusion and uncertainty as to the chronology and course of battles and campaigns, but also to enable the British Army to learn from the past in order to shape its future.

Yet while Field Service Regulations governed reporting at the general level, the specifics of completing a daily war diary were distilled into the pages of the *Field Service Pocket Book* issued to all serving officers. Fundamentally an *aide mémoire* for officers and those in charge of unit war diaries, the *Field Service Pocket Book* nevertheless underwent many re-drafts and revisions during the period 1909 to 1939. Unsurprisingly, this process continued into the Second World War itself, starting with the publication of the 1939 edition which was eventually updated with amendments in 1941. Yet it was to be the 1943 edition, which superseded all previous pocket books, that would end up being carried by officers of the British and Canadian armies on D-Day itself.

Instructions for the completion of war diary entries fell within Part I of the pocket book, under the heading 'Discipline, Office Work, Pay and Burial Parties'. Apart from stipulating that 'War diaries will be maintained in duplicate in the form of a day to day record of events...

by all units and establishments',[17] the *Field Service Pocket Book* reminded officers that the following points should be included in their daily entries:

- 'Daily location, movements during previous 24 hours, present dispositions. Include march tables in case of formations.
- Summary of important orders, instructions, reports, and messages received and issued, and of decisions taken.
- Nature and description of field engineering works constructed, or quarters occupied.
- Meteorological notes.
- Changes in establishment, or strength, or armament. Names of officer, and numbers of other rank, vehicle and animal casualties. Changes in stores, transport etc., L of C [Lines of Communication] units
- Important matters relating to the duties of each branch of staff.
- Names of commanders and staff'.[18]

In addition to this, war diary keepers were also obliged to supply appendices that were to contain a variety of subjects too large for the main diary itself. Consequently, officers were directed to supply the following: 'Detailed account of operations, including exact times, factors affecting the operations, maps used, condition of roads and communications, etc. Clear sketches should be given to show dispositions at important phases. Appreciations and personal impressions of commanders should be recorded'.[19] Moreover, war diary appendices should also contain:

- 'Copies of orders, instructions and important messages received from superior commanders.
- Copies of operation orders and instructions issued.
- Copies of routine orders.
- Copies of field returns AF W3008 and AF W3009.
- Opinions and recommendations by formation and unit commanders in regard weapons, equipment, tactics, organization, and inter-service co-operation likely to be of benefit for short-term research in the Army.
- Material likely to be of value later for the History of the War'.[20]

Once completed, the original copy of the war diary, chronicling the activities of those units operating overseas, was to be dispatched, 'under SECRET cover', to General Headquarters, 2nd echelon 'on the first day of the succeeding month'. From here, it would be forwarded to C7 (the Army War Diary Section) of the War Office for safe keeping. The duplicate and triplicate copies, meanwhile, would go through identical channels, although 'formations', such as British 2nd Army, had two months in which to undertake the process and individual 'units', such as battalions, three months in which to pass on their records to a 'parent or affiliated Record Office'.[21]

The ubiquitous 'Army Form C2118 War Diary or Intelligence Summary' on which all entries were either typed or hand written by a designated officer, were issued to all British and Canadian units during the Second World War. Equivalent to the US Army's 'After Action Report', copies of which reside at the US National Archives in Washington, DC, Anglo-Canadian war diaries were usually written up by a young Intelligence Officer (IO) or an appropriate subordinate deemed fit for the task by his commanding officer whose own job it was to sign-off on each daily entry. Incredibly, young officers selected to the post of unit war diarist were not specially trained to undertake such a task. Invariably fatigued, hungry and perhaps unnerved by the day's events they were, nevertheless, expected to 'pick up' the job along the way.[22]

Ironically, it was strictly against military regulations for an individual, regardless of rank, to keep a personal diary while on active service. This was due to the fact that captured diaries could reveal a significant amount about units, their strengths, casualties, morale, dispositions and a host of other useful information that could easily be exploited by German or Axis intelligence. Yet a young officer delegated with the responsibility of maintaining the regimental war diary was obliged to write up each day's events in the field, sometimes in very close proximity to the enemy. Unlike those 'diary volunteers' who, against the rules, kept a secret personal diary while in Army, officers formally appointed custodians of their regiment's daily log were 'diary conscripts', compelled to record the ebb and flow of war for official purposes.[23]

One British officer who found himself guardian of his regiment's war diary was Norman Scarfe. As a pre-war undergraduate at Oxford University, Scarfe had begun reading for a degree in history when the Second World War interrupted his studies. Commissioned as an officer in the 76th (Highland) Field Regiment Royal Artillery, an SP (self-propelled) unit operating 105mm guns mounted on the chassis of Sherman tanks, Scarfe landed on D-Day with his regiment at 'Sword' beach in support of the British 3rd Division's 8th Infantry Brigade.[24] In his magnificent post-war history of the 3rd Infantry Division, *Assault Division*, Scarfe touched upon the conflict of interest inherent in war diary keeping: 'When it was my duty to keep our official war-diary up to date, and we were in action, other duties came first. When we were not in action, there was not much to record'.[25] In other words, his first duty was to soldiering which, unsurprisingly, left little time for note taking, diary entries or personal reflection. Given the lack of opportunity afforded young officers whose job it was to faithfully record the activities and experiences of their parent unit while in the field, it is perhaps not surprising that Scarfe later mused that, '…at the Headquarters of higher formations', well away from the fighting and the daily grind of frontline duties, 'War Diaries were, doubtless, attended to more carefully…'[26]

Another British officer who landed on D-Day and, like Scarfe, would end up keeping a regimental war diary was Lieutenant Stuart Hills of the Nottinghamshire Yeomanry, nicknamed the 'Sherwood Rangers'. Already battle-hardened through its exploits in the North African theatre of operations, the Sherwood Rangers were an armoured regiment equipped with the 'Duplex Drive' (DD) Sherman tank, one of Major-General Sir Percy Hobart's specialist armoured vehicles or 'funnies'. Designed specially for the Allied invasion, the 'DD' Sherman was fitted with a waterproof, air-filled canvas screen around its hull and twin propellers working off its engines enabling it to swim ashore under its own propulsion.[27] As a member of C Squadron, Hills was responsible for swimming one of these thirty-ton tanks ashore in order to give tank support to the 1st Battalion the Dorset Regiment, whose D-Day objective was 'JIG' sector on 'Gold' beach.[28] Despite the fact that his own DD tank floundered and sank on the run-in to the beach, Hills survived his baptism of fire and would go on to fight with great distinction throughout the campaign in North-west Europe winning the Military Cross in the process.

Several decades after the war, Hills penned a vivid personal account of his wartime experiences with the Sherwood Rangers entitled *By Tank into Normandy*.[29] In this volume, Hills described how he miraculously survived the killing fields of Normandy and the subsequent lightning advance of the British 2nd Army into Belgium only to encounter a new round of grinding, attritional warfare in eastern Holland following the British defeat at Arnhem in September 1944. It was here in October of that year that he was assigned to Regimental Headquarters (RHQ) as Intelligence Officer. Aside from keeping the 'Regimental War Diary each day' and ensuring that 'the maps being used were up to date',[30] Hills defined his other duties as IO thus:

> I spent my time assimilating intelligence information, especially map work, and relaying it to the squadrons in the appropriate format, something which often entailed giving lectures about the general situation at the front. For this purpose I had to spend much of my time to-ing and fro-ing between Brigade HQ and the American HQ to find out whatever was available from air reconnaissance, wireless intercepts and intelligence summaries. At Brigade level and above, Intelligence Officers were properly trained staff officers who probably spoke German and included interrogation of prisoners in their list of duties. I was just a reasonably well-educated twenty-year-old who had to learn as he went along.[31]

Despite a lack of formal training in the arts of being an IO, which obliged Hills to 'muddle through', learning on the job as he went, he was still nevertheless expected, to provide an objective and detailed account of all military engagements fought by his regiment. This was made more difficult by the fact that RHQ was usually located behind the main action, a physical dislocation that led Hills to worry on one occasion that his war diary entries for a particular battle would subsequently lack 'immediacy and excitement'.[32]

As is evident, while some officers such as Norman Scarfe could not adequately fulfil their role as regimental war diarist while on the frontline, others like Stuart Hills had considerably more time and space in which to record the events of the day despite being somewhat removed from the thick of the fighting. Consequently, the day-to-day situations faced by 'war diary conscripts' and the context in which the diary entries were actually completed should always be at the forefront of the reader's mind when consulting the contents of 'Army Form C2118'.

In terms of content, unit war diary entries for 5/6 June 1944 vary in style, tone, detail and length. The majority are typed while a few are written in longhand. Some of the D-Day war diaries, such as those for the 2nd Battalion, The South Wales Borderers and the 90th Field Regiment Royal Artillery, are short and perfunctory in nature, one or two pages at most. Others, such as those for the 1st Battalion The Canadian Scottish Regiment and the No. 4 Commando, on the other hand, run to several pages each and display a more sophisticated style of prose on the part of the officers who wrote them. As already noted, Field Service Regulations decreed that each unit war diary would be maintained on a daily basis and that it was to record the actions and day-to-day activities of each infantry, brigade, division or Army Group. In addition, each war diary would include succinct overviews of events, casualty listings and positional map references. Appendices would enclose other information such as sketches, messages, maps and Operational Orders, passwords, patrol reports, tactical minutiae and further details concerning military engagements.[33]

USEFULNESS AS A HISTORICAL SOURCE

Yet considering their obvious historical value surprisingly little attention has been lavished upon regimental war diaries by scholars and researchers. Relegated to a second-class status by other primary evidence such as personal papers, private diaries and official reports, and eclipsed in recent years by the popularity of oral histories, war diaries have become the Cinderella of historical sources. This is remarkable in that war diaries, like their civilian equivalents '…offer us', in the words of one leading historian, 'an alternative route to the past: a close – almost physical – connection. They focus on the particular and catalogue the microcosmic'.[34] By chronicling the 'particular' and 'microcosmic', war diaries supply historians with a set of reference points by which they can orientate themselves in order to make sense of a skirmish, battle or large-scale offensive. These mental landmarks manifest themselves as a mass of detail such as the identities of battalion commanding officers, the particular mode of transport used by a regiment to enter a theatre of operations, the geography of a battlefield, map references, the names and ranks of officers, unit morale, the severity of unit casualties, the names of supporting units or relief forces, the tempo of operations, the opposition encountered and the weapon systems deployed against them by the enemy. Moreover, the immediacy of the reporting contained within war diaries and the insights they afford historians equip them to cut through the 'fog of war' that envelops the battlefield, thereby granting them a unique perspective on how a regiment or unit wages modern war.

While war diaries do not offer their readers a '"higher form" of historical source material' such as War Cabinet papers, Chiefs of Staff appreciations or Joint Intelligence Committee reports,[35] they do, nevertheless, present us with a 'worm's eye view' of a battalion, brigade or division at war. Besides verifying the sequence of events and providing an excellent check on the veracity of oral histories, regimental war diaries represent significant pieces of a historical jigsaw. Like a puzzle, when viewed together these constituent parts form a larger composite picture. They elevate the reader from the viewpoint of a worm to that of a bird surveying the limited terrain of a single battlefield or the panorama of a vast Allied invasion such as *Overlord*. Above all else, regimental war diaries offer their readership a unique 'first rough draft of history'. Yet as already noted, the relative neglect of war diaries by the historical fraternity has meant that few publications have included facsimiles or even transcripts of original diaries. To date, no single volume has brought together all the available Anglo-Canadian war diary entries for 5/6 June 1944 appertaining to those assault units who spearheaded the D-Day landings. The publication of *D-Day Documents*, therefore, aims not only to rectify this gap in the available literature, but also ventures to raise regimental war diaries to a higher ranking in the order-of-battle of historical sources.

LIMITATIONS AS A HISTORICAL SOURCE

Although undoubtedly a rich source of primary material for the military historian, war diaries, like any other set of historical records, need to be approached with some caution. Despite being written as truthfully and accurately as possible, errors of fact were bound to have entered these official accounts. As already noted, Intelligence Officers, or those designated as regimental war diarists, were just as battle-fatigued, hungry, fearful and preoccupied with other more pressing duties as any of their less literary-minded comrades-in-arms. Heavy fighting, incapacitation through wounds or ill-health or a transfer to other duties would have created gaps and inconsistencies in accounts, and therefore not all war diaries are necessarily complete or totally reliable. Consequently, when reading the official records included in this volume it must be remembered that, '…war is not fought with the convenience of military historians in mind'.[36]

Aside from basic mistakes, war diaries can exhibit a variety of other limitations. Addressing the subject of unit war diaries, albeit in the context of the First World War, the late Professor Richard Holmes reflected that:

> They are of mixed value. If a unit was in the thick of action, its adjutant or chief clerk, upon whom the writing of the diary usually devolved, might have his mind on other things. The important rubs shoulders with the commonplace: a battery diary might tell us how many shells it fired – but not what their targets were.[37]

Moreover, as one officer who maintained his own regiment's war diary has written, '…individuals have no place in a War Diary, which is a record of general activities, such as the start of an attack, the taking of an objective, the arrival of reinforcements, or the withdrawal of a unit for rest and "maintenance"'.[38] Overall, it must be remembered that regimental war diaries are but one, single historical source and, as a result, need to be complemented by memoirs, oral histories and other primary material. Only by doing this can historians fully exploit their potential to markedly enhance our understanding of what transpired seventy years ago on the beaches and in the fields of Lower Normandy.

OMISSIONS

Despite the comprehensive nature of *D-Day Documents* there are, regrettably, gaps and omissions in the volume. During the preparation of this book it was discovered that the war diaries of several units who participated in the Normandy landings were missing from the National Archives. Frustratingly, further searches in regimental museums and various other archives failed to unearth them and, as a consequence, they now appear to be lost to posterity. Consequently, those absent from the D-Day roll call are as follows: 47 Royal Marine Commando, (TNA DEFE 2/52); 61st Reconnaissance Regiment, Royal Armoured Corps, (TNA WO 166/6439); the 7th Canadian Reconnaissance Regiment, (17th Duke of York's Royal Canadian Hussars); HQ 79th Armoured Division, (TNA WO 171/583); 93rd Light Anti-Aircraft Regiment, Royal Artillery, (TNA WO 171/1124); C Company, 2nd Battalion, The Cheshire Regiment, (TNA WO 171/1276); British 3rd Infantry Division Signals, (TNA WO 171/2069); 19th Field Regiment, Royal Canadian Artillery, (TNA WO 179/3055); the 92nd Light Anti-Aircraft Regiment, Royal Artillery, (TNA WO 171/1123), who landed only one Troop, 'F' Troop, on D-Day hence no formal unit diary entry; and the 1st and 2nd SAS Regiments, who operated in France before, during and after D-Day, but whose war diaries still remain classified.[39]

To compound matters, the size and scope of this project has meant that other units who landed on 6 June have had to be airbrushed from history. Yet the rationale underpinning this editorial decision is far from arbitrary. The methodology employed to select the relevant war diary entries for *D-Day Documents* was in fact determined by Lieutenant-Colonel H.F. Joslen's authoritative *Orders of Battle of the Second World War, 1939-1945*.[40] In volume two of this seminal work, Joslen supplied his readership with a special supplement in which he listed all the Anglo-Canadian units who participated in the cross-Channel attack on 6/7 June 1944. In order to differentiate between the 'spear-head' formations that had stormed ashore first and those 'follow-up' units who had arrived later on in the day, he divided up each of the three landing beaches in the supplement into three sections entitled, 'Leading formations', 'Additional formations and units placed under command for the assault phase' and 'Sub-Area units under command for assault phase'.[41] This being the case, it was therefore decided that in the name of economy only units from the first two categories would be incorporated into this 70th anniversary publication.[42] Moreover, in the same vein it was also decided to dispense with the numerous Royal Navy Commando units, Royal Marine landing craft detachments and RAF ground crews who also played their part during the initial stages of Operation *Neptune*, the amphibious phase of *Overlord*. However, those 'Sub-Area' units and formations that have been excluded are listed in full in the relevant appendices located at the rear of this book.

CONCLUSION

Seventy years on D-Day can be viewed as a truly seismic event, one of those moments in history that change the course of World affairs forever. Notably, as much had been anticipated by the man responsible for Hitler's 'Atlantic Wall' and the defence of Western Europe,

Generalfeldmarschall Erwin Rommel, the 'Desert Fox'.[43] On 22 April 1944, while inspecting German coastal defences, Rommel confided to his *aide-de-camp*, Captain Helmuth Lang, 'Believe me, Lang, the first twenty-four hours of the invasion will be decisive…the fate of Germany depends on the outcome…for the Allies, as well as Germany, it will be the longest day'.[44] Viewed through the prism and focus of the regimental war diaries contained within the covers of *D-Day Documents*, the 6 June 1944 was indeed one of the longest and most decisive days in the history of the Second World War. Yet despite its military significance D-Day was but the first step on a long and torturous road to ultimate victory. As one Normandy veteran later wrote:

> The close of D-day was not like the close of a book that could be snapped shut, its story put from mind. When the light in the sky went out that night, the men who had survived could not jump into bed, turn over, and go to sleep. They had only completed Chapter Two: there would be no relaxation, no easy oblivion, until the war ended and the Germans surrendered.[45]

Having gained a foothold on the continent of Europe, Allied forces would take another seventy-five days to break out of Normandy. Although casualty figures for D-Day (believed to be between 8,443 and 10,865) had mercifully been far below those projected by Allied planners,[46] the numbers killed and wounded thereafter in what would be known as the Battle of Normandy exceeded even those suffered during the infamous Passchendaele offensive of 1917.[47] Casualty rates of seventy per cent in battalion rifle companies were not uncommon during the Normandy campaign, which slowly but surely acted as a suction-pump on the scant manpower resources of the British and Canadian Armies. Tragically, the butcher's bill for breaking the back of the German war machine in France was high. By the end of the Battle of Normandy, General Montgomery's 21st Army Group had calculated that, excluding casualty returns from the US 12th Army Group, the British Liberation Army (BLA) and its Canadian allies had lost a staggering 83,825 personnel killed, wounded or missing in action.[48]

A significant number of these men are buried in the Commonwealth War Graves Commission (CWGC) cemetery in Bayeux, the first major town in occupied France to be liberated by the British. The largest such site in France to hold those from Britain and the Commonwealth who fell during the Second World War, it contains the graves of 4,144 servicemen the majority of whom perished in the bitter fighting that followed D-Day. Standing opposite the war cemetery is the CWGC memorial to the 1,805 British and Commonwealth soldiers who were killed during the Normandy campaign and who have no known graves. Fittingly, this relatively simple but deeply moving monument bears the Latin inscription, *NOS A GULIELMO VICTI VICTORIS PATRIAM LIBERAVIMUS* 'We, once conquered by William, have now set free the Conqueror's native land'.[49] Drawing direct historical parallels between William the Conqueror's great seaborne invasion of England in 1066 and the launch of Operation *Overlord* 878 years later, this dedication is a fine tribute to those men and women who, seventy years ago, paid the ultimate price in freeing France, and indeed the rest of Western Europe, from the yoke of Nazi tyranny. Correspondingly, *D-Day Documents* is a humble tribute to their eternal memories.

NOTES

[3] *Never Give In! The Best of Winston Churchill's Speeches*, selected and edited by his Grandson Winston S. Churchill, (London: Pimlico, 2003), pp. 258-259.

[4] Major L.F. Ellis *et al.*, *Victory in the West, Volume I: The Battle of Normandy*, (London: HMSO: 1962), p. xvii.

[5] *The Oxford Companion to the Second World War*, edited by I.C.B. Dear and M.R.D. Foot, (Oxford: Oxford University Press, 1995), p. 853.

[6] *D-Day Then and Now*, Volume 2, edited by Winston G. Ramsey, (London: Battle of Britain Prints International Ltd, 1995), pp. 652-653.

[7] Major L.F. Ellis *et al.*, *Victory in the West, Volume I: The Battle of Normandy*, (London: HMSO: 1962), p. 1.

[8] Ibid., p. 223.

[9] Ibid.

[10] Quoted in Chester Wilmot, *The Struggle for Europe*, (London: The Reprint Society, 1954), p. 320.

[11] Michael Paris, 'Reconstructing D-Day: 6 June 1944 and British documentary films', Chapter 15, in *The Normandy Campaign 1944: Sixty Years On*, edited by John Buckley, (Abingdon, Oxon: Routledge, 2006), p. 201.

[12] Major L.F. Ellis *et al.*, *Victory in the West, Volume I: The Battle of Normandy*, (London: HMSO: 1962); Colonel C.P. Stacey, *Official History of the Canadian Army in the Second World War: The Victory Campaign: The Operations in North-West Europe, 1944-1945*, Volume III, (Ottawa, Canada: Department of National Defense, 1967); and Gordon. A. Harrison, *United States Army in World War II: The European Theater of Operations: Cross-Channel Attack*, (Washington DC: Office of the Chief of Military History, Department of the Army, 1951).

[13] Elizabeth Longford, *Wellington: Pillar of State*, (London: Weidenfeld & Nicolson, 1972), pp. 10-11.

[14] Bill Jackson and Dwin Bramall, *The Chiefs: The Story of the United Kingdom Chiefs of Staff*, (London: Brassey's, 1992), p. 43.

[15] John Dunlop, *The Development of the British Army 1899–1914*, (London: Methuen, 1938), pp. 292-293.

[16] *Field Service Regulations Part II: Organisation & Administration 1909*, General Staff, War Office, (London: HMSO, 1909), pp. 137-138.

[17] *Field Service Pocket Book*, Part I – Pamphlet No. 13, 'Discipline, Office Work, Pay and Burial Parties', 19th June 1943, (London: HMSO, 1943), p. 14.

[18] Ibid., p. 14.

[19] Ibid.

[20] Ibid., pp. 14-15.

[21] Ibid., p. 15. While all British Army war diaries were deposited with the Army War Diary Section, in the aftermath of the Second World War all British divisional war diaries were deposited at the Cabinet Office in Whitehall under the care of a Mr C.V. Owen. See Norman Scarfe, *Assault Division: A History of the 3rd Division from the Invasion of Normandy to the Surrender of Germany*, (Staplehurst, Kent: Spellmount Ltd, 2004), p. xv.

[22] Andrew Holborn, *The 56th Infantry Brigade and D-Day: An Independent Infantry Brigade and the Campaign in North West Europe, 1944-1945*, (London: Continuum, 2010), p. 4

[23] Richard J. Aldrich, *Witness to War: Diaries of the Second World War in Europe and the Middle East*, (London: Doubleday, 2004), p. 9.

[24] The regiment's war diary can be located in TNA WO 171/976, 'Royal Artillery, Field Regiments. 76 Regt'.

[25] Norman Scarfe, *Assault Division: A History of the 3rd Division from the Invasion of Normandy to the Surrender of Germany*, (Staplehurst, Kent: Spellmount Ltd, 2004), p. xi.

[26] Ibid., p. 18.

[27] See Richard Doherty, *Hobart's 79th Armoured Division at War: Invention, Innovation & Inspiration*, (Barnsley, South Yorkshire: Pen & Sword Books Ltd, 2011).

[28] It is notable that the famous Second World War poet, Captain Keith Douglas, author of *Selected Poems* and *Alamein to ZemZem*, was on attachment to the Nottinghamshire Yeomanry from the 2nd Derbyshire Yeomanry on D-Day. Having already fought with the Sherwood Rangers at the Second Battle of El Alamein in October 1942, Douglas was a member of A Squadron on 6 June 1944. Prior to the cross-channel assault, Douglas wrote to his old Oxford tutor, Edmund Blunden, the notable First World War poet, who had served as a Lieutenant in the 11th Battalion, The Royal Sussex Regiment, 'I've been fattened up for the slaughter and am simply waiting for it to start'. Having entered the charnel house of the Normandy battlefield, Douglas's prophecy was realised on 9 June when he was 'hit in the head by a piece of mortar shell as he was running along a ditch towards his tank' during the battle for Hill 103 near the village of Tilly-sur-Seulles. See Antony Beevor, *D-Day: The Battle for Normandy*, (London: Viking, 2009), p. 10 & p. 177. One of Britain's other great Second World War poets, Major John Jarmain, also fought in the Western Desert at Second El Alamein and served in Normandy with the 61st Anti-Tank Regiment of the 51st Highland Division. Like Douglas, Jarmain was killed in action by a German mortar round on 26 June 1944 while on a reconnaissance mission at Ste-Honorine La Chardonnerette. See John Jarmain and James Crowden, *Flowers in the Minefields: John Jarmain - War Poet - 1911-1944: A Short Appraisal of His Life and Work*, (Somerset: Flagon Press, 2012).

[29] Stuart Hills, *By Tank Into Normandy: A Memoir of The Campaign in North-West Europe From D-Day to VE Day*, (London: Cassell & Co, 2002). An alumnus of Tonbridge School, Hills was a contemporary and school friend of Sandy Smith who, as a Lieutenant in the 2nd Battalion, the Oxfordshire & Buckinghamshire Light Infantry, won a Military Cross on D-Day while commanding a platoon during the famous *coup de main* glider assault on 'Pegasus Bridge'. Ibid., p. 71.

[30] Ibid., p. 193.

[31] Ibid., p. 198.

[32] Ibid., pp. 199-200.

[33] Andrew Holborn, *The 56th Infantry Brigade and D-Day: An Independent Infantry Brigade and the Campaign in North West Europe, 1944-1945*, (London: Continuum, 2010), p. 3.

[34] Richard J. Aldrich, *The Faraway War: Personal Diaries of the Second World War in Asia and the Pacific*, (London: Doubleday, 2005), p. 5.

[35] Richard J. Aldrich, *Witness to War: Diaries of the Second World War in Europe and the Middle East*, (London: Doubleday, 2004), p. 17.

[36] Norman Scarfe, *Assault Division: A History of the 3rd Division from the Invasion of Normandy to the Surrender of Germany*, (Staplehurst, Kent: Spellmount Ltd, 2004), p. xi.

[37] Richard Holmes, *Complete War Walks: British Battles from Hastings to Normandy*, (London: BBC World Wide Ltd, 2003), p. 14.

[38] Norman Scarfe, *Assault Division: A History of the 3rd Division from the Invasion of Normandy to the Surrender of Germany*, (Staplehurst, Kent: Spellmount Ltd, 2004), pp. 18-19.

[39] However, they are now available in a limited edition volume entitled *SAS War Diary, 1941-1945*, (London: Extraordinary Editions, 2011).

[40] Lieutenant-Colonel H.F. Joslen, *Orders of Battle, Volume II: United Kingdom and Colonial Formations and Units in the Second World War, 1939-1945*, (London: HMSO, 1960).

[41] Ibid. See pages 578-589.

[42] That said, other painful editorial decisions concerning participating units have had to be made. These include the exclusion of the following regiments and corps who, despite being part of the 'leading formations', were deemed too small to justify entry into *D-Day Documents*: Survey Battery, 9th Survey Regiment RA and 'B' Flight 652nd Air Op Squadron, who landed on 'Sword' beach; 474th Search-light

Battery RA, 155th AA Ops Room RA, 160th AA Ops Room RA and 'A' Flight 652nd Air Op Squadron, who operated on 'Juno' beach; and 152nd Anti-Aircraft Ops Room, 356th Search-light Battery RA and 662nd Air Op Squadron, who came ashore at 'Gold' beach. Ibid., p. 585, p. 583 & p. 581.

[43] *Hitler's Generals*, edited by Correlli Barnett, (London: Weidenfeld & Nicolson, 1989), p. 310.

[44] Cornelius Ryan, *The Longest Day: The D-Day Story*, (London: Victor Gollancz Ltd, 1982), p. 12.

[45] Norman Scarfe, *Assault Division: A History of the 3rd Division from the Invasion of Normandy to the Surrender of Germany*, (Staplehurst, Kent: Spellmount Ltd, 2004), p. 90.

[46] British 21st Army Group predicted that out for every 70,000 men landed on D-Day, 9250 would be casualties including 3000 men drowned. See Colonel C.P. Stacey, *Official History of the Canadian Army in the Second World War: The Victory Campaign: The Operations in North-West Europe, 1944-1945*, Volume III, (Ottawa, Canada: Department of National Defense, 1967), p. 119 & p. 651.

[47] Gary Sheffield, 'Dead Cows and Tigers: Some aspects of the experience of the British Soldier in Normandy, 1944', Chapter 9, in *The Normandy Campaign 1944: Sixty Years On*, edited by John Buckley, (Abingdon, Oxon: Routledge, 2006), p. 121.

[48] Major L.F. Ellis *et al.*, *Victory in the West, Volume I: The Battle of Normandy*, (London: HMSO: 1962), p. 493.

[49] This inscription refers to the Duke of Normandy, William the Conqueror, who in October 1066 landed at Hastings and defeated the Anglo-Saxon army of King Harold thereby becoming England's first Norman King.

D-DAY DOCUMENTS

TNA AIR 40/1959

'PHOTOGRAPHIC INTELLIGENCE FOR OPERATION OVERLORD' – DOUVRES LA DELIVRANDE

Crucial to the planning of Operation *Overlord* was the intelligence supplied by Photographic Reconnaissance (PR) sorties flown over the Dutch, Belgian and French coastlines. Prior to D-Day, millions of aerial photographs were taken of Hitler's 'Atlantic Wall' and its defences in an effort to monitor their construction and development. To ensure the security of *Overlord,* for every PR sortie flown over Normandy two were undertaken over the Pas de Calais area.[50] Such was the volume of PR photographs that 80 per cent of all intelligence on the subject derived from this one source.[51] Of particular interest to Allied planners would have been the sprawling German radar station at Douvres, the focal point for countless Allied PR sorties during the months and weeks leading up to the Normandy landings.

Positioned three miles south of Saint-Aubin-sur-Mer, a coastal town located on 'Juno' beach, the two *Luftwaffe* manned complexes which made up the Douvres La Delivrande site were a key component of the *Kammhuber* Line, a chain of radar stations across Europe designed to track British bombers en route to targets deep inside Nazi Germany. By plotting the bombers' course, height and speed on special Seeburg plotting tables, and then passing on the data to an Anton fighter direction centre buried deep inside a two-storey L479 bunker at Douvres, this radar station could co-ordinate the interception of enemy raiders by German night-fighters.[52] Codenamed *Distelfink* ('Goldfinch')[53] by the Germans, the Douvres installation became operational in August 1943 and was the largest radar site in Normandy covering twenty-five acres. Commanded by *Oberleutnant* Kurt Egle, the defending garrison comprised approximately 238 men of 8 *Kompanie Luftnachrichten-Regiment 53,*[54] later reinforced by the 8th and 12th Companies of 736th Grenadier Regiment and men from 192nd Panzergrenadier Regiment.[55]

Although technically linked, the north site at La Delivrande and the larger site south at Douvres La Delivrande were separated by a road running from Bény-sur-Mer to the village of Douvres. The northern site consisted of a Siemens *Wassermann* long-range early warning system, in essence a 36 metre high antenna mounted on a revolving stand and code named 'Chimney' by Allied intelligence, which was heavily defended by barbed wire, minefields, trenches, Tobruk emplacements, and machine-gun nests.[56] The southern installation was even more formidable consisting of two *Freya* medium range aerials and a Giant *Würzburg Riese* radar parabolic antenna protected by minefields, barbed wire, five 50 mm guns, six machine-guns and one 50 mm heavy mortar. Additional protection came in the form of Tobruk emplacements, trench systems, bunkers, personnel shelters and four-storey deep concrete casemates. Unsurprisingly, the Germans referred to these fortified positions collectively as *Stützpunkt* (strong-point) Douvres.

Alerted to their presence and function by photographic intelligence, the Allies consequently launched repeated aerial attacks by fighter-bombers on the two complexes from mid May until D-Day itself. Yet despite the intensity of these raids the individual radar antennae were still active up to 17 June when *Luftwaffe* personnel destroyed the sets prior to capture.[57] Conscious of the need to secure these sites quickly on D-Day, Allied planners allocated this task to one British Commando unit and one Canadian infantry battalion. No. 48 Royal Marine Commando would land in 'Nan' sector on 'Juno' beach at around 0900 hours on the morning of 6 June.[58] Their primary job was to capture the area surrounding and including Langrune-sur-Mer, while their secondary objective later in the day was Dourves. They would be aided in this endeavour by the Canadian 8th Brigade Group's North Shore (New Brunswick) Regiment.[59] Yet after fierce fighting and numerous delays it was evident by the evening of D-Day that Douvres was not going to fall to the Allies that day and consequently 8th Brigade was ordered to contain the two sites until first light when they were to be assaulted.[60]

Attacked at 0700 hours on 7 June, the defences of the two fortified radar sites were considerably stronger than the Canadians had anticipated making progress slow. Despite the support of 19th Field Regiment Royal Canadian Artillery, Sherman tanks from the Fort Garry Horse and the battalion's mortars the position remained impervious to the Allied assault.[61] The North Shore's war diary entry for 7 June recorded:

> The Radar station was found to be stronger than had been anticipated and was engaged by 19 Cdn Fd Regt, which was in support of us. Our mortars also took on the Station but as the concrete works were rather thick and well dug-in, little or no damage was done. The day was fast drawing to a close and a decision was finally made and B[riga]de permission obtained to by-pass the Station and move to the B[riga]de RV.[62]

Ironically, Intelligence estimates supplied to British I Corps (under whose aegis Canadian 3rd Division operated) prior to D-Day had stated that by the time Allied forces encountered *Stützpunkt* Douvres, air and naval attacks would have so severely damaged the two sites that *Luftwaffe* radar specialists would not have 'the stomach to fight'. As it was, these predictions would prove to have been wildly optimistic.[63]

Thwarted, the North Shore (New Brunswick) Regiment eventually withdrew and the task of containing the radar station fell to the 51st (Highland) Division, one of whose regiments, the 5th Battalion, The Black Watch, in conjunction with Armoured Vehicles Royal Engineers (AVRE) from 80th Assault Squadron RE,[64] also failed to dislodge the occupants of these

Stützpunkte.[65] Despite being ordered to disengage from the enemy and pull back, the commanding officer of the battalion, Lieutenant-Colonel Thompson, proposed to renew the offensive by attacking the German garrison from the rear. Frustrated, however, by continued German resistance and the slowness of the Allied advance, senior commanders issued fresh instructions stating that Douvres was once again to be by-passed and 'left to be shelled by the Navy'.[66]

From 7 to 10 June the job of investing and harassing the garrison at Douvres fell to Nos 46 and 48 Royal Marine Commandos of the 4th Special Service Brigade supported by the Royal Navy and RAF. On 10 June responsibility for the radar stations and their fortifications was passed to yet another unit, No. 41 Royal Marine Commando. Considered to be 'More of a hindrance than a nuisance' at this time, *Stützpunkt* Douvres slowly developed into something of a thorn in the flesh of the Allies.[67] This was due to the fact that the installation held a commanding position overlooking the Anglo-Canadian beach head enabling the Germans manning these mini-fortresses to report on troop movements and naval activity to German forces defending Caen.[68] Moreover, the German LXXXIV Korps responsible for Lower Normandy viewed this position as a 'valuable pivot' for future offensive operations designed to 'drive the Allies back into the sea'. Consequently, *Oberleutnant* Egle was urged by his superiors via a surviving telephone line to hold out and await relief.

However, this defiant stand simply induced British I Corps to wage a campaign of attrition against Egle's men. RAF Typhoon fighter-bombers were called upon to strafe, bomb and rocket Douvres, while No. 41 Royal Marine Commando employed Centaur tanks, PIAT bombs, machine-gun fire and snipers to produce a 'harassing fire programme' designed to undermine the morale of the garrison, keep them pinned down and prevent *Luftwaffe* technicians from venturing into the open to fix damaged radar equipment.[69] Determined to help their besieged comrades weather this storm of steel, the *Luftwaffe*, on the night of 14 June, executed a parachute supply drop over the Douvres sites. Yet despite the audacity of the German Air Force, the dropped supply canisters, which contained breech blocks for anti-tank guns, ammunition, booby traps and technical equipment, were quickly intercepted by British Commandos thereby denying them to their intended recipients.[70]

The 14 June was to mark a turning point in the fortunes of Egle's garrison. Worried about mounting casualties among the besiegers and frustrated by the resilience of the defenders, British commanders ordered Lieutenant-Colonel Eric Palmer, commanding officer of No. 41 Royal Marine Commando, to storm the radar stations and finish the job once and for all. Over the next couple of days Palmer formulated a plan of attack which would include the employment of forty-four armoured vehicles to support his Commandos. The assault duly commenced at 1630 hours on 17 June with a thirty minute naval and artillery bombardment.

Just before H-Hour, set for 1700 hours, 77th Squadron RE launched a diversionary attack south of the main radar site enabling 'B' and 'C' Squadrons 22nd Dragoons with their flail tanks and 5th Assault Squadron RE with its AVREs to deploy against the two strong-points. While the flail tanks or 'Crabs' thrashed a path through the minefields, the AVREs blasted bunkers and casemates with their 290 mm Petards and assault engineers placed 70 lb 'beehive' charges on armoured doors and reinforced roofs of German dug-outs.[71]

At 1720 hours 'B', 'P' and 'X' Troops from No. 41 Royal Marine Commando attacked the main complex while 'A' Troop assaulted the smaller northern site. 'Y' Troop remained in reserve.[72] Covered by tank fire, Marine Commandos attacked and methodically cleared the labyrinth of trenches and bunkers inside the two complexes with grenades and small arms fire. Despite putting up a spirited defence by 1830 hours the German defenders were compelled to capitulate in the face of this overwhelming onslaught. In total, six officers and 214 other ranks were taken prisoner.[73] Although No. 41 Royal Marine Commando suffered just one casualty during the battle, the Germans killed three Sappers, wounded seven and destroyed four AVREs and damaged another three.[74] Minefields claimed four 'Crabs' from 'B' and 'C' Squadrons 22nd Dragoons but damaged little else. Yet by skilful planning and a clever use of armour and infantry, Lieutenant-Colonel Palmer achieved what his predecessors could not, namely the elimination of *Stützpunkt* Douvres as a point of major resistance.

NOTES

[50] F.H. Hinsley *et al.*, *British Intelligence in the Second World War: Its Influence on Strategy and Operations*, Volume 3, Part 2, (London: HMSO, 1988), p. 42.

[51] Ibid., p. 16.

[52] See Steven J Zaloga, *D-Day Fortifications in Normandy*, (Botley, Oxford: Osprey Publishing, 2005), p. 30 and Tim Saunders, *Battleground Europe: Normandy: Juno Beach Canadian 3rd Infantry Division & 79th Armoured Division*, (Barnsley, South Yorkshire: Pen & Sword Books Ltd, 2004), p. 165.

[53] *D-Day Then and Now*, volume 2, edited by Winston G. Ramsey, (London: Battle of Britain Prints Ltd, 1995), p. 563.

[54] Colonel C.P. Stacey, *Official History of the Canadian Army in the Second World War: The Victory Campaign: The Operations in North-West Europe, 1944-1945*, Volume III, (Ottawa, Canada: Department of National Defense, 1966),p. 70.

[55] Ken Ford, *Battle Zone Normandy: Juno Beach*, (Stroud, Gloucestershire: Sutton Publishing Ltd, 2004), pp. 164-165.

[56] *D-Day Then and Now*, volume 2, edited by Winston G. Ramsey, (London: Battle of Britain Prints Ltd, 1995), p. 563.

[57] Tim Saunders, *Battleground Europe: Normandy: Juno Beach Canadian 3rd Infantry Division & 79th Armoured Division*, (Barnsley, South Yorkshire: Pen & Sword Books Ltd, 2004), p. 167.

[58] Major L.F. Ellis *et al.*, *Victory in the West: The Battle of Normandy*, Volume I, (London: HMSO, 1962), p. 183.

[59] Colonel C.P. Stacey, *Official History of the Canadian Army in the Second World War: The Victory Campaign: The Operations in North-West Europe, 1944-1945*, Volume III, (Ottawa, Canada: Department of National Defense, 1966), p. 77 & p. 79.

60 Ibid.,p. 111.

61 Ibid.,p. 134.

62 Tim Saunders, *Battleground Europe: Normandy: Juno Beach Canadian 3rd Infantry Division & 79th Armoured Division*, (Barnsley, South Yorkshire: Pen & Sword Books Ltd, 2004), p. 168.

63 Ibid.

64 Richard Doherty, *Hobart's 79th Armoured Division At War: Invention, Innovation & Inspiration*, (Barnsley, South Yorkshire: Pen & Sword Books Ltd, 2011), p. 91.

65 Colonel C.P. Stacey, *Official History of the Canadian Army in the Second World War: The Victory Campaign: The Operations in North-West Europe, 1944-1945*, Volume III, (Ottawa, Canada: Department of National Defense, 1966), p. 134.

66 Tim Saunders, *Battleground Europe: Normandy: Juno Beach Canadian 3rd Infantry Division & 79th Armoured Division*, (Barnsley, South Yorkshire: Pen & Sword Books Ltd, 2004), p. 171.

67 Ibid.

68 Ken Ford, *Battle Zone Normandy: Juno Beach*, (Stroud, Gloucestershire: Sutton Publishing Ltd, 2004), p. 78.

69 Tim Saunders, *Battleground Europe: Normandy: Juno Beach Canadian 3rd Infantry Division & 79th Armoured Division*, (Barnsley, South Yorkshire: Pen & Sword Books Ltd, 2004), p. 171.

70 Ibid., pp. 171-172.

71 Ken Ford, *Battle Zone Normandy: Juno Beach*, (Stroud, Gloucestershire: Sutton Publishing Ltd, 2004), p. 163.

72 Tim Saunders, *Battleground Europe: Normandy: Juno Beach Canadian 3rd Infantry Division & 79th Armoured Division*, (Barnsley, South Yorkshire: Pen & Sword Books Ltd, 2004), p. 176.

73 Colonel C.P. Stacey, *Official History of the Canadian Army in the Second World War: The Victory Campaign: The Operations in North-West Europe, 1944-1945*, Volume III, (Ottawa, Canada: Department of National Defense, 1966), p. 144.

74 Richard Doherty, *Hobart's 79th Armoured Division At War: Invention, Innovation & Inspiration*, (Barnsley, South Yorkshire: Pen & Sword Books Ltd, 2011), p. 94.

TNA AIR 40/1959–PR Photograph of the Luftwaffe Radar Stations at Douvres La Delivrande

TNA CAB 106/312

VICTORIA CROSS CITATION FOR COMPANY SERGEANT MAJOR STANLEY HOLLIS, 6TH BATTALION, THE GREEN HOWARDS

4390973 Company Sergeant Major (CSM) Stanley E. Hollis, (1912-1972) of the 6th Battalion, The Green Howards, holds the distinction of winning the only Victoria Cross (VC), Britain's highest award for gallantry in the face of the enemy, on D-Day.[75] Moreover, he achieved the double distinction of being recommended for this prestigious decoration twice on 6 June. As General Sir Peter de la Billière, author of a notable work on the VC, has observed, 'The award of a Victoria Cross has always marked out a winner as someone special and elevated above his peers in terms of prowess on the field of battle'.[76] As his citation attests, Sergeant-Major Stan Hollis was no exception to this rule.

The Victoria Cross was instituted by a Royal Warrant signed on 29 January 1856 by Queen Victoria, who personally 'endorsed the proposition that bravery should be recognised in every rank of the armed forces'.[77] Prior to 1856, senior officers could receive the Order of the Bath, or a mention-in-despatches, whereas other ranks were without a gallantry award until the Crimea War of 1854-1856 when the Distinguished Conduct Medal (DCM) and Conspicuous Gallantry Medal (CGM) were introduced for the Army and Navy respectively.[78] The creation of the VC therefore ensured that from this time onwards any member of the British armed forces, regardless of rank, who committed an act(s) of heroism on the battlefield would now receive official recognition.

Since 1856, the Green Howards have won a total of eighteen VCs, as well as three George Crosses, the highest award granted to civilians and soldiers for acts of bravery while not in sight of the enemy.[79] Having won the regiment's seventeenth VC,[80] which was gazetted in the *London Gazette* on 17 August 1944,[81] and Hollis was duly decorated by King George VI at Buckingham Palace on 10 October 1945.[82] Yet the bestowing of the Victoria Cross was merely the pinnacle of a military career that had already been characterised by heroism, selflessness and devotion to duty on the part of the recipient.

A former merchant navy man from Middlesbrough, Stan Hollis had volunteered for the 4th Battalion, The Green Howards, a Territorial regiment, in May 1939. On mobilisation in September 1939, he helped form the new 6th Battalion, The Green Howards, a unit in which he would spend his entire military service.[83] Landing in France in April 1940 with the British Expeditionary Force (BEF), Hollis experienced his first combat during Hitler's

Blitzkrieg through the Low Countries and France, which by late May had pushed the BEF back to the Channel ports of Calais, Boulogne and Dunkirk. It was during the terrible retreat to the beaches of Dunkirk that Hollis underwent an experience that was instrumental in shaping his attitude to the war, and in particular the Germans. While moving towards the coast, he discovered hundreds of old men, women and children machine-gunned by the *Luftwaffe*, who had deliberately strafed vast columns of refugees in order to impede the progress of Anglo-French troops. Unsurprisingly, this cemented inside him a deep-hatred for the Germans and would be one of the motivating factors for Hollis's deadly efficiency on the battlefield thereafter.[84] Although wounded en route by a mortar bomb, Hollis finally reached Dunkirk in early June, but was subsequently forced to swim 'virtually naked, wounded and exhausted many yards from the beaches to a waiting navy vessel' thereby escaping capture by the 'skin of his teeth'.[85]

Having recovered from his wounds, Hollis was posted to the Middle East with the 6th battalion, which saw service in Iraq, Palestine and Cyprus. As part of the 69th Brigade, a sub-unit of which the 50th (Northumbrian) 'Tyne & Tees' Infantry Division, the 6th battalion took part in the Western Desert campaign and played an active role with Montgomery's 8th Army at the Battle of El Alamein in October 1942. It was while in North Africa that Hollis was again wounded, this time being made a prisoner-of-war by the Germans, which led to a remarkable meeting with *Generalfeldmarschall* Erwin Rommel, the 'Desert Fox', who congratulated him personally on his heroism. However, after several failed escape attempts, the first of which resulted in his being badly beaten by his German captors, Hollis eventually made a home-run back to British lines subsequently rejoining his regiment for the Allied push into Tunisia and final victory over *Generaloberst* von Arnim's *Heeresgruppe Afrika* (Army Group Africa) in May 1943. Yet Hollis and his battalion would go on to fight with great distinction in Sicily. It was during the very heavy fighting around Primosole Bridge that Hollis was nominated not only for a mention-in-despatches but also a DCM for a succession of heroic acts and outstanding leadership. Yet in keeping with an earlier recommendation for a Military Medal (MM) for bravery during the withdrawal to Dunkirk,[86] both submissions were inexplicably turned down.

Although Hollis's distinguished service throughout the Sicily campaign had not been formally recognised, his parent division, however, suffered no such indignity. So impressed was General Montgomery with the fighting record of the 50th Division and its sub-units, that he personally selected them to lead the initial assault wave for the planned invasion of Europe.[87] Consequently, almost four years to the day since he had been forced to swim for his life at Dunkirk, Sergeant-Major Hollis found himself at the spear-point of an Allied invasion force poised to liberate Western Europe and reverse the humiliation of June 1940. Commanded by Major-General Douglas Graham, the 50th Division comprised the 231st Brigade, 151st

Brigade and 69th Brigade.[88] It was under the latter brigade that the 6th Battalion, The Green Howards and her sister battalion, the 7th Green Howards, were to land on 'Gold' beach on 6 June, becoming, in the process, one of only two regiments in the British Army to land two assault battalions on D-Day.[89] Having sailed for Normandy in the *Empire Lance*, a cargo ship converted into a Landing Craft Infantry (LCI), the 6th battalion was to cover the last seven miles to shore by means of the British-made and Royal Marine crewed Landing Craft Assault (LCA) vessel. As Company Sergeant Major of D Company, 6th Green Howards, which had been designated the left-hand assault battalion, Hollis was in the vanguard of the first assault wave destined for 'King Green' sector of 'Gold' beach situated near the village of La Rivière.[90] Landing at 0725 hours, the battalion's main objective was the German artillery battery at Mont Fleury, situated on the ridge at Ver-sur-Mer. Equipped with 122 mm Russian artillery pieces captured by the Germans on the Eastern Front, and manned by elements of the 1260th Army Coastal Artillery Detachment, this position posed a serious threat to the landings in this sector necessitating a swift neutralisation by British ground forces.[91]

Yet prior to the landings, Hollis had noticed from previous briefings in England based on photographic reconnaissance images, a German pill box on the sea wall which began to worry the seasoned veteran. If it were a machine-gun nest then it had the potential to lay down withering fire on Hollis's men as they left their landing-craft, turning the assault into a bloodbath. Having long ago decided to take pre-emptive action during the final run in to shore, Hollis grabbed a Bren gun from one of his men and balancing it on the ramp of his LCA fired a full magazine into the pill-box to dissuade any Germans hidden therein from reacting to the landing. Yet on nearing the shoreline he injudiciously picked up the Bren gun by its barrel, which was still scolding hot, and received a nasty burn to the palm of his hand, which, in Hollis's own words, was 'A self-inflicted wound, quite the most painful I had during the entire war, it took weeks to heal and the battle hadn't even started.'[92] In fact, what Hollis had thought an enemy position was in reality a shelter for passengers using a tramline that ran along the coast behind the sea wall. This belated discovery elicited from one of his men the cry it's "'only a bloody bus shelter, Sarn't Major!'".[93]

Having thus executed a relatively unopposed landing, Hollis and his battalion moved off to capture the Mont Fleury battery. However, en route they encountered a couple of very real pill boxes, whose deadly automatic fire ensured that the unit's line of advance to the battery was effectively blocked. As the citation for his VC makes plain, Hollis was obliged to take the initiative and clear the first one with hand grenades and automatic fire from his Sten gun. Advancing still further through a series of enemy trenches, Hollis encouraged the occupants of another pillbox to surrender capturing, in the process, twenty-five to thirty prisoners.[94] For these gallant actions, Hollis was recommended by the battalion Commanding Officer (CO), Lieutenant-Colonel Robin Hastings, for a Victoria Cross.

Following the action at the Mont Fleury battery, Hollis was ordered to take command of 16 Platoon which was leaderless due the deaths of its commanding officer, Lieutenant J.A. Kirkpatrick and the platoon sergeant, J.J. 'Rufty' Hill.[95] The battalion's ultimate D-Day objective was the St. Léger feature five miles inland. On the way, however, lay the small village of Crépon. Not wishing to be drawn into a prolonged fight for the village, Lieutenant-Colonel Hastings ordered B and C companies to bypass Crépon, while D Company was tasked with clearing it of Germans. In reserve was A Company positioned to aid her sister companies if they ran into difficulties.[96] On clearing the village, Hollis and his platoon encountered a German machine-gun nest and field gun concealed in an orchard. Having informed his Company CO, Major Ronnie Lofhouse, of this discovery, Hollis was subsequently ordered to eliminate this point of resistance in order that it should not hold up D Company's advance. Selecting two men with Bren guns to accompany him, Hollis chose a PIAT [Projector Infantry Anti-Tank] anti-tank weapon to destroy the artillery piece.[97]

Crawling through a rhubarb patch in order to get a clean shot at the target, Hollis had ordered other members of his platoon to rush out into the middle of the orchard and give covering fire to his group. Yet on emerging from cover, they had all been killed by accurate enemy fire from a fully-alert enemy. Pressing on nevertheless CSM Hollis got into a suitable firing position and launched his PIAT bomb, which missed. Now attracting very heavy fire from entrenched positions, Hollis exclaimed: 'No, to hell with this; I'm getting out of here'.[98] Believing his Bren gunners to still be with him, Hollis withdrew quickly and rejoined D Company. It was only belatedly that Hollis and Lofthouse realised that the two men were still in the orchard pinned down by the Germans. As his citation recounts, Hollis then volunteered to extricate his two comrades. He did this by charging into the orchard firing a Bren gun from the hip in order to distract the Germans from concentrating on the two soldiers. Ignoring a fusillade of fire aimed at him, Hollis carried on firing until the two men had withdrawn at which point Hollis himself sprinted out of the orchard and to safety.[99] By executing this incredibly brave and selfless act, Hollis had undertaken his second VC action of D-Day.[100]

This was not, however, to be the last heroic act CSM Hollis committed while fighting in Normandy. On 11 June, the 6th Battalion, The Green Howards put in an attack on the village of Cristot held by strong German forces. Encountering a machine-gun nest located in a narrow, sunken lane which was holding-up D Company's advance, Hollis quickly evaluated the situation and decided to act. Having established that the enemy machine-gunner took cover every time he had fired a long burst down the lane, Hollis resolved to take advantage of such a pause to close with the enemy and destroy him. Timing his move exactly, Hollis threw a grenade at the Germans and charged the position using his Sten gun to finish them off.[101] This was his third such valorous act since D-Day. Yet in mid August Hollis's luck finally ran out when he received his fifth and most serious set of wounds to date from a mortar bomb during fierce fighting around Falaise.[102] Evacuated back to the UK as a serious casualty, his numerous wounds ensured that Hollis would take no further part in the fighting in North-west Europe.

Although a professional, dedicated soldier, who was wounded on five occasions during the war, Hollis was never a natural peacetime or barrack-room soldier. Promoted and demoted with regular frequency, Hollis appears to have been in his element while in the field fighting an enemy he loathed. Due to his experiences at Dunkirk and in other campaigns, Hollis evolved into a cold, calculating killer on the battlefield, personally dispatching one hundred and two enemy soldiers during the Second World War. Yet Hollis was no mindless murderer.[103] Instead, he had much in common with '…many of those who achieved a VC over a series of actions or a period of time', namely being 'dedicated to fighting the enemy and exercising care and sacrifice for their fellow servicemen' while possessing 'almost fanatical patriotism'.[104] This was confirmed by his Commanding Officer, Lieutenant-Colonel Hastings, who attested that, 'He was absolutely personally dedicated to winning the war – one of the few men I ever met who felt like that'.[105] Yet, as one authority had remarked, 'away from exploding shells, the threat of anti-personnel mines and the stammer of German machine guns, Hollis was a quiet, likeable Englishman – just the sort with whom to enjoy a pint in the local'.[106] It was perhaps fitting, therefore, that after pursuing several forms of employment, Stanley Hollis ended his days running a village pub in Loftus in North Yorkshire passing away aged 59 years on 8 February 1972.[107]

NOTES

[75] Mike Morgan, *D-Day Hero: CSM Stanley Hollis VC*, (Stroud, Gloucestershire: Sutton Publishing, 2004), p.vii.

[76] General Sir Peter de la Billière, *Supreme Courage: Heroic Stories from 150 Years of the Victoria Cross*, (London: Little, Brown, 2004),p. 354.

[77] Ibid.,p. 1.

[78] Ibid., p. 2.

[79] Roger Chapman, *Beyond Their Duty: Heroes of the Green Howards*, (Richmond, Yorkshire: The Green Howards Museum, 2001), p. i & p. iii.

[80] Geoffrey Powell and John Powell, *The History of the Green Howards: Three Hundred Years of Service*, (Barnsley, South Yorkshire: Pen & Sword Books Ltd, 2002), pp. 282-283.

[81] Roger Chapman, *Beyond Their Duty: Heroes of the Green Howards*, (Richmond, Yorkshire: The Green Howards Museum, 2001), p. 91.

[82] Ibid., p. 78.

[83] Ibid.

[84] Mike Morgan, *D-Day Hero: CSM Stanley Hollis VC*, (Stroud, Gloucestershire: Sutton Publishing, 2004), p. 100.

[85] Ibid., p. 5.

[86] Ibid., pp. 23-27.

[87] Major Ewart Clay M.B.E., *The Path of the 50th: The Story of the 50th (Northumbrian) Division in the Second World War, 1939-1945*, (Aldershot, Hants: Gale & Polden Ltd, 1950), p. 218.

[88] Andrew Holden, *The 56th Infantry Brigade and D-Day: An Independent Infantry Brigade and the Campaign in North West Europe, 1944-1945*, (London: Continuum, 2010), pp. 74-76.

[89] Geoffrey Powell and John Powell, *The History of the Green Howards: Three Hundred Years of Service*, (Barnsley, South Yorkshire: Pen & Sword Books Ltd, 2002), p. 259.

[90] Christopher Dunphie and Garry Johnson, *Battleground Europe: Normandy: Gold Beach: Inland from King – June 1944*, (Barnsley, South Yorkshire: Pen & Sword Books Ltd, 2002), p. 29.

[91] Simon Trew, *Battle Zone Normandy: Gold Beach*, (Stroud, Gloucestershire: Sutton Publishing, 2004), pp. 123-124.

[92] Christopher Dunphie and Garry Johnson, *Battleground Europe: Normandy: Gold Beach: Inland from King – June 1944*, (Barnsley, South Yorkshire: Pen & Sword Books Ltd, 2002), p. 44.

[93] Mike Morgan, *D-Day Hero: CSM Stanley Hollis VC*, (Stroud, Gloucestershire: Sutton Publishing, 2004), p. 56.

[94] Winson G. Ramsey, *D-Day: Then and Now*, volume 2, (London: Battle of Britain Prints International Ltd, 1995), p. 440.

[95] Simon Trew, *Battle Zone Normandy: Gold Beach*, (Stroud, Gloucestershire: Sutton Publishing, 2004), p. 128.

[96] Christopher Dunphie and Garry Johnson, *Battleground Europe: Normandy: Gold Beach: Inland from King – June 1944*, (Barnsley, South Yorkshire: Pen & Sword Books Ltd, 2002), p. 50.

[97] Simon Trew, *Battle Zone Normandy: Gold Beach*, (Stroud, Gloucestershire: Sutton Publishing, 2004), p. 129.

[98] Winson G. Ramsey, *D-Day: Then and Now*, volume 2, (London: Battle of Britain Prints International Ltd, 1995), p. 450.

[99] Christopher Dunphie and Garry Johnson, *Battleground Europe: Normandy: Gold Beach: Inland from King – June 1944*, (Barnsley, South Yorkshire: Pen & Sword Books Ltd, 2002), pp. 54-58.

[100] Mike Morgan, *D-Day Hero: CSM Stanley Hollis VC*, (Stroud, Gloucestershire: Sutton Publishing, 2004), pp. 62-67.

[101] Christopher Dunphie and Garry Johnson, *Battleground Europe: Normandy: Gold Beach: Inland from King – June 1944*, (Barnsley, South Yorkshire: Pen & Sword Books Ltd, 2002), pp. 89-92.

[102] Mike Morgan, *D-Day Hero: CSM Stanley Hollis VC*, (Stroud, Gloucestershire: Sutton Publishing, 2004), pp. 102-103.

[103] Ibid., p. 107.

[104] General Sir Peter de la Billière, *Supreme Courage: Heroic Stories from 150 Years of the Victoria Cross*, (London: Little, Brown, 2004), pp. 356-357.

[105] Max Hastings, *Overlord: D-Day and the Battle for Normandy 1944*, (London: Michael Joseph Ltd, 1984), p. 110.

[106] General Sir Peter de la Billière, *Supreme Courage: Heroic Stories from 150 Years of the Victoria Cross*, (London: Little, Brown, 2004), p. 40.

[107] Roger Chapman, *Beyond Their Duty: Heroes of the Green Howards*, (Richmond, Yorkshire: The Green Howards Museum, 2001), p. 78.

115

COPY

THE VICTORIA CROSS

No. 4390973 Warrant Officer Class II (Company Sergeant-Major) Stanley Elton Hollis, The Green Howards (Alexandra, Princess of Wales's Own Yorkshire Regiment)

In Normandy on 6th June, 1944, during the assault on the beaches and the Mont Fleury Battery, C.S.M. Hollis's Company Commander noticed that two of the pill boxes had been by-passed, and went with C.S.M. Hollis to see that they were clear. When they were 20 yards from the pillbox, a machine gun opened fire from the slit and C.S.M. Hollis instantly rushed straight at the pillbox, firing his Sten gun. He jumped on top of the pillbox, re-charged his magazine, threw a grenade in through the door and fired his Sten gun into it, killing two Germans and making the remainder prisoner. He then cleared several Germans from a neighbouring trench. By his action, be undoubtedly saved his Company from being fired on heavily from the rear and enabled them to open the main beach exit.

Later the same day, in the village of Crepon, the Company encountered a, field gun and crew armed with Spandaus at 100 yards range. C.S.M. Hollis was put in command of a party to cover an attack on the gun, but the movement was held up. Seeing this, C.S.M. Hollis pushed right forward to engage the gun with a P.I.A.T. from a house at 50 yards range. He was observed by a sniper who fired and grazed his right cheek, and at the same moment the gun swung round and fired at point-blank range into the house. To avoid the fallen masonry C.S.M. Hollis moved his party to an alternative position. Two of the enemy gun crew had by this time been killed, and the gun was destroyed shortly afterwards. He later found that two of his men had stayed behind in the house and immediately volunteered to get them out. In full view of the enemy who were continually firing at him, he went forward alone using a Bren gun to distract their attention from the other men. Under cover of his diversion, the two men were able to get back.

Wherever fighting was heaviest, C.S.M. Hollis appeared and in the course of a magnificent day's work, he displayed the utmost gallantry and on two separate occasions his courage and initiative prevented the enemy from holding up the advance at critical stages. It was largely through his heroism and resource that the Company's objectives were gained and casualties were not heavier, and by his own bravery he saved the lives of many of his men.

TNA CAB 106/312 – CSM Stan Hollis's Victoria Cross Citation

TNA WO 219/5120

GENERAL DWIGHT D. EISENHOWER'S 'ORDER OF THE DAY'

General of the US Army, Dwight D. Eisenhower (1890-1969) was, according to one of his biographers, 'not born great, nor did he achieve greatness. But when greatness was thrust upon him, he met the challenge'.[108] During the prelude to D-Day, Eisenhower would face one of the greatest challenges of his career, namely to order, in the face of poor weather conditions, the launch of the largest amphibious assault in history, Operation *Neptune/Overlord*. Rising to the occasion, he undoubtedly took one of the most important and courageous command decisions of the Second World War. Yet had he miscalculated, Eisenhower may very well have been confined to the dustbin of military history, a name destined to be forever synonymous with a catastrophic disaster. As it was, Eisenhower's historic decision was fully vindicated changing not only the course of world history but his own career path, which would eventually lead to his becoming in November 1945 US Army Chief of Staff, commander of NATO forces from 1950-1952, and a year later the thirty-fourth President of the United States.[109]

A regular, professional soldier, who had attended the prestigious military academy at West Point, Eisenhower was not at first singled out for great things. Although he had not seen action with General John Pershing's American Expeditionary Force (AEF) during the First World War, Eisenhower nevertheless rose slowly but surely up the promotion ladder later, coming to the attention of the then Army Chief of Staff, General George C. Marshall, who placed his name on a list of chosen men destined for higher command in what Marshall expected to be the next global conflict.[110] As one of Marshall's protégés, Eisenhower would enjoy a meteoric rise during the Second World War being 'catapulted from the obscurity of the American peacetime Army' into the stratosphere of high command. On 25 June 1942, he was appointed commanding general of the European Theatre of Operations, followed in November 1942 by command of the Allied landings in North-West Africa, Operation *Torch*. In the same month Eisenhower was promoted Commander-in-Chief, Allied Forces in North Africa and thereafter Commander Allied forces in the Mediterranean, overseeing the campaigns in Tunisia, Sicily and Italy.[111]

On Christmas Eve 1943, he was appointed Supreme Commander of Allied forces for the forthcoming invasion of Europe. Consequently, Eisenhower would lead what can be regarded seventy years on as the 'most high-powered, experienced, intelligent, volatile, strong-minded and colourful cast of military and political characters ever assembled to make history'.[112] A natural diplomat and 'team player' in the Marshall mould, Eisenhower's talents would, nevertheless, be sorely tested in the months following D-Day due to deep-seated mistrust, jealousy and varying degrees of xenophobia within the Allied camp. As Supreme Allied Commander Eisenhower would be heavily criticised, particularly by the British, for his 'broad front' policy of attacking the Germans all along the frontline of western Europe, a strategy at odds with the 'single thrust' approach favoured by figures such as General Sir Bernard Montgomery. Yet it was the series of unilateral decisions he was obliged to take between the 3 and 5 June 1944 on whether or not to initiate, postpone or cancel the liberation of Europe that tested his true mettle as a coalition commander.

Having moved his headquarters from Bushy Park just outside London to Southwick House, Portsmouth, Naval HQ of Admiral Sir Bertram Ramsay, mastermind of Operation *Neptune*, on 2 June, Eisenhower set the stage for the final countdown to D-Day. Living sparsely in the grounds of Southwick House in a trailer he called 'my circus wagon',[113] Eisenhower would nevertheless visit the house regularly in order to consult with his Naval, Army and Air Force commanders, and more importantly his Chief Meteorological Officer, Group-Captain James Stagg of the RAF. Aside from the Germans the greatest threat to *Overlord/Neptune* was the weather in the English Channel. A low pressure front moving in from the Atlantic ensured that stormy weather began to jeopardize the entire venture placing Eisenhower in the unenviable position of being at the mercy of volatile weather patterns. In order to base his final launch decision upon the most up-to-date weather reports available, the Supreme Commander consulted Group-Captain Stagg twice a day, once in the early hours of the morning (0415 hours) and then later at night (2130 hours).[114] Rarely in history has a four-star general relied so heavily upon the specialist advice of a subordinate officer in order to commence an operation.

Yet the ramifications flowing from a postponement order were colossal. As one authority on the D-Day landings has reflected:

> Secrecy would be lost. Assault troops would be unloaded and crowded in barbed wire, where their original places would already have been taken by those to follow in subsequent waves. Complicated movement tables would be scrapped. Morale would drop. A wait of at least 14 days, possibly 28, would be necessary – a sort of suspended animation involving more than 2,000,000 men...The good weather period available would become still shorter and the enemy's defences would become still stronger...[115]

It was perhaps not surprising, therefore, that on 3 June Eisenhower confided to his diary: 'Probably no one who does not have to bear the specific and direct responsibility of making the final decision as to what to do can understand the intensity of these burdens'.[116] The situation, however, was to get a lot worse for the Supreme Commander, who at his 0415 hours meeting on the morning of 4 June, was informed by Stagg that no sign of an improvement in the weather had materialised. Consequently, Eisenhower was forced to postpone D-Day for twenty-four hours fully conscious of the attendant risks to the vast Allied armada bottled-up in British ports. Yet at 2130 hours that evening in the library at Southwick House, Stagg was in a position to promise a period of 'relatively good weather' over the next day or so.[117] At 0415 hours on the morning of 5 June, Eisenhower and his subordinate commanders met again for what would be their last meeting prior to the landings. Satisfied with Stagg's latest forecast, which was more optimistic than his previous reports, General Eisenhower uttered the immortal words: 'O.K., we'll go' thereby ordering the launch of the cross-Channel attack for Tuesday 6 June.[118]

Prior to the actual assault on Hitler's *Festung Europa* (Fortress Europe), every member of the Allied Expeditionary Force was issued General Eisenhower's 'Order of the Day'. The Supreme Commander had started to compose the edict in February 1944 and during the protracted drafting stage he made numerous amendments to it. As a consequence, he left his own very personal stamp on this historic document.[119] The final version, which was printed in May 1944 by Supreme Headquarters Allied Expeditionary Force (SHAEF), was designed so that it could easily be carried in a wallet or breast pocket by Allied servicemen, who, it was hoped, would draw upon it for inspiration and motivation during the testing times to come. As is evident, the wording of the document not only reflects the righteousness of the Allied cause, but also the profound confidence SHAEF placed in the vast forces at its disposal: 11,000 aircraft, 7,000 ships and 175,000 men for the initial assault.

Yet in the mind of the Supreme Commander, D-Day was anything but a foregone success. Worried sick by the unpredictable nature of the weather in the English Channel and the strong possibility that the Germans could intervene swiftly and turn *Overlord* into a bloodbath for the Allies, Eisenhower penned, after lunch on Monday 5 June, a press release to be used in the event of an Allied defeat on the beaches of Normandy:

> Our landings in the Cherbourg-Havre area have failed to gain a satisfactory foothold and I have withdrawn the troops. My decision to attack at this time and place was based upon the best information available. The troops, the air and the Navy did all that bravery and devotion to duty could do. If any blame or fault attaches to the attempt it is mine alone.[120]

The message was quite simple: Eisenhower would take full responsibility for any defeat on 6 June. Yet as history records, Operations *Overlord/Neptune* were, aside from the crisis on 'Omaha' beach and the inability of British 2nd Army to capture Caen on D-Day, a success. As a consequence of this great victory, Ike forgot all about the alternative press release kept in his wallet since before the invasion. Rediscovering it two weeks later, Ike, according to his naval aide, Captain Harry C. Butcher USN, 'pulled it out, laughed, and commented that thank goodness he had not had to issue it'.[121] Butcher, then witnessed his boss proceed to throw this piece of paper into a wastebasket thereby relegating it to the 'what ifs' of history.

NOTES

[108] Don Cook, 'General of the Army Dwight D. Eisenhower' in *The War Lords: Military Commanders of the Twentieth Century*, edited by Field Marshal Sir Michael Carver, (London: Weidenfeld & Nicolson, 1976), p. 509.

[109] Barrett Tillman, *Brassey's D-Day Encyclopedia: The Normandy Invasion A to Z*, (Washington DC: Brassey's Inc, 2004), p. 86.

[110] See Thomas E. Ricks, *The Generals: American Military Command from World War II to Today*, (London: The Penguin Press, 2012), pp. 17-58.

[111] Forrest C. Pogue, *United States Army in World War II: The European Theater of Operations: Supreme Command*, (Washington DC: Office of the Chief of Military History, Department of the Army, 1954), p. 8.

[112] Don Cook, 'General of the Army Dwight D. Eisenhower' in *The War Lords: Military Commanders of the Twentieth Century*, edited by Field Marshal Sir Michael Carver, (London: Weidenfeld & Nicolson, 1976), p. 509.

[113] Carlo D'Este, *Eisenhower: Allied Supreme Commander*, (London: Weidenfled & Nicolson, 2002), p. 518.

[114] Ibid., pp. 519-525.

[115] Winston G. Ramsey, *D-Day: Then and Now*, Volume 1, (London: Battle of Britain Prints International Ltd, 1995), pp. 156-157.

[116] Carlo D'Este, *Eisenhower: Allied Supreme Commander*, (London: Weidenfled & Nicolson, 2002), p. 519.

[117] Antony Beevor, *D-Day: The Battle for Normandy*, (London: Viking, 2009), p. 21.

[118] Forrest C. Pogue, *United States Army in World War II: The European Theater of Operations: Supreme Command*, (Washington DC: Office of the Chief of Military History, Department of the Army, 1954), p. 169 and Carlo D'Este, *Eisenhower: Allied Supreme Commander*, (London: Weidenfled & Nicolson, 2002), p. 526.

[119] Ibid.

[120] Ibid., p. 527.

[121] Stephen E. Ambrose, *D-Day: 6th June 1944: The Battle for the Normandy Beaches*, (London: Pocket Books, 2002), p. 595n.

Soldiers, Sailors and Airmen of the Allied Expeditionary Force!

You are about to embark upon the Great Crusade, toward which we have striven these many months. The eyes of the world are upon you. The hopes and prayers of liberty-loving people everywhere march with you. In company with our brave Allies and brothers-in-arms on other Fronts, you will bring about the destruction of the German war machine, the elimination of Nazi tyranny over the oppressed peoples of Europe, and security for ourselves in a free world.

Your task will not be an easy one. Your enemy is well trained, well equipped and battle-hardened. He will fight savagely.

But this is the year 1944! Much has happened since the Nazi triumphs of 1940-41. The United Nations have inflicted upon the Germans great defeats, in open battle, man-to-man. Our air offensive has seriously reduced their strength in the air and their capacity to wage war on the ground. Our Home Fronts have given us an overwhelming superiority in weapons and munitions of war, and placed at our disposal great reserves of trained fighting men. The tide has turned! The free men of the world are marching together to Victory!

I have full confidence in your courage, devotion to duty and skill in battle. We will accept nothing less than full Victory!

Good Luck! And let us all beseech the blessing of Almighty God upon this great and noble undertaking.

Dwight Eisenhower

TNA WO 219/5120 – General Eisenhower's 'Order of the Day'

TNA AIR 14/2041

OPERATIONS *TAXABLE* AND *GLIMMER*

In order to fulfil Winston Churchill's requirement that Operations *Overlord* and *Neptune* be protected by a 'bodyguard of lies', the British London Controlling Section (LCS), whose job it was to formulate and co-ordinate strategic deception, devised a host of tactical deception operations scheduled to be launched before, during and after D-Day. Code-named *Paradise One* through *Five*, *Big Drum*, *Taxable*, *Glimmer* and *Titanic I* through *IV*,[122] these *ruses de guerre* were concocted to disorientate and fool the *Oberkommando der Wehrmacht*, Hitler and Army Group B as to true Allied intentions before, during and after the launch of the Allies' Second Front. Two of the most sophisticated, elaborate and technically challenging operations were *Taxable* and *Glimmer*. Now largely forgotten, these missions were flown respectively by four-engine Lancaster and Short Stirling bombers of 617 and 218 Squadrons of the RAF.

Formed in March 1943, 617 Squadron – the famous 'Dambusters' – was an elite unit within RAF Bomber Command who, on the night of 16/17 May 1943, participated in Operation *Chastise*, a low-level, pin-point attack with aerial mines on the Möhne, Eder and Sorpe dams in central Germany. These strategically important dams supplied water and electricity to the Third Reich's industrial heartland, the Ruhr valley, and were therefore regarded as high value targets. Consequently, nineteen specially adapted Lancaster bombers led by Wing Commander Guy Gibson were dispatched to execute the mission. Although eight Lancasters were lost, the squadron succeeded in breaching the Möhne and Eder dams.[123] The squadron's specialised flying skills displayed during these raids therefore made them the ideal choice for Operation *Taxable*.

The aim of *Taxable* was to simulate, through electronic deception, a large 'ghost' convoy of ships approaching the coast at Cap d'Antifer, north of Le Havre. Designed partly to convince enemy radar stations (which had deliberately been left intact) that the Allies were in fact attempting a landing north of the Seine,[124] it also served to complement and reinforce the grand deception being practised on the Germans by the LCS, namely that the bulk of Allied forces in the form of the notional First United States Army Group (FUSAG), commanded by General George S. Patton, were based in the south-east of England and were poised to invade the Pas de Calais.[125]

Yet a lack of available heavy shipping to undertake this deception necessitated the use of aircraft employing Radio Counter Measures (RCM) in the form of 'Window'. 'Window' was the code name for an electronic counter-measure based on aluminium foil strips which when dropped from aircraft jammed German radar stations by creating false targets on their receiver screens. First employed by RAF Bomber Command on the night of 25 July 1943 during a raid on the German city of Hamburg (Operation *Gomorrah*) it proved to be highly successful in confusing the *Luftwaffe* as to the true number and position of attacking aircraft.[126] Consequently, it was seen as the perfect tool with which to conjure up for the benefit of the Germans a phantom fleet bound for the Pas de Calais.

Having received orders that the squadron would participate in the operation, the commanding officer of 617 Squadron, Group Captain Leonard Cheshire, put his aircrews through a period of intensive training beginning on 7 May 1944.[127] In tandem with a naval component, Special Task Force 'A', who would be using a variety of RCMs to fool the Germans, 617 Squadron would employ sixteen Lancaster bombers on the mission. The flight plan devised by the squadron to accomplish their mission was later explained by Cheshire:

> The tactics…were to use two formations of aircraft with the rear formation seven miles behind the leaders, each aircraft being separated laterally by two miles. Individual aircraft flew a straight course of seven miles, turned round and flew on the reciprocal one mile away. On completion of the second leg it returned to its former course and repeated the whole procedure over again, advancing far enough to keep in line with the convoy's speed of seven knots.[128]

What Cheshire did not describe, however, was the manner in which 'Window' was dispatched over the target area. Flying elliptical courses between Dover and Cap d'Antifer at an altitude of 3000ft and at a speed of 200 miles per hour, the releasing aircraft formed a 'box' 12 miles wide and 8 miles deep.[129] During the long legs of their orbit, which entailed flying either towards or away from the coast, the bombers would release a bundle of 'Window' every five seconds, or one bundle for every 400 metres flown. The overall effect of this complicated process was to create a large cloud of 'Window' measuring sixteen by fourteen miles. As each orbit took seven minutes and moved the formation of aircraft one mile further on, this cloud of 'Window' gave the impression of a vast invasion fleet 200 square miles in size moving towards the coast of France at a speed of 8.5 knots.[130] Having taken off at 2300 hours on 5 June, 617 Squadron would maintain this routine throughout the night until dawn on D-Day when they returned to base.

The naval component of *Taxable*, Special Task Force 'A', was commanded by Lieutenant-Commander Calder,[131] and comprised eight Harbour Defence Motor Launches from Portsmouth Command, which not only emitted fake radio traffic and produced low-level jamming, but also towed barrage balloons fitted with radar reflectors codenamed 'Filbert'.[132] Designed to 'simulate echoes given off by a large ship',[133] 'Filbert', in conjunction with 'Window', was employed to convince the Germans that a naval convoy travelling at seven knots across a 140 mile front was carrying an Allied force tasked with landing between Bruneval and Fécamp on the morning of 6 June. Commencing operations at 0037 hours on 6 June, Special Task Force 'A' sailed towards the French coast using radar and radio equipment to announce its presence to German radar operators. From a point seven miles off shore, Commander Calder's motor launches raced towards the coastline in order to simulate a landing. Stopping short by two miles, the flotilla then headed back to its original start point using smoke to cover its withdrawal. Having carried out its primary task, Calder's force laid a minefield off Capd'Antifer withdrawing shortly before dawn to avoid enemy fire.[134] Succeeding in avoiding any casualties or battle damage en route home, the force eventually sailed into the port of Newhaven at 1200 hours on D-Day. However, despite the professionalism and skill with which the Royal Navy and RAF performed their respective deception work, Operation *Taxable* did not achieve its ultimate aim, namely to draw a sharp reaction from the Germans. This failure was mainly attributed to the adverse weather conditions experienced in the English Channel that night.[135]

Taxable's twin operation, *Glimmer*, which was also launched during the night of 5/6 June, was carried out by 218 'Gold Coast' Squadron RAF. Commanded by Wing Commander R.M. Fenwick-Wilson, this squadron flew Short Stirling four-engine bombers and between 20 and 31 May conducted specialised training in preparation for their mission. Aside from flying different types of aircraft and being assigned separate targets (six Stirling bombers from 218 Squadron were ordered to fly circuits back and forth between the Straits of Dover and Boulogne) there were several differences between how each squadron performed their respective duties. In contrast to their sister squadron, 218 chose a different navigational flight plan, and as Fenwick-Wilson was not granted relief aircraft, each of his Stirlings would have a crew consisting of two pilots, three navigators and four crewmen to drop 'Window' at selected times.[136] However, in all other respects the techniques utilised by the two squadrons to simulate the sailing of two vast 'ghost' fleets towards France were identical.

In support of 218 Squadron was Special Task Force 'B' commanded by Lieutenant-Commander W.M. Rankin. Comprising twelve Harbour Defence Motor Launches and one Air Sea Rescue launch from Dover Command this naval force would split up into two smaller units during the execution of *Glimmer*. One group left Dungeness in order to target the beaches off Boulogne, while the second left the Thames and sailed towards the beaches of Dunkirk and those between Boulogne and the Somme.[137] As with *Taxable*, each launch would tow a barrage balloon with reflectors and would use RCM equipment and radio traffic to create the illusion that a large convoy was operating in the English Channel.[138] Commencing their work at 0110 hours, Commander Rankin's force, in conjunction with 218 Squadron flying over head dropping 'Window', spent the next few hours before dawn ensuring their presence was detected by German radar stations. Unlike *Taxable*, no mines were to be laid on this mission,[139] but by 0554 hours Special Task Force 'B' had completed its work and reached home port at 1300 hours on 6 June. A post-action report submitted by RAF Bomber Command stated that, in stark contrast to Operation *Taxable*, the Germans had indeed accepted the *Glimmer* deception sending E-Boats out into the Channel to investigate the phantom fleet.[140] Yet unlike their counter-parts in Special Task Force 'A', Rankin's force conducted their activities far to the north-east where the weather in the Channel was more conducive to such a complicated electronic deception operation.

NOTES

[122] Thaddeus Holt, *The Deceivers: Allied Military Deception in the Second World War*, (London: Weidenfeld & Nicolson, 2004), p. 578.

[123] See Paul Brickhill, *The Dam Busters*, (London: Pan, 1954).

[124] *D-Day Then and Now*, Volume 1, edited by Winston G. Ramsey, (London: Battle of Britain Prints International Ltd, 1995), p. 251.

[125] See Roger Hesketh, *Fortitude: The D-Day Deception Campaign*, (London: St Ermin's Press, 1999).

[126] *The Oxford Companion to the Second World War*, edited by I.C.B. Dear and M.R.D. Foot, (Oxford: Oxford University Press, 1995), p. 332.

[127] Mary Barbier, *D-Day Deception: Operation Fortitude and the Normandy Invasion*, (Westport, Connecticut: Praeger Publishers, 2007), p. 109.

[128] Hilary St George Saunders and Denis Richards, *Royal Air Force, 1939-45: The Fight is Won*, Volume III, (London: HMSO, 1954), p. 109.

[129] Major L.F. Ellis *et al.*, *Victory in the West: The Battle of Normandy*, Volume I, (London: HMSO, 1962), p. 160.

[130] *The Oxford Companion to the Second World War*, edited by I.C.B. Dear and M.R.D. Foot, (Oxford: Oxford University Press, 1995), p. 333. See also Jock Haswell, *D-Day Intelligence and Deception*, (New York: Times Books, 1979), p. 176.

[131] Mary Barbier, *D-Day Deception: Operation Fortitude and the Normandy Invasion*, (Westport, Connecticut: Praeger Publishers, 2007), 109.

[132] Jock Haswell, *D-Day Intelligence and Deception*, (New York: Times Books, 1979), pp. 175-176.

[133] Hilary St George Saunders and Denis Richards, *Royal Air Force, 1939-45: The Fight is Won*, Volume III, (London: HMSO, 1954), p. 109.

[134] Mary Barbier, *D-Day Deception: Operation Fortitude and the Normandy Invasion*, (Westport, Connecticut: Praeger Publishers, 2007), p. 71.

[135] Ibid.,, pp.109-110.

[136] Ibid., p. 110.

[137] Ibid., p. 71.

[138] Major L.F. Ellis *et al.*, *Victory in the West: The Battle of Normandy*, Volume I, (London: HMSO, 1962), p. 160.

[139] Mary Barbier, *D-Day Deception: Operation Fortitude and the Normandy Invasion*, (Westport, Connecticut: Praeger Publishers, 2007), p. 71.

[140] Ibid., p. 111.

TOP SECRET
APPENDIX "B"
to BC/TS.31627/Sigs dated 8ᵗʰ May 1944.
OPERATIONAL RESEARCH SECTION (B.C.)

NOTES ON THE SIMULATION OF SHIPPING BY WINDOW

GENERAL METHOD

1. It has been found that the illusion of a mass of shipping can be produced on ship-watching radar by the release of WINDOW along trails spaced 2 miles apart, provided that the height of release is less than 3,000 feet, the size of bundle is increased as the coast is approached and the WINDOW is replenished every 7 minutes.

2. A single aircraft making a series of elliptical orbits, each of 7 minutes duration, should be able to maintain two of the necessary trails, each of length about 8 miles. Thus two aircraft could maintain two trails of length 16 miles, and a total of eight aircraft flying in two boxes of four could cover the requirement of a breadth of 16 miles and a depth of 15 miles.

3. It is hoped that the movement of shipping can be simulated by advancing the positions of orbits gradually towards the coast. The exact procedure to be followed on an operation will be developed in training but the following paragraphs indicate a possible method.

SUGGESTED OPERATIONAL PLAN

4. The aircraft would fly in boxes of four. Those in each box would fly on straight tracks four miles apart and of length about 8 miles along GEE lattice lines towards the coast. They would then make an accurate rate 1 turn through 180° on to a course parallel to and 2 miles from their inward course, finally completing the orbit, with a rate 1 turn, within 7 minutes. The required form of orbit is illustrated in the attached Fig. 1.

5. One box of four aircraft would begin patrol on the length 30–38 miles from the coast and the second four on the length 38-46 miles away. The front four would fly at 3,000 feet and the rear four at 2,500 feet.

6. In order to represent the forward movement of shipping, the turning points (T_1 and T_2 on Fig. 1) would be moved nearer to the coast every orbit by an amount sufficient to produce an advance of the front at a rate of 5 knots. This represents a move forward every orbit of about 0.7 miles which should be made with an error of less than 0.25 miles. It is suggested that turning points should depend on the time for which the operation has been in progress. A suggested navigator's chart designed to facilitate this is shown in Fig. 1.

7. In order that the Radar shall "see" a uniform initial approach, the front box would attempt to approach the starting-line 30 miles from the coast in line abreast

/from .....

-2-

from 55-60 miles from the coast, but there would be no necessity thereafter for the aircraft to keep precisely in step. Both boxes should be on their starting-lines at the same time and there should be no gap and as little overlap as possible between the two boxes.

8. WINDOW would be released on the straight runs only during the progress of the operation, but the front box would also release during the 25-30 mile run up to the starting line. 12 bundles would be released during each one third of every straight run, the size of bundle being larger for the portions of the run nearer the coast. A schedule of the changes in WINDOW sizes required as the coast is approached is shown in Fig.2. The number of bundles required for each aircraft is shown in an Appendix.

SPECIAL REQUIREMENTS

9. The required rate of WINDOW launching is about 12 bundles per minute. In view of this high rate and the necessity for changes in bundle size, it is recommended that two WINDOW chutes be fitted to each aircraft and two aircrew be used for launching. One would release WINDOW during the inward run and one during the outward run, each using his rest period to position his supplies conveniently.

10. The WINDOW will be supplied in parcels containing twelve bundles of the same size i.e. one parcel will be released wholly before the next bundle size change. The bundle will require no manipulation before placing in the chute. Supplies of the correct material will be available for three full-scale trials, but standard WINDOW could be used for any necessary preliminary practices.

11. The success of the operation depends largely on the accuracy with which the general mass of WINDOW moves forward. The required accuracy in track-keeping is 0.5 miles, but it is essential that the turning points should be within 0.25 miles of the required position. The operation will allow aircraft to home on GEE lattice lines to the turning points and it is considered that the required accuracy can be maintained. Since, however, a concentrated effort lasting for 4 hours may be called for, it is most desirable that a relief navigator should be provided in every aircraft. The resting navigator would be usefully employed in checking the number of orbits completed and in giving the WINDOW droppers their directions.

12. In order to ensure that the change over between navigators takes place without any hiatus in the maintenance of accuracy and in order to cover the possibility of a GEE set becoming unserviceable, the provision of an extra GEE set in each aircraft is a necessity.

13. The GEE sets used will need to have the expanded strobe time-base together with the calibrated scales essential to its accurate use.

SCB/MTA

BC/S.31380/ORS   6/5/44

TNA AIR 14/2041 – Operations Taxable Glimmer – Air and Sea Deceptions operations, 5/6 June 1944

TNA WO 205/532

'G.S.I.21 ARMY GROUP WEEKLY NEPTUNE REVIEWS'

Between 1 February 1944 and 30 June 1944 some of the most vital operational intelligence reports concerning Operation *Overlord* were produced by British 21st Army Group. Entitled 'Weekly Neptune Intelligence Reviews', these appreciations were compiled by General Sir Bernard Montgomery's chief of intelligence at 21st Army Group, Brigadier E.T. 'Bill' Williams, one of the most gifted intelligence analysts of the Second World War.

At the outbreak of hostilities in September 1939, Williams was an embryonic Oxford don at Merton College where he held a Junior Research Fellowship in modern history. Having already been commissioned into the 1st King's Dragoon Guards (KDG) in June of that year as a special reserve officer, Williams deployed with the regiment to the Western Desert in late 1940. In February 1941, Williams had the distinction of being the first British soldier to make contact with Rommel's *Deutsche Afrika Korps* when his armoured car collided accidentally at night with a German half-track vehicle. In reporting this incident to his superiors (the first such confirmation that Rommel had landed in North Africa) Williams had unknowingly initiated a career in intelligence. Although subsequently promoted to the intelligence branch of the 1st KDG with the rank of Major, Williams was later posted to General Headquarters (GHQ) in Cairo due to the growing strain placed upon already weakened eyes by the intense African sun. It was there that he came to the attention of Colonel Freddie de Guingand, Director of Military Intelligence in the Middle East, who in 1942 transferred him to his intelligence staff in Cairo.[141]

When de Guingand became Chief of Staff to General Bernard Montgomery, the new commander of British 8th Army, in August 1942, Williams was asked to join him. So impressed was Montgomery by Williams' talents that he promoted him to be his head of intelligence in the field, a post Williams would serve in throughout later campaigns in Tunisia, Sicily and Italy.[142] On being designated Land Forces Commander for the Normandy landings in December 1943, Montgomery requested that Williams, now a Brigadier, serve as Chief of intelligence for 21st Army Group.[143] After the war Montgomery paid handsome tribute to Williams in his memoirs, stating that, 'Intellectually he was far superior to myself or to anyone on my staff...He saw the enemy picture whole and true; he could sift a mass of detailed information and deduce the right answer'.[144] In the months and weeks prior to D-Day these skills and qualities would be tested to the full.

As Montgomery's General Staff (Intelligence) (GS(I)), Brigadier E.T. Williams had access to all sources of top secret intelligence including ULTRA, the product of Bletchley Park's successes in breaking German and Axis high-level ciphers. Through 'all-source' analysis Williams prepared weekly intelligence summaries for 21st Army Group HQ on German dispositions and intentions. Not only were these seen by Montgomery they were also circulated to the Supreme Commander, General Eisenhower, and his staff at SHAEF and to Montgomery's subordinate commanders in 1st US Army (Lieutenant-General Omar N. Bradley), and British 2nd Army (Lieutenant-General Sir Miles Dempsey). In terms of the vast intelligence machine the Allies relied upon to aid their planners in formulating the *Overlord/Neptune* operations, Williams was a vital but relatively small cog. Higher up the intelligence hierarchy existed the Joint Intelligence Committee (JIC), the apex of British intelligence, which produced high-level assessments for Churchill, the War Cabinet and the Chiefs of Staff Committee. Higher still, in the stratosphere of the Allies' command structure, was COSSAC and its successor, SHAEF, both of which possessed their own intelligence staffs. Yet despite being a middle-ranking intelligence officer, Williams' 'product', namely his 'Weekly Neptune Review', carried a disproportionately higher weight than other rival papers. This was due to the fact that from January 1944 onwards 21st Army Group had come to 'dominate' operational planning for D-Day. Consequently, as the blueprint for *Overlord* was 'refined and applied between April and June 1944', intelligence assessments flowing from Williams' pen grow in importance.[145] However, in the weeks preceding D-Day Williams would produce, in light of the costly American landings at 'Omaha' beach, two of the most portentous intelligence estimates of his wartime career.

Issued weekly to all senior commanders in order to keep them abreast of developments in the dispositions and order-of-battle of German forces in France, Williams' Neptune Intelligence Reviews contained the most up-to-date intelligence the Allies possessed on these subjects. Having already disseminated on 23 April one of his weekly reviews in which he indicated that a significant reinforcement of 'Omaha' and 'Gold' beaches by German units had taken place, Williams issued on 14 May 1944 weekly Neptune Review No. 14. Narrowing his focus upon the Allies' intended assault area, Williams stated bluntly that:

> ...it is a most unsatisfactory state of affairs that we cannot specifically identify all the elements which go to make up the sector we are proposing to assault...This much [however] is evident – that we shall on D day make contact immediately with 716, 709 and 243 [divisions], the fringe of 711 and within a very short time 352 Infantry and 21 Panzer Divisions.[146]

Three weeks later on the morning of 4 June, the day Eisenhower postponed *Overlord/Neptune* by twenty-four hours due to appalling weather conditions, Williams circulated his final pre-assault Neptune Review. Once again, special emphasis was placed on the whereabouts in Lower Normandy of particular German divisions and their potential to thwart the landings.

As the official history of wartime British intelligence records, with regards pinpointing the exact location of the elusive 352nd Infantry Division, Williams 'came close to divining the truth' when he wrote:

> The evidence about 352 Division is…flimsy. For some time now in other areas coastal divisions have been narrowing their sectors while divisions, the role of which had hitherto been read as layback, have nosed forward into the gap provided by the reduced responsibility of the coastal divisions. 711 Division on the extreme left of 15 Army is a case in point, for it is apparent that elements of 346 Division have eased themselves into its former holding on the right just West of the Seine. The evidence that the same has happened on the left in the case of the 716 Division is slender indeed. A single soldier from 352 Division is reported to have been making for Arromanches in March…That 716 Division has followed the pattern of coastal readjustments is not substantiated; yet it should not be surprising if we discovered that it had two regiments in the line and one in reserve, while on its left 352 Division had one regiment up and two to play.[147]

Yet we now know that Montgomery's star Intelligence Officer was ultimately wrong about 352nd Division having 'one regiment up and two to play', for its commanding officer, Generalleutnant Dietrich Kraiss had committed two regiments to coastal defence duties and had kept one, *Kampfgruppe Meyer*, back as his strategic reserve.[148] The significance of these intelligence estimates, therefore, is that they deal with one of the greatest controversies and mysteries of the Normandy landings, namely the failure of Allied intelligence to pin-point the whereabouts of a crack German infantry division, the 352nd, prior to the Normandy landings.

The 352nd Infantry division, some of whose sub-units had already seen active service in North Africa and on the Eastern Front, was formed in France in November 1943 following the issuing of Führer Directive No. 51, which anticipated a major Allied offensive in the West.[149] Initially stationed at St Lô, the new 352nd Division, which comprised nine full strength battalions, was subsequently ordered by *Generalfeldmarschall* Erwin Rommel, commander of Army Group B, on 14 March 1944 to redeploy to the coast of Normandy.[150] By doing so, Kraiss's field division reinforced the static 716th Infantry Division led by *Generalleutnant* Wilhelm Richter whose area of responsibility stretched from the town of Carentan in the west to the mouth of the River Orne in the east. Entrusted with strengthening the left of Richter's sector (an area running from Carentan to the seaside resort of Asnelles in the east), Kraiss and his division effectively increased German forces on 'Omaha' and 'Gold' beaches by 150 per cent.[151] Yet despite possessing the 'best intelligence in the history of warfare',[152] Allied code-breakers and spy chiefs initially missed this fateful redeployment.

During the months leading up to D-Day, Allied intelligence came to rely heavily upon three sources of intelligence for up-to-date information on the development of the 'Atlantic Wall' and its defences. The first was ULTRA, the code name given to the signals intelligence (SIGINT) produced at Bletchley Park, the home of the Government Code & Cipher School (GC&CS), by means of the breaking of high-grade enemy ciphers and the analysis of intercepted signals. One of the strengths of ULTRA as a source of intelligence was that it was able to supply its restricted readership with the unit identities, orders-of-battle and dispositions of the German Army in the field. Prior to D-Day, the locations of fifty-six of the fifty-eight German divisions stationed in France had been identified by British intelligence by means of ULTRA. The two notable exceptions were the 352nd Infantry Division and the 21st Panzer Division both of which were to intervene decisively on 6 June.[153] Yet few historians have sought the reasons for why these two units succeeded in evading what has sometimes been thought of, mistakenly, as the all-seeing eye of ULTRA.

An exception was Ralph Bennett, a veteran of Bletchley Park and later an authority on wartime signals intelligence (SIGINT), who explained many years after the war that, although 'ULTRA was absolutely reliable when it appeared, it could not be relied on always to appear when needed or to answer every question explicitly'.[154] Certain factors outside the control of Allied intelligence against the successful interception and decryption of German and Axis radio traffic such as deliberate wireless silence on the part of the enemy; adverse weather conditions or 'fading', which could severe a radio link while a message was being transmitted; face-to-face meetings between enemy commanders and their subordinates; the use of couriers to convey messages between units; and the failure of Allied bombing to cut landlines prior to *Overlord*.[155] This last factor, in particular, would contribute greatly in rendering the Allies blind as to the locations and duties of specific German divisions for, as long there existed operable telephone networks, static divisions manning coastal defences were not obliged to communicate via their ENIGMA machines. This in turn thwarted Allied eavesdroppers, the 'Y' Service, whose job it was to pluck from the ether the Morse-code transmissions emitted by ENIGMA and to then pass them on to GC&CS for deciphering.

In light of these points, it is safe to conclude, therefore, that one or more of these factors did indeed help mask the presence of the 352nd division for, in the six month period preceding D-Day, the division was mentioned only once in an ULTRA decrypt dated 22 January 1944. While alerting the Allies to its existence and the fact that its position in the German order of battle placed it under the control of the Commander-in-Chief West, *Generalfeldmarschall* Gerd von Rundstedt, the decrypt failed, however, to divulge exactly where in France it was garrisoned. Yet, as has already been noted, this gap in Allied knowledge was not unique. Apart from the 21st Panzer Division, ULTRA knew even less about the 352nd Division's sister units, namely the 716th and 711th divisions who, aside from a brief reference to the incorporation of a Fusilier battalion into the latter division on 23 May, failed to appear in any decrypt prior to the Normandy landings.[156]

Even less helpful was the second source of intelligence the Allies relied on, specifically Photographic Reconnaissance (PR). Although millions of photographs of Hitler's 'Atlantic Wall' were taken by specialist squadrons in the years and months leading to Operation *Overlord*, PR could only record and monitor the proliferation of German defensive positions along the coast. When it came to identifying exactly which unit was manning specific coastal defences, PR was of little use to Anglo-American intelligence and their military 'customers'. It was indeed fortunate, therefore, that 'Bill' Williams was most likely alerted to the presence of *Generalleutnant* Kraiss's division behind the bluffs and beaches of 'Omaha' and 'Gold' by Human Intelligence (HUMINT), the work of spies. In terms of clandestine intelligence gathering in France, the British relied upon three covert organisations: the Special Operations Executive (SOE), formed in July 1940 to conduct sabotage, espionage and reconnaissance in occupied Europe in addition to the co-ordination of local resistance movements;[157] the Secret Intelligence Service (SIS), popularly known as MI6, who since 1909 had constituted Britain's main foreign intelligence agency; and the French Resistance which worked closely with both organisations.

Although much has been written on the SOE and the Resistance, the wartime activities of SIS, however, still remain shrouded in secrecy despite the recent publication of an authorised history.[158] That said, we now know from this history that two of the most important conduits of intelligence on German coastal defences and the static units garrisoning them were Colonel Claude Dansey's (Assistant Chief of SIS) French agent networks, which he had built-up over a period of two years in anticipation of D-Day,[159] and Commander Wilfred 'Biffy' Dunderdale's P.5 (French and Polish) networks.[160] Unsurprisingly, one of the greatest obstacles to both organisations in their pursuit of timely intelligence was German field security. Fully conscious of Allied efforts to spy on their activities, the *Wehrmacht* 'screened' all those who entered restricted zones and physically prevented any civilians from straying too close to their lines. Yet through a combination of stealth and guile, the SIS and the Resistance succeeded in surmounting these problems enabling them to send back to London a steady stream of HUMINT.

One of the methods employed by local resistance groups in the Normandy area to convey intelligence about German units and fortifications to the UK was by means of specially-trained carrier pigeons known as 'flying postmen'. In the context of the controversial landings at 'Omaha', this form of secret communication bred a persistent post-war myth in Lower Normandy, namely that shortly before D-Day the local Resistance group used carrier pigeons to warn the Allies of the arrival of the 352nd Division behind 'Omaha' and 'Gold' beaches. Yet legend has it that German soldiers armed with shot-guns downed these birds in flight thereby preventing the Allies from learning of the arrival of this crack unit. This tale, however, fails to take into account the fact that French Resistance cells, the SOE and the SIS all possessed Wireless Transmitters (W/T) through which they communicated vital information back to their superiors in the UK. It is therefore highly unlikely that any of the aforementioned covert intelligence services would have jeopardised the safe arrival of such vitally important intelligence by relying upon this highly-vulnerable form of messenger.[161]

Yet thanks to the declassification of WO 205/532 and the 'Weekly Neptune Reviews' contained therein, we can tentatively conclude that snippets of HUMINT on the 352nd Division and its location must have reached the desk of Brigadier Williams for him to have 'discovered the presence of 352nd Division' behind the beaches of 'Omaha' and 'Gold'.[162] But this in turn begs the real question, namely, why was this intelligence not acted upon by senior commanders at the time? One school of thought has it that Williams' report was so potentially explosive that it was consequently withheld from the lower ranks for fear that it would seriously undermine their morale.[163] Seventy years on we know this to be a myth. Williams himself later admitted to the official historian of the cross-Channel attack that despite deducing on 4 June that 'Omaha' had most likely been reinforced by Kraiss's crack field division, he simply 'could not warn the troops in time'.[164]

Nevertheless, the reason for this tragic breakdown in communication between 21st Army Group HQ and its subordinate units is still a matter of conjecture amongst historians. While some record that Williams' report *was* eventually circulated to all Allied corps and divisional commanders, albeit after they had put to sea with the invasion force,[165] others such as the notable historian, Carlo D'Este, author of *Decision in Normandy*, disagree. D'Este asserts that Williams' final pre-assault intelligence estimate never reached Major-General Leonard Gerow's US V Corps before D-Day owing to the fact that Colonel B.A. 'Monk' Dickson, head of intelligence for US 1st Army, was prevented from alerting V Corps to these changes in the German order-of-battle due to the strict wireless silence imposed aboard his command vessel and across the Allied armada in general.[166] Whatever the true reasons behind this intelligence *débâcle*, the ignorance surrounding this scrap of intelligence would have fateful consequences for the US V Corps on D-Day, who would suffer terribly at the hands of the 352nd Division.

During the build-up to the invasion, the men of V Corps's subordinate divisions, namely the US 29th Infantry Division (the 'Gray and the Blue'), the US 1st Infantry Division (the 'Big Red One') and the 2nd and 5th US Ranger battalions had been briefed by Intelligence Officers that the only resistance they would encounter on D-Day would be from the static 716th Infantry Division, which was plagued by low morale and comprised mostly of Poles, Russians and other nationalities press-ganged into service by the *Wehrmacht*. The poor calibre of this division, so it was claimed, meant that it would not seek prolonged combat and would certainly be in no position to launch a major counter-attack against the Allied spearhead.[167] Yet at 0630 hours (H-Hour) on the morning of 6 June, the 'Big Red One', the 'Blue and the Gray' and their counterparts in the US Rangers encountered devastating artillery, mortar and small-arms fire as the ramps of their landing-craft were lowered. The ensuing carnage and subsequent loss of momentum were so bad that at 0830 hours, General Omar N. Bradley, Commander of US 1st Army, whose HQ was aboard the USS *Augusta*, considered withdrawing troops from the beaches and re-directing the follow-up waves to land at 'Utah' beach and at the British beaches to the east, namely 'Gold' and 'Sword'.[168]

Thanks to the intervention of the 352nd Division, the slaughter on what would eventually be referred to as 'Bloody Omaha' was, in relative terms, colossal. Virtually every unit that landed on 'Charlie', 'Dog', 'Easy' and 'Fox' sectors of 'Omaha' beach in the initial assault waves were badly mauled. Some units such as A Company of 116th Regiment, 29th Infantry Division, were virtually wiped out.[169] Yet astonishingly uncertainty still surrounds the exact number of casualties incurred by V Corps on D-Day. Estimates vary from 2,000, as stated by the US official history of the cross-Channel attack to 2,374 as recorded in the *V Corps History*.[170] Stephen E. Ambrose, meanwhile, calculates them to be approximately 2,200.[171] Nevertheless, these figures are, in the opinion of the US Army's official history, 'frankly a guess', as 'under the Army's…casualty reporting system, it is unlikely that accurate figures of D-Day losses by unit will ever be available'.[172]

The destructive power of Kraiss's troops was not confined solely to 'Omaha'. The 352nd Division also inflicted heavy casualties on elements of the British 50th (Northumbrian) Infantry Division landing on 'JIG' sector of 'Gold' Beach, and was instrumental in seriously disrupting Operation *Aubrey*, the British mission to capture the strategically important fishing port at Port-en-Bessin. Marking the boundary between the US 1st Army and the British 2nd Army, Port-en-Bessin should have been captured on D-Day by No. 47 Royal Marine Commando. Instead, the Commando was obliged to fight a desperate three-day battle against a strong German garrison which they had not expected to meet.[173] Although Anglo-American units would eventually overcome such stubborn resistance, the 352nd Division did achieve one notable success on D-Day, namely preventing the US V Corps and British 2nd Army from achieving a number of objectives set by Allied planners. Yet this was something of a Pyrrhic victory as by midnight on 6 June the 352nd Infantry Division had almost ceased to exist as a coherent fighting force due to the loss of its strategic reserve (*Kampfgruppe Meyer*) to Allied fighter bombers, and the crippling casualties its battalions suffered along the Normandy coastline. Moreover, just two months later its erstwhile leader, *Generalleutnant* Dietrich Kraiss would die near St. Lô of wounds sustained during the Battle of Normandy.[174]

Yet the failure to convey to the assault divisions the presence of the 352nd Division begs the question: what if the intelligence had reached V Corps in time? One historian has asserted that, 'sure knowledge of the location of 352 Division could have done nothing to stem the slaughter at Omaha beach', observing that while this omission did indeed 'cost lives' it did not lose the battle'.[175] Nevertheless, if the course of events had gone against the Allies on the morning of 6 June, failure at 'Omaha' could have created a vast gap between US VII Corps at 'Utah' beach in the west and the British XXX Corps at 'Gold' beach in the east, a situation that could so easily have been exploited by the Germans. Moreover, the ignorance of US V Corps as to the calibre of the enemy they were to face on 'Omaha' ensured that the risks attendant of such an amphibious assault multiplied dramatically. Through the absence of timely intelligence on the subject, a basic precept of warfare was broken, specifically to 'know one's enemy'. In hindsight, pre-knowledge of the enemy would, at the very least, have given US forces a fighting chance on D-Day. Not only would this have allowed them to prepare mentally for the assault, it would also have granted them the chance to alter their fire plans, employ suitable weaponry, change tactics and to request longer naval and air bombardments prior to H-Hour. That said, even if Major-General Gerow's corps had been notified as to the presence of the 352nd Division, his men faced a still greater obstacle to a successful seaborne landing, namely geography.

As early as January 1944, US 1st Army HQ was acutely aware of the magnitude of the physical defences on 'Omaha' through the work of British Combined Operations Pilotage Parties (COPP), who had landed on this strip of coastline at night in order to reconnoitre it. Captain Scott-Bowden, a Royal Engineers officer attached to COPP, had participated in these covert operations and as a consequence was summoned to Norfolk House, St James's Square, HQ of SHAEF, to brief General Bradley as to the state of German defences at 'Omaha'. Before leaving this briefing, however, Scott-Bowden turned to Bradley and said, 'Sir, I hope you don't mind my saying it…but this beach is a very formidable proposition indeed and there are bound to be tremendous casualties' to which Bradley replied somewhat ominously, 'I know, my boy, I know'.[176] Quite simply, the geography of the Lower Normandy coastline dictated that V Corps could not land anywhere else other than the area already designated for the landings. The sheer complexity of *Overlord/Neptune* meant that 'operations and operational intelligence' became 'prisoners of prior planning' precluding any change to the agreed blueprint for the seaborne assault.[177] As a consequence, the men of the US 1st and 29th infantry divisions faced a *fait accompli* and would pay a very heavy price on D-Day for the rigidity of Allied planning and the absence of Williams' intelligence appreciation.

NOTES

[141] See C.S. Nicholls, 'Williams, Sir Edgar Trevor [Bill] (1912-1995), University administrator and Intelligence Officer', *Oxford Dictionary of National Biography*, (Oxford: Oxford University Press, 2004).

[142] Ibid.

[143] Nigel Hamilton, *Monty: Master of the Battlefield, 1942-1944*, (London: Hamish Hamilton, 1983), p. 529.

[144] *The Memoirs of Field Marshal The Viscount Montgomery of Alamein, K.G.*, (London: Collins, 1968), p. 167.

[145] John Ferris, 'Intelligence and OVERLORD: A Snapshot from 6 June 1944', Chapter 14, in *The Normandy Campaign 1944: Sixty Years On*, edited by John Buckley, (Abingdon, Oxon: Routledge, 2006), p. 186.

[146] TNA WO 205/532, 'G.S.I. 21 Army Group Weekly Reviews, Bigot Top Secret', 'GSI 21 Army Group Weekly Neptune Review, No. 14, Based on information available to 0900 hrs 14 May 44, Bigot Top Secret', p. 2.

[147] TNA WO 205/532, 'G.S.I. 21 Army Group Weekly Reviews, Bigot Top Secret', 'GSI 21 Army Group Weekly Neptune Review, No. 17, Based on information available to 0900 hrs 4 June 44, Bigot Top Secret', p. 1

[148] F.H. Hinsley *et al.*, *British Intelligence in the Second World War: Its Influence on Strategy and Operations*, Volume 3, Part 2, (London: HMSO, 1988), pp. 842-843.

[149] *Hitler's War Directives, 1939-1945*, edited by Hugh Trevor-Roper, (Edinburgh: Birlinn Ltd, 2004), pp. 218-224.

[150] F.H. Hinsley *et al.*, *British Intelligence in the Second World War: Its Influence on Strategy and Operations*, Volume 3, Part 2, (London: HMSO, 1988), p. 842.

[151] John Ferris, 'Intelligence and OVERLORD: A Snapshot from 6 June 1944', Chapter 14, in *The Normandy Campaign 1944: Sixty Years On*, edited by John Buckley, (Abingdon, Oxon: Routledge, 2006), p. 196.

[152] Christopher Andrew, 'Bletchley Park in Pre-war Perspective', Chapter 1, in *Action This Day: Bletchley Park from the Breaking of the Enigma Code to the birth of the modern computer*, edited by Michael Smith and Ralph Erskine, (London: Bantam Press, 2001), p. 1.

[153] Noel Annan, *Changing Enemies: The Defeat and Regeneration of Germany*, (London: Harper Collins, 1995), p. 101.

[154] Ralph Bennett, *Ultra in the West: The Normandy Campaign of 1944-45*, (London: Hutchinson & Co Publishers Ltd, 1980), p. 35.

[155] Ibid., pp. 35-36.

[156] Ibid., p. 55.

[157] See M.R.D. Foot, *SOE In France: An Account of the Work of the British Special Operations Executive in France, 1940-1944*, (London: HMSO, 1966), p. 8.

[158] See Keith Jeffery, *MI6: The History of the Secret Intelligence Service, 1909-1949*, (London: Bloomsbury, 2010).

[159] Ibid., p. 476.

[160] Ibid., pp. 529-536.

[161] Jock Haswell, *The Intelligence and Deception of the D-Day Landings*, (London: B.T. Batsford Ltd, 1979), pp. 145-146.

[162] Gordon A. Harrison, *US Army in World War II: European Theater of Operations: Cross-Channel Attack*, (Washington DC: Office of the Chief of Military History, Department of the Army, 1951), p. 319n.

[163] Jock Haswell, *The Intelligence and Deception of the D-Day Landings*, (London: B.T. Batsford Ltd, 1979), pp. 145-146.

[164] Gordon A. Harrison, *US Army in World War II: European Theater of Operations: Cross-Channel Attack*, (Washington DC: Office of the Chief of Military History, Department of the Army, 1951), p. 319n.

[165] John Ferris, 'Intelligence and OVERLORD: A Snapshot from 6 June 1944', Chapter 14, in *The Normandy Campaign 1944: Sixty Years On*, edited by John Buckley, (Abingdon, Oxon: Routledge, 2006), p. 197.

[166] Carlo D'Este, *Decision in Normandy*, (London; Robson Books, 2000), p.113n.

[167] F.H. Hinsley *et al.*, *British Intelligence in the Second World War: Its Influence on Strategy and Operations*, Volume 3, Part 2, (London: HMSO, 1988), p. 843.

[168] Stephen E. Ambrose, *D-Day: June 6, 1944: The Battle for the Normandy Beaches*, (London: Pocket Books, 2002), p. 360. See also, Antony Beevor, *D-Day: The Battle for Normandy*, (London: Viking, 2009), p. 104.

[169] Ibid., p. 112.

[170] Gordon A. Harrison, *US Army in World War II: European Theater of Operations: Cross-Channel Attack*, (Washington DC: Office of the Chief of Military History, Department of the Army, 1951), pp. 330-330n.

[171] Stephen E. Ambrose, *D-Day: June 6, 1944: The Battle for the Normandy Beaches*, (London: Pocket Books, 2002), p. 541.

[172] Gordon A. Harrison, *US Army in World War II: European Theater of Operations: Cross-Channel Attack*, (Washington DC: Office of the Chief of Military History, Department of the Army, 1951), p. 330n.

[173] See John Forfar, *From Omaha to the Scheldt: The Story of 47 Royal Marine Commando*, (East Linton, East Lothian: Tuckwell Press, 2001).

[174] Barrett Tillman, *Brassey's D-Day Encyclopedia: The Normandy Invasion A to Z*, (Washington DC: Brassey's Inc, 2004), p. 132.

[175] John Ferris, 'Intelligence and OVERLORD: A Snapshot from 6 June 1944', Chapter 14, in *The Normandy Campaign 1944: Sixty Years On*, edited by John Buckley, (Abingdon, Oxon: Routledge, 2006), p. 197.

[176] Antony Beevor, *D-Day: The Battle for Normandy*, (London: Viking, 2009), pp. 8-9.

[177] John Ferris, 'Intelligence and OVERLORD: A Snapshot from 6 June 1944', Chapter 14, in *The Normandy Campaign 1944: Sixty Years On*, edited by John Buckley, (Abingdon, Oxon: Routledge, 2006), p. 193n.

BASED ON INFORMATION AVAILABLE
TO **0900** HRS **14** MAY **44**

SEEN

Brig	....
G1 (A)	....
G1 (B)	....
G2 (A)	....
G2 (B)	....
G3(A)	....
PA(B)	....
PA	....

1. DEVELOPMENTS IN THE WEST

From a very confusing week emerges a clear reinforcement of the NEPTUNE area. Late last month and continuing into May a drastic redisposition of enemy armour was proceeding. The areas where the enemy seems most worried may be judged only by the shape of his layout and from what we know of recent movements. The Pas de Calais and the mouth of the Seine are both stiff with infantry, while it is to the area between the Seine and the Loire that his armour has been coming. Of the ten Panzer type divisions in the West four are within this circlet, a fifth on the banks of the Seine and what should be the best of the remainder is disposed either side of the Somme. Although Rundstedt is the Commander-in-Chief, it is becoming increasingly apparent that the somewhat elderly infantryman has handed over, or has had wrenched from him, the command of the two Armies from Brittany to Holland and that within this area the majority of the best Panzer divisions is assembling. Rundstedt appears directly to command the Biscay and Mediterranean Armies and to exercise a general suzerainty only over the younger and more favoured Field-Marshal What Geyr is doing it is difficult to see. Nominally Panzer Group West controls the armoured formations in France directly under Rundstedt. Yet it is difficult to see how, with the majority of them in what has become so evidently Rommel's sphere of influence, Geyr can be very much more than a general who sees that the armour is ripe for a battle in which it will be commanded by somebody else. Geyr is Rundstedt's tank man, perhaps, before the advent of Rommel, intended by the Commander-in-Chief to fight the armoured battle for him. But Hitler's Panzer protege is unlikely to brook much interference and it is far more likely that Rommel will be early at Caen and Bayeux, exercising a very personal command while Geyr bellyaches to Rundstedt and Rommel sidetracks them both because of his favour with the Führer.

21 Panzer Division has moved up into the area just South of the beaches. From 29 April onwards important troop movements have been reported towards Caen, Falaise and Argentan by road and rail through Domfront and Sées. All appear to have included tanks and tracked carriers. On 7 May a large concentration of armoured vehicles was reported in the Foret de Cinglais between Caen and Falaise. 21 Panzer Division has moved from its station at Rennes to a new one in Calvados, close South of Caen, and with its tanks apparently East of the River Orne. The appearance of elements of 21 Panzer Division on the railway East of Granville, which excited mild curiosity last week, now reveals its true purpose. The exact area occupied by the division, and its dispositions within the area, are not yet known; but on any reckoning it now lies but a short run from the Eastern beaches of the Neptune area.

Deeper inland the railways have been very busy. A movement of two heavy tank battalions from Mailly was reported last week. One went to the area of 179 Panzer Training Division North of Paris; one to Thouars. A simultaneous movement to Thouars, now known to have been a similar series of tank trains, is probably that same movement as was previously reported to be carrying a heavy tank battalion from Wezep in Holland into France. These movements to Thouars were assumed to be reinforcements for 17 SS Panzer Grenadier Division. That is now most unlikely. Thouars was a transit station only, and the two tank battalions presumably went on to the South. Furthermore, before the arrival of 17 SS Panzer Grenadier Division was, on 30 April, reported by one aeurce to be "moving to the West". This is not yet confirmed; but if true may mean that 17 SS has made a knight's move by way of Nantes to Rennes to replace 21 Panzer Division. This demands confirmation.

Nor is this the whole of the movement to West France. From 3 May onwards a large movement of 79 trains, no less than 34 of which are reported as of the type which carries heavy tanks and equipment, ran into France through Orleans to Chateau du Loir. Most went on to an unknown destination; but 11 trains discharged at Chateaudun and one each at Orleans and Chateau du Loir. The contents of this movement, which must be comparable in size with a complete armoured division, are not known. The only single movement hitherto recorded as having so many heavy tank trains is that which, in March, carried a great assembly of armoured units away from Eastern France at the time of the crisis in the Ukraine and South-East Europe. The most obvious explanation is that those troops, some at least of whom were Panzer demonstration units, and who were at the time reported as a Panzer division, have now been brought back to the West. And if 17 SS Panzer Grenadier division has moved North-West to replace 21 Panzer Division around Rennes, this new arrival may in its turn replace it by the Loire. The net result of this readjustment is to add a Panzer division to the immediate reinforcement of the Neptune beaches, so that 21 Panzer Division is now poised behind the right of 716 Division just as 352 Infantry Division is available to seal off any penetration through its left.

A further movement into North-West France, though less remarkable, is equally obscure. From 3 to 9 May 23 trains, seven of which were tank trains, came from Germany (which, it must be remembered, includes for this purpose Alsace and Lorraine) through Tours westwards, perhaps in the direction of Nantes. It is impossible to say what this movement carried. It is too small for an infantry division, which in any case should have no need of tank trains; and much too large for a tank battalion. One more unknown is added to our anthology.

Reports of Tiger tanks with the crossed keys sign at Aumale seem to confirm the presence of I SS Panzer Corps between the Somme and Seine, though further East than we expected. Its Corps troops seem to be widely distributed over the Department of Seine Inferieure - for some of the trains which brought them in ran as far as Mantes and possibly Rouen too. Where the Panzer Corps to control the Panzer divisions in the Neptune area is to be found is not yet evident. Though Rommel may command them direct, they will need a Corps HQ for administration.

In last week's Review the mysterious train movement away from Bayeux and Caen could not be explained. It is still regarded as most unlikely that 716 Division which, for all its deficiencies, knows the area bunker by bunker, could have been taken away at this juncture. Whatever left - and we can only hope for reports from Brittany telling us what arrived there - it is apparent that the defences in the sector of 716 Division exhibit a front of three regiments each with two battalions forward and apparently all their companies in the line; and some 4,000 yards inland the reserve battalions digging defences aimed to give landward depth to the crust just as the underwater obstacles extend it seaward. If the camera cannot tell a lie it never yields the whole truth and it is a most unsatisfactory state of affairs that we cannot specifically identify all the elements which go to make up the sector we are purposing to assault, nor are we able to say what was put in the trains which so recently left it. This much is evident - that we shall on D day make contact immediately with 716, 709 and 243, the fringe of 711 and within a very short time 352 Infantry and 21 Panzer Divisions. It should not be long before 12 SS Division has moved up from Lisieux and if 17 SS Panzer Grenadier has replaced 21 Panzer Division around Rennes, it will be on the move so soon as the shape of our assault is evident.

The infantry division which recently arrived upon the coast at Fecamp is now identified with 84 Division, previously at Rouen; and 331 Infantry Division, identified last week in the Pas de Calais, seems to be the same as the division lately held unidentified at Lille. The unlikely formation reported at Laon is dropped for lack of further evidence. But against these reductions we must add two new formations, both somewhat dubious: whatever left Calvados for the Cotes du Nord at the end of April, and that which came in from an Easterly direction through Tours at the beginning of May.

Movement is still going on within Rundstedt's command and the enemy is still not at his action stations. But the pattern is formulating and, with a time lag, clarifying, and from it we can see that Rommel is gaining his way and organising as many of the sixty division as he can get his hands on to meet one of three main eventualities: assaults upon the Pas de Calais; astride Le Havre; or either side of the Cherbourg peninsula.

GSI 21 ARMY GROUP
WEEKLY NEPTUNE REVIEW
NO. 17

BASED ON INFORMATION AVAILABLE
TO 0900 HRS 4 JUNE 44

1. DEVELOPMENTS IN THE WEST

The chief gaps in our knowledge of the enemy in the Neptune area are the strength and location of 21 Panzer Division, the location of 352 Division and whether 245 Division is in the area. Nothing more has come to light about 21 Panzer Division; but there is slowly growing evidence in photographs of tank tracks North of Caen – Bayeux lateral. The evidence about 352 Division is as flimsy. For some time now in other areas coastal divisions have been narrowing their sectors while divisions, the role of which has hitherto been read as layback, have nosed forward into the gap provided by the reduced responsibility of the coastal divisions. 711 Division on the extreme left of the 15 Army is a case in point, for it is apparent that elements of 346 Division have eased themselves into its former holding on the right just West of the Seine. The evidence that the same has happened on the left in the case of 716 Division is slender indeed. A single soldier from 352 Division is reported to have been making for Arromanches in March, and in late May Vire was reported empty of troops. That 716 Division has followed the pattern of coastal readjustments is not substantiated; yet it should not be surprising if we discovered that it had two regiments in the line and one in reserve, while on its left 352 Division had one regiment up and two to play. Were this so, the suspicion that 245 Division is in the area would grow likelier; elements were reported at St Lô in February and have not been mentioned since. If 352 has adopted a partly positional task the need for another layback division is obvious. In the same way in the Contentin peninsula it is suspected that 709 Division has reduced its coastal holding to the Eastern coast while 243 Division has taken over from the Western responsibility. 91 Division may look both ways in the meantime and be ready to seal off penetration into either flank. 352 Division may have a task like 243's, 245 (if it be there) like 91's: which is all very neat and tidy but rationalised beyond our evidence.

While the allied offensive in Italy has continued to prosper there is still no substantiation of the move of 9 Panzer Division over the border, a move which grows less likely as the avenues are blocked by our bombing, reinforcements arrive from other theatres and Overlord draws nearer.

From First Army's zone comes the suggestion that 273 Panzer Training Division has become 11 Panzer Division and it seems probable in view of the earlier report of 9 Panzer that, rather than the Panzer Training Divisions being renumbered as we have suggested, they have been poured wholesale into battered Panzer divisions from the Eastern front, which have taken over their operational responsibilities at the same time as they have absorbed their personnel. What returning division 179 Panzer Training Division North of the Seine will be tipped into remains to be seen: the Viennese association of "16 Grenadier and 10 Panzer" with "9 Panzer" (which has in fact arrived) throws up two possibilities. Another point which arises is that of some of the puzzling train moves into France may perhaps now be explained as the arrival of these hungry skeletons: one in particular, which is in the second week in May came to rest in the same area as the troops of I SS Panzer Corps, and adjoining those of 179 Panzer Training Division.

The similar conversion of infantry training divisions seems to have been carried now as far as is intended. 156 was known to have become 47; and it is now established that 171 and 191 have become 48 and 49 respectively. There is no evidence that any others have been converted in the West. Two reports of a 43 Division at Laon in March seemed for a time to hint at it: but the report is not supported by evidence of troops in the area.

The increase in the number of infantry divisions in Fifteenth Army has for some time called for a further Corps Headquarters: and documentary evidence has now been received that LXVII Corps commands the divisions on each side of the River Somme: the same Headquarters, it seems, as formerly, under the title of LXVII Reserve Corps, was responsible for the Western half of Nineteenth Army in the South. There is however no indication of any new Infantry Corps Headquarters in Seventh Army. The increase in its infantry divisions has perhaps not been enough to call for one; and its principal need would seem to be rather a Headquarters to replace II SS Panzer Corps, which left Alençon in March. To some extent this role might be filled by II Para Corps; which, though last located at Melun in March, is likely to have moved West with the general flow of paratroops into Brittany. A Parachute Corps is of course quite capable of commanding other troops, including armour. In fact the command of I Para Corps in Italy has lately consisted of two infantry, one parachute and one Panzer Grenadier divisions: and in the first counter-attacks against the Anzio bridgehead it commanded Panzer divisions as well. Nevertheless there would seem to be scope for both II Para Corps and a Panzer corps West of the Seine.

2 THE ATTACK ON ENEMY COMMUNICATIONS IN THE WEST

Since the beginning of March our air attacks have been directed in considerable measure against enemy rail communications in France and Belgium. In the last two weeks they have turned also to road communications. As these attacks reach their climax it is pertinent to examine the effect produced on the enemy's ability to move his reserves by road and rail and to supply them in battle.

The attacks may be divided into a strategical phase, when our target was the rail facilities of Northern and Eastern France and Belgium, and a tactical phase where the policy of attrition was supplemented by one of actual interdiction, by attacks on bridges and viaducts and by straightforward line cutting. The two phases have been dovetailed, for attacks on locomotive servicing facilities and marshalling yards succeeded in imposing some delay in the overall speed of rail movement and facilitated the work of tactical attack by imposing a reduction on the flexibility of the system as a whole.

The capacity of any system of rail routes depends on four things: the existence of through lines for the trains to run on; the existence of waggons to make up the trains; locomotives to haul them; and facilities to service the locomotives spaced at reasonable intervals along the routes. The importance of the last must not be overstressed, for maintenance in the open is always possible and in fact prevalent in military rail working.

The normal capacity of the lines running from North and North-East into the NEPTUNE area is about 700 trains per day. Of the 13 main lines running into the area not more than six have been cut by the strategic bombing at any one time. Allowing for slow working, hand signalling etc on the running lines reopened through damaged yards and general operating disorganisation, it is fair to assess that the capacity of the lines from the North and North-East has been reduced to about 400 trains per day. This will be more than adequate for the peak troop and supply movement likely to be carried over these lines. The greatest tightening in this area has occurred in the last week as a result of extraordinarily successful attacks on Seine railway bridges and the Paris-Ceinture junctions.

With the exception of the bridge at Conflans St Honorine, which is damaged, all rail bridges over the Seine below Paris are now down and likely to remain so for the first three weeks of June. The result will be that the enemy will be forced to detrain North of the river or attempt to move slowly through the damaged Paris junctions.

The total line capacity into the NEPTUNE area from the South and South-West is estimated at 400 trains per day for steam working. In view of the lesser degree of disorganisation to rail centres in the area compared with the situation in the North and North-East (apart from interference with electrified working for which allowance has been made) it is considered that on the average only one line (equivalent to the capacity of 60 trains) is likely to be unusable at any one time, and that the capacity of the remainder will be reduced by 25 per cent. That leaves a capacity of say 250 trains which will easily cover all required traffic.

The waggon situation is not really strained. At the end of 1943 there were in France and Belgium about 250,000 waggons (98,500 covered, 120,000 open and 33,500 flat). In addition at any one time there are at least 50,000 German waggons in circulation in France and Belgium and about 15,000 German waggons made up in standard troop trains and used for that purpose. A precise estimate of the number of waggons which has been put out of action in air attacks during 1944 to date is not possible, but consideration of the loading of yards attacked and the scale of the damage inflicted, together with the difficulty of organising rapid repair under present conditions, leads to the conclusion that the total number now out of action is about 25,000, or only 8 per cent of stocks. There should be an ample margin over essential requirements.

The locomotive situation is very similar. It is estimated that at the end of 1943 there were in France and Belgium about 13,400 locomotives. About 1,800 of them have become total losses, leaving 11,600. A further 25 per cent of these must be considered to be in service sheds for running repairs. Consequently, there are about 9,000 fully operational locomotives in France and Belgium. It is estimated that not more than 1,200 of them, or 13 per cent, will be required for peak military requirements during OVERLORD.

Locomotive servicing facilities have been hard hit but not vitally. In the general area covered by the attacks, the locomotive running sheds have an aggregate maximum servicing capacity of about 20,000 locomotives. It is estimated that capacity equal to 3,400 locomotives (17 per cent to total) is now destroyed, and an additional 10 per cent is still out due to impairment of access tracks. Remaining capacity within the general area of attacks is 73 per cent of pre-raid capacity. The peak requirement for OVERLORD is six per cent only.

It is clear from the above that the strategic bombing of rail centres to date has not reduced rail capacity to below the enemy's essential military requirements for movement and supply. There has, however, been a not inconsiderable general weakening of the system, which will cause some delays. Delay imposed on a division moving from the French/Belgian frontier with high priority to the Seine area may be about 6 - 12 hours. Delay to divisions from South and South-West will be less. The greatest delay will result from the cutting of the Seine bridges and the bombing of the Grand Ceinture junctions. If the Paris junctions can be kept out the great bonus is that the enemy will have to detrain North of the Seine, and then move into the battle area by road.

His movement by road will be far from easy, for outstanding success has been achieved in attacks on the Seine road bridges. Of the 13 road bridges between Paris and the sea, one (Le Mesnil Ande) has been down since 1940). Of the remaining 12, three only are now serviceable, the West bridge at Rouen (slightly damaged), the bridge at Courseulles-Sur-Seine, and that at Rangiport. Repairs are in progress to the bridges at Elbeuf, Le Manoir and to the East bridge at Rouen. The enemy will have to fall back on the Seine ferries, of which there is a limited number (several below Rouen). This method will be slow and will produce bottlenecks which will result in 'tails' vulnerable to strafing.

Catalogue of German Divisions in France and the Low Countries at 4 June 44:

PANZER

2, 9, 11, 21, (179), Lehr	
1 SS, 2 SS, 12 SS	9

PANZER GRENADIER

17 SS	1

PARACHUTE

3, 5, ? 6	2	+	? 1

INFANTRY

331,			
84, 85, 91			
352, 353			
319, 326, 338			
242, 243, 244, ? 245			
265, 266			
271, 272, 275, 276, 277			
343, 344, 346, 347, 348			
708, 709, 711, 712, 716, 719			
16, 17, 18, 19, GAF			
47, 48, 49 = 37 + 1?			
Dieppe, St Malo, Pyrenees	40	+ ?	1

INFANTRY TRAINING

148, 157, 158, 159, 165, 182, 189	7		
	....		
	59	+ ?	2
	....		

Main Headquarters,
21 Army Group,

No 1 APDC,
LONDON, W.1.

McK.   BGS 'I'

TNA AIR 27/1648

OPERATIONS RECORD BOOK NO. 297 SQUADRON RAF - 1-8 JUNE 1944

Seventy years on the D-Day landings can be regarded as the 'apotheosis' of combined operations, a potent 'fusion of maritime, aerial and land power' designed to penetrate Hitler's 'Atlantic Wall', overwhelm its defences and establish the Allies firmly on the continent of Europe.[178] An integral part of the Allied blue-print for this combined offensive was the overall Air Plan devised by Air Chief Marshal Sir Trafford Leigh-Mallory, Commander-in-Chief of the Allied Expeditionary Air Force. Outlined within this set of operational orders were Leigh-Mallory's 'principal air tasks' for *Overlord*, namely: the attainment of air superiority *vis-à-vis* the *Luftwaffe*; continuous photographic reconnaissance of enemy 'dispositions and movements'; the disruption of the enemy's lines of communication, supply and reinforcement; the support of Allied amphibious landings and subsequent breakout operations; the elimination of enemy naval forces; the neutralisation of the enemy's coast and beach defences; the protection of the landing beaches and shipping concentrations from attack by the *Luftwaffe*; the dislocation of the enemy's communications and control during the assault phase; and the provision of 'air lift' for airborne forces.[179]

Unsurprisingly, much ink has been spilt by historians in discussing the role of the Allied tactical and strategic air forces in softening-up Normandy and the rest of France in preparation for the launch of the Allies' Second Front. In order to realise Leigh-Mallory's air plan, RAF Bomber and Coastal Commands, the 8th and 9th United States Army Air Forces (USAAF), and the British 2nd Tactical Air Force (TAF), clocked-up thousands of flying hours bombing and strafing selected enemy targets in Western Europe. Despite the heavy butcher's bill incurred by the RAF and its American cousins while carrying out this preparatory work,[180] on D-Day itself a staggering 171 RAF and Commonwealth squadrons were operating over Normandy flying a total of 5,656 sorties against the enemy.[181] In stark contrast to their opponents in the *Luftwaffe*, who could muster just two FW-190 Focke Wulf fighters on 6 June,[182] the Allies' air forces were, in the words of the RAF's official history, 'omnipotent, omnipresent [and] overwhelming'.[183] Yet the unsung heroes of the Normandy air campaign are those aircrews from the US IX Troop Carrier Command and RAF Transport Command who on the night of 5/6 June 1944, and in the face of heavy anti-aircraft fire, bad weather and navigational problems, flew into battle the US 82nd and 101st Airborne Divisions and their British counter-part, the 6th Airborne Division.

One of the 15 RAF squadrons involved in supplying the air lift capability for the 6th Airborne Division was No. 297 Squadron.[184] Formed at Netheravon on 22 January 1942 from the old Parachute Exercise Squadron, 297 initially flew obsolete de Haviland Tiger Moth two-seater bi-planes and twin-engine Armstrong Whitworth Whitely Mark V bombers, the latter of which had been specially converted to train fledgling parachutists. Following a series of airborne exercises, the squadron became fully-operational in October 1942 participating thereafter in leaflet drops to France and tactical night bombing missions over Europe. In April 1943, 297 began using troop-carrying gliders for 'transport work' in the UK but this experiment was curtailed in August of that year when it set about converting to the twin-engine Armstrong Whitworth Albemarle. Yet on 2 September 1943 the squadron used its old Whitleys to parachute members of No. 12 Commando onto a Drop Zone (DZ) near St. Valerie en Caux in France. This episode was then followed by a period of further parachute exercises in the UK. From February 1944, when the squadron had fully converted to Albemarles, until the eve of D-Day the squadron participated in operational supply drops to the Special Operations Executive (SOE) in France.[185]

During the *Overlord* planning phase British air chiefs had selected No. 38 Group RAF (Airborne Forces) commanded by Air Vice-Marshal L. N. Hollinghurst, and No. 46 Group RAF (Transport Command), commanded by Air Commodore A.L. Fiddament, to carry out the task of flying-in the entire 6th Airborne Division on D-Day.[186] The overall plan dictated that the main body of the 3rd Parachute Brigade, commanded by Brigadier James Hill, would be dropped into Normandy from 108 Dakota transport planes flown by Nos. 48, 233, 271, 512 and 575 Squadrons. At the same time the 5th Parachute Brigade, commanded by Brigadier Nigel Poett, would fly to France in 129 aircraft from Nos. 38 and 46 Groups. In all, 4,310 parachutists would be dropped during the early hours of 6 June while over 250 Horsa and 30 Hamilcar gliders of Nos. 1 and 2 Glider Pilot Regiments would bring-in 493 troops, 17 field guns, 44 jeeps and 55 motor cycles.[187]

This vast airborne armada would take-off from eight RAF airfields, namely, Blakewell Farm, Brize Norton, Broadwell, Down Ampney, Fairford, Harwell, Keevil and Tarrant Rushton, which were all located in southern England.[188] In order to achieve its various objectives in the Orne River area, 6th Airborne division would land on a series of Drop Zones (DZs) - 'K', 'N' and 'V' - and Landing Zones (LZs) - 'W', 'X' and 'Y'. Yet despite committing 470 troop carrier aircraft and 1,120 gliders to the task, RAF Transport Command still could not provide enough air lift capacity obliging 6th Airborne Division to be flown-in in two lifts, the first during the early hours of the sixth, codename *Tonga* and the second, late on the evening of D-Day, codenamed *Mallard*.[189]

As part of No. 38 Group, 297 Squadron was stationed at RAF Brize Norton in Oxfordshire where it had been operating since 14 March 1944.[190] This is confirmed by the squadron's Operations Record Book (TNA AIR 27/1648), compiled by Flight Officer Morell and Flight Lieutenant E. R. Petman, which also records that this relatively obscure squadron employed 25 of its Albemarle bombers to transport parachutists and glider-borne troops to Normandy during the night of

5/6 June. Yet hidden away among the squadron's numerous log entries for the period 5-7 June are three separate missions which were crucial to the overall success of *Overlord* and its amphibious phase, *Neptune*.

The first sortie involved the employment of a single specially converted Albemarle bomber in which a 'stick' of 10 men from the elite 22nd Independent Parachute Company would emplane for France in order to act as a reception party for 6th Airborne Division. Known as 'Pathfinders', the operational role of these highly-trained parachutists, who were commanded by Major Francis Lennox-Boyd, was to land behind enemy lines long before the first wave of parachutists and gliders appeared overhead in order to mark-out DZs and LZs. Having taken off from Brize Norton at 2300 hours on the night of the fifth, Lennox-Boyd's men jumped from their Albemarle at 0020 hours the next morning, thereby becoming some of the first Allied soldiers to land in occupied Europe.

Once on the ground, the Pathfinders quickly set-up their Eureka homing beacons and a variety of other visual aids designed to control the approach of troop carrying aircraft. Part of the 'Rebecca-Eureka guidance system', Eureka beacons emitted signals to incoming aircraft which were equipped with Rebecca receivers configured to emit their own response signals when activated. By means of this ingenious system Pathfinder units could communicate with pilots and vice versa enabling RAF Transport crews to locate their correct DZ or LZ at night. Despite the scattering of some Pathfinders during the drop, the landing of airborne forces on incorrect DZs and a lack of guidance to some RAF pilots due to damaged Eureka beacons, the Pathfinders were largely successful in their nocturnal work playing a critical role in ensuring the success of Operation *Tonga*.[191]

As documented in 297 Squadron's Operations Record Book, the squadron also had the distinction of participating in one of the most famous and daring actions of the Normandy landings, namely the airborne assault on the German artillery battery at Merville. Early in 1944 Photographic Reconnaissance (PR) had alerted British planners to the construction of four casemates near the village of Merville situated east of the Orne River between Cabourg-les-Bain and Ouistreham. Planning staff estimated that these casemates could house four 150 mm artillery pieces which, in the event of an Allied landing, could rain down deadly fire onto 'Sword' beach, the D-Day objective for the British 3rd Infantry Division. Having identified this potential threat it was decided by senior officers that the Merville battery had to be neutralised during the early hours of 6 June if it was not to cause heavy British casualties. Consequently, it was regarded as the primary task of Brigadier James Hill's 3rd Parachute Brigade, which was instructed, 'To ensure that the battery 800 yards south of Merville is silenced by 30 minutes before dawn' and that '...no other commitment must jeopardise success in this enterprise'.[192] This daunting task was duly assigned to the 9th Battalion, The Parachute Regiment and its redoubtable Commanding Officer (CO), Lieutenant-Colonel Terence Otway.

Yet the Merville battery posed a significant challenge to any would-be attacker. Protected by anti-tank ditches, barbed-wire, minefields, anti-aircraft guns, mortar-pits and machine gun nests it also possessed a garrison of 130 men housed in a series of fixed fortifications. Given a free-hand to devise his own plan of attack against the battery's formidable defences, Otway settled on a brilliant but highly-complex scheme. As a preparatory measure around 0030 hours on the morning of the sixth, 100 four-engine Lancaster bombers would blast the battery with 1000 pound bombs. At 0050 hours Otway's battalion, which consisted of 620 men, would parachute onto DZ 'V' two kilometres west of the battery. Met by a reception party on the DZ, which would organise the battalion after its jump, Otway and his men would then await news from his advance reconnaissance party whose task it was to assess the battery's defences following the bombing raid. Working from this intelligence, a 'taping' party would then proceed to clear paths through the surviving minefields and barbed wire.

Having gotten into position, A and C companies, which constituted the main assault force, would await the arrival of three Horsa gliders which had been towed across the English Channel by Albemarles from No. 297 Squadron. Named 'Force G-B' after its leader Captain Robert Gordon-Brown, these glider-borne troops would affect a *coup-de-main* landing inside the battery's perimeter at 0430 hours. At this precise moment, the main assault force would detonate Bangalore torpedoes placed through the barbed-wire defences and would rush through the gaps to join Gordon-Brown's men in clearing the position and destroying the guns. If for any reason the assault were to fail, at 0530 hours the cruiser HMS *Arethusa* would shell Merville from the sea in order to neutralise its guns.[193]

However, through a series of unfortunate incidents Otway's plan would be left in tatters. Helmuth von Moltke, the famous Prussian Field Marshal, once observed that 'no battle plan survives first contact with the enemy'. On the morning of D-Day Otway's plan was to be no exception to this rule of war. Following a chaotic airborne descent due to high winds, Flak, navigational errors and thick smoke generated by inaccurate bombing on the part of RAF Lancasters, which had missed the battery completely, the men of the 9th Battalion found themselves dispersed over an area of 50 square miles. Consequently, only one-hundred-and-fifty men reached the initial RV forcing Otway to revise his original plan of battle. Furthermore, bad luck was to dog 'Force G-B'. Having already lost one glider shortly after take-off due to a broken tow-rope, which had obliged it to force land in Britain, the force's other two gliders ended-up missing their intended target: Gordon-Brown's glider landed east of the battery and the third Horsa also missed landing 500 yards east of the German position. Despite these set-backs Otway launched his attack at 0430 hours. During the next half an hour his men, aided by 'Force G-B' which engaged German forces outside the perimeter wire, managed to disable or destroy the battery's guns, which were in fact 100 mm Czech guns, far smaller in calibre than the artillery pieces the Paras had expected to find. Finally, at 0500 hours the battalion had accomplished its mission but out of the 150 men who started only 75 men remained standing.[194]

Two nights after the launch of Operation *Overlord*, 297 Squadron took part in what its Operations Record Book would refer to as a 'relatively small operation but an important one' nonetheless.[195] In conjunction with its sister squadrons, Nos. 295 and 296, 297 would employ two of its Albemarle bombers to undertake a special duties flight to the Brittany Peninsula. Codenamed *Cooney* this clandestine operation would involve flying 58 members of the FAR 4 ème BIA 4 ème Bataillion de l'Air (4 French PARA or 4 Special Air Service) to a series of 17 DZs in the area St Brieuc-Dinan-Redon-Pontivy onto which they would drop 'blind' i.e. parachuting in without the help of reception parties on the ground.[196] Divided-up into 16 operational parties of three men and two parties of five men, this force of SAS troops planned to link-up with the local 'underground' movement, the *Maquis* (French Resistance forces) in order to cut vitally important railway lines linking Brittany and Normandy.[197] Their orders were clear and precise: 'to impose the maximum delay on the movement of German reinforcements to Normandy, and thereafter to assist in the arming and training of the *Maquis* and to harass the Germans'.[198] Although relatively little is known about this mission the concerted efforts of British and French SAS teams after D-Day were indeed successful in impeding the movement of German troops by rail to the Normandy beachhead.[199] Yet this clandestine work came at a cost with casualties amongst these Special Forces troops being relatively high.

Following the critical role it played during Operations *Tonga* and *Mallard*, 297 Squadron went on to tow Horsa gliders into eastern Holland during the ill-fated Operation *Market Garden* in September 1944, which ended in British defeat at Arnhem. Having converted from Albemarles to four-engine Handley Page Halifax bombers in October 1944, the squadron flew SOE sorties into Europe and conducted tactical night bombing raids behind German lines. In March 1945, 297 took part in Operation *Varsity*, the airborne element of Operation *Plunder*, the British crossing of the Rhine river, during which it towed thirty Horsa gliders to LZ 'P' inside Germany. After this operation the squadron resumed SOE flights and also flew British troops to Norway and Denmark in the wake of the unconditional surrender of Nazi Germany in May 1945. Continuing into peace time as one of the few units still employed to train airborne forces, 297 was eventually disbanded on 1 April 1946 only to reform the same day from No. 295 Squadron RAF. Having converted from Halifaxes to Handley Page Hastings in December 1948, the squadron used the latter type of aircraft to fly in coal to the beleaguered city of Berlin during the famous Russian blockade which lasted from 26 June 1948 to 12 May 1949.[200] After a brief period as an airborne support unit, No. 297 squadron was finally disbanded at Topcliffe airfield on 15 November 1950.[201]

NOTES

[178] Paul Kennedy, *Engineers of Victory: The Problem Solvers Who Turned the Tide in the Second World War*, (London: Allen Lane, 2013), p. 216.

[179] *D-Day Then and Now*, Volume 1, edited by Winston G. Ramsey, (London: Battle of Britain Prints International Ltd, 1995), p. 134.

[180] Nearly two thousand Allied aircraft were lost during the period 1 April to 5 June 1944. See *The Oxford Companion to the Second World War*, edited by I.C.B. Dear and M.R.D. Foot, (Oxford: Oxford University Press, 1995), p. 853.

[181] Hilary St. George Saunders and Denis Richards, *Royal Air Force, 1939-45: The Fight is Won*, Volume III, (London: HMSO, 1954), p. 113.

[182] Cornelius Ryan, *The Longest Day: June 6, 1944*, (London: Victor Gollancz Ltd 1982), pp. 200-202.

[183] Ibid., pp. 112-114.

[184] Carl Shilleto, *Battleground Europe: Merville Battery & The Dives Bridges: British 6th Airborne Division Landings in Normandy D-Day 6 June 1944*, (Barnsley, South Yorkshire: Pen & Sword Books Ltd, 2011), p. 36.

[185] John D.R. Rawlings, *Coastal Support and Special Squadrons of the RAF and their Aircraft*, (London: Jane's Publishing Company Ltd, 1982). pp. 195-196.

[186] Major L.F. Ellis *et al.*, *Victory in the West: Volume I: The Battle of Normandy*, (London: HMSO, 1962), p. 559.

[187] Ibid., pp. 107-108. See also Lloyd Clark, *Battle Zone Normandy: Orne Bridgehead*, (Stroud, Gloucestershire: Sutton Publishing Ltd, 2004), p. 38.

[188] Carl Shilleto, *Battleground Europe: Pegasus Bridge & Merville Battery: British 6th Airborne Division Landings in Normandy D-Day 6 June 1944*, (Barnsley, South Yorkshire: Pen & Sword Books Ltd, 1999), p. 29.

[189] Major L.F. Ellis *et al.*, *Victory in the West: Volume I: The Battle of Normandy*, (London: HMSO, 1962), p. 138.

[190] James J. Halley, *The Squadrons of the Royal Air Force & Commonwealth, 1918-1988*, (Tonbridge, Kent: Air Britain (Historians Ltd), 1988), p. 353.

[191] Lloyd Clark, *Battle Zone Normandy: Orne Bridgehead*, (Stroud, Gloucestershire: Sutton Publishing Ltd, 2004), pp.44-45.

[192] Ibid., p. 216.

[193] See Carl Shilleto, *Battleground Europe: Merville Battery & The Dives Bridges: British 6th Airborne Division Landings in Normandy D-Day 6 June 1944*, (Barnsley, South Yorkshire: Pen & Sword Books Ltd, 2011), pp.57-92.

[194] See Neil Barber, *The Day the Devils Dropped In: The 9th Parachute Battalion in Normandy – D-Day to D+6: The Merville Battery to the Château St. Côme*, (Barnsley, South Yorkshire: Pen & Sword Books Ltd, 2002), pp. 15-97.

[195] TNA AIR 27/1648, Operations Record Book of No. 297 Squadron RAF, 7-8 June 1944, p. 3.

[196] Ibid., p. 254.

[197] Ibid., p. 86.

[198] Ibid., p. 251.

[199] Ibid., p. 252.

[200] Ibid., p. 196.

[201] Ibid., p. 353.

TNA AIR 27/1648

NO. 297 SQUADRON RAF OPERATIONAL LOG BOOK ENTRY FOR 5/6 JUNE 1944

Place	Date	Time	Summary of Events SECRET	References to Appendices
Brize Norton	1.6.44		Little flying took place during the day. Two aircraft were engaged on heavy glider towing and a further two aircraft proceeded to Netheravon and subsequently dropped 'guinea pigs' on the Div.D.Z. – as training for two new crews. The dropping was done very successfully. In addition and aircraft was flown to and from Pershore.	
	2.6.44	14-00	All personnel confined to camp till further notice; this includes persons who were living out. The reasons given by the Station Commander was 'Security' although he said this might be a false alarm.	
			4 fighter affiliation sorties were carried out during the day with the Unit at Aston Down and one of the Squadron's new pilots received dual instruction in glider towing. Apart from 3 additional air tests no more flying took place.	
	3.6.44		Briefings all day but security good. Only aircrew learnt their DZ & L.Z. etc. Various meetings and parades to get all ground personnel into Fire, Gas Defence parties etc. F/Lt. Allison & F/O. Grimshaw were both married today. As a concession both were allowed a '48 hours' but no one else could attend their weddings.	
			Three aircraft were engaged on ferrying gliders, from Tarrant Rushton and this was the only flying which took place. The servicing Echelon were thus given every opportunity to work on the aircraft – A.E.F. markings being placed thereon.	
	4.6.44		There was no flying whatsoever during theday, and the ground crews worked very hard throughout the day and night to bring aircraft serviceability to 100%. There was an air of expectancy about the Station as 'gen' on forthcoming operations was awaited.	
	5.6.44		D-Day at last! Final briefing at 18.30, when aircrew finally learnt that tonight was the night. The first aircraft took off at 23.00 hours. Even at 23.00 hours very few besides the aircrew knew that the day had arrived. The security has been good. A few airmen have been placed in the GUARD ROOM for careless talk. After two years of training the honor of opening the Second Front in France has fallen to 297 Squadron.	
			The moral of the Squadron has jumped to 100%.	
			PHASE I. Paratroops were landed near the East Bank of the RIVER ORNE, approx 6 miles.	
			PHASE II. Additional paratroops were dropped on the D.Z.	
			PHASE III. 2 Gliders were also successfully landed on the Coast between Cabourg-les-Bains and Ouistreham to silence a coastal battery, in case it has not been knocked out previously by bombing. A very successful start. For full particulars see F. 541.	
			News came through to the Station shortly before lunch that the long awaited SECOND FRONT was to begin early the following morning. Briefs for the various phases of the forth- coming nights operations had already been prepared and the briefings proceeded throughout the afternoon culminating in one main briefing at 18.30 hours for all crews concerned – 26 in all from the Squadron.	
	6.6.44	18-50	20 aircraft took off to tow gliders to yesterdays D.Z. F/O. Long and crew were reported missing. Another very successfull operation; for full details see Form 541.	
			There was no flying activity during the morning as the aircrews were making up some lost sleep following their strenuous efforts of the previous night.	
			In the afternoon, the briefing and general preparation for operation 'Mallard' took place which was laid on for the evening.	

SECRET

BY No. 297. Squadron, R.A.F.
FOR THE MONTH OF June 1944

DATE	AIRCRAFT TYPE & NUMBER	CREW	DUTY	TIME UP	DOWN		DETAILS OF SORTIE OR FLIGHT	REFERENCES
5/6. 6. 44	Albemarle N. P.1383	W/O. Riokard W.A. F/S. Escott E .R. F/S. Buist J. F/S. Pomfrey W.C. Sgt. Hinksman F.	(Br) Pilot (Br) Nav. (Br) W/Op. (Br) A/G. (Br) B/A.	23.00	02.00	3.00	OPERATION – TONGA – OVERLORD. Phase I. One aircraft (plus 1 A/C of 296 Squadron) took off at 23.00 hrs. each with sticks of 10 troops of the 22nd Independent Para. Coy. to act as pathfinders for the main paratroops and glider forces which were following.	
5/6-6-44	Albemarle Mk 2. V. 1716	F/O. W.H McCutcheon F/S. Bowers J. F/O. T.F. Bayliss F/S. Sanders F. F/S. Perkins E.J.	(Can) Pilot Br. Nav. Br W/Op. Br A.G. Br B/A.	23.00	02.00	3.00	A further 3 aircraft (plus 2 of 296 Squadron) also took off at the same time each with sticks of 10 troops to drop on the same D.Z. at the same time. In a sense these aircraft were also pathfinders as there were no Radar or light aids. The object of the dropping of these 5 sticks was to supply troops to hold off any attacks which might be made on the D.Z.	
5/6-6-44	Albemarle I P. 1400	F/O. M.L. Godden. F/O. I Miller Sgt. Froman B. F/O M. F. Carlson F/O. F.R.W. Bagshaw	(Br) Pilot (Br) Nav. Can B/A. Br. W/op. Br A.G.	23.30	02.00	3.00	whilst the Independent troops were laying down their Radar and light aids. The D.Z. was situated near the EAST bank of the River Orne approx. 6 miles N.E. of CAEN, and the time for the troops to drop was 00.20. hours. The 2 pathfinders dropped down the Eastern side of the D.Z. & the	
5/6-6-44	Albemarle I P. 1384	F/S. Roberts K.J. F/O. B.O. Green Sgt. Creak J.C. W/O. Johnson (B flt) Sgt. Pearson J.P.T.	(Br) Pilot. (Br) Nav. (Br) W/Op. (Br) A.G. (Br) B/A.	23.07	02.22	3.15	5 specials down the Western side, where they were to take up positions guarding approaches from the main road & river running to CAEN. All dropping carried out successfully. 2 aircraft had to make 2 runs over as the troops had difficulty in opening the jumping aperture door. No casualties.	
5-6/6/44	Albemarle II V.1700	F/L. I.W. McCall F/S. Kidd H.W. F/O. A.W. Crouch F/S. McCormick T. P/O. J.W. Irvine	(Br) Pilot (Br) Nav. (Br) W/Op. (Br) A.G. (Br) B/A.	23.45	02.50	3.05	Phase II. The main paratroop force comprising 9 Aircraft (plus 10 aircraft of 296 Squadron) commenced taking off at 23.38 hours and there was a hold up in the course thereof as 2 aircraft of 296 Squadron went U/S. It was too late to replace them and only 17	
5-6/6/44	Albemarle V.1812	S/L. D. Emblem F/L. A.W. Slipper F/O. D. Pickard F/L. B. Bullivant P/O. D.A. Brook	(Br) Pilot (Br) Nav. (Br) B/A. (Br) W/Op. (Br) A.G.	23.50	02.50	3.00	aircraft subsequently got away. These flew to the same D.Z. as above and dropped their troops and containers at 01.01 hours. All containers had not to be dropped on the D.Z., and certain aircraft jettisoned theirs on a position about 3/4 mile South of the D.Z. immediately after dropping the troops.	
5-6-6-44	Albemarle P.1365	F/S. Miller J.D. F/O. C.J. Heffernan Sgt. Hodges F. F/S. Beddow E.R. Sgt. Page W.A.R.	(Br) Pilot (Br) Nav. (Br) B/A. (Br) W/Op. (Br) A/G.	23.50	02.50	3.00	This phase was very successful (lights & Eureka laid by Independents were used successfully), and all troops were dropped on the D.Z. One 297 Squadron aircraft (Pilot, F/S. Miller) was unable to jettison the containers and had to return to BASE with them. Owing to the concentration and consequent congestion over the D.Z., some	
5-6-6-44	Albemarle V.1743	F/O. J. Coxell P/O. J.W.E. Challis Sgt. Coley R.R. Sgt. Jones D. T. Sgt. Wiles L.E.	(Br) Pilot (Br) Nav. (Br) B/A. (Br) W/Op. (Br) A.G.	23.50	03.00	3.10	aircraft	

/OVER.

DATE	AIRCRAFT TYPE & NUMBER	CREW	DUTY	TIME UP	TIME DOWN		DETAILS OF SORTIE OR FLIGHT	REFERENCES
5/6. 6. 44	Albemarle MkI P.1367	F/O. T.R. Shortman Sgt. Clements V.V. F/S. Jenkins T.G. F/S. Peppitt J.W. F/O. B.C. Easton	(Br) Pilot " Nav. " W/Op. " A.G. " B/A.	23.50	03.00	3.10	(continued) had to make 2 runs in order to get their troops away. There were a few cases of superficial damage and F/O. Brott had to land at FORD with one engine.	
5/6. 6. 44	Albemarle V.1772	F/L. Watkins W.S. F/O. G.L. Scott Sgt. Jenkins A.J. Sgt. Yorke J.G. Sgt. Stephenson L.L	(Br) Pilot " Nav. " B/A. " W/Op. " A.G.	23.55	02.55	3.00		
5/6. 6. 44	Albemarle V.1742	Sgt. F lavell J.T. F/S. Campbell J.C. Sgt. Breingan M.M. Sgt. Graynoth R.N. F/S. Entwhistle J.M	(Br) Pilot " Nav. " B/A. " W/Op. " A.G.	23.55	02.55	3.00		
5/6. 6. 44	Albemarle MkI P.1471	F/L E.A. Allison P/O. K.B. Moore F/S. Harris C.C. F/S. Bindon M.R. F/O. J.N. Tattam	(Br) Pilot " ? Nav. " W/Op. " A.G. " ? B/A.	23.55	02.55	3.00	Operations "Bigot"	
5/6. 6. 44	Albemarle MkI P.1378	F/S. Busbridge A. F/S. Mowan B. Sgt. Morris D. Sgt. Flack A. Sgt. Insley W.F.	(Br) Pilot " Nav. " W/Op. " A.G. " B/A.	23.59	02.45	2.46		
5/6. 6. 44	Albemarle V.1781	F/L. B. Cowderoy F/S. Fletcher H.M. Sgt. Wood W.J. W/O. Thomson A.S. F/O. E.C. Ellis	(Br) Pilot " Nav. " B/A. " W/Op. " ? A.G.	01.10	04.50	3.40	Phase III. The main glider force comprising 9 combinations (plus 8 of 296 Squadron) commenced taking off at 01.10 hours and all managed to get away except one (P/O Jaspsr) whose glider had to release at BASE shortly after becoming airborne as the aelerons were U/S. The gliders were released at 03.20 hours at a position adjoining the D.Z. described above and then went into land on the D.Z., the lighting having been laid down in the form of a strip by the pathfinder troops. This phase of the operation was again very successful. One or two cases of superficial flak damage were reported. The Weather was not too good and crews reported large banks of cloud over the D.Z. with a base of 2000. Fortunately the visibility was good. All gliders were heavily loaded with troops and equipment. Tow ropes were jettisoned over the enemy (we Hope !!!).	
5/6. 6. 44	Albemarle V.1823 Glider cast off at French Coast.	F/O. E.D. Halpin F/S. Sloan C.H.P Sgt. Taylor P.W. Sgt. Smith J.H.L. Sgt. Sharpe R.W.	(Br) Pilot " Nav. " B/A. " W/Op. " A.G.	01.10	04.40	3.30		
5/6. 6. 44	Albemarle V.1778 Glider u/s no operation	P/O. T.W. Jasper F/S. B urnett D.H. F/S. Meynell S. F/S Dodd R.G. F/S. Arnold J.C.P.	(Br) Pilot " Nav. " B/A. " W/Op. " A.G.	01.15	01.40	0.25.		
5/6. 6. 44	Albemarle V.1825	F/S. Littlemore J.W F/.O. A.E. Doyle F/S. Wilson J. Sgt. Pursell J.W. Sgt. Brough D.S.	(Br) Pilot " Nav. " B/A. " W/Op. " A.G.	01.15	04.55	3.40		

APPENDIX
SECRET

For the Month of June 1944   By No. 297 Squadron, R.A.F.

DATE	AIRCRAFT TYPE & NUMBER	CREW	DUTY	TIME UP	DOWN		DETAILS OF SORTIE OR FLIGHT	REFERENCES
5/6-6-44	Albemarle P. 1396	Sgt. Flavell E. F/O. D. Russell Sgt. Edwards R.O.J Sgt. Layden J.F. Sgt. Clancy J.	(Br) Pilot " Nav. " B/A. " W/Op. " A.G.	01.20	04.00	2.40		
"	Albemarle V V.1771	S/L. R.F. Trim P/O. P. Boddington F/L. P. Lee W/O. Organ R.K F/O. J.D.Grimshaw F/O. J.G. Cox	(Br) Pilot " Nav " A.G. " W/Op. " B/A. " Tail gunner	01.20	04.55	3.35	Operations "BIGOT"	
5/6-6-44	Albemarle I. P.1651	F/O. C.S. Brott Sgt. Davis W.L. Sgt. Mills E. Sgt. Griffith R.J. F/O V.J. Marsh	(Br) Pilot " Nav. " W/Op. " A.G. " B/A.	01.25	04.22	2.57	V2	
"	Albemarle I P. 1409	F/O. R. Wharmby F/S. Cooper R. W/O. Marsh F.J. Sgt. Smith J.E. Sgt. Waters E.J.	(Br) Pilot " Nav. " W/Op. " A.G. " B/A.	01.26	04.56	3.30		
5/6-6-44	Albemarle V. V.1769	F/S. Cunningham G.W. F/O. A. Roddan Sgt. Forbes W.M. Sgt. Cowden T.A.W. F/O. T.E. Reilly.	(Br) Pilot " Nav. " W/Op. " A.G. " B/A.	01.45	05.05	3.20		
"	Albemarle V. V.1773	F/L, R .H. Thomson F/O. A.P. Ludwick F/O. L.E. Blundell F/S. Flynn P. W/O. Taylor D.E.	(Br) Pilot " Nav. " A.G. " W/Op. " B/A.	02.30	06.00	3.30	Operations "D" <u>2nd Part of Phase III.</u> The intention was to release 3 gliders on the French Coast between Cabourg-les-Bain and Onistreham at 5000' the gliders then having to fly on set courses so as to land	
5/6-6-44	Albemarle V. V.1782	F/O. K.T. Garnett F/S. T-Kerrick A. Sgt. Peacock H. F/O. C.A. Shaw Sgt. Gould D.J.	" Pilot " Nav. " W/Op. " A.G. " B/A.	02.31	05.56	3.25	on a position adjoining a Battery of enemy coastal guns. This Battery was situated approx 2½ miles N.N.E. of the D.Z. and was bombed earlier in the phase of operations by 100 Lancasters (just before the main para. force went in. In case the Battery had not been	
"	Albemarle V. V.1776 Glider broke off returned to Base	F/S. Richards D.M. P/O. A.R. Reitzner F/S. Webster C. F/S. Howells M.S. F/S. Ward J.E.	(Br) Pilot (Czech) Nav, (Br) B/A. " W/op. " A.G. i	02.30	04.00	1.30	completely wiped out by the bombing, the 3 gliders were to provide re-inforcements for attacking it. The 3 combinations took off at 02.30 hrs. and 2 were subsequently released on time at 0 4.30 hours. The release had to be made at 1000' owing to the low cloud Base, the cloud lowering as the evening progressed, and consequently the gliders were flown nearer to the target. The third glider (tug pilot F/S. Richards) had to land in this country as the tow rope broke before the English Coast was reached on the outward trip. A rather dejected crew made an early return to Base.	

(7472) Wt. 24229/1650. 180M. 8/40. P.I. 51-7751.

84

DATE	AIRCRAFT TYPE & NUMBER	CREW	DUTY	TIME UP DOWN	DETAILS OF SORTIE OR FLIGHT	REFERENCES
6/7/ 6. 44	Albemarle V.1781.	F/O M. L. Godden F/O. L. Miller Sgt. Froman B.P/O.M.F. Carlson F/O. F.R . W. Bagshaw	(Br) Pilot " Nav. " B/A. " W/Op. " A.G.	18.50 22.20 3.30	OPERATION – MALLARD – OVERLOAD. The intention of this operation was to provide glider-borne re-inforcements of troops and equipment, the glider landings to be made on the same L.Z. as previous. The Squadron provided 20 combinations and the first take-off following quickly afterwards. The main wheels of F/O, Coxell's glider fell off as soon as the glider was	
6/7/ 6. 44	Albemarle P. 1395 rope Tow attachment u/s landed near Whitchurch	F/O. A.W. Milroy F/S. Ashdown K.F. Sgt. Richards H.J. Sgt. Powell S. W/O. Oliver J.W.	(Br) Pilot " Nav " B/A. " W/Op. " A.G.	18.50 19.55 1.05	airborne and caused a temporary obstruction of the runway. These were soon removed, however and little delay was causedt to subsequent take-offs. The rope of F/O. Milroy's aircraft became detached from the tug on the outward trip to the English Coast and the glider had to make a forced landing.	
6/7/ 6. 44	Albemarle V.1778	P/O. T.W. Jasper F/S. Burnett D.H. F/S. Meynell S. F/S. F/S. Dodd R.G Arnold J.C.P.	(Br) Pilot " B/A. " W/Op " A.G.	18.50 22.50 4.00	The remaining 19 combinations reached the L.Z. on time (21.12 hours) and the concentration was excellent, all gliders releasing in approx 1½ minutes.	
6/7/ 6. 44	Albemarle P. 1460	F/O. J.G.Y.Hodge Sgt. King D.A. Sgt. Jenkins A.J. Sgt. Yorke J.G. Sgt. Stephenson	(Br) Pilot " Nav. " B/A. " W/Op. " A.G.	18.55 23.35 3.40	There was some light flak, and F/O. Long's aircraft was hit and is thought to have crashed somewhere approximating the L.Z. area, he and his crew are now posted missing. This flak came up from an area supposed to be held by us, probably one or more isolated pockets. A few aircraft received superficial damage, one having	
6/7/ 6. 44	Albemarle V.1823	F/O, E.D.Halpin F/S . Sloan C.H.P. Sgt. Taylor. P.W. Sgt Smith J.H.L. Sgt. S. Harpe R.W.	(Br) Pilot " Nav. " B/A " W/Op. " A.G.	18.55 22.35 3.4.0	a square foot knocked out of the leading edge of the starboard tail-planem otherwise the operation was a complete success. The cloud base was 2/3000 feet, varying in places, and the visibility was approx. 15 miles. A good trip. The whole of the Royal Navy appeared to be off shore and fortunately did not interfere. The aircraft flew in at 750'. 15 Fighter Squadrons provided cover for the Channel crossing and these were joined by further Squadrons when the French Coast was reached.	
6/7/ 6. 44	Albemarle V.1812	S/L. D. Emblem F/L. A.W.- Slipper F/O. D. Pickard F/L. B. Bullivant P/O. D.A. Brook F/Lt. Light (Passenger)	(Br) Pilot " Nav. " B/A. " W/Op. " A.G.	18.55 22.50 3.55		
6/7/ 6. 44	Albemarle V.1776	W/Cdr. J.G. Minifie. F/L. E.R. Petman F/L. S. Burnham F/S. Eunnell E. F./S. Brettel V.R. G/Capt. Homer (Passenger)	(Br) Pilot " Nav. " B/A. " W/Op " A.G.	18.55. 22.45 3.50		
6/7/ 6. 44	Albemarle 1 P.1378	F/S. Busbridge A. F/S Mowan B. Sgt. Insley W.F. Sgt. Morris D. G Sgt . Flack A.R.	(Br) Pilot " Nav. " B/A. " W/Op. " A.G.	18.59 22.39 3.40		
	Albemarle V.1743	F/O. J. Coxell P/O. J.W.E. Challis Sgt. Coley R.R. Sgt. Jones D.T. Sgt. Wiles L.E.	(Br) Pilot " Nav. " B/A. " W/Op. " A.G.	19.00 22.40 3.40		

APPENDIX
SECRET

FOR THE MONTH OF June1944

By No.297 Squadron, R.A.F.

DATE	AIRCRAFT TYPE & NUMBER	CREW	DUTY	TIME UP	TIME DOWN		DETAILS OF SORTIE OR FLIGHT	REFERENCES
6/7-6. 44	Albemarle V. V.1773	F/O. R.H. Long F/O. S.P. Cooper Sgt. Aparicio W. Sgt. Chatterton H.J. Sgt. Muir R.T.	(Br) Pilot " Nav. " B/A " A.G. " /Op.	19.00			Operations Mallard – Missing from this operation	
6/7-6. 44	Albermarle I P.1409	F/O. R. Wharmby F/S. Cooper R. Sgt. Waters E.J. W/O. Marsh F.J Sgt. Smith J.E.	(Br) Pilot " Nav. " B/A. " W/.Op " A.G.	19.02	22.32	3.30	Operations "Mallard"	
6/7-6. 44	Albemarle V.1825	F/S. Richards D.M P/O. A.R. Reitzner Sgt. Webster C. F/S. Howells M.S. Sgt. Ward J.E.	(Br) Pilot Czech Nav. " B/A. " W/Op. " A.G.	19.05	22.55	3.50	Operation "Mallard"	
6/7-6. 44	Albemarle V.1772	F/L. W.S. Watkins F/O. G.L. Scott Sgt. Richardson H.J. F/O I.L. Jacques Sgt. Rhodes G.W.	(Br) Pilot " Nav. " B/A. " W/Op. " A.G.	19.05	23.00	3.55	Operation "Mallard"	
6/7-6. 44	Albemarle V. V.1769	B/S. Cunningham G.W. F/O. A. Roddan F/O. T.E. Reilly Sgt. Forbes W.M. Sgt. Cowden T.A.W.	(Br) Pilot " NSV " B/A. " W/Op. " A.G.	1905	22.55	3.50	Operation "Mallard	
6/7-6. 44	Albemarle V. V.1782	F/O. K.T. Garnett F/S. Tabbs.-Marrick A. Sgt. Gould D.J. Sgt. Peacock H. F/O. C.A. Shaw	(Br) Pilot " Nav. " B/A. " W/Op. " A.G.	19.03	22.33	3.30	Operations "Mallard"	
6/7-6. 44	Albemarle I. P.1471	F/L. E.A Allison F/O. K.B. Moore F/O. J.W. Tattam F/S. Harris C.C F/s. Bindon M.R.	(Br) Pilot " B/A. " W/OP. " A.G.	19.04	22.24	3.20	Operations "Mallard"	
6/7-6. 44	Albemarle 2 V.1841	Sgt. Taylor D.J. Sgt. Straehan W.E. Sgt. Smith G.A. Sgt. Bunker R.F. Sgt. Ayers J.	(Br) Pilot " Wav. " B/A. " W/Op. " A.G.	19.04½	22.49½	3.45.	Operations "Mallard"	
6/7-6. 44	Albemarle I P. 1378	F/S. Roberts K.J. F/O. B. Green Sgt. Pearson J. Sgt. Creak J. W/O. Johnson R.	(Br) Pilot " Nav. " B/A. " W/Op. " A.G.	19.03½	22.33½	3.30	Operations "Mallard"	

DATE	AIRCRAFT TYPE & NUMBER	CREW	DUTY	TIME UP	TIME DOWN		DETAILS OF SORTIE OR FLIGHT	REFERENCES.
6/7/6 44	Albemarle 2. V.1716	F/O. W.H.McCutcheon	(Br) Pilot	19.07	22.32	3.25	Operations "Mallard"	
		F/S. Bowers J.	" Nav.					
		F/S. Perkins E.J.	" B/A.					
		F/O. T.F. Baylis.	" W/Op.					
		F/S Sanders F	" A.G.					
"	Albemarle I P.1376	F/O. T.R. Short man	(Br) Pilot	19.50	22.50	3.00	Operations "Mallard"	
		F/S. Clements V.V.	" Nav.					
		F/O. B.C. Easton	" B/A.					
		F/S. Peppitt J.W.	" A.G.					
		F/S. Jenkins T.G.	" W/Op.					
7/8 6 44	Albemarle I P.1383	W/O. Rickard W.	(Br) Pilot	22.40	02.45	4.05	Operations "Cooney" A realtively small operation but an important one. French Troops were dropped with the object of making contact with the "Underground Movement, the object being to blow up various Railway Bridges in a day or two.	
		F/S. Escott E.R.	" Nav.					
		Sgt. Hinksman F.	" B/A.					
		Sgt. Buist J.	" W/Op					
		F/L. Light	" A.G.					
		F/S. Humberstone D.	" Passenger					
		Sgt .Wieklow	" Dispatcher.					
"	Albemarle 2. V.1841.	F/L. R.H. Thomson	(Br) Pilot	23.00	3.30	4.30	Operations "Cooney" Weather conditions were not perfect 5/10 - 8/10 cloud at 2,000 covered most of the route with slight ground, mist over the target areas, hence the crews found a little difficulty in identifying their DZ's. Each crew had two targets in the Brittainy Peninsular. Flak opposition was moderate, but not as extensive as on the two previous nights. No enemy Fighters were encountered and there were no incidents. F/Lt. Thomson was handicapped in that his GEE box was U/S GEE successfully until reaching the operation was successfully completed.	
		F/O. A.P. Ludwick	" Nav.					
		W/O. Taylor D.E.	" B/A.					
		F/S. Flynn P.	" W/Op.					
		F/O. L.E.Blundell	" A.G.					

TNA ADM 179/475

REPORT ON OPERATION *GAMBIT* – HM SUBMARINE X-23

The midget submarines X-20 and X-23 and their crews hold the distinction of being the first units of the Allied Expeditionary Force to position themselves off the coast of Normandy in preparation for the launch of Operations *Neptune/Overlord*. The danger and uncertainty surrounding their hazardous mission was encapsulated by the code word assigned to the operation namely, 'Gambit', which in chess terms means 'throwing away the opening pawns' in a game.[202] The use of midget submarines or 'X-Craft' for operational purposes was inspired in part by Admiral Sir Max Horton, one-time Flag Officer Submarines, and later Commander-in-Chief Western Approaches. Each X-Craft weighed twenty-seven tons, had a speed of six knots, measured 15 m x 1.75 m and had a complement of four crew members.[203] X-Craft first saw active servicein late September 1943 during Operation *Source*, a planned attack on the German battleship *Tirpitz* and her sister warships *Scharnhorst* and *Lütsow*. Hiding in north Norwegian fjords in an attempt to avoid detection by the Royal Navy and RAF, the *Tirpitz* was attacked by three X-Craft using side-mounted demolition charges which left her severely damaged and immobilised. The other three X-Craft employed on the mission, however, failed to engage their targets.[204]

In stark contrast to the offensive role that had been assigned to their sister craft during Operation *Source*, HM submarines X-20 and X-23 had been detached from the 12th Submarine Flotilla in early 1944 to act as navigational beacons for the Normandy landings.[205] For this sort of mission each midget submarine carried a crew of five: two Naval lieutenants, one engine room Artificer and two officers from the Combined Operations Pilotage Party (COPP), which specialised in covert beach reconnaissance work.[206] In the build-up to D-Day X-20 had been tasked with conducting reconnaissance missions of French beaches selected by Allied planners as likely landing sites for the invasion. Between December 1943 and January 1944, X-20 undertook several operations that were instrumental in helping piece together a detailed picture of Hitler's 'Atlantic Wall' along the coast of Calvados. One such assignment was code-named Operation *Postage Able* which lasted from 17 to 21 January 1944. This operation entailed members of COPP 1 Naval Party 750 swimming ashore at night in order to: identify minefields; bring back samples of mines; record details of beach obstacles; assess the gradients of beaches, as well as acquire shingle and sand samples in order to confirm whether they would support tanks and heavy vehicles.[207] The stretch of beach on which they conducted these cloak-and-dagger activities would later be codenamed 'Omaha', the scene of some of the heaviest and bloodiest fighting experienced by US 1st Army on 6 June.

Operation *Gambit* commenced on Friday 2 June when X-20 and X-23 sailed from their home base, HMS *Dolphin* in Gosport, to act as navigational markers for naval Forces 'J' and 'S' whose respective objectives were 'Juno' and 'Sword' beaches.[208] X-Craft had been selected for this clandestine work primarily because the profile of their superstructures were so small that German radar could not detect them. This made them the ideal choice of craft with which to spearhead the vast naval armada which had been assembled in a multitude of ports along the south coast of England. Their subsequent passage to Normandy was slow and broken down into two initial phases. Phase one entailed their being towed by Royal Naval trawlers (HM Trawler *Darthema* for X-20 and HM Trawler *Sapper* for X-23) from Gosport to a point beyond the Isle of Wight. From this location in the English Channel phase two commenced whereby the two craft proceeded, fully-submerged, to the Calvados coastline under their own power, a full twenty-four hours ahead of any other Allied naval forces.

Having parted company at this point, the two X-Craft proceeded to their respective designated areas: X-20 to 'Juno' beach, where the 3rd Canadian Infantry Division would land, and X-23 to 'Sword' beach, final destination for the British 3rd Infantry Division. After arriving at their allotted stations at daybreak on Sunday 4 June, the captains of both submarines were to fix their positions 7,000 yards off shore by rising to periscope depth and taking bearings from the shoreline. Once they had established their exact locations, they were to weigh anchor and rest on the sea bed for the rest of the day. The overall plan for the employment of X-20 and X-23 envisaged that just before dawn on the morning of D-Day, they were to surface and commence signalling by means of coloured lights seaward to Forces 'J' and 'S'. This was critical to the success of Operation *Neptune* in these areas in that both beaches were hard to identify, especially in the dark, and lacked recognisable landmarks. Moreover, rocky outcrops off-shore at 'Juno' and mud flats stretching seaward east of 'Sword' made accurate navigation essential.[209] Although the crews of both craft had been briefed that D-Day was set for Monday 5 June, at 0100 hours on the 5th X-20 and X-23 both received wireless messages containing the code word 'Pretty' signalling that Operation *Overlord* had been postponed for twenty-four hours and consequently they were to remain submerged for another day.[210]

Remaining submerged off a hostile coast while awaiting further orders was a nerve-racking and testing experience. Both crews had to contend with hot, stuffy and claustrophobic conditions coupled with a serious underlying concern over ever decreasing levels of oxygen inside the midget submarines. In an effort to pre-empt oxygen starvation, twelve captured *Luftwaffe* oxygen bottles had been stored onboard the two X-Craft enabling the crews to breathe properly while submerged for prolonged periods of time.[211] The crew of X-23, which consisted of Sub-Lieutenant J.H. Hodges RNVR and ERA George Vause accompanied by two COPPists, Lieutenant Geoffrey Lyne RN and Lieutenant James Booth RNVR, who constituted S/COPP9,[212] experienced all of these sensations while awaiting the arrival of the largest amphibious invasion force in history. Captained by twenty-six year old Lieutenant George Honour RNVR, who had volunteered for 'hazardous service' while serving in the Western Desert with the Royal Naval Volunteer Reserve,[213] X-23 was positioned one mile off the port of Ouistreham, the furthest point east on 'Sword' beach. By identifying several key landmarks in and around Ouistreham, such as the lighthouse, the town church and the church spires in the villages of Langrune and St. Aubin-sur-Mer,[214] Navigation officer, Lieutenant Lyne, had managed to place the craft exactly where Honour had been briefed to do so.

Having been in receipt of the code word 'Pomade', which meant that the 'operation will take place' today,[215] X-23 surfaced at 0507 hrs on Tuesday 6 June, checked her position and rigged her mast with a lamp and radar beacon.[216] In addition to this, Honour's men also laid out rubber dinghies fitted with searchlights which were to be operated by a member of the crew as mark positions. Approaching ships would therefore be able to ascertain the exact positions of 'Gold', 'Juno' and 'Sword' beaches by taking bearings on the lights displayed by the dinghies and midget submarines.[217] For nearly two and a half hours on the morning of D-Day these two midget submarines sat on the surface exposing themselves fully to the Germans. However, in order to grant the crews of X-20 and X-23 a chance of successfully evading capture if their vessels were sunk by enemy fire, each member of the crew wore a rubber frogman's suit and carried false French papers.[218]

Risks aside, the operational details for *Gambit* were as follows. To successfully guide Naval Force 'S' to the right quarter of 'Sword' beach, X-23 would switch on a green signal light and would 'commence flashing until first assault forces arrived'.[219] The mechanics of this task obliged X-23 and her dinghy to 'flash coloured lights to seaward between bearings 350° and 030°'. In order to mark her own position, 'DD', X-23 was instructed to flash the letter 'D' for 'Dog' for 'ten seconds every forty seconds from H-140 (i.e. one hundred and forty minutes before H-Hour, which at 'Sword' beach was 0725 hours) until daylight, when she [would] show flag D for Dog'. To mark the position of her dinghy, 'HH', X-23 had to flash the letter 'H' for 'How' for 10 seconds every 40 seconds from H-80 until daylight when she [would] show flag H for How'. To aid the navigation of 'S' Force, X-23 used the following series of lights: Amber signified 'position accurate'; Green indicated 'position within 300 yds'; and Red signalled 'position within 1,000 yds'. Other navigational aids employed by Honour's men on the morning of D-Day were a rod sounder and Type 78 T Beacon, the latter of which X-23 used to transmit 'G' for 'George'.[220]

One of the main roles allotted to the X-craft on D-Day was to guide the Duplex-Drive (DD) tanks (amphibious Sherman tanks fitted with waterproof, air-filled canvas screens around their hulls and twin propellers working off their engines, which enabled them to swim ashore under their own propulsion) to their correct launch positions thousands of yards off shore.[221] Having ensured that the DD tanks were on target, the work of X-23 and her sister ship, X-20, was complete. At this point, the pre-arranged post-action extrication plan came into effect. Once the landings had taken place a Royal Navy landing craft would escort X-23 to Force 'S' HQ ship, HMS *Largs*, where it would await the arrival of HM Trawler *En Avant* at H+85 minutes. HMS *En Avant* would then tow X-23 back across the English Channel to *HMS Dolphin* where her crew could enjoy a well-earned rest,[222] having spent seventy-six hours at sea, sixty-four of these under water which, in the opinion of the British official history of the Normandy landings, had been a 'severe test of nerve, skill and endurance'.[223] For his outstanding seamanship and dedication to duty during Operation *Gambit*, Lieutenant George Honour was awarded the Distinguished Service Cross (DSC). Other gallantry awards went to Lieutenant Ken Hudspeth RANVR, Captain of X-20, who received a bar to his DSC; Lieutenant James Booth, who was awarded a French Croix de Guerre; and to various members of both submarine crews, who werementioned-in-despatches.[224]

NOTES

[202] Cornelius Ryan, *The Longest Day, June 6 1944*, (London: Victor Gollancz Ltd, 1982), p. 43.

[203] Bernard Ireland, *Jane's Warships of World War II*, (London: Harper Collins, 1996), p. 189.

[204] Patrick Bishop, *Target Tirpitz: X-Craft, Agents and Dambusters: The Epic Quest to Destroy Hitler's Mightiest Warship*, (London: Harper Press, 2012), pp. 215-272.

[205] Ian Trenowden, *Stealthily By Night: The COPPists: Clandestine Beach Reconnaissance and Operations in World War II*, (Midsomer Norton, Avon: Crécy Books Ltd, 1995), p. 136.

[206] Major L.F. Ellis *et al.*, *Victory in the West: The Battle of Normandy*, Volume I, (London: HMSO, 1962), p. 140.

[207] Donald McLachlan, *Room 39: Naval Intelligence in Action 1939-45*, (London: Weidenfeld & Nicolson, 1968), p. 331. See also Ian Trenowden, *Stealthily By Night: The COPPists: Clandestine Beach Reconnaissance and Operations in World War II*, (Midsomer Norton, Avon: Crécy Books Ltd, 1995), pp. 80-88.

[208] Ibid., p. 137.

[209] Major L.F. Ellis *et al.*, *Victory in the West: The Battle of Normandy*, Volume I, (London: HMSO, 1962), p. 141.

[210] TNA ADM 179/475, 'Operation Gambit – Operational Order', Bigot –Top Secret, 24th May 1944, p. 4.

[211] Ian Trenowden, *Stealthily By Night: The COPPists: Clandestine Beach Reconnaissance and Operations in World War II*, (Midsomer Norton, Avon: Crécy Books Ltd, 1995), p. 138.

[212] Ibid., p. 136.

[213] Cornelius Ryan, *The Longest Day, June 6 1944*, (London: Victor Gollancz Ltd, 1982), pp. 40-41.

[214] Ibid., p. 42.

[215] TNA ADM 179/475, 'Operation Gambit – Operational Order', Bigot – Top Secret, 24th May 1944, p. 4.

[216] Major L.F. Ellis *et al.*, *Victory in the West: The Battle of Normandy*, Volume I, (London: HMSO, 1962), pp. 160-161.

[217] Cornelius Ryan, *The Longest Day, June 6 1944*, (London: Victor Gollancz Ltd, 1982), p. 42.

[218] Ibid., p. 43.

[219] TNA ADM 179/475, 'Report on Operation "Gambit" from the Commanding Officer, H.M. Submarine "X.23" to Captain (S), Fifth Submarine Flotilla, "H.M.S. Dolphin", Top Secret, 9th June 1944, p. 2.

[220] Ibid., p. 3

[221] Stephen E. Ambrose, *D-Day: June 6, 1944: The Battle for the Normandy Beaches*, (London: Pocket Books, 2002), p. 54 & p. 509.

[222] TNA ADM 179/475, 'Operation Gambit – Operational Order', Bigot – Top Secret, 24th May 1944, p. 5.

[223] Major L.F. Ellis *et al.*, *Victory in the West: The Battle of Normandy*, Volume I, (London: HMSO, 1962), p. 161.

[224] Ian Trenowden, *Stealthily By Night: The COPPists: Clandestine Beach Reconnaissance and Operations in World War II*, (Midsomer Norton, Avon: Crécy Books Ltd, 1995), p. 144.

TNA ADM 179/475

OPERATION 'GAMBIT'

TOP SECRET

SUBJECT

REPORT ON OPERATION "GAMBIT".

FROM... THE COMMANDING OFFICER, H.M. SUBMARINE "X.23".

DATE.... 9ᵗʰ June, 1944.

TO....... CAPTADI (C), FIFTH SUBMARINE FLOTILLA, H. M. S. "DOLPHIN".

I have the honour to submit the following report on the conduct of H. M. Submarine "X.23" in operation "Gambit".

Friday, 2ⁿᵈ June.	2120.	C.O.P.P. and X-Craft personnel embarked.
		Lieutenant L.G. Lyne, R.N. – C.O.P.P.9.
		Lieutenant G.B. Honour, R.N.V.R. (C.O. H.M.S/M "X.23"
		Sub Lieutenant H.J. Hodges, R.N.V.R., (1ˢᵗ Lieut.)
		Lieutenant J.M. Booth, R.N.V.R. – C.O.P.P.9.
		E.R.A. G.B. Vause.
	2140.	Slipped from Fort Blockhouse and proceeded to East Gate.
	2225.	Passed through gate and rendezvoused with H.M.S. "Sapper".
		Some difficulty was experienced in passing the tow owing to the swell and the phones were very faint.
	2310.	Proceeded towed by H.M.S. "Sapper".
Saturday, 3ʳᵈ June.	0120.	"F" Buoy. Owing to the phones it was decided to remain on the surface as good speed was being made.
	0230.	Stopped while H.M. Submarine "X.20" cleared dan buoy mooring wire, that had fouled herscrew.
	0250.	Resumed course.
	0435.	Slipped tow in position 164° "F" Buoy 15.2 miles and proceeded on engine.
	0521.	Stopped engine and dived course 172° 650 revs. 30 feet.
	1025.	Raised Induction and guffed through.
	1525.	Raised induction and guffed through.
	1930.	Raised induction and guffed through.
	2320.	Surfaced and proceeded on engine with running charge.
Sunday, 4ᵗʰ June.	0300.	Broke charge increased to full ahead.
	0400.	Bottomed.
	0830.	Periscope depth ran to the East. Churches identified and fix obtained.

1100.   Bottomed........

TOP SECRET

-2-

Sunday, 4th June. (Continued).	1100.	Bottomed.
	1725.	Periscope depth and obtained further fixes.
	1940.	Bottomed
	2315.	Surfaced. No message received on wireless. Ran to final position on tant string and anchored.
Monday, 5th June.	0100.	Message received operation postponed twenty-four hours. Message was very faint and gyro repeater had to be switched off to receive message.
	0300.	Bottomed.
	2315.	Surfaced and commenced wireless watch. Message received operation taking place, but reception was very difficult and master gyro was stopped during the reception of the message which caused it to become unsettled and useless. However, as we were already in our marking position, this did not prove so serious as it might have done.
Tuesday, 6th June.	0445.	Surfaced.
	0507.	Commenced flashing until first assault forces arrived. Proceeded to H.M.S. "Largs".
	1205.	Rendezvoused H.M.T. "En Avant" and tried to pass tow, without success, owing to the high seas. H.M.T. "En Avant" towing wire passes and tow back commenced on surface. As we had no phones and there was a large amount of traffic in the channel, I decided it far better to carry on, on the surface.
		The passage crew had a very bumpy journey back, but kept in high spirits the whole journey.
Wednesday, 7th June.	0730.	Berthed alongside Fort Blockhouse.

I would like to stress the good work and cheerfulness of E.R.A. G.B. Vause, throughout the whole trip, he was continually attending to the hundred and one odd jobs that crop up in X-Craft and it was largely due to him that I was able to report 'No defects' on return. It is considered that his efforts are well worthy of Official recognition and he is recommended for such award as may be thought appropriate.

LIEUTENANT, R.N.V.R.

TNA WO 252/583

I.S.I.S. REPORT ON FRANCE: NORMANDY WEST OF THE SEINE, VOLUME 2 – INTER-SERVICE TOPOGRAPHICAL DEPARTMENT, PART VIII (A) PHOTOGRAPHS OF PART V (A) COAST, BEACHES AND EXITS, APRIL 1943

Photographs 37 to 45 represent snap-shots from a larger, comprehensive volume containing hundreds of photographs and postcards depicting the coastline and countryside of Lower Normandy. Selected by the British Inter-Service Topographical Department (ISTD), these images show the seaside town of Arromanches-les-Bains and the beach and cliffs of Longues-sur-Mer, a small village three miles to the west of Arromanches. Both geographical sites were located in the 'Gold' beach sector, a ten-mile strip of coast on which the British 50th Infantry Division would land on 6 June.[225] The historical importance of these snapshots stems from the fact that prior to D-Day they were instrumental in helping Allied planners select appropriate landing areas for men and war *materiel* in the 'Gold' beach sector. Working from a wealth of accumulated material, the ISTD played a leading role in selecting Arromanches to become the site for the famous artificial 'Mulberry' harbour 'B', later re-named 'Port Winston' in honour of the British Prime Minister. Operational from 14 June, 'Mulberry B' would eventually supply the British 21st Army Group with 6,000 tons of supplies per day.[226]

High above the beach at Longues-sur-Mer which, due to precipitous cliffs, was not suitable for amphibious landings, was sited a major German *Kriegsmarine* (German Navy) coastal battery consisting of 4 x Skoda 152 mm naval guns, which could engage enemy shipping up to a range of fourteen miles. Designated a *Stützpunkt* or strongpoint, the battery had a garrison of one-hundred and eighty men and was engaged by HMS *Ajax*, FFS *Georges Leygues* and HMS *Argonaut* on the morning of D-Day. Drawn into a long-range artillery duel with these warships for most of the day, the battery was finally neutralised at 1800 hours having fired only 150 shells. However, the position remained in German hands until it was finally captured by 2nd Battalion the Devonshire Regiment on the morning of 7 June following a direct infantry assault supported by naval, air and artillery bombardments.[227]

Geographical locations aside, the surprising presence of civilian photographs and postcards in War Office files is a direct result of the famous appeal orchestrated in 1942 by Admiral John Godfrey, the Director of Naval Intelligence (DNI). Through the medium of BBC radio, Godfrey broadcast to the nation requesting that listeners send in private photographs and holiday postcards of 'places of potential military interest' on the coast of Europe. The response to this clarion call was incredible. It had been estimated that perhaps as many as 10,000 people might reply to this official supplication. In fact, over 80,000 replies were received from listeners who had holidayed in France or who had lived there prior to the war. Due to the enthusiasm and patriotism of the British public, the ISTD was able to create a comprehensive photographic library from the material sent in, which by war's end was employing hundreds of staff.[228] This collection was, in the opinion of former member of the Naval Intelligence Division (NID), by 'far and away the largest and most valuable of its kind ever assembled in Britain...' or anywhere else in the world.[229] This vast archive of photographic evidence was of immense value to Allied planners for 'pictures taken at eye level can be more informative than obliques taken from aircraft' mainly because they can 'show the gradient [of a beach], whether the surface is sand or shingle', as well as indicate the 'height and construction of sea walls, groins and breakwaters'.[230] From this public appeal the ISTD was able to produce, for its military customers, a series of handbooks on different geographical areas along the Western coast of France, Lower Normandy being one of them. In conjunction with their efforts to acquire images of pre-war French beaches, the staff of the ISTD also searched libraries, universities and institutions for 'every kind of botanical, geological, mineral, agricultural, medical detail that might affect the efficiency of a force operating abroad'.[231]

Yet despite undertaking such crucial preparatory work, the ISTD remains one of the unsung heroes of D-Day. This is due largely to the fact that very little has been written by historians about its work, a situation compounded by the organisation having been somewhat overshadowed by the 'cloak and dagger' exploits of the Combined Operations Pilotage Parties (COPP), a specialist unit created in December 1942 to undertake, inter alia, the covert beach reconnaissance of the Dutch, Belgian and French coastlines.[232] Pre-dating the establishment of COPP, the ISTD had been created during the autumn of 1940 following the disastrous Norwegian campaign earlier in the year. Lamenting the lack of topographical information available to them at that time, the British Chiefs of Staff subsequently ordered the Joint Intelligence Committee (JIC), Britain's highest intelligence forum, to create a body that could manage the 'collection, analysis and distribution of topographical intelligence'. As a result, the Naval Intelligence Division's topographical section was reconfigured to supply relevant data to other Service departments, eventually moving out of London to Manchester College, Oxford in October 1940. There it evolved into the ISTD, operating under the aegis of the Admiralty for the duration of the war.[233]

Although headed by Colonel S.J. Bassett RM, who presided over an eclectic mix of Naval hydrographers, RAF specialists, Royal Engineers, academics and those from the worlds of publishing and advertising, the ISTD was, in actuality, the brainchild of Admiral John Godfrey. As one of his former subordinates has written, the ISTD was 'conceived, nurtured and brought to maturity, in the face of initial apathy in other departments, almost entirely as a result of Godfrey's vision, drive and enthusiasm'.[234] Starting out with just one member of staff, by the end of 1944 the department had swollen to 541 members,[235] who ensured that 'from June 1940 onwards, no single Commando, hardly an agent of SOE and certainly no major Allied force set foot on German or Italian held territory without the benefit of detailed information about the terrain and its natural and man-made features and characteristics'.[236]

The apogee for the ISTD and its product, however, occurred during the years 1942 to 1944 when the strategic balance began to shift in favour of the Allies. Suddenly critical to the process of operational planning, the ISTD became a crucial component of the Allied planning machinery for offensive operations against Hitler's *Festung Europa* (Fortress Europe). Divided into country sections, the ISTD was called upon to provide detailed background information for Commando raids such as the one on the dry-docks at St-Nazaire in March 1942 (Operation *Chariot*); the ill-fated Anglo-Canadian assault on Dieppe in August 1942 (Operation *Jubilee*); and Operation *Torch*, the Allied landings in North-west Africa in November of that year. Its greatest task, however, was the preparation of topographical intelligence for Operation *Overlord*. In doing so, the ISTD was obliged to draw upon a disparate collection of intelligence sources, both 'open' and 'secret'. These ranged from accounts by refugee aliens, reports from foreign governments-in-exile, covert intelligence supplied by the Secret Intelligence Service (SIS) and Photographic Reconnaissance (PR) images to captured documents, prisoner-of-war interrogations, details from underwater reconnaissance missions, information gained during commando raids and geological surveys. By means of this 'all-source analysis', the ISTD was able to supply its Whitehall customers with topographical intelligence on terrain, beaches, ports and transport communications. Moreover, by utilising over one million photographs of intended landing areas, the Inter-Service Topographical Department was able to furnish the Allied Expeditionary Force with up-to-date charts, maps and coastal silhouettes of German coastal defences.[237] Unsurprisingly, this was of inestimable value to Allied planners during the months and weeks leading up to D-Day.

NOTES

[225] Max Hastings, *Overlord: D-Day and the Battle for Normandy*, (London: Michael Joseph, 1984), p. 106.

[226] See Guy Hartcup, *Code Name Mulberry: The Planning, Building & Operation of the Normandy Harbours*, (Barnsley, South Yorkshire: Pen & Sword Books Ltd, 2011).

[227] Tim Saunders, *Battleground Europe: Gold Beach – JIG: JIG Sector and West – June 1944*, (Barnsley, South Yorkshire: Pen & Sword Books Ltd, 2002), pp. 131-142.

[228] See TNA ADM 223/90, Memo on Handbooks, Naval Intelligence Division, para. 81 and Donald McLachlan, *Room 39: Naval Intelligence in Action 1939-45*, (London: Weidenfeld & Nicolson, 1968), p. 315.

[229] Patrick Beesly, *Very Special Intelligence: The Life of Admiral J.H. Godfrey C.B.*, (London: Hamish Hamilton, 1980), p. 212.

[230] Jock Haswell, *The Intelligence and Deception of the D-Day Landings*, (London: B. T. Batsford Ltd, 1979), p. 93.

[231] Donald McLachlan, *Room 39: Naval Intelligence in Action 1939-45*, (London: Weidenfeld & Nicolson, 1968), p. 46.

[232] See Ian Trenowden, *Stealthily By Night: The COPPists: Clandestine Beach Reconnaissance and Operations in World War II*, (Midsomer Norton, Avon: Crécy Books Ltd, 1995).

[233] F.H. Hinsley *et al.*, *British Intelligence in the Second World War: Its Influence on Strategy and Operations*, Volume 1, (London: HMSO, 1979), p. 161.

[234] Patrick Beesly, *Very Special Intelligence: The Life of Admiral J.H. Godfrey C.B.*, (London: Hamish Hamilton, 1980), p. 205.

[235] Ibid.

[236] Ibid.

[237] F.H. Hinsley *et al.*, *British Intelligence in the Second World War: Its Influence on Strategy and Operations*, Volume 3, Part 2, (London: HMSO, 1988), p. 90.

I.S.I.S. REPORT ON

FRANCE

VOLUME 2

NORMANDY

WEST OF THE SEINE

C.B. 4096 J

*This book is invariably to be kept locked up when not in use and
is not to be taken outside the ship or establishment for which it is
issued without the express permission of the Commanding Officer*

INTER-SERVICE TOPOGRAPHICAL DEPARTMENT

January 1943

C.B. 4096 J (20)

I.S.I.S. REPORT ON

FRANCE

VOLUME 2

NORMANDY
WEST OF THE SEINE

PART VIII (A)

PHOTOGRAPHS OF PART V (A)
COAST, BEACHES, AND EXITS

INTER-SERVICE TOPOGRAPHICAL DEPARTMENT

April 1943

37 Between Asnelles and Arromanches

38 Arromanches-Les–Bains, Looking East

39 Arromanches-Les-Bains: The Sea Wall

40 Arromanches-Les-Bains: The Sea Wall

41 Arromanches-Les-Bains: The Sea Wall

42 Arromanches-Les-Bains: The Hard and Sea Wall

43 The Cliffs West of Arromanches

44 Landing 33. Longues-sur-Mer, Looking East

45 Landing 33. Longues-sur-Mer: The Beach

TNA ADM 53/120730

HMS *WARSPITE* – SHIP'S LOG TUESDAY 6 JUNE 1944

HMS *Warspite*, a dreadnought battleship of the Queen Elizabeth Class, is considered to be one of the most distinguished ships ever to have served in the Royal Navy. Referred to as the 'Grand Old Lady', she was commissioned in March 1915 and weighed 30,600 tons. In June 1944 her main armament consisted of 8 x 15 inch guns, while her secondary armament comprised 20 x 4.5 inch and 32 x 40 mm anti-aircraft guns. With a ship's complement of 1,184 men her top speed was 24 knots and she measured 195.0 x 31.7 x 9.4 m.[238] While serving in the Grand Fleet's 5th Battle Squadron she saw her first action at the Battle of Jutland on 31 May 1916 during which she suffered severe damage from German naval fire. Forced to limp back to Rosyth for urgent repairs, *Warspite* would later suffer further damage through a series of collisions and accidents ensuring that she took no further part in naval operations during the First World War.[239]

Having survived the serious cuts inflicted upon the Royal Navy in the aftermath of the 1914-1918 war, *Warspite* continued to serve throughout the inter-war years despite undergoing a series of modifications, reconstructions and refits to her engines, armaments and super-structure.[240] In 1937 she became the flagship of the Mediterranean Fleet but at the outbreak of war she was ordered back to the UK to join the Home Fleet tasked with hunting down German capital ships. Over the next five years *Warspite* would see action at the Second Battle of Narvik (13 April 1940); the Battle of Cape Matapan (27-29 March 1941); the landings in Sicily (Operation *Husky*, 9 July 1943) and at Salerno in September of that year (Operation *Avalanche*) where she was nearly sunk by German radio-controlled glider-bombs.[241] Furthermore, she would go on to provide naval gun support to the amphibious assault on the island of Walcheren in November 1944 (Operation *Infatuate*). In all, HMS *Warspite* earned ten battle honours during the Second World War, adding to a record number of such awards unsurpassed by any individual ship in the Royal Navy.[242]

Such distinctions aside, on the morning of Tuesday 6 June 1944, HMS *Warspite* (with X turret and No. 4 boiler non-operational due to damage sustained at Salerno) was but one of 1,213 naval warships positioned off the Normandy coast.[243] As part of the Eastern Naval Task Force commanded by Rear-Admiral Sir Philip Vian RN, *Warspite*, in conjunction with her sister ships HMS *Ramillies*, another Queen Elizabeth class battleship, and the monitor HMS *Roberts*, both armed with 15 inch guns, constituted the heavy guns component of Bombarding Force 'D' tasked with supporting the landings by Assault Force 'S' on 'Sword' beach.[244] Bombarding Force 'D', directed by Rear-Admiral W.R. Patterson RN aboard his flagship HMS *Mauritius*, comprised two Battleships, one Monitor, five cruisers and thirteen destroyers.[245] Their job was to engage and neutralise selected German coastal batteries and enemy communications in order to 'assist in ensuring the safe and timely arrival of [land] forces…and to support the assault and subsequent operations ashore'.[246]

As related by the official history of the Royal Navy during the Second World War, at 0530 hours 'along the whole fifty-mile front the warships' guns opened up with what was up to that time the heaviest rain of shells ever to be poured on land targets from the sea'.[247] *Warspite's* log for 6 June records that from 0530 hours onwards she engaged German coastal batteries at Villerville, Benerville and Houlgate to the east of 'Sword' beach.[248] Like her sister ship *Ramillies*, *Warspite* could 'lob' a shell weighing nearly a ton over a distance of 32,000 yards or 18 miles.[249] This reach meant that she could successfully engage the distant 155 mm gun battery at Le Havre which, instead of targeting vulnerable landing ships off 'Sword' beach, wasted her shells in a long-range duel with the old dreadnought.[250] The unforgettable experience of being aboard the mighty battleship when she fired salvo after salvo from her 15 inch guns was recorded by an imbedded American journalist, who wrote:

> When the guns fired at once the great 35,000-ton [*sic*] battleship gave a tremendous shudder. Everything on board that can fall or break loose has to be fastened or battened down when the ship goes into action. Cabin doors in the bridge have to be removed or the blast that rushes from end to end of the ship when she fires would splinter the panelling. Ears have to be plugged with cotton-wool'.[251]

The accuracy of Allied naval gunfire on D-Day relied heavily upon 104 specially trained Mustang and Spitfire pilots.[252] Prior to the launch of Operation *Neptune*, each pilot trained intensively with the particular ship he would observe for. To ensure the success of this naval-air partnership, the observers flew in pairs – one acting as a fighter escort while the other concentrated on observing the fall of shot.[253] One such pilot employed on this specialised work was Wing Commander L.C. Glover RAF, who was assigned spotter to *Warspite*. Glover spent the morning of D-Day flying half-way between *Warspite* and the Norman coastline observing the fall of shot aimed at an enemy battery at Villerville. However, during the course of his sortie Glover nearly had his plane destroyed by two shells fired from the battleship, an episode he later recounted:

> I called out the order 'fire' and turned slowly broadside on to the shore to wait for the fall of shot. Suddenly, in the clear sky my aircraft experienced a most violent bump which practically shook me out of my wits. At the same moment, I saw two enormous objects moving rapidly away from me toward the shore and immediately realized that I had flown at right angles through the slipstream of *Warspite's* two ranging 15-inch 'bricks.[254]

Unfortunately, not all of Glover's comrades were so lucky. During the opening phase of *Neptune* two Allied spotter planes were hit and obliterated by naval shells.

Remarkably, the only attempt by *Kriegsmarine* surface vessels to attack the Allied armada on D-Day came from three German E-Boats who launched a torpedo attack on Bombardment Force 'D' at 0530 hours. Taking advantage of cover afforded them by a smoke screen laid by Allied aircraft to shroud the bombarding squadron from German shore batteries, the three E-Boats fired a number of torpedoes. Although two passed harmlessly between *Warspite* and *Ramillies*, one did hit the Norwegian S-Class destroyer H.Nor.M.S *Svenner* sinking her.[255] However, *Warspite's* log notes that at 0604 hours she 'engaged twelve enemy destroyers in Mouth of Seine' and that at 0612 hours the battleship 'Hit and sank' one of these enemy destroyers thereby dissuading other surface ships from attempting any further offensive action against the fleet.[256]

Having undertaken twenty 'shoots' between 6 and 7 June, firing a total of 314 shells from her main armament, *Warspite* was obliged to return to Portsmouth in order to replenish her magazines.[257] Returning to action on 9 June, she was tasked with providing naval gun support not only to the US VII Corps at 'Utah' beach, but also to the British 50th Infantry Division in the 'Gold' beach area.[258] During this period of consolidation, Allied warships such as *Warspite* were instrumental in breaking-up or disrupting German counter-attacks aimed against the Allied beachhead. *Generalfeldmarschall* Erwin Rommel, Inspector-General of the Atlantic Wall and commander of Army Group B, complained to Adolf Hitler on 11 June that 'the effects of heavy naval bombardment are so powerful that an operation either with infantry or armoured formations is impossible in an area commanded by his rapid [naval] firing artillery'.[259] Yet on 11 June *Warspite* was once again obliged to leave her gun-line in order to restock on ammunition consequently sailing to Portsmouth where it was discovered that her 15 inch guns were worn out and needed replacing. En route to a refit at Rosyth naval base she was severely damaged by a magnetic mine thereby preventing any further participation in Operation *Neptune* which ended on 30 June. It was not until 25 August that *Warspite* returned to service when she resumed her bombardment duties this time against the fortresses at Brest and Le Havre.[260] Following her last action at Walcheren, HMS *Warspite* sailed to Portsmouth where she was placed into category C reserve in early November 1944, paid off into reserve in February 1945 and finally sent for scrap in April 1947 thus ending a long and distinguished life.

NOTES

[238] Bernard Ireland, *Jane's Warships of World War II*, (London: Harper Collins, 1996), pp. 106-107

[239] Captain S.W. Roskill D.S.C., R.N., *HMS Warspite: The Story of a Famous Warship*, (London: Futura Publications, 1974), pp. 102-140.

[240] Ibid., pp. 154-192.

[241] Bernard Ireland, *Jane's Warships of World War II*, (London: Harper Collins, 1996), p. 107.

[242] Paul Kennedy, *Engineers of Victory: The Problem Solvers Who Turned the Tide in the Second World War*, (London: Allen Lane, 2013), p. 253.

[243] *The Oxford Companion to the Second World War*, edited by I.C.B. Dear and M.R.D. Foot, (Oxford: Oxford University Press, 1995), p. 853.

[244] Bombarding Force 'D' was one of five bombardment forces committed to Operation *Neptune*, the others being 'E' for 'Juno', ' K' for 'Gold', 'C' for 'Omaha' and 'A' for 'Utah'.

[245] Captain S.W. Roskill, D.S.C., R.N., *The War At Sea 1939-1945: The Offensive, 1st June 1944 – 14th August 1945*, Volume III, Part II, (London: HMSO, 1961), p. 32.

[246] Ibid., p. 30.

[247] Ibid., p. 43.

[248] TNA ADM 53/120730, Ship's Log HMS *Warspite*, 6 June 1944. See also Major L.F. Ellis *et al.*, *Victory in the West: The Battle of Normandy*, Volume I, (London: HMSO, 1962), p. 162.

[249] *D-Day Then and Now*, Volume 2, edited by Winston G. Ramsey, (London: Battle of Britain Prints International Ltd, 1995), p. 521.

[250] Paul Kennedy, *Engineers of Victory: The Problem Solvers Who Turned the Tide in the Second World War*, (London; Allen Lane, 2013), p. 270.

[251] Robert J. Kershaw, *D-Day: Piercing the Atlantic Wall*, (Hersham, Surrey: Ian Allen Publishing Ltd. 2004), p. 98.

[252] In addition to these pilots, thirty-nine 'Forward Observers Bombardment' (F.O.Bs) landed with British assault troops thereafter directing naval gunfire from ashore. See Captain S.W. Roskill, D.S.C., R.N., *The War At Sea 1939-1945: The Offensive, 1st June 1944 – 14th August 1945*, Volume III, Part II, (London: HMSO, 1961), p. 33.

[253] Ibid., pp.32-33.

[254] Stephen E. Ambrose, *D-Day: June 6, 1944: The Battle for the Normandy Beaches*, (London: Pocket Books, 2002), pp. 268-269.

[255] Major L.F. Ellis *et al.*, *Victory in the West: The Battle of Normandy*, Volume I, (London: HMSO, 1962), pp. 162-163.

[256] TNA ADM 53/120730, Ship's Log HMS *Warspite*, 6 June 1944.

[257] Captain S.W. Roskill, D.S.C., R.N., *The War At Sea 1939-1945: The Offensive, 1st June 1944 – 14th August 1945*, Volume III, Part II, (London: HMSO, 1961), p. 45.

[258] Ibid., p .62.

[259] Ibid.

[260] Captain S.W. Roskill D.S.C., R.N., *HMS Warspite: The Story of a Famous Warship*, (London: Futura Publications, 1974), pp. 282-283.

HMS *WARSPITE* – SHIP'S LOG, TUESDAY 6 JUNE 1944

Initials of the Officer of the Watch	H.M.S											Tuesday 6th day of June, 1944.	
	From							*To*				*or At* Sea	
	Time	Log (Stating type)	Distance Run through the water		True Course	Mean Revolutions per minute	wind		Weather and Visibility	Sea and Swell	Corrected Barometric Pressure in Millibars	Temperature (°F)			LEAVE GRANTED TO SHIP'S COMPANY
			Miles	Tenths			Direction (true)	Force (0-12)				Dry Bulb	Wet Bulb	Sea	REMARKS
	0100	016.3	13	0	160°	146.7									0120 Sighted Leader buoy of Channel 10 Co. 160° Force D proceeded by 40 M.S. to the coast of France
	0200		13	0	160°	151.5									
	0210		2	0	160°										0210 A/C to 170° in wake of sweepers
	0300	040.6	10	5	170°	144.2									
			5	5	170°										
	0400	052.3	8	0	160°	151.2	E	3	c/5	31					
	0500	059.7	7	5	160°	82.7									0525 Stopped in bombardment billet
	0525		2	5	160°										250° 11 ½ miles from cap D La Havre. 0530 Opened
	0600	NR.	0	2	as req	43.3									fire on enemy shore battery 3 ? 0545-0558
	0700	063.6	1	5	"	30.0									Bombarded battery at villerville. 0604 Engaged twelve enemy destroyer in Mouth of seine
	0800	064.1	1	5	"	31.5	E	3	c/5	31					0612 Hit and sank one enemy destroyer. 0612 - 0647 commended bombarding villervill
	0900	065.3	1	5	"	34.0									shore battery. 0733 First wave of assault troops touched down on beaches. Co and speed
	1000	068.0	5	5	"	62.5									as reg for remaining in bombardment area. 0738-53 Bombarded shore battery at commerville 0755-0821 Bombarded battery at
	1100	069.5	1	5	"	29.8									Villerville 0901-0938 Re engaged Villerville battery. 0945 Working party embarked in L.C.T. 0952-1012 Bombard battery
	1200	069.5	3	0	"	40.6	SE	3	bc/6	23					at Benerville 1112-1200 Villeville battery agained bombarded 1219-1229 Bombarded Benerville battery w/r C.B is correct

Distance run through the Water	Position		Latitude N		Longitude W		Depending on	Currents experienced		ANCHOR BEARINGS
232.2	0800		° ′ 49° 24		° ′ 00 18		hand fix			2305 - St ? Lt. 132°. Predever Lt. 222°.
	1200		49 22		00 15		"			
Zone Time kept at noon -2	2000		49 23		00 17		"	Number on Sick List	3	

Time	Distance	Pos		Course / Lat	value	Wind	force	weather	current	ANCHOR BEARINGS
1300	70.5	3	0	as req.	42.0°					1309-1335 Benerville battery re-engaged 1315 A/Raid message R. 1331 air raid message W.
1400	70.5	0	5	"						1440-1503 Bombarded concentration of enemy vehicles (tanks lorries etc.)
1500	70.5	0	0	"	12.6					1520-1545 Bombard German H.Q. and shore battery.
1600	71.0	3	5	"	43.7	W	3	bc/7	23	1551-1621 Bombard Villerville shore battery
1700	71.0	2	0	"	35.5					
1800	71.7	6	0	"	70.2	W	3	bc/7	23	1710-1814 Re engage Villerville battery assisted by formation of aircraft.
1900	73.7	3	5	"	41.9					
2000	74.9	2	0	"	36.6	W	3	bc/1	31	1931 Assumed 3rd° readiness 2005 air raid message R.
2100	74.9	3	0	"	45.9					
2200	78.2	5	5	"	59.8					
2300	88.0	9			108.5					2305 Came to st?d ? with six shackles in ? Air Raid message W. (312° St Aubins Lt 3.8 miles)
2400						W	4	bc/5	21	

TNA DEFE 2/253

'RAID ON QUINÉVILLE – REPORT ON INTELLIGENCE OBTAINED' - OPERATION *HARDTACK 21*

The story of the Army Commandos began in the summer of 1940 when Prime Minister Winston Churchill ordered that a specialist force be raised to undertake 'butcher-and-bolt' raids along the coastline of Nazi-held Europe. Eventually formalised into individual, battalion-sized units designed to operate behind enemy lines as self-contained groups, each Army Commando, whose unit designations numbered from No. 1 Commando to No. 12 Commando, comprised around 500 men.[261] Well trained, highly-motivated and superbly fit, these men would participate in some of the most famous raids of the war such as Operations *Claymore* (4 March 1941); *Anklet* and *Archery* (26-28 December 1941) launched ostensibly to destroy shipping, warehouses and stocks of fish oil, paraffin and kerosene on the Lofoten Islands and at Vaagsö in Norway;[262] Operation *Chariot*, the audacious raid on the huge dry-dock at St Nazaire in March 1942; and Operation *Jubilee*, the disastrous amphibious assault on the seaside town of Dieppe in August of that year.

Yet more obscure and little known are the series of Commando raids launched in late December 1943 against selected targets on the Channel Islands and along the Dutch and French coasts. Orchestrated by the British Combined Operations HQ they were code-named *Hardtack* and heavily involved No. 10 (Inter-Allied) Commando. Created at a meeting at the War Office on 26 June 1942, this truly international Commando would eventually comprise six sections made up of volunteers from France, Holland, Belgium, Norway, Poland and Yugoslavia. In addition, it had on its strength a secret unit, X Troop, which consisted of German nationals and German-speaking Jews and eastern Europeans, who had escaped from Nazi occupation and persecution during the early years of the war.[263] These men were of particular value to their British counterparts in that they could interrogate prisoners-of-war, translate captured documents and participate in psychological warfare against their former countrymen.

The antecedents to *Hardtack* raids began during the spring of 1943 when GHQ Home Forces was directed to make every effort to deceive the Germans into thinking that the Allied invasion would be unleashed against the Pas-de-Calais. Consequently, small-scale Commando raids were orchestrated against chosen targets on the Dutch-Belgian coast and that of northern France. To aid Allied deception measures 'Raid commanders', according to one authority on the subject, were 'not told of the strategic nature of the operation but were instructed to gather intelligence, capture prisoners and leave evidence of visits with beach navigation markers'. Unsurprisingly, this was against the spirit and indeed the letter of the classic Commando reconnaissance which aimed to infiltrate a target and then withdraw from it without leaving a clue as to its recent presence.[264]

By mid 1943, and with Allied planning for *Overlord* well under way, the Chief of the Imperial General Staff (CIGS), General Sir Alan Brooke, instructed that all small raids were now to be co-ordinated by the Chief of Staff to the Supreme Allied Commander (COSSAC), with the details of each operation to be worked out by the Small Scale Raiding Committee at Combined Operations HQ.[265] Having devised the *Hardtack* series of missions, this committee selected 1 Troop (French) of No. 10 (Inter-Allied) Commando to execute their plans. Selected primarily for their local knowledge and linguistic skills, these French Commandos trained throughout the early autumn of 1943 mounting their first *Hardtack* raid (*Hardtack Dog*) against Biville, a French commune in Lower Normandy, between 24-27 November.[266] Throughout late December numerous other *Hardtack* raids were launched by men of No. 10 Commando, supported on occasions by other units such as the Special Boat Squadron (SBS) and Nos 4 and 12 Commandos.[267]

In keeping with the activities of the Combined Operations Pilotage Parties (COPP), whose *raison d'être* was to acquire beach intelligence through stealth and guile, the men of No. 10 Commando were also tasked with collecting valuable intelligence on German coastal defences. Yet the job of Army Commandos sent on *Hardtack* missions differed in one crucial respect from that of their contemporaries in COPP, namely the capture of German prisoners for interrogation. Always fraught with the potential to 'go noisy' if German personnel resisted capture or fought their attackers, *Hardtack* raids were, nevertheless, designed to probe covertly different sectors of Hitler's 'Atlantic Wall' prior to the launch of Operation *Overlord*. Yet by landing *Hardtack* missions in different geographical areas, Combined Operations HQ ensured that the German high command would remain guessing as to the intended location of the main Allied landings.

For Operation *Hardtack 21*, a reconnaissance mission to Quinéville, a small village on the east coast of the Cotentin Peninsula, an entirely French patrol was selected comprising five men from one (French) Troop No. 10 Commando commanded by Sub-Lieutenant Francis Vourc'h. Their target was situated in an area Allied planners would later designate 'Peter' sector of 'Utah' beach[268] on which the US VII Corps, commanded by General J. Lawton 'Lightning Joe' Collins, would land the US 4th and 90th Infantry Divisions on D-Day.[269] The German unit responsible for the stretch of coastline from Quinéville southward was the 919th Hessian-Thüringian Grenadier Regiment from the 709th Infantry Division commanded by *Generalleutnant* Karl-Wilhelm von Schlieben.[270] In the days following D-Day, Quinéville and its surrounding area would become the focal point for fierce fighting.[271]

Hardtack 21 had originally been intended to be launched on the night of 25/26 December 1943 but due to bad weather was postponed until the following night. Transported to a position off the Normandy coast by a Motor Torpedo Boat (MTB) operating out of the port of Newhaven, Vourc'h's men infiltrated close to shore using a Dory, a twenty-foot rowing boat powered by an out-board motor. Coxswained by a Royal Naval rating and accompanied by a Commando signaller, whose job it was to remain in radio contact with the MTB, the Dory towed a smaller craft, a RAF dinghy which Vourc'h's patrol paddled towards a stretch of beach just north of Quinéville.[272]

Once ashore the raiding party spent from 2350 to 0245 hours reconnoitring this particular stretch of coast with the aim of reporting back on 'inundations and beach obstacles'. In the process they took note of coastal defences such as 'Element C', collected sand and mud samples and recorded the types of vegetation, terrain and enemy activity encountered.[273] They also hoped to catch a prisoner, duly setting up an ambush to achieve this end. Nevertheless, despite very close proximity to the enemy the patrol was not challenged or fired upon and no German prisoners were captured. In recognition of the patrol's success in bringing back invaluable intelligence on German defences in the Quinéville area, data that was fed directly into Allied planning for 'Utah' beach, Vourc'h was awarded the Military Cross by the British, the first officer in No. 10 Commando to be decorated for such work.[274]

Yet despite such successes, *Hardtack* raids came to an abrupt end in January 1944 due to growing concern within COSSAC that further missions would inevitably draw German attention to Normandy as a likely point of invasion. Despite protestations from Admiral Sir Bertram Ramsay, mastermind of Operation *Neptune*, the seaborne phase of *Overlord*, that this type of operation should indeed continue albeit elsewhere in Europe, other figures such as Montgomery's Chief of Staff, Major-General Freddie de Guingand, shared COSSAC's anxieties. Ultimately, the SHAEF Raids and Reconnaissance Committee had the final word on the matter decreeing that, with the exception of COPP who were to continue to reconnoitre selected assault beaches, all other Commando units were now forbidden from operating along the Belgium and French coasts.[275] Yet despite this embargo men from No. 10 (Inter-Allied) Commando would go on to participate in another series of beach reconnaissance missions prior to D-Day codenamed Operation *Tarbrush*, which were executed between 14-19 May in response to Allied concerns about the sowing of German mines on beaches.[276] The Commando's two French Troops, Nos 1 and 8, would go on to participate in Operation *Overlord* itself, landing on 'Red' sector of 'Sword' beach at 0820 hours on D-Day, their mission being: to eliminate the Cassino strongpoint (*Wiederstandnest* 10) at Riva Bella near Ouistreham.[277]

NOTES

[261] *The Oxford Companion to the Second World War*, edited by I.C.B. Dear and M.R.D. Foot, (Oxford: Clarendon Press, 1995), p. 1152.

[262] See F.H. Hinsley *et al.*, *British Intelligence in the Second World War: Its Influence on Strategy and Operations*, Volume II, (London: HMSO, 1981), p. 200.

[263] Nick Van Der Bijl, *Commandos in Exile: The Story of 10 (Inter-Allied) Commando 1942-1945*, (Barnsley, South Yorkshire: Pen & Sword Books Ltd, 2008), p. 10 & pp. 13-14.

[264] Ibid., p. 75.

[265] Ibid., p. 79.

[266] Ibid., p. 80.

[267] Although thirty-one *Hardtack* raids were planned under the aegis of Combined Operations HQ, only ten left the drawing board. See TNA DEFE 2/236 - DEFE/258 and TNA DEFE 2/345; and Nick Van Der Bijl, *Commandos in Exile: The Story of 10 (Inter-Allied) Commando 1942-1945*, (Barnsley, South Yorkshire: Pen & Sword Books Ltd, 2008), Appendix 4: 'No. 10 (Inter-Allied) Commando Raiding Table', pp. 198-200.

[268] 'Utah' beach was sub-divided by Allied planners into several different landing sectors. These began in the north with 'Peter' at Quinéville moving southward through 'Queen', 'Roger', 'Sugar', 'Tare', 'Uncle', 'Victor' to 'William' sector at the mouth of the Vire estuary. See *D-Day Then and Now*, volume 2, edited by Winston G. Ramsey, (London: Battle of Britain Prints Ltd, 1995), p. 377.

[269] Gordon A. Harrison, *US Army in World War II: European Theater of Operations: Cross-Channel Attack*, (Washington DC: Office of the Chief of Military History, Department of the Army, 1951), p. 182.

[270] Stephen Badsey, *Battle Zone Normandy: Utah Beach*, (Stroud, Gloucestershire: Sutton Publishing Ltd, 2004), p. 30.

[271] Gordon A. Harrison, *US Army in World War II: European Theater of Operations: Cross-Channel Attack*, (Washington DC: Office of the Chief of Military History, Department of the Army, 1951), pp. 390-395.

[272] Nick Van Der Bijl, *Commandos in Exile: The Story of 10 (Inter-Allied) Commando 1942-1945*, (Barnsley, South Yorkshire: Pen & Sword Books Ltd, 2008), pp. 75-76.

[273] TNA DEFE 2/253, 'Raid on QUINEVILLE – Report on Intelligence Obtained', Combined Operations Headquarters, 'Most Secret', 30 December 1943, pp. 1-3.

[274] Nick Van Der Bijl, *Commandos in Exile: The Story of 10 (Inter-Allied) Commando 1942-1945*, (Barnsley, South Yorkshire: Pen & Sword Books Ltd, 2008), p. 83.

[275] Ibid., pp. 83-84.

[276] Ibid., p. 90.

[277] Ken Ford, *Battle Zone Normandy: Sword Beach*, (Stroud, Gloucestershire: Sutton Publishing Ltd, 2004), p. 42 & p. 55.

Combined Operations Headquarters,
1a, Richmond Terrace,
Whitehall, S.W.1.

3 0 DEC 1943

T.I.S.

COPY NO. 12

C.O.S.S.A.C.

Raid on QUINEVILLE – Report on Intelligence Obtained.

Reference maps GSGS 4347 Sheet 31/20 NE and GSGS 4250 Sheet 6E/3 & 4.

SUMMARY.

1.   Half a dozen Special Service Troops reconnoitred an area north of QUINEVILLE, on the east side of the COTENTIN peninsula, on night 26/27 December 43. They penetrated between two occupied strong points only 500 yards apart, reconnoitred unobserved an "Elements C" anti-tank obstacle and an inundation. They brought back specimens of mud from the inundation and from a marshy patch on the beach, and a fragment of a new wire fence. The enemy showed occasional S.Ls and Verey Lights but did not fire on the patrol or the M.T.B. carrying it. The force were ashore for nearly 3 hours (2350 to about 0245).

BEACH.

2.   The beach was 1,000 yards wide at the time and place (about 373107) of landing, and composed of firm sand, of which a specimen (BAG A) was brought back.

3.   Near high-water mark there was an extensive marshy area, with some green or yellowish vegetation growing on it, into which men sank up to their ankles and sometimes to their knees. A specimen (BAG B) of the mud in the marsh was recovered.

(Comment: the vegetation shows clearly in air
photographs, e.g. print 2067 of 140 Sqn. sortie
R.A.853 . The marsh is NOT mapped).

4.   The bed of the little stream which runs across the beach from 363108 was also very soft going, though sand and not mud.
(Comment: This stream is NOT mapped. See also 12 below).

OBSTACLES.

Underwater Wire.

5.   At 365108 the force crossed a wire fence running in the marsh parallel to the shore and about 200 yards from high-water line. This was a very old, jumbled entanglement, apparently suffering from constant immersion, and was cut without difficulty.

New Wire?

6.   There is an incomplete and discontinuous apron fence
just   inland of the coastal track, parallel with the shore,
running from 363110 to 363108. A short specimen is attached (packet D).

(Comment: this is the same type of wire as has
previously been recovered from other areas, and as
is illustrated on plate 11A of M.I.10's "Notes on
Enemy Obstacles No.1"; but specimens we have seen
before have been in much rustier condition.
Suggest this is a new fence in course of erection,
replacing the fence which has been seen here on photographs
Elements C.   for some months).

7.   The force met at several points the Elements C obstacle
which runs from 363110 to 363107 (clearly visible on air photographs),
and subsequently recognised it as such from ground photographs.
They measured its height as 7 ft. 10 ins. and the width of one
section as 9 ft. 1 in.

(Comment: these are 3 ins. and 8 ins. over the
accepted measurements, but the accepted figure
for width (8 ft. 5 ins) does NOT include the thick
side bolts for attaching each section to its
neighbour.
This may be an indication of the degree of
accuracy of measurement to be expected from parties
working in these conditions - i.e. pitch dark night
and very near the enemy).

8.   The obstacle was not in any way fixed or stapled into the
ground, and here and there could be moved slightly by two or three
men.

9.   Where the obstacle crossed the road at 363108, one section
had been left wheeled back to allow vehicles to pass: two men
could move this about easily and fairly quietly (cf print 4028 of
400 Sqn sortie R41).

10.   The obstacle was not seen to be complicated in any way
by wire or booby traps, and two men climbed over it without
difficulty.

TRACKS AND FLOODING.

11.   The track parallel with the shore just inland of high-water
mark (363109 northwards) is a beaten earth track 9 ft. wide.
Heavy vehicle tyre ruts, two or three inches deep, were visible in
places.

12.   The road running eastward to the shore at 363108 has a
macadamised surface, in good condition and 13 ft. wide. On its
north side runs a stream; on its south side a grass verge, about
12 ft. wide, shelves into the flood. The road surface seemed to
be rather under 3 ft. above water level.

13.   Two men waded into the flooded area, from the seaward side,
at 363108 (inside blue square on map) and 363109. They reported
the ground very soft and muddy underfoot: a specimen of mud from
363109 was recoevered (BAG C). The water was about 18 ins. deep
at 363109 and 6 ins. to 9 ins. in the southern field 363108.

ENEMY ACTIVITY.

Light Signals.

14.   At 2325 hrs, while the dory was approaching the beach, a
Verey Light signal (Green over Red over Green) was fired from
QUINEVILLE 3703. One or two single red lights were fired at the

/same time..

same time. While the dory was withdrawing single red and single white signals were fired. More details may later be obtainable.

Searchlights.

15.   While the dory was withdrawing a single searchlight exposed from about FORT ST MARCOUF 388062 directly onto the waiting M.T.B. remained stationary for over two minutes, swung inland and doused. About 10 minutes later it again exposed, this time sweeping out to sea across the M.T.B. and back onto it; held it for a minute; resumed its sweep and doused. The beam passed over the dory, without halting, about four times during these sweeps. Thirty minutes later it exposed several times straight along the beach with a stationary beam.

Fire was not opened by either side.

Verey Lights were NOT fired while the S.L. was exposed.

16.   A strong steady torch was shown from QUINEVILLE to seaward from 2307 to about 2335 and about 2355 to 0015.

Movement Ashore.

17.   While the force were crossing the beach on their way in they heard a dog bark from the direction of the strong point 363114, and thought they heard a Frenchman call to it "Vas tu te taire".

18.   While they were reconnoitring the road at 363108 they saw a torch and heard a dog and voices about 200 yards to their southeast.

19.   Four of them went as far north as the old weapon position at 362113 - i.e., almost on top of the strong point at 363114 - without notice being taken of them. The weapon position was a square pit about 10 ft. across, the sides of which - reinforced by stone - had started to fall in.

20.   Comment: The force did in fact land 1,150 yards north of where they had intended. On previous information it would not normally have been recommended as feasible to send the force in through a gap of only 480 yards between occupied strong points: possibly the date (26 Dec) had its influence on enemy state of readiness?

G. G. RICE

Major G.S
for S.I.O.
to Chief of Combined Operations.

HARDTACK 21.

This raid against QUINEVILLE was originally mounted on the night 25/26 Dec 43 but cancelled due to unsuitable weather although raids against the Channel Islands took place this night.   The following night the raid was again mounted and carried out.   The object was to make a reconnaissance of inundations.   The Force landed at a point other than that intended but were able to reconnoitre a stretch of coast 500 yards long between the two strongpoints and to report on inundations and beach obstacles.

No German patrols were encountered and although occasional searchlights were exposed and verey lights fired there was no further German reaction.

DEFENCES.

General.

All defences as interpreted from air
photographs up to 24 Oct 43. and reports from ground
sources, are shown on the defence tracing.

Infantry Defences   (described from South to north)

QUINEVILLE is quite strongly held and the
defences extend a mile or more south of the River
SINOPE.   To the north of the SINOPE the northern
edge of the QUINEVILLE defences is at 374087. This
defence area may be expected to contain a few heavier
weapons such as small A/Tk guns, light infantry guns
and French 75 mm in addition to the usual light
and heavy MGs. (Searchlights, although not shown,
will certainly be present in the area) Mines are
reported along the coast in area 3807-3708

The defences here include also several
obstacles such as Element "C", as well as rail
tetrahedra set in concrete as under-water obstacles
between 374086 and 573088.

A house known as the MAISON ROUGE is at
370093 and may be a small defence area of sorts.   There
are one or two possible weapon pits and a just possible
minefield.   There may be wire surrounding the grounds
but this cannot be seen on air photos. Troops could,
of course, live in the house itself.

Just north of the MAISON ROUGE a road comes
down to the coast at 368096, where there is probably
a derelict defence post.   A possible pill-box is
marked, as well as two weapon-pits and some slit trenches,
but it is not active, although some old wire may be
found in the area.

At 363109 and 363115 are small defence positions
each of which may contain one weapon heavier than a
MG. - that at 363115 is definitely reported to contain one
37 mm A/Tk gun (and also two AA MGs)

At 363128 is an area where some activity is
visible and where there are one or two huts as well as
trenching and weapon pits.   Wire possibly surrounds
the site.

At 367145 is the MORSALINES strongpoint which
will contain, in addition to MGs, one or more A/Tk guns
or light guns up to 75 mm calibre.

The breakwater at ST. VAAST (3814) as well as
the Port itself are quite heavily defended and may be
expected to include light guns and searchlights as well
as lighter weapons.

/ILES ST. MARCOUF.

ILES ST. MARCOUF.

These islands were once suspected of
containing a watchpost, but no activity
has been seen there for a year and they are
presumed, in default of other evidence, to be
deserted. They are connected by cable to
the mainland. The lighthouse on the island
is thought to be operated by remote control
from the mainland.

Troop Dispositions.

The MORSALINES strongpoint 367145 is
reported probably manned by about 20 men. In
MORSALINES village and the immediate neighbouhood
there are about 150 gunners who form the crew of the
battery at 354139.

Over 100 troops are reported in QUINEVILLE
village where there is a Battalion Headquarters,
probably in the Chateau at 370077. About 50 of
these men are likely to be allotted between the
three strongpoints along the built up area from
the mouth of the SINOPE to the mouth of the
TAREST.

The remaining strongpoints seem to be held
by about an infantry section (12 to 15 men) plus
half a dozen men for any heavy weapon such as an
anti-tank gun that may be present - perhaps 20 men
in all.

Patrols and Readiness.

Positions will normally be actually
manned at all times by half of their allotted
strength, the remainder being available almost
immediately.

Patrols of two men between strongpoints
must be expected at night, but no details of
routes and times are known.

GLOSSARY OF TERMS

52 LI	52nd Light Infantry (2nd Ox & Bucks)
AA Fire	Anti-Aircraft fire
AA&QMG	Assistant Adjutant & Quartermaster General
AAC	Army Air Corps
AARR	Airborne Armoured Reconnaissance Regiment
AB	Armoured Brigade
A/Borne	Airborne
AC	Aircraft
ACC	Army Catering Corps
Adjt	Adjutant
Admin	Administration
ADMS	Assistant Director Medal Services
Adv	Advance
AFHU	Airborne Forces Holding Unit
AFV	Armoured Fighting Vehicles
AGRA	Army Group Royal Artillery
Airfd	Airfield
Airtps	Airborne Troops
A/L	Airlanding
ALB	Airlanding Brigade
Amb	Ambulance
Amn	Ammunition
AO	Administrative Officer
AOD	Advance Ordnance Depot
AOP	Air Observation Post
A/P	Anti-Personnel
APIS	Army Photographic Interpretation Section
Armd	Armoured
ARP	Ammunition Refilling Point
Arty	Artillery
Ass	Assault
ASSU	Air Support Signal Unit
A/TK	Anti-Tank
Att	Attached
AVRE	Armoured Vehicles Royal Engineers

AWD	Advanced Workshop Detachment
AWOL	Absent Without Leave
BC	Battery Commander
Bde	Brigade
BDS	Beach Dressing Station
Bdy	Boundary
Bdr	Bombardier
BLA	British Liberation Army
Bldg	Building
BMA	Beach Maintenance Area
BM	Brigade Major
Bn/bn	Battalion
Bombrep	Bomb Report
Br	British
Brhead	Beachhead
Brig	Brigadier
Bty	Battery (heavy calibre artillery guns)
BW	Black Watch
Cam	Camouflage
Capt	Captain
Cas	Casualties
C/Attack	Counter-Attack
CBO	Counter-Battery Officer
CCS	Casualty Clearing Station
CD	Coastal Defence
Cdn	Canadian
Cdo	Commando
CF	Chaplain to Forces
C-in-C	Commander-in-Chief
Civ	Civilian
CM	Counter Mortar
Cmdrs	Commanders
CMO	Chief Medical Officer
CO	Commanding Officer
Coln	Column
Comn	Communications
Comp	Composite
Conc	Concentration

Co-ord	Co-ordination
Coy	Company
CP	Command Post
Cpl	Corporal
CPO	Command Post Officer
CRA	Commander Royal Artillery
CRASC	Commander Royal Army Service Corps
CRE	Commander Royal Engineers
CSM	Company Sergeant Major
CSO	Chief Signals Officer
'D' Day	Allied Planning term for the day on which an operation was launched
DADOS	Deputy Assistant Director Ordnance Services
DCM	Distinguished Conduct Medal
DD	'Duplex Drive' amphibious tanks
Def	Defence
Dem	Demolition
Dep	Deputy
Det	Detachment
Dev	12th Battalion, Devonshire Regiment
DF	Defensive Fire
DFC	Distinguished Flying Cross
DID	Detail Issue Depot
Disposn	Disposition
Dis	Disable
Div	Division
DLI	Durham Light Infantry
DMA	Divisional Maintenance Area
Docs	Documents
D of W	Died of Wounds
DR	Despatch Rider
DSO	Distinguished Service Order
DZ	Drop Zone
88 mm	German dual-purpose anti-aircraft/anti-tank gun
East Yorks	5th Battalion, East Yorkshire Regiment
Ech	Echelon
En	Enemy
Eqpt	Equipment
ETA	Estimated Time of Arrival

Est	Establishment
Evac	Evacuation
Excl	Excluding
FB	Firm Base
Fd	Field
FDL	Forward Defended Locality
FDS	Field Dressing Station
FFI	*Forces Françaises de l'Intérieur*
Flak	German Anti-aircraft fire
F/L	Flight Lieutenant
Fm	Farm
F/O	Flying Officer
FOB	Forward Observer Bombardment
FOO	Forward Observation Officer
FOP	Forward Observation Post
FSP	Field Security Personnel
FUP	Forming-up Place
Fus	Fusilier
FW	Focke-Wulf
GAF	German Air Force
GB Force	Captain Gordon-Brown's coup-de-main glider force for the Merville Battery
Gd	Ground
Gen	General
GHQ	General Headquarters
GOC	General Officer Commanding
Gold	Landing beach for 50th Infantry Division
GPO	Gun Position Officer
GP	Group
GR	German Grenadier Regiment
GREN	Grenadier
Grn	Garrison
H	Hour
HAA	Heavy Anti-Aircraft
HD	Highland Division
HE	High Explosive
HF	Harassing Fire
HMS	His Majesty's Ship
Hosp	Hospital

How	Howitzer
HQ	Headquarters
HW	Heavy Weapons
IA	Inter-Allied
Indep	Independent
Inf. Bde	Infantry Brigade
Int	Intelligence
Intrep	Intelligence Report
IO	Intelligence Officer
I/S	In support
ISUM	Intelligence Summary
Juno	Landing beach for Canadian 3rd Infantry Division
KIA	Killed-in-Action
KO	Knocked Out
KSLI	2nd Battalion, King's Shropshire Light Infantry
L.A.A.	Light Anti-Aircraft
LAD	Light Aid Detachment
L.C.A.	Landing Craft Assault
L.C.G.	Landing Craft Gun
L.C.S.	Landing Craft Ship
Ldg	Landing
LMG	Light Machine Gun
LO	Liaison Officer
L of C	Lines of Communication
LSI (H)	Landing Ship Infantry (Heavy)
LSI (L)	Landing Ship Infantry (Light)
LST	Landing Ship Tank
Lt-Col	Lieutenant-Colonel
Lt	Lieutenant
L.Z.	Landing Zone
Mag	Magazine
MC	Military Cross
MDS	Main Dressing Station
ME	ME 109 Messerschimitt fighter
Med	Medical
MG	Machine Gun
Minefd	Minefield
Misc	Miscellaneous

M	Mortar/Missing
MMG	Medium Machine Gun
MM	Military Medal
MO	Medical Officer
Mov	Movement
MP	Multi-purpose
MR	Map Reference
M/S	Message
MTO	Motor Transport Officer
Mulberry A	American Artificial Harbour facility (St-Laurent-sur-mer)
Mulberry B	British Artificial Harbour facility (Arromanches)
NBW	*Nebelwerfer* rocket launcher
NCO	Non-Commissioned Officer
Neptune	Allied codeword for the Naval phase of Operation *Overlord*
Nr	Near
NTR	Nothing to Report
OBD	Ordnance Beach Detachment
Obj	Objective
OC	Officer Commanding
Offr	Officer
O Group	Orders Group
OO	Operations Order
Ops	Operations
OP	Observation Post
Ord	Ordnance
OR's	Other Ranks
Oxs & Bucks	2nd Battalion, Oxfordshire and Buckinghamshire Light Infantry
Pan	Pannier
PARA	Parachute Battalion/unit
Paratp	Paratroops
Pet	Petrol
PGR	Panzer Grenadier Regiment
Ph	Phase/Photograph
PIAT	Projector Infantry Anti-Tank
Pl	Platoon
Pnr	Pioneer
P/O	Pilot Officer
Posns	Positions

Prelim	Preliminary
Pt	Point
Pte	Private
Pty	Party
PW	Prisoner of War
Pz/Pzr	German Panzer
QMS	Quartermaster Sergeant
RA	Royal Artillery
RAC	Royal Armoured Corps
RAF	Royal Air Force
RALO	Royal Artillery Liaison Officer
RAMC	Royal Army Medical Corps
RAOC	Royal Army Ordnance Corps
RAP	Regimental Aid Post
RASC	Royal Army Service Corps
RCA	Royal Canadian Artillery
RCE	Royal Canadian Engineers
Rd	Road
Rds	Rounds of ammunition
Recce	Reconnaissance
Recd	Received
RE	Royal Engineers
REME	Royal Electrical and Mechanical Engineers
Ref	Reference
Regt	Regiment
Regn	Registration
Rep	Representative
Res	Reserve
Rfts	Reinforcements
RHQ	Regimental Headquarters
RHU	Regimental Holding Unit
RK	Rank
RMAS	Royal Marines Armoured Support
RM	Royal Marines
RN	Royal Navy
Rpg	Rounds per gun
RTU	Returned to Unit
RUR	1st Battalion, Royal Ulster Rifles

RV	Rendezvous
SA fire	Small arms fire
SAS	Special Air Service
SB	Stretcher Bearer
SDZ	Supply Dropping Zone
Sec	Section
SFCP	Support Fire Control Post
Sgt	Sergeant
Sigs	Signals
Sitrep	Situation Report
6 pdrs	Six pounder gun
S/L	Squadron Leader
SL	Start Line
Smk	Smoke
SO	Staff Officer
SOS	Struck off Strength
SP	Self-Propelled gun
Spandau's	German machine guns
Sqn	Squadron
S.S. Bde	British Special Service Brigade (Commandos)
Sta	Station
Star Shell	Flare/illumination
Steel Hedgehog/ Element C	Beach obstacles
Str	Strength
Strat	Strategic
Strongpt	Strong-point
Sups	Supplies
Svy	Survey
Sword	Landing beach for British 3rd Infantry Division
Tac	Tactical
TAF	Tactical Air Force
TCV	Troop Carrying Vehicle
Tgt	Target
Tk	Tank
TO	Transport Officer
TOS	Taken off Strength
Tp	Troop

Tpt	Transport
Twds	Towards
2 i/c	Second- in-Command
U/C	Under Command
U/S	Un-Serviceable
US	United States
USS	United States Ship
UXB	Un-exploded Bomb
VC	Victoria Cross
Veh	Vehicle
W	Wounded
W/C	Wing Commander
WD	War Diary
W/draw	Withdraw
WE	War Establishment
Wef	With Effect
Wksps	Workshops
WL	Wagon Lines
WO	Warrant Officer
W/Proofing	Water Proofing
Wt	Weight
W/T	Wireless Telegraphy
X-Country	Cross-Country
X Roads	Crossroads
Yeo	Yeomanry

WAR DIARY ENTRIES FOR 5/6 JUNE 1944

ORIGINAL

WAR DIARY

or

INTELLIGENCE SUMMARY

(Delete heading not required).

Army Form C. 2118.

Unit 1st Bn. The Hampshire Regt.

Commanding Officer Lt. Col. C.H.R. Howie

Month and Year JUNE, 1944

Place	Date	Hour	Summary of Events and Information	References to Appendices
BEAULIEU	1		Bn. briefed for the pending operations.	
SOUTHAMPTON	2		Bn. embarked as per operational orders	
"	3 – 5		Spent on the sea	
LE HAMEL	6		Two assault coys and two reserve coys landed, as per operational orders, on the Jig Green Beach east of the village of LE HAMEL. The aerial bombardment did not seem to have been as effective as expected. Enemy machine-gun nests survived the aerial, naval and Arty bombardment and made the fullest use of their underground, well-concealed and well-built positions. The narrowness of the beach and the presence of mines added to the difficulties of Bn's task. In spite of heavy casualties, however, the Bn. drove the enemy from the beach and captured the villages of LE HAMEL and ASNELLES-SUR-MER, inflicting heavy casualties on the enemy. Lt. Col. H.D. NELSON-SMITH, M.C., O.C. Bn., became a casualty +	

WAR DIARIES SECTION
No
18 JUL 1944
G.H.Q. 2nd Echelon

WL.47734.928 2,000,000 3.43 W. H. & S. 51/6975

Instructions regarding War Diaries and Intelligence
Summaries are contained in F.S. Regs., Vol. I.
Monthly War Diaries will be enclosed in A.F.
C.2119. If this is not available, and for
Intelligence Summaries, the cover will be
prepared in manuscript.

ORIGINAL

WAR DIARY

or

INTELLIGENCE SUMMARY

(Delete heading not required).

Army Form C. 2118.

Unit 1st Bn. The Hampshire Regt.

Commanding Officer Lt. Col. C.H.R. Howie

Month and Year JUNE, 1944

Place	Date	Hour	Summary of Events and Information	References to Appendices
LE HAMEL	6		was removed to the R.A.P. ARROMANCHES – LES-BAINS was then stormed. Enemy 88mm guns and Spandau teams, which put up a determined resistance, were ultimately wiped out. Bn. reorganised and attacked TRACY-SUR-MER where enemy resistance was stubborn. The nature of the country, infested with woods orchards gave the enemy snipers good cover. Bn. H.Q. was established at ST. COME DE FRESNE.	
ST. COME DE FRESNE	7		Lt. Col. C.H.R. HOWIE took over the command of the Bn. The enemy resistance at TRACY-SUR-MER was overcome and MANVIEUX was entered without opposition. After having cleared the LE HAMEL – ASNELLES SUR MER – ARROMANCHES LES BAINS – TRACY SUR MER – MANVIEUX perimeter, the Bn. moved to RUBERSY and arrived there at about 1830 hrs. A number of snipers were reported to be in the area of the village of BUHOT. A patrol of 4 Jeeps was sent to winkle them out. Two	

WL.47734.928 2,000,000 3.43 W. H. & S. 51/6975

An example of an original war diary (WO 171/1305)

6TH AIRBORNE DIVISION AND THE ORNE BRIDGEHEAD

'There was a rush of air from the slipstream; we were on static lines and the chutes opened automatically as we dropped from about 600 feet. The anti-aircraft fire looked like fireworks, coming lazily up, and didn't look particularly dangerous; I was concentrating on getting myself right. Weapons stuck through my equipment, ammunition, explosives, a kitbag on my leg with more ammunition, which had to be released so that it landed first...I [landed in a tree] but trees can be a good landing. There was a quarter moon. I cut myself down with my fighting knife, fell and was badly bruised...Where was I? I hadn't a clue but I knew I wasn't where I should have been.'

Sergeant Tom Wood, 12th Battalion, The Parachute Regiment.[278]

113

6TH AIRBORNE DIVISION AND THE ORNE BRIDGEHEAD

(FROM THE CAEN CANAL IN THE WEST TO THE RIVER DIVES IN THE EAST)

German Defenders:
7th Army commanded by *Generaloberst* Friedrich Dollmann and 15th Army commanded by *Generaloberst* Hans von Salmuth
(Lower Normandy defended by LXXXIV Korps commanded by General der Artillerie Erich Marcks)

Coastal Defence:
716th Infantry Division commanded by *Generalleutnant* Wilhelm Richter

German Units in the Orne Region:
21st Panzer Division commanded by *Generalmajor* Edgar Feuchtinger
711th Infantry Division commanded by *Generalleutnant* Josef Reichert
346th Infantry Division commanded by *Generalleutnant* Erich Diestel

Allied Attackers: British 1st Corps commanded by Leiutenant-General Sir John Crocker
Assault Division: 6th Airborne Division commanded by Major-General R.N. Gale

Operation '*TONGA*' (Night Drop and Landings during 5/6 June)
Operation '*MALLARD*' (Resupply Mission on evening of D-Day)

H-Hour: 0020 hrs

Parachute Drop Zones (DZs):

'K'	Toufréville:	3rd Parachute Brigade
'N'	Ranville:	5th Parachute Brigade
'V'	Varaville:	3rd Parachute Brigade

Glider Landing Zones (LZs):

'K'	Toufréville:	3rd Parachute Brigade
'N'	Ranville:	6th Airlanding Brigade
'V'	Varaville:	3rd Parachute Brigade
'W'	St-AubinD'Arquonay:	6th Airlanding Brigade
'X'	Caen Canal Bridge:	3 x Horsa gliders 2nd Battalion Oxs & Bucks Light Infantry
'Y'	River Orne Bridge:	3 x Horsa gliders 2nd Battalion Oxs & Bucks Light Infantry

D-Day Divisional Objectives: (i) Secure the bridges over the Caen Canal ('Pegasus' Bridge) and the River Orne ('Horsa' Bridge). (ii) The destruction of the German coastal gun battery at Merville. (iii) The destruction of four bridges over the River Dives; one bridge over the River Divette and a culvert at Robehomme. (iv) To hold the general area between the River Orne and the River Dives in order to prevent German reinforcements from the 15th Army threatening the landings on 'Sword' beach and the Allies' Eastern flank.[279]

Casualties on D-Day: 1500 (Killed, Wounded and Missing)[280]

NOTES

[278] Lloyd Clark, *Battle Zone Normandy: Orne River Bridgehead*, (Stroud, Gloucestershire: Sutton Publishing Ltd, 2004), p. 17.

[279] Carl Shilleto, *Merville Battery & The Dives Bridges: British 6th Airborne Division Landings in Normandy D-Day 6th June 1944*, (Barnsley, South Yorkshire, 2011), pp. 32-34.

[280] *D-Day: Then and Now*, Volume 2, edited by Winston G. Ramsey, (London: Battle of Britain Prints International Ltd, 1995), p .620.

3RD PARACHUTE BRIGADE

WO 171/593
Intelligence/war diary
3RD PARACHUTE BRIGADE HQ

Month and Year June 1944   Commanding Officer Brig. S.J.L. HILL DSO, MC.

Place	Date	Hour	Summary of Events and Information	References to Appendices
Field.	5	2320	Bde HQ flew to DZ "V" near VARAVILLE.	
Northern	[6	0056	Bde HQ dropped, sticks scattered widely. Bde. Comd. Wounded]	
France.		0600	Lt HAIG THOMAS, 4 Cdo att, killed near BAVENT.	
[LE MESNIL]	[6	0900	Bde HQ opened area LE MESNIL X-rds area 141728 (Sheet 75/2 1/50,000). 1 CDN PARA BN in same area protecting HQ. Bde. Comd. wounded in early morning by bomb fragment.] Maj W.A.C. COLLINGWOOD, BM; Maj A.A.K. POPE, DAA & QMG; Rev. J. McVEIGH, CF 4th Class; Capt W.E. CHURCH, MO, and Lt D.J. KIPPIN, SLO, missing Capt J.T. WOODGATE assumes duties of DAA & QMG, and Capt A.T. WILKINSON duties of BM. [Capt J.A. WILKS, Sigs Offr 1, and Lt S. GYTON, Provost, missing. Strength (Bde HQ) 9 Offrs 12 ORs; (Def Pl) 1 Offr 26 ORs. 9 PARA BN under comd 1 SS BDE.	
		2300	BM and SLO rejoin having come in with glider force.	
		[0400	Considerable number of PW taken from BREVILLE area together with approx 40 rifles of varying types, 1 MG 34 and amn.]	
	[7	0900	Total PWs number 152, chiefly POLES and RUSSIANS; sent to Div.	Posns as at Appx "A".
		1400	Commandos withdraw from VARAVILLE forcing us to withdraw Cdn Coy under cover of darkness from ROBEHOMME.	
		1700	Div Comd arrives, orders patrols to TROARN on infm of CSM 13 Bn.]	
		2100	Enemy snipers in vicinity, no casualties sustained.	Dall. Thy

Wt 43550/1614 560M 3/41 BPL 51/8792

WO 171/1240

Intelligence/war diary

8TH BATTALION, THE PARACHUTE REGIMENT

Month and Year June 1944   Commanding Officer Lt. Col. ? S. PEARSON DSO. MC.

Place	Date	Hour	Summary of Events and Information	References to Appendices
BLAKE HILL FM. AIRFD. TRANSIT CAMP	4	–	All preparations for operation OVERLORD completed and Bn ready to emplane in evening. Later in day message received putting D-day to 6 Jun and Bn is stood down for 24 hrs.	
-ditto-		–	D-1 and all preparations complete.	
-ditto-		1930	Major. G. Payne with two Bn "path finder" sticks move off for HARWELL AIRFD.	
-ditto-		2115	Bn moves from Transit camp to BLAKE HILL FM AIRFD.	
BLAKE HILL FM. AIRFD.	5	2240	GLIDERS TAKE-OFF. (HORSA GLides – TUGS C.47s.)	
-ditto-		2311	C. 47 Para chute A/C. TAKE-OFF.	
	6		D-day.	
[NORMAN DY TOUFFRE VILLE		0020	PATHFINDER STICKS arrive on D.Z.	
-ditto-		0045	GLIDERS arrive on L.Z, but are widely dispersed	
-ditto-		0050	BN MAIN BODY - Time of 1st DROP on D.Z.]	

Wt.47724/993 2,000,000 3/43 W. H. & S. 51/6375.

SHEET 2

Place	Date	Hour	Summary of Events and Information	Remarks, references to Appendices and initials
[DZ	6th	0020	TWO RECCE PARTIES OF 8th PARA BN WERE DROPED ON D.Z. SLIGHT OPPOSITION WAS MET AT R.V. WHICH WAS QUICKLY OVERCOME AND ONE GERMAN KILLED. ONE GERMAN ON A BICYCLE WAS TAKEN PRISONER.	
		0045	O.C. RECCE PARTY SAW GLIDERS COME OVER VERY WIDELY DISPERSED. HE WAS ONLY ABLE TO LOCATE TWO OF THEM.	
		0050	SAW MAIN BODY ARRIVE AND STATES THAT AIRCRAFT WERE FLYING IN EVERY DIRECTION AT DIFFERENT ALTITUDES AND ALL FLYING WELL ABOVE DROPPING SPEED.	
		0120	C.O. ARRIVED AT R.V. AND SITUATION WAS AS FOLLOWS. THERE WERE ABOUT 30 MEN PRESENT AND ONE R.E. JEEP AND TRAILER. IT WAS REPORTED BY RECCE PARTY THAT BN APPEARED TO BE VERY WIDELY DISPERSED AND THAT NO CONTAINER A/C HAD DROPPED ON D.Z._ NOTE THE R.V. SIGNAL WAS A RED AND GREEN VEREY LIGHT PUT UP AT FREQUENT INTERVALS WHICH COULD BE SEEN A CONSIDERABLE DISTANCE AWAY. [ACTUALLY IT WAS SEEN ON RANVILLE D.Z.]	
		0145	SGT. FESQ OF F.S.P. WAS SENT INTO TOUFFREVILLE TO GET INFORMATION FROM THE LOCAL INHABITANTS. HE REPORTED THAT TROARN WAS HELD AND ALSO ESCOVILLE.	

SHEET 3

Place	Date	Hour	Summary of Events and Information	Remarks, references to Appendices and initials
DZ	[6		AND SANNERVILLE. THE PRISONER WAS ALSO INTERROGATED AND HE CONFIRMED THE STATEMENTS OF THE LOCAL INHABITANTS. HE REPORTED THAT THE FMN IN TROARN WAS A MOBILE COY WITH HALF-TRACKS — STRENGTH OF ABOUT 200 AND THAT ALL MAIN RDS WERE COVERED BY MG FIRE. DURING THIS PERIOD ELEMENTS OF THE BN. WERE ARRIVING SLOWLY AT THE R.V. AND THERE WAS CONSIDERABLE M.G. FIRE ON THE D.Z. EVERYBODY REPORTED THAT THEY HAD BEEN FIRED ON ON THE WAY TO R.V.	
		0330	SITUATION AS FOLLOWS:—	
			BN STRENGTH	
			11 OFFICERS AND ABOUT 130 0Rs. 1 OFFICER AND 2 0Rs WERE WOUNDED AND 6 0Rs HAD D.Z. INJURIES AND WERE NOT IN A CONDITION TO FIGHT. THE C.O. WAS WOUNDED IN THE HAND.]	
			DETAILED STRENGTH WAS:—	
			"A" COY 4 0Rs	
			"B" COY 2 OFFICERS 27 0Rs 1 L.M.G.	
			"C" COY 3 OFFICERS 78 0Rs NO L.M.G.	
			[1 OFFICER CASUALTY]	

SHEET 4

Place	Date	Hour	Summary of Events and Information	Remarks, references to Appendices and initials
DZ	6		BN. HQ 6 OFFICERS AND APPROX 30 O.Rs CONSISTING OF AND BDE SIGS COMPLETE, A PORTION A TK PL WITH 2 HQ COY P.I.A.T.S, A FEW R.A.M.C. AND BN HQ PERSONNEL	
			1 OFFICER AND 7 O.R.s GLIDER PILOT REGT	
			TPT 2 R.E. JEEPS AND TRAILERS AND 6 R.E.S	
			SIGNALS 2 BDE SETS AND 2 × 18 SETS	
		[0300	C.O. APPRECIATED SITUATION AS FOLLOWS:—	
			1. FROM REPORTS FROM RECCE PARTY IT APPEARED THAT REMAINDER OF BN. HAD DROPPED TO THE NORTH OF THE D.Z. IN AREA REANVILLE AND LE MESNIL.	
			2. THAT BN. WAS NOT STRONG ENOUGH TO CAPTURE TROARN AND THAT WE HAD NO R.E. ASSISTANCE TO DESTROY THE BRIDGE.]	

SHEET 5

Place	Date	Hour	Summary of Events and Information	References to Appendices
			(3) THAT WE HAD SUFFICIENT STRENGTH AND EXPLOSIVES TO DESTROY THE BRIDGES AT BURES WHICH WAS OF A SINGLE SPAN TYPE AND COULD BE DESTROYED WITHOUT MUCH TECHNICAL ASSISTANCE. (4) THAT IF A POSITION WAS TAKEN UP IN AREA X RDS 146695 AND TRACK RUNNING EAST TO BURES SUFFICIENT FORCE COULD BE COLLECTED TO ATTACK TROARN LATER IN THE DAY FROM THE NORTH. THEREFORE THE PLAN WAS AS FOLLOWS :- (1) STRONG FIGHTING PATROL OF 1 PL FROM "C" COY WOULD MOVE TO TROARN TO MAKE A RECCE AND REPORT ON DEFENCES AT WEST END OF TOWN. (2) REMAINDER OF BN WOULD MOVE TO AREA X RDS 153700 LEAVING TWO DETS P.I.A.T.s AND COVERING FORCE IN AREA X RDS 146695 TO COVER ANY MOVEMENT OF ENEMY NORTH AND TO GUIDE ANY STRAGGLERS TO BN POSN. (3) 1 OFFER AND 2 ORS TO REAMISN AT R.V. TILL FIRST LIGHT TO GUIDE ANY STRAGGLERS WHO	

SHEET 6

Place	Date	Hour	Summary of Events and Information	References to Appendices
	6	0400	MAY HAVE ARRIVED AT R.V. AFTER BN HAD LEFT.	
		0430	BN MOVED OFF	
			BN ARRIVED AT POSN X TRACKS 153700. RECCE PATROL SENT OFF AT ONCE TO RECCE BURES AND ANOTHER WITH I.O. AND MAJ. WILSON TO RECCE NORTHERN APPROACHES TO TROARN FOR PURPOSE OF ATTACKING IT.	
		0500		
		0530	CAPT. SHOPPEE WHO HAD BEEN DETAILED AS TROWBRIDGE PARTY ARRIVED AT BURES. HE HAD LANDED AT BRIQUEVILLE 173722 AND MOVED STRAIGHT TO BURES WHICH HE FOUND UNOCCUPIED AND RECCE'ED BRIDGES. AT 0545 hrs HE MET R.E. PARTY AND REPORTED. HE ALSO MET RECCE PATROL FROM BN AND A RUNNER WAS DISPATCHED TO BRING UP PL FOR PROTECTION OF R.E. PARTY AND JEEPS LANDED WITH R.E. STORES.	
			LT. THOMPSON REPORTED TO BN HQ. HE STATED THAT HE HAD LANDED ON THE RANVILLE D.Z. WITH THE MORTARS AND M.M.Gs HE LANDED AT 0100 hrs AND COLLECTED 3 M.M.G. DETS. AND 3	

SHEET 7

Place	Date	Hour	Summary of Events and Information	References to Appendices
			WITH 2 MORTARS AND 3 M.M.Gs AND SOME 50 O.Rs FROM "A" COY. AT 0200 hrs HE LEFT DZ WITH THE OBJECT OF MAKING FOR TROARN. IN RANVILLE HE MET A FRENCHMAN WHO SAID HE WOULD ACT AS A GUIDE AND HE MOVED VIA RANVILLE – LE MENSIL X RDS TO RD JUNC 140704 WHERE HE MET AT 0450 MAJ. ROSEVEARE R.E. AND 1 OFFR. AND 20 O.R.s OF THE BN AND A PARTY OF R.E.S. LT. THOMPSON HAD 1 OFFR CASUALTY WITH HIM. MAJ. ROSEVEARE TOOK COMMAND OF THE PARTY AND ORDERED THEM TO HOLD A FIRM BASE ON THE RD. JUNC. AS HE HAD NO IDEA WHERE THE BN WAS. HE WITH A PARTY OF R.E.s WAS GOING TO TRY TO BLOW THE BRIDGE AT TROARN. LT. THOMPSON ORGANISED THE DEFENCE OF THE RD. JUNC. THEN MOVED DOWN THE RD TO MAKE A RECCE, WHEN HE MET THE FORCE AT X RDs 147695 WHO DIRECTED HIM TO BN H.Q. THE C.O. DIRECTED HIM TO BRING HIS	

SHEET 8

Place	Date	Hour	Summary of Events and Information	References to Appendices
			FORCE TO THE BN AREA AND IT ARRIVED AT 0615 hrs.	
		0630	P.I.A.T. DET. AT X RDS 147695 REPORTED SIX HALF-TRACK VEHS MOVING ON RD TROARN – LE MESNIL AND APPROACHING THEIR POSN. THEY OPENED FIRE AND SCORED HITS ON ALL SIX VEHS CAUSING THEIR CREWS TO DISMOUNT AND TAKE UP POSN ON THE FAR SIDE OF THE RD. A FIRE FIGHT THEN ENSUED AND AFTER A SPIRITED ACTION THE ENEMY WITHDREW WITH THEIR CASUALTIES LEAVING 3 DEAD WHO WERE IDENTIFIED AS 21 PZ DIV AND SIX HALF-TRACKS, FOUR OF WHICH WERE INADEQUATELY DESTROYED AS THEY WERE RECOVERED BY THE ENEMY THAT NIGHT.	
		0900	PATROL ARRIVED BACK FROM TROARN. PATROL COMD STATED THAT HE HAD MOVED TO TROARN STA. AND WAS FIRED ON FROM THE HIGH GROUND TO THE SOUTH OF THE STA. PATROL COULD NOT	

SHEET 9

Place	Date	Hour	Summary of Events and Information	References to Appendices
			GET ON AND LAY UP AND OBSERVED HALF-TRACK VEHS MOVING NORTH ON TROARN – LE MESNIL RD AND TROARN – BANNEVILLE RD.	
			C.O. THEN APPRECIATED THAT MOST OF MOBILE COY HAD PROBABLY LEFT TROARN AND THAT AS SOON AS R.E. PARTY WERE FINISHED WITH BURES BRIDGES TROARN BRIDGE COULD BE DEALT WITH.	
		1000	CAPT. JUKES R.E. REPORTED TO BN HQ THAT BRIDGES HAD ALSO BLOWN AT 0915 AND THAT HE THOUGHT THAT TROARN BR. HAD ALSO BEEN BLOWN. HE ALSO STATED THAT THERE WAS AN A TK GUN AND JEEP AND A GLIDER AND 3 CASUALTIES IN THE RIVER. C.O. WENT TO BURES AN ATTEMPT WAS MADE TO EXTRACT THE A TK GUN BUT THIS WAS FOUND TO BE IMPOSSIBLE.	
		1200	R.E.s RETURNED FROM BURES AND IT WAS DECIDED TO SEND R.E. PARTY WITH JEEP AND EXPLOSIVES AND ONE STRONG PL INTO TROARN TO BLOW BRIDGE OR, IF ALREADY BLOWN, TO WIDEN GAP.	
			REMAINDER OF BN WOULD MOVE TO ROAD JUNC	

SHEET 10

Place	Date	Hour	Summary of Events and Information	References to Appendices
			HE MET BN AT 143702. HE STATED THAT HE HAD BEEN LANDED ON RANVILLE DZ AND GATHERED TOGETHER 51 MEMBERS OF THE BN. HE SAW IN THE DISTANCE THE GREEN AND WHITE VEREY LIGHTS BEING FIRED AT THE BN R.V. AND DECIDED TO MAKE STRAIGHT FOR THEM. HIS ROUTE TOOK HIM THROUGH HEROUVILLETTE WHERE THEY RAN INTO THE ENEMY AND HAD TO FIGHT THEIR WAY THROUGH THE VILLAGE. FORCE SUFFERED 6 CASUALTIES.	

SHEET 11

Place	Date	Hour	Summary of Events and Information	References to Appendices
			140704. NO WORD HAD BEEN RECEIVED OF PATROL THAT HAD GONE TO RECCE NORTHERN APPRAOCHES TO TROARN. FORCE TO BLOW BRIDGE AT TROARN WAS TO MOVE VIA BURES AND THEN DOWN AXIS OF ROAD SOUTH TO TROARN.	
		1230	O.C. "A" COY AND SIGS OFFR. REPORTED TO BN HQ. THEY HAD BEEN DROPPED SOME 5 MILES SOUTH OF THE D.Z. THEY BROUGHT ONE MAN WITH THEM. MAJ. WILSON'S PATROL ARRIVED BACK AT THE SAME TIME. MAJ WILSON STATED THAT HE HAD MET NO OPPOSITION TO THE NORTH OF TROARN, BUT ON MOVING FURTHER WEST DOWN RLY. LINE THEY RAN INTO A STRONG GERMAN POSN AT 159678 WHICH PINNED THEM DOWN BY FIRE. WHEN THEY STARTED TO WITHDRAW THE I.O. MOVED BY A DIFFERENT ROUTE FROM THE REMAINDER OF THE PARTY AND HAS NOT BEEN SEEN SINCE.	
		1300	BN MOVED TO NEW POSN AND FORCE MOVED TO TROARN.	
		1330	O.C. "C" COY ARRIVED WITH 4 OFFRS AND 51 ORs.	

SHEET 12

Place	Date	Hour	Summary of Events and Information	References to Appendices
140704	6	1400	BN IN AREA RD JUNE 140704 AND BN DISPOSED IN FOLLOWING AREAS :- "A" COY – AREA 140707 (RESERVE COY) "B" COY – AREA 139703 "C" COY – AREA 142705 BN HQ – 140706 MORTAR PL – "C" COY AREA M.M.G. PL – IN POSNS BY DAY IN "B" COY AREA FIRING TO WEST OVER D.Z.	
		1700	BY NIGHT PL WITHRAWN TO BN HQ AREA A TK PL – SECS UNDER COMMAND OF COYS LT. BROWN RETURNED FROM TROARN. HE STATED THAT THEY HAD MET A LITTLE OPPOSITION IN TROARN WHICH HAD BEEN DEALT WITH AND THE R.E.s HAD INCREASED THE GAP IN THE BRIDGE TO 40 FEET. 7 PRISONERS WERE BROUGHT BACK FROM A M.G. POST WHICH WAS ATTACKED. THEY WERE	

SHEET 13

Place	Date	Hour	Summary of Events and Information	References to Appendices
140704	6		IDENTIFIED AS 21 PZ DIV.	
		1740	ATTACK MADE ON "B" COY POSN BY 5 A.F.V.s.	
			ATTACK BEATEN OFF AND ONE ENEMY 6-TON TRUCK FULL OF STORES CAPTURED.	
		1800	STREGNTH OF BN APPROX 17 OFFRS 300 O.R.s.	
			<u>WEAPONS</u>	
			BN VERY SHORT OF L.M.Gs.	
			2 x 3 MORTARS AND ONE CAPTURED GERMAN	
			3 M.M.Gs.	
			6 P.I.A.T.s	
			<u>SIGS</u>	
			2 x 68 SETS	
			4 x 18 SETS WHICH ALLOWED COMN WITH COYS. BY 2000 hrs LINE WAS LAID TO ALL COYS.	
			DURING THE NIGHT D/D+1 LOCAL PATROLS WERE SENT OUT. NO CONTACT MADE WITH ENEMY EXCEPT FOR SNIPERS AND SMALL PATROLS. BN CONCENTRATED ON GETTING WELL DUG IN.	

WO 171/1242

Intelligence/war diary

9TH BATTALION, THE PARACHUTE REGIMENT

Month and Year June 1944   Commanding Officer Lt. Col. N. T.B.H. OTWAY

Place	Date	Hour	Summary of Events and Information	References to Appendices
BROADWELL	4	0830	Bn. to take into action. This was done and the flag was dedicated by the padre, the Rev. T. GWINNETT C .F. at the last Church service.	
"	5	0800	Word received that the operation was definitely on. Morale rose to 100%.	ajmp
			In the afternoon compulsory rest was ordered.	ajmp
		2000	Glider parties (Adm jeeps & 6 pdr A/Tk guns) left for HARWELL Airfield. Recce party consisting of Major Smith, Major Parry, CSMI's Miller and Harold, Sgt's Knight, Eas lea, Pinkus and Lukins and Ptes Adsett and Mason, left also for HARWELL.	
		2115.	Main body of Bn. left transit camp for BROADWELL Airfield, collected parachutes and emplaned at 2245 hrs.	ajmp
[HARWELL.		2310	Path-finder A/C took off.	ajmp
		2312	Adm and A/Tk gun gliders took off.	ajmp
BROADWELL		2312	Main body took off.	ajmp
NORMANDY	6	0020	TROWBRIDGE (Recce) party dropped on D.Z. accurately and proceeded to carry out appointed tasks. There were no losses from this A/C.]	ajmp

Wt. 47724/993 2,000,000 3/43 W.H. & S 51/6375.

SHEET 2

Commanding Officer Lt. Col. T.B.H. OTWAY.

Place	Date	Hour	Summary of Events and Information	References to Appendices
NORMANDY	6	0030	OBOE of 100 Lancasters bombed D.Z. area. Some of Recce party were caught in this OBOE but suffered no casualties.	aJup
" "	[6	0050	Main body ef the Bn. dropped over a wide area.	aJup
" "	6	0235	110 All ranks had reported at the RV by this time.]	aJup
" "	6	0250	Strength of Bn. now approximately 150 all ranks. B.n Commenced march to first objective.	aJup
" "	6	0400	C.O. summoned "O" Group and issued orders for the assault on the Battery.	aJup
" "	6	0415	Assualt commenced - immediately previous to which one glider was seen to circle the Battery position and crash land in an orchard in the area of the Firm Base. Casualties:- 10 Officers killed. 2 Coy. Comds, Adjutant & one other officer wounded.	See App "A" & "B".
" "	6		Success signal put up. Bn. commences withdrawal.	aJup
	0600	6	Bn reorganised prior to move to LE PLISM. Strength now approximately 80 all ranks. Battery shelled by enemy.	aJup
" "				aJup
" "	6	0730	Bn commenced move to LE PLIEM and was caught in bombing of hostile targets.	See App "c" aJup

Wt.47724,993 2,000,000 3,43 W. H. & S. 51/6375.

SHEET 3

Commanding Officer Lt. Col. T.B.H. OTWAY.

Place	Date	Hour	Summary of Events and Information	References to Appendices
MERVILLE NORMANDY	[6	0930	Bn. arrived at LE PLIEN, took up positions in the area CHATEAU D'AMFREVILLE and engaged the enemy. Heavy Mortaring throughout the day.] Lt. Halliburton wounded and subsequently died.	see App "C" ajmp
LE PLIEN	7		Bn. attacked by the enemy. Considerable sniping which caused some casualties. C.O. visited Brigadier Lord Lovatt Commanding ISS Bde.	
[LE PLIEN	7	2130	Bn relieved by 1 SS Bde and proceeded to LEMESMIL where temporary positions were taken up. In this area the Bn reverted to Brigade control and were given orders to hold the high ground South of ST C??ME.]	see App "C" ajmp
[ST COME	8	1200	Attack by enemy infantry developed on the right flank and was repulsed.	see App "C" ajmp
ST COME	8		Further enemy attacks launched during the latter part of the day. Ground	see App "C" ajmp
[ST COME	9		held.] During the night 8/9 June two 3" mortars were received also 3 Vickers MGs. Up to this time the Bn's sole heavy weapon had been one Vickers MG. In the early morning a determined enemy attack was launched following a heavy mortar concentration. This attack and others that followed were repulsed with very heavy losses to the enemy. During the afternoon a counterattack.]	see App "C" ajmp

Wt.47724/993 2,000,000 3/43 W.H. & S. 51/6375.

Intelligence/war diary
1ST CANADIAN PARACHUTE BATTALION

Place	Date	Hour	Summary of Events and Information	Remarks, references to Appendices and initials
[Carter Bks. Bulford	6 June 44		The initial stages of operation OVERLORD insofar as the 1st. Cdn. Parachute Battalion was concerned, were divided into three tasks. The protection of the left flank of the 9th Para Battalion in its approach march and attack on the MERVILLE battery 1577 was assigned to "A" Company. The blowing of two bridges over the RIVER DIVES at 1872 and 1972 and the holding of feature ROBEHOMME 1873 was assigned to "B" Company with under command one section of 3 Para Sqdn Engineers. The destruction of a German Signal Exchange 1675 and the destruction of bridge 186759 plus neutralization of enemy positions at VARRAVILLE 1875 was assigned to "C" Company.	M
			The Battalion was to drop on a D.Z. 1775 in the early hours of D Day, "C" Company dropping thirty minutes before the remainder of the Battalion to neutralize any opposition on the D.Z. The Battalion emplaned at Down Ampney Airfield at 2250 hours on the 5th June, 1944. "C" Company travelled in Albemarles and the remainder of the Battalion in Dakotas (C-47). The flight was uneventful until reaching the French Coast when a certain amount of A.A. fire was encountered. Upon crossing the coastline numerous fires could be seen which had been started by the R.A.F. bombers. Unfortunately the Battalion was dropped over a wide area, some sticks landing several miles from their appointed R.V. This factor complicated matters but did not deter the Battalion from securing its first objectives.	M
			Protection of Left Flank of 9 Para Bn – "A" Company	
			"A" Company was dropped at approximately 0100 hours on the morning of 6th June, 1944. Lieut. Clancy, upon reaching the Company R.V. found only two or three men of the company present. After waiting for further members, unsuccessfully, of the Company to appear, he decided to recce the village of GONNEVILLE SUR-MERVILLE 1676. Taking two men he proceeded and penetrated the village but could find no sign of the enemy. He then returned to the Company R.V. which he reached at approximately 0660 hours and found one other Officer and twenty Other Ranks of the Battalion and several men from other Brigade Units waiting. The entire body then moved off along the pre-arranged route to the MERVILLE battery. Encountering no other opposition en route other than heavy R.A.F. Bombardment at GONNEVILLE SUR-MERVILLE. Upon completion of the 9th Battalion task the Canadian party acted first as a recce patrol to clear a chateau 1576 from which a German M.G. had been firing and then as a rear guard for the 9th Battalion withdrawal toward LE PLEIN 1375. The party left the battalion area (9th Battalion) at LE PLEIN at 0900 hours and reached the 1st Cdn. Para. Bn. position at LE MESNIL BAVENT crossroads 139729 at 1530 hours on the 6th June, 1944.]	M

Place	Date	Hour	Summary of Events and Information	Remarks, references to Appendices and initials
[Carter Bks. Bulford.	6 June	44	**ROBEHOMME - "B" Company** Two platoons of "B" Company were dropped in the marshy ground south and west of ROBEHOMME. Elements of these platoons under Sgt. OUTHWAITE then proceeded toward the Company objective. En route they encountered Lieut. TOSELAND with other members of "B" Company making a total of thirty All Ranks. They were guided through the marshes and enemy minefields to the ROBEHOMME bridge by a French Woman. On arriving at the bridge they met Capt. D. GRIFFIN and a further thirty men from various sub-units of the Battalion, including mortars and vickers Platoons. MAJOR FULLER who had been there for some time had left in an attempt to locate Battalion Headquarters. Capt. GRIFFIN waited until 0630 hours for the R.E.'s who were to blow the bridge. As they failed to arrive explosives were collected from the men and the bridge successfully demolished. A guard was left on the bridge and the main body withdrawn to the ROBEHOMME hill. Although there were no enemy in the village there were several skirmishes with enemy patrols who were attempting to infiltrate through the village and some casualties were suffered by the Company. An OP was set up in the church spire. An excellent view was obtained ? the road from PONT DE VACAVILLE 2276 to VARRAVILLE. Artillery and infantry could be seen moving for many hours along this road from the East. It was particularly unfortunate that wireless communication could not be made with Bn. HQ as the subsequent fighting of the Battalion was carried out in such close country that observation of enemy movement was almost impossible. At 1200 hours on the 7th June, 1944, it was decided to recce the route to Bn. HQ. Upon the route being reported clear orders were issued for the party to prepare to join Bn. HQ Lieut. I. Wilson, Bn. I.O. came from LE MESNIL to guide the party back. The move was made at 2330 hours, the strength of the party by this time being 150 All Ranks, the addition having been made by stragglers of various units who had reported in. The wounded were carried in a civilian car given by the cure, and a horse and cart given by a farmer. The route was BRIQUEVILLE 1872 to BAVENT road 169729, through the BOIS DE BAVENT and on to LE MESNIL cross roads. Near BRIQUEVILLE the lead platoon was challenged by enemy sentries. The Platoon opened fire killing seven and taking one prisoner. Shortly afterwards this same platoon was fortunate enough to ambush a German car which was proceeding along the road from BAVENT. Four German Officers were killed. Bn. Headquarters was reached at 0330 hours on the 8th June, 1944.]	M M M

Place	Date	Hour	Summary of Events and Information	Remarks, references to Appendices and initials
[Carter Bks Bulford	6 June	44	VARRAVILLE – "C" Company The majority of "C" Company was dropped west of the RIVER DIVES, although some sticks were dropped a considerable distance away including one which landed west of the RIVER ORNE. Due to this confusion the Company did not meet at the R.V. as pre-arranged but went into the assault on the Chateau and VARRAVILLE in separate parties. MAJOR McLEOD collected a Sgt. and seven O.R.'s and proceeded towards VARAVILLE. En route they were joined by a party under Lieut. WALKER. One of the Sgts. was ordered to take his platoon to take up defensive positions around the bridge that the R.E. sections were preparing to blow. This was done and the bridge was successfully demolished. MAJOR McLEOD and Lieut. WALKER with the balance of the party then cleared the chateau and at the same time other personnel of "C" Company arrived from the DZ and cleared the gatehouse of the chateau. The gatehouse then came under enemy M.G. and mortar fire from the pillbox situated in the grounds of the chateau. The pill-box also had a 75 mm A/Tk. Gun. The whole position was surrounded by wire, mines and weapon pits. MAJOR McLEOD, Lieut. WALKER and five O.R.'s went to the top floor of the gatehouse to fire on the pillbox with a P.I.A.T. the enemy 75 mm A/Tk. Gun returned the fire and the shot detonated the P.I.A.T. ammunition. Lieut. WALKER, CPL. OIKLE, PTES. JOWETT AND NUFIELD were killed and MAJOR McLEOD and PTE. BISMUKA fatally wounded. PTES. DOCKER and SYLVESTER evacuated these casualties under heavy fire. CAPT. HANSON, 2 i/c of "C" Company was slightly wounded and his batman killed while proceeding to report to the Brigade Commander who had arrived in the village from the area in which he dropped. "C" Company, together with elements of Brigade HQ and the RE's took up defensive positions around the village and a further party encircled the pill-box in order to contain the enemy. A further party of "C" Company under Lieut. McGOWAN who had been dropped some distance from the DZ arrived in VARAVILLE in time to catch two German Infantry Sections who were attempting to enter the town. Lieutl McGOWANSS' platoon opened fire causing casual and the remainder of the enemy surrendered. This platoon took up firing positions firing on the enemy pillbox. "C" Company HQ which was located in the church yard pinned an enemy section attempting to advance in a bomb crater killing at least three. The chateau was evacuated by our troops and left as a dressing station. An enemy patrol re-entered the chateau and captured the wounded including Capt. BREBNER, the Unit M.O., and CSM Blair of "B" Company. This patrol although attacked by our own troops managed to escape with their prisoners. Heavy enemy Mortar Fire and sniping was brought to bear on our positions from the woods surrounding VARAVILLE. During this time the local inhabitants were of great assistance, the	M M M

SHEET 4

Place	Date	Hour	Summary of Events and Information	Remarks, references to Appendices and initials
[Carter Bks Bulford	6 June	44	<u>VARRAVILLE – "C" Company</u> (Cont'd) Women dressing wounds and the men offering assistance in any way. One Frenchman in particular distinguished himself. Upon being given a red beret and a rifle he killed three German Snipers. This man subsequently guided the Brigade Commander and his party towards LE MESNIL. Although it is believed that he was a casualty of the bombing attack that caught this party enroute to LE MESNIL. At approximately 1030 hours the enemy pill-box surrendered. Forty-two (42) prisoners were taken and four of our own men who had been captured were released. From 1230 hours on artillery was brought to bear on VARAVILLE from the high ground east of the RIVER DIVES. At 1500 hours cycle troops of the 6th Commando arrived and at 1730 hours on 6 June, 1944, "C" Company proceeded to the Bn. Area at LE MESNIL. The green prisoners giving evident satisfaction to the French population enroute.]	M
			<u>VICKERS PLATOON – Initial Stages</u> The Vickers platoon was dropped in four sticks of ten or eleven each being a total of forty-one (41) All Ranks. For the first time their M.G.'s were carried in Kit Bags, a number of which were tore away and were lost. The Platoon was dropped over a wide area, a part of them joining "C" Company's attack on VARAVILLE, part joining "B" Company at ROBEHOMME and part joining Bn. H.Q.. Casualties on the drop totaled twelve missing and three wounded. One of the missing, PTE. PHIPPS, was identified in a photo in a German newspaper found on a P.W. After the initial Company tasks had been accomplished the platoon was deployed to the companies as single gun detachments or as Sections.	M
			<u>MORTAR PLATOON – Initial Stages</u> The Mortar Platoon was dropped over a wide area and suffered very heavy loss in equipment due to kit bags breaking away and a great majority of the men landing in the marshy ground. As the platoon dropped they attached themselves to the nearest company they could find and assisted in the capture of the objectives. One detachment commander landed on top of the German pill-box at VARAVILLE. He was made prisoner and spent the rest of the time in the pill-box until the Germans surrendered to "C" Company. A point of interest was that the P.I.A.T. Bombs did definite damage to the interior of the pill-box and had a very towering effect upon the morale of the defenders.	M

SHEET 5

Place	Date	Hour	Summary of Events and Information	Remarks, references to Appendices and initials
Carter Bks Bulford	6 June	44	MORTAR PLATOON (Cont'd) Some of the Mortar Platoon which joined "B" Company at ROBEHOMME were detailed to guard the approaches to the destroyed bridge. Three enemy lorries full of infantry appeared on the other side of the bridge. The guard opened fire knocking out the truck killing most of its occupants. The other two lorries were able to withdraw. One of our own men who was a prisoner in the lorry was able to make good his escape. Upon the detachments arriving at LE MESNIL they were re-grouped as a platoon and given three mortars which had arrived by sea. These mortars were set up in position in the brickwork where they engaged the enemy. [BATTALLION HEAD QUARTERS – Initial Stages The Commanding Officer, 2 i/c, Signals Officers and the Intelligence Officer and a small portion of the Battalion Headequarters together with elements of 224 Para Fd. Ambulance and other Brigade Units met at the Battalion R.V. in the early hours of the morning of 6th June, 1944.] The Signals Officer was detailed to look after the Enemy Signal Exchange near the R.V'.. He went into the house and found a certain amount of Signals equipment which he destroyed but he found no Germans. The Intelligence Officer set out with two men to recce VARRAVILLE and bring back a report on the situation. In the Battalion Headquarters meantime the party moved off to LE MESNIL taking with them many scattered elements including 6 Pdr. A/Tk. Gun and crew. Upon reaching the Chateau 1574 they encountered part of the Brigade Headquarters. The party there upon split up into unit parties and continued until they reached the orchards 141729 where they came under heavy sniping fire from nearby houses. This fire caused several casualties including one officer. The enemy were forced to withdraw from the buildings after an attack by the party. The party reached the Battalion area at approximately 1100 hours on 6th June, 1944	M M
	7 June	44	In the early hours of the morning German infantry of the 857 and 858 Grenadier Regiments supported by S.P. Guns and a number of MK. IV Tanks attached "B" and "C" Companies positions. Our mortars in the brickworks were given an ideal target as the German infantry formed up in close groups along a road in the apparent belief that we possessed no mortars. Heavy casualties were inflicted on the enemy and the main force of the attack broken, however casualties were inflicted on our own Battalion by the S.P. Guns and tanks. One tank penetrated to within one hundred yards of the "C" Company position but withdrew before the P.IA.T.'s could fire effectively on it. Some of the enemy infantry also attempted to assault our forced positions but were driven off.] [It was learned	M

5TH PARACHUTE BRIGADE

WO 171/595
Intelligence/war diary
5TH PARACHUTE BRIGADE HQ

Month and Year June 1944   Commanding Officer Brig. J.H.N. POETT

Place	Date	Hour	Summary of Events and Information	References to Appendices
BRIZE NORTON FAIR-FORD	1-4 5 (D-1) 6(D)	2300 2340 0015	Bde HQ in HARWELL TRANSIT CAMP. Comd Post and 'Coup de Main' Force take off. Bde HQ takes off Comd Post lands on DZ 'N' NORTH of RANVILLE	
			Coup de Main Force lands in glider on LZs adjacent to BENOUVILLE and PONT TOURNANT Brs. 5 out of 6 gliders land close up to brs. Br garrison surprised & brs captured intact.	
		0100	Bde HQ lands. Major part dropped off & to the EAST of DZ 'N']	
		0215	30% Bde HQ at RV 112745. HQ opens here. Clearing of obstructions on DZ 'N' begins	
		0300	60% Bde HQ at RV.]	
			Lt G ROYLE, 2 i/c Bde Sig Sec, killed	
		[0330	4 A/L A TK Bty & Bde gilder element lands on LZ 'N' A TK guns move quickly into posn. 9 x 6 pdr & 2 x 17 pdr landed safely	
		0200	7 Para Bn. (approx one coy in strength) move from Bn. RV., cross brs & est tight bridgehead on WEST of Canal	
		0400	LE BAS DE RANVILLE occupied by 12 Para Bn. (Str approx about 2 coys) PWs from 736 Gren Regt taken]	

Wt.47724/993 2,000,000 3/43 W. H. & S. 51/6375

SHEET 2

Place	Date	Hour	Summary of Events and Information	References to Appendices
	[6 (contd)	0530	Bde HQ moves to Fm 106741 & is later joined by Comd Post.	
		1100	7 Para Bn extend bridgehead posns on arrival of further tps which had been dropped off DZ. Series of counter attacks begin against 7 Para Bn. from NW & SOUTH. Elements of 736 Gren Regt & 192 PZ Gren Regt identified & supported by light tks & a few SP guns. All attacks successfully beaten off.	
		1200	Patrols and recce elements of 126 PZ Gren Regt attack 12 Para Bn. from the SOUTH, attacks continuing during the afternoon with considerable losses to enemy. Some PWs taken. Tks and SP guns seen. All attacks repulsed.	
		1300	1st S S Bde, seaborne tps, reach and cross brs BENOUVILLE & PONT TOURNANT. 3 Cdo remains area brs to reinforce 12 Para Bn. if necessary.	
		1330	Tks of 13/18 HUSSARS arrive at brs.	
		2100	Glider borne forces land. RUR on LZ 'N' & Move to LONGUEVAL, 2 OXF & BUCKS on LZ 'W' & move to HEROUVILLETTE. Two glider casualties.	
	7 (D+1)	2300	Resupply by air.	
		0100	7 Para Bn. relieved on brs by WARWICKS and move into Bde reserve.	
		0300	12 Bn. comes under comd 6 Airldg Bde].	

Wt.47724/993 2,000,000 3/43 W. H. & S. 51/6375

WO 171/1239
Intelligence/war diary
7TH BATTALION, THE PARACHUTE REGIMENT

Month and Year June 1944   Commanding Officer Lt Col. R.G. PINE-COFFIN, MC.

Place	Date	Hour	Summary of Events and Information	References to Appendices
TILSHEAD	1	1000	CO briefs Bn for operation OVERLORD cinema TILSHEAD.	HHds
		1500	Div. Int Conference HARWELL - escape cards issued.	
	2		Coy. Briefing - 1800 hrs conference at BDE HQ HARWELL.	HHds
	3		Coy. Briefing - 1800 hrs Conference at BDE HQ HARWELL.	HHds
		2100	Co-ordinating conference with Major HOWARD "D" Coy X2 oxf & Bucks.	
	4		Visit to FAIRFORD Airfd to fit chutes and meet aircrew and return to TILSHEAD. 1800 hrs Conference at BDE HQ HARWELL.	HHds
	5		Bn. moves to rest camp in FAIRFORD PARK where short service was held by Rev PARRY - 1900 hrs Bn. moves to airfd - 2320 hrs Bn. takes off.	HHds
[RANVILLE	6	0100	Bn. completed drop but went into action with Coys. at half normal strength due to some plane loads being dropped in wrong places and one load not dropping at all.]	HHds
[LE PORT AND BENOUVILLE	6	0325	Bn occupied objective and held it against various counter-attacks "A" and "B" Coys. being heavily engaged. Cas - killed 3, Officers.]	appdx I HHds

Wt.47724/993 2,000,000 3/43 W. H. & S. 51/6375

SHEET 2

Month and Year June 1944   Commanding Officer LT-COL R.G. PINE-COFFIN, MC.

Place	Date	Hour	Summary of Events and Information	References to Appendices
LE PORT & BENOUVILLE	6		Capt. Parry (Padre), Lt. Bowyer and Lt Hill, [and 16 O Rs.] [wounded 4 officers,] Major TAYLOR, Capt. WEBBERA Lt. HUNTER & Lt. TEMPLE [and 38 ORs:] [Missing, 170 ORs. did not RV after drop.]	
		[1325	Bn of Commandos passed through bn posns.]	
		2200	Stick from a/c which failed to drop arrived by glider - included Major TULLIS and Lt THEOBALD and R.M.O. (Capt. Young).	
		[2230	Bn. of Royal Warwicks arrived and put in an attack on BENOUVILLE.]	HHds
	[7	0015	Bn. relieved by Royal Warwicks.	
		0045	Bn. arrived in Bde res and rest area at 105734. Odd ptys of men rejoined the Bn. at various times during the day.	
[LE HOM		1330	Bn. moved out and tookup a defensive posn in area 112735 (Div res).]	
			Bn. posns shelled and mortared at various times during the day, some times heavily.]	HHds
	8			
		[2100	Bn. seaborne pty arrived.]	
	9	1111	Shell burst in area of Bn. HQ. 3 ORs killed - 8 ORs wounded.	HHds

Wt.47724/993 2,000,000 3/43 W. H. & S. 51/6375

WO 171/1245
Intelligence/war diary
12TH BATTALION, THE PARACHUTE REGIMENT

Month and Year Jun 44   Commanding Officer Lt. Col. A.P. Johnson

Place	Date	Hour	Summary of Events and Information	References to Appendices
KEEVIL	2	1240	Bn. addressed by corps comd. Sgt Browning C.B.D.S.O	
KEEVIL	3	1250.	Bn. addressed by Bdr Comd. Brigadier Pratt	
[RANVILLE	6]	0100 hrs	OPERATION OVERLORD [Bn] landed in CHERBOURG PERNINSULAR [took up posns in LE BAS DE RANVILLE and high ground SOUTH. B & C Coys. fwd A Coy. NORTH covering rear and watching Bridges] Maj Mayfield, Capt. Twinbull Lt Sharp, Lt Austin and 100 ORs missing. Lts (TOTTENHAM) - Smith & Campbell & 12 ORs wounded.	
[LEBAS DE RANVILLE		1200	Capt (SIM) and 7 ORs fought very gallant action area HEDGEROW S.W of Bn. Posn. Held off attack by Enemy Coy supported by 3 S.P. guns. 4 ORs killed Tiger Tank destroyed B coy area.	
		2100 hrs	Bn came into RANVILLE under and 6 airldy Bn. A Coy. moved fwd area X rds 105727].	

Wt 47724/993 2,000,000 3/43 W.H. & S 51/6375.

WO 171/1246

Intelligence/war diary
13TH BATTALION, THE PARACHUTE REGIMENT

Month and Year June 1944   Commanding Officer Lt. Col. P.J. LUARD.

Place	Date	Hour	Summary of Events and Information	References to Appendices
[RANVILLE	6	0050	13th Bn. (Lancashire) The Parachute Regiment, forming part of 5th Parachute Brigade dropped from DAKOTA and ALBEMARLE a/c on D.Z. 'N' – NORTH of RANVILLE, near CAEN, Dept of CALVADOS.	
		0230	Bn. moved off from R.V., having rallied on the Bn. hunting horn call (L for Lancaster), and formed in Companies½.	
		0300	Village of RANVILLE now cleared of enemy. Very few enemy were found, as from infm received from inhabitants, it appears that the main body of the enemy were away, and that the majority of those left behind departed with all speed when they saw parachutists. Those PW taken were wounded and seemed very young. Identification from PW, dead and documents, was 7/11 Pz Gren Regt 125.	
		0320	Glider party arrived on L.Z. 'N', now cleared of poles by 'A' Coy. Party consisted mainly of A/Tk guns, which moved rapidly into posn.]	
		0510	British aircraft observed attacking posns in area LE PLEIN - OUISTREHAM.	
		0600	Patrol to HEROUVILLETTE reported village in enemy hands.	
		0855	Report received from Bde HQ that news from seaborne tps is that they have broken through first line of defs.	
		0900	12 Para Bn. outpost heavily mortared.	
		[1005	Enemy S.P. guns reported on 'A' Coy front.	
		1020	'A' Coy. attacked by about 40 men and 3 SP guns.	
		1032	'A' Coy's. last LMG wiped out.]	

Wt.47724/993 2,000,000 3/43 W. H. & S. 51/6375.

SHEET 2

Place	Date	Hour	Summary of Events and Information	References to Appendices
[RANVILLE	6	1033	'A' Coy. reported attack repulsed. A/Tk guns knocked out 3 S.P. guns incl 2 destroyed. PW identified as 125 Pz Gren Regt (21 Pz Div).]	
		1120	Infm received of counter-attacks against 7 Para Bn and 12 Para Bn. All these attacks are being held.	
		1200	Arty conc put down on HEROUVILLETTE RACECOURSE to assist 'A' Coy.	
		[1210	'A' Coy. reported one more S.P. gun knocked out.	
		1212	'C' Coy. put in limited counter-attack to assist 'A' Coy. Enemy cas reported as l Offr and 42 ORs killed and 6 ORs captured.	
		1230	7 Para Bn. report one Pl of enemy wearing Brit airborne smocks and red berets penetrated part of our line.	
		1330	1 S.S. Bde Commando tps passed over BENOUVILLE BRS and through Bde posns towards FRANCEVILLE PLAGE.]	
		1650	4 Schmeisser machine pistols and amn found in RANVILLE sent to 'A' Coy.	
		[1710	'A' Coy. again attacked by approx 50 of 3/I/Pz Gren Regt 125. Attack again repulsed.]	
		1800	5 Para Bde report 7 Para Bn not yet relieved on BENOUVILLE BRS and 12 Para Bn. repulsed number of enemy attacks.	
		2100	Main glider party 6 Airldg Bde, landed on L.Z. 'N'	
		2100-2130	L. Z. shelled from SOUTH.	
		[2330	Dakota a/c dropped supplies by parachute. 13 Para Bn casualties for 6 Jun 44 Killed - 1 OR, Wounded 25 ORs, Missing 2 Offrs and 56 ORs.]	

Wt.47724/993 2,000,000 3/43 W. H. & S. 51/6375.

6TH AIRLANDING BRIGADE

WO 171/591
Intelligence/war diary
6TH AIRLANDING BRIGADE HQ

Month and Year June 44   Commanding Officer Brig. Hon. H.K.M. Kindersley MBE MC

Place	Date	Hour	Summary of Events and Information	References to Appendices
[BAS DE RANVILLE	6	2215	Bde HQ est 107734.	Div & Units informed 01.
	7	0135	Have received report enemy captured 1 Sub unit of 12 Para and are wearing their uniforms (From 1 RUR.)].	Brigadier informed.
Coy 2 OXF	BUCKS	0231	DR despatched.	
		0515	Situation and Identifications as at 2400 hrs 6 Jun 44. (From Div and repeated units).	See message (3)
		[0800 1000	2 OXF BUCKS occupied HEROUVILLETTE and trying to push fwd to ESCOVILLE].	Map marked.
		1005	1 RUR occupied LONGUEVAL.	Map marked.
		1115	2 OXF BUCKS occupied ESCOVILLE.	Map marked.
			Col. RG PARKER called at Bde HQ for infm regarding own tps for GOC :- 1 RUR in LONGUEVAL and moving on to St HONERINE. 2 OXF BUCKS occupy HEROUVILLETTE 0800 hrs and ESCOVILLE 1005 hrs. Col PARKER reports.	
		1130	1 SS Bde putting in attack NORTHWARDS.	
		1130	2 OXF BUCKS report trouble with AFV in ESCOVILLE. 2 OXF BUCKS in ESCOVILLE on objectives.]	Map marked.

Wt.47724/993 2,000,000 3/43 W. H & S. 61/6375

WO 171/1279

Intelligence/war diary

12TH BATTALION, THE DEVONSHIRE REGIMENT

Month and Year June 44   Commanding Officer Lt. Col. G.R.Ste?s

Place	Date	Hour	Summary of Events and Information	References to Appendices
	1/2		Bn. (less A Coy) stationed marshalling camps at GRAYS (personnel party) and PURFLEET (vehicle party) awaiting move to theatre of operation 'OVERLORD'.	
	3	0900	Bn. (less A Coy) left marshalling camps. and	
		1200	" " " " embarked at TILBURY	
		1430	Ships at anchor off SOUTHEND	
	4	1100	LCIs (carrying Personnel party) sailed to SHEERNESS	
		1630	Troops allowed ashore to visit camp.	
		1940	Troops reembarked	
		2020	LCIs returned to SOUTHEND	
	5		Ships at anchor inside Thames Estuary Boom.	
	6	0445	Ships sailed in convoy.	
			Convoy shelled in STRAITS OF DOVER.	'A'
			A Coy under comd Major J.Rogers emplaned in gliders at FARRINGDON aerodrome and flew to area of operation. One glider crashed in sea 8 miles off French coast. 6 ORs missing	
			Gliders landed in FRANCE in area F/7 1273 assembled and moved to HEROUVILLETTE Village held until arrival of Bn on 7 June. No casualties.	
	7	Day	LCIs and Transport ships landed on coast of FRANCE off OUISTRENEM. All personnel landed safely. Some equipment drowned.	
		1600	Bn regrouped in unit assembly area 'HOMER'	
LE BAS DE RANVILLE		1700	Moved to Concentration Area Le Bas de RANVILLE and took up	Capt. ? Adjutant

Wt 47724/993 2,000,000 3/43/ W.H. & S 51/6375.

WO 171/1357
Intelligence/war diary
2ND BATTALION, THE OX & BUCKS LIGHT INFANTRY

Month and Year June 1944   Commanding Officer

Place	Date	Hour	Summary of Events and Information	References to Appendices
	[6th		The Regt Less bridge assault party of Letter 'D' Coy and 2 plns of "B" Coy, took off from Harwell and Keevel airfields at 1840 hrs and 1910 hrs respectively. The trip was rather bumpy over land but all became very calm over the sea. At approx 2055 hrs we approached the French coast and could see a large fleet of ships standing off shore and occasional bursts of fire coming from their guns. It was very easy to pick out the River and canal below and ahead of us and we knew there had been no mistake in navigation. All gliders except four landed on or somewhere near the L.Z. although in most cases crash landings	Appx 'A' (Br assault by glider)

Wt 43550/1614 560M 3/41 BPL 51/8792.

SHEET 2

Page 3

Month and Year   Unit
       Commanding

Place	Date	Hour	Summary of Events and Information	References to Appendices
			occurred and many collisions took place, a certain amount of flax as gliders ran in added to the many difficulties of the Glider Pilots who in the majority of cases did magnificently. There was a certain amount of firing on the L.Z. and some snipers still seemed to the holding out in the area of the bridges at BENOUVILLE. After some delay, due to the fact that some gliders landed rather a long way south and also some were very badly smashed which made unloading difficult, the Regt formed up in the area. of Rd june 098754 at Le Port.	
		2215	The Regt. began to move forward to cross	

Wt 43550/1614 560M 3/41 BPL 51/8782.

SHEET 3

Month and Year

Unit

Commanding

Place	Date	Hour	Summary of Events and Information	References to Appendices
			the bridges to the pre-arranged concentration area at 108744. At this time four glider loads had failed to land, comprising BNHQ. No 5 1 Rifle Platoon 'B' Coy, ½ 'B', Coy, HQ, 1 Mortar Pln glider. A few people had been hurt in crash landings including the Comd Offr who managed to carry on and the loading Offr who had to be evacuated. Major Howard commanding the Bridge assault force reported to the Comd Offr and said that the route to the concentration area was clear. Despite the darkness of the night the Regt moved quickly into the concentration area and a temporary HQ was set up at 109744.	
		2300	The Comd Offr met the Brigade Comd.	

Wt 43550/1614 560M 3/41 BPL 51/8792.

SHEET 4

Month and Year

Unit

Commanding Officer

Place	Date	Hour	Summary of Events and Information	References to Appendices
			6 Airldg Bde on the bridge at BENOUVILLE and was taken forward to the area of the Church at RANVILLE 116734. The Comd Offr recieved orders to move forward into the area of the 13 Parachute Bn. at RANVILLE with intention of occupying HEROUVILLETTE 122724 as soon as possible and then to move on to occupy ESCOVILLE as was originally intended.	
	[7 JUNE	0130	Regt passed S.P. 110739 moving forward to the Chateau in RANVILLE a temporary HQ was set up there. The remainder of the Regt moved into the area of the Chateau grounds and took up a position of all round defence. Elements of the Bridge]	

Wt. 47724/993 2,000,000 3/43 W. H & S. 51/6575.

WO 171/1383
Intelligence/war diary
1ST BATTALION THE ROYAL ULSTER RIFLES

Month and Year June 1944

Place	Date	Hour	Summary of Events and Information	Remarks and references to Appendices
BROADWELL TRANSIT CAMP	5th	1700	Loading completed.	
		1900	All Ranks informed that D-Day for operation 'OVERLORD' would be 6 JUNE 1944.	
		2100	Party of officers and ORs proceeded to Broadwell airfield to watch the departure of 9 Para.Bn commanded by Lt. Col. T.B.H. otway. Take off commenced 2250 hrs and all aircraft away by 2350 hrs.	
			<u>Meteorological</u>. Slight wind, cloudy, warm.	
		1000	Final preparations for operation; morale high.	
		1615	Bn. parades for searching prior to move to airfields.	
	[6th	[1500	All personnel taking part provided with a fatless meal to prevent or reduce air sickness.Tea and water provided in gliders and all Ranks instructed to drink as much as possible before Landing.]	
		"	Information received from Broadwell airfield that 9 Para Bn. had been dropped to correct DZs and that landing strips for gliders of LZs had been clearly visible.	Wheldon Capt

(3110) Wt 35842/1764 1000M 12/39 BPL 51/5684.

SHEET 2

Month and Year June 1944

Place	Date	Hour	Summary of Events and Information	References to Appendices
BROADWELL TRANSIT CAMP	6th	1500	Information also received from Blakehill farm that Major Drommond and who had taken off with HQ 6 Air Div the previous night from Harwell airfield had forced landed and was returning to Blakehill farm.	
		1700	Bn. moved to take off airfield Broadwell and Down Ampney. All arrangements proceeded according to plan, except the load in the spare gliders at Broadwell. A/tr Pe load had to be changed for M.M.G load at last moment, but completed in time before take off.	
		1832	1st combination off from Broadwell airfield. For the first hour of the flight which took place over England the weather was showery and flying conditions bumpy. After crossing the coast at approx 2000 hrs flying conditions improved.	
RANVILLE		2100	Glider no 1 (Major. G. Rickcord. B Coy HQ.) touched down, 6 mins before time scheduled. LZ N 1/25000 sheet CAEN 116749	
			Slight enemy opposition on LZ from mortars and M.G.s, and difficulty in securing tails of vehicle carrying gliders was reported.	
			Bn. check point. X Rds 111739.]	Wheldon Capt

(3110) Wt 35842/1764 1000m 12/39 BPL 51/5684 Forms C2118/22.

SHEET 3

Place	Date	Hour	Summary of Events and Information	Remarks and references to Appendices
[RANVILLE]	6th		Capt Gordon reported one with a Pl glider on fire after landing.	
		[2230	Bn. HQ established Le Bas de Ranville. Farm buildings 105734 and Bn. reported complete less one R&L missing from the glider which caught fire on LZ (R&L Woodburn F Coy) DR reported Bde HQ established at 106731.	
			Information received that enemy in following areas:-	
			(a) Snipers in area RANVILLE.	
			(b) '30' Contour between RANVILLE and STE HON ORINE.1072	
			(c) Longueval 0872. Strength not known.	Appx 'A' (account of C
	[7	2349	C Coy ordered to seize and occupy Ring Contour '30'.]	Coy ops D/D+1 by
		0200	C Coy report in position on Ring Contour '30'. no opposition encountered. One Pl M.M.G. in support.	Capt Wheldon)
			Bn. task of seizing STE HONORONE and LONGUEVAL confirmed.	
			Orders issued GP CO.	
			C Coy to remain on 'Hill 30' as fire support.	
			A and B Coys. assaulting Coys. A. B left. D Coy in reserve.	
			F.U.P. Copse 095727.	
			Route. Ranville - track June. 102734 - track June 102734 – FUP.	
		0600	Bn. moves from Le Bas de Ranville.]	Wheldon Capt

(3110) Wt 35842/1764 1000ᴍ 12/39 BPL 51/5684 Forms C2118/22.

DIVISIONAL
TROOPS

WO 171/425
Intelligence/war diary
6TH AIRBORNE DIVISION HQ

In lieu of AF C 2118.

Month and Year June 1944

Commander - Maj. Gen. R.N. GALE, OBE, MC.

Serial	Date	Time	Event	Action taken	Remarks
1	6	0020	"Coup de main" party of 6 plns 2 OXF BUCKS with dets RE landed by glider between brs over CANAL de CAEN and R. ORNE.	Both brs captured intact with slight opposition – close brhead est on WEST bank of canal brs.	Little flak encountered over coast or ldg. One glider broke tow rope, rest landed in close proximity to brs. Brs were prepared for demolition but charges were not in posn. Later found stored in neighbouring hut.
2	6	0050	(a) 7 Para Bn. dropped - task to consolidate the brhead est by the "coup de main" party.	Bn was dropped somewhat wide of correct DZ. There was consequently delay in re-org and Bn. did not reach br until 0300 hrs.	One Coy. had been lightly equipped to double to the brs - to reach it within one hr of drop. In fact this Coy. dropped furthest astray and reached the brs last.
			(b) 12 and 13 Para Bns dropped on DZ " ". Tasks		
			(c) 9 Para Bn. landed on DZ " ". Tasks		
			(d) 8 and 1 Cdn Para Bns landed on DZ " ". Tasks		
3	6	0335	Div HQ and 4 A Tk Bty landed.		
4	6	0755	Infm from 5 Para Bde that brs had been captured intact.	Airtps infm	No news of 3 Para Bde.
5	6	0825	Br at 114762 reported intact.	1 Corps infm	
6	6	0915	Unconfirmed report that bty 155776 had been destroyed.	1 Corps infm accordingly	Later confirmed that bty was destroyed by 0500 hrs.
7	6	1230	Sitrep. Div HQ est Le BAS de RANVILLE 1073. 5 Para Bde seized brs intact with little opposition and now firmly est. Some enemy activity incl small counter		

........./2.........

SHEET 2

Serial	Date	Time	Event	Action taken	Remarks
		(77 mm SP	attack area SE of RANVILLE. 3 enemy guns destroyed. 3 Para and 1 SS Bdes not yet contacted, but latter believed to be now approaching brs. 8 Inf Bde making good progress.		Enemy identifications. HQ 2 Bn. and 8 Coy 125 Pz Gren Regt at COLOMBELLES 0770. 7 Coy 125 Pz Gren Regt in area RANVILLE on anti-para tp patrols night 5/6 Jun. 711 Engr Coy HEROUVILLETTE 7271. 30 tks POUSSY 1356.
8	[6	1300	Strong enemy attempt at infiltration 500 yds SOUTH of PONT TOURNANTsp by SP guns caused a critical situation.	Brilliant action by Brig Poett and most determined fighting by 7 and 12 Para Bns repulsed the attack. "One" Cdo temporarily diverted to assist clear up situation.	By 1400 hrs all ground lost in the brhead area had been regained.]
9	[6	1353	1 SS Bde crossed the brs - unit of 8 Inf Bde now at brs - situation completely in hand.	1 SS Bde came under comd 6 Airborne Div on crossing.]	
10	6	1610	3 Para Bde report area at LEMESNIL held by 1 cdn Para Bn. Approx 130 enemy entering BREVILLE.		
11	6	1700	3 Para bde reported that brs at VARAVILLE ROBEHOMME and BURES had been successfully blown.		This bde was dropped over an enormous area and is now about one third str.
12	6	1700	Situation on div front comfortably in hand.		
13	6	2100	Glider ldg of 1 RUR, 2 OXF BUCKS, Armd Recce Regt and 211 Lt Bty.		
14	[7	0001	Sitrep. Continual attacks from SOUTH all held - now known that brs at TROARN and VARAVILLE were successfully blown. Owing to strong resistance 1 SS Bde were unable to adv beyond line BREVILLE -		

........./3.........

WO 171/1249

Intelligence/war diary
22ND INDEPENDENT PARACHUTE COMPANY

Month and Year June 1944   Commanding Officer Capt. J. Vischer

Place	Date	Hour	Summary of Events and Information	References to Appendices

Field -U.K.	1
	3
	5
		
		1200
		1800
		2300
			Opening day of briefing of all ranks for Operation 'OVERLORD'.
			First briefing with RAF crews for Operation 'OVERLORD'.
			Final briefing of all ranks for Operation 'OVERLORD'.
			All Offrs attended final briefing of RAF crews.
			Two sticks commanded by Maj. F.G.L. LENNOX-BOYD, 2IC Lt M. MOORE Capt I.A. TAIT)
			
			Four sticks commanded by Lt. R.E.V de LATOUR)
			                Lt. D. C. E. WALLS)
			                Lt. R. MIDWOOD)
			                Lt. J. VISCHER)
				All map references in this war diary refer to Map FRANCE 1:50000 Sheet TROARN 7 F/2
				
				} emplaned and took off at BRIZE NORTON airfd in ALBEMARLE a/cs For N
				
				} emplaned and took off at HARWELL airfd in ALBEMARLE a/cs For N + K

		2330	One stick commanded by No. 910946 Sjt HULME, W. emplaned and took off from KEEVIL airfd in STIRLING a/c	
	6	0020	The following pathfinder sticks were dropped on the following DZs in NORMANDY, France EAST of the R. ORNE	

		0035
		0040
			(i) <u>DZ "V" ref map. 1776</u>
			Two sticks commanded by Lt. R.E.V. de LATOUR and Lt. D.C.E. WELLS
			One OR No. 319425 Pte. DEAKIN received jumping injury (broken leg) on landing and was later evacuated.
			One "EUREKA" set up on DZ coding channels "C/A".
			'T' set out on ground using holophane lights and coding letter 'V'.
			One OR wounded No. 1100814 Pte. CHRISTIE, P. and later evacuated.
			
			<u>Comment on drop:</u> Sticks dropped well over DZ by RAF. Stick assembly slowed up by:
			      (a) extra heavy load carried on men, taking up extra space in a/c and resulting in cramped positions when running in
			      (b) dykes filled with water on extremeties of DZ
			      (c) noise and confusion created by RAF bombing of enemy battery posn at SALLANELLES refmap 1376
			Some kitbags broke away under the shock of the chute developing and were lost. Of the four 'EUREKAS' dropped on this DZ three were retained intact, the fourth was put out of action by the drop and detonated on the DZ.
			                                    ...../-2	

SHEET 2

COMMANDING OFFICER: Capt. J. VISCHER

Place	Date	Hour	Summary of Events and Information	References to Appendices
In the Field	6	0145	Both sticks assemble at 9 Para Bn. RV wood refmap 168757 with A Coy. 9m Para Bn. to set out lights and 'EUREKA' for gliderlanding on enemy battery posn refmap 1577.	
		0405	'EUREKA' switched on, channels C/A immedeately east of battery posn.	
		0415	Seven holophane lights set out on ground marking 'T', coding letter "A" (A).	
		0600	Sticks moved off to company conc area LE BAS RANVILLE refmap 1073, contacted 9 Para Bn. in area LE PLEIN refmap 1275, assisted in giving covering fire for Commando attack on AMFREVILLE refmap 1274 No. 3663154 L cpl HOWARTH, L. killed by enemy action.	
		2000	Both sticks reported in to company conc area at LE BAS RANVILLE+	
			(ii) <u>DZ 'N' ref map1174</u>	
			Two stick commanded by Capt. I.A. TAIT and Lt. M MOORE dropped on SE corner of DZ	
		0023	Major F.G.L. LENNOX-BOYD premature and accidental exit from a/c SE of DZ refmap Eastings 15–20 Northings 70-75 Major F.G.L. LENNOX-BOYD has not been seen since and is reported missing.	
		0020	One stick commanded by Lt. J. VISCHER dropped across SE corner of DZ. This stick should have dropped on DZ 'K' refmap 1269 but owing to navigational error by RAF crew the stick was released over DZ 'N'.	
		0035	Stick under Lt. J. VISCHER assembled on DZ contacted part of Capt. I.A. TAIT's stick and set up 'EUREKA'-beacon and 'T' of 5 lights. 'EUREKA' switched on to channels D/C, holophane lamp coding letter 'K'.	
		0130	All three sticks assembled at Xroads refmap 125740 under Capt. I.A. TAIT with exception of Maj. F.G.L. LENNOX-BOYD and one OR (No. 14416184 Pte. NEWTON, R. who rejoined the company two days later).	
			<u>Comment on drop:</u> All three sticks were dropped somewhat off the DZ across the SE corner Sticks were slow. This was due to heavy loads and cramped spacing in the a/c. Stick assembly on the ground consequently took longer than intended. A number of kitbags broke loose during the drop and were lost. No jumping injuries were sustained by any of the three sticks. No 'EUREKAS' were compromised on this DZ but three were damaged by the drop.	
		0350	Marking of LZ 'N' for night glider landing – Div HQ tps - under Capt. I.A. TAIT	
			Three sticks commanded by Capt. I.A. TAIT, Lt. J.VISCHER, Lt. M. MOORE set out lights on three separate landing strips Two 'EUREKAS' were set up.	
		0700	<u>Comment on landing:</u> Successful landing was made by most gliders, some overshooting the lights. It was later reported that the lights were clearly visible.	
			The party made its way to company conc area near Div HQ at LE BAS RANVILLE.	

SHEET 3

Place	Date	Hour	Summary of Events and Information	Reference to Appendices
In the Field	6	0020	(iii) <u>DZ 'K' refmap 1269</u> One stick commanded by Ltt R. MIDWOOD dropped on DZ.	
		0035	One 'EUREKA' set up coding channels D/C, one holophane lamp coding letter 'K'.	
			Five of the stick failed to report to stick RV. Four of these have not been seen since and are reported missing (No. 3654430 L sjt BOARBMAN, A., No. 14301912 L Cpl STOODLEY, R., No. 5124865 P te. NAUGHTON, L Cpl. HACKMAN, R.)	
			No. 1435752 L Cpl. O'SULLIVAN, E.D. killed by enemy action on DZ	
		0130	Remainder of stick assembled under Lt. R. MIDWOOD at 8 Para Bn. RV, Road and track junc refmap 132690 A thorough search of DZ was carried out.	
		0530	Remainder of stick moved off under Lt. R.MIDWOOD to company conc area at LE BAS RANVILLE	
		1230	Lt. R. MIDWOODAND four ORs reported to company conc area at LE BAS RANVILLE	
			<u>Comment ondrop :</u> Slow stick on account of heavy loads. Stick came under enemy fire immedeately after landing. One 'EUREKA' carried by N sjt BOARDMAN is missing and must be considered as probably compromised. This DZ has been in the hands of the enemy since D-Day. It has therefore not been possible to establish the exact fate of this 'EUREKA'. Search of the DZ is at present impossible. Owing to enemy opposition one 'EUREKA' was abandoned on the DZ after being detonated.	
		0100	One stick of twenty men commanded by Sjt HULME dropped with the mainbody on DZ 'N' ° Three ORs sustained jumping injuries (No. 1305139 Pte. KING, R. – fractured leg, No. 3663662 Pte. STEPHENS, J. – fractured leg, No. 14408455 Pte. ALLCOCK, H. - twisted ankle.), and were later evacuated.	
		0130	The stick assembled at xroads refmap 125740 and reported to Capt. I.A. TAIT.+	
		2130	<u>Daylight glider landing on LZ 'N'.</u> Ground aids set up by one stick commanded by Capt. I.A. TAIT.	
			<u>Daylight glider landing on LZ 'W'</u> Ground aids set up by one stick commanded by Lt. J. VISCHER.	
			<u>Comment on Landings</u>: Both landings were highly successful.	
		2200	Lt. DCE WELLS wounded by mortar fire in area LE BAS RANVILLE and evacuated.	
		2330	<u>Night supply drop on SDZ 'N'</u> SDZ marking carried out by one stick commanded by Capt. I.A.TAIT.	
			Lt. R.E.V. de LATOUR re-promoted temporary Capt.	

WO 171/1017

Intelligence/war diary

53RD AIRLANDING LIGHT REGIMENT, RA

Month and Year June 1944   Commanding Officer Lt Col ADM Teacher.

Place	Date	Hour	Summary of Events and Information	References to Appendices
BULFORD	1 to 6 6		Preparation for Action D-Day; the Regiment less 211 A/L Bty received its orders to move to the marshalling area. 211 A/L Bty went into action by glider from FAIRFORD aerodrome - passed over Bulford Camp at approx 2000 hrs towed by Stirling aircraft.	For details of activities of 211 Bty from 6-15 Jun. see Appx I.
	7		Movement order for the regt to move to marshalling area were issued. Regt cleared up Bulford Camp preparatory to evacuation.	See "Movement Instr No 1 (Road) APPX II.
	8	0200	Regimental vehicle parties left Bulford for rendezvous at Staines Middx. Met Metropolitan Police who escorted convoy through London on the North Circular Road to marshalling area.	

*5973. Wt.22661/1499. 300M. 8/42 Wy.L.P. Gp.656.

WO 171/959

Intelligence/war diary
3RD AIRLANDING ANTI-TANK BATTERY RA

Month and Year June 44

Commanding Officer Major W.R. CRANMER.

Place	Date	Hour	Summary of Events and Information			References to Appendices
GOSPORT	1	0600	Bty arrives to embark.	Bws dr	J.W. Captain	
		1500	Bty completely embarked on LSTs.	Bws dr	J.W. Captain	
		1700	LSTs move to RYDE ROADS.	Bws dr	J.W. Captain	
AT SEA	2		At anchor.	Bws dr	J.W. Captain	
AT SEA	3		At anchor.	Bws dr	J.W. Captain	
			AF W 3008, 3009 rendered.	Bws dr	J.W. Captain	Appx A
AT SEA	4		At anchor.	Bws dr	J.W. Captain	
AT SEA	5	1830	Ship sails; personnel briefed for operation.	Bws dr	J.W. Captain	
RANVILLE	6	0100	Para party of 4 dropped near RANVILLE.	Bws dr	J.W. Captain	
		0230	Atp less 2 guns land near RANVILLE by glider.	Bws dr	J.W. Captain	
LION SURMER		1300	Bty commences to disembark & move to assembly area COLVILLE.	Bws dr	J.W. Captain	
				Bws dr	J.W. Captain	
COLVILLE	7	0500	Bty completely assembled.	Bws dr	J.W. Captain	
		0600	Move to RANVILLE Airborne parties met.			
			Casualty and strength return 16 ORs missing & 4 wounded	Bws dr	J.W. Captain	
					J.W. Captain	

Wt 13474/1805 1,200,000 7/40 BPL 51-7171 Forms C2118/22

WO 171/960

Intelligence/war diary

4TH AIRLANDING ANTI-TANK BATTERY RA

Month and Year June 1944   Commanding Officer MAJ. T H P DIXON MC RA.

Place	Date	Hour	Summary of Events and Information	References to Appendices
TARRANT	1-5		Bty under comde 6 Airlanding Bde at Fransit Camp.	PRD
RUSHTON	6	0055	Recce party landed in area RANVILLE NORMANDY with 12th & 13th Para Bns.	PRD
RANVILLE		0330	Main Glider party arrives 11 Guns and 2 1/Q mey Guns into action.	PRD
RANVILLE AREA		1030	4 S.P. German guns destroyed.	PRD
RANVILLE AREA		1400	Forward ATK gun lost, 2 glider pilots and 1 gunner killed and 2 wounded. Sgt Woodridge in attempting to rejoin unit lost gun and jeep.	PRD
-do-	7		Sgt Guest and 3 guns killed in action. Gun knocked out by German S.P. which was subsequently knocked out by 17 per of 3rd Bty attached to as	PRD
-do-	8		B.C. and 1 Tp Comde and Glider party rejoined Bty after having been landed East of R. Dives.	

Wt.47724/993 2,000,000 3/43 W. H. & S. 51/6375.

WO 171/435
Intelligence/war diary
6TH AIRBORNE ARMOURED
RECONNAISSANCE REGIMENT

Month and Year June 1944   Commanding Officer Lt / Col G.R.de C. Stewart.

Place	Date	Hour	Summary of Events and Information	References to Appendices
Tarrent Rushton & Brise Norton. do.	1/5 6	-	Regt. in transit camps. A Sqn. and R.H.Q. at TARRANT RUSHTON & B & H.Q. Sqns AT Brise Norton. Loading Gliders and awaiting instructions to emplane. Regt. enplaned from airfields as above on Operation OVERLORD, B & H.Q. Sqns at 1900 hrs, A Sqn & R.H.Q. at 1925 hrs. One Horsa with 2 i/c forced to cast off and made successful landing area Winchester. No further episodes in flight. Hamilcars and Horsas arrived over D.Z. area Ranville 1173, 2100/2130 Hrs. All Horsas landed without incident, one Hamilcar in landing crashed into Tank unloading from another causing both to become Z Cas. Some Mortar fire on D.Z. during landing, one Hamilcar hit. Regt. R.V. in harbour at 123734.	
123734	7	0700	Move from Harbour area, via LE MESNIL, to new harbour area Rd. Junc. 137707.	INSERT: Light Tank cas on Enemy mine 135706, approx 1200 hrs. Crew missing. Light hit by S.P.Gun at 135708, 1 cas X Tank cas Z.
		0930	Recce patrol engaged 4-wheel Armd. Car in wood 137706, Jeep set on fire by incendiary bullet and blew up, no Cas. personnel.	
137707		0930/ 2100	Recce patrols operating in area TOUFFREVILLE, SANNERVILLE, BANNEVILLE LA CAMPAGNE. Enemy movements seen in TOUFFREVILLE and SANNERVILLE and area 1168/1169. incl.inf, small numbers tanks and S.P. Guns. 192 Pz. Gren Regt.	

Wt.47724/993 2,000,000 3/43 W. H. & S. 51/6375.

WO 171/1510
Intelligence/war diary
3RD PARACHUTE SQUADRON RE

Month and Year June 1944   Commanding Officer Major J. C. A. Roseveare.

Place	Date	Hour	Summary of Events and Information	References to Appendices
BLAKEHILL FARM	1/2		Sqn. in Transit Camp. Recreational trg and final preparation of eqpt. 3 Tp at DOWN AMPNEY.	Outline Plan and Summary of events Appx "A".
	3		All ranks briefing with models, maps and photographs.	
	4/5		First date for op. cancelled due to weather.	
	5/6		D-Day.	
			For events from night 5/6 Jun to night 7/8 Jun see Appx "A" attached.	
			All map refs refer to Sheet 7F/2 France 1/50.000.	
Le MESNIL de BAVENT 140728	8		Repeated attacks all day by enemy particularly EAST of X rds. 1 Tp at X rds 133726. 3 Tp replace 2 Tp EAST of X rds. HQ take up 3 Tp posns on NE of perimeter. 2 Tp into res for rest.	
		2200	L Cpl PERRY and marching personnel arrive with 3 Lt wt MCs and 2 FCs.	
	9		Enemy sit remains same. Continued mortar and shell fire.	
		1530	Cpl THORNE and veh party arrived location. Cpl GREEN and sec from 2 Tp.	
		1700	Booby trapped covered approach to posns EAST of X rds.	
			Lt SHAVE and sec from 2 Tp det to join 8 Para Bn area 140705 for patrols and RE work.	

Wt. 10570/2039 1,280M. 5/44 W. H. & S. 51-8686

APPENDIX A
OPERATION "NEPTUNE"
3 PARA SQN RE

OUTLINE PLAN AND SUMMARY & EVENTS

1. 3 Para Sqn. were under comd 3 Para Bde for the op with the task of assisting the bde to carry out their initial tasks and subsequently were to revert to comd CRE.

2. Sqns tasks were as follows:-

(i) Destruction of brs by H + 2 hrs at

(a) TROARN	177680	5 span masonry arch
(b) BURES	173698	girder
(c) BURES	175702	girder (rly br)
(d) ROBEHOMME	195726	girder
(e) ROBEHOMME	193743	culvert
(f) VARAVILLE	186758	masonry single span

(ii) Mining of rds at:- 140702
141728

(iii) Route Recce in area
RANVILLE BREVILLE Rd Jun 140702
ESCOVILLE HEROUVILLETTE LE MARIQUET

(iv) Recce for RE stores in Jettison drops.

3. OUTLINE PLAN. D-Day 6 Jun 44. P-hour 0520 hrs.
H-hour 0715 hrs. 3 para Bde gp were dropping on two DZs:-

DZ V Area 1775 - Bde Gp less 8 Bn. Gp.
DZ K Area 1289 - 8 Para Bn Gp.

Sqn. less No 3 tp and aet Sqn HQ were to drop with 8 Para Bn. on DZ K at P-4' hrs 30 min with task of destroying brs at TROARN and BURES.

No 1 Tp was to destroy TROARN br covered by a coy of 8 Para Bn. in Ste SAMSON and a coy in TROARN and No 2 Tp was to destroy brs at BURES covered by a pl of 8 Para Bn.

No 3 Tp and a det of Sqn. HQ were to drop under comd l Cdn Para Bn. on DZ V at P-4 hrs 26 mins with the task of destroying the brs at ROBEHOMME and VARAVILLE. One coy of 1 Cdn Bn. were to deal with enemy in VARAVILLE area and the ROB EHOMMS brs were to be covered by one pl.

Two gliders were allotted to the sqn on DZ K and one glider on DZ V for the carriage of additional explosive and ongr eqpt. The two gliders on DZ K carried the necessary stores for attacking the piers of the TROARN br.

ACTUAL HAPPENINGS

4. The AIR PLAN - 8 Bn Gp

Take off and flight to the coast were uneventful. It was remarkable at the airfd that there were little signs of nervous strain than before many exs. Everyone was eager to get on with the task and no one had any thoughts of being dropped in the wrong place. Hot tea was served from Thermos flasks during the flight and no one was troubled by air-sickness. Sqn. loss 3 Tp and two gliders took off from BLAKEHILL FARM and 3 Tp and one glider took off from DOWN AMPNEY.

There was some last minute confusion at the latter airfield as one a/c went u/s and, had to be replaced at the last moment.

PTO/Sheet 2/During

SHEET 3

During flight there was no sign of any of our own A/C or EA and it was noticeable that the promised beating up of the flak on the coast did NOT take place. On crossing the coast some fairly close flak came up. On DZ K the first six A/C in were to be 3 Sqn. (Nos 224 to 229) followed by mortar and MMG pls of 8 Bn. followed by Rifle Coys.

5. On baling out at 0050 hrs there was flak and SA fire on DZ. As far as can be ascertained all six A/C dropped reasonably near the Indep Para Coy lights which were located at 124737. From cross-examination of stick comds I think all six A/C commenced to drop within grid square 1273. The sticks were fairly long in some cases duo to men falling over due to the violent evasive action taken by some pilots. My A/C 224 was steady and applied flap before dropping. Direction of run-in appeared to be NE - SW to NNE - SSW. Just before the green a glider was released just above my A/C.

On landing I suspected we were in the wrong posn as I could see no high ground to the EAST and STIRLING A/C were running in from all directions dropping paratps. Several gliders landed close by - they were not RE ones. My stick comd Lieut LACK and the SSM set about collecting the stick at the containers which were well conc and illuminated by the THOMAS devices which worked well.

Paratps dropping around appeared to belong to every Para Bn. in the div. I contacted Capt TAIT of the Indep Para Coy who said he had been dropped in the wrong place and this was DZ K". I found this hard to believe. We rallied as many 8 Bn. and 3 Sqn. men as possible and kept them moving down to a track junc 123734. There I contacted Capt JUCKES and we re-organised. Considerable signs of battle were coming from the SW and it was obvious that the later Nos in the sticks must have struck trouble in the area RANVILLE - LE MARIQUET. Our posn was confirmed by a signpost at the X-rds at 121732.

6. On taking stock we appeared to have a recce boat, a Mk II Camouflet set, 4/500 lb of plastic explosive and 45 gen wade charges besides an adequate number of accessories, beehives etc, and the HQ link 68 set and one 18 set. We only had 6 trolleys however, sufficient anyway to carry out some form of demolition on our 3 brs. The following Offrs were present - OC., Capt JUCKES, Lieuts SHAVE, FORSTER, BREESE, WADE and LACK. No 8 Bn. offrs were apparent but some 20/30 ORs chiefly from the mortar and MMG pls. About 60 sprs and NCOs were present.

7. I then endeavoured to org the party for the approach march. In the absence of any 8 Bn. Offrs it proved rather difficult to persuade the 8 Bn. ORs to take the lead even under Spr offrs so eventually the point sec consisted of Capt JUCKES, myself and few stout-hearted Sprs who were not hauling the trolleys. As we moved off to the accompaniment of Mortar and MMG fire, a jeep and trailer with Med stores joined the party. The time was about 0230 hrs. approx. The route followed was HEROUVILLETTE - ESCOVILLE - Rd June 140703. The march, which was fortunately unopposed, was a feat of endurance by the Sprs hauling the heavily laden trolleys. Many were limping with DZ Injuries but they all pulled their weight on the trying gradient up to the Rd. junc.

8. On reaching the road junc at about 0400 hrs two 8 Bn. Offrs, materialized, one was the Mortar Offr. I ordered them to take up a def posn with all the 8 Bn. personnel and hold the area of the rd junc. We then redistributed the stores amongst the tpt available. All the wet stores were unloaded in the timber yard, and all Gen Wade charges were loaded on the jeep and Tlrr. All plastic explosive and the camouflet set were loaded on the trolleys and I ordered Capt JUCKES

to proceed..........

SHEET 4

to proceed at once with the main body of the Sprs to attack his brs at BURES and I took Lt BREESE and 7 NCO's and sprs with me in the jeep and Tlr to attack the TROARN Br.

9. TROARN BR

We set off down the road at a moderate pace with everyone ready with a Bren and several Stens for any trouble. Just before the level crossing we ran slap into a barbed wire knife rest rd block. One Bosche fired a shot and then went off. It took 20 minutes hard work with wire cutters before the jeep was freed. We then proceeded on, leaving behind, it transpired later, Spr. MOON. Two scouts were sent ahead to the cross rd 160676. As they arrived a Bosche soldier cycled across complete with rifle. On being dragged from his bicycle he protested volubly and we made the mistake of silencing him with a Sten instead of a knife.

The Town was now getting roused so we lost no time and everyone jumped aboard while I tried to make the best speed possible, as the total load was about 3000 lbs we only made about 35 mph. At the corner 163678 - here the fun started as there seemed to be a Bosche in every door way shooting like mad. However, the boys got to work with their Stens and Spr. PEACHEY did good work as rear gunner with the Bren. What saved the day was the steep hill down the Main Street as the speed rose rapidly and we careered from side to side of the road as the heavy tlr was swinging violently. We were chased out of the town by an M.G. 34 which fired tracer just over our heads.

On arrival at the br which was not held, we found Spr. PEACHEY and his Bren were missing. 39 Gen. Wade charges were immediately placed across the centre span, a cordtex lead connected up, and the charges fired. The demolition was completely successful - the whole centre span being demolished giving a gap of 15 to 20 feet. The time taken was about 5 minutes.

I decided TROARN would not be a healthy spot to return to so we drove the jeep up a track due NORTH towards BURES as far as possible and then ditched it. Lieut BREESE made a recce of BURES which led him to believe it was occupied. It was now about 0500 hrs. The party therefore swam several streams SOUTH of BURES and took to the woods. A good deal of M.G. 42 fire from the direction of the rd junc 140703 made me alter my plan and I decided to make for LE MESNIL which was reached at 1300 hrs.

10. BURES BRS

Capt JUCKES led his party through the BOIS DE BURES and reached the brs unopposed at about 0630 hrs. Work was immediately commenced on the demolition of the brs. Lt. SHAVE and one sec worked on the track br and the remaining 2 Tp. Sprs amounting to about 1½ Secs with Lt. FORSTER on the Rly. Br. Local protection was provided by Sprs of No. 1 Tp.

While this was proceeding, the main body of the 8 Bn. were arriving in the area of the track junc. 158699 being less than 100 strong but having been dropped on the correct DZ. They had with them the two jeeps and tlrs loaded with explosive and the small RE party which had landed in the correct place and at the correct time in their two gliders.

Lt. WADE was sent back from the brs to find Lieut. LACK and his

trolley.........

SHEET 5

trolley which had fallen behind owing to the infirmities of the Sprs pulling it. On the way he contacted a Jeep and tlr. which was on its way to the BURES brs. Information had reached the C.O. 8 Bn that 2 Tp were working there and he despatched this Jeep and Tlr to them. Lt. WADE then attempted to reach the TROARN br with the Jeep and tlr. on his own. On nearing the town however, FRENCH locals warned him that the Germans were on the alert and that there was no possibility of him getting through alone. Lt. WADE therefore returned to the BURES brs. with the Jeep and tlr. and then proceeded to Recce the Troarn br on foot. On the way he found the ditched jeep used by OC and party and found the br. demolished. Finding no sign of life, he then returned to BURES.

Both brs were blown by 0930 hrs and a steel punt was also sunk. The tps were all pretty tired by now and Capt. JUCKES decided to have breakfast before moving off. He himself reported back to 8 Bn. in the Jeep and the CO visited the br sites. An attempt was made to unload a jeep and 6-pdr. gun which were in a crashed glider 100^x from the Rly. Br. in the river. The CO put a time limit on these efforts and the tps withdrew to the 8 Bn. area by 1215 hrs.

The CO 8 Bn. then decided it would be a good idea to attack the TROARN br again but would only release a Pl for the purpose. The party formed up in the following order of march under comd of Capt. JUCKES:-

One Pl 8 Para Bn. comd by Lieut C.BROWN.

Protective det RE under Sgt SHRUBSOLE.

Jeep and tlr with 40 Gen. Wades and Lieut. Wade & 6 Sprs.

Rearguard dot. RE under Lieut. SHAVE.

Route taken was EAST to BURES and then down rd SOUTH towards TROARN. A firm base was established at rd track crossing 166683 with the working party and Lt. SHAVE'S party. At about this pt some sniping had commenced and alarmist reports were received from the FRENCH of the action the Germans would take to cut off the party. However, it was decided to proceed and the Pl of 8 Bn. pushed on into the Town and proceeded to drive the enemy up the street in a WESTERLY direction. The rear gd was then brought in to the ORCHARD immediately NORTH of the houses. Sgt. SHRUBSOLE'S party were then pushed into the Town and worked their way down the hill towards the brs. They came under fire and a small battle ensued in which one German was killed and five surrendered. The way was now clear to the br and the working party on the Jeep proceeded straight down to the br and laid their charges across the next span to that already destroyed and successfully demolished it. The total gap was now about 35/40 feet as the pier was almost completely demolished by the second explosion. The sluice was not attacked as it did not afford a passage to vehs. Some boats and punts were sunk. The party then withdrew in good order through TROARN by the route they came. The Inf. Pl. was withdrawn through Lt. SHAVE'S rear guard and the return march was completed successfully. The br was blown at about 1500 hrs and the party were back at 8 Bn. by 1630 hrs.

11. STRAGGLER PARTIES

Tps jumping towards the ends of sticks and who landed in the RANVILLE area became closely engaged with the enemy at once. There was considerable firing and confusion and there are many reports of Sprs being captured and subsequently escaping. Individual reports all show that extremely offensive action was taken against the German in all cases.

The late........

SHEET 6

The late Sgt. JONES killed eight of his captors with their own weapons. Spr. THOMAS although wounded (He was shot during his descent) killed 3 Germans with two 36 Grenades. SQMS BROWN, although injured on the drop killed a large number of Germans with his Sten.

A small party of 5 sprs with Sgt. DOCHERTY and Lieut. BEAUMONT moved off with Major HEWETSON of the 8 Bn. and about 20 Inf. towards HEROUVILLETTE where they met Captain FOX and 8 Sprs with one trolley of explosive. The combined party was heavily engaged by M.G. fire in the Town and only escaped by climbing several walls and leaving the trolley. The Inf. suffered about 10 casualties here. The RE suffered 2 cas. The party made their way x-country to the rd. junc 140703. An enemy armd C. and tk were engaged SOUTH of this pt and contact was made with 8 Bn. at about 1400 hrs.

Other individuals and small parties made their way to either Rd junc 140703 or X-rds 140728 in accordance with the pre-briefed plan. Captain A.J. JACK, who was captured immediately on landing in the Anti-paratp Kommando HQ, escaped in the early morning and arrived at LE MESNIL at 0900 hrs.

The only Offr missing was Lieut E.V.KNOX who was known to have been shot during his descent but who was alive on landing. No trace has been discovered of this Offr since.

12. MINELAYING.
Immediate steps were taken at Bde HQ at LE MESNIL by the Bde Staff and the RE present to locate A.Tk. mines for the blocking of the rd. junc 140703. The jettison drop appeared to be scattered over a wide area and a large number of containers were in enemy occupied territory. Some Mk.V. mines began to arrive early evening time and at 2200 hrs. minelaying was commenced by 2 Tp with about 80 Mk. V. A.Tk. mines. The fd. was completed by about 2359 hrs and No. 2 Tp then returned to Sqn. HQ at LE MESNIL at 0200 hrs D+1.

13. Dets. of HQ and 1 Tp not involved in the minelaying moved out of the 8 Bn. Area to Sqn. HQ arriving about 1600 hrs D.Day.

14. MINELAYING.
During D+1 day further supplies of Mk. V. A.Tk. mines were made available from Div. and a minefield was laid in LE MESNIL during the night by HQ personnel of the Sqn. under Lt. WILLIAMS and Sjt. SHRUBSOLE. About 100 mines were laid in a road and across a field under S.A. fire. No cas. were sustained.

3 TP. ACTIVITIES.

15. Three a/c with paratps and one glider with Jeep and tlr were involved. The dropping again was extremely inaccurate, the majority being dropped about 1 km EAST of the DZ in flooded areas and outside the village of VARAVILLE. One a/c took such violent evasive action that the paratps all fell down in the a/c and the stick stretched from VARAVILLE to ROBEHOMME, the last man out Lieut. WILLIAMS landed on top of the hill SOUTH of the church at ROBEHOMME - surely a record length of stick about 3 km.

As the whole area ....

SHEET 7

As the whole area was flooded and intersected with ditches, it was impossible for sticks to RV at their containers. The THOMAS lighting devices worked well and indicated the posn of the containers submerged 2 to 3 ft.

16. Lieut. INMAN collected 12 sprs and 3 containers of explosive and after much hard work in crossing numerous ditches reached VARAVILLE where he found Lt. BAILLIE who was alone. 5 sprs and 200 lbs of explosive and accessories were left with Lt. BAILLIE who proceeded to destroy the br. successfully making a gap of 15 ft. This was completed at 0440 hrs.

17. Lt. INMAN having handed over the explosive left at once for ROBEHOMME with 7 Sprs and one trolley. In VARAVILLE at 181757 he contacted Capt. SMITH and Lieut. HOLLOWAY and 3 Sprs. Capt SMITH went back to the br at VARAVILLE, and the remainder (2 Offrs and 10 OR's) proceeded through PETIVILLE where infm was obtained that BAVENT was held. The party therefore took to the flooded fds and after 1 km. left the trolley and carried the explosive on their backs. At 0900 hrs, ROBEHOMME was reached and Sgt. POOLE contacted. It was then learned that Sgt. POOLE who had dropped nearby had destroyed the br with 30 lbs of explosive collected from Cdn. Inf. The party proceeded to the br and blew two craters on the home side at 1100 hrs. The covering Cdn. Inf. Party patrolled the river bank and left one Bren Gp for protection of the working party. They were not present when the main attack came in the form of some enemy Lorry-borne inf. before the job was complete. The demolition was successful but the working party were pinned by fire. By use of their own Bren Guns however, the party were able to withdraw to ROBEHOMME at 1300 hrs.

18. L/Cpl. HILL reported that glider with Jeep and trailer were in 3 ft. of water at 178724 near BRICQUEVILLE. Attempts to recover equipment that day were frustrated by enemy fire from BAVENT direction.

Strength of tps at ROBEHOMME now about 120. Det of 32 from 12 Bn. attempted to move through BAVENT and were captured.

Minor enemy attacks were beaten off.

D+1 DAY.

19. Tps now org as 3 pls mixed inf and Sprs under Capt GRIFFIN (1 Cdn Para Bn). 2 Pl attack on BAVENT unsuccessful. Lt. HOLLOWAY comd mixed pl containing inf and 21 sprs.

Recces of routes NORTH and SOUTH of BAVENT carried out during day. L/Cpl. HILL and party despatched at 1300 hrs to recover equipment from glider. Returned successfully at 2000 hrs with all equipment except m/c's and camouflet tubes.

1600 hrs. L/Sgt. WREN and 7 Sprs blew two craters at rd june 193736 LE HAIN being unable to find correct site of culvert at 198743 owing to floods. Rd blocks of MK. V mines were laid at 182727 and 184727 to render feature tank proof.

At 2000 hrs Cdn. Recce patrol returned having contacted Bde HQ at LE MESNIL and brought orders for party to return by night.

Rd blocks were lifted and Cdn. Pl proceeded to silence MG post at 168724 at 2300 hrs. Main body 162 all ranks moved off at 233c hrs.

Arrived ....

WO 171/1652
Intelligence/war diary
591 PARACHUTE SQUADRON RE

Month and year June 1944   Commanding Officer Capt. G.F. DAVIDSON RE.

Place	Date	Hour	Summary of Events and Information	References to Appendices
FAIRFORD	5	2330	Sqn. less 27p and 10 sec Emplaned at FAIRFORD, BERKS in six STIRLING A/C for flight to CAEN - CHERBOURG peninsula on operation NEPTUNE. DZ - area of RANVILE - LE HOM west of the bridges over the CAEN-A-MER CANAL & R.ORNE.	
BROADWELL		2315	2 Tp - 7 sec ÷ emplaned in Horsa glider with 9 Para Bn. for assault on heavy Coastal bty at MERVILLE.	
			5,6,8 sec - Emplaned in DAKOTA a/c with 9 para Bn. for follow -up assault on bty post at MERVILLE.	
RANVILLE	6	0100	Sqn landed by parachute on D.Z and carried out main task of clearing area of poles for a L.Z for the glider borne assault at 0330. Sgt Thomas received by bullet wounds in shoulder 2 ORs injured during drop.	
		0500	Sqn completed further landing strips and then moved into Bascle Ranville area and dug in defensive positions Two aircraft had failed to drop their sticks on the DZ and these sticks were still missing O.C. "2 1/c were among those missing.	

Wt.47724 993 2,000,000 3/43 W. H. & S. 51/6375.

SHEET 2

Month and Year June 44   Commanding Officer Major G.F. DAVIDSON.

Place	Date	Hour	Summary of Events and Information	References to Appendices
RANVILLE	6	0730	1 Tp, 3Tp salvaged containers for remainder of morning.	
		1300	1 Tp laid A.P. minefield 3Tp laid A.Th minefield.	
		2000	2 1/c and his steel arrived at sqn HQ and took over command.	
	7	0130	3 Tp Checkered up mine belt laid during afternoon and completed belt later in day. 2 ORs injured due to shelling during laying.	
	7	0800	Sqn. on salvaging containers - equipment from glider.	
	8	0800	Sqn. on salvaging equipment. No 2 Tp less 16 men reported to Sqn. HQ.	
	9	0800	Sqn. on salvaging equipment and general engineer tasks 3 ORS killed and 3 ORs injured due to shell fire.	
	10	0800	4 officers major wood capt jackson St Best and St Oliveira and 27 ORs now considered missing. The crews of their aircraft reported dropping them in correct place. Sqn on general engineer tasks. 1 OR killed. 1 officer Sgt Fish and 3 ORs injured due to shell splinter.	
	11	0800	General engineer work and salvaging containers from german minefield. 1 OR killed due to S. mine. S.S.M - 1 OR casualties due to shell shock.	

Wt 13474/1805 1.200,000 7/40 BPL 51-7171 Forms C2118/22.

WO 171/429
Intelligence/war diary
6TH AIRBORNE DIVISION SIGNALS.

Commanding Officer Lt. Col. D. S. Tew? SIGNALS.

Place	Date	Hour	Summary of Events and Information	References to Appendices
	3		Capt Mc Master, Capt Westwood and 37 ORs embarked at SOUTHAMPTON. Gliders loaded.	
	4		Parachutes loaded in planes.	
			Operation OVERLORD postponed 24 hours due to weather Conditions.	
	5		Emplaned and took off from numerous aerodromes in S. ENGLAND CO, Adjt, Capt. Pinnell, Lt. Jenkins, 36 ORs J and K Secs by parachute; Major Fenton, Lt. Bradshaw, Lt. Bayliss and 570 Rs by glider.	
			Operation orders attached.	
	6		Landed in NORMANDY area HAUGER - RANVILLE Parachutists 0100 hrs gliders 0330 hrs. DIV HQ est in LE BAS DE RANVILLE at chateau 106737 by 0700 hrs.	

Wt.47724/993 2,000,000 3/43 W.H. & S. 51/6375

SHEET 2

Commanding Officer Lt. Col. D. S. Tew? SIGNALS.

Place	Date	Hour	Summary of Events and Information	References to Appendices
	6		Considerable bombardment heard in direction of coast, but little enemy activity locally until attack on RANVILLE Sp by AFVs. Successfully repulsed at 1045 hrs.	
			Contact with 1 Corps est 0716 hours and live contact to 5 Para Bde.	
			Contact est with UK 0755 hours.	
			3 Para Bde were deficient of nearly all signal eqpt on landing and contact was not est until 1235 hours 6 Airldg Bde incl L Sec landed by glider at 2100 hours. Contact est with 6 Airldg Bde at 2150 hours, 50 mins after bde landed.	
			Air resup brought sig stores during night 6/7 Jun having been demanded during day on Q Base link from U.K.	
			Cas Lt Royle and 2 ORs killed, May Fenton and 4 ORs	

Wt.47724/993 2,000,000 3/43 W.H. & S. 51/6375

SHEET 3

Commanding Officer Lt. Col. D. S. Tew? SIGNALS.

Place	Date	Hour	Summary of Events and Information	References to Appendices
	6		wounded, Capt. Wilks, Lt Gilbert and 72 ORs missing.	
	7		More eqpt salvaged from DZ.	
			Enemy activity increasing; Div HQ stood to 1145 hrs.	
			Lines frequently cut by shell and mortar fire.	
			Enemy armd UG cable blown by Lines offr.	
			Cas 1 OR Killed, 3 ORs wounded, 7 ORs believed missing now located.	
			Report on D and D + 1 attached.	
	8		Maplay and codewords from 1 Corps compromised.	
			Confusing over codesigns with 3 Br. Div.	
			Cap. Mc Master with Capt. Westwood and 37 ORs arrived 1815 hours as first follow up by sea, which included spare WT sets, cable and MT spares. Maj. Donald arrived having landed with HQ 1 Corps.	
			Cas Capt. Pinnell and 4 ORs wounded, 9 ORs believed	

Wt.47724,993 2,000,000 3/43 W. H. & S. 51/6375

WO 171/2525
Intelligence/war diary
716TH COMPANY RASC
(AIRBORNE LIGHT COMPANY)

Month and Year June 1944   Commanding Officer Major E.C. Jones R.A.S.C.

Place	Date	Hour	Summary of Events and Information	References to Appendices
Field	1st		H.Q. consisting of 4 Offrs & 59 ORs leave concentration area and embarked on SS MONOWAI.	Ecj
	5th		Sailed from COWES Roads.	Ecj
	6th		Landing operation commence Seaborne party 4 Offrs & 59 ORs no casualties. 4 Offrs & 59 ORs land by parachute - 276553 Lt Silvert & 1 OR killed in action, 2 wounded & 2 missing.	Ecj
			1 Offr & 9 ORs also land by Parachute – 300583 Lt Hale wounded. 1 OR wounded. 12 ORs missing from detachment in the Field.	
	7th		D.M.A. set up under command 210076 Capt. I.J.A. McKittrick R.A.S.C. 1 OR wounded, 3 missing.	Ecj
			Seaborne party at Assembly area 1 ORs accidently injured. Further Seaborne party 1 Offr & 29 ORs land - no casualties.	
	8th		2 ORs wounded at D.M.A. Seaborne party move to D.M.A. - move completed without incident. 2 further parties land Seaborne 1 Offr & 65 ORs 1 Sjt & 34 ORs - no casualties.	Ecj

Wt.47724/993 2,000,000 3/43 W. H. & S. 51/6375

WO 177/831

Intelligence/war diary

224 PARACHUTE FIELD AMBULANCE RAMC

Month and Year June 1944   Commanding Officer Lt. Col. D.H. THOMPSON RAMC

Place	Date	Hour	Summary of Events and Information	References to Appendices
LE MESNIL (France 1/50,000 Sheet 7F/2 Map Reference 137728)	6		1 Canadian Parachute Bn. Major YOUNG saw the farm (M. BARBEROT) & was immediately given accommodation for affected wounded.	
			Unit dug in on edge of wood.	
		1200	M.D.S. is up in farm on instruction of levied officer in Bde. farm (LT. COL. A.S. PEARSON D.S.O. M.C. 8 Bn. the parachute Regt.)	
			Number of casualties treated 5 officers & 47 O.Rs. (& 2 civilian's) number of operations fulfilled by Capt. GRAY 10.	
		2330	Lieut. PHILO with Cpl. Cummings, Dod. Hurly & a captured German medical orderly went & BREVILLE (134745) & captured 63 Germans O.Rs. 5 wagons, 1 MK & approximately 30 blankets.	
			In the late afternoon & evening the M.D.S., which was together with Bde. H.Q. & H.Q. 1 canadian Parachute Bn. was constantly under fire but the Field Ambulance suffered no casualties.	
			Approximately two thirds of the unit were still unaccounted for including the following officers:- Lt. Col. THOMPSON, Major J.S. DARLING, LT.(QM) R.F. HARDER, Capt. D.H. NELSON, Lieut. R.M. MARQUIS, Capt. I.F.B. JOHNSTONE. No news had been received of the 9th Bn. the Parachute Recd. Capt. C. BREBNER RCAMC RMO 1 Canadian Para. Bn. was known the wounded & a	

SHEET 2

Commanding Officer Major A.D. YOUNG. RAMC

Place	Date	Hour	Summary of Events and Information	References to Appendices
LE MESNIL (France 1/50,000 Sheet 7F/2 Map Reference 137728)	6		Prisoner of War & Capt. R.E. HOLTAN R.A.M.C. R.M.O. 8 Bn. the Parachute Regt was missing. There was therefore in the Bde. H.Q., 1 Canadian Para, Bn. & 8 Bn. the Para. Regt. only the following R.A.M.C. officers:- Major YOUNG, Capt. GRAY & Lieut. CUNNINGHAM. The other attached Fd. Amb. Officers were found Lieut. G.C.G. PHILO R.A.S.C. Rev. A.L. BECKINGHAM R.A.Ch.D. & Capt. C.A. CHAUNDY A.D. Corps.	
	7.	0600	Enemy within 300 yds. of M.D.S. on north, West, & East. Spasmodic sniping & M.G. fire which continued throughout the day.	Ady
		0940	Lieut. PHILO contacted A.D.M.S. of 195 Airlanding Fd Amb. in R.A.NVILLE (113735) the road between LE MESNIL & RAVILLE under occasional mortar fire & continuous sniping.	
		1030	Major MacDonald R.A.M.C. 8 Fd Amb. command clearing casualties in 4 amb cars from LE MESNIL & 8 Fd Amb. in COLLEVILLE-SUR-ORNE (O83786)	
		1200	Capt. F. RUTTER R.A.M.C. 195 Airlanding Fd Amb. & Capt. W.J. ATKINSON R.A.M.C. (ex Parted Form) reported for duty as G.D.O. & surgeon respectively.	
		1400	Div. Thompson R.A.S.C. & Pts Garret & launch RAMC blown up on own minefield 300 yds. E. A cross road at LE MESNIL whilst collecting casualties.	Ady

WO 177/833
Intelligence/war diary
225 PARACHUTE FIELD AMBULANCE RAMC

Month and Year June 44   Commanding Officer Lt. Col. E.I. BRUCE HARVEY

Place	Date	Hour	Summary of Events and Information	References to Appendices
KEEVIL	5	1100	The unit, less No 2 & 3 sec paraded and marched to the airfield, for final fitting of parachutes, and for stowing kit to the a/c.	
		1400	Compulsion test.	
		1900	Hot meal. Following this the unit paraded and messages from C-in-C 21 Army and Allied supreme LTQ were read out. Rev. Briscoe said a few short prayers.	
		2130	Tps embarked for airfield.	
		2230	Tps Emplaned 2245 In Take off	
FRANCE	6	0105	HQ flight carried the coast at CABOORG. Some flak was experienced. Pilot failed to see the DZ lights so flew to sea and made a second run in. At 0120 hrs the green light went on and the unit dropped on DZ.	E.I. Bruce Harvey

M3524/1218 1200M 10/41 H.B. & Co. Ltd. 51-1541.

SHEET 2

Month and Year June 44   Commanding Officer Lt. Col. E.I. BRUCE HARVEY

Place	Date	Hour	Summary of Events and Information	References to Appendices
LE BAS de RANVILLE	6	0230	Majority of unit made R.V. in copse 113745 (map france 7 F/2) There was some confusion on the DZ owing to enemy action and the use of coloured lights by them. Some opposition was experienced and there was some mortoring in the later stages. Unit proceeded in sea of 12 para Bn to LE BAS de RANVILLE. C.O. with Capt Wilson and 4 RASE carried out recce of chakean at 105732. The inhabitants were useful and were friendly. Then German officer of TODT organisation was captured in bed.	
		0415	The unit was fought in and an MDS established some DZ casualties were treated at once and by 0400 casualties began to come in from various units	E.I. Bruce Harvey

M3524/1218 1200M 10/41 H.B. & Co. Ltd. 51-1541.

SHEET 3

Commanding Officer Lt. Col. E.I. BRUCE HARVEY

Place	Date	Hour	Summary of Events and Information	References to Appendices
LE BAS de RANVILLE	6	0430	At sun light 0430 C.O. visited No 3 sec. at church in RANVILLE (109736). There was some sniping going on and one of the section had been targeted by enemy LMG. Capt Tibbs had organised his section to clean the DZ. This work he continued till 1400 hrs this day. His section worked well, often under considerable S.A. & mortar fire, and fought in all wounded. Four of his section were wounded and two killed. Capt Tibbs conduct was of a high order and worthy of recognition.	
		0700	C.O. proceeded to Br. (104745) to visit R.A.P of Conp-de-main party who had landed in France alongside both troops. Capt Jacob RAME had established an RAP in ditch on mark 102747. He had some dead & 15 casualties. The parties cover being warily sniped. Arrangements were made to evacuate these casualties to MDS.	E.I. Bruce Harvey

M3524/1218 1200M 10/41 H.B. & Co. Ltd. 51-1541.

SHEET 4

Commanding Officer Lt. Col. E.I. BRUCE HARVEY

Place	Date	Hour	Summary of Events and Information	References to Appendices
LE BAS de RANVILLE	6	0920	ADMS visited MDS, and proceeded up to br with C.O. br. Under enemy M.G. fire and covered by snipers. Infrmt received that No 2 see (Capt Wagstaff) having established ADS at BENOVVILLE 095746 were cut off together with 'A' by 7 Para Bn. Several of No 2 sec were missing at RV, S/DGT MARSDEN an his stick being missing. An RAP. under Capt WRQHEART was Established in Estaminet at Bn. site 098748 to collect casualties from 7 Para Bn & 'A' Coy OXF Bucks still holding eastern Bn.	
		1400	Capt TIBBS reported DZ clear of casualties S/Sqn HODGSON and 5 SB's detached to 13 Para Bn. in Chateau 735114 remainder No. 3 see came in to MDB.	E.I. Bruce Harvey

M3524/1218 1200M 10/41 H.B. & Co. Ltd. 51-1541.

SHEET 5

Month and Year June 44

Commanding Officer Lt. Col. E.I. BRUCE HARVEY

Place	Date	Hour	Summary of Events and Information	References to Appendices
LE BAS de RANVILLE	6		Considerable sniping by enemy tps occurred ? the day & one of whom appeared to be covering the M.D.S. Some mortar fire was experienced and in travels.	
			Casualties flowed in large nimbus, they had the foreman and afternoon, Snipeal teams was working constantly from time of opening.	
			Capt Young RAMC was mining from 7 Para Bn. All personnel not employed in MOS digging slit trenches.	
		1600	Contact officer from 8 Fd Amb of 3 Bn. Div repute to RAP at Bn.	
		1730	C.O. visited Bn. to find Capt Wagstaff and part of his sactin new made then way barke from A Coy location. Tpt was pounded and casualties from A Coy.	Eulm Harvey

M3524/1218 1200M 10/41 H.B. & Co.Ltd. 51-1541.

SHEET 6

Month and Year June 44

Commanding Officer Lt. Col. E.I. BRUCE HARVEY

Place	Date	Hour	Summary of Events and Information	References to Appendices
LE BAS de RANVILLE			Evacuated to RAP. at Bn. This was soon full and Capt WAGSTAFF establishes & second post 200 ydrs up the road.	
	6	2100	By 2100 his Tpt under Major MacDonald of 8 Fd Amb reported and Starts to clean casualties from Bn to FDS in beach area. Some 50-60 casualties were evacuated in this way.	
		2200	The ? was ? intermittent merlan fire and continuously sniped, but my Macdonald established aces at Fm 109742 and Evact of MDS Began. By this time then some some 280 casualties admitted to M.D.S.	
			Twice fighting continued throughout the night.	Eulm Harvey
	7		An attack by ME 109's just light caused some casualties.	

M3524/1218 1200M 10/41 H.B. & Co.Ltd. 51-1541.

WO 177/793
Intelligence/war diary
195 AIRLANDING FIELD AMBULANCE

Month and Year June 1944   Commanding Officer Lt. Col. IAULHILILAND RAMC.

Place	Date	Hour	Summary of Events and Information	References to Appendices
Field	1		In sealed camp. Briefing of N. CO's & OR's commenced, Capt. WEST detached. G.O.C.s unit.	
	2		Main briefing completed. Detailed study of photographs in briefing tout.	IG.
	3		Gliders loaded.	IG.
	4		Gliders checked over. Gusty wind reaching almost gale force. D.C.I.G.S visited camp. Gliders issued, bulke to sect, 1, 10 off & 114 OR's by air.	IG.
	5		Met glider pilots at airdrone with Senior glider passengers. High wind continues.	IG.
	6		Emplaned by 1900hrs. Perfect take off. Unchallenged journey to coast. 1 glider hit by flack & 1 OR killed. 1 crashed on landing Q Sqt ? fractured pelvis. Remainder intact. Some difficulty in finding RV as landing effected were South of LZ. Reached woods in BAS DE RANVILLE by midnight.	IG. IG.
FRANCE	7		Moved to house in RANVILLE after Rece by CO. M.D.S [FRANCE, Sheet 7 7/2 115735] established in slightly cramped house at 1100. Very busy 154 casualties admitted up to midnight 23 surgical cases dealt with.	
	8		Evacuation started 0700 hrs. Billet clear by 1200. Flow of cases ceased considerably in afternoon. Some close mortar fire. Occasional casualties only in afternoon. Some civilians from shelling. Visit from GOC. Heavy direct shelling at 1800. 1 on building & 8 outside 3 RAMC casualties.	IG.
			All patients evacuated out surgical next out to shelter. Seaborne party armed. 2 unit RASC casualties Total casualties for day 102. 28 Surgical operations performed. Seaborne lolt & 51 OR's.	IG.
			Quiet morning. 2 Hours constant shelling in afternoon. 1 direct hit. 2 Rome of one	

WO 171/432

Intelligence/war diary

6TH AIRBORNE DIVISION WORKSHOPS REME

Month and Year June 1944   Commanding Officer Major E.B. BONNIWELL

Place	Date	Hour	Summary of Events and Information	References to Appendices
ARDINGLY, SUSSEX	5		moved from ardingly to camp J2 at Falmer move completed by train at 20 00 hrs. personnel accommodated in tents for the night.	Appx "A" (A. Fs W 3008 & 3009) for month of June 1944 ?
FALMER, SUSSEX	6		(D-Day) Day spent in completing Embarkation Rolls, showing foreign enemy nations, maps etc. all personnel of HQ have been allocated to one craft - R20; these personnel together with 44 from 1 corps make a total craft load of 79. Personnel briefed in the operation generally all are extremely keen to get on with the job, and disappointed that they were unable to go to war by air.	
FALMER, SUSSEX	7		Left camp J2. at 15 00 hrs by T.C.V. for part of embarkation, arrived Newhaven 18 00 hrs, embarked at once on L.C.T. 89+. craft sailed from land at once & laid up off Newhaven to await forming up of convoy. Convoy consisting of 1 LCI & 9 L.C.Ts left Newhaven 23 00 hrs.	

*5973. Wt.22661/1499. 300M. 8/42. 6253. Wt.38126/345. 200M. 11/42. Wy.L.P. Gp. 656.

WO 171/1234
Intelligence/war diary
NO.1 WING THE GLIDER PILOT REGT. AAC

Month and Year June 1944   Commanding Officer Lt. Col. I.A. Murphy.

Place	Date	Hour	Summary of Events and Information	References to Appendices
Base	6 June 44 8 June 44		Operation 'NEPTUNE' see attached Appendices. All crews not taking part in Operation 'NEPTUNE' ordered to stand by for next operation.	

Wt.13474/1805 1,200,000 7/40 BPL 51-7171 forms C2118/2?.

Month and Year June 1944   Commanding Officer Lt. Col. John W Place

Place	Date	Hour	Summary of Events and Information	References to Appendices
CRICKLADE	1			
	2		All ranks confined to camp.	
	3			
	4			
	5			
	6		Operation TONGA. 19 crews of NO: 2 Wing took part.	
			Operation MALLARD. 108 crews of NO: 2 Wing took part. The operations were brilliantly successful and glider pilots received high praise.	
	7			
	8		The Majority of crews returned from NORMANDY, disembarking at NEWHAVEN. After de-briefing and re-kitting at FARGO they returned to	
	9		airfields.	
	10			
	11		Crews briefed for Ex. WILDOATS.	
	12			
	13		Ex. WILDOATS postponed - later cancelled.	
	14			
	15			
	16			
	17			
	18			
	19			
	20			
	21			
	22		RUSHY WEIR CAMP, near BAMPTON, established for the benefit of "F" Squadron. "E" Squadron have set up a similar one near CHELTENHAM.	
			48 hour passes for those ex Operations and 24 hours (within radius of 25 miles) for remainder, started.	

*5973. Wt.22661/1499. 300M. 8/12. Wt.41231/636. 250M. 12/42. Wy.L.P. Gp.658.

'SWORD' BEACH

'Nearer and nearer we drew to the shore…Trembling, my rifle tightly clenched, I crouched awaiting the dreaded shout, "Ramps down!" We seemed to inch in, in between craft already beached, some of which were burning.
The diesels went into reverse, the bows ground into sand and pebbles and we came to a standstill. "Ramps down!"
This was it, I was determined to present myself for the minimum time as a target at the top of the ramp and being one of the first to go I had a clear run.

[The beach was a] complete shambles…Against a backdrop of smoke, gutted blazing buildings were several burning knocked out DD tanks and strewn about from the water's edge to the seawall were sodden khaki bundles staining red the sand where they lay. The thought that for them the day was already done appalled me'.

PRIVATE RICHARD HARRIS, 1st Battalion, The Suffolk Regiment ('Queen White' Beach) [281]

'SWORD' BEACH

(From the Orne Estuary at Ouistreham in the East to the village of St-Aubin-sur-Mer in the West)

German Defenders: 7th Army Commanded by *Generaloberst* Friedrich Dollmann

(Lower Normandy defended by LXXXIV Korps commanded by *General der Artillerie* Erich Marcks)

Coastal Defence: 716th Infantry Division commanded by *Generalleutnant* Wilhelm Richter and 21st Panzer Division commanded by *Generalmajor* Edgar Feuchtinger based around Caen

Allied Attackers: British 1st Corps commanded by Lieutenant-General Sir John Crocker

Assault Division: 3rd British Infantry Division commanded by Major-General T.G. Rennie

Naval Forces: Force 'S' commanded by Rear-Admiral A.G. Talbot RN and Bombardment Force 'D' commanded by Rear-Admiral W.R. Patterson RN

H-Hour: 0725 hrs

Landing Sectors: 'OBOE', PETER', 'QUEEN', 'ROGER'[282]

D-Day Divisional Objectives: (i) Pierce and overwhelm shoreline defences. (ii) Secure landing areas and capture the high ground of the Pèriers Ridge inland. (iii) Advance West and East to link-up with the 3rd Canadian Infantry Division on 'Juno' beach and British 6th Airborne Division at the Orne River. (iv) Secure river crossings over the Orne River and Caen canal. (v) The capture of the city of Caen by means of a rapid advance and the establishment of a bridgehead south of the city.

Casualties on D-Day (Beaches only): 630 (Killed, Wounded and Missing)[283]

NOTES

[281] Tim Kilvert-Jones, *Sword Beach: British 3rd Infantry Division/27th Armoured Brigade*, Battleground Europe series, (Barnsley, South Yorkshire: Pen & Sword, 2008), pp. 106-107.

[282] Only 'QUEEN' sector was used for the actual landings.

[283] *D-Day: Then and Now*, Volume 2, edited by Winston G. Ramsey, (London: Battle of Britain Prints International Ltd, 1995), p. 620.

8TH INFANTRY BRIGADE

WO 171/611

Intelligence/war diary

8TH BRITISH INFANTRY BRIGADE HQ

Month and Year June 1944   Commanding Officer Brig. E.E.E. CASS, OBE, DSO, MC.

Place	Date	Hour	Summary of Events and Information	References to Appendices
LA BRECHE	[6	0720	Two leading Coys 1 S LAN R touched down at beaches at LA BRECHE and although met by MG and Mortar fire made satisfactory progress.	
		0725	Two leading Coys 2 E YORKS touched down on left of 1 S LAN R, also encountering some opposition.	
		0745	Second waves of the two leading Bns touched down, met by small arms and mortar fire. Lt. Col. Burberry 1 S LAN R was killed whilst directing operations on the beach and Major Stone took command of the Bn.	
			One Coy of 1 S LAN R proceeded to deal with a strong point to the right of the bridgehead.	
		0810	1 S LAN R overcame all opposition on the immediate beaches, except for the occasional sniper and started to move towards HERMANVILLE-SUR-MER	
		0825	The reserve bn 1 SUFFOLK touched down on the beaches at	

22293 Wt. 33096/1140 1,000m 12/40—McC & Co Ltd–51-8212 Forms C2118/22

SHEET 2

Month and Year June 1944   Commanding Officer Brig. E.E.E. CASS, OBE, DSO, MC.

Place	Date	Hour	Summary of Events and Information	References to Appendices
	6		LA BRECHE and quickly moved to the assembly area, a wood 900 yds inland. This Bn only suffered about two casualties on the beach itself from enemy shell fire.	
		0900	1 S LAN R reported HERMANVILLE taken and their Bn. HQ established there, the Bn consolidating the area.	
		0930	1 SUFFOLK assembled in the woods N.E. of HERMANVILLE-SUR-MER and one Company moved off to cover the Bn. up to COLVILLE-SUR-ORNE. This village was soon cleared by another Company of this Bn.	
		1200	B Company 1 SUFFOLK prepared to attack the first Bn. objective – a coast defence bty of 10.5 cm guns	
		1300	First locality taken by 1 SUFFOLK – the enemy surrendering after a few rounds had been fired by the covering troops.	
		1320	'A' Company 1 SUFFOLK moved forward through the village to attack a strong point immediately South of COLLEVILLE.	

22293 Wt. 33096/1140 1,000m 12/40—McC & Co Ltd–51-8212 Forms C2118/22

SHEET 3

Commanding Officer Brig. E.E.E. CASS, OBE, DSO, MC.

Place	Date	Hour	Summary of Events and Information	References to Appendices
	6	1330	2 E YORKS reported the defences on the left of the bridgehead cleared.	
		1430	Col. Huchinson, 2 E YORKS was wounded by Mortar fire and Major R.H. Sheath assumed command of that Bn. Reorganisation of the Bn. was taking place preparatory to their attack on the next line of defences to the EAST of the bridgehead.	
		1500	'A' Company 1 SUFFOLK were unable to capture the strong point at the first attempt due to heavy MG fire from the strong point.	
		1800	2 E YORKS captured their second objective, taking a few prisoners.	
		2000	2 E YORKS proceeded to take up a defensive position in ST AUBIN d' ARQUENAY.	
		2100	1 SUFFOLK finally succeeded in taking the strong point south of COLLEVILLE after stiff opposition and a large number of prisoners were taken. The Bn then proceeded to consolidate	

22293 Wt. 33096/1140 1,000m 12/40—McC & Co Ltd–51-8212 Forms C2118/22

SHEET 4

Commanding Officer Brig. E.E.E. CASS, OBE, DSO, MC.

Place	Date	Hour	Summary of Events and Information	References to Appendices
	6		the area around this last feature.	
		2130	2 E YORKS were relieved by 1 KOSB and the Bn. drawn into Bde reserve West of COLVILLE-SUR-ORNE.	
		2300	1 SUFFOLK were well dug in on their position and were sending out patrols to contact the enemy.	
			The other two Bns were carrying out local patrolling during the night.	
COLLEVILLE	7	0615	1 SUFFOLK were put under command of 9 British Inf Bde to support their attack on the right flank. 2 LINCOLNS came under command of this Bde.	
		1130	1 S LAN R sent two platoons to secure PLUMETOT and CRESSERONS.	
		1300	1 S LAN R captured PLUMETOT and CRESSERONS with very little opposition.	
			2 E YORKS took over the defensive position on the PERIER ridge from 1 R.U.R. and carried out patrolling during the hours of	

22293 Wt. 33096/1140 1,000m 12/40—McC & Co Ltd–51-8212 Forms C2118/22

WO 171/1381

Intelligence/war diary

1ST BATTALION THE SUFFOLK REGIMENT

Month and Year June 1944   Commanding Officer Lt. Col. R.E. GOODWIN.

Place	Date	Hour	Summary of Events and Information	References to Appendices
AT SEA	6th	0640	1/Suffolk, which formed the reserve battalion of the 8th. Bn. Inf Bde (an assault Bde), left their L.S's just after dawn had broken and embarked on 18 LCAs. They joined up with the L.C. Is at the lowering position and the run in to the French coast commenced.	
		[0700	The voyage in was uneventful until within about half a mile of the beach. The day was dull and the sky overcast - the sea had a heavy swell and was rough for the L.C.As. There was no sea sickness. As the Bn. approached the beach it came under light and sporadic shell fire and occasional snipers shots. The two assault Bns of the Bde who had landed at H + 5 mins (0725 has) were still fighting on the beaches as the Bn. approached.	
		0825	The Bn. touched down 5 mins behind time and rapidly disembarked. They ran up the beach and]	

Wt.47724,993 2,000,000 3/43 W. H. & S. **51/6375**

SHEET 2

Month and Year June 1944   Commanding Officer Lt. Col. R.E. GOODWIN.

Place	Date	Hour	(Continued) Summary of Events and Information	References to Appendices
OUISTREHAM	[6th	0825	assembled under the lee of the sand dunes and houses just inland. Shortly afterwards they made their way inland to their prearranged assembly area which was approx 900 to 1000 yds inland.] The landing beach was approx 2 miles to the WEST of the small town of OUISTREHAM in NORMANDY, which lies at the mouth of the River ORNE and a small canal running out to the sea from the larger industrial town of CAEN. The landing of the 3rd Br Inf Div. was on the EAST of the Army front with the 6th AIRBOURNE DIV and No 1 SS Bde containing the left flank of the Div. front. [The beach itself was a flat sandy beach immediately between LA BRÈCHE and LION-SUR-MER. The beach was covered by German strong points, and the sandy foreshore had various	

Wt.47724,993 2,000,000 3/43 W. H. & S. **51/6375**

SHEET 3

Month and Year June 1944

Commanding Officer Lt. Col. R.E. GOODWIN.

Place	Date	Hour	(Continued) Summary of Events and Information	References to Appendices
OUISTREHAM	[6	0825	types of beach obstacles consisting of iron "Hedgehogs", wooden stakes and ramps. All of them were equipped with the normal Teller mines or shells attached to the top. Landing craft generally managed to avoid these obstacles, which at the moment of landing were partially covered by the sea, and in no case so far as is known was any of the battalions damaged by these obstacles. In one case at least the obstacle collapsed when hit by the LCA which ran on and beached dry.

The L.C.I. containing rear Bn H.Q. was hit by a shell when beaching and an account of the heavy sea running the landing ramp came adrift. The craft again put to sea and the personnel were transferred to an L.C.I (S) and eventually ran in and beached at about 0920 hrs. At least two of the LCAs | |

Wt.47724, 993 2,000,000 3/43 W. H. & S. 51/6375

SHEET 4

Month and Year June 1944

Commanding Officer Lt. Col. R.E. GOODWIN.

Place	Date	Hour	(Continued) Summary of Events and Information	References to Appendices
OUISTREHAM	[0825	6th	were hit by shells immediately after the troops had disembarked. The battalion suffered about two casualties (wounded) on the beaches.]	9.w.ad.
	6th	0930	The Bn. duly assembled in the woods N.E. of HERMANIVILLE-SUR-MER, and D Company less two platoons moved off as a right flank guard and firm base for the future move of the Bn up to COLLEVILLE-SUR-ORNE. They reached their posn and "C" Company moved off to carry out their task of clearing that village.	
	6th	1200	This was soon done, as it had already been partially cleared by troops of the Airborne Division, and by about midday "B" Company, with one pl D coy under command, moved up to attach the first main enemy locality consisting of one troop (4 guns) 10.5 cm coast defence guns.	9.w.ad.

Wt.47724,993 2,000,000 3/43 W. H. & S. 51/6375

SHEET 5

Month and Year June 1944

Commanding Officer Lt. Col. R.E. GOODWIN.

Place	Date	Hour	(Continued) Summary of Events and Information	References to Appendices
COLLEVILLE-SUR-MER.	6th	1300	This locality had already received heavy bombing by the RAF and after only a few rounds had been fired the garrison of about 60 Germans came out and surrendered. "B" Coy then moved in and occupied the posn.	
COLLEVILLE-SUR-MER.	6th	1320	"A" Company, with one pl "D" Coy under comd for breaching, then moved up through the village to attack and capture the second locality just to the SOUTH. Details of this attack are shown in the attached Appendix. "B"	Appendix "B"
		1340	"D" Coy, less 2 pls, who were still in their original covering posn and who were being mortared were drawn out to rejoin their pl. who had been operating with "B" Coy in COLLEVILLE-SUR-MER.	
		1500	By this time the Bn. were distributed as follows - Adv HQ and "A" Coy were still attacking	OR

Wt.47724,993 2,000,000 3/43 W. H & S. **51/6375**

SHEET 6

Month and Year June 1944

Commanding Officer Lt. Col. R.E. GOODWIN.

Place	Date	Hour	(Continued) Summary of Events and Information	References to Appendices
COLLEVILLE-SUR-MER	6th	1500	the enemy posn. "B" Coy in posn in the gun posn to the WEST of the village: "C" Coy guarding the S.E. approaches. "D" Coy less 1 pl (still with "A" Coy) were in the centre of the village with the R.A.P. The Mortar pl. who had landed at about 1000 has with the A/Tk pl., were in various supporting posns to the NORTH of the village.	
		2100	The enemy posn being now under control "B" and "D" Coys (the latter having collected its breathing pl) moved fwd to the S.W. and S.E. of the village respectively to take up a def. posn for the night. "B" Coy moved up without any further interference and were established by about 2215 hrs. "D" Coy on moving up were confronted by a farm house locality about 300 yds ahead of their consolidation area	

Wt.47724,993 2,000,000 3/43 W. H. & S. **51/6375**

SHEET 7

Commanding Officer Lt. Col. R.E. GOODWIN.

Place	Date	Hour	(Continued) Summary of Events and Information	References to Appendices
COLLEVILLE-SUR-MER	6th	2100	this was held by the Germans and was therefore cleared by the leading pl (17). After a short engagement with small arms fire the garrison surrendered and 2 officers and 38 ORs were sent back as prisoners.	
		2300	The Bn. were dug in on their consolidation area, and "D" DAY came to a close with patrols moving out fwd to contact the enemy. Casualties suffered by the Bn. on 6 JUN 44 were KILLED - Captain R.G. RYLEY - Lieut. T.J.F. TOOLEY and 5 other ranks. WOUNDED - 24 other ranks. MISSING - 4 other ranks.	

Wt.47724,993 2,000,000 3/43 W. H. & S. **51**/6375

WO 171/1397

Intelligence/war diary

2ND BATTALION, THE EAST YORKSHIRE REGIMENT

Month and Year June 1944   Commanding Officer Lt. Col. C.F. Hutchinson

Place	Date	Hour	Summary of Events and Information	References to Appendices
Field	1-2		Final briefing of all tps was carried out and dispersal of Bn. to conc areas prior to embarkation.	this is untrue. The pike was provided by Lt Col Hutchinson. The RM badge was subsequently sweated onto the pike - head on board HMS GLENEARN
"	3		Bn. moved from conc areas to embarkation hards. Assaults Coys embarking in "EMPIRE BATTLEAXE". Reserve Coys in HMS GLENEARN with Bn H.Q. Weather was fine freshening towards evening. Rt Hon W.S. Churchill P.C. M.P. and Gen Smuts reviewed the invasion fleet. Lt. Col. C.F. Hutchinson presented Capt. Hutchinson with a silver bugle inscribed with the Regtl crest and in return the ships company presented the Bn with a pike which bore the Regtl badge of the Royal Marines. The Bn H.Q. Flag made by the ladies of WATERLOOVILLE was then attached to the pike and an anchor signifying the part played by the HM Navy sewn to the flag.	
			Supreme Commander postponed the operation 24 hours.	
	4	P.M–	The day was spent resting on board the craft, the M.O. making a final examination of the feet of all ranks followed with the Padre collecting all letters and addresses which may be of use to the enemy.	

Wt.10570/2039 1,280M. 5/44 W. H. & S. 51-8686

SHEET 2

Month and Year June 1944   Commanding Officer Lt. Col. C.F. Hutchinson.

Place	Date	Hour	Summary of Events and Information	References to Appendices
Field	5		The sealed bundles of maps were broken and distributed to Comds of all craft. The assault Coys were visited by the C.O. and addressed by him. Rev V.A. Price gave a short blessing.	
		2100	The L.S.I. weighed anchor and set sail taking its place in the gigantic convoy.	
	6	0430	No enemy were encountered on the trip over and no interference received by sea of air. Landing craft were quickly loaded and lowered in accordance with the timetable. The assault Coys sailed past and were cheered by the remainder of the Bn. who were waiting to be loaded.	
		0600	All were afloat and ready to run in.	
		0735	Wireless silence broken A & B Coys reported heavy opposition but the operation was proceeding according to plan.	
		0755	Reserve Coys and Bn H.Q. touched down.Some difficulty experienced in negotiating the underwater obstacles in the increasing swell but on the whole beaching was extremely good. Cross fire and sniping was fairly considerable and accurate enemy. Mortar and shell fire was causing some casualties.	

Wt.10570/2039 1,280M. 5/44 W. H. & S. 51-8686

SHEET 3

Commanding Officer Lt. Col. C.F. Hutchinson.

Place	Date	Hour	Summary of Events and Information	References to Appendices
Field	6	0755	cont. The difficulty of evacuating casuaties was increased by the rapidly rising tide, fire, and the fact that the M.O. was hit on disembarking. The clearance of the beach perimeter was going on and C Coy were despatched to the O.P. posn SOLE. D Coy lost their Coy Comds when a mortar bomb burst among the Coy H.Q. and some difficulty was experienced in collecting them. The move across the open marshy ground towards SOLE was slowed by the nature of the terrain and was under observation and mortar fire throughout. Nothing had been seen of F.00.B. and party since landing but Arty fire was readily available from 76 Fd Regt on call. SOLE proved to be more strongly held than originally anticipated but the posn was secured by C Coy. A Coy by this time having cleared the beach had assisted in the consolidation. B Coy rejoined the Bn. and the attack on the gun posn of DAIMLER prepared. Bn. O. Gp held just NORTH of SOLE came under considerable mortar fire and the R Gp in moving to a posn from which to make a suitable recce was caught by a salvo in a sunken lane Lt. Col. C.F. Hutchinson was hit in the arm and in the absence of Major G.W. Field.	

Wt.10570/2039 1,280M. 5/44 W.H. & S. **51-8686**

SHEET 4

Commanding Officer Lt. Col. C.F. Hutchinson
                                                                                                      Maj. S. R. Sheath

Place	Date	Hour	Summary of Events and Information	References to Appendices
Field	6 (cont)		who was collecting the track vehicles on the beach, the comd passed temporarily to Maj S.R.Sheath. The attack on DAIMLER was put in by A & C Coys supported by 76 Fd Regt and B Sqn 13/18 H and was quickly secured for little loss. Some 70 P.Ws of the Arty coastal Bn surrendered and considerable enemy weapons captured of 4 × 7.5 cm several 40 mm AA Guns and numerous small arms. By this time the mortars, AA guns and some carriers had come ashore but had suffered some casualties from shell and mortar fire on the first lateral. The Bn. moved on to ST AUBIN D'ARQUENAY which was not held and in ruins. Here, it took up defensive posn until relieved by the 1 K.O.S.B. and withdrew to a posn WEST of HERMANVILLE where it dug in, in a cornfield. In the hrs of darkness some enemy aircraft attacked the beaches but were met with considerable AA fire.	
"	7		Cas for 6 June:- Killed 5 Offrs & 60. Wounded 4 Offrs & 137. Missing 3 ORs. Shortly after first light another attack was made by Ju 88 on the beach dropping A.P. and H.E. bombs. Six were seen to be destroyed. The morning was spent in	

Wt. 10570/2039 1,280M. 5/44 W.H. & S. **51-8686**

WO 171/1332
Intelligence/war diary
1ST BATTALION,
THE SOUTH LANCASHIRE REGIMENT

Month and Year June 1944   Commanding Officer Major J.E. ST?

Place	Date	Hour	Summary of Events and Information	References to Appendices
[LANDING BEACH QUEEN' REO] (App. A.)	6	0545	First wave (A & C Coys) lowered and left ISI.	Casualties.
		[0720	First wave beached and although met by heavy MG fire and mortaring made satisfactory progress. Communications with A & C Coys established by wireless on run-in, and progress report obtained by Bn HQ.	KILLED. Ltcol RPH Burbury. T/Maj RH Harrison. Lieut. RC Bell-Walker
		0745	Second wave (Bn HQ, HQ Coy, B & D Coys) touched down, met by small arms fire, mortar and 88 mm. Landing made almost on strongpoint COD, which was still active. Bn HQ moved towards sand-dunes near 88 mm gun posn, and whilst (endeavouring to) direct operations, the CO, Ltcol RPH Burbury, was killed. Major Stone assuming command of the Bn. B Coy proceeded to deal with strong-point COD; their Coy Comd, Major RH Harrison, was killed immediately on landing. Lt RC Bell-Walker assumed command, but was killed during attack on pillbox. Opposition overcome, apart from isolated snipers. B and D Coys advanced towards HERMANVILLE-sur-MER. Bn HQ followed along main axis, up main road. During the period on the beach, contact was lost with coys due to losses sustained by signalers, or wireless becoming detached, with their operators.	Lieut. C Relph. Lieut. WGH Allen. and 13 ORs. WOUNDED. T/Maj JF Harward. Capt. AH Eggeling. Lieut. NT Parry. Lieut. RW Pearce, MC. Lieut. FR Ashcroft. Lieut. G Wilson.
[HERMANVILLE -SUR-MER. (M.S. 40/18SW) 074802]		0900	HERMANVILLE taken, and Bn HQ established area church, communications working with B, C and D Coys, who fulfilled their roles according to plan, and commenced to consolidate. A coy out of contact, and not till late in day till they were extricated from street-fighting. Odd snipers still active around the village.]	and 83 ORs MISSING.
		1300	LOB parties arrived and dispersed to Coys.	19 ORs.

Wt.52938/1102 660M. 2/44 W.H. & S. 51-9071

SHEET 2

Commanding Officer Major J.E.ST.

Place	Date	Hour	Summary of Events and Information	References to Appendices
HERMANVILLE	6	1800	Reinforcements contacted and brought up for allocation to Coys. Enemy jamming experienced on wireless. Considerable numbers of Allied Airborne troops in gliders brought in low over sea by their tug-planes and released SE, with supplies dropped by parachute.	119 Reinforcements (ORs) received from 103 RHU.
		—	Local patrols carried out night D-day/D+1; quiet.	
HERMANVILLE [Reg: M.S. 40/16 N.W.]	7	0900	Naval bombardment of PLUMETOT (040793) and CRESSERONS. (040798).	
		1130	1 Pl B Coy and 1 Pl C Coy moved off to secure PLUMETOT and CRESSERONS.	Casualties.
		1300	Both places taken, opposition not very stiff. Remainder B and C Coys followed up, mounted on S.P. guns, for consolidation. Two prisoners taken at PLUMETOT, identified as 328 Inf GREN Regt.	KILLED:- 2 ORs. WOUNDED:- 9 ORs. MISSING:- 7 ORs.
		1445	B Coy established at LA DELIVERANDE. (027812) 1 Offr & 30 O.Rs captured, P.O.W.	
		1700	Bde HQ inform of expected counter attack at BIEVILLE, and warn CO that Bn. must be prepared to move at moment's notice.	
		1720	Brigadier countermands these instrs - orders B Coy to clear LUC SIMER (042825), in cooperation with RM Commando. This is achieved successfully, and B Coy move to a posn near LION-sur-MER, containing enemy strong-point TROUT, which still holds out.	App. 'A'
		2330	C Coy withdrawn to old posn once more. (HERMANVILLE)	

Wt.52938/1102 660M. 2/44 W. H. & S. 51-9671

9TH INFANTRY BRIGADE

WO 171/616
Intelligence/war diary
9TH BRIGADE HQ

Month and Year June 1944   Commanding Officer Brig. A.D.G. ORR, DSO.

Place	Date	Hour	Summary of Events and Information	References to Appendices
	1 3 4 5		By June 1st all briefing for Operation OVERLORD was complete and HQ 9 Br Inf Bde was sub-marshalled into craft loads. Two days of relaxation with everything done by the staff of the static camps followed, and on the evening of June 3rd embarkation began. News was received on 4 June that D-day had been postponed for 24 hours, and it was not until 1815 hours on 5 June that the convoy actually set sail.	SPECIAL NOTE: all appendices for Operation 'OVERLORD' dispatched before Bde left England.
	6		[Main HQ of 9 Br Inf Bde crossed the Channel during the night 5/6 June in the LOCUST and immediately before landing transferred to the Standby Craft 366 LCT(IV). At 1300 hrs the party landed and in a very short time HQ was established in the Assembly Area NORTH of HERMANVILLE-SUR-MER.	
			It was here that the enemy struck a severe blow. A mortar bomb, falling in the HQ, severely wounded Brig. JC CUNNINGHAM, MC; the G. III, the IO and one LO, and killed the 'I' Sjt. As a result, command of the Bde was taken over by Lt. Col. ADG ORR, DSO. HQ was moved about ¾ mile inland.	
			By this time, 2 LINCOLNS had gained contact with the enemy, who were established in some strength in a strong point in LION SUR MER, while 1 SUFFOLK of 8 Br Inf Bde had attacked and captured a strongly held enemy position on the ridge between PERIERS SUR LE DAN and COLLEVILLE SUR ORNE.	} WD/JUN/1.
			Comd 3 Br Inf Div therefore issued orders that 9 Br Inf Bde (less 2 LINCOLNS) with under command 1 SUFFOLK should move to the left of the bridgehead for the night 6/7 June and establish itself in a position to cover the bridges at BENOUVILLE and RANVILLE, and the main approaches to them from the WEST. Thus, the night of D-day found the Bde disposed as in attached Trace 'A', with 1 KOSB at ST AUBIN d'AROUENAY, 2 RUR on the high ground NE of PERIERS SUR LE DAN, 1 SUFFOLK covering the exists from COLLEVILLE SUR ORNE, and Bde HQ in the village itself.	

*6391. Wt.48123/1073. 319M. 2/43. Wy.L.P. Gp.656.

WO 171/1334

Intelligence/war diary

2ND BATTALION, THE LINCOLNSHIRE REGIMENT

Month and Year June 1944 Commanding Officer Lt. Col. C.E. WELBY-EVERARD

Place	Date	Hour	Summary of Events and Information	References to Appendices
GRANVILLE HOUSE, HAMBLEDON.	1 & 2		Battalion resting in Marshalling area.	
	2	2030	Craft serials 399, 400, 401, 402, 403, 404 (consisting Carriers, A tk, Mortars and duplicate Battalion HQ) moved to GOSPORT for embarkation.	
		2350	Above serials embarked.	
Camp A.2. EMSWORTH COMMON HANTS.	4		Main body of Battlion - craft serials 394, 395, 396 imbussed in preparation for move to PORTSMOUTH. Operation postponed 24 hours and Battalion returned to Camp.	
	5		Main body again moved to PORTSMOUTH and embarked in LCI(L). Remainder of day and night spent at sea.	
FRANCE	6	0725	Capt PHW Clarke. CSM Haycox, Lsjt F. Smith, Lcpl W. Barnes, Cpl w Kington, Lcpl C. Martin landed with Inf 185/Bde in Order to recce Bn. Assembly Area.	
	[6	1200	Main body Bn. landed, very wet landing, waist deep in water. Beach being slightly shelled. Bn. moved to assembly area in Southern outskirts of LION. Snipers very active], 6 enemy aircraft attacked beaches - all brought down by AA fire.	

M3524/1218 1200M 10/41 H. B. & Co.Ltd. **51**-1541)

SHEET 2

Month and Year June 1944 Commanding Officer Lt. Col. C.E. WELBY-EV?.

Place	Date	Hour	Summary of Events and Information	References to Appendices
FRANCE	6	1210	Patrol, from A Coy Commanded by Lt AF Henry sent off to reach CRESSERONS.	
		1300	First casualty Pte Harmer C. 14391886 wounded by snipers bullet.	
		1415	Vehicle Party (Craft loads 399, 404) disembarked and joined main body.	
		1700	Lt Henry's patrol returned - unable to reach CRESSERONS owing to enemy strong point at LION SUR MER. 4801296 Pte Newsome E. killed by shell-fire. first fatal casualty.	
		[1800	Bn. placed under Command 8 Br Inf Bde with task of holding flank of beach head Days' casualties 2 OR killed, 1 OR wounded.]	
	6/7		Night spent in assembly area.	
	7		Lt J. Harrod appointed Bde 10 in place of Capt Baptiste (Wounded)	
	[7	1400	Comd 8 Br Inf Bde visited CO and gave orders for attack on beach strong point at LION SUR MER.] Capt DRF Hart MC wounded.	
		[1520	Bn. moved to attack strong point. Phase 1 A & B Coys to take Chateau at HT LION Phase 2 C & D Coys to capture strong point. Phase 1 successful but Phase 2 abandoned owing to Bn. moving at very short notice to ST AUBIN d' ARQUENAY.]	

*5973. Wt.22661/1499. 300M. 8/42. Wy.L.P. Gp.656.

WO 171/1318
Intelligence/war diary
1ST BATTALION,
THE KING'S OWN SCOTTISH BORDERERS

Month and Year June 1944   Commanding Officer Lt. Col. G.D. ?nny

Place	Date	Hour	Summary of Events and Information	References to Appendices
	1-3		Bn. in marshaling area	
	4-5		Serials commenced embarkation and the operation was postponed for 24 hrs.	
	6 (D Day)		Bn. assault scale landed between 1145 hrs. and 1445 hrs. The move to the assembly area just North of HERMANVILLE-SUR-MER was carried out without incident. At 1735 the 'R' group moved off to COLLEVILLE-SUR-ORNE followed by the Bn. main body. After about half an hour the Bn. moved to ST. AUBIN D'ARQUENAY where the night was spent. Several prisoners were brought in and many papers & documents from enemy dug-outs, etc. were sent back.	
	[7.		At 0830 the Bn. moved to PÉRIERS SUR LE DAN where the attack on CAZELLE was	

Wt. 34859,1676 800,000 11/43 W.H. & S. 51-7676

WO 171/1384
Intelligence/war diary
2ND BATTALION, THE ROYAL ULSTER RIFLES

Month and Year June 1944   Commanding Officer Lt. Col. I.C. HARRIS

Place	Date	Hour	Summary of Events and Information	References to Appendices
WATERLOOVILLE	1st		Bright sunny day devoted to preparation for impending operations. Organised Inter-Company Football matches in afternoon, remainder of day devoted to rest.	Icn
GOSPORT	3rd		Loading of LCTs took place in the evening at GOSPORT. The weather was again bright and sunny. LCTs sailed and moored off Southsea.	Icn
SOUTHSEA	4th		LCI parties proceeded from WATERLOOVILLE for leading at SOUTHSEA but returned to Camp A7 at WATERLOOVILLE, loading having been postponed for 24 hrs owing to bad weather conditions.	Icn
SOUTHSEA	5th		LCI parties embarked during the morning at SOUTHSEA and moored off SOUTHSEA. Instead of the expected high tension in face of such a mighty undertaking the feelings appeared to be calm, as if yet another of the many exercises on similar lines was about to take place. Food on board was very satisfactory, fresh vegetables and bread being supplied to augment the "Compo" rations. LCTs slipped their moorings and headed for the open sea, followed later by the LCIs(L).	Icn
		1730		
	[6th.]		The journey across was uneventful, the sea being comparatively calm until approximately two hours before the landing, when it became rather choppy and made a number of people seasick, though tablets to prevent this had been issued which proved a great help to some. The huge convoy of which the Battalion was part, and the enormous number of Allied Aircraft seen making for the Continent kept spirits bouyant. [Just before the convoy turned inwards to the shore, German coastal batteries opened fire and shells fell in the convoy; this delayed the landing slightly whilst the assault brigade put them out of action.]	Icn
		[1200	At 1200 hrs the Landing Crafts Infantry containing the Battalion touched down on the beach of NORMANDY at LION SUR MER, slightly West of OUISTREHAM,	Icn
			(to Sheet Two)	

Wt 13474/1805 1,200,000 7/40 BPL 51-7171 Forms C2118/22

SHEET 2

Month and Year June 1944

Commanding Officer Lt. Col. I.C. HARRIS.

Place	Date	Hour	Summary of Events and Information	References to Appendices
[LION-SUR-MER (France)	6th. (Contd)		a wide sandy beach fringed with sand dunes. Here the Battalion caught first sight of the enemy as batches of snipers with hands over their heads were being rounded up from the houses and sand dunes lining the beach. By this time the sea had developed a considerable swell. The Battalion was well used to wet landings when carrying out exercises, but this was without doubt the wettest on record, most people landing in at least four feet of water and many in as much as five and a half feet. The majority became soaking wet from the top of their heads. Although the beaches had been almost cleared of the enemy, hostile shells and mortar bombs were falling in fair quantities. Consequently, even though the Battalion formed part of the reserve brigade in the Assault Division, the landing was made very difficult and uncomfortable. Many of the Rifleman being small in size were finding it difficult to get ashore, particularly in view of the fact that over and above their normal kit - heavy enough - they were each carrying a bicycle. Few casualties only were experienced on the beach, to those there were, being from shell and mortar fire.	Icn
		1645	The Battalion quickly made its way to the Assembly Area, the small village of LION-SUR-MER about half a mile inland, where they were met by Captain M.D.G.C. RYAN, OC "HQ" Coy, and his party of guides who had landed an hour previously with one of the assault brigades to make a reconnaissance of the Assembly Area. Shell and Mortar fire was still coming down resulting in a further few casualties. The Brigade Commander, Brigadier J.C. CUNNINGHAM, M.C., was wounded and evacuated, our Commanding Officer, Lieut Colonel I.C. HARRIS, assuming temporary Command of the Brigade. Major B.J. FITZ G. DONLEA, M.C., assuming temporary Command of the Bn.] Whilst in the Assembly Area Capt A.G. SEELERS, the Mortar Platoon Commander, was wounded in the legs by small arms fire, probably from a sniper, and evacuated. Having assembled and sorted itself out from the inevitable tangle which such <div align="right">(To Sheet Three) ....</div>	Icn

Wt 13474/1805 1,200,000 7/40 BPL 51-7171 Forms C2118/22

SHEET 3

Commanding Officer Lt. Col. I.C. HARRIS.

Place	Date	Hour	Summary of Events and Information	References to Appendices
[Periers sur le Dan (France)	6th. (Contd)		a landing makes, the Battalion was ordered to occupy the high ground at a point slightly North East of PERIERS le DAN, where it dug in for the night in readiness for a quick move forward.	Icn
			Lieut Colonel I.C. HARRIS returned to the Battalion, the Brigade having been taken over by Colonel A.D.G. ORR, DSO, who had acted as the Brigade Second in Command for a few months prior to D Day.]	
			Seven German Snipers and ten others were captured with a fair quantity of weapons and equipment.	
	[7th.		The Battalion was ordered to move in a South Westerly direction to capture CAMBES, a small village thickly wooded, approximately six miles inland from the coast. The Bn. moved via Le Mesnil] with "D" Company, Commanded by Caption J.R.StL. ALDWORTH, as vanguard. [It was believed that CAMBES was lightly held, but as the two woods surrounding it were themselves surrounded by walls some ten feet high, it was not possible to observe the enemy's actual dispositions. "D" Company was ordered to proceed forward and capture CAMBES with the rest of the Battalion closely following in reserve.]	Icn
		[1700.	"D" Company moved forward supported by one Squadron of tanks (East Riding Yeomanry); the rest of the Battalion remained halted at the side of the wood.]	See Appendix I
		⋆	Four enemy fighters suddenly appeared and machine gunned the rear companies, causing no casualties. During the battle "D" Company Commander, Captain J.R.StL. ALDWORTH, was Killed; Captain H.M. Gaffikin - OO Carrier Platoon - wounded, remaining with the Battalion, and Lieut H. GREENE wounded and evacuated. The attack had cost "D" Company one Officer and fourteen other Ranks Killed, one Officer and eleven Other Ranks Wounded and four Other Ranks Missing, with two Stretcher Bearers from the Medical Section Killed whilst tending the wounded.	Icn
			(to Sheet Four)...............	

Wt 13474/1805 1,200,000 7/40 BPL 51-7171 Forms C2118/22

185TH INFANTRY
BRIGADE

WO 171/702
Intelligence/war diary
185TH INFANTRY BRIGADE HQ

Month and Year June 1944   Commanding Officer Brig K.P. Smith, OBE.

Place	Date	Hour	Summary of Events and Information	References to Appendices
COLLEVILLE	6/7		D-day and D + 1 recorded in detail. Bde HQ at COLLEVILLE-SUR-ORNE where it had been est since evening D-day. Some trouble experienced with alleged snipers in the village and Def P1 was sent out to round up any Germans or 'Collaborateurs' who where everywhere suspected of firing on our tps. No results. Comns with fwd units were difficult at times, particularly with 2 WARWICK who lost their M14 Rear Link in LEBISEY WOOD. The rather depressing news from the front was lightened on the morning of JUNE 7 by the arrival OBERST KRUG and his staff, who had been running the German battle from the strong point at HILLMAN. He was commanding 736 Grenadier Regt and surrendered to 1 SUFFOLK. Much saluting and heel clicking accompanied his farewells to his staff.	Appx 1

COLLEVILLE	8		Posn of units first light 8 JUNE was :- 2 WARWICK – BEUVILLE
			            1 NORFOLK – Woods NW of BIEVILLE
			                 with one coy in BEAURECIARD.
			            2 KSLI – BEUVILLE.
			
			 These posns, although we did not expect it there, were to remain static for several weeks.	

		0800	Report received from 2 WARWICK that enemy in LEBISEY had tanks and assault guns in rear areas of woods and many MG posns. Posn believed held by 125 Pz Gren Regt which had moved into the posn just before our attack.	
		0800	2 WARWICK report their FOB and party are missing.	
BEUVILLE 066756		1010	Bde HQ moved to a field near BEUVILLE. Shortly after our arrival a party of Canadian airmen turned up. They had been held prisoner in the German HQ and BEUVILLE and had brought 61 of the captors captive to us. During the morning some targets of German armour near LEBISEY were engaged by STAFFS YEO and by naval units and some casualties inflicted.	
BEUVILLE 085751		1400	Bde HQ moved to new location at BEUVILLE Chateau. Shortly after our arrival	

Wt 13474/1805 1,200,00 7/40 BPL 51-7171 Forms C2118/22

SHEET 2

THE OPERATIONS OF 185 INF BDE ON D DAY AND D + 1

D Day

At 0945 hrs Advance Brigade HQ left the HQ ship in a LCI(S) and touched down at 1000 hrs. At that time, as the LCI(S) approached the shore the beach was under hy mortar fire, sporadic shelling and light automatic fire. Brigade HQ then moved on towards HERMANVILLE-SUR-MER.

At about 1010 hrs (1 NORFOLK possible earlier) LCIs carrying infantry touched down. Two of 2 WARWICK and one of 2 KSLI's LCIs were hit by shells and mortars and battalions suffered a small number of casualties before disembarking.

On touching down units proceeded immediately to their assembly areas, the move taking place under sporadic shell and mortar fire and at least two salvoes from multi-barrelled flame producing weapons.

2 WARWICK reached their assembly area by 1100 hrs losing a number of men, chiefly through sniper fire, on the way. On reaching their assembly area the two Westernmost companies came under accurate LMG fire from German positions towards LION-SUR-MER and CRESSERONS, suffering a number of casualties, and the CO prepared a plan for attacking these positions pending approval by Brigade.

2 KSLI reached their assembly area by 1050 hrs suffering a small number of casualties en route.

1 NORFOLK reaching assembly area by 1040 with some casualties.

Brigade Tac HQ established itself near the Church in HERMANVILLE at 1105.

At that time, the situation as it appeared to Comd 185 Infantry Brigade was that the infantry of the brigade less their support weapons were in their assembly areas; STAFFS YEO being held up by congestion of the beach exits; 1 S LAN R (8 Bde) at the x rds SOUTH of HERMANVILLE; COLLEVILLE-SUR-ORNE not yet cleared of the enemy; the German strong points HILLMAN and MORRIS reported very strongly held but were to be attacked by SUFFOLK.

The Brigade Commander called 'O' Group at 1200 hrs - 2 KSLI were ordered to commence moving forward on axis HERMANVILLE - BEUVILLE – CAEN; STAFFS YEO to get clear of beaches as soon as possible and catch up and marry up with 2 KSLI vide original plan; 2 WARWICK were ordered to disengage from enemy in their original assembly area and to re-assemble in woods EAST of HERMANVILLE church, 1 NORFOLK were ordered to proceed towards COLLEVILLE-SUR-ORNE ready to pass through 8 Bde directly HILLMAN and/or MORRIS were taken.

At 1215 hrs Commander 185 Inf Bde received information of enemy ta? NORTH of CAEN, of fire from position atn PERIERS-SUR-LE-DAN and of heavy fighting on 8 Canadian Bde front, which caused him to decide to put, into operation ? alternative plan of moving 2 WARWICK on to the EAST of the axis behind ? thus taking advantage of the anti-tank obstacle.

Meanwhile 2 KSLI moved off and was met by, and dealt with successfully, opposition from many enemy MGs and mortars on the high ground astride the road EAST of PERIERS-SUR-LE-DAN.

At 1430 hrs Brigade Commander moved to COLLEVILLE where he found that 8 Bde had been unable to capture HILLMAN and that MORRIS was still held by enemy.

Situation at this time:- 2 KSLI and STAFFS YED approaching LE HOMME leaving a company to deal with the enemy battery at PERIER-SUR-LE-DAN which was dominating the main axis. 2 WARWICK moving into their second assembly area, some delay having been caused by difficulty in disengaging from the enemy in their original assembly area. No battalions at this time had yet got any support weapons with them, owing to the congestion on the beaches.

At 1500 hrs HILLMAN was still holding out. MORRIS and SOLE were still reported to be held by the enemy. Brigade Commander ordered 1 NORFOLK to bypass HILLMAN and make good high ground EAST of BEUVILLE.

2 WARWICK ordered to ST AUBIN D'ARQUENAY and follow up behind 1.NORFOLK, or to move up axis of canal road, one company to take over bridge at BENOUVILLE

2W 0955.

2K. 1010

1N. 0950.

........./from

SHEET 3

free Airborne Div as 8 Bde had been unable to do so. As 1 NORFOLK received heavy casualties in bypassing HILLMAN Brigade Commander decided after referring to Div Comd that 2 WARWICK should move up axis of canal road. No opposition coming from MORRIS.

On approaching BENOUVILLE heavy small arms fire directed on leading 2 WARWICK company and 2 WARWICK were ordered to put in an attack at about 1900 hrs. Attack was successful several enemy being killed and about ten PW being taken. 2 WARWICK then advanced towards BLAINVILLE meeting some opposition from an enemy mob coln fighting a delaying action, suffering some casualties and having their FOOs tank knocked out. 2 WARWICK halted for the night on NE outskirts of BLAINVILLE.

Meanwhile 2 KSLI made good progress until they reached BEUVILLE where the leading company came under heavy fire from snipers in the village. The CO decided to by-pass BEUVILLE and to attack as his next objective the enemy strong point and HQ in BEUVILLE. This was completed by 1600 hrs.

About 1615 hrs about 20 enemy tanks were seen approaching on the right flank. At 1630 hrs 8 of them attacked, four and possibly six, were knocked out by STAFFS YEO and anti tank guns of 2 KSLI. This action was over by 1730 hrs, meanwhile a company of 2 KSLI which was out of communication with the CO had pushed on towards LEBISEY, the outskirts of which they reached about 1730 hrs. One company was consolidating the right flank of BIEVILLE against further tank attacks, one company was moving forward to BEUVILLE and the fourth company was still engaged in stiff fighting with the battery at PERIERS-SUR-LE-DAN. This they finally captured putting all the guns out of action and destroying or capturing most of the garrison by about 2100 hrs.

About 1800 hrs CO 2 KSLI re-established communication with company which had reached outskirts of LEBISEY. He was informed that casualties were heavy, that the company commander was killed and that they were unable to pentrate the wood owing to its thick nature, concealed MGs and snipers and that a party of the enemy were in process of encircling them. The +CO considered that to commit his two available companies (already considerably depleted by casualties) into this extensive and obscure objective and without a firm base behind him would be running the risk of defeat in detail. This was passed back to the Brigade Commander who agreed to the withdrawal of the company from LEBISEY and ordered 2 KSLI to establish a firm base SOUTH of BIEVILLE. This withdrawal was carried out after dark without undue loss. Situation at nightfall therefore was three companies 2 KSLI digging in at BEUVILLE. 2 WARWICK on outskirts of BLAINVILLE and 1 NORFOLK on the high ground EAST of BEUVILLE.

1 NORFOLK had some difficulty in disengaging two companies pinned down by HILLMAN but finally consolidated on the high ground EAST of BEUVILLE by 1900 hrs. A number of enemy snipers were mopped up on this feature.

Brigade Commander warned CO 2 WARWICK that night that he would have to carry out an attack on LEBISEY as early as possible on D + 1 and that orders for the attack would be issued at 0730 hrs on D + 1. 2 WARWICK secured BLAINVILLE at first fight and carried out the necessary recces of routes forward, all routes then being reported clear of enemy.

D + 1

Brigade Commander issued orders at 0730 hrs. Zero to be at 0945 hrs. The attack to be supported by three field regiments (less one battery) and one cruiser. CO 2 WARWICK completed his orders by about 0830 hrs and companies moved towards their assembly positions. During this move A Company (left forward company 2 WARWICK) came under heavy fire from houses on the canal road towards BEUREGARD which had apparently been clear of enemy during previous recces. This caused considerable delay. CO 2 WARWICK requested postponement of H hour. Bde Comd referred the matter to Div Comd who, in view of the importance of capturing LEBISEY as quickly as possible, ordered that delay should not be more than half an hour. This information passed by Brigade Commander to CO 2 WARWICK and supporting arms. Meanwhile, right forward company (B company 2 WARWICK) and reserve company (C Company) proceeded to assembly area and owing to breakdown of communications did not receive orders for postponement. They then proceeded to attack at the original hour, unsupported, reached the forward edge of the wood with few casualties, and reported that they were in the wood. Fourth Company (D Company) was still on the bridge at BENOUVILLE.

........../ Acting on this

WO 171/1387

Intelligence/war diary

2ND BATTALION, THE WARWICKSHIRE REGIMENT

TOP SECRET

Month and Year June 1944   Commanding Officer Lt. Col. H.O.S. HERDON.

Place	Date	Hour	Summary of Events and Information	References to Appendices
FRANCE	4 JUNE		'S' COY — Maj M RYAN -OC	
			Capt PB WATERWORTH -OC Carrier Pl	
			Lt AR ALLEN -2 IC Carrier Pl	
			Lt PM HEALEY -OC Mortar Pl	
			Capt AJM BANNERMAN -OC A Tk Pl	
			Lt J BINDLESS -2 IC A Tk Pl	
			Lt AG WILSON -Assault Pnr Pl Comd	
			'HQ'COY — Maj TL BROCK -OC	
			Lt JR CLARKE -SO	
			Lt AP ROBERTS -TO	
			Capt SJ WILLIAMS -QM	
			Capt JHT LAWTON -MO	
			Capt(Rev) J AUSTIN -Padre	
			BN HQ — Lt. Col. H.O.S. HERDON -CO	
			Maj RG KREYER -2 IC	
			Capt W PIKE -ADJT	
			Lt PWF LAMB -IO	
			FOB — Capt J LEE	
			An uneventful passage across the channel in the direction of NORMANDY	
	5 JUNE [6 JUNE		'D' DAY - 'H' HOUR = 0725 hours.	
			The marching personnel and the three LCIs were due to touch down at 0955 hours. The three LCIs approached the beach at LION-SUR-MER, on time, together. Beach was under mortar and shell fire and there were still some snipers left in the houses along the promenade. 'C' Coy's LCI hit a mine on the beach, and was also hit by a shell, whilst 'D' Coy's LCI had both its ramparts shot away. This and the sniping and shelling on the beach caused a certain amount of confusion in disembarkation, and the Battalion suffered a few casualties; but by 1130 hours, all four companies and Bn. HQ were concentrated in an Assembly Area about ½-mile SOUTH of LION-SUR-MER.] 'A' and 'C' Coys came under accurate small arms and MG Fire in the Assembly Area from German positions to the WEST.]	
			/3	

Wt 43550/1614 560M 3/41 BPL 51/8792

TOP SECRET

Month and Year June 1944   Commanding Officer Lt. Col. H.O.S. HERDON.

Place	Date	Hour	Summary of Events and Information	References to Appendices
FRANCE	[6 JUNE		The Brigade Plan was then altered and the Battalion was ordered to disengage to the EAST and proceed to another Assembly Area EAST of HERMONVILLE. 'A' and 'C' Coys suffered some casualties in the Cemetery at LION-SUR-MER whilst disengaging. Lt R PRATT was wounded at this time. [The German Strong Point SW of COLLEVILLE-SUR-ORNE was still holding out and 2 KSLI and 1 NORFOLK, who were advancing by the original axis, had suffered casualties from this position. For this reason the Battalion was ordered to advance along the axis COLLEVILLE-SUR-ORNE - BENOUVILLE - BLAINVILLE. BENOUVILLE was found to be held and 'A' Coy put in a successful attack on this position at about 1830 hours. 'D' Coy was now ordered to take over the defence of the bridges over the ORNE from the Airborne Division. The rest of the Battalion continued on towards BLAINVILLE, meeting opposition the whole way from a German Mobile Delaying Force armed with MGs and A tk Guns. The Battalion halted for the night on the outskirts of BLAINVILLE at midnight, having had four killed and thirty-five wounded.]	CR
	[7 JUNE		During the night the Battalion received a Warning Order that they would attack a German position in LEBISEY WOOD at 0945 hours. 2 KSLI had been held up by this position the previous day, but it was not thought to be strongly held. At 0730 hours Lt. Col. HERDON gave out orders for the attack as follows:-	

'A' COY LEFT   } To attack EASTERN half of the WOOD
'B' COY RIGHT

'C' COY   - To follow up, pass through and clear
                              the WESTERN half

'D' COY   - To follow up as soon as they had been
                              relieved on the Bridges at BENOUVILLE]

/4

Wt 43550/1614 560M 3/41 BPL 51/8792

Intelligence/war diary
1ST BATTALION, ROYAL NORFOLK REGIMENT

Month and Year June 1944   Commanding Officer Lt. Col. R.H. BELLAMY.

Place	Date	Hour	Summary of Events and Information	References to Appendices
			back to craft.	
			At about 2300 hrs a Naval signal comes to the effect that the force in this port will slip anchor to-morrow morning.	
			Weather - changeable. Bright periods. Rain at night.	
LCI/317	5	1000	Our LCIs together with the rest of the force sailed out of harbour, anchored for a few hours and then set sail with the rest fo the naval force for France. Tps very seasick.	HH.
In the Fd	[6]	0725	"H" hr and D day for the SECOND FRONT. [This Bn being part of the follow up Bde, landed at H + 150, but was landed 5 mins early at 0950.] [Beach under fairly heavy mortar & shellfire - Bn. moved to conc area and on to take over from SUFFOLKS at approx 1200 hrs. Unfortunately HILLMAN part of the initial bridgehead, held out for almost the whole day & this Bn. had to go round]	

Wt.52938/1102 660M. 2/44 W.H . & S. 51-9071

SHEET 2

Month and Year June 1944   Commanding Officer LT. Col. R.H. BELLAMY.

Place	Date	Hour	Summary of Events and Information	References to Appendices
			[the left flank, losing several casualties in 2 Coys from our own tks which thought they were enemy getting out of HILLMAN and fired on them. These two Coys A & B were finally extracted and the Bn. consolidated for the night on ROVER some way short of CAEN which was budgeted as D day objective for 185 Inf Bde. Gp.]	Lt. Toft killed, Capt. Kelly Lt. Ward, Capt. Lang RAMC wounded
In the Fd	[7		During the day a general advance was maintained by the Bde. Gp. and the WARWICKS became heavily involved in a posn VERMOUTH overlooking a large area to the NORTH and a step to the last posn overlooking CAEN. This Bn. intended to attack in front of VERMOUTH and found it to be a well prepared def posn, contrary to expectations. Under very heavy fire of all kinds, the CO remained in posn until dark and then drew out]	HH.

Wt.52938/1102 660M. 2/44 W.H. & S. 51-9071

WO 171/1325

Intelligence/war diary

2ND BATTALION, THE KING'S OWN

SHROPSHIRE LIGHT INFANTRY

Month and Year June 1944   Commanding Officer Lt. Col. F.J. MAURICE.

Place	Date	Hour	Summary of Events and Information	References to Appendices
NEWHAVEN	3	1000	The marching personnel of the Bn (i.e. a small Bn. HQ and four Rifle Coys) leave Camp J 3 and embark in three LCI (L)'s for operation "OVERLORD".	
	4		Operation postponed for 24 hrs owing to a strong Westerly Wind.	
	5		Operation "ON" The convoy composed chiefly of LCI's and LCT's assembles outside NEWHAVEN at 1100 hrs and sails for FRANCE at 1400hrs. Still an unpleasant strong West Wind and a grey sky. - Meanwhile the various vehicle parties of the Bn had been assembling and embarking at PORTSMOUTH and the LONDON DOCKS in LCT's, LST's and MT Ships.	
AT SEA	6		The voyage proved uneventful. Soon after 0800 hrs news came that 8 INF BDE had touched down and later we learned that they had secured the immediate beachhead. We were cheered by the news that 6 AIRBORNE DIV had captured intact the bridges over the CANAL DECAEN and R. ORNE.	
[LA BRECHE		1010	The LCI's carrying the Bn. touched down very much as planned at LA BRECHE D'HERMANVILLE. It was NOT an easy landing, 4 to 5 ft of water and a sea running. The beach was still under shell fire.]	(Contd Sheet 2).

M3524/1218 1200M 10/41 H.B. & Co.Ltd. 51-1541)

SHEET 2

Place	Date	Hour	Summary of Events and Information	References to Appendices
LA BRECHE (Continued).	6	1010	However with the aid of ropes carried ashore by the Navy the heavily-laden men struggled ashore with few casualties and little loss of equipment. One LCI shortly after we had disembarked was hit by Shell Fire and sunk. [All Companies then moved forward to the Assembly Area as ordered whilst mopping up operations were still going on in houses adjacent to the beaches.]	
[HERMANVILLE		1100	By 1100 hrs the Bn (less "SP" Coy) had assembled in the orchards immediately North of HERMANVILLE as planned. Every Officer and man had carried ashore a sandbag labelled with his name and in there was placed gasmasks, cardigans and some other items of clothing to lighten our load and then dumped by Coys. This was well worth while and 95% were recovered in MT on the following day, the missing 5% having been destroyed by shelling. The STAFFS YEO (Sherman Tks) riding on the tanks of which unit, the Bn. was supposed to advance on CAEN, were landing but making little progress forward, owing to congestions on the roads.]	
		1115	The Bde Comd passed the Assembly Area on an airborne bicycle to be joined by the C.O. on a similar mount.	(Contd Sheet 3).

Wt.34859,1676 800,000 11/43 W. H. & S. 51-7676

SHEET 3

Place	Date	Hour	Summary of Events and Information	References to Appendices
[HERMAN VILLE]	6	1130	C.O. leaves Brigadier to find out situation with Staff Yeo.	
		[1200	C.O. reports to Bde Comd in HERMANVILLE that only about one and a half Squadrons of STAFFS YEO are clear of beaches and that a large minefield apparently covered the right flank of HERMANVILLE across the axis of advance originally planned for the tanks.. Bde Comd then orders the Bn. to advance on foot along main axis. The STAFFS YEO to marry up as soon as possible.]	
		1230	Bn. Advance in the following order X,W,Y,Z Coys. - Major REA (Bty Comd 7 Fd Regt) and Capt GOWER (FOB) travelled with C.O. - [FOO's from 7 and 33 Fd Regt's had reported and been allotted to the leading Coys and STAFFS YEO. 7,33 and 76 FD REGTS were in support as far as available but 33 and 76 FD REGTS were still involved in the 8 INF BDE Battle.]	
		[1300	X Coy came under fairly heavy Mortar and Artillery Fire on the forward slopes of the ridge South of HERMANVILLE (to be known as the PERIERS RIDGE).	
		1315	X Coy report enemy posts in the fields on top and just beyond PERIERS RIDGE, in particular M.G. posts holding them up from the right.]	(Contd Sheet 4).

Wt.34859, 1676 800,00 11/43 W.H. & S. 51-7676

SHEET 4

Place	Date	Hour	Summary of Events and Information	References to Appendices
HERMANVILLE	6	1315	C.O. orders W Coy to come up on the right and take on M.G. post. Adjutant reports to C.O. in A.C.V. having just got forward from the beaches.	
		[1330	Advance continues on two Coy fronts, leading coys still meeting enemy parties in the fields on the reverse slopes.]	
		[1400	W Coy overcomes some opposition in Church Area West of PERIERS SUR-LE-DAN FOO sent forward to X Coy who take LE HOMME]	
		[1425	CO orders Z Coy to attack enemy battery at PERRIERS-SUR-LE-DAN which is holding up the tanks on the right and dominating the main axis.]	
		1430	X Coy held up by accurate sniping from BEUVILLE.	
		1450	CO arrives and decides to by-pass with W and Y Coys. Sp Coy priority vehicles arrive - A Tk Pl, 2 Sections Carriers and Mortar Pl.	
		1545	W and Y Coys reaches forward edges of BIEVILLE. Y Coy report no opposition during advance on left W Coy having received some casualties on the way proceed to "Mop Up" area of Chateau.	
		[1615	Sp Coy arrive on Right Flank - German tanks seen approaching from West.]	Contd Sheet 5.

Wt.34859,1676 800,000 11/43 W. H. & S. 51-7676

SHEET 5

Place	Date	Hour	Summary of Events and Information	References to Appendices
[HERMANVILLE	6	1630	Counterattack by German Tanks from Right Flank.	
		1700	Counterattack successfully driven off. Two enemy tanks accounted for by 6 prs. Enemy Tanks seen to be moving on round right flank.	
		1730	Reported that Y Coy had reached Northern Outskirts of Woods in LEBISEY. Wireless communication difficult.	
		1800	Y Coy report held up by Cross Fire from enemy M.Gs in wood and snipers amongst trees also enemy party of approx 40 trying to get round their flank.	
			Situation reported back. Decision made to establish firm base at BEUVILLE and withdraw Y Coy after dark.	
		2000	Firm base established with strong A Tk defence on right.	
		2315	Y Coy withdraw successfully without further casualties.]	
[BIEVILLE	7	0930	With the Battalion as a firm base, 2 WARWICKS attacked LEBISEY from the left flank but meet stiff opposition and are unable to complete capture and consolidation.]	Contd Sheet 6.

M3524/1218 1200M 10/41 H.B. & Co.Ltd. 51-1541)

DIVISIONAL
TROOPS

WO 171/410
Intelligence/war diary
BRITISH 3RD INFANTRY DIVISION HQ

BB Informed in
MAG Gen. T.G. Renn?

Place	Date	Hour	Summary of Events and Information	References to Appendices
ASHLING HOUSE HEN M Road 12	June 1/4 4		EMBARKATION of Troops proceed according to plan – All D-Day Troops were embarked at Southampton – Parsifal awl and Newhaven on HQ left for LARGS. Owing to bad weather D-Day (1st day) was postponed and it was thought as the earliest possible day would be 9 or 10 June.	
	5		However weather improved and it was decided to assault at 0725 6 June. D-Day. Voyage uneventful rough but no overt enemy opposition and on ships carrying troops. One or two destroyers sunk by mines.	
	6		Assaults went in as planned but some 7 minutes late. DDO launched from 5000 yards under cover smoke owing to bad weather.	

(3110) Wt 35842/1764 1000M 12/39 BPL?

SHEET 2

Place	Date	Hour	Summary of Events and Information	References to Appendices
La BRÊIN	6 JUNE	[0930	Div Comd - CRA. G? A-se left LARGS in LCM which came off GORILAND and contained CRA: heard - The LCM carrying GOC. never turned up.]	Appx 1 One copy of Log attached for general information
		[1030	The Div party landed on Red Beach in appx H + 3 and moved in land to wood 082 804 where General was to meet up with Bng casse, & Bde Ground-	
		1130	No Sign of Bng Casse - The vessel had to drop behind owing to traffic congestion and Div party proceeded on foot to meet up with Comd 185 Bre.	
		1200	Met Brig Smith in Hermanville-SUR-MER and reported safe arrival of Div Party and locative ashore to G1 on HMS LARGS.	
		1300	Div Count moved to Div HQ at 072 803 Battle continued as planned.	
		1600	Div HQ shelled - Div Co ordered move to alternative HQ at Colleville-SUR-ORNE. Div G1 and remainder of Div party on HQ ship and standby Ship came ashore.	

(3110) Wt.35842/2764 1000M 12/39 BPL 51/5684 Forms C2118/22.

SHEET 3

Place	Date	Hour	Summary of Events and Information	References to Appendices
COLLIERVILLE SUR ORNE	6 June	1830	Att Div parties of first and second tide in – one orderly casualty. Div HQ dug in at Colleville	Appx 2 & 3 For course of all build see Log.
	7		3 Bn Inf Div Int Summaries number 1 and 2 att	
	8		Div Comd A-C att Comd Post fwd and forces battle from here – see log attached	
	9	2210	Alternative Div HQ raised at Periers-Sur-le-Dan – Ex German strongpoint	
			Div HQ bombed – one 1000lb and many anti personnel bombs – Three officers and ten OR hit including Sigs. Officers Div QMG Major BRENNAN killed – SIQ – Capt BLYTHE wounded – LO – Lt TAVERSHAM wounded.	
			3 Div Int Summaries No. 3 att Approx 4 Q	
	10		Day special instructions Div in reorganising – Div HQ dug in deep! – CV1-RHQ office – CV5 and Sigs Comd vehicle bulldozed in.	
			Peaceful night.	

13140 Wt. 35842/1764 1000M 12/39 BPL 51/5684 Forms C2118/22.

WO 171/969
Intelligence/war diary
7TH FIELD REGIMENT RA.

Month and Year: June 1944   Commanding Officer Lt. Col. N.R.H. TAB

Date	Hour	Event	Ref to Appendices
Jun 1-6		During the last few days of May the Regiment was in camp at WYKEHURST PARK, BOLNEY, SUSSEX. Terrific activity in welding and fixing armour plating to SPs guns and carrying out wireless modifications to OP tanks. There was a great shortage of welders and electricians as most of the Division specialists had to return to their units and the Regimental LAD had to be waterproofed and go to their concentration area. However, Division managed to provide specialists from static resources.	
May 31		Regimental main parties moved off to concentration area near GOSPORT.	
Jun 1		This was spent in marshalling camp carrying out final stages of waterproofing.	
2		The Regiment loaded into LCTs at GOSPORT Ferry and except for guards disembarking personnel were returned to marshalling camp.	
3		Regiment embarked for Operation OVERLORD. The Operation was postponed one day but troops remained on board.	
4		On board LCTs.	
5		LCTs started out of PORTSMOUTH to form up with invasion shipping. The invasion forces set out about midday.	
6		After a quiet night craft approaching the French coast near OUISTREHAM for the invasion.	
	0644	Ranging started on run-in targets for assault on Northern FRANCE.	
	0655	Fire for effect on targets.	
	0725	H-Hour for invasion.	
	0935	Regiment's recce parties landed.	
	1045	24 guns landed but held up on beaches.	
	1155	Regiment established at HERMANVILLE SUR MER. In support of 185 Inf Bde. 24 guns in action.	
	1320	Bde approached PERIERS-SUR-LE-DAN.	
	1830	Counter attack by Regiment of 21 Pz Div in area BIEVILLE. Counter attack driven off.	
	2155	Regiment in action area COLLEVILLE.	
		One Officer (Capt R.N. de Courcy Thompson) and six other ranks wounded.	
7	1600	Regiment moved to new position North of BIEVILLE.	
	1730	Regiment in action in support of 2 WARWICK in LEBISEY WOOD.	
	1900	9 Bty position shelled. Moved to alternative positions. One officer (Capt. R.B. Gregory) and two other ranks injured, and two ORs killed.	
8	0800	9 Bty hit by AP bombs, several casualties. One officer (Lt. D.G. Turney) and twenty other ranks injured and two ORs killed.	
	0930	16 Bty captured three PW, in Tower overlooking gun position.	

WO 171/971
Intelligence/war diary
33RD FIELD REGIMENT RA

Month and Year June 1944   Commanding Officer Lt. Col. T.E. Hussey RA.

Place	Date	Hour	Summary of Events and Information	References to Appendices
GOSPORT.	2	0600	First vehicles loaded on LCT's for operation 'Overlord' small guard left on board and personnel return to Marshalling Camps.	
PORTSMOUTH	4		Personnel embark.	
	5		D-day postponed 24 hours, operation notified as on 1200 hrs. 5 June and sail at 1230 hrs. Weather Choppy and nearly all in LCTs are sick.	
at sea	6	0430	Stand to. Uneventful but rough crossing. H-go synchronise watches for run in short. Comns food but no Communication with Foo who is to contact quu in bombardment. Adft orders ho in ML to go forward to observe. Fire for effect opened at H − 30 & results reported found. Continue firing until H hour 0725 hrs. when 6 LCT	

Wt 43550/1614 560M 3/41 BPL 51/3792.

SHEET 2

Month and Year   Commanding Officer

Place	Date	Hour	Summary of Events and Information	References to Appendices
			Craft turn away to waiting position. No activity from GAF. Co. lands at H+70 and reports beach not under shell fire except at few isolated places(.) Regt due to land on Red & White beaches but are landed at H + 155 further west on Red beach between LA BRECHE 0980 and LION-SUR-MER. Beach now being subjected to shellfire, mortaring and incendiary rockets. Shells fall near several craft on way in but no casualties until landing. Beach exits not were prepared and guns have to remain on beach for 20 mins approx. 76(H) & A Regt in action on beach(.) 109 Bty first off the Beach and but in action in cornfield 300 yds from beach 074808. 113/114 in action on beach. RHQ and 101 in action 079800. Amer brought ashore his SP's MIH and in Porpoises, (metal troughs caused by SPs; these are mostly left on beach as they	
		1100.		

Wt 43550/1614 560M 3/41 BPL 51/3792.

SHEET 3

Place	Date	Hour	Summary of Events and Information	References to Appendices
			Casualties on beach. Lt K.W. Bellingham killed by direct hit from shell while driving 'Weazle' gur wade 101 and 5ORs wounded(.) Vehicle casualties Z tank and one MIH 101 drowned.	
			Capt D.I. Gower, in support KSLI, killed by 88 mm which pierced his tank killing also Bde Bain 101 and injuring 2 others. Tank completely destroyed. Progress slow and was only ½ way to CAEN by dusk. A raid at night which is first appearance of GAF. RAF Cores is complete. 2 Para Bdes land at dusk. 113/114 & C Bty moved up to from rest of Regt.	
	7		Night 6-7th heavy combing of beaches, but disembarkation continues.	

Wt 43550/1614 560M 3/41 BPL 51/3792.

WO 171/976
Intelligence/war diary
76TH FIELD REGIMENT RA

Month and Year June 1944   Commanding Officer Major H.B. Pirie RA.

Place	Date	Hour	Summary of Events and Information	References to Appendices
West of RIVER ORNE	6	0740 0835	D = Day for Assault. H = Hour. 0720 hrs. O.P. Parties, CPOs Recce Party & U.L.O. party landed. Gun Troops. A. & B. came in to land. A.C. (S.P.) was hit by shell and set on fire. This blocked ship and only enabled 3 guns, 1 Sherman OP, 2 Half-Tracks and 2 AOPs to land. A.1. & M.2 were drowned. During the landing of the vehicles the battery sustained its first casualty = L/Bdr. Drummond R., killed by shell. B. Troop (LCT 273) coming in to land, struck a mine which blew a hole in the ramp. A shell hit the top of the ramp. Door was dropped and first 2 guns beached. The wreckage of the ramp was so bad that only H. Truck (AOP) was able to beach. A.5 (Half-track) stuck on the ramp. It was decided to reverse the LCT into deeper water and try to dislodge the Half-Track. When reversing, the LCT	

Wt 13474/1805 1,200,000 7/40 BPL 51-7171 F orms C2118/22.

SHEET 2

Month and Year June 1944   Commanding Officer Major H.B. Pirie R.A.

Place	Date	Hour	Summary of Events and Information	References to Appendices
West of RIVER ORNE	6		again struck a mine, which blew the engine room. The skipper of the LCT ordered the ship to be abandoned. Some of the crew and Troops remained aboard in the hope that the LCT would eventually be high and dry and the vehicles would be able to land.	
	6	0840	5 SP guns came into action on beach. Persistent enemy shelling on beach scoring 4 more hits of B. Troop's LCT and many near misses.	
		0915	Recce parties proceeded forward to position A.	
		0920	By this time the beach was crammed full of all types of vehicles and armour. During its action on the beach, the guns of the Battery fired an average of 50 rounds each.	
		1130	As Beach exits were all inclined to be choked, A. Troop sent a party of one NCO & 9 men to clear a path up through the dunes to the first road. This was done and eventually	

Wt 13474/1805 1,200,000 7/40 BPL 51-7171 Forms C2118/22.

SHEET 3

Month and Year June 1944   Commanding Officer Major H.B. PIRIE R.A.

Place	Date	Hour	Summary of Events and Information	References to Appendices
West of RIVER ORNE	6.		completed by bulldozers.	
		1600	Remainder of B. Troop beached with the help of an Armoured Recovery vehicle. The beach was still under heavy shellfire. These vehicles moved direct to position "A" joining up with A. Troop on the way.	
HERMANVILLE-SUR-MER		1630	Battery in action in Area A. (east of HERMANVILLE-SUR-MER). In this position the Battery fired on enemy strongpoint code name DAIMLER resulting in the capture of this point by our own Troops with hardly a shot being fired against them. Only a short time was spent in this position before moving to Area B. in the vicinity of COLLEVILLE-SUR-ORNE. Bsm. Mcleve was wounded about this time by a sniper whilst on his way from the beach to the position with ammunition. Gnr. French, one of the Amms. Nos., was also wounded.	
COLLEVILLE-SUR-ORNE	6	1900	Battery arrived at Area B. and went into action in direct	

Wt 13474/1805 1,200,000 7/40 BPL 51-7171 Forms C2118/22.

SHEET 4

Month and Year June 1944   Commanding Officer Major A. LYELL. R.A.

Place	Date	Hour	Summary of Events and Information	References to Appendices
COLLEVILLE-SUR-ORNE	6	1900	support of the 6th Airborne Division. During the evening Major H.B. Pirie and Capt. D.P.D. Featherstone (FOO) were wounded L/Bdr. Smith and Dor./op. Macdonald of B.C.S party were also wounded all except Major Pirie were evacuated to England. The Battery fired at least 200 rounds per gun in this position.	
	7		Major Pirie was again wounded and returned to England.	
	8		During the night 8/9th. AP bombs were dropped in the vicinity of Battery position. No casualties. Casualties were sustained by the other 2 Batteries of the Regiment.	
	9	1600	Tank Alert was given. This proved to be a false rumour.	
			Captain A. Lyell was promoted Major and took over command of the Battery. Lieut. N. Fraser was promoted Captain and became 'B' Tp Cmdr. Lieut. O. Rolland was promoted Captain and became 'A' Tp Cmdr. Lieut. A. Morrall took over duties of C.P.O from Capt. Fraser. Boms. Same & Sgt. Wilson were promoted Bsm. and Bsm. Morris became Battery Sergeant Major. Bsm. Powell	

*5973. Wt.22661/1499. 300M. 8/42. Wy.L.P. Gp. 656.

WO 171/913

Intelligence/war diary
20TH ANTI-TANK REGIMENT RA

Month & Year June 1944   Commanding Officer Lt. Col. G.B. THATCHER, RA.

Place	Date	Hour	Summary of Events & Infm
	6	0810	Bty HQ & E Tp 67 Bty plus I Tp 45 Bty land in sp 8 Br Inf Bde.
LA BRECHE	"	1045	CO & party touch down White Beach under mortar fire.
HERMANVILLE	"	1100	CO establishes HQ 073802.
""""	"	1200	41 Bty land complete in sp of 185 Inf Bde.
"	"	1100-1700	CO visits 41 & 67 Btys, KINGS, & BUCKS A tk Pls.
"	"	1700	101 Bty less M Tp land in sp 9 Br Inf Bde.
"	"	1800	41 67 & 101 Btys all ashore (Casualities :- Maj AM ONIONS RA, Capt GF GREENBANK RA, Capt IW DANBY RA, and 3 ORs).
"	"	1900	CO co-ordinates Beach Gp guns.
"	"	2000	CO goes to Div to get infm of 9 Br Inf Bde attack. 185 Inf Bde are apparently held up on line of HILLMAN - CROSSLEY.
"	"	2100	41 Bty at 081780, 67 Bty 083774.
"	"	"	Div HQ moves to COLLEVILLE but in view of the danger to the right flank of the 8 Br Inf Bde beach-head, the CO remains at HERMANVILLE during the night of D/D - 1, to co-ordinate the A tk defences, using 5 KINGS, 1 BUCKS, & S LAN R. The LINCS subsequently appear to be holding a firm base containing the enemy within LION & HT LION, & fit in admirably with their 6 x 6-prs with the CO's desired A tk lay-out.
"	"	2345	RHQ settle down to get a little rest, but it is necessary to maintain a strict watch owing to the instability of the situation.
	7	0500	RHQ Stand To & prepare to rejoin DIVHQ CO inspects 5 KINGS A tk lay-out at first light, & rejoins RHQ at COLLEVILLE at 0730 hrs, it having been established at the new location at 0600 hrs. Digging & camouflage claim first priority.
CAZELLE	"	0900-1200	41 Bty located at LE HOMME 67 Bty at COLLEVILLE 101 Bty at COLVILLE. CO subsequently inspects gun posns & learns new Div attack plans - 9 Br Inf Bde, KOSB & RUR going right to CAZELLE (with 2 SP Tps A tk & 1 Tp 6-pr);
			8 Br Inf Bde (S LAN R) attacking CRESSERONS & PLUMETOT. (LINCS) pressing in on LION & HT LION. It is also believe that the GOC plans to send WARWICKS or NORFOLKS round extreme left, flanking to attack CAEN itself
"	"	1300	Corps Comd & Div Comd leave Div HQ for BEUVILLE to implement the proposed plans. We await developments with rising exuberance
"	"	1600	Within 2 hrs the 185 Inf Bde attack on VERMOUTH has definitely achieved no success, & all at the cost of severe casualities, particularly to the WARWICKS & NORFOLKS. These 2 Bns. are withdrawn in some confusion but the A tk defences of 41 Bty remain firm & intact.
"	"	1700	RHQ 2nd Tide parties arrive, & vehs are allotted an adm area orchard COLLEVILLE, next to Div HQ.
"	"	1700	The situation on the brs BENOUVILLE & RANVILLE needs careful watching. The need is for A tk guns, so 3×6-prs of 45 Bty by now just landed, are pushed down forthwith under comd 6 Airborne Div, together with E Tp 67 Bty. E Tp is, by 2200 hrs, subsequently withdrawn, as the threat is considered by the Div Comd to have decreased.

WO 171/1518
Intelligence/war diary
17TH FIELD COMPANY RE

Month and Year June 1944   Commanding Officer Major L. SCOTT-BOWDEN. DSO., MC., RE.

Place	Date	Hour	Summary of Events and Information	References to Appendices
LION-SUR-MER	6		The Company less No.2 Pl disembarked on beaches between H + 120 & H + 360 and proceeded to BENOUVILLE. No.2 Pl under Command of 185 Br Inf Bde assaulted with infantry and fought to, and consolidated around Chateau de Beauville. No.3 Pl constructed FBE Rafts on canal. No.1 Pl prepared Bailey Br bank seats. O.C. Major DJ Willison wounded in head by an 88 mm shell fragment. Lt Dixon was hit in the arm by a bullet, and Lt Clarke wounded by shellfire.	
BENOUVILLE	7		Unloading Bailey Bridging eqpt and construction of FBE Ferry commenced. Capt. CW Watson 2i/c killed by air bombing.	
"	8		Cl 70 Raft and west bank landing bay constructed.	
"	9		Canal br completed. Un loading stores and work on approaches and bankseats for River ORNE Br commenced.	
"	10		Canal Br maintained. Constructed floating pier for River ORNE Br.	
BEAUVILLE	9		No.2 Pl sent fighting patrol to clear up BEAUVILLE.	
"	10		No.2 Pl laid hasty A/Tk minefield.	
BENOUVILLE	11		River ORNE Br completed. 2 Pl minelaying and searching CHATEAU DE BEAUVILLE buildings for booby traps. Lt McColl & Ralph, and 14 O.R's joined Company as reinforcements.	
"	12		Major L. Scott-Bowden takes Command of Company. 1 and 3 Pls recce tank forward routes and roads. Company start laying Le-Homme minefield (over 5750 A/Tk mines).	
"	13		LE-HOMME minelaying completed. Clearing tracks for tanks.	
"	14		Minefield primeter wire completed. BEUVILLE minefield laid (1275 A/Tk mimes).	
"	15		Work on tank routes and roads. Laying silent sentries (improvised trip flares) in front of FDLS.	
"	16		Construction of tank tracks from BENOUVILLE to BEAUVILLE completed. Minefield at Bde HQ laid (1250 A/Tk mines). Enemy minefield swept and found to be dummy.	

Wt.47724/993 2,000,000 3/43 W. H. & S. 51/6375

WO 171/1604
Intelligence/war diary
246TH FIELD COMPANY RE

Month and Year June 44   Commanding Officer Maj R.M.S. MAUDE RE

Place	Date	Hour	Summary of Events and Information	References to Appendices
FRANCE	6		3 Div landed on Beaches of France north of CAEN at 0720 hrs. Coy deployed as follows:- No 1 Pl. 2 Secs on White Beach } for clearance of forward routes 2 Secs on Red Beach ∫ through BMA and main lateral to proposed Bridging site at BENOUVILLE. No 2 Pl. 4 Assault Demolition teams and 2 mine Clearance Teams with 2 E YORKS and 2 Mine Clearance Teams with 1 SUFFOLK. No 3 Pl. As above with respectively 1 S Lan R and 1 SUFFOLK. The assault was successful and opposition lighter than expected but mortars and shell fire on the beaches caused casualties and congestion for some hours. By the evening the company was assembled in the southern edge of ST AUBIN prepared to move to the bridge sites when they were cleared. The Bridges were captured intact by 6 Airborne Div. By midnight casualties appeared to be 12 Wounded including	

SHEET 2

Month and Year June 44   Commanding Officer Maj R.M.S. MAUDE RE

Place	Date	Hour	Summary of Events and Information	References to Appendices
FRANCE	6		1 Sergeant and one L/Sgt and six sappers missing. (Four of these returned by D3)	
	7		After a fairly quiet night the coy stood to at dawn and was employed in clearing routes of mines in the areas between COLLEVILLE and ST AUBIN. During the night 2 pl constructed a Class 40 Raft across the river ORNE 200 yds south of the RANVILLE Bridge. This raft was not used.	
	8		No 1 Pl replaced No2 Pl at raft site and worked on booms and approaches. Some mortar and shell fire, especially during the night and caused trouble and the raft was damaged by a direct hit when all troops had withdrawn. No 2 Pl reorganized and rested with No 3 Pl, and the Coy moved to an area south of COLLEVILLE where they dug in and prepared a defensive role to protect Div HQ if necessary. No 3 Pl constructed a water storage plant in COLLEVILLE.	

WO 171/1606
Intelligence/war diary
253RD FIELD COMPANY RE

Month and Year June 1944   Commanding Officer Major J.P. ASHER R.E.

Place	Date	Hour	Summary of Events and Information	References to Appendices
	1st		Unit split up into craft serials situated at various Concentration Camps. HQ at Camp J 2 Red nr Brighton, Sussex.	
	3rd		D-Day personnel depart concentration Camps for embarkation hards - HQ under comd Capt. E.J. HOADLEY - Officer i/c Craft - embark SHOREHAM 1400 hrs. Move direct to sea.	
	4th		Arrive NEWHAVEN 0830 hrs. On board for remainder of day.	
	5th		Notification of 'D' Day as 6th June. Maps issued and final preparations made. Cruising on Channel off coast for remainder of day and overnight.	
	6th		'D' Day - H 0725 hrs. Unit land at various H + times during the day. HQ land at Red Beach near Hermansville 1215 hrs. 3 ton office truck strikes A/T mine near beach exits. Arrive RV with OC Unit before HERMANSVILLE 1430 hrs.	
			No. 1 Platoon suffer casualties on landing at 0950 hrs - 5 ORs. wounded by mortar fire.	
			Nos. 1 & 2 Pls. employed on route clearance with 1 NORFOLKS and 2 WARWICKS respectively under comd 185 Inf. Bde.	
			No. 3 Pl. land on Queen White Beach with 2 RUR at 1300 hrs mounted on bicycles. This Pl. held in reserve under comd 9 Br. Inf. Bde.	
	7th		Casualties - No. 1 Pl. 5 ORs. No. 2 Pl. 1 OR. TOTAL – 6	
			After quiet night moved off to COLLIEVILLE-SUR-ORNE 1230 hrs. Nos. 1 & 2 Pls continued route clearance in advance of 185 Inf. Bde. No. 3 Pl. jion HQ at this location 1800 hrs. Digging in - preparing for counter attack which did not materialize. Casualties/......	

22293 Wt. 33096/1140 1,000m 12/40—McC & Co Ltd-51-8212 Forms C2118/22

Month and Year June 1944   Commanding Officer Lt. Col. G.P.L. ON, OBE.

Place	Date	Hour	Summary of Events and Information	References to Appendices
DITCHLING	1st		Bn. HQ and "D" Coy. moved to Camp J.1. at MIDDLETON, Nr. DITCHLING, this morning; part of "C" Coy. also moved to this Camp, while "C" Coy. HQ moved to Camp J.2. This completed marshalling into craft loads. - A lovely day, except for slight showers in the morning.	P.A. Carrilogh
"	2nd		The Commanding Officer joined Bn. HQ in Camp J.1 having completed the briefing of the Detachments marshalled in the London Area.	P.A. Carrilogh
SHOREHAM	3rd	1000	Bn. HQ embarked on L.C.T. 337 about 1000 hrs. at SHOREHAM. "C" & "D" Coys. also embarked during the course of the morning, at the same place. The day is spent moored in the Harbour. In the evening the LCT Convoy sailed from SHOREHAM and anchored off NEWHAVEN.	P.A. Carrilogh
NEWHAVEN	4th		Owing to a strong wind, operation OVERLORD was postponed 24 hrs and the LCT Convoy tied up alongside in NEWHAVEN+during the course of the morning. Baths and showers were arranged in the Naval Quarters and in the afternoon those who wanted went to Camp J.2 for 2½ hrs where an excellent meal was provided. Another lovely day.	P.A. Carrilogh
"	5th		The Newhaven Convoy moved out during the course of the morning and lay at anchor off the port. Shortly after mid-day, it weighed anchor and sailed for the ISLE OF WIGHT, where the Main Convoy formed up and sailed. Operation OVERLORD is on.	P.A. Carrilogh

Wt.?7724/993 2,000,000 3/43 W.H. & S. 51/6375

SHEET 2

Commanding Officer Lt. Col. G.P.L., OBE.

Place	Date	Hour	Summary of Events and Information	References to Appendices
HERMANVILLE-SUR-MER	6	0725	H hour was 0725. The first detachment of the Bn. to land was the Traffic Control Party, 4 Officers and 9 ORs., under the 2 i/.c., Major H.M.F. Langley. This party landed on QUEEN White Beach at H + 20 and were responsible for controlling the traffic through the Beach Exits. "A" Coy., under Command 8 Br. Inf. Bde (The Assault Bde) landed between H + 20 and H + 120. On the Beaches they came under heavy mortar and arty. fire and suffered a number of casualties. No.1 Pl. gave some useful assistance to 41 Royal Marine Commando in clearing houses on the front, and Lieut. Betts, the Pl. Comd., was wounded in the leg. On the Left, No.3 Pl. (Lieut. A.J. Milne), on reaching the second lateral, came under fire from an A/Tk. gun and suffered serious casualties, only one Carrier and 11 men escaped unwounded. "C" Coy and two Pls. "D" Coy, under Comd. 185 Inf. Bde. (the Follow-Up Bde) landed shortly after H + 240. At this time, the Beach Exits were all temporarily closed and the Beach became very congested. The Two Bn. HQ vehicles only just managed to get ashore as the tide was beginning to fall and the LCT could not wait on a falling tide. After some delay on the beaches, which were being intermittently shelled, one of the exits was opened and tpt started moving inland. On reaching HERMANVILLE-SUR-MER, about 1300 hrs., Bn. HQ was temporarily established first in the Square and then in the grounds of a nearby house, whilst the Commanding Officer went forward to visit "A", "C" and "D" Coys. now in action. There was slight excitement in HERMANVILLE, due to snipers and also on account of the shelling of the Div. HQ area - Not far distant.	P.A. Carrilogh
		1800	At 1800 hrs. Those at HQ listened to the BBC News of the Battle and at 2100 hrs to the King's speech.	

Wt.47724/993 2,000,000 3/43 W. H. & S. 51/6375

contd Sheet 3.

SHEET 3

Commanding Officer Lt. Col. G.P.L , OBE.

Place	Date	Hour	Summary of Events and Information	References to Appendices
HERMANVILLE	6	2200	At about 2200 hrs. Bn. HQ moved up to the vicinity of Div HQ, now established at COLLEVILLE-SUR-ORNE, where it spent a comparatively quiet night. During the late afternoon and evening, "A" Coy. established a defensive M.G. Belt along the line HERMANVILLE-SUR-MER - COLLEVILLE-SUR-ORNE. One Pl. of Mortars went into action at Bn. HQs and One Pl. about a mile away on the left flank. "C" Coy. protected the right flank of the KSLI during their advance to BEUVIELLE, with two Pls. established on the right of the Main Rd. HERMANVILLE - BEUVIELLE. During this phase, Lieut. Dixon's Pl. (No.9) successfully supported an attack by a Coy. of the KSLI against a 4 gun battery, which was holding up the advance from the PERIER-SUR-LE-DAN AREA, under the Command of the Pl. Sgt., Sgt. Rawling, as Lieut. Dixon was hit, and later died, of shrapnel wounds in the head. This Pl. then advanced to BEUVIELLE, the furthest point of our advance, and engaged an enemy M.G. posn, killing 10 men and taking one prisoner. No. 8 Pl. remained in posn on the Main Rd. on top of the ridge all night and were heavily shelled. No.7 Pl. remained in Bde. reserve. Sgt Rawling who personally killed 3 German & was later wounded was recommended for the MM. Casualties. Officers - 240154 Lieut. H. Dixon. "C" Coy. Died of wounds in the A.D.S. 278352 Lieut. R.B. Betts, "A" Coy., Wounded in the leg. 1 O.R. Slightly Wounded - remains at duty. Other Ranks. "A" Coy. 2 Killed. 20 Wounded. 7 Missing. "C" Coy. 3 Wounded. "D" Coy. 1 Wounded. Weather - a glorious day, but there was a slight swell on the beach and landing conditions were not ideal.	P.A. Carrilogh

Wt.47724,993 2,000,000 3/43 W.H. & S. 51/6375

WO 177/688
Intelligence/war diary
8TH FIELD AMBULANCE RAMC

Month and Year June 1944   Commanding Officer Lt. ?L D.M. AHERN

Place	Date	Hour	Summary of Events and Information	References to Appendices
UK	1 June		Unit marshalled in PORTSMOUTH area with main residue at ALDERSHOT.	Nubben
PORTSMOUTH	5 June		Embarkation of unit (less residues) completed	Nub
NORMANDY	6 June	0745 hrs.	Landed under coma 8 Pre Inf Bde.	Nub
			Preparation and plans for the assault and experiences of the unit are given in offices A B and C.	
COLLEVILLE		1300hrs	ADS est in a farm and its land NORTH of COLLEVILLE.	Nub
			Per Evaluation to 20/21 FDS commenced.	
		2000hrs	Evac from 6 Airborne Div Commenced. CCPs est EAST and WEST of RO ORNE at BENOUVILLE	D.
COLLEVILLE	7 June		Evac from secs and 6 Airborne Div. Evacuation was either to CEP n FDS according to the situation prevailing at the time.	Nub
			In the evening secs were withdrawn from bus.	
COLLEVILLE	10 June		B Coy lot at CAZELLE in 8 Bde area.	Nub

22293 Wt. 33096/1140 1,000m 12/40–Mcc & Co Ltd-**51-8212** Forms C2118/22.

WO 177/690
Intelligence/war diary
9TH FIELD AMBULANCE RAMC.

Month and Year June 1944   Commanding Officer Lt. Col. E.H.P. LAEN. RAMC.

Place	Date	Hour	Summary of Events and Information	References to Appendices
DROXFORD	1		Unit already split into craft loads and submarshalled into various camps in "A" Marshalling area.	
	3		LCT craft load embarks late in the evening.	
	5		LCI craft loads embark, a delay of 24 hours having held up embarking.	
	6		Crossing of Channel – rough – many personnel sick.	
			Advance party, with Capt Hutton, land at 1150.	
			LCI craft loads landed at 12.00 hrs on Queen White beach immediately opposite Assembly Area and marched to Assembly area without incident. Cpl Yeudall of 26th Fd. Hygiene Section wounded by mortar fragment while returning to beach.	
			Assembly area located at road junction 080809 – sheet St. Aubin.	
			LCT Craft load landed at 13.30 at junction of Red and White beaches. Heavy seas resulted in Cpl. Riley – NCO i/c Wheeled stretcher party – being swept away. Believed to have been picked up by Navy.	
			Party mortared while marching to Assembly Area. Pte. Meadows hit by splinter in buttock. Q.M. left on beach to guide in arriving vehicles.	
			All marching personnel rendezvoused at Assembly Area with the above exceptions. Assembly area in LION-SUR-MER.	
			It was decided that the ADS would have to open in Assembly Area as there was delay in taking objectives. Sections passed through Assembly Area and reported to Battalions as under:	

Wt.52938/1102 660M. 2/44 W.H. & S. 51-9071.

SHEET 2

Place	Date	Hour	Summary of Events and Information	References to Appendices
			A.1 - Capt Riley to 1 KOSB.	
			A.3 - Lt. Lewis to 2 Lincs.	
			B.5 - Lt. Searle to 2 R.U.R.	
			ADS established in Church with personnel in neighbouring gardens.	
			HQ. 9 Br. Inf. Bde. hit by a bomb about 1600 hrs and Brigadier and several casualties brought into ADS. All tide 1 vehicles (less 1 Jeep and A3 15 cwt lost on beach) reported during evening.	
			Slight bombing during the night - probably due to houses on fire in area. Snipers active in area - but appeared to respect Red Cross Evacuation of casualties to CEP.	
	7		Moved to new location in HERMANVILLE during morning. Snipers still active. Relatively few casualties coming in. Site of ADS in wooded park with 20ft pits dug by Germans in use as treatment centre.	
			Slight enemy air activity during the night.	
			2 LINCS, with attached section, switched to 8 Br. Inf. Bde.	
			front and ordered to evacuate to 223 Fd. Ambulance.	
			Vehicles due to land Tide 3 - 2 x 4 Stretcher Amb. Cars and	
			1 x 15cwt Water Truck failed to land. Subsequently learned that	
			the ship carrying them was sunk.	
			cont.	

Wt.52938/1102 650M. 2/44 W. H. & S. 51-9071.

WO 177/830

Intelligence/war diary

223RD FIELD AMBULANCE RAMC

Month and Year June 1944   Commanding officer Lt. Col. J.A.D. JOHNSTON. MC RAMC.

Place	Date	Hour	Summary of Events and Information	References to Appendices
CHAILEY SUSSEX.		1	The large portion of the unit leaves this location for Camp J2 where it arrives at 1225 hours.	Dr
CAMP J2		2	Individual rations etc. for operation OVERLORD are drawn.	Dr
		3	The major portion of the unit proceeds to Newhaven and embarks on LCTs and LSIs. The night is spent in harbour.	Dr
NEWHAVEN		4	The craft proceed to anchorage outside Newhaven.	
AT SEA		5	The weather deteriorates, there is rain, high seas, and wind, making life on board very uncomfortable. During the afternoon, the craft sail on operation OVERLORD. Heavy seas are shipped by the open craft and sea-sickness is the rule even though alleviated by hyoscine.	Dr
				Dr
		6	Sleeping on board is awkward and the men cannot rest as they should since water swills about in the decks of the open ships and spray repeatedly drenches them. During the early daylight hours of this (D)Day the coast of France is sighted and landings begin. Enemy opposition in the form of mortar fire and shell fire is encountered both at sea and on the beach, but despite this, all personnel and vehicles of this unit scheduled to land on this day actually did so. By 1200 hours, HQ Coy, B Coy, and Transport are assembled and advance to Hermanville sur Mer, north of Caon, where an ADS is established and the evacuation of casualties begun. This ADS is sited in the avenue of a chateau, and is under canvas, utilising two very large pits dug by the enemy, which provide excellent cover.	Detail of vehicle loads of equipment carried on the man attached on Appendix I.
			Forward of this, Nos 1, 2, and 3 sections are draining the casualties of their respective battalions. The local population afford us quite a good, friendly, if rather reserved, reception. Since it is impracticable to move the ADS further forward, evacuation is carried out largely direct from CCPs to 21 and 22 F.D.Ss which are only half a mile behind the ADS Despite this, the casualties passing through the ADS on this day numbered 35.	Dr
HERMANVILLE SUR MER		7	The early morning saw casualties still coming through, fairly fast, and a good deal of Luftwaffe activity mainly directed at the beaches. All battalions of 185 Inf Bde had now suffered fairly heavily in their attempts to reach their	Dr

Wt.47724/993 2,000,000 3/43 W.H. & S. 51/6375.

WO 171/423
Intelligence/war diary
3RD BRITISH INFANTRY DIVISION
PROVOST COMPANY

Month and Year June 1944   Commanding Officer Capt S.D. SHILLINGTON DAPM.

Place	Date	Hour	Summary of Events and Information	References to Appendices
A & J Marshalling areas	3		Embarkation effected from the various camps, the Coy being dispersed on 36 different landing craft spread over the first three tides.	Appendix "A" SDS
	4		D-Day postponed 24 hours.	SDS
Aboard craft	5		Craft sailed – fair sea running.	SDS
Aboard craft FRANCE	6	07.25 (H. hour)	D-Day sections touched down in the following order No. 6. (att 8 1.B.) at H + 45, No.4. (att 185 1.B.) at H + 185, No 5 (att 9 1.B.) at H + 240, Det No.3. (Bridging) at H + 120 and elements of Coy HQ (wil 21/c) at H + 185, together with NCOs 1, 2 & 3 sections. all landed safely on Beaches but losses were sustained in transport 4 untangles (hit by shrapnel) and three jeeps (drowned).	SDS
		11.30	Coy HQ was established at Rd June 075802 (sheet 7E/5 (1:80.000 France)).	SDS
		22.30	Coy HQ moved to map Ref 079789/sheet 7.5/1 (1:80.000 France) all section NCOs reported to previously planed RV points	SDS

*5973. Wt.22661/1499. 300M. 8/42. 6253. Wt.38126/345. 200M. 11/42. Wy.L.P. Gp. 656.

SHEET 2

Commanding Officer Capt S.D. SHILLINGTON DAPM.

Place	Date	Hour	Summary of Events and Information	References to Appendices
France	(D71)		and then ensured that the passage forward of the assault Transport and supporting Tanks was controlled. By the end of the day one section sqt had been evacuated to the F.D.S. and one L/cpl. reported as missing. 2nd Tide personnel were unable to land according to plan. Coy HQ location unchanged Bde sections carried on with the routing of Bde maintence Routes, Patrols, Traffic Routs in Bde areas and controlled the general advance of maint vehicles to the forward areas and Bde "A" ech areas Further landings were made by Div Troops and supporting Troops of Bdes. Traffic Points within the B.M.A. were warned by NCOs of the Coy owing to the number of casualties to NCOs of the beach Pro Coy.	SDS
		13.00	2nd Tide personnel, with remainder of coy HQ and section load carrying vehicles commenced to land on the beaches.	

*5973. Wt.22661/1499. 300M. 8/42. 6253. Wt.38126/345. 200M. 11/42. Wy.L.P. Gp. 656.

UNITS ATTACHED TO BRITISH 3RD INFANTRY DIVISION FOR THE ASSAULT

WO 171/623
Intelligence/war diary
27TH ARMOURED BRIGADE HQ

Month and Year June 44				Commanding Officer Brig. G.E. PRIOR-P?

Place	Date	Hour	Summary of Events and Information	References to Appendices
PETWORTH	1		First Tide parties of all units moved to marshalling areas. Staff Offrs of this HQ moved to HQ 3 Br Inf Div at DENMEAD. BM visited Staffs Yeo in their marshalling area, and Bde Comd returned from LONDON.	
DENMEAD	2		Bde HQ remained at DENMEAD all day. Final preparations (incl waterproofing Stage 2) were carried out in readiness for embarkation.	
DENMEAD			Certain unit parties loaded on LST today.	
	3		Bde HQ moved out from DENMEAD and embarked on GOSPORT hards at 1500 hrs. Bde Comd and BM remained ashore for one additional night. Embarkation was rather slow owing to the grounding of LCTs and one or two vehicle failures at the foot of the ramp.	
STOKES BAY	4		Made fast all day off STOKES BAY. Operation postponed 24 hrs.	
SOUTHAMPTON	5		Weather deteriorating.	
FRANCE	[6		Sailed from SOUTHAMPTON at 1750 hrs in a fresh breeze which increased as darkness fell.	
			Arrived off the lowering posn at 1100 hrs after a rough but otherwise undisturbed voyage. Touched down at 1200 hrs - an hour early. The beach was very much congested, but was neither bombed or shelled at that time. Moved to RV at 072802 where the Bde Comd and BM who had landed earlier were waiting. A rather sticky battle followed, progress was difficult and the day drew to a close with the Bde hemmed in with their backs to the sea and the canal and no contact with the Canadians on the right. Bde HQ passed the night just WEST of COLLEVILLE SUR ORNE.]	
COLLEVILLE	[7		Expected counter attack by armour did not materialize, so at 1000 hrs approx the advance was resumed towards CAEN, 185 Inf Bde supported by C Sqn Staffs Yeo reached the line COUVRE-CHEF - HEROUVILLE and there met stiffening opposition. At about 1600 hrs TIGERS with a Bn. of Inf were reported as approaching RANVILLE Br. Hasty readjustments were made and two Sqns of 13/18 H were despatched to held the crossing. By 1900 hrs the	

M3524/1218 1200M 10/41 H.B. & Co.Ltd. 51-1541.

WO 171/845
Intelligence/war diary
13TH/18TH ROYAL HUSSARS

Place	Date	Hour	Summary of Events and Information	Remarks and references to Appendices
NORMANDY FRANCE	[6		After 17 1/4 hrs sailing in roughish sea the Assault Bns. of 8 Inf Bde (1 S. Lancs and 2 E Yorks) touched down at H hour -0725 hrs with 'A' and 'B' DD Sqns touching down in QUEEN Sector RED and WHITE Beaches at H - 7 1/2 mins, with full naval and air support. Not all DD Tanks were able to swim and some which did were swamped by LCTs. Opposition on RED Beach was particularly strong. E Yorks suffering heavy casualties. Beach clearing operations not very successful and considerable delay experienced in getting off the beaches.	
			RHQ and 'C' Sqn. landed at H + 45 mins on WHITE beach to find beaches still uncleared and considerable shelling and mortar fire encountered. Eventually by 0900 hrs tanks were able to pass through and marry up with their Inf and enemy defences were mopped up after considerable shelling and sniping from the houses.	
		0930	1 S Lancs Regt captured HERMONVILLE-SUR-MER with 'A' Sqn. in support - little opposition.	
		1130 hrs	Lieut Coker, with 5 tanks 'B' Sqn. began to support 1 SS Bde ever onto Bridges at BENOUVILLE over the CANAL-DE-CAEN and the RIVER ORNE, which were taken over intact from 6 Airborne Div. Two 'B' Sqn. Tanks knocked out by 88 south of BENOUVILLE.	
		1200	'C' Sqn, with 1 Suffolks captured locality Morris at COLLEVILLE-SUR-ORNE and prepared to support Inf onto locality Hillman 1/2 mile south. Enemy in Morris surrendered with white flag 40-50 prisoners. Considerable opposition from Hillman and progress slow. First attack failed.	
		1545	Locality SALE, S.E. of OUISTREHAM captured by 'B' Sqn. and 2 E. Yorks. Locaility "Daimler" 1 mile S.E. Strongly held. Naval support asked for but could not be given.	
		1600	30-40 prisoners surrendered from Sale.	
		1700	Hillman still intact. 2 Tks of 'C' Sqn knocked out by anti-tank gun. Staffs Yeo take up position to cover Hillman. RHQ in position 1 mile S.E. HERMONVILLE in orchard.	
		1900	Daimler captured by 'B' Sqn and E. Yorks.	
		2000	Tank State - 'A'-6; 'B'-10; 'C'-13; R.HQ-3; Recce - 8. 31 Vehicle casualties.	
		2100	Hillman captured and consolidation begun.	
		2200	RHQ moved to southern outskirts of HERMANVILLE. Sqn drawn in to harbour. Losses inflicted on enemy estimated at-- Killed 60, captured 40, two 88 mms destroyed, 1 Staff car captured, two m/cs destroyed. Own casualties; 12 ORs killed, 12 wounded. Capt. Denny, Lts. Jonnison, Harold, Anderson and Burgess and 78 ORs missing.	
		2300	General posn. 8 Br Inf Bde with the regt in sp reached all objectives by 2100 hrs, rather later than anticipated. 185 Bde held up on high ground North of Caen. 9(th Bde covering flanks against armd threats. Armour reported to the South and West, probably 21 Pz Div.]	

WO 171/862
Intelligence/war diary
1ST EAST RIDING YEOMANRY

Month and Year June 1944   Commanding Officer Lt. Col. T.C. WILLIAMSON DSO.

Place	Date	Hour	Summary of Events and Information	References to Appendices
Field	1 June		A Sqn and 1 Tp B Sqn embarked on LSTs at GOSPORT.	
	2 June		LAD and 3 Fitters M.14 Half Tracks embarked on LSTs at GOSPORT.	
	3 June		The remainder of the Regt. embarked on LCTs at GOSPORT.	
	4 June		The CO and IO embarked on HMS LOCUST, 9 Bde HQ Ship.	
			Owing to a gale warning the sailing was postponed for 24 hrs.	
	5 June		Lt. D.S. BELLMAN RHQ Tp Ldr was disembarked suffering from boils.	
			The convoy sailed for France at 1730 hrs.	
D Day	[6 June]	1315	LCTs came under fire from enemy coast guns. The craft withdrew out of range.	
		[1412	LCTs touched down and the tanks commenced to move across the beach to the assembly area at 073808.	
		1440	Arrived in Assembly Area.] Tanks dewaterproofed and took up posns as planned.	
		1730	Enemy posns as follows:- in strength in CRESSERONS, PLUMETOT, LION-SUR-MER in OUISTREHAM. 21 Pz Div has been identified as being in the area.	
		[1735	B Sqn has adv tps in the outskirts of LION-SUR-MER.] Four PW of 726 Gr. Regt 716 Inf Div have been captured by 4 Tp. Lt. GOODWIN was wounded when mounting Maj MATTHEWS' Tank to give him information.	
		1930	A Sqn arrived in assembly area and took over B Sqn posns. 1 Tp A Sqn destroyed one enemy half tracked carrier. C Sqn moved to area 070770. Destroyed one A Tk gun believed to be 88 mm and two light AA posns. C Sqn in this operation lost one Sherman and two men.	
		[2015	Regt. ordered to move via HERMANVILLE and COLVILLE to a concentration area at 084779.	
		2130	Moved to new posn.	
		2245	Arrived in new posn.]	
D + 1	[7 June	0400	Reveille. Quiet undisturbed night.]	
		0515	C.O. and Sqn Ldrs carry out a recce of high ground 0777 with a view to taking up posns there.	

M3524/1218 1200M 10/41 H.B. & Co.Ltd. **51-1541**.

WO 171/863
Intelligence/war diary
THE STAFFORDSHIRE YEOMANRY Q.O.R.R.

June 1944

VOLUME 54

1st   Tanks and personnel moved out to Marshalling Area at 0815 hrs. Reveille 0500 hrs. The remaining personnel were sealed in Camp Area.

2nd   All the remaining personnel of the Regt. moved out to camp J. 6. at 1200 hrs. arriving at approx. 1300 hrs by route via HAYWARDS HEATH, camp J.10 is sealed but provided with an excellent NAAFI and a cinema. Tanks remained in J.2. Everyone had a good rest.

3rd   At 1600 hrs the D + 2 and D + 4 personnel left J.6. to proceed to Marshalling Area D-Day vehicles and personnel in NEWHAVEN, leading tank leaving marshalling area at 1500 hrs. Loading commenced at 1800 hrs and was completed the same day.

4th   Bad weather made it impossible to sail on this day and the whole operation was postponed for 24 hours.
In the afternoon personnel returned to T.C.V. to J.2. where they had a hot meal and a shower and went back again.

5th   Reveille - 0700 hrs. Craft moved out at 0830 hrs and anchored about 3 miles outside the harbour. We finally sailed at 1230 hrs. Sea was rough and some personnel were seasick.

[6th   D Day

Touched down at 1030 hrs on White beach and had practically speaking a dry landing A terrible jam on the beach - where no organisation appeared to be operating and no marked exits were to be seen. The majority of our tanks remained stationary for approx. 1 hour. Spasmodic shelling and a considerable amout of sniping. Traffic control seemed non-existent and even after leaving the beach vehicles remained head to tail for long periods on the only available routes. It was then decided not to proceed to the arranged Assembly Area and Sqns were ordered to rally in the area of the X rds South of HERMANVILLE. In order to save time O.C.2 KSLI decided that his Bn. should proceed on foot instead of riding on the tanks. Porpoises were dumped in the Assembly Area.

The C.O. appreciated that the ridge in the vicinity of Pt. 61 was ground vital to us and ordered "C" Sqn. to seize it forthwith. They galloped for it and shortly after reported it clear of the enemy. At this juncture Comd. 185 Bde ordered "A" Sqn. to proceed on a special task in connection with the clearing up of the strongpoint HILLMAN which was still holding out. RHQ and "B" Sqn. then proceeded on the axis of advance. "B" Sqn. was engaged by an 88mm A/Tk gun from the right flank which destroyed 2 "Fascine" Tanks, 2 other Sherman IIIs and a Sherman V (O.P. tank) the M.O's half track. "B" Sqn. engaged and the gun was silenced. The CO then ordered "B" Sqn. to take up battle positions on the Pt. 61 feature with tasks to the S.W. in case an outflanking attack by enemy armour should develop.

"C" Sqn. was now engaged, by a Bty of 122 mm guns firing East from the wooded area around PERIER-SUR-LE-DANS, and temporarily held up. The KSLI were now fighting hard in BEUVILLE but the CO asked for a Coy. to clear up the wooded strip to our right flank. His request was acceded to by Cpl. Maurice and in spite of running the gauntlet the tank advance continued without further loss.

Nos. 1 and 2 Tps. "C" Sqn. and elements of the Recce Tp. moved on fast on the right flank and succeeded in crossing the natural anti-tank obstacle S.W. of BEUVILLE.

No.4. Tp. on the left was held up at the obstacle as there was no possible crossing in that area.

No.1. Tp. then succeeded in working forward into LEBISEY with the leading infantry. CO KSLI then decided to launch an attack on LEBISEY at 2114 hrs. No. It was at 1615! Recce Tp. now reported enemy tanks advancing North from the direction of CAEN. It was ab 1615!

CO asked for the immediate release of "A" Sqn. who arrived just in time to take up battle positions to the West of BEUVILLE. The enemy tanks advanced very fast and were engaged when they reached the Western end of the A/Tk obstacle. Two were K. OD and the remainder moved West into the wooded country in the direction of LE LANDEL Two troops "A" Sqn. moved across to our right flank and when the German tanks emerged No.1 Tp. engaged and destroyed four. Other enemy tanks swung still more to the West and moved fast for the high ground above PERIER-SUR-LE-DAN. "B" Sqn. ordered 3 17 pdr tanks and one Sherman III to engage and 3 more German tanks were destroyed. No other enemy tanks then from the woods.

Neither the 2 WARWICKS or 1 NORFOLKS were available to assist on the attack on LEBISEY and in view of the very heavy losses sustained by the K.S.L.I. in a lard days fighting Col. Maurice decided not to attack that night.

At last light the regiment rallied and leagured West of BEUVILLE but in spite of innumerable snipers in the adjacent woods we were not seriously disturbed the 3½ hrs in Leaguer.]

SHEET 2

Note In the encounter with enemy tanks only 2 hits were scored on our tanks and neither of them was put out of action. The enemy K.?d. one M.10 S.P. A/Tk. gun. We destroyed seven and K. OD two enemy tanks all Mk. IV Specials. Some of which were wrongly described as Mk. VI tanks owing to the additional armour plates fitted.

Our Casualties were Lieut. D.F. Alexander and Winter halder Killed.

Troopers. Rowse, Furnivall, Bradbury, Roberts, and Issott killed.

Cpl. Knight, Tprs, Bailey, Samuelson wounded.

Cpl. Ducker, Tpr. Wright, Cpl. Cowley, L/Cpl. Wyatt, Tprs.

Sugden and Harkness missing.

[7th D + 1

At first light the regiment less one Sqn. was ordered back to the high ground North of PERIER-SUR-LE-DANS and took up battle positions facing South and South West. "A" Sqn. remained in the area BEUVILLE and throughout the day supported attacks by 2 WARWICKS and 1 NORFOLKS, on LEBISEY. The enemy appeared to have reinforced strongly during the previous night and all the attacks were unsuccessful, the infantry suffering heavy casualties.

The ground to the East of BEUVILLE was unsuitable for the purpose of the required support and it was found that there were no possible crossing places of the natural A/TK obstacle between the main axis and the road.

BLAINVILLE - CAEN

185 Bde eventually decided to consolidate North of the obstacle No.1. Tp. "A"] Sqn. destroyed a Staff Car in the LE LANDEL area and machine-gunned a party of 10 Germans. The only survivor surrendered. They may have been manning two 105 mm S.P. guns which were formed intact and which had moved up during the night. [The remainder of the Regiment stayed in battle positions all day but although a few enemy tanks were seen near the Western extremity of the A/Tk obstacle shortly before last light they did not advance.]

We were shelled intermittently during the day but casualties were light amounting to one killed and two wounded.

Casualties No tank casualties.

Personnel – Trooper Gillingham killed

Cpl. Taylor and Tpr. Webster wounded.

[8th Location unaltered. Back at first light to Battle positions on Pt. 61 Range we were machine-gunned as we came out of out leaguer by Focke-Wolfs, but no damage was done. A certain amount of enemy movement was seen around LEBISEY, but it was discussed down through Gazelle towards ST CONTEST assisted by the Armd Bde.]

A small batch of POW Were brought in by Lt. Kennedy's Tp. "C" Sqn. And despatched to POW Cage.

[Now discovered Canadians had hardly advanced at all the 1st Day leaving our right flank completely exposed. Canadians apparently now making good progress South and a reasonable West to East line established.]

Echelon build up now commenced and HQ Leaguer formed North of the 61 Ridge IN the lower ground.

Pulled back at last light behind the ridge and leagured a short way in front of the "B" Vehicles. Casualties - Tanks NIL, Personal Sgt. Evans "C" Sqn. wounded.

[9th Location unaltered. Beaches again bombed in the night but AA defences now very much stronger. An intense barrage put up and searchlights in operation. Higher appreciation still appears to believe a large counter-attack by armour will try to cut us off from the Canadians, or in any case try to push round our Div. flank and secure the high ground on which we are sitting. At first light therefore we pushed up again to our position on Pt. 6l ridge. Little enemy movement was seen, but the 9th Bde Assisted by ERY managed to take CAMBBS. The CO went to watch the Battle with the Brigadier.]

Spasmodic shelling but only slight on our own position. Pulled back into same leaguer at last Night.

Casualties Vehicles - NIL, Personnel - NIL.

Dennis Manning the Recce Tp. Ldr. had trouble with his wireless set so changed tanks with Sgt. Watson and sent his own tank home by itself. It did not arrive in Leaguer that night.

[10th Location unaltered. Beaches again bombed in night and attacked by fighter bombers one small party only who were fortunate in brewing the whole of Sector Stores dump of ammo and petrol, which burnt hard the whole of the morning and caused dense volumes of black smoke. Apparently the whole of the Petrol and ammo were packed in one tight area. It was reported that parachutists dropped on PLUMETOT in the middle of the morning, but this later proved entirely untrue. Pulled back into same Leaguer at night.

Cas. Vehs. NIL. Capt Manning wounded Tprs. Smith "C" and the remainder of that Honey Crew less Cowell RECCE wounded L/C. Humphreys Recce killed L/C. Humphreys the DOL who had been killed returned across country to say that their tank had been KO near DOUVRES. Capt. Manning went to investigate and was sniped in the arm. We later found that the RADAR STATION had never fallen, and Bde had never told us. The enemy had driven straight up the main road to within 100 yds of the RADAR STATION and was KO at point blank range.

DEFE 2/53
Intelligence/war diary
1ST SPECIAL SERVICE BRIGADE

Month and Year June 1944   Commanding Officer Brig. THE LORD LOVAT DSO.MC.

Place	Date	Hour	Summary of Events and Information	References to Appendices
FRANCE 6th June	D Day		4 Cdo with Adv Bde HQ landed at LA BRECHE at H + 30. They were 500 strong and their objective was the coastal Bty at OUISTREHAM. 4 Cdo had suffered 40 casualties while landing including the CO. C Tp of the Cdo engaged the defences and gained the main coast rd, followed by the rest of the Cdo. Fighting French Tps led the Cdo towards OUISTREHAM, coming under by fire. They over ran the casino area and the assault on the Bty commended. After severe fighting the posn was taken. Casualties on both sides were heavy. Meanwhile Adv Bde HQ contacted the CO 2 Bn. E Yorks. R/T contact by Bde HQ was made with 6 Airborne Div and it was learnt that the brs which the Bde intended to use were intact. Bde HQ and 6 Cdo landed at 0840 hrs under hy gun and mortar fire. 6 Cdo took the lead when the rd was gained and the adv to the brs commenced. Progress was slow because of the marshy ground and enemy mortar fire. The forming up pt was reached in 1 hr, by which time 3 and 45 RM Cdos had landed and they caught up with 6 Cdo. They had suffered few casualties. The brs were reached at 1230 hrs and contact made with 6 Airborne Div. 6 Cdo crossed the brs and sent their cycle Tp fwd to capture LE PLEIN. Bde HQ halted E of the river br. 45 RM Cdo passed over the brs towards their objectives at MERVILLE and FRANCEVILLE PLAGE. 3 Cdo who had been held up, crossed the brs at 1530 and were diverted to protect Div. HQ. Thus the original plan was abandoned and the Bde comd decided to hold the high ground from MERVILLE to BREVILLE. 45 RM Cdo were ordered to remain at MERVILLE for the night. Bde HQ moved to ECARDE and 6 Cdo consolidated in LE PLEIN.]	

Wt.47724,993 2,000,000 3/43 W. H. & S. 51/6375

SHEET 2

Commanding Officer Brig. THE LORD LOVAT DSO.MC.

Place	Date	Hour	Summary of Events and Information	References to Appendices
FRANCE	D + 1 7th June		[4 Cdo re joined the Bde at 2000 hrs, and dug in at HAUGER they had suffered hy casualties in fighting during the day. At the end of the day, 3 Cdo were still detached. [At 0300 hrs 3 Cdo re joined the Bde. At 1200 hrs Maj. Gen Gale Comd 6 Airborne Div. visited Bde HQ and ordered 45 RM Cdo to take FRANCEVILLE PLAGE. The Cdo suffered hy casualties in the assault, and after bitter fighting withdrew to MERVILLE. Two Tps of 3 Cdo on loan to 45 RM Cdo joined them, after suffering casualties while silencing a gun bty. 45 RM Cdo were out of touch with Bde.	
[FRANCE	D + 2 8th June		The enemy attempted to penetrate the Div. area but was repelled. 6 Cdo were being mortared and a patrol was sent to clear BREVILLE. This was done, prisoners and weapons being captured. At 1900 hrs 3 Cdo moved to LE PLEIN to join up 4 & 6 Cdos. Enemy attempts to infiltrate were reported at 2130 hrs. This was prevented.] In the early hours, runners arrived at Bde HQ from 45 RM Cdo, who were still cut off. Before assistance could be sent to 45 RM Cdo, an enemy attack in force developed during which a Tp of 4 Cdo were forced to withdraw. Eventually a counterattack by 3 to infiltrate were prevented. 45 RM Cdo had suffered heavily during the day and they were withdrawn inside the Bde posns. It was decided to hold the ridge of ground from HAUGER to BREVILLE at all costs. A large-scale attack was expected. Bde HQ moved from ECARDE to LE PLEIN.]	
[FRANCE	D + 3 9th June		Infiltration attempts were made throughout the day. 45 RM Odo moved into posns in AMFREVILLE to complete a defensive ring round the high ground. The Bde was still isolated from 6 Airborne Div. GONNEVILLE and LE BAS DE BREVILLE were heavily shelled during the day, being likely enemy forming up points. FRANCEVILLE PLAGE was bombarded by rocket.]	

Wt. 47724, 993 2,000,000 3/43 W. H & S. 51/6375

WO 218/65
Intelligence/war diary
NO. 3 COMMANDO

Month and Year June 1944   Commanding Officer Lt. Col. P. YOUNG DSO MC.

Place	Date	Hour	Summary of Events and Information	References to Appendices
C. 18	1		Briefing of all ranks.	WJW
Camp	2		Briefing for Operation.	WJW
	3		Briefing for operation.	WJW
	4	1000	Church Parade for all Denominations.	WJW
	5	1030	Bridgadier The Lord Lovat, DSO, MC. addresses whole Brigade.	WJW
		1400	Unit embusses in TCVs and proceeds to WARSASH.	
WARSASH		1630	Unit embarks in LCI(S) 289, 290, 291, 292 and 293.	
AT SEA		1730	Flotilla slips and ties up at CALSHOT.	
		1900	Flotilla slips and ties up at STOKES BAY.	
		2130	Slip and sail in convoy with Force "S".	WJW
	6	0830	In convoy move to off beaches of NORMANDY. Sporadic shelling by enemy. Monitor and warship in area replying.	
		0905	Touch down after run-in, the last half of which was under shell fire. LCI (S) 289 and 290 hit near the beach – both in sinking condition. Some casualties in 6 Troop (LCI 290). Further casualties occur on beach. Beach under shell fire.	See Appx 'A' No 1
LA BRECHE			Commando form up under CO and move to first check point.	WJW
		0930	Bde 46 set DIS.	
		1000	Contact 45 (RM) Commando in Bde first FUP All troops in less one section of 6 Troop. Only one Vickers and one mortar. Area of FUP being mortared. Enemy rocket propelled projectiles land to WEST of FUP Lt Cowieson treated for wounds and sent back to beach. Major JBV Pooley MC joins, and reports his batman missing. He himself is suffering from blast.	WJW

M3524/1218 1200M 10/41 H.B. & Co. Ltd. 51-1541.

SHEET 2

Commanding Officer Lt. Col. P. YOUNG DSO MC.

Place	Date	Hour	Summary of Events and Information	References to Appendices
LA BRECHE	6	1110	Adjt contacts R.M. near COLVILLE. Posn just NORTH of COLVILLE had held up 6 Commando but now eliminated. Bde now pushing on with help of 13/18 Hussars.	WJW
		1200	45 (RM) Commando reach COLVILLE, followed by this Unit. COLVILLE BEING shelled desultorily.	WJW
		1230	Move on to Bridge - 1074 - 5 Troop and remainder hold up by snipers (one OR killed) C.O. meets Brigadier. Role now changed to deference of defence of BAS DE RANVILLE under Brigadier Powett with 6 Airborne Div.	WJW
		1530	3, 5, 4, 6 and some of 2 Troop across the bridge and taking up defensive posns at BAS DE RANVILLE. AO with Admin staff also arrive.	WJW
		1540	Lieut Wills arrives with one jeep.	WJW
		1600	Lieut A. Wardle reports 1 Troop HQ and remainder of 2 Troop crossing Brdge under smoke.	WJW
		1715	4 enemy tanks reported on contour SOUTH of cross roads 104727. Engaged by Airborne 3" mortars. 5 Troop have laid Hawkins 75 mines across the road running SOUTH from BAS DE RANVILLE.	WJW
		1800	Snipers reported in village. Sporadic shooting but no snipers found. Bde report Lieut Ponsford and 3 Troop in LE PLEIN with remnants of a Para Bn.	See Appx 'A' No 2 WJW
		1830	Tanks reported to have withdrawn from ridge to SOUTH, FOB directs 20 rounds on Enemy Infantry digging in at 092721, front edge of wood from HMS SERAPHIS.	WJW
		1900	Residue of 5 Troop under Cpl White report attack going in against 3 Div on West side of River ORNE. CO returns from visiting HQ of Brigadier Powett and reports R.U.R. landing by glider at 2130 hours tonight to relieve us. We are then to revert to 1 SS Bde. 4 Commando captured OUISTREHAM.	WJW
		2000	German fighter-bombers fly over one village – no aggresive action.	WJW
		2050	Gliders towed by D.Cs start to come in, (Troop carriers).	WJW
		2115	Large gliders carrying A/T guns and tanks coming in, towed by Liberators. Terrific fighter cover. Considerable LAA opposition from the enemy.	WJW WJWarde

SHEET 3

Commanding Officer Lt. Col. P. YOUNG DSO MC.

Place	Date	Hour	Summary of Events and Information	References to Appendices
BAS DE RANVILLE	6	2220	Bde want 2 i/c or Adjt to report to Bde immediately to recce night posn.	WJW
	7	0005	2 i/c returns. Unit to hand over to RUR and go to area SOUTH of Bde HQ and to be in posn by 0430 hrs.	WJW
			Activity from SOUTH. 3 Casualties from 1 Troop. Tanks and infantry reprted.	
		0230	CAEN area bombed by our heavies.	
		0315	C.O. 2 i/c and Troop Cmdrs leave by jeep to recce new area.	WJW
		0330	Unit leaves by road (march route) for new area.	
		0430	Troops allotted areas. HQ established at 114746 in orchard.	
		0800	ORQMS Wardle visits Bde HQ for posns of other units.	
		0900	Bde I.O. reports some A/TK guns to be placed under command.	
		0915	B.M. and A/Tk Officer arrive. CO goes with them to site two guns, one with 4 Troop and the other with 5 Troop.	
		1000	Raid by enemy fighter bombers on beach area.	
		1015	Airborne Bty of 75 mm Fld Guns open fire from field next to our posn.	
		1100	4 ME 109's fly over – no offensive action.	WJW
		1300	Message from Bde - "2 i/c with two Troops yo support 45 (RM) Commando in their attack on FRANCEVILLE PLAGE. 4 & 5 Troops set off with 2 i/c, FOB and CO with party of RAMC under Sjt Spears.	See Appx 'A' No's 3 & 4 WJW
		1415	Enemy Bty ranging on our guns in adjoining field.	WJW
		1445	Shells and mortar bombs falling in our area.	
		1500	Reported - "tanks seen in numbers on SOUTH ridge SOUTH of RANVILLE"	
			Stragglers of RUR and DEVONS coming back. 6 Troop astride road with two 6 pdrs in support. HQ in stand-to posns astride road. 1 Troop bring section into field. MTO mounted on jeep with, 55 Browning (camouflaged. under glider) covers gap between 1 Troop and HQ.	WJW WJW
		1515	Adjt visits Lord Lovat who has organised Bde HQ in better posns.	WJW
		1545	4 Tanks burning SOUTH of RANVILLE.	
			A coy of DEVONS join us for a short time and then go back to RANVILLE.	
		1615	RANVILLE reported in our hands. Shermans reported to be in action.	WJW

1622/PMEA/1–500,000–9/41.

DEFE 2/40
Intelligence/war diary
NO. 4 COMMANDO

Month and Year June 1944   Commanding Officer Lt. Col. R.W.P. DAWSON. DSO.

Place	Date	Hour	Summary of Events and Information	References to Appendices
[LA BECHE	6 June 44	0750	A fiercely opposed beach landing during which No. 4 Commando took over the role previously allotted to an earlier wave of Infantry which had been pinned down by enemy fire; the storming of heavy fortifications at OUISTREHAM; street fighting through areas infested with snipers; a forced fighting march with men carrying up to one-hundred and forty pounds and finally, after a further eight hours the taking over of a defensive position which was to withstand heavy mortaring, repeated enemy attacks, shelling and dive bombing - these were the highlights of the first days of No. 4 Commando after their D-Day landing in FRANCE. The Commando, five hundred strong, landed in two waves from HMS Princess Astrid and the SS Maid of Orleans and touched down on RED QUEEN Beach, a mile to the WEST of OUISTREHAM, at LA BECHE. The original intention of the British landings had been for 8 Bde, which consisted of the Suffolks, East Yorks and South Lancs to take the beach and form a beach head through which No. 4 Commando was to pass and take the Gun Batteries at OUISTREHAM. The County Regiments, landing at 0750 hrs, found intense opposition from the strongpoint on RED QUEEN Beach and were pinned down by concentrated machine gun and mortar fire at the water's edge, some being in 2 ft of water when No. 4 Commando's first wave of LCAs went in at 0820 hrs. Mortar bombs were falling in and around the LCAs and as the Commando landed there were 40 casualties, including the Commanding Officer, Lt. Col. R.W.P. Dawson, who was wounded in the leg. Rapidly forming up under concentrated fire, No. 4 Commando fought their way from the beach to the forming up area, putting out of action several of the enemy strong positions and enabling Units of 8 Bde to pass through. 'C' Tp, under command of Capt. D.C.W. Style MC, (later seriously wounded), pushed past the East Yorks, who were lying at the water's edge, and successfully engaged about a dozen of the enemy in slit trenches and a few more in pillboxes, afterwards moving up in orderly fashion to the Assembly Area.]	KCW

Wt.47724/993 2,000,000 3/43 W. H & S. 51/6375.

SHEET 2

Commanding Officer Lt. Col. R.W.P. DAWSON. DSO.

Place	Date	Hour	Summary of Events and Information	References to Appendices
[LA BECHE	6 June 44		Lt. Col. R.W.P. Dawson moved forward to contact 2nd Bn. East Yorks Regt. and was wounded in the head. He was, however, sufficiently able to order the Commando to move off from the Assembly Area, relinquishing command of the Commando when the Second in Command passed him, saying that he intended, if it was possible to follow on behind. The Second in Command ordered the medical orderlies to give him some morphine. Col. Dawson was again seen on the road after the Battery had been taken, he was then sent by the Medical Officer to the BDS. On the evening of D plus 1 (7 June 44) Col. Dawson arrived in a Jeep at Commando defence positions at HAUGER, and stayed there until D plus 3 when he was ordered to be evacuated by the ADMS.	KCW
			'C' Tp waited for the remainder of the Commando to position itself, and then moved on behind 1 and 8 (Fighting Frenchs) Tps along the OUISTREHAM road to the Check Pt, being harassed by snipers and machine gunners in houses. Tanks greatly helped in clearing this opposition. From the Check Pt, 'C' Tp again took the lead and established a route to the Battery - The Commandos main task. Invaluable assistance was given to the leading Tp by a French Gendarme member of the Underground Movement, who helped the Commando to by pass other enemy strongpoints and reach their objective without unnecessary delay. Great help was also afforded the Unit by 4 Centaurs which gave cover from snipers. On arrival at major tank obstacles covering the inland side of the Battery strongpoint, and still under enemy fire, a search was made and two suitable bridges made. Here, a machine gun post and mortar position were silenced by PIAT fire.	
			Together with 'A' Tp, under command of Capt A.M.Thorburn, 'C' Tp then gave covering fire to enable 'D' Tp, (commanded by Major P.A.Porteous VC) to pass through 'E' Tp, (commanded by Capt. H.Burt) and 'F' Tp (commanded by Capt. L.N.Coulson), were then covered across. Continued sniping and mortar fire inflicted further casualties.]	

Wt.47724/993 2,000,000 3/43 W. H & S. 51/6375.

SHEET 3

Commanding Officer Lt. Col. R.W.P. DAWSON. DSO.

Place	Date	Hour	Summary of Events and Information	References to Appendices
[LA BECHE	6 June 44		The heavy rucksacks carried by the Commando had been dumped under HQ and the Mortar Section. Under orders by Unit wireless, mortar fire was brought to bear on the Flak Tower at the EAST of the Gun Battery and covering the whole area. The French Detachment, commanded by Capt. P. Kieffer, who was later evacuated severely wounded, over-ran the Cassino area on the WEST of the strongpoint. Then the assault went in on the Battery, all Tps moving according to plan, Heavy casualties were inflicted on the enemy who put up a very stiff resistance from their strong fortifications and cunningly camouflaged block houses commanding excellent fields of fire. The concrete emplacements had withstood severe Naval bombardment exceedingly well, and although out numbered, the Germans were in excellent defensive positions and had advantages of emplacements which had successfully withstood a terrific pounding from the sea and air. Several prisoners were taken when the Germans surrendered after their position had become untenable. Casualties on both sides had been high and after the engagement medical orderlies from opposing sides worked side by side succouring the wounded. One of the outstanding features of the defence of the Battery by the enemy was the careful sighting of their positions, and from the Commando's view point, the difficulty of finding points of enemy fire power during the mopping up stages, so well had the emplacements been prepared. But at least one point of Hitler's Western Wall had proved vulnerable under determined enough attack. No. 4 Commando then withdrew to the area where the ruck-sacks had been left and prepared for a strenuous and back breaking 9 miles march under constant sniping and mortar fire to HAUGER across the CAEN Canal and the River Orne. A stick of bombs dropped by a German plane caused no casualties, but mortar fire and sniping occurred at the bridges after the majority of the Unit had safely crossed them. It was here that Lieut. P.M. Mercer Wilson - the only]	KCW

Wt.47724/993 2,000,000 3/43 W. H & S. 51/6375.

SHEET 4

Commanding Officer Lt. Col. R.W.P. DAWSON. DSO.

Place	Date	Hour	Summary of Events and Information	References to Appendices
[HAUGER	6 June 44		casualty of the crossing of the bridges - was killed during a minor action against the enemy. Continuing unmolested the Unit reached the CROSS ROADS (121755) on the RANVILLE - SALLENELLES RD, where Brigadier The Lord Lovat DSO, MC, Commanding No. 1 Special Service Brigade was contacted. The Brigadier ordered the Unit to move forward and take up defensive positions in and around the village of HAUGER on the extreme left flank of the Allied landings and in direct contact with the enemy. Headquarters was established at a small farm in the village at 2130 hrs and troops were allotted their defensive areas and carried out digging slit trenches and weapon pits, a task which took until the early hours of D + 1 (7 June 44), the area having been reconnoitred by Major P.A.] Porteous VC.	
[HAUGER	7 June 44		It was to be four days and nights before the Unit had opportunity to rest. Proved to be fairly quiet, but the Unit continued digging in and the camouflage of weapon pits.] The digging in operations, tiresome and wearying as they were in the hard ground of many Tp areas, were however to prove of inestimable value. Lt. Col. R.W.P. Dawson had remained behind at the assembly area to have his wounds attended to and he rejoined the Commando remaining in command until 9 June 44 when Major R.P.Menday assumed command of the unit. [Two Sections of 'D' Tp, under Lieut. J.S. Hunter Gray, moved off to patrol in the SALLENELLES direction and made contact with a cycle patrol of No. 6 Commando. The patrol met with intermittent sniping during the afternoon, further patrols went out at night, but no contact was made with the enemy,] who, it later appeared, must have been regrouping to launch counter attacks. [At 2130 hrs 'A' Tp reported enemy moving in the fields about 300 yds from their position and trying to infiltrate through the open fields into the Woods in their rear. The enemy were engaged until darkness and after dark, a very thick hedge where the enemy was thought to be digging in for amortar or infantry gun position, was sprayed with K gun fire. MG and mortar fire were directed at]	KCW

Wt.47724/993 2,000,000 3/43 W. H & S. 51/6375.

WO 218/68
Intelligence/war diary
NO. 6 COMMANDO

Month and Year June/44   Commanding Officer Lt. Col. A.D. MILLS. ROBE? DSG. M.C.

Place	Date	Hour	Summary of Events and Information	References to Appendices
Camp C18	1 2&3		Commando remains in camp and continues to study Operational plans	
Camp C18	4		Operations postponed 24 hours.	
Camp C18	5		Commando embarks for 'Overlord' at Warsash 1/9	
In the field	6		Commando lands on QUEEN RED at 0840 hrs and marches to the positions at LE PLEIN taking en route one German battery 16 prisoners and killing 24. Our casualties Capt Pyman MC killed, Major Coade wounded, 4 O.R's killed and 28 wounded. Total casualties first day 3 and 32. Action of the Commando Grand. Appendix 'A'.	
In the field	7		Commando is mortared 4 casualties Capt Robinson and 1 Troop comes in and tells us Lieut Fazan killed. Lieut Stalker and 10 O.R's wounded. We bombard enemy position with aid of Major Seligmann. At noon 2 +Troop 3 Troop and 6 Troop attack gun battery after second bombardment. 8 prisoners are taken. See appendix 'B'. Signals and booby traps completed. Appd 'C & D'	

Wt.47724/993 2,000,000 3/43 W.H. & S. 51/6375.

APPENDIX 'A'

ACTION OF No. 2 TROOP

Date	Time	Report
6/6/44	1015	2 Troop assumes lead, and made contact with tanks (SHERMANS) at 084792.
	1020	2 Troop comes under mortar fire from area 065791. Leading tanks, left to liquidate mortars.
	1035	Leading section 2 Troop under fire from German L.M.G firing from road 085787. Position attacked and gun crew wiped out.
		Then came under fire from 2 LMG's in pill boxes and trenches.
		Major Coade wounded recceing for an attack on these. Were eliminated with help of SHERMANS which re-joined at this point. Casualties 1 GR killed, 1 OR wounded.
	1100	Advance continues —
		Supposed minefield crossed under enemy LMG fire. 2" Mortar smoke used to cover crossing (No casualties).
	1110	2 Troop contacts enemy in dug-out at 093786 who withdraw.
	1130	Lt. Cruden shot through sholder at 091793 on path. Sniper shot, believed killed.
	1135	Party of approx 12 enemy at 093783 (rd) on being attcked scattered and ran.
	1200	Forward guns of battery at 094778 observed by leading section.
		2 Troop attack immediately Battery was in hedge behind thick scrub.
		7 prisoners taken, others wounded and killed. Scrub did not delay advance of troop pushing on to ST AUBIN-D'ARQUENCY. Following troop to 4 further prisoners, where remaining guns of battery had been withdrawn (88 mm?). Advance continues down road 093767 to road junction 098753, where cycle troop was contacted, tp bridge - to LE PLAIN. The 7 prisoners handed over to Brigade HQ on EAST bank of river.
	1900	Commando sniped at from AMFREVILLE.
	2000	Patrol composed of 1 Sec 2 Troop sent to clear village.
	2100	Village cleared and patrol returns.

WO 218/70
Intelligence/war diary
NO. 10 TROOP, (INTER-ALLIED) COMMANDO

APPENDIX "A"

Month and Year June 44   Commanding Officer E.R.F. Langley, 2/Lt.

Place	Date	Hour	Summary of Events and Information	References to Appendices
Eastbourne	3.6		Static Troop HQ of 90Rs moved to location of Commando HQ.	WRLy
	6.6		Officer and 43 ORs take part on initial assault on Western Europe. As far as it can be ascertained when compiling the diary for June, the casualties were: - 1 Officer P.o.W. (Major Hilton Jones), 4 ORs killed, 3 ORs missing, 5 ORs wounded.	WRLy
	7.6		2/Lt. K.J. Griffith (322333) QORWK. posted to 3 Troop and reported for duty.	WRLy
	12.6		E.R.F. Langley serving with this Troop since formation is granted immediate Emergency Commission as 2/Lt.,posted to 3 Troop as Admin Officer vice Lieut. G.H.C. Emmet who is promoted Captain and taken on strength of Commando HQ retrospective 15.5.44.	WRLy
	20.6		Received notification that Lieut. G. Lane of this Troop is P.O.W. in German Hands.	WRLy
	30.6		2/Lt. Griffith, L/Cpl. Andrews, L/Cpl. Terry and Pte. Turner ordered to stand by to join B.W.E.F.	WRLy

Wt 43550/1614 560M 3/41 BPL 51/8792.

DEFE 2/48
Intelligence/war diary
NO. 41 ROYAL MARINE COMMANDO

Month and Year June 1944   Commanding Officer Lt. Col. E.C.E. PALMER, R.M.

Place	Date	Hour	Summary of Events and Information	References to Appendices
C.19 Camp SOUTHAMPTON WARSASH AT SEA	25 May to 4 June 5 June 6th June	 1515 2130 0745 0750 0825	(2 Hunt class Destroyers, 1 Fleet Destroyer). Briefing continued until June 4th. Unit embarks in 5 L.C.I. (S) at Warsash. Craft sail in convoy. Until 0745 hrs. when the coast became dimly visible and our naval craft could be seen firing on the land targets the sea passage had been uneventful. Message received by H.Q.L.C.I.(S) that the beaches were not under fire. Coastline now perfectly visible and Troop Commanders were able to identify their beach from previous study of low obliques during the briefing. The beach appeared a bit of a shambles. It was littered with dead and wounded and burnt out tanks and with flails flailing through wire and mines, bulldozers clearing gaps etc. The beach was quite obviously	

Wt.52938/1104 660M. 2/44 W. H. & S. 51/9071

SHEET 2

Month and Year June 1944   Commanding Officer Lt. Col. E.C.E. PALMER, R.M.

Place	Date	Hour	Summary of Events and Information	References to Appendices
At Sea	6th June	0825 0830 0840 [0845	still under fire as mortar bombs and shells were crashing down fairly plentifully. It appeared however that Red Beach was getting a better share of this fire than White. Shells started falling around the craft and several near hits were reaching ship damaging ramps etc. on some craft but caused no casualties to personnel. Due to land. Touch down about 200 yards out to sea on Red Beach with our proper Beach, White, 300 yds. away on the left. Whilst still coming in, Lieut. Colonel Gray had foreseen this and did his best to get the craft to slew right on to the proper beach which was in fact drawing less fire than Red. In the general confusion, however, his efforts were unsuccessful.] 'P' Troop commanded by Captain B.J.B. Sloley with a neucleus of Advance HQ moved swiftly across to White Beach and within about 5	 (2)

Wt.52938/1102 660M. 2/44 W.H. & S. 51-9071

SHEET 3

Month and Year June 1944

Commanding Officer Lt. Col. E.C.E. PALMER, R.M.

Place	Date	Hour	Summary of Events and Information	References to Appendices
	6th June	0845	minutes were off the beach almost complete. Within another 5 minutes a section of A.Troop with Captain C.N.P. Powell, DSO, Troop Commander had followed. Lieut. Colonel Gray then decided to move this body up to the first lateral and to find a more suitable spot for assembly.	
		0920	P. and A. Troops halted at road junction 080809 and waited there for the remainder of the Commando.	
		0940	By this time a dozen men of 'X' Troop/had joined up and reported that their Troop Commander Captain H.E. Stratford, M.C. had been wounded on landing and that they had also lost about 25 men killed and wounded, on the beach. 'Y' Troop reported that the 2 i/c Major D.L. Barclay had been killed and that the Signal Officer Lieut. A.G. Aldis M.M. was a casualty.	
			Lieut. Colonel Gray then decided to push on with the troops he had collected and P. Troop followed by Y. troop and	

Wt.52938/1102 660M. 2/44 W.H. & S. 51-9071

SHEET 4

Month and Year June 1944

Commanding Officer Lt. Col. E.C.E. PALMER, R.M.

Place	Date	Hour	Summary of Events and Information	References to Appendices
	6th June	0940	A. started to move into LION. Civilians contacted and gave information that the Germans had left at about 0700 hrs. that morning, and the French seemed quite pleased to see us. P. Troop were then ordered to push on and occupy the strongpoint, Y. following them in.	
		1020	B. Troop were contacted and reported that Capt. H.F. Morris Troop Commander was a casualty on the beach. Lieut. Colonel Gray then decided that since Force II had lost its commander, Major D.L. Barclay and both troop commanders he would take both forces under his own command and employ them as far as possible in their original role. P. Troop then reported held up by LMG fire and snipers from houses on each side of strong point. At the same time the S. LANCS contacted us and reported that they were held up by opposition from the strongpoint at Cross Roads 068816. B. Troop under Lieut.Sturgis	

Wt.52938/1102 660M. 2/44 W.H. & S. 51-9071

SHEET 5

Place	Date	Hour	Summary of Events and Information	References to Appendices
LION-SUR-MER	6th June	1020	were ordered to moved up road to Chateau as far as 065814 there to contact laterally the S. LANCS, A.Troop were to follow. This was with a view to ultimately outflanking the strongpoint. Wireless contact by this time had been established with 8 Br. Inf.Bde. The code word "TROUT" (contact S. LANCS) was passed. The FOB signalmen were all wounded on the beach and their sets destroyed, the FOB's own set was damaged hence no contact with naval support. FOO Lieut. Miller R.A. and party wounded on beach but R.A. Rep. Capt. J.C. Clough was up with HQ unable however to assist since the Centaurs attached had apparently been knocked out.	
		1040	P.Troop still held down. S. LANCS at this time were drawing mortar and M.G. fire and were having casualties.	
		1050	Lieut. Colonel Gray ordered Y. Troop to prepare to back up the S. LANCS and if possible to assault through them. Just	

*5973. Wt.22661/1499. 300M. 8/42. 6253. Wt.38126/345. 200M. 11/42. Wy.L.P. Gp. 656.

SHEET 6

Place	Date	Hour	Summary of Events and Information	References to Appendices
LION-SUR-MER	6th June	1050	at this time 3 Avre tanks contacted us and informed us that 8 Br. Inf. Bde. had put them under command to assist where required. They were immediately put in support of Y.	
		1100	Accordingly, firing their Besas the tanks moved up the road Y. Troop following. Withing 100 yards of the strongpoint, unidentified gun, which later proved to be a 50 mm PAK, opened fire at very short range and knocked out the first tank. Within 5 minutes all 3 tanks were put out of action and enemy mortars had ranged on Y. Troop. Y. Troop suffered casualties including Captain P.T.H. Dufton killed. The remainder of the Troop occupied the houses on each side of the road.	
		1140	B. Troop reported that they had pushed ahead as far as Cross Roads 062814 and that they had suffered casualties from mortar fire and from some unidentified mobile gun operating in area 059813 and that (temporarily) without some support on the	

*5973. Wt.22661/1499. 300M. 8/42. 6253. Wt.38126/345. 200M. 11/42. Wy.L.P. Gp.658.

SHEET 7

Commanding Officer Lt. Col. E.C.E. PALMER, R.M.

Place	Date	Hour	Summary of Events and Information	References to Appendices
LION-SUR-MER	6th June	1140	Chateau area they could not push on. The S. LANCS had not been contacted. Since no support was available our own 3" Mortars having expended all their ammunition on the strongpoint. B. Troop were told to remain where they were.	
		1300	Up to 1300 hrs. the position remained virtually unchanged with both sides sitting where they were engaging any targets that presented themselves. No Arty or other support was available. The LO (Lieut. Kay) was sent to 8 Br.Ind. Bde. to report this fact.	
		1310	A. Troop report that they had got as far as houses in area 065814 where they had been mortared and fired upon from the left flank. Capt.C.N.P.Powell DSO was a casualty. B.Troop at almost the same time reported that the enemy were counter attacking about 60 strong on the left flank with mortars and an infantry gun in support. Lieut.Colonel Gray	

*5973. Wt.22661/1499. 300M. 8/42. 6253. Wt.38126/345. 200M. 11/42. Wy.L.P. Gp.656.

SHEET 8

Commanding Officer Lt. Col. E.C.E. PALMER, R.M.

Place	Date	Hour	Summary of Events and Information	References to Appendices
LION-SUR-MER	6th June	1310	then appreciated that a counterattack on the commando might become general and decided to withdraw all Troops to the line of the lateral road running from the sea to the beach 070813 thence to road junction 067812 which was an easier line to defend.	
		1330	By this time B. Troop and a section of A. Troop had withdrawn to the line, 1 Section of A. Troop was missing. P. and Y. Troops conformed. X. Troop, the smallest in numbers was attached to Y. Troop. The general appreciation was that there was about 80 enemy in the strongpoint and 100 in the Chateau.	
			By this time the majority of casualties had been evacuated to the Beach by the 6 Jeeps which had landed at about 1000 hrs. The FOB's Jeep with the Bombardier and wireless set also arrived and contact was made with the destroyers. HQ moved from the Church to Orchard about 074813.	

*5973. Wt.22668/1499. 300M. 8/42. 6253. Wt.38126/345. 200M. 11/42. Wy.L.P. Gp. 656.

SHEET 9

Month and Year June 1944   Commanding Officer Lt. Col. E.C.E. PALMER, R.M.

Place	Date	Hour	Summary of Events and Information	References to Appendices
LION-SUR-MER	6th June	1500	Contact 9 Inf. Bde. who had landed at H + 6 hrs and had detached two Battalions to assist in coastal sector. 41 Cdo came under command the 9 Inf. Bd. and the Brigadier ordered the 5 Lincolns and a battalion of the RUR to complete the perimeter partly formed by 41's present positions to the sea; with the Lincos directly on 41's left.	
		1600	By 1600 hrs. the Lincos were in position with a dividing line inclusive to 41 road LYON-LUC-SUR-MER. German aircraft dropped 1 bomb which fell on a small track about 50 yards from the HQ cratering it and rendering it unusuable. (this was presumably unintentional).	
		1800	Between 1600 and 1800 hrs. there was intermittent mortar and shell fire from the enemy. The navy had carried out a shoot on the strongpoint and the Chateau between 1700-1800 hrs.	
		1930	Lieut. Stevens reported to HQ that he and the missing section of A. Troop had returned having been cut off in area	

*5973. Wt.22661/1499. 300M. 8/42. 6253. Wt.38126/345. 200M. 11/42. Wy.L.P. Gp. 656.

SHEET 10

Month and Year June 1944   Commanding Officer Lt. Col. E.C.E. PALMER, R.M.

Place	Date	Hour	Summary of Events and Information	References to Appendices
LION-SUR-MER	6th June	1930	065814. He himself on the way back had knocked out a german armoured car (presumably the mobile gun referred to) with a grenade. Except for sniping and LMG fire from the houses where Germans had been left behind, all was quiet during the rest of the light. Casualties for the day were approximately 140 killed, wounded and missing. Officers killed - Major D.L. Barclay, Captain P.T.H. Dufton. Missing - Lieut. J.C. Pearson and Lieut. A.G. Aldis, M.M. Wounded - Captain H.F. Morris, Captain H.E. Stratford, M.C. and Capt. C.N.P. Powell, D.S.O.	
LION-SUR-MER	7th June	1105	All quiet except for snipers and occasional shell fire up to 1105 hrs. [At that time 3 Heinkels with Spitfires on their tails suddenly swooped out of the clouds and dropped 3 sticks of anti personnel bombs one of which straddled HQ orchard killing the FOB Capt. P.C. Dixon RA and 2 men, and wounding	(3)

*5973. Wt.22661/1499. 300M. 8/42. 6253. Wt.38126/345. 200M. 11/42. Wy.L.P. Gp. 656.ss

DEFE 2/51
Intelligence/war diary
NO. 45 ROYAL MARINE COMMANDO

Place	Date	Hour	Summary of Events and Information		References to Appendices
Filed	6/30 June 44	-	45 RM Commando Summary of Events.	WHG	A
"	19 Jun	-	Operation "Jolly".	WHG	B
"	24 Jun	-	Operation "Charles James".	WHG	C
"	29 Jun	-	Operation "Vilen".	WHG	D
"	1/30 June	-	Arrivals & Departurs, Officers.	WHG	E
				W.H.G?Y.	
				Lt. Col. R.M.,	
				Conid 45 R.M. Comma?	

(3110) Wt 35842/1764 1000M 12/39 BPL 51/5684 Forms C2118/22

SHEET 2

SUMMARY OF EVENTS
45 R. M. COMMANDO

6 JUNE

0910 – 45 RM Cdo landed at LA BRECHE WEST of the R. ORNE as part of the 1 SS Bde. The Bde was to push inland and contact the 6 Airborne Div who were holding the bridges across the CAEN CANAL and the R. ORNE. By 1415 the Bde had reached the bridges over the CAEN CANAL and contacted the 6 Airborne. Snipers were proving themselves a nuisance in this area and while 45 RM Cdo was between the two bridges LT. COL. RIES was wounded in the left leg by a sniper and MAJ. CRAY took command of the Cdo. After crossing the R. ORNE 45 RM Cdo now swung NORTH to its objective, to clear the enemy out of FRANCEVILLE-PLAGE and hold a defensive position to the EAST of the village. On entering SALLENELLES the Cdo came under fire from a strong point in the area of the PIT 135773. As time was getting on the CO decided to by pass this position and push on to FRANCEVILLE. Word was then received from Bde not to proceed further than MERVILLE but to dig in and consolidate for the night.

ADM 202/304

Intelligence/war diary

5TH INDEPENDENT ROYAL MARINE ARMOURED SUPPORT BATTERY

Month and Year June 1944   Commanding Officer. Captain F.B. Marshall, R.M.

Place	Date	Hour	Summary of Events and Information	References to Appendices
EMSWORTH STOKES BAY	June 2nd 3rd	p.m. p.m.	Battery (4 Sherman & 16 Centaur Tanks & Crews) marshalled. Battery Embarked in 8 LCT(A)'s. Battery commander Major R.J. Freeman, R.M. Embarked in LCT IV.	
CUISTREHAN	6th	0720	"D" Day "S" Tp. (capt. J.D. Scott, RM) & "T" Tp. (Capt. E. Elliott, R.M.) landed on Queen Red Beach. Half "V" Tp. under Lt. John Pogson, RM & half of "W" Tp. under Lt. C.K. Brown, (S.A.U.D.P.) landed on Queen White Beach. Capt. J.L. Bryan, RM Troop Comdr. of "V" Tp. with 1 Shermen & 2 Centaur broke down a few hours sail from England & never reached France.	89
			Capt. L.H. Carnier, RA Tp.Comdr. Of "A" Tp. also broke down but his craft eventually brought him in on D+1.	
			"S" Tp. carried out several indirect shoots in support of 4 Cdo while partially immersed. Owing to an unexpectly rapid rise in the tide all three of Capt. Scott's tanks were drowned. Lt. A.C. Badenoch R.M. tank had a burnt out Clutch and was unable to leave the beach. This left only 1 Centaur in fighting order in "S" Tp. The two Centaurs of "V" Tp. under Lt. Pogson tore their waterproofing on going down the ramp and were drowned. The two centaurs under Lt. Brown were put off into water that was far too deep and also drowned. Lt. Brown and his guns crews had to swim ashore. "T" Tp. was the only Tp. to land complete. Capt. Elliott established communications with his FOO but these were broken immediately owing to causes unknown. All guns fired at direct targets on the run in. All Tps. were under fire before landing and "T" Tp. came under particularly heavy fire which caused 3 casualties among the Amn. No's when re-amunntioning L/Cpl. Youngaan was killed. "S" Tp. suffered one wounded casualty. Major R.J. Freeman & his H.C. came under very heavy fire immediately on landing at H + 45 and all were wounded. B.S.H. Betts & Cpl. West only received slight wounds but Major Freeman was wounded in the leg. He carried on for 2 days	

Wt 13474/1805 1,200,000 7/40 BPL 51-7171 Forms C2118/22.   cont/.... 2

SHEET 2

Commanding Officer Captain F.B. Marshall, R.M.

Place	Date	Hour	Summary of Events and Information	References to Appendices
OUISTREHAM	6th		but then had to be evacuated to the U.K. Brigadier Mears (C.R.A. 3 Brit Div) put Capt. Elliott and his guns under command 33 Fd. Regt., R.A. Capt. Elliott took up a position in support about 1 kilometre R.E. of HERMANVILLE (080800).	
	7th	a.m.	Capt. L.H. Carnier, R.A. with 1 Sherman & 2 Centaurs landed and joined Capt. Elliott. One of his Centaurs (C/Sgt. Davies) struck a mine and was practically imobilised and after reaching the HERMANVILLE position proceeded no further. Capt. F.B. Marshall, R.R. (2 i/c) landed a.m. and joined Major Freeman.	
		p.m.	"i" Tp. together with Capt. Garnier in his Sherman & 1 Centaur (Sgt. Allen) moved forward to a position south of HERMANVILLE (066784) beside the road HERMANVILLE-PERRIERS-SUR-LE-DEN. No targets were engaged except a direct shoot by capt. Elliott's Sherman on a sniper in HERMANVILLE Church Tower.	
	8th	p.m.	Major R.J. Freeman, R.M. was evacuated with the other wounded to U.K. Capt. F.B. Marshall, R.M. on orders form Col. A.J. Harvey, R.M. assumed command of the Battery. A party of 4 Officers (Capt. Scott, Lt. Badenoch, Lt. Pogson & Lt. Brown) and 50 OR's who had no operational tanks - including seven. No's who had been unable to return to U.K. owing to their craft catching fire- was formed on Queen Red Beach and established themselves in abandoned German dug-outs. They were attached to 101 Beach Group and assisted in unloading vessels on the beach.	
	9th	a.m.	Sgt. Cook in his Centaur which had broken down on the beach joined Capt. Elliott. Capt. Elliott's party now consisting of his own & Capt. Garnier's Sherman & 6 Centaurs moved forward to a position near Perriers - sur - le - Den. (055765) to engage enemy mortars. The FOO provided by 33 Fd. Regt. R.A. could not locate the mortrs and the Shoot did not take place.	
	10th		Good work was done by the Beach Party in unloading a record amount of Stores on the beach. Capt. Eliott's party failed to get a shoot owing to being out of range. It was impossible to move forward owing to the proximity of enemy tanks.	

Wt 13474/1805 1,200,000 7/40 BPL 51-7171 Forms C2118/22.

cont/.... 3.

DEFE 2/49
Intelligence/war diary
ROYAL MARINE ENGINEER COMMANDO

Month and Year June 44   Commanding Officer Major E.T. GILBERT RM.

Place	Date	Hour	Summary of Events and Information	References to Appendices
STEYNING	3		Lieut. M.R. McLaren to Canadian Military HQ p.m. 3 Jun.	
	3		Pe/x 106504 Mre C.H. Atkins awarded 1st G.C.B. w.ef. 3 Jun.	
	5		Pe/x 106706 Mre L.W. Hunter awarded 1st GCB w.e.f. 5 Jun.	
			<u>OPERATIONS IN FRANCE D-DAY</u>	
	6		RM Engn Cdo Detachment HQ 1 SS Bde commanded by Lieut. Denis Nevile RM disembarked H + 75.(Detachment consisted of 1 Lieut. 1 Sgt. 5 Cpls & 32 marines)	
			<u>RM L.C. O. C. U.</u>	
			Team 7 under command Capt. A.B. Jackson RM disembarked H + 20.	
			Team 8 under command Csm D.J.R. Marss RM disembarked H + 20.	
			Team 9 under command Lieut. D.J. Cogger RM disembarked H.	
			Team 10 under command L/Sgt. P.H. Jones RM disembarked H.	
			Team 11 under command Lieut. D.J. Smith RM disembarked H +20	
			Team 12 under command L/Sgt. K.M. Briggs RM disembarked H + 20.	

M3524/1218 1200M 10/41 H.B. & Co. Ltd. 51-1541.

SHEET 2

Month and Year June 44   Commanding Officer Major E.T. GILBERT RM.

Place	Date	Hour	Summary of Events and Information	References to Appendices
STEYNING	6		<u>Battle Casualties</u>	
			The u/m ranks killed in action 6th June, 1944.	
			Ch/x 104901 Mre HWG Rosson (RMLCOCU No 10).	
			Ch/x 109879 (T) Mre A. Evans (RM Engn Cdo Detachment attached HQ 1 SS Bde).	
			<u>Missing</u>	
			The u/m rank 'MISSING' Delieved seriously wounded 6th June, 1944.	
			Ex 4507(T) Cpl (Ty) Robert Clark (RM Engn Cdo Detachment attached HQ 1 SS Bde).	
			<u>Wounded</u>	
			The u/m ranks wounded 6th June. 1944.	
			Pe/x 102045 L/Cpl. F. P. Carolan (RM Engn Cdo Detachment attached HQ 1 SS Bde).	
			Ch/x 105451 Mre Edward Darby (RMLCOCU No.10).	
			Ch/x 103959 Mre K.W. Lewis (RM LCOCU No.9).	

M3524/1218 1200M 10/41 H.B. & Co. Ltd. **51-1541.**

SHEET 3

Commanding Officer Major E.T. GILBERT RM.

Place	Date	Hour	Summary of Events and Information	References to Appendices
STEYNING	6 (contd)		Ch/x 109879 (T). Mre A. Evans & Ch/x 104901 Marine H.W.G. Rosson D.D to Chatham Division RM 6 Jun 44.	
	6		Ex 4507 (T) Cpl (Ty) Robert Clark discharged 'Missing' to RM Depot, Lympstone, 6 Jun 44.	
	6		Lieut. R. L. Nicholson from HMS Apple done pm 6 Jun 44.	
	8		Course. Results. The u/m obtained qualifications as stated in No.49 Bomb Disposal Course at SME Ripon.	
			Lieut. HAP. Milligan RM - Above average	
			Ch/x 1442 C/sgt. W.M. Clifford - Above average	
			Ch/x 105568 Sgt. Roy Break - Above average.	
	10		The u/m rank wounded 10th June 1944.	
			Ch/x 109901 Mre. D.M. Greer.	
	12		Lieut. S. Richardson R.E. from HMS Apple done 12 Jun 44 (tempy attached to this unit from H.O.C.)	
	13		Major E.T. Gilbert RM to Co HQ on duty pm 13 Jun 44 returning on completion.	

M3524/1218 1200M 10/41 H.B. & Co. Ltd. **51-1541.**

WO 171/841
Intelligence/war diary
22ND DRAGOONS (ROYAL ARMOURED CORPS)

Month and Year June 44   Commanding Officer Lt. Col. G.H. GROSVENOR D.S.O.

Place	Date	Hour	Summary of Events and Information	References to Appendices
Normandy Frances	6	0730	3rd & 4th Troop B sqn (Lieut W. Shaw & Civil Burbidge) touch down on Mike sector, the location in some six foot of water. Enemy opposition so far not very great apart from small gun fire & a few shells. All tanks made shore safety and begin SWEEPING their allotted lane.	
		0800	3rd Troop B squadron finish sweeping their two lanes & having crossed the A.TK Ditch over which 2 Fasciurs had been laid rally at first lateral road.	AV
		0805	First Troop B squadron Lieut. I Hammerton) touches down & begin flailing two lanes each with two tanks, the fifth tank giving fire support.	AV
		0815	4th Troop "B" Sqn has now swept its	AV

Wt.47724/993 2,000,000 3/43 W. H. & S. 51/6375.

SHEET 2

Month and Year June 44   Commanding Officer Lt. Col. G.H. GROSVENOR D.S.O.

Place	Date	Hour	Summary of Events and Information	References to Appendices
Normandy Frances	6	0815	lanes having encountered an embankment of Belgian Box & German Teller mines & also much wire which tended to interfere with the motion of the rotar.	
		0820	2nd Troop B Sqn Touches down on Mike sector Rotar of our tank is blown off on craft just before touching down. An error of navigation on the part of the navy made this troop touch down on Mike 2 instead of Mike1 and in consequence the lanes were swept on this beach. M.G. opposition is engaged by tank without Rotar.	AV
		0830	2nd Troop B Sqn passes through sand dunes & on sweeping a further lane through a minefield two tanks become casualties due to	AV

Wt.47724 993 2,000,000 3/43 W. H. & S. 51/6375.

SHEET 3

Commanding Officer Lt. Col. G.H. GROSVENOR D.S.O.

Place	Date	Hour	Summary of Events and Information	References to Appendices
NORMANDY FRANCE	6	0830	to founding on mines. Mortar fire in this area is still very heavy and is engaged by these tanks immobilized in the mine field.	AV
AALIC		0840	Our 75 mm which has been a source of considerable annoyance has been knocked out by our of 2nd troop B sqn Tanks at 900 yards ranges.	AV
AALIC		0850	Troop Sergeant 2nd Troop B squadron in wounded by mortar fine & evacuated to RAP.	
AALIC		0855	1st Troop B squadron finishes its allotted tasks (i.e. Sweeping two lanes) & reports to 8 Beach GP. HQ for the allotment of any further tasks.	AV
AALIC		0900	Troop leader 2nd troop B Sqn. (Lieut. M. Barraclough) ditches his tank in attempting to cross a bridge on Sqn duties. Only two tanks (one without a motor survive in this troop	AV

Wt.47724 993 2,000,000 3/43 W. H. & S. 51/6375.

SHEET 4

Commanding Officer Lt. Col. G.H. GROSVENOR D.S.O.

Place	Date	Hour	Summary of Events and Information	References to Appendices
NORMANDY FRANCE	6	0930	Fourth Troop B Squadron having now cleared its allotted sections on the beach as well as the other lanes move off along first lateral. Owing to density of traffic movement because impossible and the troop pull off road into a garden to do some necessary maintenance on rotar & Chains.	AV
		Aalic	Second Troop B Squadron is still engaging enemy mortar fire & snipers in its sector.	AV
		1025 Aalic	Our tank of 2nd Troop, the only remaining one capable of flailing is sent to our sector to clear lanes which has so far not been completed. The remainder dismounted assisting REs to fill a water-logged ditch with rubble to make it passable for Traffic.	AV

Wt.47724 993 2,000,000 3/43 W. H. & S. 51/6375.

SHEET 5

Commanding Officer Lt. Col. G.H. GROSVENOR D.S.O.

Place	Date	Hour	Summary of Events and Information	References to Appendices
NORMANDY FRANCE	6	1030	Fourth Troop Continues movement to Bernieres sur Mer (TF/1 99 85).	AV
		1135	Third Troop B Sqn has so far found no trace of 2 cdn A and Bdr HQ under whose command they are now supposed to be.	AV
			A union at squadron R.V. & Troop leader goes off on his own to look for this Bde HQ.	AV
		1225	Fourth Troop B Sqn learns Bernieres sur Mer with tanks of 2 Cdn Armd Bdr to RV with I Inf Bdr (Cdn).	AV
	Aalic	1330	The remaining Flailing Tank of 2nd Troop B Squadron, now in hour sector is hrt by an anti-tank gun & put out of action.	AV
	Aalic	1600	Second, Troop B Sqn baron Sqn R.V. and lueets Bds coned I Cdn Inf Bde in BENY-SUR-MER who informs them that they are under his command as from now	

Wt.47724 993 2,000,000 3/43 W. H. & S. 51/6375.

SHEET 6

Commanding Officer Lt. Col. G.H. GROSVENOR D.S.O.

Place	Date	Hour	Summary of Events and Information	References to Appendices
NORMANDY FRANCE	6	1600	Progress of Fourth Troop is very slow due to extensive minefields & they have only reached a position just North of BENY-SUR-MER.	AV
		1610	Third Troop joins in column of Ins Bde in the advances on CARPLQUET (7F/16997).	AV
		1930	Fourth Troop goes into harbour approx 2½ miles NORTH of BENY-SUR-MUR.	
		2005	Second Third Troop B Sqn harbour at X Rds NE of Villous les Burnous (7F/1 0075) The Extent of the advances having been approximately two miles. B sqn H.Q. could not be located.	AV
	?lie	2330	1st Troop B Sqn having been unleased by (8) Beach GP HQ. Now gun into harbour with 4th Troop which they had previously colluded 2nd Troop remain in their location on the beach.	

Wt.47724 993 2,000,000 3/43 W. H. & S. 51/6375.

SHEET 7

Place	Date	Hour	Summary of Events and Information	References to Appendices
NORMANDY FRANCE			Their Tanks Casualties to Personnel – 1. O.R Wounded Casualties to Tanks – 2 Counts – Offs. 5 Y or Z Casualties.	 AV

Wt.47724 993 2,000,000 3/43 W. H. & S. 51/6375.

SHEET 8

Place	Date	Hour	Summary of Events and Information	References to Appendices
NORMANDY FRANCE	6	0735	D-Day : Four Troops of A Sqn & 2 Troops of C Sqn (attached) Touch down on Queen sector approximately ten minutes behind scheduled times (4. hour bring fixed for 0725 hrs). All Troops are under Command of 5 ARE. The following Troop an on Red Beach (LEFT OF QUEEN Sector) and are under command of 79 Sqn acts on 5 ARE. 3 Troop C Sqn (Lieut J.L.A Allan) No 1 Lane. 3 Troop C Sqn (Sjt. Wood) No 2 Lane. 4 Troop C Sqn (Sjt. Cocluane) No 3 Lane. 4 Troop C Sqn (Lient. V. Boat) No 4 Lane. The following Troops are on WHITE Beach (Right of QUEEN Sector) under Command of 77 Squadron 5 ARE.	

Wt.47724 993 2,000,000 3/43 W. H. & S. 51/6375

SHEET 9

Month and Year June 44

Commanding Officer Lt. Col. G.H. GROSVENOR D.S.O.

Place	Date	Hour	Summary of Events and Information	References to Appendices
NORMANDY FRANCE	6	0735	1st Troop A Sqn (Lieut. D. Robertson) No 5 Lane. 1st Troop A Sqn (Sjt Turner) No 6 Lane. 3rd Troop A Sqn (Sjt Surythe) No 7 Lane. 3rd Troop A sqn (Lient. D. Kaapp) No 8 lane. Remaining Troop of A Squadron assist 5 ARE in beach clearances as follows: 2nd Troop (Lieut C. Mindy) RED Beach 4th Troop (Lieut P.T.S Sadler) WHITE Beach.	
		0755	All lanes are now swept clear of mines and the infantry pass through the gaps onto the first lateral. MG. fire still prevails from the houses & other enemy positions.	
		0805	Flail Troops return to the beaches and continues widening lanes. There is still much opposition from MG. & rifle fire which is systematically	

Wt.47724 993 2,000,000 3/43 W. H. & S. 51/6375.

SHEET 10

Month and Year June 44

Commanding Officer Lt. Col. G.H. GROSVENOR D.S.O.

Place	Date	Hour	Summary of Events and Information	References to Appendices
NORMANDY FRANCE	6		engaged.	AV
		1028	A Squadron leader (Major P.E.S. Clifford) & R.I.C. A Sqn which is all there in of A squadron HQ travelling both in the same tank touch down on QUEEN Sector White Beach under command of Staffs Yeomanry.	AV
		1230	A Squadron HQ with two troops of Flails of the Westminster Dragoons under command union in Staffs Yeomanry assembly area. 3d Troop A Sqn (Lieut. D. Kaapp) now with only two tanks is met as arranged.	AV
		1300	Staffs Yeomanry move south towards CAEN with Flail Troops (2 Tps W.D. + 1 Tp 22D) and A Sqn HQ in Rrar of Staffs Yeo. RHQ.	AV

Wt.47724 993 2,000,000 3/43 W. H. & S. 51/6375.

SHEET 11

Commanding Officer Lt. Col. G.H. GROSVENOR D.S.O.

Place	Date	Hour	Summary of Events and Information	References to Appendices
NORMANDY FRANCES	6	1430	A Sqn HQ & troops under command reach BRUVILLE.	AV
		1445	Sufficiently wide lanes have now been swept on this beach & opposition has died down.	AV
		1500	Capt T. Wheway rallies Troops approximately 1 mile inland. The following casualties have so far been sustained: Killed - 4 ORs, missing believed killed, 1 Offr (Lieut J.L.A. Allen) & 4 ORs, Missing 5 ORs (Cpl Birtherton Crew & tank which may have returned to England after craft had embarked). Wounded 6 ORs Tank. Casualties are more serious: 5 Tanks written off 8 Tanks Y – Z casualties, 2 Tanks X casualties which only have 11 Tanks in number.	AV

Wt.47724 993 2,000,000 3/43 W. H. & S. **51**/6375

SHEET 12

Commanding Officer Lt. Col. G.H. GROSVENOR D.S.O.

Place	Date	Hour	Summary of Events and Information	References to Appendices
NORMANDY FRANCES	6	1535	Capt T. Whewhy takes the Eleven tanks which are still running to the East Rising Yeomanry concentration area. Most troops now coming under command of 27 Amd Bde where mines are suspected. The mines are blown up without harm to our tanks and the area is cleared.	
		1700	Enemy area is encountered by Staffs Yeomanry, with whom and A Sqn HQ & their troops, and is engaged spasmodically.	
		2100	The Eleven Tanks with Capt T. Whewhy move into harbor South of Lion Sur Mer	
		2208	Staffs Yeomanry engaging enemy area	
			A sqn H.Q. & their troops, move into harbor with Staffs Yeomanry ½ miles West of BEUVILLE (7F/10674).	

Wt.47724/993 2,000,000 3/43 W. H. & S. 51/6375.

WO 171/1055
Intelligence/war diary
53RD MEDIUM REGIMENT RA HQ

Month and Year June 44				Commanding Officer Lt. Col. H.E. FERNYHOUGH
Place	Date	Hour	Summary of Events and Information	References to Appendices
NORMANDY	June 6 D-DAY		Recce parties had their first view of the FRENCH coast shortly after dawn(.) Streams of LCs A & LC's I went last in the early hours(.) The coast soon became recognisable from our table of landmarks & large-scale maps(.) Lines of splashes mediated shelling of the beach & beached LCT's, beach-signs & beach – group personnel at work became identifiable(.) The sea remained choppy & the wind combined to interfere with the performance of rhino ferries(.) Maj J.E. Marsham went ashore with one rhino – load from his craft in the afternoon & found everything proceeding ashore except the rhinos(.) The line of seaside dwellings appeared intact from afar but was later seen to be only a facade amid ruins(.) Sniping & MG fire from several houses was dealt with by (contd)	

M3524/1218 1200M 10/41 H.B & co.Ltd. 51-1541).

SHEET 2

Month and Year June 44				Commanding Officer Lt. Col. H.E. FERNYHOUGH
Place	Date	Hour	Summary of Events and Information	References to Appendices
NORMANDY	June 6 "D-DAY"		(Contd) small fighting ships of the corvette or Frigate type(.) Continuous sp was provided by larger naval units incl at least one battleship(.) The tank-deck of LST 383 Hrs having been cleared (the DURWS swimming & other vehicles forming a rhino-load) a bomb dropped about 50 yards from the ship damaged the elevator mechanism, & the 3 Inr lorries remaining on the main Deck were off loaded across an improvised gangway on to the main Deck of LST 385(.) The Vehs of this Regt had already been lowered to the 1h deck(.) It became evident that we would not to able to unload our vehicles that day due to rhino troubles & after watching the glider - borne this pass over & cut loose above the ORNE br-head we retired for the night(.) Most of the ships pulled away from the coast & made smoke(.) W'less contact was est with other parties who had all arrived off shore during the day and with CRA 3 Dw HQ ashore.	Hes Hes

M3524/1218 1200M 10/41 H. B .& Co.Ltd. 51-1541).

WO 171/1121
Intelligence/war diary
73RD LIGHT ANTI-AIRCRAFT REGIMENT RA

Month and Year June 44   Commanding Officer Lt. Col. J.A. ARMSTRONG RA.

Place	Date	Hour	Summary of Events and Information	References to Appendices
SLINFOLD LA BRECHE HERMANVILLE CALVADOS NORMANDY HERMANVILLE	1-5 1-30 6	 1630	RHQ, 218, 220 322 Btys in concentration and marshalling areas prior to operation OVERLORD. Sub-units split into their assualt Groups. 296 Bty, phased back, remains in concentration area. OC 218 with L Cp, A/218 has two guns, C/218 less two guns, landed on WHITE and RED beaches respective as H+ 45, in time Beach under heavy fire 229673 Capt. T.E. DALE, OC ATP, was wounded in the arm by mortar fire and was evacuated after completing his recce. Bty Comd. also suffered minor wounded in hand from mortar splinter. Remaining guns of ATP landed at H + 240 & of CTP at H + 120. All guns are ashore by H + 300; BHQ established in first lateral by H + 360. C.O. work R Cp. landed at H + 240 & set up AARC as Beach Command Post. 2/1/C with R Cp landed at H + 530 (200 min cate) & recce Reg which was embarked by 101 B.S.A. by 1930 hrs.	ap ap ap

*6391. Wt.48123/1073. 319M. 2/43. Wy.L.P. Gp.656.

SHEET 2

Month and Year June 44   Commanding Officer Lt. Col. J.A. ARMSTRONG RA.

Place	Date	Hour	Summary of Events and Information	References to Appendices
LA BRECHE HERMANVILLE	6		RMO landed at H + 60 (on time) He was clearly wounded in the back from mortar fragments, but set up a BDS in a German strongpoint. In view of RAME casualties, medical orderlies of A and C TPs 218 had to be called in. The BDS continued to function here for the next two days where I was absorbed in to the FDS had moved inland. OC 220 Bty & RCP landed at H + 530 (200 mins late) but recce of the area allotted was impossible to the ground which was still in enemy hands. BHQ was eventually established with RHQ OC 6TP 322 Bty landed at H + 45 & carried out recce. First guns began to come ashore at H + 430 and were all in action by H+510. As recce party of H/322 and I/322 had not landed OC 6TP recced then also located strong pts on the beach were still holding out & individual detachments were involved in mopping up ops.	ap ap

M3524/1218 1200M 10/41 H.B. & Co.Ltd. 51-1541.

SHEET 3

Place	Date	Hour	Summary of Events and Information	References to Appendices
	6		In the instance a Boters was need to neutralise a sniper's post.	ap
			<u>SMOKE</u>	
			As the main smoke parties of 112 Inr Smoke Coy did not arrive at expected time an improvised organisation was formed out of Balloon crews & A parties from B/273/86 L A A Regt. They were not able & operate during the night of D + 1 - D + 2 owing to the fact that supplies of generators were not landed in time	ap
			<u>CASUALTIES</u>	
			Total casualties for D day were 1 Offr wounded, 1 OR killed 5 ORs wounded and 1 OR missing.	
HERMANVILLE	7		Regt. remained under come HQRA 3 Brit but DIV as Comas with 80 Bdr in Mike Ndn sector was still impassible adgt. landed with padre at 1400 hrs, a head of A Cp.	ap
			Oc 220 Bty carried out recce for new gun position for his troops	

M3524/1218 1200M 10/41 H.B. & Co.Ltd. 51-1541.

WO 171/1800
Intelligence/war diary
5TH ASSAULT REGIMENT RE HQ

Month and Year June 44   Commanding Officer Lt. Col. A.A.B. COCKS.

Place	Date	Hour	Summary of Events and Information	References to Appendices
At sea	5	0830	Sailed from SOUTHAMPTON. Rough but uneventful personnel very ill.	CS
	6		D-Day. See Regt Records at Appx Bug. G.L WATKINSON Comd /aset Bdire comes with us.	CS
ST AUBIN	7		Set up HQ at 0186 supervision of Sqn rally. No contact possible with main RNQ. So unsuccessful in attack on RADAR sta at DOUURES.	CS
	8		Establish comn with RHQ Capt P.J. DRAPER killed at 2100 hrs whilst attempting to neutralize German Reigel nine 43.	CS
	9		Visited by Adjt.	CS
	10		Regiment embarked & set HQ pened with main RHQ.	CS

22293 Wt. 33096/1140 1,000m 12/40—McC & Co Ltd—51-8212 Forms e2118/22.

WO 171/1806
Intelligence/war diary
77TH ASSAULT SQUADRON RE

Month and Year June 44   Commanding Officer MAS. K. du B. FERGUSON RE.

Place	Date	Hour	Summary of Events and Information	References to Appendices
Beaches NORTH of HERMAVILLE-SUR-MER	6	0735	Visibility good, sea rough with cross swell from ATLANTIC ocean. DD this made slow going. AVRE overtook them 2000X from shore, then waited to allow them to pass. DD touched down to flank. giving little or no fire sp. Rockets from LCT (R) fell among houses and several had near misses on LCT AVRE. LCT (AVRE) touched down at H hr simultaneously with inf (1 S LAN R) who were due at H+5 mins. Craft drifted due to wait for DD and 2 Tp beached 100ˣ WEST of 1 Tp who were on correct gap. LCT 109 (4 Tp and CRE) hit after coding flail had disembarked and second flail became jammed in doorway, having been knocked out. Craft further damaged by fire and was ordered back to UK. Capt FAIRIE reported this by R/T at H+4 hrs approx, stating that heavy casualties sustained incl CRE, Lt col ADB COCKS killed and Lt CHARLTON wounded. (No Confirmation get of safe return or detailed casualties). See detail 29 JUN.	Separate and special reports of HQ 5 ASLT REGT RE of whole op. Ref maps throughout JUN 44 FRANCE 1:50,000 7 E/5 and 7 F/1. Corresponding 1:25,000 scale maps.
		0745	Gapping on remaining three gaps in progress. 2 Tp and 3 Tp met dunes	R? Ferguson Maj

22293 Wt. 33096/1140 1.000m 12/40—McC & Co Ltd-51-8212 Forms C2118/22.

SHEET 2

Month and Year June 44   Commanding Officer MAS. K. du B. FERGUSON RE.

Place	Date	Hour	Summary of Events and Information	References to Appendices
Beaches NORTH of HERMAVILLE-SUR-MER	6 (contd)		6-8 ft high; 1 Tp came onto rd running inland above soft sand. Obstacles on beach were ramp-type (2 rows) with Tellermines on top, stakes with shells on top, and hedgehog with shells on leg facing towards sea (2 rows in echelon). Bottom row ramps in 4'6" water approx at H hr. Clearance went slowly as mines difficult to reach and disarm. Sea choppy and difficult to work in.	R Ferguson Major
		0900	Gaps completed (approx time) and taking by traffic inland. 1 Tp improved surface of soft sand and cleared mines from adway. Lt1 FAIRLIE killed when he ran over mine and knocked out, after being wounded by shellfire while clearing mines by hand. Tp rallied fwd in orchard 076805. 2 Tp dropped bridge on to 50mm gun posn. Crew killed, gun fortunately sited to fire to flank. Considerable work on improvement involving blowing of turin Bangalore and dropping of log carpet. Sgt MYHILL killed by shellfire while working dismounted, SPR SPIERS wounded.	

22293 Wt. 33096/1140 1.000m 12/40—McC & Co Ltd-51-8212 Forms C2118/22.

SHEET 3

Place	Date	Hour	Summary of Events and Information	References to Appendices
	6 (contd)		3 Tp used br and made alternative route through dunes. Capt CARRUTHERS wounded in hand, but worked until gap complete. An obstacle clearance Lt. DICKINSON wounded and evacuated. OC's hit and set on fire while clearing obstacles. L Sgt SPENDER killed, Sprs JOHNSTONE and SETTERFIELD wounded. Fire extinguished by driving into deep water.	R Ferguson Major
		1000	(approx) Sqn rallied with ITP less Lt DICKINSON's crew, Sgt NLITLEY, and L sgt BARCLAY left & complete clearance beach obstacles. Several ths damaged by shellfire etc, but only two destroyed on beaches.	
		1130	Capt. How with one other AVRE recced towards LION-SUR-MER with a view to assisting 1 S'LANR or 41 R M COMMANDO in clearance.	
		1230	Capt McLENNAN took Capt CARRUTHERS' AVRE to join Capt. How in sp 41 RM COMMANDO. Petard and besa used against mortar posts and empers etc until 50 mm Atk gun knocked out all three. CAPT MCLENNAN, CPL SHEA SPS MANWEL, TREADREA killed (confirmed 9 JUN) and Sprs MORRIS, ELLIOTT, SAMSON, Cpl PARSONS wounded.	

22293 Wt. 33096/1140 1.000m 12/40—McC & Co Ltd-51-8212 Forms C2118/22.

SHEET 4

Place	Date	Hour	Summary of Events and Information	References to Appendices
	6 (contd)	1600	OC, assuming duties CRE visited Div HQ netted set to HQRE 3 Br Inf Div. Remnants Sqn moved to 077794. OC visited 79 Sqn Lea. OLIISTREHAM, who are clearing town.	
			Final state AURE fit 3 X 1Y4Z5. 16 casualties. Lo flails lost on Sqn front, though two Cmdo (both 3 Tp) killed. One b/d failed to get off craft. One ran over mine. Two fit.	RF
077794 near HERMANVILLE	7		Salvaged 2 brs from beach, one o.k. and dismantled ready for carriage fwd, other buckled. Ordered to send 4AVRE 79 Sqn to BENOLIVILLE. Strong – pt at LION-SUR-MER holding firm. Capt FORD and B vehs arrived. RHQ and LHD arrived.	RF
	8		11 AURE 79 Sqn took part in clearance of LION. not actively engaged. OC recced area 0776 with CO 1 MX with view to AURE covering gap between E YORKS and NORFOLKS. 9 AURE 79 Sqn moved to area farm 071768. 2T/c regt MAS SIMPSON visited div from 3 CON Div. 26 and 80 Sqn had had negligible casualties. OC, 2T/c and RSM WALSH recced	RF
	9		from 071768 for reg rally.	R Ferguson Maj

22293 Wt. 33096/1140 1.000m 12/40—McC & Co Ltd-51-8212 Forms C2118/22.

WO 171/1807
Intelligence/war diary
79TH ASSAULT SQUADRON RE

Month and Year June 1944   Commanding Officer Major J.G. HANSON

Place	Date	Hour	Summary of Events and Information	References to Appendices
PORTS MOUTH HARBOUR	4	1200	Operation OVERLORD (EX NEPTUNE) is postponed 24 hours. No interference by hostile aircraft. A press correspondent is with us on 114A.	
	5	1230	All serials slip moorings. The sealed maps and photos are opened - we are due to land at LA BRECHE. The sea is rough and most people are sick. The Bridge is reshackled. An uneventful night.	
	6	0500	Reveille.	
		0600	Little enemy interference except one destroyer is seen cut clean in half and sinking amidships. All serials are up in two columns.	
ENGLISH CHANNEL	6	0650	Bombardment begins by Div Arty. It is just possible to pick out Landmarks and we believe we are going in dead on our pre-arranged exits. The wave Top Photographs are most useful. Serials move into line.	
		0715	All Serials have to go full speed astern as the rocket salvoes are falling short and one or two very nearly hit Serial 114.	

Wt.47724/993 2,000,000 3/43 W. H. & S. 51/6375.

SHEET 2

Month and Year June 1944   Commanding Officer Major J.G. HANSON RE.

Place	Date	Hour	Summary of Events and Information	References to Appendices
RED BEACH LA BRECHE		0725	All Serials touchdown. CRE orders 'SEARCH FRONT' over the air. There is a large explosion on Serial 109, on which the CRE and 4 Tp 77 Sqn are carried. Flails and AVRE disembark and wade out in good order. The sea is rough and a cloud of smoke overhangs hedgehog COD. For a minute or so there is no fire from the enemy. From the water's edge up to the back of the beach is about 250 yds not 400 yards. The first 100 yards is thick with obstacles. First two rows of Ramp Type obstacles every alternate one mined with a 1935 Tellermine on top is in four feet of water. Then two or three rows of heavy Pit Props sunk into the ground again each alternate one fixed on top with a Tellermine. And inland of these, rows of reinforced concrete Tetrahedra and steel girder hedgehogs with alternate obstacles wired up with Shells with German Push Igniters DZ.35. Flails and AVRE were unable to drive in between the obstacles. Sqn Ldr's AVRE is out of touch with the CRE. 13/18 Hussars (DDs) have not	

Wt.47724/998 2,000,000 3/43 W.H. & S. 51/6375.

SHEET 3

Month and Year June 1944   Commanding Officer Major J.G. HANSON RE.

Place	Date	Hour	Summary of Events and Information	References to Appendices
			touched down and no Infantry LCAs are in sight.	
		0735	Flails of 22 Dgns are working at top of the beach. Lt. BOAL's and Cpl AGNEY's on 1 Tp lane both received direct hits from an A/Tk gun and are put out of action. Sjt COCHRANE's of 2 Tp is also knocked out and the Bridge AVRE receives a direct hit and the Bridge drops flat. Lt. ALLEN's	
		0805	Flail in 4 Tp lane is also knocked out - Four out of eight of the 22 Dgns Flails are put out of action before getting into the Hedgehog.	
		0830	1 Tp and 4 Tp have received a Flail each from the Beach Clearance Teams. Sjt MANNING's Flail IN 2 Tp gets a track blown off by A/Tk Mine in his lane. 2 Tp lane is completely stopped with both Flails out, the Bridge out and the Troop Leader Capt DESANGES killed – the Tp Officer is wounded. 1 Tp is doing well.	
		0832	10K reports SUNRAY killed (Capt AYERS). Sqn Ldr's AVRE commences jamming reinforced concrete Tetrahedra successfully, but after first row steel wire rope cables for Beach Clearance get firmly wedged	

Wt.47724/993 2,000,000 3/43 W.H. & S. 51/6375.

SHEET 4

Month and Year June 44   Commanding Officer Major J.G. HANSON RE.

Place	Date	Hour	Summary of Events and Information	References to Appendices
			in tracks and Sqn Ldrs AVRE is temporarily out of action. Sqn Ldr and part of crew dismounted and after close examination of Beach Obstacles decide that in view of depth of water task is now impossible, and that craft will have to risk the remaining Tellermines. (Later it was shewn that neither Tellermines nor Obstacles prevented Landing Craft from beaching and taking off.)	
		0845	1, 3 and 4 Tp lanes progressing with Infantry (2 E. Yorks) attacking across 3 and 4 Tp lanes whilst 1 Tp fights and gaps.	
		0905	1 Tp reports CLEAN having made a gap and cleared the lateral right handed as far as 3 Tp 77 Sqn. 3 Troop is progressing but having difficulty. Sjt WOOD 22 Dgns (Flail) is supporting Infantry (A Coy 2 E. Yorks) into COD whilst Cpl JOHNSON flails up to lateral when in attempting to break through a wall, strips a track and breaks his jib. A DD 13/18 Hussars Tank has slipped on the bridge and blocked it. 3 Tp quickly by-passes the Bridge with a Log Carpet, but the lane is again blocked by a DD driving	

Wt.47724/993 2,000,000 3/43 W.H. & S. 51/6375.

SHEET 5

Month and Year June 44   Commanding Officer Major J.G. HANSON RE.

Place	Date	Hour	Summary of Events and Information	References to Appendices
RED BEACH LA BREACHE	6		too close to the side and going up on a mine. Sqn Ldr and Lt. HUTCHINSON checked a detour round the disabled tank whilst Infantry attacked the houses to the EAST. French Lt. Anti-Tank Mines were found and blown in situ using Mine Detectors and 808 Explosive. 4 Tp lane was also progressing steadily – The Log Carpet had been used and as a reserve the Bridge was dropped under Sqn Ldr's orders, to one side. Sjt SAWYER further to one side dropped the Bobbin Carpet to one side risking mines over the soft patch of sand, wire and sand dunes – unfortunately, the Carpet came off crooked and could not be used.	
		0940	4 Tp reported CLEAN and 3 Tp a little later. By this time, traffic had blocked 1 Tp lane and Lt. CUNNINGHAM using Mine Detectors cleared a second lane - the first vehicle however, went up on a mine. Prodding was then resorted to as the shrapnel on	
	6	1000	the ground made use of Mine Detector impractical. Cpl. ROBERTS was killed and Lcpl HOPKINS wounded whilst dealing with a Tellermine. The remnant of 2 Tp that the Sqn Ldr had	

Wt.47724/993 2,000,000 3/43 W.H. & S. 51/6375.

SHEET 6

Month and Year June 1944   Commanding Officer Major J.G. HANSON RE.

Place	Date	Hour	Summary of Events and Information	References to Appendices
RED BEACH LA BRECHE			rallied and put onto an easy bank near a metalled road exit, was doing well under Lsjt PURKISS. A further lane was put through by the Sqn Ldr Sjt SAWYER and Lsjt PURKISS, simply by guiding a S.P. Arty through the hedgehog on foot and then marking the route used.	
		1015	By this time there were five exits off the beach, but traffic was being held up on the First Lateral. Sqn Ldr then directed traffic up a narrow inland road already cleared by one Troop and reported clear.	
		0725	All attempts at Clearance of Obstacles on the Beach had proved fruitless.	
		-1000	Of the five Flails 22 Dgns on Beach Clearance, two were working on one and four Tp lanes. Two had been knocked out by Anti-Tank Guns, one just as it came off LCT 116 and the other halfway up the beach. Lt. HUNDY in the fifth had knocked every Asparagus (Pit PROPS) down in his zone that had no mines on it, tried levelling the Ramps, but the Sherman could not do this, then flailed three lanes for the Infantry through the Beach Minefield and WELL into the Hedgehog. Then at the request of a Brigadier cleared	

Wt.47724/993 2,000,000 3/43 W.H. & S. 51/6375.

SHEET 7

Month and Year June 1944   Commanding Officer Major J.G. HANSON RE.

Place	Date	Hour	Summary of Events and Information	References to Appendices
RED BEACH LA BRECHE	6	0725-1000	cleared the wire above high water mark and started a further gap into COD, followed by supporting the Infantry into the Hedgehog by shooting at the houses, from which small arms fire was coming.	
		1030	Troops were ordered to rally by half Squadrons on 1and 4 Tp Lanes. Troop Leaders continued to urge traffic forward through their lanes and improve the exits.	
			Squadron was ordered to rally at a French Farm in RIVA BELLA.	
RIVA BELLA	6	1200 1400	CO 4 Commando and remnants return from OUTSTREHAM having put the Battery out of action, but failed to take it. CO reports Lock Gates and Bridge held by the enemy. CO is wounded badly and in view of the poor state of his Unit, Sqn Ldr promises to look after the matter. Lt. HUTCHINSON is sent to Beach HQ to request Division for Infantry Support. 79 Assault Squadron is ordered to do this job itself.	
OUTSTREHAM LOCK GATES		1530	Sqn Leader and ten AVRE move off, 1 Tp working left handed and remainder right handed under Squadron Leader. Enemy are surprised and near	

Wt.47724/993 2,000,000 3/43 W.H. & S. 51/6375.

SHEET 8

Month and Year June 1944   Commanding Officer Major J.G. HANSON RE.

Place	Date	Hour	Summary of Events and Information	References to Appendices
OUISTREHAM LOCK GATES	6	1530	bank is taken easily, but enemy could not be prevented from blowing the East Span of the Bridge.	
		1630	After intensive Besa and Petard fire the enemy surrender. Six Officers, fifty one Other Ranks, three Anti-Tank Guns, and much small arms and A/Tk Minefield material captured.	
		1730	Prisoners are marched off to the Beach. Sqn Ldr deploys the Unit with AVRE on WEST bank and Bren Gun crews on EAST bank. Capture reported to Divisional HQ. Lt CUNNINGHAM is placed in charge of the position with orders to hold it, recheck the Bridge and Lock Gates for Demolition Charges and Booby Traps, count the captured material and feed the men. He does more and with much energy patrols the locality, killing and bringing in more enemy – Spr BEAN armed only with a Bren Gun surprised twenty of the enemy in a dugout, Lsjt TITLEY after being shot at by a sniper attacks the house by himself, kills two and brings back a prisoner. These are only two of similar occurrences which went on till next morning.	

Wt.47724/993 2,000,000 3/43 W.H. & S. 51/6375.

SHEET 9

Month and Year June 1944   Commanding Officer Major J.G. HANSON RE.

Place	Date	Hour	Summary of Events and Information	References to Appendices
LA BRECHE	6		Casualties sustained during the Beach Clearance and Gapping Operations were:-	
			Sqn Ldr's AVRE Tracks jammed by SWR and Shackles.	
			1 Tp. 1D and Lsjt NYE's crew lost complete with a Sqn Fitter as passenger. Bulldozer lost from a direct hit in engine.	
			2 Tp 2A Comd Capt DESANGES killed Lasjt WALKER wounded. 2B burnt out with three of crew wounded. Co-driver to Bulldozer missing. 2C Comd 2/Lt. NICHOLSON wounded and died later.	
			3 Tp Capt AYERS killed and two of 1C wounded. Co Driver to BULLDOZER wounded.	
			4 Tp CAPT POLLARD wounded, one killed and three wounded.	
			and in the attack on OUISTREHAM Lt. HUTCHINSON was wounded.	

Wt.47724/993 2,000,000 3/43 W.H. & S. 51/6375.

SHEET 10

Month and Year June 1944   Commanding Officer Major J.G. HANSON RE.

Place	Date	Hour	Summary of Events and Information	References to Appendices
LA BRECHE	6		Total: 2 Offrs and 1 killed, 1 Offr died of wounds, 1 Offr and 10 wounded, 10 missing. 4 Offrs and 21 lost from Sqn Strength.	
			Of 17 AVRE taken into action, three were burnt out or drowned, and one (1D) probably repairable.	
			22 Dgns lost six FLAILS and had three more seriously damaged out of 13.	

Wt.47724/993 2,000,000 3/43 W.H. & S. 51/6375.

SHEET 11

Month and Year June 1944

Commanding Officer Major J.G. HANSON RE.

Place	Date	Hour	Summary of Events and Information	References to Appendices
OUT STREHAM LOCK GATES	6	2000	Four AVRE under Sjt SAWYER move off to support the 2 WARWICKS at BENOUVILLE.	
	7	0400	One platoon of Infantry from Beach Bn. at last reinforces the Lock Gate position. During the night the position was mortared and bombed.	
RIVA BELLA	6	1600	Capt POLLARD establishes Sqn Harbour in Farm to South of Lateral. 2/Lt. PHILLIPS endeavours to find our DUKW with 3 tons of petrol.	
		1830	Sqn Ldr returns to Harbor and makes Major FERGUSON now A/CRE and clarifies the situation.	
	7	0900	Sjt SAWYER and four AVRE return for replenishment.	
		1130	Lt CUNNINGHAM having handed the position over to two platoons of the Beach Bn. returns with 7 AVRE, more prisoners and two civilian lorry loads of Ltb French A Tk Mines – These are placed later in 15 Fd Pk Coy. RE Dump.	
		1430	Petrol, Dustbins and Besa Ammn arrive in DUKWs.	
		1540	2/Lt PHILLIPS with four AVRE move off via COLLEVILLE-SUR-ORNE 0876 - BEUVILLE 0674 to rejoin 2 WARWICKS. Four AVRE are 1A, 3C, 4C, 4B.	

Wt.47724/993 2,000,000 3/43 W.H. & S. 51/6375.

WO 171/1528
Intelligence/war diary
71ST FIELD COMPANY RE

Month and Year Jun 44

Commanding Officer Maj. L.E. UPRON ME?

Place	Date	Hour	Summary of Events and Information	References to Appendices
NEWHAVEN	5		Operation "OVERLORD" in which unit was taking part had evidently been postponed for 24 hrs. Weather was dull, chilly and rough at sea.	
		1900	All craft serials sailed and proceeded to convoy forming up place and thence to lowering posn 10 miles off NORMANDY Coast.	
At Sea	Night 5/6		Very rough at sea. All parties less those of OC, Lts FIORI and WHYTE embarked in LCT. Remainder in LST.	
At Sea	6		D-Day for operation "OVERLORD". All parties disembarked by 1100 hrs on a shellswept and thickly occupied beach. Parties proceeded direct to RV at BENOUVILLE and all arrived complete by 1300 hrs.	
		0900	Lt GILLEN's veh party set sail in convoy from GOSPORT. Sea choppy at times, brilliant sunshine.	
FRANCE		1400	Mine clearance of respective veh harbour and Coy Harbour Areas in operation. Some snipers about, but none captured by unit.	
		1530	Enemy reported in str approx 400 yds SOUTH of BENOUVILLE. OC 3 pl and patrol 9 Sec despatched to bring him under observation. Patrol was accompanied by two DD tanks of 13/18 Hussars. This party was fired on on debouching from the SOUTH edge of the village. The second tank was hit by an 88 mm shell and knocked out. The leading tank was likewise knocked out by trying to manoeuvre on the 88 mm gun.	
		1700	One man killed from 3 pl. First casualty in the unit. Name No. 2123801 Dvr DRANSFIELD. Also wounded in this party No. 2138599 Spr Barnett and	

Wt 13474/1805 1,200,000 7/40 BPL 51-7171 Forms C2118/22.

SHEET 2

Place	Date	Hour	Summary of Events and Information	References to Appendices
BENOUVILLE	6	1700	No. 14213432 Spr SIMPSON JB.	
		1745	Patrol returned. On infm received the Coy. adopted a defensive posn near the MAIRIE in BENOUVILLE and digging-in commenced.	
		1755	Vehicles under Lt GILLEN arrived in bay off coast of NORMANDY.	
		1800	Patrol 2 R. WARWICKS with reps of patrol from 3pl recce fwd edge of BENOUVILLE for a Bn. attack.	
		1815	Glider borne rfts arrived in area of two brs over R. ORNE and the adjoining canal, which had been previously captured by 6 Airborne Div intact.	
		1900	Attack by 2 R. WARWICKS proceeds.	
		2040	0 gp at the MAIRIE in BENOUVILLE. OC 71 Fd Coy now OIC Constr of Class 40 crossing over canal and R. ORNE on evacuation of Maj WILLISON of 17 Fd Coy. through splinter wounds. 71 Fd Coy to commence offloading of 8 grillage lorries on canal site at 2300 hrs 17 Fd Coy (two pls) to construct two class 9 FBE rafts as relief for civilian br.	
		2315	Parties 71 and 17 Fd Coys deployed on site of canal crossing and offloading of eqpt put in hand. Enemy interference slight. 2IC proceeds to beach to arrange for offloading of LBVs containing bridging eqpt and despatch of loaded bridging vehs landing on second tide to offloading pt.	

Wt 13474/1805 1,200,000 7/40 BPL 51-7171 Forms C2118/22?.

WO 171/1611
Intelligence/war diary
263RD FIELD COMPANY RE

Month and Year June 1944   Commanding Officer M.H. de E'ORINE. MAJ. R.E.

Place	Date	Hour	Summary of Events and Information	References to Appendices
WICK LAM	1 3 4 5 6		Vehicle Party moved to Marshall at A.ll (DENMEAD) 1077. 210 Rks Cpt. D? 1/c. received movement order for embarkation area to move Sunday morning - this later cancelled. revised movement order for serials S. 74 & 75 to move to embarkation area. Coy. moved off 0835 hrs in TCV's & embarked on LSI(S) 74 & 75 by 1400 hrs - ferried out by S.D. Duchess of Cornwall Received maps & notification that operation was on at 2200 hrs. Craft & Sailed approx 2330 hrs. Arrived at Disembarkation Point near French Coast 0535 hrs, but LCM did not arrive until 0715 hrs. In meantime embarked on LCI(L) (both serials) & proceeded to shore. Spr. Tomkins seriously wounded by shrapnel on LSI(L). arrived on beach but too late a tide to clear beach obstacles.	 see App. "A"

22293 Wt.33096/1140 1,000m 12/40—McC & Co Ltd–51-8212 Forms C2118/22.

SHEET 2

Month and Year June 1944   Commanding Officer M.H. de E'ORINE. MAJ. R.E.

Place	Date	Hour	Summary of Events and Information	References to Appendices
COLLVILLE-SUR-ORNE	6(cond)		therefore I put whole Coy. in forming of beach units & lateral roadways on beach - also clearing mines up to lateral roads & clearing snipers from Lances at back of beach. Proceeded to sites for glider Landing Strips at Ouistreham with 4 Commandoes but driven back. eventually approached strips by way of COLLEVILLE-SUR-ORNE & work was Completed by 2000 hrs. Coy went into harbour at 2330 hrs. Casualties for day were 2012066 7 Sgt SiMs. W.E. (Wounded) - 1890766 7 Sgt Williams V.J. (Wounded) - 2083451 Cpl. Beardmore D (Wounded) 1904794 Spr Britten E, (Illness) - 2010723 Spr. Burneth J. (Wounded) 5260892 Spr. Cale L.J. (Wounded)-2124133 Spr. Goodall. J. Sl (Wounded) 1944678 Spr. Greaves E.J. (Wounded) - 4928982 Spr. Miles A. (Wounded) - 14364024 Spr. Millan E (Wounded) - 14351841 Spr Parkes J.Sl. (Wounded) -14318201 Din Sargent W. (Wounded)-2004234 Spr. Smallman A. J. (Wounded)	

22293 Wt. 33096/1140 1,000m 12/40—McC & Co Ltd–51-8212 Forms C2118/22.

SHEET 3

Month and Year June 1944   Commanding Officer M.H. de E'ORINE. MAJ. R.E.

Place	Date	Hour	Summary of Events and Information	References to Appendices
COLLEVILLE-SUR-ORVE	6		H929016 Spr. Shorthouse w.(Wounded)-2010703 Spr. Swan W. (Wounded) H929003 Spr. Tomkins G. (Wounded) - 2137836 Dvn, Birrell T. (Missing) 1896460 Spr. Mckean G. (Missing)	
Do	7		Coy. moved to BENOUVILLE at 0700 hrs. commenced work on Bridge at BENOUVILLE (with 71 Fd. Coy.) also ferries Cl. 5&9 across River ORNE at RANVILLE - these later completed by 1400. Enemy attacked Bridge area at 1500 hrs & coy. Prepared Positions for defence of Bridge & Stood-to until 0400 hrs 1904794 Spr. Britten E. evacuated with cartilage trouble, 2004234 Spr. Smallman A.J. evacuated with shrapnel wound, 2083451 Cpl. Beardmore D accidentally shot himself with Sten Gun & evacuated.	
BENOUVILLE	8		Proceeded with unloading equipement & Preperartion of bank Seats for BENOUVILLE Bridge (with 71 Fd. Coy) position of bridge changed by C.E.I Caps at 1200 hrs. Recommenceds	

22293 Wt. 33096/1140 1,000m 12/40—McC & Co Ltd—51-8212 Forms C2118/22.

WO 171/1666
Intelligence/war diary
629TH FIELD SQUADRON RE

Place	Date	Hour	Summary of Events and Information	Remarks and references to appendices
Camp A 14. WICKHAM, HANTS	1		Preparations complete. Troops had very little to do. Mine clearance stores arrived and were issued to individuals. Marching party of assault residues left camp at 0400 hrs for port of embarkation.	
	2		Troops departed marshalling areas for ports of embarkation. Serial S70 of 3 troop remain and complete briefing. Sgt Soutter rejoined from hospital and was sent to join D plus 17 personnel.	
Aboard Ship	3		Troops embarked on LSIs approx 1130 hrs and allocated to troop decks. Spent the day settling in and making final preparations. Very little to report.	
	4		Sailing postponed 24 hours owing to bad weather. Troops have little to do except write last letters home. Troop Commdrs ran over various tasks to be tackled on landing and clear up small points raised by troops.	
	5		Troops commenced loading LCAs from ships magazine 0900 hrs. The task was completed late afternoon and all explosives etc. protected with plastic armour. Troops held trial loading of LCAs with personnel and adjusted stores to ensure easy disembarkation. LCAs were all overcrowded by the amount of assault stores that had to be carried. Maps were issued and troop Commdrs held final briefing.	
	6		Reveille 0400 hrs. Breakfast 0430 hrs. Troops given 'make ready' 0506 hrs. Embarked on LCAs 0545. Sea was very rough and troops, with few exceptions, were very sick, despite tablets which had been taken. Craft were scheduled to 'touch down' at 0745 hrs. In a number of cases this was not achieved, though no craft were more than 20mins late. Lt. Col. COX - CRE 5 ARE - was killed before landing and Maj F.S.Carson OC 629 Fd Sqn RE assumed command of obstacle clearance units.	App A. Plan of operation as far as it effected 629 fd Ag - RE

Lal Chand & Sons, Printers. Cal.—No. 7506 (G-389)—30-6-41—50,000 Pads.

SHEET 2

Place	Date	Hour	Summary of Events and Information	Remarks and references to appendices

QUEEN RED/WHITE BEACHES	"D" DAY 6 June		It was only possible for AVRE and CRABS to erect a few tripod markers and most of these were knocked down very soon. LCOCU were unable to see zones for this reason, but as obstacles did not hold up craft, and very few, if any, mines exploded by them, this did not matter. Contact with AVAE and CRAB teams was not easy and was only made on two of the four zones, due to AVRE casualties and inaccurate touch down. On landing it was found impossible to clear obstacles as planned owing to the state of the tide, roughness of the sea, and mortar and aimed SA fire. One of HQ Tp teams removed two rows of obstacles with the help of AVRE, but could do more because of tide. No. 2 Team of No. 3 Troop under command of Sgt Bath, with CRE 3 Br Inf Div, OC 629 Fd Sqn and Sgt Major aboard, during the approach run found obstacles ¾ covered by tide, and on trying to disembark at the first row pf obstacles found it at least 7-ft deep. Men were sent over the side of LCA to remove shells and mines from timber ramp obstacles. This task was particularly hazardous but was accomplished. The men were picked up in a very exhausted condition. On landing OC and SSM contacted other Troop teams and ascertained casualties. These had been considerable and Sqn was regrouped and put to work constructing beach exits and lateral tracks, as the tide was then too high to allow any further beach obstacles to be removed. This tack continued throughout the day under sporadic shell and mortar fire.
			
			Casualties up to 1200brs: Killed - 1 offr and 8 ORS
			                         Wounded - 2 " 31 "
			                         Missing - 8 ORS
			
			Nos 1 & 3 Troops removed beach obstacles as they were uncovered by falling tide. Task completed by nightfall. All Tps repaired exits and lateral tracks as required during the night.	

Lal Chand & Sons, Printers. cal.-No. 7506 (G-889)-30-6-41-50,000 Pads.

SHEET 3

Place	Date	Hour	Summary of Events and Information	Remark and references to appendices
QUEEN RED/WHITE BEACHES	"D" DAY 6		2 IC (Capt G .N. McDougal, MC RE) with 1 WHITE Armd Personnel truck disembarked approx. 1300hrs and was killed by shell fire on the beach within the hour. Sqn now under comd CRE 18 GHQ Tps Engrd. Total Casualties: Killed: Capt. G.N. McDougal Lieut. L.A. Hinton and 8 ORs. Wounded: Lieut. G.N. Giddings and 31 " Lieut. H.A.C. Jones Missing: 8 ORs.	
	7		One OR of No 3 Troop reported missing since 2230 hrs last night. Tps widened zones cleared of beach obstacles. This task complete by noon. No 1 Tp detailed to prove free of mines No. 2 Sector Stores Area and also took on the task of delousing GERMAN "BEETLE" Tanks. No. 2 Tp and HQ Tp remnants were combined under Lieut. Roberts and swept No. 1 Sector Stores area, laying Sommerfeld track in and out, assisted by 2 bulldozers from Beach Group. No. 3 Tp swept first lateral roadway immediately behind QUEEN WHITE beach, lifted mines, and laid Sommerfeld track and chesspaling. They were assisted late in the afternoon by No 1 Tp. Intermitten shelling and bombing – no further casualties.	
	8		No. 1 Tp assisted 84 FD Coy RE in the clearance and maint of beach exits and laterals during the morning. In the afternoon opened up new ammunition dump inland. HQ & No 2 Tp swept 1st lateral for mines and laid Sommerfeld track around BSD. In the afternoon commenced opening up exits on GREEN BEACH assisted by 84 FD Coy RE. No. 3 Tp maintained 1st lateral road behind QUEEN RED during the morning and assisted No. 1 Tp in opening up of ammn dump in the afternoon. 1 OR killed during the morning.	

Lal Chand & Sons, Printers, Cal.-No. 7506 (G-389)-30-6-41-50,000 Pads.

WO 171/2377
Intelligence/war diary
90TH COMPANY RASC
(ARMOURED ASSAULT BRIGADE)

Month and Year June 44   Commanding Officer Major J.R. Cuthbertson, RASC

Place	Date	Hour	Summary of Events and Information	References to Appendices
	JUNE 6	44	'D' Day. Major Cuthbertson(OC) and 1 OR. landed of LCT 298 with 106 Br. Coy RASC at H+2 (0925 hrs) and proceeded to agreed RV. with 6 Airborne Div. at Bridges over R. ORNE at BENOUVILLE (0974). No Airborne reps. present at 1200 hrs. 11 Vehs. of 'C' Pln. under Capt. E. Forman disembarked ex LST. 382 at 1430 hrs and reached Coy. Harbour Area S.E, of COLLEVILLE-SUR-ORNE (0877) at 1600 hrs, carrying pre-loads of Ammunition for 6 Airborne Div. Contact established with 6 Airborne Div. HQ. at RANVILLE(1174) at 1800 hrs and Ammunition preloads delivered to Airborne Div. Maint.Area in WOOD, RANVILLE at 2300hrs. Fire from, Snipers encountered at numerous points on the roads during the day. 9 Vehs of 'B' Pln under Lt. GR. Glenny loaded with Pet & Derv., disembarked at 1200hrs and proceeded to 27 Armd.	

*6391. Wt.48123/1073. 319M. 2/43. Wy.L.P. Gp.656.   Cont/Sheet 3.

SHEET 2

Month and Year June 44   Commanding Officer Major J.R. Cuthberts RASC

Place	Date	Hour	Summary of Events and Information	References to Appendices
	JUNE 44 6	contd.	Bde. A Echelon Area HERMANVILLE-SUR-MER (0679). Contact established with Capt. DE. Gray of this Coy. who landed at 1100 hrs with 1 ERY to undertake POL. Supply duties with HQ 27 Armd. Bde. Pre-Loads of Pet. & Derv delivered directed to Armd. Regts of 27 Armd. Bde. under AFV. protection in certain cases and vehs. continued throughout day and most of night 6/7 June 44 to ferry Amn. Pet.& Derv. from Beach Sector Stores Dumps forward to 'A' Echelon. 2 ORs. 'B'Pln. received injuries from Shell Splinters and evacuated to 21 F.D.S. LST 383 (carrying further 11 Vehs 'C'Pln) bombed off Shore during day – damage caused to Lift Gear. 7 Vehs. on Upper Deck were transferred at Sea to LST. 385 (already carrying 11 vehs. 'C' Pln.) Owing to delay on Beaches etc. none of these vehs were landed on 'D' Day as Scheduled.	

*6391. Wt.48123/1073. 319M. 2/43. Wy.L.P. Gp.656.

WO 171/2383
Intelligence/war diary
106TH BRIGADE COMPANY RASC

Month and Year June 1944   Commanding Officer MAJOR P.S. Bean RASC

Place	Date	Hour	Summary of Events and Information	References to Appendices
LEIGH-ON-SEA	1		Nothing to report.	RPP
	2		1624 pl in Small parties embarked on LSTs	RPP
	3		1626, 1622 and 1629 pls embarked on LSTS along with adv. HQ.	RPP
	4 } 5 }		All embarked personnel and vehicles lying off English Coast. Coy. main HQ embarked on MT Ship, sailed and dropped anchor off coast.	RPP
At sea	6	0920	D Day. 0920 hrs first vehicles of 1026 and 1629 pls landed and Proceeded to bridge site experiencing mortar fire and sniping on route to BENONVILLE. Beaching to LSTs and landing of elmainder of 1621, 1622, 1623 1624, 1629 and adv HQ.	} RPP See appendix } RPP

Wt.47724/993 2,000,000 3/43 W. H. & S. 51/6357.

'JUNO' BEACH

'My section was first from the LCA [Landing Craft Assault], and we were slaughtered. For some peculiar reason, as we approached the beach, our craft did an about turn, making a large loop, then came in for the landing...the [German] defences were manned as our craft grounded. Our support craft were knocked out so we had no heavy weapons. The DD [Duplex Drive] tanks had not come ashore. My platoon, approximately 36 strong, went through what we believe was enfilade fire from five machine guns.

We landed in our proper area, but no specialised gear reached the [sea] wall. All our assault engineers were killed in action. We were still in the water when the section was cut down... I was a Lance-Jack [Lance-Corporal], Bren crew, loaded with around a total of 300 rounds, plus 36 Mills grenades. The sea was red. One lad was hit in the smoke bomb he was carrying. Another, a human torch, had the presence of mind to head back into the water. Our flame-thrower man was hit and exploded, and we couldn't even find his body'.

LANCE-CORPORAL ROLPH JACKSON, 10 PLATOON, D COMPANY,
THE QUEEN'S OWN RIFLES OF CANADA ('NAN WHITE' BEACH)[284]

'JUNO' BEACH

(From East of La Rivière in the West to Luc-sur-Mer in the East)

German Defenders: 7th Army Commanded by *Generaloberst* Friedrich Dollmann

(Lower Normandy defended by LXXXIV Korps commanded by *General der Artillerie* Erich Marcks)

Coastal Defence: 716th Infantry Division commanded by *Generalleutnant* Wilhelm Richter

Allied Attackers: British 1st Corps commanded by Lieutenant-General Sir John Crocker

Assault Division: 3rd Canadian Infantry Division commanded by Major-General Rod F.L. Keller

Naval Forces: Force 'J' commanded by Commodore G.N. Oliver and Bombardment Force 'E' commanded by Rear-Admiral R.A. Dalrymple-Hamilton RN

H-Hour: 0745 hrs

Landing Sectors:'LOVE', 'MIKE', 'NAN'[285]

D-Day Divisional Objectives: (i) Pierce and overwhelm shoreline defences and secure the three seaside resorts of Courseulles, Bernières and St-Aubin-sur-Mer. (ii) Seize crossing points over the Rivers Mue and Seulles and capture a series of inland villages including Anguerny, Pierrepont and Colomby-sur-Thaon. (iii) Advance to a line west of Caen running along the Bayeux-Caen highway and overlooking Carpiquet airfield. (iv) Establish contact with British 3rd Infantry Division landing on 'Sword' beach. (v) A co-ordinated strike eastwards with British 3rd Division in order to capture or cut-off the rear of the strategically important city of Caen. (vi) Establish a bridgehead over the River Orne south of the city[286]

Casualties on D-Day (Beaches only): 1204 (Anglo-Canadian Killed, Wounded and Missing)[287]

NOTES

[284] *D-Day Then and Now*, Volume 2, edited by Winston G. Ramsey, (London: Battle of Britain Prints International Ltd, 1995), p. 484.

[285] Only 'Mike' and 'Nan' sectors were used for the actual landings.

[286] Ken Ford, *Battle Zone Normandy: Juno Beach*, (Stroud, Gloucestershire: Sutton Publishing Ltd, 2004), pp. 18-19.

[287] *D-Day: Then and Now*, Volume 2, edited by Winston G. Ramsey, (London: Battle of Britain Prints International Ltd, 1995), p .620.

7TH CANADIAN INFANTRY BRIGADE

WO 179/2879
Intelligence/war diary
7TH CANADIAN BRIGADE HQ

Month and Year June 1944

Place	Date	Hour	Summary of Events and Information	Remarks, references to Appearances and initials
Solent	4		Cool and cloudy. The loading is complete, and now a S.W wind has sprung up and everything postponed 24 hours. There is nothing to do but wait. All the ships and craft lie in the Solent ready to sail. A long postponement will be a pity as everyone is keyed up and the morale very high. Everyone finds it hard to realize that they are on the eve of making history. It is so like the beginning of an exercise that one's reactions are hardly different.	K.F.O
	5		Cool cloudy. The weather was poor today with a strong SW breeze and heavy clouds, but as no further postponement received the HQ ship party embarked on HMS LAWFORD by 1500 hrs, along with Captain GJ 1 and his staff. The whole armada had been sailing all day, and at 2100 hrs the Lawford set sail. The night was spent without event, everyone trying to get as much rest as possible. The passage was made without incident. Tps were told where we were going and received messages from Generals Eisenhower and Montgomery before turning in.	K.F.O
	[6		Cloudy AM, clear PM. D-DAY at last. The whole assault Gp arrived off the lowering posn and right opposite COURSELLES-SUR-SEULLES. [H Hour was set back ten minutes to 0745 hrs due to craft being later for run in. The day was dull and cloudy, threatening rain, still quite a swell, although the breeze was not quite so high. The assault went in as planned except that the AVRE teams were 20 minutes late in arriving. The poor visibility apparently prohibited the daylight bombing of the beaches. There was considerable difficulty experienced on MIKE sector in getting an exit off the beaches, for vehs. Clearance of underwater obstacles was hindered by the state of the tide. The assault itself went extremely well. While the planning timings were not accomplished it is realized these were ambitious. Once the beach defences had been overcome and mopping up completed, which took about two hours, the advance inland was done at a good pace, the opposition consisting of MMGs, 88 mm guns well sited with long fds of fire, and snipers in the fds and villages. Bde HQ was est by 1215 hrs in fm yd at GRAYE-SUR-MER after some delay in getting off the beaches. Everyone rather inclined to be rather surprised that they were in battle with the result that it took time to shake down as a HQ. By the night of D-Day the Bde was beyond the intermediate objective SOUTH of the R SEULLES with fwd tps at PIERREPONT. Bde HQ spent the night at 927808 COLUMBIERES-SUR-SEULLES, and the units dug in and prepared to move onto the final objective the next day.]	K.F.O

WO 179/2965
Intelligence/war diary
THE ROYAL WINNIPEG RIFLES

Month and Year June 1944

Place	Date	Hour	Summary of Events and Information	Remarks, references to Appendices and initials
On Board LCH 1098	6 Tue	0400	Cloudy and cool with strong NW wind and a heavy Sea. Tea and a cold snack served as breakfast for Army personnel on board.	
		[0515	LCAs manned and lowered from LSHs still ten miles from coast.]	
		[0655	Not a short from shore def although the LCH has been standing off for almost three hours. RN and arty bombardment opens up with the SP guns afloat firing short as usual.]	
		[0749	In spite of the air bombardment failing to materialize, the RN bombardment being spotty, the rockets falling short and the DDs and AVREs being late C Coy. of 1 C Scot R (Maj Desmond Crofton) under our comd, landed at the june of MIKE and LOVE for the assault on beach def and the CHATEAU VAUX, D Coy. R Wpg Rif (Maj L. R. Fulton) with u/c one Pnr see landed to the left of MIKE GREEN and B Coy (Capt P. E. Gower) with u/c No 15 Pl and two secs No 6 Fd Coy. RCE landed to MIKE RED - all within seven minutes of one another.	
Ashore Graye-Sur-Mer		[0900	The bombardment having failed to kill a single German or silence one weapon, these Coys. had to storm their positions "cold" - and did so without hesitation.] D Coy had by this time gapped the minefd at LA VALETTE and cleared GRAYE-SUR-MER, with fwd elements through towards BANVILLE.] B Coy reported RED "BAKER" and [No 15 Pl u/c B Coy had forced a crossing of the R Seulles at 964857 and cleared out the four posns on the "island".] [When A and C, the res coys landed with portions of Bn. HQ under the 2 IC and Adjt respectively, the beach and dunes were still under heavy mortar and MG fire - to the extent that, with the No 22 W/T set as a target, they (the Bn. HQ parties) were pinned down for two hours. A Coy (Maj F. E. Hodge) pushed inland towards STE CROIX-SUR-MER, starting at approx 0805 hrs, reached just short of assaulting distance before they were pinned by fire from six to eight mg posns. Simultaneously with A, C Coy. (Maj J. M. D. Jones) advanced toward their objective, BANVILLE, encountering several pockets of resistance en route but overcoming each one until just SOUTH of BANVILLE, where the enemy had dug in three MGs on commanding ground.]	

SHEET 2

Place	Date	Hour	Summary of Events and Information	Remarks, references to Appendices and initials
	6 Tue	0900	Two dets of 3# mortars, timed to land at H hr, were ordered off the LCT in twelve feet of water, the craft comd refusing to beach his craft, resulting in the loss of both weapons, the two carriers, one 10 cwt trailer and three mortar numbers drowned. [The Bn. Comd Gp, landing at 0820 hrs came under mortar and MG fire and were sniped from the left but managed to get inland by crawling over bogged AVREs and slithering along a low bank.] Seven of the original party of fifteen joined C and D Coy.s in BANVILLE for the end of Phase I of the op.	
BANVILLE		[1400	By the time C and D Coy.s had moved out from BANVILLE for TIERCEVILLE and CREULLY, the remnants of B Coy. had reported – the Coy. Comd and twenty-six ORs having survived the assault on the three casemates and twelve MG emplacements.] No 15 Pl then joined C Coy., 17 Pl which had sp C Coy. of 1 C Scot R and gapped the minefd had rejoined D and Bn was reorganized for the further advance. During this stage A Coy had asked for assistance with the enemy mgs at CROIX-SUR-MER, the resistance being much stronger than intelligence had estimated. Portions of A and C Sqns, 6 Cdn Armd Regt went to the help of A Coy with cool disregard for mines and A Tk guns, beat down the mg posns and permitted A Coy. to mop up and advance to the SOUTH. Prisoners had been brought in - a sorry lot - and escorted to the rear, five being turned out of a German ambulance from which they had sniped our tps. Throughout this advance all sub-units and Bn. HQ had come under mortar and arty fire of astonishing accuracy. The No 22 Set on it's unwieldy carriage having bogged down continually, the only comn with Bde HQ had been by a wounded LO (Lt. Harold Robson) who had landed with the Bn. Comd Gp and walked back to Bde HQ on being bandaged three hours after getting shrapnel in the leg - and by means of a captured German staff car in the hands of the Bn. I Sgt (Sgt Jorgenson).	
CREULLY		[1800	Except for the MG posn near the br at CREULLY,] which was handled skillfully and with cool dash by Lt. Mitchell of D Coy., [enemy resistance was scattered between BANVILLE and CREULLY and the Bn. area was consolidated by 1700 hrs in sq 9179, with Bn. HQ in a quarry - completing Phase II of Operation "Overlord".] During the late evening five offrs and seventy-eight ORs arrived from the rft unit and all were posted to our badly depleted B Coy.	

SHEET 3

Month and Year June 1944

Place	Date	Hour	Summary of Events and Information	Remarks, references to Appendices and initials
Creully	6 Tue	1800	It is desired to make a special note of the services rendered to the Bn during the first day of ops by our MO (Capt Robert M Caldwell) and the Bn RAP Staff – and the assault sec of 14 Cdn Fd Amb u/c Capt Harry Dixon. Not only were the wounded cared for with skill and despatch but confidence was developed and morale increased accordingly. A very special note, too, should be made about the general tone of the Bn during this day called D – 6 Jun 44. Not one man flinched from his task, no matter how tough it was – not one officer failed to display courage and energy and a degree of gallantry. It is thought that the Little Black Devils, by this days success, has managed to maintain the tradition set by former members. [Casualties for this day exceeded 130.]	
	7 Wed	0200	C Coy attacked by enemy patrol. The attack was repulsed and 19 of the patrol taken prisoner. One officer was taken but was shot on making a break for it.	
		[0615	On the move to secure our objective on line OAK at PUTOT-EN-BESSIN] with C Coy in adv gd under comd Maj J M D Jones and a flank gd composed of No 7 Pl from A Coy, two secs carriers and one sec 6 pdrs under comd Capt D B Robertson.	
		[1600	By this hour the Bn was consolidating – in spite of C Coy having advanced by the wrong route and consequently arriving one and a half hours after the Bn – (hardly an advanced gd action). [Our position was occupied with A Coy right, responsible for the bridge at the rly and rd crossing in PUTOT, C Coy north of the rly in center and D Coy left with B in res.] Snipers became pestiferous during the latter part of the day but only scattered resistance was encountered during the advance. [The flank gd became our liaison force with the 7 Green Howards at BRONAY and had an active time for the next three days.]	
Putot-En-Bessin		1900	Two USAAF air-crew bailed out from a Boston and were picked up in "no man's land" in front of D Coy.	

WO 179/2960

Intelligence/war diary

THE REGINA RIFLE REGIMENT

Month and Year June 1944

Place	Date	Hour	Summary of Events and Information	Remarks, references to Appendices and initials
HILTINGBURY CAMP C-7	1		Weather - hot and sultry. Units in the clutches of Movement Control. All movement taking place by craft leads.	JGB
	2	2200	Weather - hot and dry with occasional showers. Most of serials leave Marshalling Area C-7 for embarkation ports.	JGB
	3	2200	Weather - very hot and dry. Co's serial leaves Marshalling Area C-7 at 2200 hrs to embark.	JGB
AT SEA	4		Weather - cool and cloudy. CO visits Coy Comds aboard their craft. D-Day postponed 24 hrs due to weather.	JGB
	5	1000	All craft under way at 1000 hrs. Weather - cool and cloudy. Sea none to smooth. **D-Day**	JGB
COURSEULLES SUR-MER	[6	0805	1st Bn THE REGINA RIFLE REGIMENT, on Ex "OVERLORD" landed at NAN GREEN BEACH, COURSEULLE-SUR-MER, NORMANDY, FRANCE at 0805 hrs., with A Coy. being first in, followed by B Coy. at 0815 hrs. C Coy. landed at 0835 hrs. D Coy at 0855 hrs.	JGB
		0900	Comd Gp, with Lt-Col. F. M. Matheson, E.D., touched down at 0900 hrs.	
		0830	A Coy. report that they are held up by heavy fire.	
		0855	Two LCAs of D Coy. strike mines about 250 yds from beach and are blown up.] Major J.V. Love, Comd D Coy., Lt. R.B. Murchison, Signal Offr and a number of ORs are casualties. A number of others were rescued by RN craft, and some swam ashore.	
		[0930	D Coy., consisting of approximately 49 all ranks, under comd of Lt. H.L. Jones began advance to Reviers]	
		1000	Bn. HQ at 973655. A Coy. in particular still engaged in heavy fighting in beach area and in area behind beach.	
		1100	Bn. HQ moving to 965819. [Civilians of COURSEULLES-SUR-MER welcomed our troops with flowers. Many a bottle of wine was dug up and presented to the troops, who at that moment had a more serious task in hand.]	
		1215	C Coy. reports bridge at REVIERS clear.	
		1330	Bn HQ, followed by B Coy., moves forward to REVIERS.	

SHEET 2

Month and Year June 1944

Place	Date	Hour	Summary of Events and Information	Remarks, references to Appendices and initials
REVIERS	6	1500	Bn. HQ arrives REVIERS.	
		1555	QUEENS OWN RIFLE REGT of CANADA report that they have taken MAGNY and are advancing on BASLY.	
		1800	B Coy., followed by C Coy., with in support B Sqn 6 CATR, were ordered forward to FONTAINE-HENRY. C Coy instructions were to by pass FONTAINE-HENRY and to proceed to LE FRESNE-CAMILLY.	
LE FRESNE-CAMILLY		1850	B Sqn Comd reports that he has withdrawn his tanks after having had 6 tanks knocked out by 88 mm guns.	JGB
Sq. 9477 Sheet CAEN 7 F/1		1900	D Coy. moves direct to LE FRESNE-CAMILLY followed by Bn. HQ. A Coy. ordered to remain in REVIERS to guard approaches to river and to guard bridges.	
		1900	B Coy. reports that they are in FONTAINE-HENRY.	
		1950	C Coy. reports that they have reached LE FRESNE-CAMILLY.	
		1950	Bn. reports to Bde that Intermediate Objective on line ELM has been reached. Bn. HQ is set up in LE FRESNE-CAMILLY sq 9477.	
		2100	Bn. Ordered by Bde to consolidate for the night on line ELM sq 9578.	
		2115	B Coy. reports that they had been subjected to enemy arty fire and that Major F. L. Peters, Comd B Coy. and Lt G.D.Dickin, 2IC B Coy. were killed.	
		2115	Up to this time, approximately 150 PW were taken, over 100 of these being captured in COURSEULLES SUR-MER.	
		2200	CO goes to make recce of position to be taken up for the night.	
LE FRESNE-CAMILLY sq 9477 sheet CAEN 7 F/1	[7	0030	Bn. begins move to new position in sq 9578.	
		0300	CO and IO attend O Gp at HQ 7 Cdn Inf Bde. Days operations were discussed, and plans made to move forward to final objective on line OAK. COs of units exchanged information on the D-Day activities.	
			It was evident to all that, due to adverse flying conditions, that the air support had not been as great as been expected. Pillboxes and other emplacements were still open for business when our troops touched down.]	JGB
		0300	Bn. new in new position.	
		0500	Lt. Col. F.M.Matheson holds Bn. O Gp, and orders for the advance to final objective on line OAK are given.	
		0715	Coys move off with A and C Coy.s on right and B and D Coy.s on the left.	
		0730	Bn. HQ moves off.	
		[1200	At 1200 hrs, REGINA RIFLE REGIMENT moved into BRETTEVILLE L'ORGEULLEUSE which was clear of the enemy and the civilian population gave the troops a very friendly reception. The Bn. took a defensive position with A Coy. at 926718, B Coy at 934705, C Coy. at 923703, and D Coy. at 948703, Bn HQ set up at 927718. The Bn. dug in and things remained quiet during the afternoon. R Wpg Rif took up a position on our right at approximately 1330 hrs. Thus the REGINA RIF were out in front with no protection on our left flank, a position which we refused to vacate until relieved 11 days later by the QOR.]	

WO 179/2969

Intelligence/war diary

1ST BATTALION THE CANADIAN SCOTTISH REGIMENT

Month and Year June 1944

Place	Date	Hour	Summary of Events and Information	Remarks, references to Appendices and initials
Aboard Ship	6		Total Strength: Officers 37, OR's 815 Clear and Mild	
		0430	"Wakey, Wakey" was heard over the LSI's P.A. system and the Officers, NCO's, and men of the First Bn. Canadian Scottish Regiment arose to face the greatest day in their military career. "Now is the time," said one of the lads, "When we can tell whether our instructors knew what it was all about." There was no fuss, no sign of "jitters", the troops ate their breakfast (knowing that it would be the last proper meal for a couple of days) and then prepared to embark on ALC's	
		[0700	The ALC's were lowered from our Mother Ships. There was a strong sea running and the seven miles to shore (in 90 minutes) seemed like seventy miles.] In spite of the anti-seasick pills, which were taken by all ranks last night and this morning, bags, vomit, became, for the use of, many. [As the "Fleets" of ALC's approached the French Coast there was no sign of enemy activity, however, this calm state was soon changed.]	
		[0750	"C" Company touched down to take out a pillbox (where MIKE & LOVE SECTORS meet) under the Comand of the R. WPG. RIFS.] Their complete story will be found as and appendix to this date of the diary.	Appx. 2.
NORMANDY COAST Between the towns of VER-SUR/MER and COURSEULLES-SUR-MER		[0830	"A" Company, with the CO's party touched down about fifty yards from shore, 100 yards to the left of their beach exit, and waded through chest-deep water to the beach. Here there was a few minutes of suspense, while enemy mortar fire humed over their heads in and around the craft they had just left. Finally their beach exits were discovered and, under heavy sniping coupled with the odd burst of MG fire, this party made its way to the cross track and road junction (954857). Up to this point "A" Company had already suffered some casualties in the crafts and on the beach. "B" Company, and the 2 1/c's party touched-down on LIKE END SECTOR where they were greeted by enemy mortar fire.]	

SHEET 2

Month and Year June 1944

Place	Date	Hour	Summary of Events and Information	Remarks, references to Appendices and initials
NORMANDY COAST	[6 (cont)	0830	One of their craft received a direct hit and caused several casualties before they were able to land. "B" Company and attached troops were pinned down with a shower of directed mortar fire, which was being directed by an enemy pillbox on the extreme left of MIKE RED Beach. This pillbox was finally cleaned out by the Beach Group and a German Lieutenant with a dozen men surrendered themselves.] One of these met his doom when a "stray" bullet plugged him in the head as he stepped on to the parapit of the pillbox. This was "B" Company's first glimpse of the "characteristic pose of pinned down Huns" as they decended with their hands up. The troops were getting "hell" as the mortar fire peppered the beach causing several casualties. This episode served to reinforce the strong morale of the men, who where waiting for their beach exit to be cleared of mines. [The enemy had flooded the low-lands which lie laterally behind the sand-dunes (see map). A tank had attempted to cross this flooded area and was bogged down, so the troops were able to clamber over its rapidly sinking chassis, otherwise they would have had to swim for it.]	Appx. 9.
		0935	[Meanwhile "D" Company, with their bicycles, headed up "A" Company's exit, across an open field which was under MG Fire, to secure two bridges over the SEULLES at (953817 & 928810).] Bn. HQ, "A" and "B" Companys with "D" Company already going through them organized and started their advance through the grain fields toward the second object. A party from "A" Company under Capt. W.H.V. Matthews, M.C. and Lieut G.I. Hope routed out the MG positions and sent a dozen more prisoners on their way back to the Beach Cage, which was now becoming crowded with the small groups of Huns that were surrendering as the battalion advanced. ["C" Company again came under the Command of 1 C. Scot. R. when they met the Battalion on our axis of advance toward ST CROIX-SUR-MER. Our advance from LA VALLETE to ST CROIX-SUR-MER was a very hazardous one, as our only protection from MG and sniper's fire was the grain which was growing three to four feet high.]	

SHEET 3

Month and Year June 1944

Place	Date	Hour	Summary of Events and Information	Remarks, references to Appendices and initials
NORMANDY COAST	6	Con't	In spite of constant cross fire, the troops under noble leadership, ploughed forward only using the cover available when the MG fire became too hot. The Battalion suffered many casualties in the attack. Every man realized the necessity of reaching the Battalion objective and went "all-out". This advance in the grain fields will linger long in the minds of those who were there. Notwithstanding the fact that the R. WPG. RIF's proceeded us, there were many MG posts which had to be taken out as we advanced. Hoards of prisoners where taken and our advance was too rapid to cope with routine searching other than disarming them and sending to the Beach Cage under one or two escorts. Of course, the odd prisoner made the mistake of trying to escape and will never have the opportunity to make the same mistake again. As far as we knew at that time, ST CROIX-SUR-MER was cleared of enemy when we reached there; but when the HQ Admin Group arrived, having landed on the second tide, they had to do a bit of house clearing owing to sniping activities. Hence, a few more prisoners were taken and sent back "through the usual channels" 200 would be a conservative estimate of the prisoners taken by this battalion today. [From ST CROIX-SUR-MER to COLOMBIERS-SUR-SEULLES the Battalion moved on the axis of advance with little or no opposition.] However, from the number of wounded and dead found during the advance there was proof that the enemy had once controlled that area. Upon once arriving in COLOMBIERS, further proof of the enemy's rapid retreat was evident. Up until our entrance into the town the Germans had-had their H.A. (Q) at (927811) but they left in full retreat leaving their type-writer and office supplies behind them. [The Battalion carried on through the town after sampling various wines and ciders brought to them by the local inhabitants and stopped at the farm. (928808)]	

SHEET 4

Month and Year June 1944

Place	Date	Hour	Summary of Events and Information	Remarks, references to Appendices and initials
NORMANDY COAST	6 con't		Upon thinking about the typewriter, Sgt Woodcock, L.G., couldn't stand the thought of leaving it there, so with the aid of a jeep, driver and a co-patriot he went back and took the machine which will no doubt be used by the battalion for the duration.	
		[1830	The Battalion left the farm and reorganized in the area just south of LES PLANCHES in sqs (9280 & 9380)	
			Lt. Col. F.N. Cabeldu, E.D. wanted to push on to the Bn's final objective, but permission for this advance wasn't granted, so the Battalion consolidated in the area of PIERREPONT, with Bn. HQ just by the church at (933789)]	
		2200		
		2300	The Battalion dug in and awaited a possible enemy tank threat.	
			Patrols were sent out as per Appx. (see Appx 7)	
			[Casualties June 6 –	
			Officers	O.R's	
			Killed – Lieut. F.G. Radcliff	Killed – 22	
			Wounded – Lieut. J.H. Russell	Wounded – 58	
			Lieut. V.R. Schjelderup Missing – 1]	
			Lieut. P.E. Turnbull 4 81	LHB.
PIERREPONT	[7		Total Strength: Officers, 33 OR's 717	
			Clear and Mild	
	0400	0400	Stand To – Our first night on French soil had been spent; spent in waiting for a tank attack which didn't come. Although the troops were fatigued after what had been the most nerve-wracking day in their career; they were ready, not eager, to repulse any attack that the enemy might put in. However, with the dawn came the assurance that a panzer threat was not eminent.	
			First light appeared and the "Tommy-cookers" went into action on the second day's 24 hour ration pact. The troops prepared to push further into the Hinterland – there was no filling in of slit trenches – our "exercise" days were over.	
		0850	The Battalion closed down its present position and with "A" Coy in the lead we moved toward the objective which our Commander had set his heart on last night.	

8TH CANADIAN INFANTRY BRIGADE

WO 179/2886
Intelligence/war diary
8TH CANADIAN BRIGADE HQ

Place	Date	Hour	Summary of Events and Information	Remarks, references to Appendices and initials
Somewhere in England	June 1 - 5		Weather - fine . Enemy Air Activity - Slight. Bde HQ and all the units were split down into craft loads and passed through the "Sausage Machine" to embarkation pts, and thence to assault craft and ships. Comd Gp of Bde HQ was aboard HMS WAVENEY, a specially fitted HQ ship. D Day originally was scheduled for 5 Jun, but on 4 Jun word was received that the op had been postponed 24 hrs.	Appx 1 & 2
At Sea	6		Weather - Fine. Enemy Air Activity - NIL.	Appx 1 & 2
		[0630	D-Day. Sighted BERNIERES and ST AUBIN. The landmarks which had been carefully memorized from air photos were clearly recognizable - the jetty at the harbour of COURSEULLES - the flat expanse of marshland to the EAST - then the church steeple amid a profusion of trees, which marked BERNIERES and on down the coast to the cluster of bldgs surrounding the next church which marked ST AUBIN-SUR-MER.] As the coast drew nearer the wind increased and a heavy sea made it necessary to consider whether or not the DD tks were to be launched or should the tps go in without their immediate assistance.	
		[0700	Visibility lessening and the decision was made not to launch the DD tks.] The expectant and eager tps of the assault Coys loaded into their LCAs.	
		[0705	At this time a sig was received that the AVREs were late. H-hr for J2 was set back an additional 10 mins. To give the leading inf the sp at the correct time, orders were issued to delay fire from the SP arty to conserve amn for the assault. The armada slowly approached the shore and at 0725 LCGs opened fire on beach defs	
		0725		
		0735	followed by the SP arty who opened fire after a slight delay had occurred in transmission of order to all craft. The orders were to fire until 0807.]	
		[0745	BERNIERES and ST AUBIN receiving terrific pounding though the main effect seemed to be more inland and not on the immediate beach defs.]	J?SS

Place	Date	Hour	Summary of Events and Information	Remarks, References to Appendices and initials
At Sea		0749 0755 [0758 0800 [0810 0812 0812- 0817 0825 0850	At 0749 the rocket ships manoeuvred into posn and fired their salvoes, but owing to poor visibility and smoke the effect was not observed. A few moments later, word was received that the assault coys were ready for the dash to the shore and RM FOB ordered fire on strongpt at BERNIERES. At this time it became apparent that for some unknown reason SP arty had switched all fire to ST AUBIN. Lack of opposition from beach, however, was encouraging and assault coys were ordered in.] During the run in very little opposition was evident. No enemy AC appeared and a small number of our own AC showed up during this time. At approx 0812 AVREs were seen touching down on beach, closely followed by assault coys. As it became evident assault coys were achieving success the res coys were ordered in.] Capt J.L.S. Steven, Bde IO, landed with Bn. HQ of QOR of C. [Stiff resistance was now being encountered along the narrow coastal strip and progress was slow. By 0850 however res on had landed. Beaches were not cleared as quickly as they should have been but cas were comparatively light considering the congestion. The res Bn. finally cleared off the beach and made its way fwd to assembly area in vicinity of the church.] Brig K.G. Blackader landed and proceeded to HQ of QOR of C. He was accompanied by Lt. S. Caldecott as staff offr. As the assault Bns moved inland heavier opposition was encountered. [The first PW were identified as 726 GR of 716 Inf Div.]	Appx 1 & 2
BERNIERS-SUR-MER		0950 1030 [1054	Adv HQ party with Capts Clarke and Bickford landed and moved fwd to establish HQ in vicinity of the church in BERNIERES. 88 mm fire from posn NORTH of TAILLEVILLE – REVIERS rd knocked out three SP eqpts as soon as they cleared cover of BERNIERES. Comd Gp turned over to MBSS on beach in order to go ashore. Adv HQ opened SOUTH of church in BERNIERES.] About this time Capt Bickford, who had been well fwd, assisted in capture of 3 PW but while on his return received slight gunshot wounds. [Progress on right flank was very slow and no further gains were	JZSS

SHEET 3

Place	Date	Hour	Summary of Events and Information	References to Appendices and initials
BENY-SUR-MER	7		Noticeable. Bde HQ moved about 500 yds SOUTH of original position during the afternoon. On the left flank hy opposition was not so evident until N Shore R were close to TAILLEVILLE. Leading tps entered the village at 1352 hrs. Late in the afternoon the right flank pushed fwd slowly through BENY-SUR-MER, BASLY to LA MARE and elements of QOR of C and 10-CAR penetrated to the bde objective – ring contour 80 between ANGUERNY and ANISY.] 7 Bde reported fwd elements in CAMILLY area.	Appx 1 & 2
		1352		
		1430		
		1730		
		1953	With two Bns well fwd Bde HQ moved to BENY-SUR-MER, quite close to where the N shore R on the left flank were still engaged in TAILLEVILLE.	
		[2010	At 2010 hrs the QOR of C reported further progress on bde objective, and shortly after the R de Chaud reported moving fwd to COLOMBY-SUR-THAON. N Shore Re ordered to reorg at TAILLEVILLE.]	
		2015		
		2105		
		2200	As darkness closed in enemy air activity commenced and while fwd tps were NOT attacked in strength the rear areas in the vicinity of the beaches were subjected to hy bombing.	
			Enemy casualties were hy and approx 250 prisoners were captured by units of the bde. These were mainly from 726 Inf Regt of 716 Inf Div.	Appx 2
			Weather - fine. Enemy Air Activity - Heavy during night.	
			During the night 6/7 Jun only slight enemy patrol and mortar activity was encountered. The enemy apparently being in no posn to make any major move.	
		0710	The units were able to make good use of the time in reorg and bringing up rfts before daylight. [It is now apparent the enemy withdrawal on the 6th had been hurried and there were plenty of indications of confusion. QOR of C reported discovery of a number of vehs in good condition in the village of ANGUERNEY. In spite of determined	J?SS

Place	Date	Hour	Summary of Events and Information	References to Appendices and initials
	2 June 44	1130	J32 serial have an early lunch in order to move off at 1215.	RCR
		1200	J32 serial form up and after the roll being checked move off to the T C Vs just outside the gate.	
Chilworth 842385	3 June 44	0700	Reveille - very bright and warm	RCR
		0800	D Coy. form up and move off to the docks in T C Vs. As B HQ are the only persons in camp a very quiet day is spent by these personnel. The remainder of the Bn. are all about their respective craft and are having the usual shipboard good time.	
Chilworth 842385	4 June 44	0030	B HQ forms up and is lifted to the Royal Pier, SOUTHAMPTON DOCKS, where they board the command craft, L C H 239 after the usual amount of confusion. There are about fifty on board this time but conditions have been fixed up considerably and almost everyone has a bunk or hammock to do some snoozing in.	RCR
		1130	Word has been received that "D" day has been postponed for 24 hours. The men are very worried about an indefinite postponement. The water is quite rough and if we miss this set of tides craft will be off loaded and troops returned to respective camps which of course will be sealed. This period would last from 14 to 28 days and the lads would sooner have anything happen than that.	
ROYAL PIER Southampton	5 June 44	0900	Normal lazy shipboard day.	
		2000	As no word has been recived to the contrary, it is taken that "D" day will be tomorrow and this is officially given out to the men which is a huge relief to all concerned. The real maps are issued, grenades are primed and a good many "last" letters and written. The spirit is very high and if the Hun could have a look at our lads tonight it would shake him considerably.	RCR
		2300	One by one the ships of the convoy weigh anchor, from up and proceed out to sea. A very impressive and never to be forgotten sight.	
English Channel	[6 June 44	0315	"D" day begins with a very early reveille - spirits are very high but naturally one can feel the nervous tension in the air. Unfortunately the water is still quite rough. [Breakfast is served and all men who wish it are given a good shot of good old Navy rum.]	RCR
		0500	Men are all dressed and await the order to load into LCAs.	

Place	Date	Hour	Summary of Events and Information	Remarks, references to Appendices and initials
	6 June	0600	[Finally the word comes and the men file silently to their respective boats. After very little confusion they are packed in and the boats lower away.] Due to the waters roughness it isn't long before quite a few of them are quite sick - needless to say Capt Kirsch, the M O, is right up at the head of the list. [At this point we are still about 7 miles of the coast of France. Interrmittent gun fire can be heard but nothing tremondous has developed as yet.]	RCR
		[0715	All hell breaks loose as the artillery and various support weapons cut loose with all they have. The shore can now be seen but it is fast being obscured by smoke being caused by our shells landing in the town, BERNIERES-SUR-MER MR 7F-9965]	
		[0720	Word received at B HQ from higher formation that "H" hour has been postponed for thirty minutes. No reason is given but later it develops that the DD tanks and AVREs were behind schedule. This word only reached "C" Coy. as they were a few hundred yards of the beach at 0745 when they were beginning to think they would be assaulting the beach. Up to this time there has been no sign of action on the beach but now a few A/Tk shells begin to drop around the L C As which makes the heads go down in fast order. Unfortunately the postponement had definitely messed up the supporting fire and all that is firing now is an LCF which cruised right in close to shore and let loose with a lot of tracers.	
		0805	The assault Coy. got the word to go in. As yet no D D tanks or AVREs can be seen which looks rather ominous.]	
		[0815	A and B coy touch down - B coy immediately catch a packet of trouble as they are landed in front of a very heavily defended posn at MR 7F-998995. Several of the L C As of both coys are blown up by mines but only the front two or three men are injured on this. A coy are a little better off than B for they are at least able to get off the beach at MR 7F 989855. However, as soon as they hit the railway they come under very heavy mortar fire and are pinned down.] Their casualties here begin to mount up - Lt. P.C. Rae is wounded and Sgt Charlie Smith takes over and does a very good job in extricating his pl until he too is wounded. The balance of A coy have managed to get through and carry on with the job. B coy meanwhile have really caught quite a packet. Lt Herbert and Cpl Tessier do a damn fine job in outflanking the enemy posn and finally the remnants of the enemy surrender. The coy has suffered very heavily. Major C.O. Dalton, Lt. McLean, Lt. Herberts, C.S.M. Wallis have all been wounded while Sgt Harris and Morrisson have been killed. However some of the men under Cpl "Red" Suddes and K.F. Scott carry on with their job,	

SHEET 3

Place	Date	Hour	Summary of Events and Information	Remarks, references to Appendices and initials
			of clearing up around the beach exits although many of them are wounded to some extent.	RCR
		[0830	C and D Coys and Alternate B HQ touch down. The casualties amongst the LCAs is quite heavy almost half of them being blown up by under water mines. However, the personnel get ashore without too much trouble and pass through the assault coys on the way to their positions. By now the D D tanks and AVREs are on the beach but don't seem to be getting any place. The support all around has been very disappointing as far as we are concerned for none of the beach defences have been touched and this has caused very high casualties amongst the assaulting Coys.]	
		[0900	B HQ arrive on shore, link up with Alternate B HQ and proceed through the town where a temporary HQ is set up at MR 992848. Alt B HQ detach themselves and set up in a house at MR 994854 where they earn all rights to the house by putting out a fire and gaining the everlasting thanks of the owners. At this time it is noticed that a cafe just a hundred yards off the beach is opened up and selling wine to all and sundry.] Just about now the CO appears to be missing but after a frantic search he is found up forward with Brig K.G. Blackader who has now come ashore.	
		0940	There is considerable delay at this point while the Coys assemble. B Coy. casualties being so heavy they gather just off the beach and try to sort themselves out. A Coy. having extricated themselves from the posn on the right flank proceed to their FUP. [The R de C have now landed but are prevented from passing through us by the very accurate fire of a battery of 80 mm guns located just south of BERNIERES-SUR-MER.]	
		[1000	The 88 bty having been finally taken care of the R de C move ahead followed at a discreet distance by C and D Coys mounted on tanks and other available vehs.	
		1400	Several stops on the road before BENY-SUR-MER MR 9880 is clear enough to move in. Here there was more delay while the R de C went on to capture BASLY MR 9979.]	
		1500	C and D Coys on their tanks go forward at top speed to seize their objective and take up posns and this is accomplished without much difficulty. [B HQ and other sub-units follow up more slowly but the whole Bn is in posn by 1730 hrs. B HQ is established on outskirts of Anguerny MR 0077.] The only opposition at this time was encountered in the village of Anguerny.] Several groups of prisoners were taken in here. The Bn was isolated for some time until the R de C finally located at the	

SHEET 4

Place	Date	Hour	Summary of Events and Information	Remarks, references to Appendices and initials
ANGUERNY France 014775	7 June 44		west end of ANGUERNY and COLOMBY-SUR-THAON. The NSR regiment remained back at TAILLEVILLE - MR0082 and HQ 8 Cdn Inf Bde was at BENY SUR MER MR 9880 for the night	
		0100	Quite a bit of excitement and confusion was caused by a truck load or so of "Jerries" arriving in the centre of the village, however these were dealt with in short order. [The whole night was marked with confused bits of fighting.] An enemy patrol broke into B HQ but was dispersed, the offr in charge being taken prisoner.	RCR
		1200	HQ 8 Cdn Inf Bde set up in ANGUERNY in vicinity of our B Coy.	
		1300	Prisoners kept coming in in quite a steady stream - most of these were young fellows about 16 years of age and great amusement was caused by one of them who was wearing a great coat about 15 sizes too large.	
		1400	Alt B HQ is still established in their house at BERNIERES-SUR-MER and all their available time is spent combing the beaches for missing personnel and visiting the wounded in the B D S at MR 999855. All the lads there are quite cheerful - the walking wounded are being shifted onto various craft and being shipped back to merrie England. The lads who fell on the beach itself were rather a disheartening sight - many of them trained for years and only lasted for a few moments in action. Many a good man was lost on these beaches but they did a wonderful job. [There was much activity during the day, tracking down snipers in the village of ANGUERNY-] more prisoners were taken including a chauffer found sleeping in a German staff car. At least twelve German vehicles, half tracks and lorries were taken captive in our area and included one staff car and one armoured OP.	
ANGUERNY France 014775	[8 June 44	0300	The night still occupied with the rooting of snipers - also some shell fire landed in our areas. Contacted by the 3 Br Div with a view to their attacking tomorrow through our D coy posn. ANISY 0175.]	RCR
		1200	B Ech is now established at BASLY 9979 and Alt B HQ moves up to join them. Otherwise a fairly quiet day is spent although a certain amount of shelling still continues.	
		2000	Funeral service held in BERNIERES MR 997854 for 36 of our men killed in the initial stages of the assault - service taken by our Padre Capt J.C. Clough.	
ANGUERNY France 014775	[9 June 44	0700	With the exception of a certain amount of shelling and sniping things seem to be running along fairly normally] - men improve their slit trenches and try to catch up a bit in sleep.	RCR

WO 179/2941
Intelligence/war diary
THE CHAUDIÈRE REGIMENT

1st June 1944 to 30 June 1944

Place	Date	Hour	Summary of Events and Information	References to Appendices
ENGLAND	1/6/44		Companies B and D and the alternative HQ of the Battalion go to Southampton port. Companies D and the alternative HQ go aboard L.S.I. (Landing Ship Infantry) "Clam Lamont". Company B embarks on L.S.I. "Monowai". The port of Southampton is filled with boats of all types, which gives us a very comforting sense of power.	GPB
ENGLAND	2/6/44		Companies A and C and the general quarters of the battalion take the train to Southampton. Company A embark aboard L.S.I "Prince David". Company C and the general quarters of the battalion go aboard the "Lady of Mann". Space aboard the "Lady of Mann" is rather constrained and the hygiene leaves a lot to be desired. This can be said of the organisation as a whole.	GPB GPB
ENGLAND	3/6/44		Smooth journey. Enemy aviation and land army are conspicuous in their absence.	GPB
ENGLAND	4/6/44		Mass is celebrated on board the landing ship infantries. Almost all attend. The sea is rather choppy but the temperature is good.	
ENGLAND	5/6/44		The commander of the regiment, lieutenant colonel, Paul Mathieu mounts aboard H.M.S. "Waverney" in order to assist to a "zero" general purpose meeting of the commander of the brigade. The brigadier declares that the invasion of France would begin the following day, on the coasts of Normandy. Zero Hour will be 0745. The battalion must touch down at Zero Hour/45 on the beach "Nan White", at Bernières-sur-Mer. The maps of the invasion coasts are distributed to the officers and sub-officers around 2000 hours. All study them with a keen interest.	GPB
France	6/6/44	0430 hrs	Get up at 0430 hours breakfast and final preparations, at 0630 hours embarkation in landing craft assault barges (L.C.A.). The sea is extremely choppy and many men suffer from sea-sickness. Our advance is supported by the canons of the British marine. (Landing upon French soil of Bernières sur Mer at 0830 hours, where combat has already begun.) Between the German defences and the Queens Own Rifle of Canada, a regiment from Toronto which are part of our brigade. The beach is infested with mines. The majority of the LCAs. explode and several men are injured by the German mortars. The regiment is forced to wait on the beach for an hour under the artillery fire of the Germans because the Queens Own Rifle of Canada has not succeeded in capturing the village yet. As soon as the village has been captured, the regiment passes through the breaches made in the famous "West Wall" and cross the village, followed by tanks, the artillery and the medium machine guns in order to assemble in one of the small forests south of the village. The village of Bernières-sur-Mer is almost entirely destroyed and many of the houses are ablaze. The French are rather welcoming and many cheer us on, standing amongst the ruins of their homes. A few machine-guns and snipers are captured.	GPB

SHEET 2

Place	Date	Hour	Summary of Events and Information	Remarks, references to Appendices and initials
			Only the coastal artillery shells and mortars fall on us. In the assembly area, we come under fire from artillery and machine-guns for two hours. Lieutenant R. Lapierre and a few men are killed and others are wounded. We lose our FOOs and their SPs. Company A, under the commandment of Major H. Lapointe and supported by a squadron of tanks from Fort Garry Regt as well as one peloton of machine-guns of the Cameron Highlanders of Ottawa, launch an attack and take control of an anti-tank gun which is situated on the road and capture three prisoners. The company continues its advance and seizes the 88mm gun battery. Lieutenant Walter Moisan is wounded during this attack. Meanwhile a peloton from Company D, under the command of Lietenant J.R Gregoire and supported by a Sherman tank, does the clean-up of a small wood on the right-hand side of the road and captures 14 prisoners. (Company C, under the command of Major Georges Sévigny, captures Bény-sur-Mer and continues its advance to Basly, which they also capture) Company B under the command of Major J.F. L'Esperance branches right and seizes six German 105mm guns and takes 54 prisoners. The advance then continues in the direction of La Mare and Colomby-sur-Thaon, where we capture 18 prisoners and four German vehicles. Lieutenant L.E. Dupont is wounded entering Colomby-sur-Thaon. The Regiment consolidates itself at this latter place allowing the 9th Canadian infantry brigade to advance and to seize the objective of the division.	GPB Voir Appx 7 date 6/6/44.
France	7/6/44	[0200hrs	Around 0200 hours a German company mounted on half-tracked vehicles counter-attack company A. After fierce battle, the enemy is beaten back. We note that an entire peloton from Company A has been taken prisoner. The 2IC of Captain Pierre Vallée's company is also amongst those missing. We presume that he has been taken prisoner. Lieutenant A.P. Ladas had not wanted to surrender with his peloton prepared two grenades to throw them at the enemy but was killed instantly, along with two of his men. (Two of our anti-tank guns (6pdr) are situated near the route having engaged the German convoy and destroyed 17 vehicles. One of the canons was destroyed by the enemy) Soldier L.V Roy was killed at his post after having destroyed several enemy vehicles with his anti-tank gun. He showed splendid composure, courage and bravery. We were kept awake all night by mortar fire and German snipers situated at Colomby-sur-Thaon and Anguerny. (Up to now, the regiment has registered 32 dead and 83 wounded or missing).	GPB
France	8/6/44		Reinforcements arrive do enable us to fill the gaps. The unit sends patrols into Colomby-sur-Thaon and towards the river on our right.	GPB

WO 179/2947

Intelligence/war diary

NORTH SHORE (NEW BRUNSWICK) REGIMENT

Month and Year June 1944

Place	Date	Hour	Summary of Events and Information	Remarks, references to Appendices and initials
CHILWORTH CAMP SOUTH, ENGLAND.	1	44	Weather: Clear and warm with calm. No unit parties moved today as part of the bn is marshalling in this camp.	LD
	2	44	Weather: Clear and warm with a light SW breeze blowing. Personnel are completing marshalling and resting.	LD
	3	44	Weather: Clear and warm with a It WEST breeze blowing. At 0930 hrs Maj R.H. Daughney, Capt. J.E.H. LeBlanc, Lts Day, Fawcett and MacQuarrie moved off with C Coy. to a marshalling area. Maj. G.E. Lockwood, Capts J.R. Ross, J.A. Patterson and R.M. Hickey moved off with the alternate Bn. HQ. At 2345 hrs Lt-Col D.B. Buell, Lts B.A. Oulton and J.E. Chochinov moved out with Bn HQ to load on board the LCH 167 for the op "OVERLORD".	LD
	4	44	WEATHER: Clear and warm in the morning but showers of rain came in the evening with a SE wind. The OP was postponed 24 hrs. Tps were disembarked and paraded to a reception centre prepared on the docks. Here they were given meals, a wash, free issue of 25 cigarettes, reading and writing room. NAAFI was est and took care of the small needs of the tps.	LD
AT SEA	5	44	Weather: Cloudy and cool with a SE wind blowing. The craft sailed at 0645 hrs out around the ISLE OF WIGHT. It was a slow convoy and the swell was inducive to seasickness. It was announced at 1930 hrs that the op was on and set to land tomorrow.	LD
ST AUBIN-SUR-MER, FRANCE.	[6	44	Weather: Cloudy and cool with a It wind from the SW. H-hour was 0745 hrs. [A and B Coys touched down at 0810 hrs. Crossing the beach itself only a few casualties occurred but Lt. M.M. Keith and several of his pl became casualties in houses that were booby trapped. These houses were along the beach. Other than this A Coy. reached the line of the beachhead at 0948 hrs. Casualties numbered 24.] [B Coy. proceeded according to plan but soon discovered that no damage to the defs of the strong point at ST AUBIN-SUR-MER had been caused by the air and naval bombardment previously arranged. It appeared not to have been touched. Nevertheless, the Coy. proceeded to clear the village and allowed D Coy. to get on with their task.] Lt. G.V. Moran became a casualty on the beach. By 1007 hrs D Coy. advanced without much opposition, reached the beachhead report line. D Coy. casualties were about 4 from each platoon.	LD

SHEET 2

Month and Year June 1944

Place	Date	Hour	Summary of Events and Information	Remarks, references to Appendices and initials
ST AUBIN-SUR-MER, FRANCE	[6	44	B Coy. called on the tanks to assist in the reduction of the strong point. Later when the AVREs became available the Petards mounted on them were used to bombard the defs. The co-operation of infantry and tanks was excellent and the strongpoint was gradually reduced.] At 1115 hrs, four hrs and five mins after landing the area was cleared, then one of the ATLANTIC WALLS bastions which had taken four years to build was completely reduced. 48 Prisoners of war were taken and it is estimated that the same number were killed. This firm base having been est the 48 RM Commando began moving through to proceed with their Op. [C Coy. having formed up their group moved off along road to TAILLEVILLE and reached the road junction at 004823 before coming under fire.] The Coy. worked forward to the wall of the town and it soon became apparent that the defs of the town were much stronger than the information had reported. The position was well dug in and tunnelled in a great many places. The persistent sniping was most annoying to the attackers. [The Coy. with a tp of tanks finally cleared the defs and captured 4 Offrs and 57 ORs.] During the skirmishing in the village Maj. J.A. MacNaughton was killed. [As it was now nearing evening and the troops were weary the bn. re-organized at TAILLEVILLE for the night.] At dark the enemy bombers came and a regular fireworks display was provided as the AA opened up and the bombs dropped.	LD
TAILLEVILLE, FRANCE	7	44	Weather: Cloudy and overcast with a SW wind blowing. The bn moved off at 0700 hrs and A Coy. comd by J.L. Bellivaeu bumped into an MG post at 0730 hrs. With the co-operation of tanks the position was taken 2 offrs and 36 ORs were taken Prisoners of War. Considerable sniping in TAILLEVILLE and forward of A Coy. is very annoying and slowing up the advance. Progress is slow and the amn dump in wood (sheet 7E/5 Square 9979) blew up which temporarily halted the advance. C Coy. had been sweeping the woods and scrub an the left of the road, moved over and cleared through the HQ dug in the wood. Only four Prisoners of War were taken from this area but it was found later that they had escaped to the rear and surrendered to 9 Cdn Inf Bde HQ. This HQ position was also well dug in with underground officers, trenches, cookhouse and so on. C Coy. re-organized for the assault on the RADAR Sta. The RADAR Sta was found to be stronger than had been anticipated and was engaged by the 19 Cdn Fd Regt which was in support of us. Our mortars also took on the sta but as the concrete works were rather thick and well dug in, little or no damage was done. The day was fast drawing to a close and a decision was finally made and Bde permission obtained to bypass the sta and move on to the Bde	LD

9TH CANADIAN INFANTRY BRIGADE

WO 179/2893
Intelligence/war diary
9TH CANADIAN BRIGADE HQ

Place	Date	Hour	Summary of Events and Information	References to Appendices and initials
SOUTH-AMPTON WATER	5		Weather: Dry, cool and strong wind. Today at 0900 hrs we received the signal for which we have been waiting – the signal to go. At 1100 hrs we pulled out of SOUTHAMPTON WATER to rendezvous at CALESHOT with thousands of other landing craft and ships, spreading out as far as the eye can see. The most amazing thing so far is that in spite of the collosal concentration of ships, troops and equipment, there has been no attempt by the Luftwaffe to bomb. The answer must be that RAF has gained complete air supremacy and the first round is ours. At 1430 the convoy left anchor and we started off on our way to the coast of France. There is a strong wind and the sea is pretty rough for an LCT. Seasick tablets have been issued but in a number of instances fifty tablets would have made no difference. More than one man looks like death warmed up. Final messages from Montgomery, Eisenhower and Crerar were read to those who were able to listen and had their heads out of vomit bags. The Landing Tables, result of months of work, have stood up. We have every vehicle in its allotted place aboard the various craft - but anything else to be added would require a shoehorn.	GEO Appx 1
D-DAY	[6		[Weather: Cool, dry and a strong sea running. After an uneventful night it started to get light at 0345 hrs. 7 and 8 Bdes landed at 0730 hrs after the coast had received a terrific beating from RN ships, SP arty, rockets, hedgerows etc. Flotilla of this bde went round and round in a circle waiting in turn to land. COURSEULLES, BERNIERE and ST. AUBIN could all be seen and they were on fire in many places. A destroyer on our port hit a mine and the report came through that a cruiser astern had also been sunk. Very little fire coming from beaches out to sea from the enemy coast defence batteries. The order to land the bde on Nan WHITE was received about 1030 hrs. No part could be landed on Nan RED as planned and all personnel and vehicles had to come in on the one beach and out through BERNIERE-SUR-MER. The bde got off the beaches quickly but there was a bad traffic jam in the town which took some time to untangle.] Bde HQ suffered the first casualty on landing when Capt. Roy Gilman, BRASCO; was either killed or wounded and evacuated to England. Cpl. Kasper was the last to see him as he was riding across the beach on an M 10 SP A tk gun when a carrier in front went over a mine and nobody has seen him since. BRASCO will be sadly missed as he has been with this bde since last Christmas and is the best BRASCO we have ever had. It is possible that he has been picked up and returned to England. It is to be hoped so. [After a halt of about an hour on the road Bde HQ	GEO

Place	Date	Hour	Summary of Events and Information	Remarks, references to Appendices and initials
	6 cont		moved forward and set up its first headquarters in France at BENY-SUR-MER and awaited orders from Division for the brigade to advance, pass through 8 Cdn Inf Bde and capture the airfield at CARPIQUET. 8 Bde had not been able to get forward as quickly as had been hoped having been held up at the radar station, TREVILLE and DOUVRES. 7 Bde, contrary to expectation, had found after landing the going easier than on the left and pushed forward quickly. The position of our first HQ was not long lived as we were in a wood which was apparently ranged for mortars as a few started dropping shortly after our arrival. By hrs all units had reported they were in assembly areas and ready for the word to go. Nth NS Highrs and 27 Cdn Armd Regt led off at hrs followed by SD & G Highrs and by night Nth NS Highrs and the tanks were in the vicinity of the crossroads north of VILLONS LES BUISSONS under mortar fire and shelling. Bde HQ moved to field near church at BASLY.] There was a good deal of sniping during the night by pro-boche personnel left behind during the enemy withdrawal.	GEO
			[Strange as it may seem we must have attained surprise in the assault as we did not encounter any mines or booby traps back of the beach area and evidence that Gerry pulled out in a hurry is apparent when kit and equipment left in houses is examined. D-Day ended with all the brigade well established ashore and very few casualties incurred.]	
BASLY	7		Weather: Dry and sunny and the wind has dropped. [This has been a critical day with the brigade attacking, being counter attacked, and consolidating. A long, tiring and exacting day which ended with us further inland than any other British, Canadian or American troops except 7 Cdn Inf Bde who are even with us and going great guns.] During the night L Sec Sigs had their first casualties when the line party of Sgt. V.R.	
			Whittingham and Sigmn Cook and Johnston went out to lay line and did not return. Their jeep was found later and it is presumed that they are prisoners. Bde HQ this morning captured more prisoners of war than probably any HQ since the beginning of time. It was not through any wonderful tactical move on the part of HQ but due to the fact that our position on the line of withdrawal of enemy who had been holding out at TAILLEVILLE overnight and as they came scurrying back we roped them in and put them in a cage at the church in BASLY. The PWs did not have much fight left in them and were ready to give up. There were a lot of foreigners mixed up in them. Cpl. D. Todd, BRASCO Cpl, did particularly good work going out by himself with only a	GEO

WO 179/2936

Intelligence/war diary

THE HIGHLAND LIGHT INFANTRY OF CANADA

Place	Date	Hour	Summary of Events and Information	Remarks, references to Appendices and initials
Field	6 June 44		Operations:- Daylight broke on D-Day and presented rather a dismal picture from the weather standpoint. The sea was still rough and choppy and a fairly strong gale was blowing. The sky was dull and threatening. As the morning wore on there were slight showers. The docks were lined with tps long before daybreak. Some had got up around 0400 hrs to watch the flashes given out by the guns as the 6th Airborne Division and Commandos on our left flank attacked the strong coast batteries and vital bridges. Some were huddled in blankets in the throes of sea-sickness and not the least interested in the war. For them the war would only begin when they set foot on good old "tera firma". Others preferred sleep as an antidote to the "ol misery" in the stomach. With the light came an impressive sight. The sea as far as eye could reach was dotted with craft. Little LCIs bobbing along on the high waves, blunt nosed LCTs smashing clumsily into the swell, trim destroyers racing up and down among the fleet in search of underwater enemies and great battleships riding proudly in the distance. One felt awed by the immensity of the picture and at the same time comforted by the presense of such a large number of "big ships" ready to land the support of their powerful guns. About 0700 hrs we came in sight of the shores of France. Our tps were just getting up as they still had plenty of time before their run in. Soon we could make out the little towns along the coast and were able to get our bearings. Firing could be seen coming from some of the buildings and the presence of LCAs going through us to our rear told us that the assaulting brigades had gone in. Then came the exasperating part of the invasion for us. About 0900 hrs we were told to prepare to land. Everyone got into their eqpt and then spent the next two hours "stooging" around the channel in big circles waiting for the "run in". The 7th bde on our right flank appeared to get in with little trouble. The 8th bde front seemed to be a little slower especially on the left around ST. AUBIN where the North Shore Regt seemed to be meeting stiff opposition. Fires broke out in some of the houses on the rt flank of 8th bde.	c. OC

Place	Date	Hour	Summary of Events and Information	References to Appendices
Field	6 June	44	Shortly after 11 o'clock we were informed that HLI would not land on RED Beach in the vicinity of ST. AUBIN as the opposition had been so strong that the assault tps had not succeeded in getting far inland. We later learned that the Radar station near TAILLEVILLE was much more heavily defended than we had expected. [At approximately 1140 we made our "run in" to WHITE Beach in front of BERNIERES-SUR-MER. All the LCIs bearing the rifle coys touched down almost to-gether. The Navy did an excellent job getting us ashore as it was one of the driest landings we had managed in some time, being only knee deep. As soon as the ramps were lowered men began to stream off carrying bicycles.] The only mishap was in the beaching of B Coy. boat which carried the CO and his command gp. It came in fast, but the bow swung to the right and stove in the ramp on the neighbouring craft. It tried again and this time hit an underwater mine blowing a hole about 3 ft in diameter in the bow. No one was injured. The approaches to the beach were sown with obstacles, such as Hedgehogs, element C and poles. Teller mines were placed on top of many of these as underwater obstacles to craft. A number of LCAs from the assault wave were lying under water where they had hit these mines. [The beach itself was in a terrible confusion. There was only about 25 yds of beach in front of the promenade which was heavily wired so that there were only the exits put up by the beach gp. On the beach, which the beach gp had not had time to properly organize due to the fighting on the beaches, were jammed tps with bicycles, vehicles and tanks all trying to move toward the exits. Movement was frequently brought to a standstill when a vehicle up ahead became stuck. It was an awful shambles and not at all like the organized rehearsals we had had. More than one uttered a fervent prayer of thanksgiving that our air umbrella was so stong. One gun ranged on the beach even would have done untold damage but the 9th Cdn Inf Bde landed without a shot fired on them.] Against this welling mass of movement the Beach Gp were trying to set up and function in all its branches, but the opposition was too great. They had to be content to "nest" casualties until we had passed on.	c.o.c.

SHEET 3

Place	Date	Hour	Summary of Events and Information	Remarks, references to Appendices and initials
Field	6 June	44	We had not gone many yds inland when we met the rear elements of the 8th Cdn Inf Bde. The streets of the shattered village were blocked with rubble from the heavy preparatory shelling and bombing. In the neighbourhood of the church we were held up. We could go no farther as the roads were blocked by the transport of the assaulting bns. Well placed MG posts and snipers had caused the QOR to deploy and attack them. An 88 mm gun had knocked out three SP guns as they emerged from the village. [Every one piled up behind choking the rds, while the posns up forward were cleared.] As progress was impossible and as there was danger of the road being shelled or straffed the CO decided to pull up and wait until the road was cleared. [At approximately 1330 we pulled into an estate just behind the church and began to dig in. Here we had a chance to drink a can of self heating soup or cocoa and eat some bully beef and hard tack. Here the sun broke through and the day became quite hot and sultry. It was here too that our F vehicles met us and we were able to organize completely rather than in the Assembly Area.] We travelled with three coys riding airborne bicycles and D Coy. riding dispersed among the vehs. Our route was down the main road to BENY-SUR-MER which had been laid down as our assembly area. [Progress up ahead was still slower than anticipated and it wasn't until 1845 hrs that our advance elements reported being in BENY-SUR-MER. By 1915 the whole Bn. was in the villages and as assemblying had been completed earlier we were ready to move across the S.P. toward our objective. But the road ahead was jammed with Chaudiere vehicles.] It was in BENY-SUR-MER that our unit had its first real contact with the enemy. We were continuously mortared as we stopped in the village. There were no casualties but some dropped uncomfortably close. While awaiting the order to move tps could be seen with a book in one hand reading off French phrases much to the amusement of the inhabitants. BENY-SUR-MER had had a German barracks and the Germans were hardly out of the village before the inhabitants began to loot the place. Men struggled by with bags of flour, a wheelbarrow full of army boots, a hind leg of beef, chairs, clothes, boxes of black rye bread, butcher's saws and countless other articles. Women came by with chickens, butter, curtains, sheets, pillows, dishes, cutlery, bowls, etc. Even the parish priest was seen to carry off a set of dishes. People were all excited and friendly, offering us their best luck, glasses of milk and wine.	c.o.c

Place	Date	Hour	Summary of Events and Information	Remarks, references to Appendices and initials
Field	6 June	44	[Just as we were ready to move on, at approximately 2145 hrs, the order came to stay where we were for the night. The NNS were to stop at VILLONS-LES-BUISSON with the SD&Gs on their right and the HLI in the rear.] The 27 Armd Regt which was carrying the NNS were to support them in their area. It was fast getting dark and hurriedly dug in our defensive positions around the village. Reports of enemy armour moving north out of CAEN put us on our mettle and we prepared to receive a possible armour counter-attack earlier than we had anticipated. Thus ended D-Day our first day in Normandy. [Little sleep was had that night but no one cared. Although not a shot had been fired by our Bn. as yet, we were on enemy soil, and at the end of four years of waiting.] Some were a little disappointed that we had not as yet tangled with the enemy and felt a personal reproach that we had not succeeded in reaching the airport our objective. But war always travels more slowly than schemes as the unexpected enters in. The 8th bde on our front had reached their objective although their left flank was trailing. The 7th on our right had reached their objective with little trouble. We were in a position to push through the 8th in the morning and attack our objective so tomorrow would be another day.	c.o.c
Field	7 June	44	The night was fairly quiet. Allied planes were over and met by AA fire not comparable to that in England. Occasional mortar fire from enemy positions failed to hit anyone. Our patrols reported no enemy actively in our neighbourhood. The Brig called an "0" gp at 0545 hrs. [The Bn. was to be ready to move at 0730 hrs and carry out the remainder of the plan laid down for D day.] At 0620 hrs the first HLI prisoner was brought in by D Coy. He was a sniper caught wandering around in their area. The enemy were dropping paratroops in the area to strengthen their defences and to disrupt our organization behind the lines. Our vanguard (A Coy.) moved at 0810 hrs. B Coy. 0900 hrs. The NNS had come under fire of the enemy and were engaged in a scrap. Shortly after the SD&Gs came under fire from the left flank. At this point we were held up by enemy AFXs left turning in the road just south of COLOMBY-SUR-THAON. These had been knocked out by the Chaudiere Regt who had been surprised early in the morning. While we stopped we had good seats for an aerial dog fight in which our Spits came out victor as the Ju 88s tried to get our convoy. [At approximately 0930 hrs our carriers passed BASLY and reported progress slow due to action by the NNS up ahead.]	c.o.c

WO 179/2974
Intelligence/war diary
THE STORMONT, DUNDAS &
GLENGARRY HIGHLANDERS

Place	Date	Hour	Summary of Events and Information	Remarks, references to Appendices and initials
On Board Craft No 636 SOUTHAMPTON ROADS	June 4		always been a pleasure working with a Navy which is invariably co-operative and helpful. The IO briefed the drivers this afternoon. Sunday... how quickly the time is passing! The weather cool and cloudy, with a fresh wind. Breakfast at eight, cleaning and inspection of weapons and MT. The men are in excellent spirits. All around us lie craft of every concievable shape and size and down the navigation channel moves an endless stream of ships to their allotted areas. The Skipper (a mere boy!) informs us that 4,000 ships, not including landing craft, are to take part in this event. The magnitude of the operation becomes apparent. Wind became stronger, and rain fell during the night.	RRP
	June 5		Cloudy and fair wind today. The Serial Comd. Capt. Forman (whose birthday it is) is awakened at eight by the CO singing "Happy birthday to you", much to the amusement of all and sundry. At 1500 hrs. the Craft Comd. tells us the Invasion is "on" and an electric thrill sweeps the craft. So this is the day we sail... tomorrow we land in France! Maps are distributed to Officers, NCOs and drivers, who proceed to study same. Messages are read from the supreme Comd. and Gen. Crerar, and a pamphlet on France is distributed. The sea has a fair swell but has a promise of fine weather ahead.	RRP
BERNIERES-SUR -MER, FRANCE	June 6		Weather cool and cloudy, fresh wind. Our course due south. At 0600 hrs we are about 16 miles from the coast. [Large numbers of planes are passing over the clouds. Little to report until land is sighted. News is none too plentiful but by observation and messages received it is evident the operation is proceeding satisfactorily. We see large fires in the BERNIERES-SUR-MER sector in which we are supposed to land, and also fires are raging at ST. AUBIN-SUR-MER. So far, remarkably, no enemy planes have been sighted. Destroyers are supporting the infantry landing and dense clouds of smoke cover the beaches. At 1100 hrs we receive code word "Katnip" meaning "9 C.I.B to land in Nan sector". We touch down at 1220 hrs on WHITE beach BERNIERS-SUR-MER.]	RRP
		[1530	We are still in the town of BERNIERS-SUR-MER. The enemy strong point at ST. AUBIN-SUR-MER has not yet been destroyed. Q.O.R. are reported to be attacking enemy locations two miles south of BERNIERS-SUR-MER. The damage to the village	

Place	Date	Hour	Summary of Events and Information	Remarks, references to Appendices and initials
		[	is not so great as we has imagined it might have been and numerous civilians are seen making friends with their liberators. The marching troops are further up the road and as we have no wireless set open yet, a DR is sent forward to locate them.] The weather now is clearing and it is much warmer. We see our first Gerry plane! A couple of Spitfires are hot on its tail. Small groups of enemy prisoners are being taken to the beach.	
		1600	Our assembly area is now reported clear of enemy, with fwd troops moving on BASLY. We should be soon moving fwd. The Contact Dèt is doing a good job keeping us informed.	
		[1645	The unit is now concentrated along the road at ref. 994848 waiting for an opportunity to move fwd.] Lt. Grant reports in after acting as guide and landing with the 8th Bde.	
		1655	We move fwd again. The NNS have now reached the assembly area.	
BENY-SUR-MER		[1830	We arrive at BENY-SUR-MER and at 1900 hrs we are making ready to move again.] At 2000 hrs, fwd NNS troops are reported to have passed BASLY but are running into difficulties. It is now becoming late and the NNS are told not to proceed past VILLONS-LES-BUISSONS. This is not our objective, but we are not too dismayed or disappointed; at least we are through the much vaunted West wall and we hear the other units are also moving fwd. Enemy mortar fire and resistance becomes stronger and [we are ordered to stay where we are, in the vicinity of the church at BENY-SUR-MER.] The CO hold and "O" Group and issues orders for Coy. localities. Casualties during mortar fire are one killed and 5 wounded. The mortars are taken out and we settle in comparative calm. Air raids on the beach area at 2345.	SEE APPENDIX 4(a)
	June 1	0630	The night and early morning continued with active enemy patrolling on foot and with armour. A small patrol was shot up in "A" Coy. area. We had one OR killed, one officer, Lt R Grant wounded and 11 ORs wounded during the night. [At 0620 the CO held and "O" Gp after going to Bde. The orders are that we are to continue as per plan, endeavouring to make more speed.] Enemy air activity so far in unit area has been nil. The only confirmation of enemy units is 711 Div which was reported holding the coast.	RRO
BASLY		0830	6 enemy, including a boy of 12 years, gave themselves up. 4 enemy gliders are reported to have landed at 993783. So far, none encountered.	

WO 179/2948

Intelligence/war diary
THE NORTH NOVA SCOTIA HIGHLANDERS

Place	Date	Hour	Summary of Events and Information	Remarks, references to Appendices and initials
	6 June 1944 Tuesday		Weather: clear and warm. At 0630 hours all wireless sets were in listening watch to keep the Battalion informed of the progress of the assault battalions. [At 0804 hours the leading companies of the Seventh and Eighth Canadian Infantry Brigades touched down. At 0929 hours information had been received from the Seventh Canadian Infantry Brigade that the operation on their front was proceeding according to plan. At 1100 hours the order came through that we were to land through the Eighth Canadian Infantry Brigade according to plan. The marching troops in Landing Crafts Infantry (Large) touched down at 1140 hours on Nan WHITE beach, ST. BERNIERES, map reference 9985, sheet 7E/5 and reported "NAGA". At 1235 hours, after several landings, and finding the beach blocked by craft of the Eighth Canadian Infantry Brigade, we were able to land. Only one Mortar carrier and crew were casualties, when they ran over a mine after landing. By 1400 hours all our troops were ashore, but as the Eighth Canadian Infantry Brigade had not found the going as easy as expected, we were unable to get through the town and were unable to assemble at "ELDER", near BENY-SUR-MER as planned, and the Commanding Officer decided to assemble the battalion in a field, map reference 993845. By 1605 hours the battalion was able to move off to "ELDER", arriving there at 1644 hours after bypassing the Eighth Canadian Infantry Brigade. We had just arrived in this Assembly area when we came under shell and mortar fire, resulting in five casualties, two killed and three wounded. Word was received from the Brigadier that we were to move as soon as we were ready. The Commanding Officer gave the order to move at 1820 hours and the Battalion moved off according to plan in the following order: The Recce troop of the 27 Canadian Armoured Regiment forming a screen, followed by the carrier platoon under the command of Captain E.S. Gray, each section carrying one platoon of "C" company, followed by a platoon of Machine Guns, one troop of M 10s, 2 assault sections of pioneers and four detachments of our own Anti-Tank guns. This composed the vanguard under command of Major J.D. Learment. "A" Company was on the right of the axis on "A" squadron of tanks, "B" Company on the left on "B" squadron of tanks and "D" Company on squadron "C" tanks, bringing up the rear on the main axis. Command Post followed the vanguard, Battalion Headquarters and Support Company with "D" company. Objective – CARPIQUET Airfield. Due to the difficulty the Eighth Canadian Infantry Brigade was having in dislodging the enemy and as time was getting on, it was decided to break through their front before they had consolidated on their objective, and continue along the axis.	

Place	Date	Hour	Summary of Events and Information	Remarks, references to Appendices and initials
	6 June 1944 Tuesday (Cont'd)		[The vanguard did not encounter any serious opposition until it reached VILLONS-LES-BUISSONS, where it passed code word "DORIS". However "A" Company on "A" squadron of tanks became involved in a fight at COLOMBY-SUR-THAON. It did not last long, but held them up, as well as "D" Company which was coming along behind them on "C" squadron of tanks. By this time it was realized the battalion could not reach its objective by dark, and we were ordered by higher authority not to go beyond report line "DORIS", cross-roads map reference 007757, sheet 7F/1, but to dig in where we found ourselves and to form a firm base while there was still light. As the vanguard was already fighting in VILLONS-LES-BUISSONS, cleaning out three machinegun nests and killing most of the crews, taking prisoners and weapons, The Comd Officer decided to close up the battalion and consolidate astride the ANISY-LES-BUISSONS - CAEN cross roads. The van guard, being astride the main CAEN road, dug in and sent out patrols to ANISY and VILLONS-LES-BUISSONS. "B" company on "B" aquadron arrived one half hour later and dug in on left flank astride the road running towards ANISY.] Casualties for the day: Killed: 4 Other Ranks. Wounded: 6 Other Ranks.	

DIVISIONAL
TROOPS

WO 179/2768
Intelligence/war diary
CANADIAN 3RD INFANTRY DIVISION HQ

Place	Date	Hour	Summary of Events and Information	Remarks, references to Appendices and initials
HMS Hilary	1 to 5 Jun 44		First 3 days were spent in loading the Div. A "Trouble Shooting" Staff consisting of AA & QMG, G 2 Ops, DAQMG, G 3 (SD), PMLO and Bde Reps dealt with the many snags that were encountered. It was due, in no small measure, to this staff that the Div was completely loaded as planned. The loading was slowed down somewhat due to att units not having had sufficient driving experience, and also because our own troops had been trained throughout in driving onto LCTs, and were now suddenly comfronted with LSTs. There was no bombing of the invasion Hards or Ports. The majority of Div HQ at sea anchored off COWES on HQ Ship HMS Hilary or the Stand-in Ship HMS Royal Ulsterman. The GOC, CRA, GSO 1 and GSO 2 (L) remained at Vectis coming aboard D minus 1. The Ops Set-up at sea was divided into 2 main teams (a) The Comd Gp consisting of the Comd 9 Cdn Inf Bde (Deputy Div Comd), GSO 2 Ops, DAQMG and Deputy Heads of Arms.	
			June 5 was to have been D-Day but a 24 hr postponement was made due to weather conditions.	
	[6 Jun		This was the long awaited D-Day. The sea was much more unruly than most of us expected – probably fooling the Germans as well as ourselves. From the Hilary one could see, long before dawn, the constant flashes of exploding bombs from the coast of France.] There seemed to be a myriad of boats – all sizes and shapes tossing on the waves. [First message received was at 0618 hrs informing us that our amphibious tanks might not be launched due to heavy seas.] Subsequent messages came to the Ops desk in a steady stream, from Navy, Army and Airforce. [The DD tks were finally launched from about 4000 yds to 2500 yds on one sector, on the other sector the craft beached to unload. Rough weather was responsible for some being drowned and others arriving late on the beaches.]	
		[0809	The leading Inf touched down on both Bde Sectors.]	
		[1050	Gen R.F.L. Keller issued the order to land the reserve Bde – 9 Cdn Inf Bde – and Stand-in HQ on the left Bde Sector (the one assaulted by 8 Cdn Inf Bde). The Div Commander with half his HQ Staff left the Hilary at 1145 hrs, the other half headed by the GSO 1 Lt. Col. J.D. Mingay left at approximately 1340 hrs]	

Place	Date	Hour	Summary of Events and Information	Remarks, references to Appendices and initials
BERNIERS-SUR-MER	6 Jun	[1435	Gen Keller held a conference of Brig. Blackader and Cunningham – Commanders of 8 and 9 Cdn Inf Bdes respectively and Brig. Wyman Commanding 2 Cdn Armd Bde.	
			This first "O" Gp on French soil confirmed that the N Shore R were in TAILLEVILLE and it was decided that 8 Cdn Inf Bde would take BENY-SUR-MER. When this had been accomplished 9 Cdn Inf Bde would pass through.	
		1530	By this time BENY-SUR-MER was clear of the enemy and 9 Cdn Inf Bde had started their move forward. Meanwhile 7 Cdn Inf Bde had overcome the enemy in CROIX-SUR-MER, BANVILLE and had secured the crossing at TIERCEVILLE.	
		2200	7 Cdn Inf Bde had occupied the area LANTHEUIL, LE FRESNE CAMILLY and CAINET. 8 Cdn Inf Bde occupied area COLOMBY-SUR-THAON, AUGUERNY. 9 Cdn Inf Bde occupied area VILLONS-LES-BUISSONS – LE VEY.	
			Div HQ was situated in a small orchard at BERNIERS-SUR-MER. Everyone dug themselves in. The veh situation was very limited, consisting of wireless half-track and one jeep. Sleep was not contemplated by reason of excitement and also by heavy AA fire being put up on the beaches against enemy bombing. Our defence platoon had not landed so everyone, other than those doing immediate jobs set about guarding the HQ.]	
			SEE DAILY BATTLE LOG APPENDED FOR A DAY ONWARDS.	
BENY-SUR-MER	[7 Jun		The advance of the Div continues. [Div HQ moved up on foot to BENY-SUR-MER,] passing on its way two once active 88 mm German guns, and their crews.	
		1000	Div Commander 51 (H) Div, BGS, and DAA & QMG 1 Corps visited GOC.	
		[1020	The final objective was seized by the R Wpg Rif. N Shore R were engaged in the RADAR Station battle. This is a tough nut to crack because the station is underground and built with reinforced concrete. 9 Cdn Inf Bde encountered enemy tanks and Inf area AUTHIE. The attack was repulsed but it was decided to withdraw the Bde to more favourable ground in the area VILLONS LES BUISSONS.]	

WO 179/3050
Intelligence/war diary
12TH FIELD REGIMENT CDN

TOP SECRET

Place	Date	Hour	Summary of Events and Information	Remarks, references to Appendices and initials
Field	June 44 1		There was considerable air activity last night, one bomb fell in the wagon lines of the 13 Cdn Fd Regt which was in its standings on the FAREHAM-BOTLEY road. Five M7s and two Sherman tanks were badly damaged. Some houses were wrecked and set on fire. No one was killed, but several gunners and civilians were injured. This regiment spent the day on personal maintenance, 5 mile route marches and base ball. Some serials left for their assembly areas.	Jms
	2		Several more serials left for their assembly areas. The day was uneventful.	Jms
	3		All the gun groups left for their assembly areas except for the 11 Battery, who are assembling in the present camp. Recce parties, COs and group commanders party left for camp C 7.	
	4		Troops were loaded onto their LCTs. It was a tight fit but all were loaded without incident. The wind blew up in the afternoon and gale warnings were sent out. Exercise "OVERLORD" was postponed for 24 hours.	Jms
	5		The wind subsided somewhat, but the SOUTHAMPTON waters were fairly rough. At 2100 hrs it was officially announced to all members of the assault that exercise "OVERLORD" would take place at "H" hour at approximately 0730 hrs 6 June 44. The remaining parties who were not already briefed were briefed, and the 3 Cdn Divisional convoy sailed for its rendezvous approximately nine miles off the coast of FRANCE, our beaches being between the town of LA RIVIERE and COURSELLES-SUR-MER. 12 Fd Regiment was scheduled to land on MIKE RED.	Jms Jms
	6		The assault on the beaches was preceded by heavy bombardment from naval forces consisting of two cruisers, four destroyers of the Hunt class, rocket craft and LCGs etc as well as our own 105 mm guns who were firing 120 rounds apiece. At the last minute it was found that the Avries were late, and this caused some confusion to the landing parties, as many of the beach obstacles were not removed. Our recce parties landed at approximately H plus 15 with the leading assault companies of the infantry. They met heavy mortar fire and Major fire and Major E. PICKERING 2 i/c of the Regiment was wounded and Sigmn. SWAN was killed. Gnr. A.A. ELLMAN, batman, was badly wounded as was Major J.D. ROSS of the 16 Battery. Lt. E.C. GOTHARD, CPO of the 43 Battery was also wounded.	

SHEET 2

Place	Date	Hour	Summary of Events and Information	Remarks, references to Appendices and initials
Field	June 6		Heavy fighting took place on the beach. The enemy flooded the low land behind the beach, and the beach exists became impassible. The Engineers worked furiously with bulldozers to clear them. In the meantime the regiment landed and took up a gun position on the beach. In many cases engaging the enemy over open sights. Snipers and mortars were taking a heavy toll of the men on the beach. The WINNIPEG RIFLES managed to get forward and clear out several machine gun nests, but the REGINAS were held up for some time at the little village of GRAYE-SUR-MERE. It was approximately 1600 hrs when the squadrons of the INNS OF COURT managed to get through the beach exits and get away on their job of blowing the bridges from CAEN east and north towards the beaches. At approximately 1700 hrs 12 Fd Regiment was able to take up its position near gun area "MARY" which was between the town of BANVILLE and SAINT CROIX-SUR-MER. Prisoners began coming in and the 13 Fd regiment managed to land all their troops excepting one whose ramp door had become jammed. By 1000 hrs 7 Brigade forward companies had reached the intermediate objective which was known as code word "ELM". On this line Brigadier FOSTER decided to re-organize for attacking the following morning.	Jms
	7		The attack was launched early Wednesday morning supported by 12 and 13 Field Regiments and two batteries from the ROYAL MARINES armoured support regiment who are under command and of the 12 and 13 Fd for the invasion. The attack was slowly pressed home, and by late afternoon the WINNIPEG RIFLES were on the final objective known as "OAK" which was the railway line running from CAEN to BAYEUX. By this time elements of the 3rd A/Tk and 246 and 248 batteries ROYAL ARTILLERY plus several squadrons of armour had been landed, and were able to take part in an anti-tank role. In the centre the REGINA RIFLES were a little short of their objective while on our left flank the 9th Brigade who had come through the 8th Brigade were still short of the objective, due to stubborn enemy resistance, one of which is the RADAR Station near BENY-SUR-MER and which is still in enemy hands although surrounded.	Jms
	8		The weather became better today, and although the Luftwaffe had been pounding the beaches and our forward troops by night, more men and material had been landed, and everyone felt we were going stronger and stronger. Today was a day many of us will never forget as the enemy threw in attack after attack, the regiment firing on DF and DF SOS tasks, MIKE and UNCLE targets practically all day and all night. In the after-	

WO 179/3051
Intelligence/war diary
13TH FIELD REGIMENT CDN.

Place	Date	Hour	Summary of Events and Information	Remarks, references to Appendices and initials
PARK GATE	1 June 44		The regt is marshalled for operation "OVERLORD". The Tks and SPs of the 22 bty have been replaced and waterproofing is progressing satisfactorily by dint of hard work in their sub-marshalling area.	JWY
	2 June		The entire regt has now moved to sub-marshalling areas.	JWY
	3 June		The regt has ceased to exist as such. Some parties load.	JWY
	4 June		The remaining parties load. 5 June 44 is to be D-day.	JWY
	5 June		There is a postponement of 24 hrs.	JWY
NORMANDY, FRANCE	[6 June		D-Day with H-hr expected at 0735 hrs. It is dull morning with low clouds and poor visability, which makes the projected aireal bombardment out of the question. The wind has died down but the waves have not.	JWY
			[At 0655 hrs the 22 bty commenced ranging and soon after all guns opened fire from the LCT on the regimental concentration fired in support of the REGINA RIFLS REGT who are assaulting COURSELLES (NAN - GREEN BEACH, mr 970 855 sheet 7E/5). Major J.D. BAIRD was fire control officer. The concentration was most effective.]	
			First to land from the regt were Capt A. F. WRENSHALL and Capt J. ELSE and their OP parties. Both Capt. ELSE and his able Gnr. ROBINSON were wounded as soon as they touched down on the beach but they continued on. [Gnr. HOLTZMAN, Capt. ELSE's signaller did outstanding work in calling for fire from "S" Troop, 2 RMAS in order to engage an enemy block-house on the beach which was causing casualties to REGINAS in their attempt to clean up the town. The RMAS eliminated this nuisance.]	
			The recce party consisting of the RSO (Lt. T.C. GREENLEES) and the CPOs (Lt. J.M. DOOHAN, Lt. R.J. WALDIE, and Lt. J.T.R. BROWNRIDGE) and 3 CPOAs landed on MIKE sector at approx H.20. L/Bdr FOOTE was wounded by shrapnel. [A gun area north of GRAZE-SUR-MER was prepared.]	
			[Capt STEELE, FOO with C Coy. REGINA RIFLE REGT landed at H-40.]	
			Major G.F. RAINNIE, Unit Landing Officer, Cpl. HAUK, N.A.; Gnr. HIGGS, W.A.; and Gnr. Le. BEL, S. landed on MIKE RED. It is thought that their craft struck a mine as their bodies were later found on the beach.	

SHEET 2

Place	Date	Hour	Summary of Events and Information	Remarks, references to Appendices and initials
NORMANDY, FRANCE	6 June	44	(Cont) Capt. W. DIRKS of the 44 bty was killed when his craft struck a mine. Gnr. MOODIE, the able with Capt .Dirks, is missing but is thought to have escaped. L/Bdr FERGUSON, the signaller with Capt. Dirks, swam ashore and joined his bty.	JWY
			[Capts N.W. PICKLE & J DRAFFIN landed with 1 C Scot R at H-45 and proceeded inland in support of this unit.]	
			Major YOUNG, the Unit Deployment Officer, died of wounds as did Gnr. TAYLOR, R.F., his signaller.	
			Lt. Col. F. Le. P.T. CLIFFORD with Lt. G.H. MILSON and party landed on NAN GREEN at approx H-30 and made their way into the town of COURSEULLES.	
			Capt. J. ELSE was again wounded and later lost consciousness from loss of blood but did not return to a dressing station until he had received the third direct order to do so from the Coy. commander.	
			Capt. A.F. WRENSHALL was wounded by MG fire and brought back to REVIERS by L/Sgt. DAVIDSON.	
			[The 44 bty was the first bty to land (NAN GREEN) and occupied a posn south of COURSEULLES.]	
			[Major J.D. Baird took over as 2 IC and the first regimental gun area was taken up up at 950 838 (north of BANVILLE) at about 1800 hrs.]	
			Lt. J.M. DOOHAN was wounded and had to be evacuated.	
			GA Tank lost a track on the beach and on recovery by the 22 bty HT section it was started on its way back to the gun area. An 88 mm gun in ambush gave it two rounds and that was our first veh casualty. No lives were lost. Four snipers were rounded up by 44 bty:- I German SCD and 3 turncoat Russians. All glad to be out of the war.	
			The general impression of the prisoners being taken was their poor physique and no middle-age group.	
			[Our right flank was completely exposed as one sector of the beach was not mopped-up until later in the operation. German-air activity was apparent throughout the night but resulted in only one cas.] All ranks became eager and efficient in digging slit trenches. Only a few tgts were engaged but DF & DF SOS tasks were registered. It required all ranks xon "Stand to" to protect our area. [Very few mines were detected in our area.] Tks continued to cut OP lines.	
			Fatigue was noticiable due to 24 hr packs, the rough voyage over, lack of sleep and the natural tension of a combined operation against a prepared enemy.	

Intelligence/war diary
14TH FIELD REGIMENT RCA

Place	Date	Hour	Summary of Events and Information	Remarks, references to Appendices and initials
LCT 855 on Run-in and BERNIERES-SUR-MER Sheet 3a and 8 CHERBOURG & CAEN 1/250,000	6 June	0500 0515	Passage had been uneventful during night. Sky was clearing, and the wind had gone down to some extent. Zero hour for operation OVERLORD on our front was 0730 hrs with a postponement Later coming through of 1/2 hour. 14/19 Arty Gp under Lt. Col. H.S. Griffin was in support of the 8 CIB who were disposed on the run-in QOR on the right landing right at BERNIERES-SUR-MER and N Shore Regt on the left. Fire commenced at H-30 and continued until H 5 on the strong point at 998852 BERNIERS-SUR-MER. The concentration was NOT as tight as had been attained in some training exercises due to the running sea. The senior regt'l officers were disposed as follows:- Lt.Col. H.S. Griffin was on the Bde HQ ship HMS Waveney with Brigadier Blackader. Major Mac G. Young, the A/OC was on a LCH with the CO of the QOR, Lt. Col. Sprague. Major A.W. Duguid, regt'l fire control officer was on a LCSM. Major J.F. Kibler was unit landing officer Major G.E. Purcell was unit deployment officer. The FOOs were deployed as follows:- Assault Coy FOOs - Capt. S.H. Standen Capt. J.M. Barclay Reserve Coy FOOs - Capt. N.B. Buchanan Capt. T.L. Carter The three CPOs and the RSO, Lieuts Belyea, Lee and Flintoft and Viets and their parties landed in LC. As with the Reserve Coy. QOR at H 35. The L.C.Ts turned off after run-in and finally beached at 0925 hrs. Beach congested and exits had not been completely breached and cleared of mines - time until majority of S.P. equipments clear of beach one hour - several jeeps and one carrier and one half track drowned but all recovered subsequently.	
		1130	First Gun Position scattered in fields on right of BERNIERES-SUR-MER 200 yds off beach. RHQ in bombproof cellar at 989856. 18 guns in action, 3 on read in traffic jam and 3 destroyed by enemy action. The three SP equipments which deployed in field SOUTH of BERNIERES-SUR-MER received direct hit from a supposed 88 mm near TAILLEVILLE area and burnt out immediately.	Page 3.

Place	Date	Hour	Summary of Events and Information	Remarks, references to Appendices and initials
			Gave some support during later morning and early afternoon. Crest clearance hampered all guns.	
		1730	Brigadier PAS Todd visited the Command Post and was especially keen to get the regiment forward to Gun Area JANE.	
		1900	Recce parties went forward to area 989817 with RHQ. The order of march was 66, 81, 34 and RHQ. The regiment moved forward providing continuous support and guns were sorted out to their respective troops which had not been possible hitherto.	
		2030	Gun position was under heavy mortar fire and several casualties sustained. 66 Bty moved to gully. Position was open.	
			General picture of the part played by the FOO is as follows:	
			Capt. J.B. Lesslie went forward with R DE LA CHAUDIERRE to BASLY and engaged 105 mm bty in vicinity, later changed over to HLI and went forward to VILLONS-LES-BUISSONS in the morning 7 June. During this period engaged targets by observed shooting at GALMANCHE, ST. CONTEST and vicinity.	
			Major A.W. Duguid took over from Capt. T.L. Carter when wounded and in the early afternoon 6 June went to BENY-SUR-MER, picked up a tank troop proceeded around EAST flank of BASLY into LA MARE – Germans in occupation - engaged tgts at COLOMBY SUR THAON and Xrds 002777 and proceeded to ANGUERNY - Germans in occupation and returned to rd june 005778 to join QOR at 1700 hrs. QOR went through ANGUERNY and up to Bde intermediate objective ring contour 013769. Laid on DF SOS in the area – spent night 6/7 June in orchard m.r. 012773.	
			Capt W.L. Lawson went forward as COOP with the NNS Highrs – proceeded through BENY-SUR-MER towards BASLY and thence to Xrds NE of VILLONS-LES-BUISSONS m.r. 008759 - registered DF SOS task using smoke.	
			Night 6/7 June the regiment placed in support 9 CIB Major Young and Capt Buchanan were forward during this whole period.	
			Casualties due to battle 6 June:-	
			Killed:- Major G.E. Purcell, Capt. J.M.Barnlay, Sgt. Sciberas, R.L., Bdr. Hooton, K.J., L/Bdr. Birss, J.R., Gnr. Clavelle, A.F., Gnr. Dupuis, W.J., Gnr. Goff, R., Gnr. Massey, C.A.,	
			Wounded:- Capt. T.L. Carter, Lieut W.D. Cox, Lieut J.M. Hamilton, BSM. McCulloch, A., Sgt. Barr, A.M., L/Bdr Caverly, M., Gnr. Ballantine, K.R., Gnr. Dawson, P.C., Gar. Jordan, L.F., Gnr. Lyon, C.R., Gnr. McFeat, W.P., Gnr. Zedan, H., Gnr. Vieau, D.V.	Page 4

WO 179/3086

Intelligence/war diary

4TH CANADIAN LIGHT ANTI-AIRCRAFT REGIMENT

Place	Date	Hour	Summary of Events and Information	Remarks, references to Appendices and initials
Camp A. 22 ENGLAND	1-6-44		Clear and mild the greater part of the day. All the regiment sealed in camp including all drivers and vehs, it looks much as if we should not be in this area at for very long. Lt. Col. Woodrow came back to camp at 1400 hrs to check on how the unit is progressing. Returned to his camp at 1800 hrs. All vehs being carefully checked. This is the best stathe camp yet, the organization and staff are good. Part II Order #24 d/31 May 44	Appx. 2 mwm
Camp A. 22 ENGLAND	2-6-44		Scattered clouds, quite cool and windy. Capt. H.I. Kennedy RQM connected with a few stores today, berets, crash helmets and assault jerkins. Contact made with Lt-Col Woodrow at 1545 hrs, he gave final instructions to the Regt. Sports once again going with great gusto, the day was capped by an inter-battery game – 69 vs 100 (offrs). The men are in great physical condition and mentally ready for anything. Morale could not be higher.	mwm
Camp A. 22 ENGLAND	3-6-44		Cloudy cool, dull. Major F.A.L. Charlesworth 2 i/c contacted the Camp comdt at 1000 hrs today to try to clear up what our position is and found out that we are in the correct camp but our vehs should not be sealed with us. Movement control and static staffs have confused our position and task in the assault placing us in the same category as the small residue parties from other 3 Div units, whose main parties all landed very early in the show. Recreation and sports providing ample outlet for everyones cooped in feeling. Pictures running from 1300 hrs until 2000 hrs. Softball, soccer, volley-ball, darts, table tennis etc all provide ways of keeping everyone happy. Work proceeding along. Daily checks and examination of all eqpt and loads.	mwm
Camp A. 22 ENGLAND	4-6-44		Scattered clouds, cool, rain from 1700 hrs onwards. Voluntary church service at 1030 hrs. Afternoon sports, the main attraction being softball games 69th vs 100 Btys, 69 won 17-16. Shows, bingo and sing-song kept everyone entertained in the evening.	mwm
Camp A. 22	5-6-44		Cool scattered clouds, very quiet, only routine work and rechecking of all preparations. Route marches outside the sealed camp with full marching order. Sports entertainment and work intermingled from first to last light.	mwm
Camp A. 22	6-6-44		Scattered clouds, cool and warm, alternatley. At 0930 hrs the announcement was made over BBC that it was D-day, the great offensive had begun. News was received by the men with great spirits and everyone eager to get going. Final and complete checks of every detail in sqpt being constantly made. Personnel on sports parade at 1330 hrs watched 100 bty defeat 69th in softball in a first class game. Maps of France were issued to RHQ, 69 & 100 Btys Part II Order No. 25	Appx.2 mwm

Place	Date	Hour	Summary of Events and Information	Remarks, references to Appendices and initials
Camp A.22 ENGLAND	6-6-44		covering the area in vicinity of CAEN from 1/25000 to 1/250000 scale. Major F.A.L.Charlesworth gave the regtl offrs a brief insight into the show at 1600 hrs. The regt is under 6 hrs notice to move from 1600 hrs.	mwm
Camp A.22 ENGLAND	7-6-44		Scattered clouds, cool and dry. Normal camp routine. Maps issued to drivers at 1400 hrs. Orders to move rec'd at 1800 hrs by Major Charlesworth. to Move to camp A.11 by 1900 hrs. Crossed SP from A.22 at 1910 hrs. Vehs marshalled into craft loads on arrival at A.11 dispersal point. Personnel reed a hot meal by 2200 hrs. Part II Order No. 25A	App. 2 mwm
Camp A.11 ENGLAND	8-6-44		Cloudy dull, fairly warm. Orders received to move to boxes at 2300 hrs cancelled at 1500 hrs. Craft loads and serial commanders placed on 45 min notice to move from 2000 hrs on. Final Preparations completed and practically all of final waterproofing completed. Regiment in two craft loads:- LST 1026 – 6 guns 1 jeep from F tp 100 Bty, (also 51 pers.) 6 guns 1 jeep 51 pers from E tp 100 Bty, walking party 36 ORs from each bty i/c Lt Lavellee, Capt Waterous o.c. craft. LST 1027:- RHQ, 10 vehs 39 all ranks, 69 Bty 147 all ranks, 24 guns 3 jeeps 8-3 ton 158" WB – 100 bty 141 all ranks 24 guns 3 jeeps 8-3 ton 158" WB lorries. Total 327 all ranks from Regt. in ship. Major F.A.L. Charlesworth OC craft. All personnel issued with 1 Mae west, 2 24 hr ration packs, 1 toomy cooker & refill, 20 cigs, water sterilizers 1 emergency ration and biscuits, 2 chocolate bars and 3 vomit bags. All move orders cancelled and orders to be moving on road within 40 mins at 21 00 hrs.	mwm
Camp A.11 ENGLAND	9-6-44		Raining steadily from 0100 hrs to 2300 hrs. Regt. less 32 bty and residues on 40 min notice to move. 100 bty received 18 spare wheels for 40 mm SP.	mwm
Camp A.11 ENGLAND	10-6-44		Scattered clouds cool light wind. 4 LAA Regt craft load 1027 received order to move from A-11 camp at 2130 hrs, move across SP at 2100 hrs to move to boxes in GOSPORT. Arrive GOSPORT at 2210 hrs. Hot meal served one hour after arrival in boxes. Final state of waterproofing finished by 2359 hrs.	mwm
GOSPORT A.11 ENGLAND	11-6-44		0001 hrs - 0008 hrs clear and calm. Vehs moved to hards to load at 0300 hrs. Loading commenced at 0430 hrs into LST 308. LST loaded at 0830 hrs and at sea where we anchored in harbour waiting for convoy to form up. Major F.A.L. Charlesworth, Capt Sisson and Bty Comdrs meeting with ships officers from 0910 hrs - 1000 hrs to detail all arrangements while on board ship. Ship under way at 2030 hrs. Sea very rough.	mwm

WO 179/3121
Intelligence/war diary
6TH FIELD COMPANY, RCE.

Place	Date	Hour	Summary of Events and Information	Remarks, references to Appendices and initials
"BRIDGEHEAD" COURSEULLES-SUR-MER, NORMANDY, FRANCE	6 JUNE "D" Day	44	Weather: Bright and clear Today is D-Day for the assault of the Allied Forces into FRANCE. The assaulting companies of our brigade went in at H-Hour which was 0735 hrs. [The first tide landing of this Unit took place on MIKE and NAN beaches at COURSEULLES-SUR-MER between CHERBOURG and LE HAVRE. The assault party from No. 2 Platoon landed with the forward companies of the Regina Rifle Regiment and the Royal Winnipeg Rifles at H + 5 minutes and encountered heavy opposition from pillboxes and machine-gun nests. They assisted the infantry to get clear of the beaches and then proceeded inland with them to a position forward of LE FRESNE CAMILLY at 2300 hrs. No.1 Platoon landed at H + 75 min and found the beach under intermittent mortar fire and sniper fire. They proceeded with their task of clearing the MIKE I exit of mines. At this exit French mines were found encased in wooden boxes. On completion of this task they moved H + 75 min and found the beach under intermittent mortar fire and sniper fire. They moved inland clearing the 7 CIB route via GRAYE-SUR-MER, BANVILLE, REVIERS, AMBLIE to LE FRESNE CAMILLY. En route they had to fight through slight opposition and at BANVILLE were pinned down by sniper fire from a church steeple. An SP Gun put several rounds through the steeple before he was dislodged. A number of prisoners were captured en route and they were disarmed and sent back to the beach. Headquarters marching party met the bulldozers and tipper lorries outside BANVILLE and proceeded inland with them. [No 3 Platoon landed at H – 75 min with No. 9 and No. 10 sections and commenced mine clearance on the 7 CIB route inland.] No. 11 and No.12 sections landed at H – 135 min with two tipper lorries loaded with road repair material and worked for a short time on the NAN Green Exit. No. 3 Platoon assembled inland from COURSEULLES-SUR-MER and proceeded with nine clearance of AMBLIE. Here they assembled with No. 1 Platoon and moved to REVIERS for the night. Casualties due to the action were as follows: KILLED IN ACTION: Spr. Johnson, A.H., MISSING, BELIEVED KILLED IN ACTION, L/Sgt. Stewart, W.F., Spr. Adams, M.G., Spr. Bleoo, A., Spr. Brewer, R.N., Spr. Jackson, A.T., Spr. Lacroix, L. Spr. Martin, A.J.L., Spr. Sawdon, J.E., Spr. Sparkes, R.R. WOUNDED IN ACTION: L/Sgt. Meek, W.A., Cpl. Wilkinson, P.H., L/Cpl. Cooper, G.H. (it was subsequently learned that he had Died of Wounds), L/Cpl. Ferguson, J.T.K., (DIED OF WOUNDS), Spr. Dussault, J., Spr. Beehler, W., Spr. Bezeau, O.W., Spr. Goodrum, A.E., Spr. Jackson, R.C., Spr. Mackay, J., Spr. MacDonald, T.G., Spr. McCarthy, T.B., Spr. Poirier, J.L.W., Spr. Sopher, N., Spr. Spencer, R.C., Spr. Sweda, J.P., Spr. Tarlington, R.D., Spr. Wilkins, S.W., Spr. Zarembinski, F.	Appx 4 RJm Appx 2

WO 179/3127
Intelligence/war diary
16TH FIELD COMPANY RCE.

Place	Date	Hour	Summary of Events and Information	Remarks, references to Appendices and initials
Marshalling Area	1944 1st June		Weather: Hot and clear. Sub-Units of the Coy. were marshalled into craft loads amongst the various marshalling camps.	
	2nd June		Weather: Cloudy, warm. All craftloads waiting in marshalling areas awaiting orders for embarkation.	
	3rd June		Weather: Clear and warm. Loading of assault craft commenced.	
Aboard Craft	4th June		Weather: Cloudy, cool. Loading of assault craft completed.	
5th June	5th June		Weather: Cloudy, cool. Orders received in later afternoon that the assault on the coast of France would take place next day. H-hour to be 0745hrs. The invasion fleet weighed anchor and sailed down the Solent in the evening.	
FRANCE	6th June		Weather: Hazy and warm. [H-hour 0745hrs. The assault Sappers consisting on No. 3 Pl, landed with the assault Coys of the QOR of C and N Shore R with the specific task of assisting the Inf with the immobilization and destruction of strong points and were to stay with the Inf until the Bde objective was attained. Little call made upon these Sprs in their approved role. Passing through BERNIERES-SUR-MER, 1 Sub-Sec located 8 Booby Traps from houses and cleared them out. DZ35 and ZZ42 igniters were found. One Sub-Sec, advancing through ST AUBIN-SUR-MER found tanks held up by steel rail blocks and cut them, while under fire, allowing tanks to proceed and assist the Inf in their advance. No. 1 Sec of No. 1 Platoon landed in two parts at H/20 with Lt Cameron from HQ and Lt Peto, pl Comd. They assembled at a rendezvous some 200yds from the beach without casualty despite enemy mortars, MG's and snipers. They proceeded inland behind the leading Infantry through ST AUBIN-SUR-MER, checking the road and verges for mines.] Two of their three detectors functioned - one was wet. Lt. Peto worked to the West on the beach but could not move in at the time due to MG fire, so waited until remainder of Pl with CSM Howes and L/Sgt. Skidmore arrived in LCI(L). They hit a mine 100 yds offshore, killing Cpl. Lavigne, wounding Spr. Walsh seriously in the leg, and causing flooding of the hold. Beached in 10ft of water, most of the men swam ashore along a life-line, most of the equipment being lost. CSM Howes twice swam out to rescue men from drowning in the surf as their strength failed. Nos 2, 3 and 4 secs with one detector working, assisted Beach Group in clearing a lane of mines. Some "S" mines were	

SHEET 2

Place	Date	Hour	Summary of Events and Information	Remarks, references to Appendices and initials
France	1944 6th June	cont....	removed and two wounded infantry men recovered. As soon as possible, the party moved inland. No. 3 Sec checked the verges of the 2nd lateral to BERNIERES-SUR-MER and found nothing, but cleared trees off the road. Nos 2 and 4 Secs proceeded inland behind No. 1 Sec on the road to TAILLEVILLE. Spt. Thompson was shot in the shoulder on recce with Lt. Cameron and returned to ST. AUBIN as a cheerful walking wounded casualty. Sgt. Harrison had landed at H+60 in 5cwt and collected D7 Bulldozer, D4 Bulldozer and 2 trailers and 1 tipper lorry behind beach. One D7 was sent up the road and cleared telephone poles in the village of ST. AUBIN. Later all vehicles were brought up to TAILLEVILLE except one trailer left in ST. AUBIN. Infantry delayed in taking TAILLEVILLE so No 1 Pl collected and dug in at hay stack 500 yds North of TAILLEVILLE. Pl had intended occupying enemy trench system 200 yds North of TAILLEVILLE, but moved out because enemy shellfire in area. On D-Day No. 2 Platoon personnel landed on NAN WHITE beach at H + 65 mins and assembled there with the 5 cwt and Bulldozer (D7 Armoured) and trailer. No casualties were suffered during this landing. As no other Bulldozers were in evidence the D7 was immediately put to work constructing three wheeled vehicle exits by NAN 4 Exit. Lt. Schofield and L/Sgt. Gross went forward on recce and the platoon, organized into mine clearing parties, followed on through BERNIERES-SUR-MER sweeping the roads and vegges behind the leading infantry. Two Tipper Lorries RASC arrived at this time and Lt. Yeats dumped some roadmaking material off for the use of the Beach Gp Engineers. The Platoon continued to move forward, the Sections leap frogging each other, immediately behind the Infantry, until the latterx were held up at the crossroads just South of LA MARE. On the route up, the Platoon, besides sweeping for mines, did the following work:- (a) L/Cpl Henshall destroyed an 88 mm gun at m.r. 992822 which had been captured by the Infantry. (b) Sign posted but did not clear booby traps at 992822 reported by R de Chaud. (c) Lt Yeats and L/Sgt. Gross assisted the R de Chaud to capture one Officer and 15 OR's at LA MARE. No 2 pl plus two Secs of No 3 Pl took up defensive posns for the night in the R de Chaud area in LA MARE. The D7 and trailer remained behind in BENY-SUR-MER in HQ 9 the Cdn Inf Bde area. Maj V.C. Hamilton, landing at H+60 co-ordinated and controlled the work of No 1 and No 2 Pls on the beaches and beach exits. When the Pls followed along the two axis of advance forward, sweeping the roads and verges for mines, Maj. Hamilton, mounted on a M/C maintained personal supervision of the work. While proceeding forward to visit No 1 Platoon at 1415 hrs, he received three bullet wounds from an enemy sniper. Medical assistance was provided by an MO of the N Shore R and he was evacuated to the Beach Dressing Station. On the	

Place	Date	Hour	Summary of Events and Information	Remarks, references to Appendices and initials
France	1944 6th June	Cont.....	reporting of Maj. Hamilton as a casualty to CRE, Maj. D.W. Cunnington was immediately appointed OC of the Coy and contacting the Pls, he assumed command and set up his HQ alongside 8th Cdn Inf Bde. The HQ Officers, Lt. Cameron and Lt. Schofield, landed with L/Sgt MacInnis and 4 men of No 1 Pl with D Coy N Shore R at H+20, experiencing some MG and mortar fire. He continued through the town with the leading Pls of the N Shore R as far as Cross Roads. No enemy encountered on main street. Leaving the N Shore R, Lt Cameron recced TAILLEVILLE road for short distance and found no enemy or no obstacles of importance. Returning to beach, he met Sgt. Harrison and had him bring up D7 Bulldozer to clear main road of town of rubble and telegraph poles. Continuing his recce, he reached the outskirts of TAILLEVILLE and found no mines or obstacles, again coming under MG and mortar fire. Returning to ST. AUBIN-SUR-MER, he met Lt. Peto and passed onto him the results of his recce. Returning to TAILLEVILLE, he found the N Shore R clearing the Chateau. He blew down one door for them and was shortly after hit in the leg by a small splinter from Stick Grenade. Continuing on his recce, he found Maj. Hamilton wounded outside TAILLEVILLE, rendered first aid and procured an M.O. Returning to TAILLEVILLE, rejoined No 1 Pl for the night. It Schofield, landing at H + 60, went up as far as the square of BERNIERES-SUR-MER with the leading Pls of the QOR of C checking the roads leading into the square and to town limits. All roads apparently free of mines and debris. He then recced road as far as Rd June 992843, sending info that road OK back by runner. Waiting for the R de Chaud to assemble he came under fire of MG and snipers. Continuing to BENY-SUR-MER with the R de Chaud, they were held up by 88mm gun posn. Checking a trench under road, discovered three enemy, which he took prisoner with the assistance of Maj Carson, OC B Coy. CHofo. While R de Chuad were re-organization, South of BENY-SUR-MER, Lt Schofield checked over the town for water supply, finding two wells - also checked over German living quarters for booby traps, with negative results. He then checked over quickly a proposed ALG site on East side of town and later turned in report. Continuing to LA MARE, he joined up with NNS High. and continued South with them, returning at dusk to rejoin Coy. Capt Smith, with Coy. HQ vehicles landed about H + 7 hrs, and proceeded with convoy to Div Assembly area, sending DR from there to OC notifying arrival and asking location. The following recommendations for awards were submitted by Maj. Cunnington to CRE Military Medal:- CSM Howes, L/Cpl. Bartolacci, Spr. Foster, Spr. Duval.	

WO 179/3128
Intelligence/war diary
18TH FIELD COMPANY RCE.

Place	Date	Hour	Summary of Events and Information	Remarks, references to Appendices and initials
AT SEA, ON LAND, BUT NOT IN THE AIR	6 JUNE 44		Weather: Fair and cool. Fresh wind stiffening towards evening. Gentle swells in channel. Action stations sounded at five o'clock (dawn) as we are in enemy waters. Since unit is split up on several craft it is difficult to know what everyone is doing at the moment. The story must be pieced together later. [No. 1 Platoon landed at 0800 hrs (H-hour) on MIKE sector (Beach immediately west of COURSEILLES-SUR-MER). Clearance work started immediately. Obstacles very numerous O hedgehogs, stakes, and element C mines and shells with push igniters (2235) on most obstacles. 50 yard gap cleared in one half hour using bulldozers and pulling obstacles off beach.] Platoon Sergeant (Sgt. Romain) in charge of work since craft carrying Lt. Eddy and one section did not sail. Heavy fire experienced on beaches but by a miracle the platoon suffered only two casualties (both slightly wounded). [Platoon waited near beach until 1200 hrs. when tide was out again and cleared more obstacles. Succeeded in clearing a 400 yard gap.] While waiting on beach the platoon assisted a major and a corporal take 19 prisoners from a pillbox which had been put out of action by RN. The platoon joined rest of unit at GRAYE-SUR-MER about 1600 hrs.	CBR
			No. 2 Platoon - Recce party landed at approximately H plus 90 minutes. Car 5 cwt. drowned in nine feet of water and lost recce gear and W/T set. Therefore party had to proceed on foot and recce bridge site at PONT-DE-REVIERS (953817). Bridge found to be intact so there was no work for platoon at all. Main body of the platoon landed (with bicycles) at 1500 hrs. (should have landed at H plus 135 minutes) and proceeded to Company assembly area in BANVILLE (948830).	CBR
			No. 3 Platoon - Recce party landed at approximately H plus 90 minutes and proceeded to recce bridge site at COLOMBIERS-SUR-SEULLES (928809). Since infantry were not far enough ahead, recce had to be made on foot. Bridge found intact. Main body (with bicycles) landed at 1500 hrs and proceeded to Company assembly area in BANVILLE. Platoon commenced clearing route from COLOMBIERS-SUR-SEULLES to REVIERS. No mines were encountered and since 234 Field Company R.E. were doing same job, No. 3 Platoon stopped. OC and Lt. McKenzie and two stores lorries landed at 1400 hrs. as well as 1622 Bridging Platoon. All proceeded to Company assembly area in BANVILLE. Since bridging platoon not required due to bridges being intact, they felt rather lost and simply sat in Assembly Area.	CBR

SHEET 2

Place	Date	Hour	Summary of Events and Information	Remarks, references to Appendices and initials
AT SEA, ON LAND, BUT NOT IN THE AIR	6 JUNE 44		No. 3 Platoon recced quarry south of GRAY-SUR-MER and possible airfield sites West of BANVILLE – reports submitted to CRE. In evening company moved to bivouac area 953816. [Note: It is strange that neither bridge was blown and that roads were not mined. It seems to indicate that the enemy was completely surprised by the landing.. So D-Day ends with this unit having done little work but it isn't our fault we haven't been busy. We were certainly prepared for it.]	CBR
	7 JUNE 44		Weather: Fair and cool. Five stores lorries and eleven men (including 2 i/c) landed at 0200 hrs and proceeded to ELBOW/FRANKIE assembly area. They were joined by another craft party (4 vehicles, 20 personnel) at 0530 hrs. Company HQ located at 0630 hrs. and parties moved from ELBOW/FRANKIE to join rest of unit. Company moved to area REVIERES (964824) at 1130 hrs. Platoon all in different locations throughout village. At 1200 hrs. warned to have platoon ready to join 2 Armoured Brigade on one hour's notice. The 2nd Armoured Brigade intend to sorty out from Divisional positions and reach the high ground just north of the river ORNE. Stores loaded on two half-tracks and W/T set in Recce Car. A HQ officer will be added to platoon to be used as recce officer. C.E., 1 British Corps, visited unit during evening and requested Company to carry out airfield recce in vicinity of AMBLIE (9479). Otherwise the day was very quiet.	CBR
REVIERES	8 JUNE 44		Weather: Fair and cool. Location, REVIERS, 963822. No. 2 Platoon busy all morning checking village for snipers. None were found but there must have been at least one because an English officer was shot early this morning. Task with armoured brigade cancelled at 0630 hrs. Second tide party (11 ORs and 4 vehicles) arrived during the afternoon - a little late but quite intact. No. 3 platoon sent to clear road from BENY-SUR-MER to LA DELIVERANDE at 2130 hrs. CRE told us that 8 CIB was attacking LA DELIVERANDE which is still enemy strongpoint. However it was discovered that one of brigades of 51(H) Div. put in the attack and couldn't contact them. Road cleared as far as TAILLEVILLE when platoon came under mortar fire and were withdrawn. Fact reported to CRE. It is imperative that when sappers co-operate with infantry that close liason be established and sappers be provided with effective cover. Considerable enemy air ? during night. Our AA was fierce at times and anything but condusive to sleep. SP artillery nearby attracted the planes which dropped a few bombs but Company suffered no casualties.	CBR

WO 179/2776
Intelligence/war diary
3RD CANADIAN INFANTRY DIVISION SIGNALS

Month and Year June 44

Place	Date	Hour	Summary of Events and Information	Remarks, references to Appendices and initials
HILTINGBURY CAMP C 9 WINCHESTER AREA ENGLAND	1		Unit broken down into craft loads and marshalling. Each day sees more away.	
	2		Second day of loading unit in ships from EAST ANGLIA to SOUTHAMPTON	
	3		Last day of loading. "D-Day" almost here. Weather getting a bit rough.	
	4		24 hour postponement received. Weather still heavy but barometer rising.	
	5		Unit still sitting as is whole Army. At 1900 hrs the various skippers of the crafts announced that the Operation had commenced and we sail that night for foreign shores. D-Day is tomorrow.	
BERNIER-SUR-MER 994846 FRANCE	6		In the early morning 3 Canadian Infantry Division mounted the Assault against the Continent of Occupied Europe. After the heavy going on the beaches, we advanced into Occupied FRANCE through COURSEULLES-SUR-MER and BERNIERS-SUR-MER in NORMANDY. Adv HQ 3 Cdn Inf Div opened by our Forward Group under Major Johns ten was just south of BERNIERS at 994846. Forward Group suffered no casualties of any kind. Lieut. Murchison is reported missing possibly dead on landing. One man E See. killed and one wounded. C 75648 Sigmn Swan. E.G., E See. killed and L 64498 Sigmn Tennant, M.C., E Sec wounded. HMS HILARY and HMS ROYAL ULSTSRMAN came through safely. Main Body due to land at H plus 7 arrived in Bay at roughly 1200 hrs, but it was a day or two before they landed. Enemy resistance was heavy but fell back as Div. achieved its intermediate objective by the close of D-Day. The beaches were bombed by Huns all night but little damage was affected. Line Sec E Sec while out on a line captured 85 Huns. They were F 26373 L/Cpl Hughes, M.V., F 26408 Sigmn Martin, E.W., and G 16050 Sigmn McPhee, J.D. Two of the men were up a pole and the third one holding a Bren Gun. A Hun came out and surrendered then an officer came out with a pistol and was promptly shot. Then the rest of the Huns came out and surrendered. A copy of the statement is appended.	Appx 1

SHEET 2

Place	Date	Hour	Summary of Events and Information	Remarks, references to Appendices and initials
	6 (Cont'd)		Idno crow L See. were out laying to a Bn. and never returned. It is believed they are dead. Later the Jeep was recovered. They were H38570 L/Sgt Whittingham, V.R., B 38873 Sign Cook, A.H.C., B 398 Sign Johnston, J.R.	
			Night full of bombing of our beaches and inland.	
BENY-SUR-MER FRANCE 986808	7		The Division advanced and opened at BENY-SUR-MER 986808. Meanwhile at sea delays were still going on in unloading. Only two of the four containing the Main Body decanted today. However, enough landed to get more suitable vehicles for Div HQ. More DR machines arrived to implement the DRLS.	
			The battle continues with 7 Cdn Inf Bde being well up in their final Objective repelling continued counterattack.	
			8 and 9 Cdn Inf Bdes held up in vieinity AUGERAY and BASLY.	
			2 CAB by Div with Regts under command Bdes.	
			Line crews cut on building have trouble with snipers.	
			Periodical Air attacks on this HQ. Casualties much lighter than anticipated.	
			Sigs Billets in field across the road from Div. No casualties in Sigs Billets personnel. At night a few Air attacks and a couple of alarms at Div HQ and Billets.	
	8		Lots of D-Day Main Group landed and our assault group are in. No vehicles drowned on D-Day Group which is a record.	
			Slit trenches have been prepared for every person and everyone sleeps in them.	
			Lieut Lemieux found a French civilian who was forced to be one of the digging gang for a buried cable. This cable was found at 986813. It runs from CHERBOURG to DOUVRES. No test points can be found. No idea as to size.	
			RWRs subject to severe attack today and were badly hit.	
			LCV A5 rear end is being used as OC Sigs Office.	
			It is very evident that the training from all the exercises has been in good stead the way our troops are setting in.	
			Capt. Eckenfelder has been missing since early this morning.	
			After luneh Lieut. Grose disappeared as well. Hurried flaps took place. After supper both arrived at Billets at once. Capt. Eckenfelder had been taken prisoner at THAON and later convinced 100 Huns to surrender instead. Lieut. Gormain of 4 PRO Coy. was	

WO 179/2927
Intelligence/war diary
1ST BATTALION THE CAMERON HIGHLANDERS
OF OTTAWA (MACHINE GUNS)

Month and Year June 44

Place	Date	Hour	Summary of Events and Information	Remarks, references to Appendices and initials
	4 (cont)		BHQ and D Coy. portions left C9 at 0930 hrs and arrived on this standing at 1230 hrs after many halts and holdups. One man per veh was left in the standings and the remainder marched two miles to the camp for lunch. This Camp is even more dusty than the last one, but the grub is much better. There are two shows running daily so our wait should not be too onerous. As usual, the boys in the tpt lines are being well taken care of by the neighbours and are very content with their lot. Canvas shelters are hung between the vehs and the Drivers and Sgt. Perry i/c party are very comfortable. The bumff continues to pour in. Date in the afternoon, instrs were received to SOS a Fitter and send Pte Srtus for trades testing, fat chance of these taking place at this stage of the game! Maj. G.L. Tripp and L/Cpl N.A. Sisson of the residue party dropped in to the camp to iron out a few problems. The main 'theater' attracted full houses for two showings of "Madame Curie".	Alb
	5		Cloudy, cool, High Winds. REME personnel inspected B waterproofing of our vehs. More sups were received and sent on to HQ Coy. Lt. R.M. Watson and Rear Party, Capt. M.H. MacDiarmid Pmr and Mr Corlett YMCA Supvr arrived tonight from C9. Maj. R. Rowley 2i/c, Capt. G.A. Harris Adjt., Capt. R. Ferrie Sigs Offr., Lt. Morriss I.O., and Lt. Adams Sigs Offr of D Coy. practiced MAYLAY and UNICODE during the AM before visiting the veh standings. Embarkation docs are now complete for all concerned. Four Compo packs were obtained at the DID in the afternoon In the evening the big show was Unit D of the Cdn Entertainment Party and the 'Ritz' was packed for both houses.	Alb
	6		Clear & warmer, SW wind. It's come at last! Offrs and men crowded about radios as first news of the invasion came over and Gen Eisenhower spoke. The PA system blared forth the communiques and knots of men grouped about the speakers. While many had figured that this would be D-Day it came as a surprise as there had been very little aerial activity as heard in this area during the night. Immediately following the announcement seals were broken on the maps and the sheets were set up so that progress could be followed. FFWs failed to pick up any of the broadcasts of the joint forces on the continent. We had to rely on the newspapers and the BBC for all news of stirring events taking place. Following supper in the Offrs mess 2000-2100 hrs the Offrs grouped around the radio and listened to the KING as he called the nations to prayer, and urged them to	

SHEET 2

Place	Date	Hour	Summary of Events and Information	Remarks, references to Appendices and initials
	6 (cont)		carry on the crusade for the liberation of despotically occupied countries. We are naturally concerned about the CO and the Coys who landed on the beaches in the initial assault. All the coys have definitely dangerous roles to play, especially the MMGs and Mortars as they are scheduled to go out with the "Jock" coloumn tonight. from 9 CIB. Gen Eisenhowerst Order of the Day (App 3) was circulated to all tps after embarking for the continent.	(APP 3)
	7		Partly Cloudy, cool. Satisfaction reigns as the news came over the BBC that the Cdns are ahead of schedule The Pmr, Rear Pty Sgt and YMCA Super with party and equipt left for the residue Camp this afternoon. Nothing doing about camp. Just eating sleeping and lazing around waiting for the signal to get under way and get over ourselves.	Alex
	8		Cool, showers. Continue to loaf about camp continually speculating about the progress our lads are making in NORMANDY. Considerable irritation and annoyance finding voluble expression regarding the small amount of direct publicity allotted to the magnificent showing 3 Cdn Inf Div is making. Our Div is the only one keeping away out ahead of schedule and is obviously taking the enemy completely in its stride. More annoyance caused by the Boche claiming that the 2nd Div. was involved and no correction was made! Announcement to the effect that a Bde was going on in on bicycles and tks proof that the Highland Bde is filling its follow-up role.	Alex
	9		Heavy rain, clearing at noon. BHQ with D5 tps of A B & D Coys still sitting tight with nothing to do and no word yet of a move.	Alex
	10		Rain, clearing at noon. Still no word of move, and tomorrow is D5 the day we are supposed to land.	Alex
	11		Overcast, scattered showers. At last something has happened. Warned to be prepared to move on ½hrs notice but also told that we might not get under way for two days yet: 24 hr rations, emergency rations,	Alex

WO 179/3370

Intelligence/war diary

14TH CANADIAN FIELD AMBULANCE RCAMC

Place	Date	Hour	Summary of Events and Information 14 CANADIAN FIELD AMBULANCE, R.C.A.M.C.	Remarks, references to Appendices and initials
On Board Ship	1 June 1944		Warm and pleasant. Majority of serials loaded on craft as assigned. Unit is now split into craft loads and as no facilities exist for communication the Diary will be very general until D-Day.	Jnn
On Board Ship	2 June 1944		Serials on craft and ships. Weather rather windy and cool.	Jnn
On Board Ship	3 June 1944		Weather continues cool with gusts of rain and rather windy. We rather wonder if the weather is not going to turn against us.	Jnn
On Board Ship	4 June 1944		Very windy with white caps in the Solent where we are at anchor. There are many ships about.	Jnn
On Board Ship	5 June 1944		Weather still rough, but shows signs of clearing. We sailed about 1830 hrs the shipsleaving the protection of the anti-submarine met one after the other. The signal was flashed that the operation was on at approximately 2000 hrs. Real maps were issued and everyone feels much relieved that at last the long period of waiting is over. Let us hope the operation, vast as it is, will be a success.	Jnn
NORMANDY BEACHES	6 June 1944		D-Day, A day to remember. Our first sign that the Second Front was starting came from a large number of heavy bombers which passed overhead about 0600 hours We were not attacked by hostile sea or air forces throughout the journey. About 1100 hrs those in the LST's could see the French coast. H hour being 0720 hrs we could see a number of fires, the navy was shelling and large numbers of landing craft were in evidence. The scene was almost peaceful. (We found out later that the beaches had been anything but peaceful.) The Rhino ferries were manoevered into position forward, the operation taking some hours. The sea was running fairly fast and considerable time was lost. Eventually about 1500 hrs the Tank Deck of the LST's had been transfered to the Rhinos. On serial 1148 our vehicles were on the tank deck. The OC decided to go ashore on foot with the first trip as serial 1151 had its vehicles on the first Rhino trip and he wanted to get ashore as soon as possible.	Jnn

SHEET 2

Place	Date	Hour	Summary of Events and Information	Remarks, references to Appendices and initials
PIERREPONT NORMANDY	7 June 1944		The assault sections had landed on schedule, 5 & 6 sections at 0740 and 4 sec. about 0800 hrs. The beach defences were strong and a number of casualties were suffered by the assaulting infantry. Our casualties were 7 men from No. 6 section who are missing possibly drowned and G47114 Sgt. Lutes, D.H. 5 section who was wounded. The missing are as follows; G45429 Pte. Atkinson, L.L., G27177 Pte. Crossman, L.W., G27926 Pte. Duguay, J.G., B72218 Pte. Gardiner, W.A., G47208 L/C pl Herman, H.T., B91239 Pte. Pickford, P.S.F., M100390 Pte. Ware, E. Serial 1151 landed and proceeded to our assembly area near BANVILLE 944829 The OC borrowed a push bike and went up to the area. Our Recce officer Major Norton had the situation will in hand. An RDS on wheels was set up and a few casualties evacuated. They were mostly German wounded as the majority of the 7 Bde casualties occurred on the beaches and were evacuated tp either the Beach Dressing Station or 1 - 2 FDS. We dispatched 2 heavy ambulances to the FDS to assist with this work. The OC recced the surounding areas, contacted Bde HQ and generally got the picture. The immediate objective was in our hands and while the operation was not up to schedule, was going quite satisfactorily. Contact was made with No. 5 section and No. 3 section sent to relieve No. 6 section with the Regina Rifles. No. 4 section with the 1 C Scot R could not be located as they were moving forward. The night was quiet. There was some bombing of the beaches but it was not severe. Casualties admitted to ADS - 8. Everyone up early. Recces were continued. The O.C. located a possible area for ADS in Pierrepont 933789 - a house used by the Germans as a Bn or Coy HQ and RAP It is filthy, and has been well gone over both by our troops and by the French civilians but it will do. Serial 1149 reported in, having landed late on D-Day. No vehicle or personnel casualties. No. 4 section reported in having lost contact with the 1 C Scot R who advanced quite rapidly during the late hours of D-Day. No. 5 section was later withdrawn as the jeep had not come in. About 1400 hours the unit moved to Pierrepont 933789 and set up an A.D.S. in the house. Casualties were coming in but with only 2 jeeps it was hard to clear them. About 1800 hours serial 1148 reported in without suffering any casualties. Jeeps were sent forward to the 3 batallions and the normal	Jnn

Place	Date	Hour	Summary of Events and Information	Remarks, references to Appendices and initials
SOUTHAMPTON	1944 1 June		THURSDAY:- Cool, showery. Very quiet day. Meeting of all serial commanders of 1555 LST II. in lecture tent for instruction re rations, movement etc.	Grog
SOUTHAMPTON	2 June		FRIDAY:- Fine cool moderate S.E. wind. Serial moved off from camp C 2 and passed S.P. at 1610 hrs, began loading on LST 65 at 2300 hrs, loading of main deck completed at 0100 hrs without incident. Accomodation for ORs practically nil, most of them sleeping on, in or under vehicles on main deck.	Grog
LST 65	3 June		SATURDAY:- Cloudy, cool, moderate north west wind. LST 65 moved off to anchorage off ISLE OF WIGHT at 0530 hrs. Quiet day, meals are good, ablution and sanitary arrangements on board are good.	Grog
LST 65	4 June		SUNDAY:- Cloudy, strong north westerly wind, heavy rain in evening. Voluntary church parade at 1030 hrs. Very quiet day. All troops in excellent spirits.	Grog
LST 65	5 June		MONDAY:- Cloudy, wind dropping. Uneventful day. Moved off in very large convoy at 1930 hrs for cross channel run. Slight swell in channel.	Grog
Beny sur Mer France	6 June		TUESDAY:- Section 2 under Lieut J.L. Heaslip landed with C and D Coy. if N Shore R on NAN RED beach by ST. AUBIN-SUR-MER at H 20, 0805 hrs. The beach was under enemy small arms and mortar fire and the section sought protection by a sea wall and established a casualty nesting post there. The section stayed there until 1045 hrs rendering emergency first aid and collecting wounded from the immediate beach area. The whole area was exposed to small arms and mortar fire continually with the result that Pte. Henderson, G. and Pte. Vermette, A.R. were killed by mortar shell on the beach and Cpl. MacDonald, D.B. was severely wounded about the eyes and left arm. Pte. Stewart, A.A. was very slightly wounded on the nose. The section left at 1045 hrs leaving Pte. Marshall, L.S. behind as nursing orderly to the 60 or 75 wounded, and proceeded to sweep the town of ST. AUBIN-SUR-MER for casualties which were nested at convenient places. The section then moved 2 miles further south to vicinity to TOILLEVILLE and helped with evacuation of N Shore R casualties. Lieut. J.L. Heaslip went to BERNIERES-SUR-MER and contacted Major G.P. Tanton at 2300 hrs 6 Jun 44. The section stayed by TOILLEVILLE until 1400 hrs 7 Jun 44 collecting and evacuating wounded and then rejoined the ADS at BENY-SUR-MER. Major A.D. MacPherson of 22 Cdn Fd Amb recce party was met on the beach at 0930 hrs also Major Chapman RAMC of FDS at the same time. A BDS was later extablished by the sea wall at	

SHEET 2

Place	Date	Hour	Summary of Events and Information	Remarks, references to Appendices and initials
BENY-SUR-MER, FRANCE	1944 6 June		<u>TUESDAY (continued)</u>:- approximately 1200 hrs. Approximately 20 civilian casualties were treated in ST. AUBIN-SUR-MER. Section 1 under Capt L.E. Cowan landed with C and D Coy. QOR of C on NAN WHITE beach by BERNIERES-SUR-MER at H 20, 0805 hrs 6 Jun 44. The section collected wounded on the beach which was under heavy enemy mortar and small arms fire. After an hour and a half, the section proceeded to BERNIERES-SUR-MER and collected and nested casualties throughout the town. Capt L.E.Cowan took 13 surrounding German prisoners in the town. The section worked in BERNIERES until about 1400 hrs and then proceeded, nesting casualties along the route to BENY-SUR-MER which was reached at 1700 hrs. An improvised CCP was set up there and about 25 casualties treated, which were evacuated by ADS ambulance at 0300 hrs D 1, 7 Jun 44. This was the first contact made with HQ 22 Cdn Fd Amb. Capt L.E. Cowan, seriously ill with perforated peptic ulcer returned with same ambulance to FDS at BERNIERES and was operated on. The section continued treating casualties until 0900 hrs 7 Jun 44 when HQ arrived at BENY-SUR-MER 3/4 Section 5 under Capt. I. Winkler assembled on beach at BERNIERES-SUR-MER approximately H + 45 hrs with the Chaudieres group, commended picking up casualties and evacuating them to BDS working in small groups, Pte. LeBar, D.L. was wounded when LCA in which he was landing hit a mine. Pte. White, E.H. was wounded by a sniper bullet when rescuing a casualty from the water. The rest of section did a casualty sweep, nesting some and evacuating others to BDS at BERNIERES. Section 5 proceeded south along road to BENY-SUR-MER, outskirts reached about 1900 hrs, worked during night in village and contacted HQ on their arrival at 0600 hrs D + 1 in BENY-SUR-MER. The recce party consisting of Major C.E. Baker, Major A.D. MacPherson (7 Cdn FDS) and Pte. Etherington, F. T. landed in jeep at about 0900 hrs 6 Jun 44. Under heavy shell fire Major C.E. Baker and Pte. Etherington, F.T. were wounded, with jeep a total loss. Major C.E.Baker became sererated and was last seen at 0930 hrs 6 Jun 44. Serial 1554 comprising 72 ORS and Major G.P. Tanton, H/Major J.M. Malone, Capt. G. Scattergood, Capt. J.W. Latimer, Capt. R.D. Reid (CDC) from their LST sited land at about 1000 hrs. Capt. J.W. Latimer was disembarked by Rhino and proceeded to assembly area at about 1630 hrs. Remainder of party at about 2230 hrs. Contact with other part of Fd Amb was made and with 33/34 FDS. Part of the serial steed at the FDS area, the other part preceded them to assembly area. From serial 1555 Lt. Col. M.R. Caverhill disembarked by duk at 1730 hrs. Due to confusion caused by smoke screen, part of the party with difficulty got to the assembly area, those remaining disembarked and made their way to the ADS at BENY-SUR-MER. A recce was done by Lt. Col. M.R.Caverhill and a site chosed at BENY-SUR-MER m.r. 988810 sheet 7E/5.	appy Grog

WO 179/3375
Intelligence/war diary
23RD CANADIAN FIELD AMBULANCE RCAMC

1 June 44 to 30 June 44

Place	Date	Hour	Summary of Events and Information	Remarks, references to Appendices and initials
In the field	1 June		Weather Scattered cloud, some rain. "B" Coy moved off to marshalling area, C9 at Chandlerford, at 1030 hours. Remainder of craft loads moved off at different hours during the afternoon to the same marshalling camp. Upon arrival at camp, men were soon settled down. Meals at this camp reported to be good, far better than A22.	
	2 June		Bright and sunny. Day spent quietly, personnel attend shows or sing-songs in the evening.	
	3 June		Weather: Bright Sun and hot. Early part of day spent quietly, nothing to do but rest. Warned during the day to be ready to move out this evening or during the night.	
	4 June		First craft load left at 0130 hours after drawing 24 hours ration, emergency ration, vomit bag and sea-sick tablets. Efficient handling of out going parties by the camp staff was noted. Upon reaching vehicle stands, were notified of delay in moving time. Various craft loads moved of at different times to SOUTHAMPTON yards. All aboard ships in time for the evening meal. Spent night in the harbour, Weather Scattered clouds and warm.	
	5 June		Cloudy and cool. Day spent in harbour, everyone getting plenty sleep. Ships got under way at approximately 2330 hours. Maps of invasion coast given to senior NCO's and Officers.	
	6 June		Clear and cool; D-Day. Coast of France sighted at approximately 1500 hours by craft load made up of Personnel from HQ and "A" Coy. "B" Coy. landed on French coast at 1100 hrs. following HLI of C battalion, established an advance ADS at BERNIERS-SUR-MER. Worked there until 1600hrs. Moved up to BENY-SUR-MER and set up in church in centre of village (986805 7 E/5). Worked there all night.	
	7 June		Clear and cool. "B" Coy. moved up to BASLY (992793 7 F/1) and set up section in school. They are getting lots of work and are doing a good job. Remainder of assault section still off the coast of France. LST with Craft load 1743 came in at about 1630 hours and began unloading. Lt. Col. Loree landed at 1730 hours and is located at quarries (953816 M Y E/5) west of REVIERS.	

UNITS ATTACHED TO CANADIAN 3RD INFANTRY DIVISION FOR THE ASSAULT

WO 179/2839

Intelligence/war diary

2ND CANADIAN ARMOURED BRIGADE HQ

Place	Date	Hour	Summary of Events and Information	References to Appendices
SOUTHAMPTON Hants	3 June continued	44	sequence for craft stowage. The reshuffling was completed by 0500. Orders to move again from the halt did NOT come until noon, when the convoy moved the remaining mile and a half to the hards, and loaded aboard 1740. Stowage of vehicles on the craft carrying the BM's headquarters party was supervised by Maj. E.G. PALLISTER, DADME, and OC Troops for the voyage; Maj. ROTHSCHILD; Capt K.M. PACK. Ship's officers proved much more friendly and helpful than those encountered on amphibious exercises.	
COWES ROADS	4 June	44	During the night 3/4 June, LST 1740 moved from SOUTHAMPTON to anchorage in COWES ROADS, where it lay in company with invasion vessels of every type. Shipboard life slipped into a quite tolerable routine. Cooperation with the ship's crew continued to be excellent, to the degree of producing from ship's stores a generous rum ration for all other ranks aboard. In keeping with naval custom, an army officer stood by the queue to witness the actual quaffing of the rum.	
COWES ROADS	5 June	44	The restful shipboard holiday continued until 2030 hours, when the naval signal was received that the operation was on, with H-hour set as 0735 hours 6 June. The OC tps, Maj. E.G. PALLISTER, immediately opened the stack of sealed map bundles which had been carried in 2 Cdn Armd Bde's ACV, and dealt out maps to all unit parties on the craft. Because of the necessity of blacking out the lower, or tank, deck of the LST, it was NOT possible to get on with the task of mounting maps in the ACV, and the officers' accomodation space on the upper deck became a confusion of maps for several hours until the 35 officers aboard had their map bundles sorted, distributed to vehicles and other ranks, -and folded, arranged, and marked their map boards. By midnight order reappeared out of chaos, and all ranks of HQ 2 Cdn Armd Bde turned in for a good night's sleep. Immediately after dark LST 1740 shipped anchor and began to move.	
ENGLISH CHANNEL	6 June	44	At H-hour LST 1740 was moving south out of sight of any land. Ignorance of what was going on was complete, by orders of the ship's captain, all wireless sets were switched off. Sunlight was brilliant, the sea was studded with companion craft, and occasional flights of Spitfires and Lightnings passed overhead. All ears were intent for the sound of gunfire ahead, but the only evidence of enemy action was given by occasional mines bobbing by just outside the marked swept channel.	

SHEET 2

Place	Date	Hour	Summary of Events and Information	Remarks, references to Appendices and initials
ENGLISH CHANNEL	6 June 44 continued		Aboard LST 1740 the wireless silence continued until 1115 hours, when the ship's captain announced that the ship was within ten miles of FRANCE, and gave permission for wireless to be switched on. Wireless equipment in ACV and command tank stayed out of action, because they were on the lower, or tank, deck, and two 5-cwts FFW on the top deck were used to listen on brigade and divisional command nets. First word of the battle received on 1740 was a report from 10 Cdn Armd Regt. at 1115 that forward troops had reached report line YEW, 1000 yards inland. At 1126 the other forward unit, 6 Cdn Armd Regt, reported its RHQ location ashore as map ref 954858. At 1140 6 Cdn Armd Regt. reported RHQ had NOT Yet moved forward, being held up by a gap in the road, and did NOT know the position of the leading squadrons. 10 Cdn Armd Regt reported its RHQ and reserve squadron beaching at 1148 hours. On the divisional net, first definite news came at 1200 hours, with an intercept from divisional tactical headquarters to control, reporting Tac HQ beaching at that time. At 1252 Tac HQ confirmed with a message that it was ashore.	
			From this message it was inferred, by the BM's party aboard LST 1740, that the brigade commander, Brig. R.A. WYMAN, was ashore from the divisional headquarters ship.	
			A picture of the progress of the infantry brigades began to appear at 1202, when an intercept on the divisional net reported HQ 8 Cdn Inf Bde at map ref 993847. At 1220 the first report heard from 7 Cdn Inf Bde announced their forward elements in the outskirts of GRAYE-SUR-MER. At 1225 9 Cdn Inf Bde reported themselves ashore.	
			From the flow of wireless interceptions, a situation map was maintained at one of the 5cwts on the top deck of LST 1740. At the same time a large operations map was kept up by officers of HQ 1 Brit Corps, in the wardroom of the ship, and a third map by a phantom detachment working in the ship's captain's cabin. Information was exchanged among the three news-collection centres.	
			At 1226 hours word came on the brigade net that 27 Cdn Armd Regt. had touched down. From then until 1800 hours no sitrep came from units of the brigade; at 1800 10 Cdn Armd Regt reported forward troops at ELM, the intermediate objective.	

Place	Date	Hour	Summary of Events and Information	Remarks, references to Appendices and initials
ENGLISH CHANNEL	6 June 44 continued		In the early afternoon LST 1740 anchored about two miles off COURSEULLES-SUR-MER, but little information could be acquired from direct observation of the beaches, and the divisional command net provided most of the news received during the afternoon. Maj. R.P. ROTHSCHILD was the first to make identification of landfall, when he spotted the watertower at COURSEULLES.	
			In mid-afternoon the Rhino ferry which had been towed across channel was cast off from the stern. Two hours were consumed in manoeuvring it around to the bow; meanwhile the ship moved from anchorage off COURSEULLES to anchorage off BERNIERES-SUR-MER. Loading of the Rhino from the LST consumed about 30 minutes, and took a third of the vehicles on the ship; the first Rhino load included only two scout cars of the 2 Cdn Armd Bde party, for Brig. R.A. WYMAN and Col. J.F. BINGHAM, who were already ashore on feet from headquarters ships. Soon after the Rhino had started its journey to beach the remainder of the HQ, waiting impatiently for it to return to take its second load, saw it instead strand on a sandbar. As time wore on it became apparent that the Rhino was NOT going to get a second load off the LST before dark 3/4. Meanwhile the alternate HQ went ashore, and assumed control of the brigade wireless net at 2000 hours. At midnight the group left stranded on LST 1740 learned from wireless listening that Brig WYMAN had ordered 6 and 10 Cdn Armd Regts, each less one squadron, to concentrate in the area BENY-SUR-MER, and that commander 3 Cdn Inf Div had ordered 9 Cdn Inf Bde to retain 27 Cdn Armd Regt. overnight.	
			Alternate HQ	
			Meanwhile, on LST 1741, the alternate HQ group, headed by Maj. G.S.L. BUTLER add Maj. D.N.D. DEANE-FREEMAN, kept similar listening watch until 1320 hours, when they got ashore the half-tracked command vehicle and two tanks. The Rhino's ship-to-shore journey was delayed when the Rhino hit underwater rocks, and it was NOT until 1700 hours that the three vehicles touched down on the beach, and proceeded to an assembly area two miles inland. There they met Brig. R.A. WYMAN, and went to work as the functioning brigade headquarters.	

Place	Date	Hour	Summary of Events and Information	Remarks, references to Appendices and initials
ST-AUBIN-SUR-MER	6 June 44 continued		Capt N.M. Macdougall, battle captain of HQ Sqn, who was Tank Unit Landing Officer for the headquarters group, was scheduled to land with 27 Cdn Armd Regt at H plus 180. The craft in which he had made the sea passage actually put in to shore at H plus 60, but was turned back by the beachmaster. He landed finally at about noon at BERNIERE-SUR-MER, and went through the village to its EAST end, and established a Brigade Headquarters report centre, which for a short time consisted of Capt. Macdougall and his jeep FFW.	
			The brigade commander, Brig. R.A. WYMAN, and the alternate brigade commander, Col. J.F. BINGHAM, landed on foot late in the morning from the divisional headquarters ship and the alternate divisional headquarters ship, respectively, and reached the report centre at the EAST end of BERNIERES-SUR-MER at about 1330 hours. Brig. WYMAN and Col. BINGHAM made personal reconnaissances in the areas in which fighting was in progress to gain first-hand information; in the early afternoon they became mounted when the two scout cars came ashore from LST 1740; Brig. WYMAN and Col. BINGHAM then continued to effect personal liaison with divisional and infantry brigade headquartes', and with forward battalions.	
			Wireless communication became difficult in the late afternoon, and control was taken over by Brig. WYMAN and Col. BINGHAM, using Capt. Macdougall's 5 cwt FFW as the control vehicle. Thereafter the ACV, still afloat, became completely a side-issue in the war. In the early evening Brig. WYMAN and Capt. Macdougall made a reconnaissance of BENY-SUR-MER, and selected a night harbour area next door to the RHQ of the HLI of C. The vehicle party from LST 1741 joined Brig. WYMAN and Col. BINGHAM at about 2200 hours, and wireless control was transferred to the M14 half-track, which Brig. WYMAN and Col. BINGHAM employed as their command vehicle until the arrival of the vehicle party from LST 1740 the following day.	
			The beach group of 2 Cdn Armd Bde Wksp RCEME landed D-Day, was attached to 23 Beach Recovery Section REME, and began at once to put drowned vehicles back on the road. With long hours daily, the beach group put 100 vehicles on the road in four days time.	

WO 179/2989
Intelligence/war diary
6TH CANADIAN ARMOURED REGIMENT
(1ST HUSSARS)

Place	Date	Hour	Summary of Events and Information	Remarks, references to Appendices and initials
FORT MONCKTON	1 June Thu	44	Fair and warm. Briefing on bogus maps-all NCOs down to Crew Cmdrs are new briefed. Quarter stores open wide to get rid of odds and ends.	EDhn
ENGLAND	2 June Fri	44	Fair and warm. Last minute preparations are being made and loads are being marshalled. Some "B" vehicles are being sent to other marshalling camps but all our "F" echelon vehicles are being loaded from here or BAY HOUSE. "A" and "B" Sqns loaded.	EDhn
SOUTHAMPTON DOCKS	3 June Sat	44	Generally clear and some rain. "RHQ and "C" Sqns loaded on LCT IV's and proceeded to Southampton Docks where we were tied up. The men were marched down to the NAAFI in Southampton where they saw a show or wrote letters. The remainder stayed on board and rested or sun-bathed.	EDhn
	4 June SUN	44	Windy but clear. Men again went for a route march around the docks but of course nobody is allowed outside.	EDhn
AFLOAT	5 June Mon	44	Clear and warm with strong winds. Convoy for the invasion left Southampton at 1000 hours and by Midnight all Personnel had been briefed with the maps to be used on the invasion.	EDhn
PIERREPONT Sheet 7F/1	6 June Tue	44	Early morning fresh winds, then fair and warm. Cooler at night. After a very rough crossing sub-units of this Regt. arrived off the NORMANDY COAST, FRANCE, to participate in the initial assault that will eventually free the peoples under the yoke of the Germans. "H" hour had been posponed one hour thus we started the assault at 0735 hrs. Our two "DD" Sqns "A" and "B", arrived off "MIKE" (Red and Green) and "NAN" (Green) Beaches between LA RIVIERE and COURSEULLES both inclusive, sheet 6E/5. Due to the roughness of the seas the LCT's had to run our "DD" Sqns close inshore and when 2000 to 5000 yards off shore, our "DD" tanks were launched. All of the 19 "B" Sqn	EDhn

SHEET 2

Place	Date	Hour	Summary of Events and Information	Remarks, references to Appendices and initials
PIERREPONT sheet 7F/1	6 June Tue	44	Cont'd. tanks commanded by Major J.S. DUNCAN were launched, but only ten of Major W.D. BROOKS ("A" Sqn) left the LCT's for the assault. During the run in seven tanks were sunk by shell or mortar fire and at least one of them was run down by our Rocket Ships. The remainder on touching down and deflating their canvas, engaged the Beach Defenses and were successful in destroying the remaining gun positions and MG's, at least 4-75 mm and 13 MG's. Captain J.W. POWELL, 2 IC of "A" Sqn, had his tank hit by a 75 mm located in a concrete fort but he was able to move forward and destroy it. THE R WPG R and the REGINA R supported by "A" and "B" Sqns respectively moved accross the beach but our tanks were unable to follow them immediately inland as the exits had not been cleared. "A" Sqn was especially held up. When our tanks landed on the beach they found teller mines on the posts driven into the beach, which normally are covered at high tide, had not been dealt with. They also found far more heavy calibre weapons than they had anticipated. At 0820 hours "C" Sqn under command of A.D'A. MARKS, and "RHQ" with the Commanding Officer, Lt Col. R.J. COLWELL, touched down in their LCT's and dis-embarked onto the beach, "MIKE" sector. On arriving there and finding the exits not open and a considerable number of obstacles on the beach, The CO and Major F.E. WHITE, the 2 IC, left their tanks and walked the length of the beach endeavouring to find an exit. It can be noted here that everybody was calm and one would think that this was just another exercise. In the meantime the traffic was beginning to pile up so certain troops were dispatched to engage the snipers and MG positions. They were located on the crest of the hill behind the beach and were well dug in and were successfully hindering and ENGINEERS endeavouring to clear the exits. At one exit an armoured car was hit and it was necessary to move it by brushing it to one side, this was accomplished by Lt. G.W. GORDON, who charged it with his tank. While on the beach the Regt. was under continual mortar and shell fire but fortunately was suffered very few casualties among "B" vehicle personnel. On completion of the exits the Regt. moved inland to rally at GRAYE-SUR-MER, but on the way through the exit the CO's tank struck a mine, blowing off a track, thereby-forcing him to take command of his Regt. from the 2 IC's tank. As the Infantry began to move inland they ran into opposition so all available tanks were rushed to support them. "A" Sqn with the R WPG R, "B" Sqn with the REGINA R and "C" Sqn in support of the 1 C SCOT R. It may be noted here that	Appx 4 Appx 5 Appx 6 Appx 7 Appx 8 Appx 9

SHEET 3

Place	Date	Hour	Summary of Events and Information	Remarks, references to Appendices and initials

PIERREPONT Sheet 7F/1	6 June	44	(Cont'd)
			that Major J.S. DUNCAN's tank was unfortuneatly sunk and he and his crew were reported by an eye-witness to be last seen climbing into an RAF dingy. This automatically made the 2 IC Captain H.L. SMUCK temporary OC of "B" Sqn.
			    "B" Sqn on the EAST bank of the R. SEULLES helped the Inf to clean up COURSELLES and "A" Sqn did likewise the LA RIVIERE. "C" Sqn started to advance and cleaned out some of the villages on the way to BANVILLE.
			    It must be taken into consideration that all future actions were always in support of the Inf although they may not be mentioned every time.
			    In the afternoons fighting some of "B" Sqns found themselves ahead of our own Inf. They had some tough luck with a couple of 88 mm, losing 5 tanks to them, until Sgt. Gariepy LR, was able to silence them. Lieut. E.L. PEASE was killed in this engagement.
			    The action on this day was so intense and fast that the tactical picture was hard to visualize, except to advance with the Inf and consolidate. By nightfall we had completed PHASE 11 of our objective. PHASE 11 was the establishing of the 7 CIB (Cmd by Brig. H.W. FOSTER) on a line running through FONTAINE-HENRY, PIERREPONT and ST. GABRIEL. That night "F" Echelon harboured at PIERREPONT, excepting "C" Sqn. who harboured alittle further inland.
			    "A" Echelen arrived at BANVILLE at 1630 hours and harboured there for the night. This Ech under Captain H.R. HERBERT carried supplies of POL, Ammunition and also reinforcement tank crews.
			    After checking up on the number of tanks left, it was found that "B" Sqn. had only four tanks in fighting condition and "A" Sqn only nine, so the CO decided to put "B" Sqn under command of Major W.D. BROOKS and make it a composite Sqn.
			    On reviewing the days action, we found that we did not meet up with any of the enemy's armour but we had inflicted very severe losses on the German Inf, staff and armoured cars and at least eight 88 mm A/tank guns and many smaller A/tank weapons. Two troops of "C" Sqn advanced as far as our objective, namely, BRETTEVILLE-L'ORGULLEUSE, sheet 7F/1, withdrawing without loss after inflicting casualties on the enemy inf. These troops it is believed were the only troops of the ALLIED FORCES to reach their objective on "D" DAY on the whole NORMANDY battlefront.
			    So we close this great day satisfied that we have accomplished all that was possible and lived up to our motto "HONDIE NON CRAS".	

WO 179/2993
Intelligence/war diary
10TH CANADIAN ARMOURED REGIMENT
(FORT GARRY HORSE)

TOP SECRET

APPX "B"

NARRATIVE
10 CDN ARMD REGT

1. In this short account it is impossible to incl many of the actions of individuals and sub-units, though they may have had much bearing upon the larger view.

2. All ranks of the regt showed up well and gave a very good account of themselves. The Op was not an easy one - amphibious Ops never are. Only two men had been under fire before and the requirements of the early landing assault waves had caused some useful types of vehs to be left behind.

3. Due to unavoidable delay on the beach, all vehs carried in LSTs on the first tide did not get ashore until the evening of D-Day. This delay and a consequent phasing back of second tide vehs, presented problems, particularly in regard to the important type of "individual vehs", without which we had to make.

4. The D plus five loads were, of course, not available on this day, due to the same cause.

5. A long period of trg prior to the op was of much value as was our close knowledge of and co-operation with the inf bns. Exercise FABIUS was especially valuable. A tribute is due to the excellent int provided for the op period. It was unfortunate that more time for trg with out op vehs could not have been provided for A sqn (the non DD sqn) and the recce tp; especially the latter, who had not had chance to drive their new STUARTS prior to embarkation. However, due to careful handling no cas were incurred.

6. All ranks were carefully briefed beforehand on the bogus maps, according to instrs and were given the substance of Gen MONTGOMERY's address. On board after sailing, they were read the messages from Gens EISENHOWER, MONTGOMERY and Lt. Gen. CRERAR.

7. The assault wave consisted of:

RHO	- CO and Adjt in LCT (with A Sqn HQ) 2IC and RHQ tp leader later in on LST Complete duplication being ensured.
A Son	- (Non DD) Sqn HQ in two alternative halves. Five tps of two SHERMAN IIIs and one Vc each. These tps were in some cases a little broken up due to shipping problems. A spare tk to come in on D plus 8.
B & C Sons	- (DD Sqns). These decided to swim in two spare tks each, making up scratch crews and a total each of 20 tks. After beaching, two SHERMAN Vc tks who were working initially under the RN were att to B Sqn. Other than these two tks B and C Sqns had no Vc tks.
HO Son	- Only three light tks were allowed on the loading table and these were kept in hand by the CO throughout. Certain other B vehs – the Sqn leader's 4 x 4 5 cwt, etc., and a VALENTINE br layer from 2 Cdn Armd Bde, a SHERMAN rec tk (A Sqn) and a scout car for the Regt int offr and one for the Regt Sigs offr (these latter did not arrive till the evening of D-Day).

8. <u>INTERCOMN</u>

RHQ was in contact with 8 Cdn Inf Bde and 2 Cdn Armd Bde throughout. The alternative HQ also, before and after landing.

SHEET 2

9. VOYAGE

The expedition left the boom outside PORTSMOUTH about 1700 hrs having cast off in SOUTHAMPTON water about 1500 hrs. There was a fresh wind blowing up channel and quite a sea running. The LCT in which RHQ was sailing was very heavily laden, not a spare foot of deck space being available. Quite a few of the men were seasick and a restless night was spent by all.

10. GEN

The plan is known and will not be described here. On account of the sea running, the DSOAG of the DD Sqns gp – Comd R.E.D. RYDER, V.C., asked the Senior Sqn leader if he wished to launch at the previously decided distance of 7000 yds or to move in closer. It was decided to close to 2000 or 3000 yds and eventually the Sqns were both launched close inshore, though inflated. H hr being 0745 hrs, DD time on 6 Jun 44. RHQ CO and Adjt only) and A sqn HQ together with A Sqn touched down at about 900 hrs.

11. It was found that several centres of resistance along the beach had not been touched by the preliminary air or SP arty bombardment and soon came to life. This was especially so on the front of C Sqn and the N shore R on the LEFT.

12. The AVREs came in late (note at H hr), though the assault inf were in on time on the beach. The assault Sqns RE being late and having difficulty in making their gaps kept the tks in most cases on the beach until about 0930 hrs, on NAN RED and WHITE beaches.

13. Visibility was good from 0800 hrs onwards from the sea.

14. The arrangements by the RN both for security in convoy over the channel and in sp of the landing seemed excellent.

15. Beach defs were found to be very much as foreseen by int. The teller mines on the stakes, hedgehogs, etc, were found to be shells but with a limited damaging effect, however.

D DAY (6 JUNE)

16. ACTION ON LEFT FLANK

C Sqn (Maj BRAY) found the beach fairly quiet on landing except for sniping, occasional shells on their left, where on LCT with some of their tks aboard had been sunk by fire from ST. AUBIN-SUR-MER direction. The LCT with AVRE on board were late coming in and the SP arty barrage soon moved inland. By the time the inf assault companies got in, the situation had become much more lively and the tks were giving supporting fire in all directions. The tks had now lost four and were down to sixteen; crew comds directing fire were subjected to sniping and several were lost here.

17. By H plus 45, the SP companies of inf were coming in and the assault REs had still made no gaps; so the Sqn leader made the decision to push through the minefd himself. This he did losing three more tks but he led the reminder through the minefd and got on and helped the inf now fighting in ST. AUBIN-SUR-MER.

18. Sporadic fighting took place here but, dominated by the tks, the inf soon satisfactorily cleared the town except for one strong pt where the enemy held out stubbornly. A tp was allotted to the inf but the posn held out all day until finally giving in at about 2000 hrs that night. Sgt. WALTERSON distinguished himself here; finally charging in with his tk and compelling surrender.

19. The remainder of the Sqn helped the inf in this town on many occasions during the day.

SHEET 3

20. Meanwhile the N Shoe R had asked for a det to assist them in overrunning TAILLEVILLE to the SOUTH. One, and later another tp were sent up. Capt CHRISTIAN (2IC C Sqn), to comd. This little force had a good party for awhile overrunning and destroying an 88 mm, a 75 mm and about 50 inf. They seized the high ground beyond the village before the def there developed. The siezing of TAILLEVILLE developed much stiff fighting during the day in which Capt. CHRISTIAN, Lt. LITTLE and Sgt. FIDLER distinguished themselves. Considerable damage was done to enemy material and personnel; the enemy held out stubbornly.

21. That night orders were sent out to conc the regt in BENY-SUR-MER but the N Shore R appealed against it as they found the tks invaluable and the gen situation fluid and unsatisfactory. Eventually the Sqn remained.

22. <u>ACTION ON RIGHT</u>

(Tps landing on NAN WHITE – RHQ, B QOROJE and A Rdcc. Sqns in sp of QOR of C and R de Chaud). This DD sqn Bsgn (Maj. J.A. MEINDL) had a similar experience to C Sqn on the LEFT in landing. After the inf landed, however, enemy fire opened up and one coy of the QOR suffered severely before B sqn could suppress it. The tks remained upon the beach until almost 0930 hrs. No gaps were made till then, as the RE Coy. were late on this beach also. Considerable sniping took place and sporadic shelling came down.

23. When they were able, B Sqn moved through BERNIERS-SUR-MER near HQ of QOR of C. This Sqn undoubtedly performed valuable service in supporting the QOR of C from the beach and later took several MGs and two 88 mm guns to the SW of the town.

24. At about 0900 hrs RHQ (two tks) and A Sqn beached. Unfortunately the LCT carrying RHQ and A Sqn HQ hit a mine, damaging the ramp and craft put to sea again still loaded. It did not beach until almost 1000 hrs. The remainder of Sqn however got to shore and joined with B Sqn still on the beach.

25. R de Chaud had landed in good shape, pushed through to their rally point and were subsequently joined by A Sqn less Sqn HQ. 8 Cdn Inf Bde were also ashore and had moved forward to the southern outskirts of BERNIERS.

26. When the CO, Adjt and Sqn leader and RL of A sqn landed and pushed fwd to 8 Cdn Inf Bde's fwd HQ a confusing picture presented itself. BERNIERS was jammed with vehs and tks of all sorts, the adv had been held up by minefds and 88 mm guns, the R de Chaud were forming up but could not get on and A sqn were pushing our tps too cautiously ahead. Into this mass, the 9 Cdn Inf Bde began landing and the Bde 2IC arrived. The rds were plugged with zealous soldiers impatient to get on, Fortunately the enemy did not shell the town.

27. As soon as possible the Sqn leader took charge and A sqn moved on. Meanwhile the CO had ordered a move fwd and though tks were lost the momentum was regained. R de chaud followed on the centre line towards BENY-SUR-MER.

28. After their losses on the beach, fortunately the QOR of C had little difficulty in clearing BERNIERS and with B Sqn followed on the centre line towards BASLY.

29. A Sqn supported by R de Chaud encountered considerable resistance about BENY-SUR-MER. The inf in front seemed slow cleaning such opposition as snipers and battle patrols. The QOR of C trying to push on behind complained of this. By about noon the Bde 2IC ordered another Sqn to converge on the high ground COLOMBY-SUR-THAON from the WEST. So B sqn were taken away temporarily from the QOR of C and put fwd around BASLY.

30. About 1400 hrs RHQ who were following up the rd behind A & B Sqns able to inform 8 Cdn Inf Bde that A sqn was on the bde objective but wanted inf badly. However, none were to be forthcoming for a while. To RHQ pushing fwd, the leading R de Chaud coy seemed to be consolidating in BASLY while the fwd Sqn was wanting inf. It was impossible, however, short of abduction, to get any fwd, even lifted on tks.

SHEET 4

31. That afternoon plenty of skirmishes went on as the inf began to arrive - the QOR of C in ANGUERNY and R de Chaud in the COLOMBY-SUR-THAON posns whilst patrolling was carried on by the tks. One interesting affair was a patrol by RHQ to the LEFT towards the third Brit Div bdy. A Coy. HQ was attacked and overrun and cas inflicted.

32. By nightfall A and B sqns had assisted their bns on to their posns and were supporting them there as well as doing patrol work. Orders now came to concentrate the regt for rest and replenishment in BENY-SUR-MER and infm received that the remainder of RHQ were ashore.

33. None of the inf wished to relinquish their sqns and finally RHQ and A sqn only reached BENY-SUR-MER by about 0100 hrs. B Sqn came in much later whilst C Sqn never reported in till the afternoon of D plus 1. An 0 gp was held at Bde HQ in BENY-SUR-MER that night.

Cas: Killed - Lt N.H. BROWN, B Sqn and 4 ORs.

Wounded - Maj J.A. MEINDL, Lt W.D. LITTLE and 10 ORs.

Missing - 9 ORs.

Tks knocked out – 11.

D PLUS 1 (7 JUNE)

34. <u>LEFT SON</u>

C Sqn near TAILLEVILLE in sp of N Shore R. After a restless night, the Sqn was on the move by 0700 hrs. Considerable action took place in supporting the N Shore R in their attack upon the RADAR STA. In these actions three amn dumps were blown up and over 30 prisoners taken.

35. The German def of this place was very strong and by the evening of this day further attack by fwd inf was discontinued. The place did not fall until the 18th June after hy air and arty bombardment.

36. About 1500 hrs the sqn left to rejoin the regt then positioned about COLOMBY-SUR-THAON. Lt. AINUTT killed en route.

37. <u>REGT. LESS C SON</u>

As noted, the Regt. 2IC, the sig offr and the Regt. IO, both in scout cars had now joined, together with certain other important vehs. The RHQ tp leader, Lt. THEOBALD, had drowned his tk in landing and had not come fwd as yet.

38. The Regt. was in res during the day. An interesting recce was sent out under come of Capt GOODMAN to see if the lateral rd from BENY THAILLEVILLE to LA DELIVRAND was clear of enemy. Useful infm was secured for the GOC in this regard. Several enemy were killed, an amn dump destroyed and a large coastal gun, engaged in harassing new landings, was shelled and put out of action near LA DELIVRAND.

39. A certain amount of sniping was prevalent here and on the move up. Part of the 9 Cdn Inf Bde were in this town. The civil population, it was noted, appeared friendly but not enthusiastic; they had been, on the whole, well treated in this important agricultural province of NORMANDY. Also, it was felt that we might not succeed.

40. The Regt. moved up to the high ground to dominate and hold, SOUTH of COLOMBY-SUR-THAON by BASLY and LA MARE, C Sqn joining later.

41. The CO and Adjt recced fwd to LES BUISSONS where the 27 Cdn Armd Regt and NNS Highrs were offering a stiff resistance to enemy attack. 27 Cdn Armd Regt. wished no immediate help. Informed CO that we stood firm behind also earmarked a Sqn to move fwd and assist if required.

D PLUS 2 (8 JUNE)

42. Recced fwd with Adjt's tk. Engaged in brief battle with Brit Armd Regt who fired first. SHERMAN armour good.

43. Pushed B Sqn (now under comd Capt J.F.M. HALL) towards VILLONS-LES-BUISSONS. About noon they reported being in action against an enemy attack.

WO 179/3010

Intelligence/war diary

27TH CANADIAN ARMOURED REGIMENT (SHERBROOKE FUSILERS)

Place	Date 1944	Hour	Summary of Events and Information	Remarks, references to Appendices and initials
Aboard LCT 759 ENGLISH CHANNEL	0506	1900	Light rain during the night, partly cloudy and cool during the day visibility fair with a brisk NW wind and choppy sea. D-Day was postponed one day because of the bad weather but in spite of the wind the flotilla set sail at 1415 hrs and passed the boom into the open sea at 1730 hrs. Maps of France which had been sealed up to this time were opened and distributed to be fitted under talcs which had previously been marked. No maps of the coast area itself of 1:50,000 scale were included, therefore at least half of the trace on the talcs was useless and only a few vehicles had maps showing the assembly area. Seasick pills were given out every four hours on most craft and proved very good, but in spite of these many of the men were violently sick, as the craft pitched and tossed badly. Most of the craft are very heavily loaded and the decks are awash with water. Weather in the Channel is windy and cold.	Lmf
Aboard LCT 759 Serial 1723 Offshore from BERNIER-SUR-MER	[0606	1200	[The flotilla moved southwards across the channel all night towards the coast of France and at 1000 hrs land could be sighted.] At 1030 hrs a wireless message was received that the Queens Own Rifles of Canada and the North Shore Regt had reached YEW at 1020 hrs. [At 1130 hrs the craft started the run in to the beach after circling off shore from BERNIERE-SUR-MER, ST. AUBIN and COURCELLES, waiting for the order to beach. There is no air opposition and the landing is well covered by our own aircraft. Some fires can be seen burning on the shore and small arms fire is still coming from isolated strongpoints.] Naval shelling is going on on a small scale. The troops on board have stowed all equipment and vehicles have been unchained. The men are sitting up on top of their vehicles watching the shore and seem quite calm about the whole thing.	Lmf
MR 9 881 SHEET 7F/1 1:50000 BENY-SUR-MER, FRANCE	0606	1800	[The Regt. landed at 1215 hrs on NAN WHITE Sector, just west of BERNIERE-SUR-MER and moved through the town. There was much congestion on the beach and in the town and a long wait resulted while this was cleared. During a short halt on the road at 993844 marching infantry of the NNS Highrs loaded on the tanks and porpoises and rode the remaining distance to the assembly area ELDER, 9881, arriving at 1800 hrs.] The porpoises loaded with ammunition unloaded very well from the craft except for a few which came unfastened in the water, these were unhooked and will be left in the assembly area. [All tanks and vehicles on LCTs arrived at the assembly area, those on LSTs did not beach. There were no casualties to personnel up to this point.]	Lmf

SHEET 2

Place	Date 1944	Hour	Summary of Events and Information Sheet 3 27 Canadian Armoured Regiment (Sher Fus R) Serial 1044/1	Remarks, references to Appendices and initials
MR 9881 NORTH OF BENY-SUR-MER FRANCE	0606 D Day	1900	Major F.H. Baldwin, OC HQ Sqn. with two ORs, landed in a jeep with 8 Cdn Inf Bde as TULO for this Regt. The craft he was on struck a mine and a 15-cwt was jammed in the doorway. The craft had to back into deep water where the 15-cwt was pushed off, it then beached with a bad list and decks awash. On landing he was unable to accomplish his task as TULO because of the congestion on the beach and the main road inland where traffic was held up by an 88 mm gun positioned on high ground inland. When the unit landed, Major Baldwin made contact at BERNIERE-SUR-MER and accompanied them to the Assembly Area ELDER near BENY-SUR-MER.	Lmf
			Lt. W.F. Grainger and one OR landed in a jeep with 7 Cdn Inf Bde as spare TULO to recce an alternative route and Assembly Area in case plans had to be changed and assembly area could not be used at ELDER.	Lmf
LA MARE, FRANCE MR 006756 Sheet 7F/1	[0606	2300	The Recce Troop, under Lt. G.A. Kraus, led off the 9 Cdn Inf Bde Group from ELDER at 1900 hrs, followed by C Coy. of the North Nova Scotia Highlanders on their carriers, A Coy. on A sqn's tanks, B Coy. on B Sqn's tanks and D Coy. on C Sqn's tanks. The unit moved through BENY-SUR-MER and BASLY to LA MARE MR 003783. Opposition was met on the right flank in the form of enemy mortars and A/Tk guns which were taken out by Sgt. Beardsley's tank. A Sqn moved on the right, B Sqn. on the left and C Sqn. centre. The head of the column reached LA MARE at dusk, and together with the North Nova Scotia Highlanders, the unit formed a fortress based on the high ground around the crossroads at 006756 between ANISY and VILLONS-LES-BUISSONS.]	Lmf
			Lt. C.C. McLachlan has been appointed A/Capt and QM with effect from 1 Jun 44 to replace Capt. I. Echenberg.	Lmf
			D-46001 SSM MacLeod, D.E. has been appointed A/RSM with effect from 1 Jun 44 to replace RSM Dufault who was SOS prior to embarkation.	Lmf
			8 ORs of the 85 LAD attached to this unit are reported missing. Their craft has been reported sunk off DOVER by enemy action.	Lmf
			Attached at Appx 3 is a list of 9 Cdn Inf Bde and 3 Cdn Inf Div Code Names.	Lmf
			Attached at Appx 3 are photographs of the beach and maps of the area.	Appx 3 Lmf

WO 171/854

Intelligence/war diary
C SQUADRON THE INNS OF COURT REGIMENT
(ROYAL ARMOURED CORPS)

Month and Year June 1944   Commanding Officer Lt. Col. R.A.G. BINGLEY.

Place	Date	Hour	Summary of Events and Information	References to Appendices
	June 4th 1944		C Sqn. plus special force of R.E. personnel (5 Offrs & 35 Ors) embarked PORTSMOUTH June 4th 1944 in two LCT Mk IVs as follows Load I: Major G.H.P. Strakosch, Lt. E.B. Young, Lt. A.O. Hunt, Lt. R. Wigram, Lt. L.T. Yodaiken, Lt. O.J. Sinnatt, Lt. P.R.D. Shaw, Lt. W.I.H. Gwynne-Jones, Lt. D.W. Lofts (R.E.) Lt. J. Symm (R.E.), plus 59 ORs; Load II: Lt. Col. R.A.G. Bingley, Capt., W.L. Warren, Revd. J. du B. Lance, C.F., Lt. K. Black, Lt. P.E. Reeve, Lt. A.T. Corke, Lt. P.S. Wall, Lts. J.D. Petworth (R.E.), R. Bridgett (R.E.), P.M. Taylor (R.E.), plus 65 ORs. Capt. S.H. Gill travelled with R. Winnipeg Rifles in another craft. Lt. Kaye travelled with 50 Div.	
	June 6th 1944		Both craft touched down at 0830 hrs on beach at COMSEULLES, NORMANDY. Casualties by a mine under water on Load II were: Humber S/Car (Padre), 2 White ½-tracks, 1 Daimler S/Car, 1 Sgt. wounded.	21

Wt.47724/993 2,000,000 3/43 W. H. & S. 51/6375.   Contd Sheet 2.

SHEET 2

Month and Year June 1944   Commanding Officer Lt. Col. R.A.G. BINGLEY.

Place	Date	Hour	Summary of Events and Information	References to Appendices
		1030 hrs	Daimler A/Car hit by A/Tank Weapon at 954857. Lt. Shaw killed and driver. Operator wounded.	
		1200 hrs	Daimler S/Car blown up on mine leaving beach. No personnel injured.	
		1500 hrs	2a, 4a, 1, 5 Tps crossed R. SEULLES. 6 Tp later.	
		1600 hrs	4a, Daimler A/Car knocked out at LA RIVIERS by A.T. rifle. Lt. O.J. Sinnatt killed and operator. Lt. Sinnatt was trying to eliminate German defence post. SHQ harboured for night area Vienne en Bessin 8579.	
	June 7th 1944		La crossed SEULLES 8474, 2 & 6a at 8471. Thunderbolts bombed 4, 5a Tps at 8773 - casualties: Lt. Gwynne Jones killed, Lt. Lofts R.E. killed, Lt. Reeve wounded and 5 ORs killed and 5 wounded. 1 & 5 reached railway area BRONAY, 2a - NORREY-EN-BESSIN, la2 & 6 ST. MARGUERITE. Enemy tanks at Bronay reported by 6.	22

Wt.47724/993 2,000,000 3/43 W. H. & S. 51/6375.   contd Sheet 3.

DEFE 2/46
Intelligence/war diary
4TH SPECIAL SERVICE BRIGADE HQ

Month and Year June 44

Commanding Officer Brigadier B.W. LEICESTER

Place	Date	Hour	Summary of Events and Information	References to Appendices
SOUTHAMPTON	1-4		Briefing in C.19 Camp.	
WARSASH	5	1600	Embark in LSI(S) Serials 1519 and 1520.	
[ST AUBIN-SUR MER	6	0900	Landed at high tide in face of Imping and MG fire.	Appx 'E' and Annx 1
LA RIVE	6	1000	Bde HQ assembles 005850.	
LA RIVE	6	1130	Tac HQ moves into ST. AUBIN, area 015855. Rear HQ remains LA RIVE.	
ST. AUBIN	7	1100	46 RM Cdo landed NAN RED. Assembled in area LA RIVE under Comd 4 SS Bde.	A. p.7/1 Serial 5
			Immediate task to adv through LUC-SUR-MER.	
LION-SUR-MER	7	1100	Lt. Col. T. M. GRAY, Commanding 41 RM Cdo wounded, Maj D. BARCLAY, 2 ic.	A. p.7/2 Serial 17
ST. AUBIN	8	1130	Killed. Major J.A. TAPLIN therefore assumed comd.	A. p.8/2 Serial 14
ST. AUBIN	9	0925	Bde Comd returns from visit to 1 Corps with infm concerning future Cdo tasks.	A. p.9/1 Serial 12
ST. AUBIN	9	1130	46 RM Cdo to proceed to agreed line in LA DELIVRANDE GOC 51 (H) Div considering move 4 SS Bde complete to LA DELIVRANDE-DOUVRES] area.	A. p.9/1 Serial 17

Wt.47724/993 2,000,000 3/43 W.H. & S. 51/6375

DEFE 2/52
Intelligence/war diary
NO. 48 ROYAL MARINE COMMANDO

Month and Year June 1944				Commanding Officer Lt. Col. J.L. MOULTON RM

Place	Date	Hour	Summary of Events and Information	References to Appendices
SASH	5	1330	The Commando left the Marshalling area in TCV's for WARSASH where after a brief wait in a field, it Embarked from the Jetty on LCI (S) of 202 Flotilla.	
		1400		
		1900	That Evening, after lying alongside during the afternoon, the flotilla sailed for its RV with the convoy. The Cdo was informed that the operation was on, maps were distributed and troops told their objective.	
Sea	5/6		The crossing was rough since there was a stiff NW breeze and a high proportion of the troops were seasick. The hyoscine issued had little effect as a sedative. The night passed without incident.	
		0500	The next morning we reached our RV off the French coast and circled the HQ ship, HMS HILARY awaiting the time to land. It was postponed 15 minutes. About 0730 the Flotilla moved in towards the shore, men put on their Equipment and Camouflaged their faces and hands.	
			At first it appeared that the landing would be unopposed and most craft dismounted the 2" mortars which were prepared to move, the landing with smoke. Then MG's opened up from the strong point at ST. AUBIN which was almost opposite the Easternmost landing craft and perhaps 200 yds from the Westernmost and	

Wt.52938/1102 660M. 2/44 W. H. & S. 51-9071

SHEET 2

Month and Year June 1944				Commanding Officer Lt. Col. J.L. MOULTON RM

Place	Date	Hour	Summary of Events and Information	References to Appendices
	6		the craft were subjected to mortar and shell fire; the Z' Tp craft received a direct hit amidships. The Derlikons replied and HQ craft put down smoke on the beach with 2" mortars.	
ST. AUBIN NAN RED (010853)		0843	Beach obstacles had not been cleared and was well below the water when the Cdo landed. Two craft (Y and Z Tps) struck obstacles and were unable to beach. HQ craft struck an obstacle but was fairly close inshore. The majority of landing ramps failed, Either because their inshore ends floated or because the movement of the craft on the obstacles shook them off the craft. A, B, X and HQ Tps were able to wade ashore in about 3 feet of water, but Y and Z Tps could only get ashore by swimming. Many Offcrs and men attempted to swim ashore from their craft and a high proportion of these were lost through drowning. Some got ashore (Major de stacpoole just made the beach although wounded before he left the craft; Capt Lennard, a strong swimmer was drowned; TSM Travers was carried far to the East and landed under the guns of the strongpoint at LANGRONE. On reaching the shore, troops made for the cover of the Earth cliff and sea wall [SEE SKETCH APPX 'A'].	

Wt.52938/1102 660M. 2/44 W.H. & S. 51-9071

SHEET 3

Commanding Officer Lt. Col. J.L. MOULTON RM

Place	Date	Hour	Summary of Events and Information	References to Appendices
	6		here they found a confused situation. The cliff and sea wall gave some protection from SA fire, but any movement away from them was under NG fire. The whole area meanwhile was under heavy mortar and shellfire. Under the sea wall was a jumble of men from other units including many wounded and Dead; the beach was congested with tanks, SP guns and other Vehicles, some out of action, others attempting to move from the beach in the very confused space between the waters edge and the sea wall. LCT's were arriving all the time and attempted to land their loads adding to the general confusion.	
			A quick recce showed that the beach Exit to the right of the isolated houses was free from aimed SA fire Except for occasional shots and that a gap had been cleared through the mines. As this was the quickest way to the assembly area, orders were immediately passed for troops to move up to the assembly area by this route, B Tp led followed by A, HQ, and X, but in the conditions prevailing, it was largely a question of telling sub sec Comdo and individual men the way to move.	

Wt.52938/1102 660M. 2/44 W. H. & S. 51-9071

SHEET 4

Commanding Officer Lt. Col. J.L. MOULTON RM

Place	Date	Hour	Summary of Events and Information	References to Appendices
ST. AUBIN	6	0900	The Assembly Area was much quieter and Tp RV's were quickly established and Cdo HQ set up. The CO returned to the beach to contact Y and Z Tps. A considerable number of men of mixed Tps were found still under the cliff and these were moved off to the right. He found Y Tp attempting to get ashore from an LCT to which they had transferred from their LCT. Lieut Fouché was already ashore and he was ordered to fan men along to the right as they came ashore out he was hit almost immediately, by mortar, fragments and seriously wounded; his orderly was killed, However, the landing of Y Tp was very slow and few men managed to get ashore before the LCT (as was later discovered) shoved off, taking with her about 50 men of its Cdo to England despite their Energetic protests. Z Tp was more fortunate and about 40 men were eventually, collected in the Assembly Area. These had got ashore now up transferred first to an LCT, then to an LCA. The LCA made two trips under a stout hearted young leading seaman. In the ASS area it was found on calling for reports that A, B and X Tps call had about 50-55 men available (Capt. Reynolds A Tps returned to duty although wounded). S 'Tp had one 3" moves and one crew det (MMG's were to come later in Tps). HQ had had about 20 casualties but was working Satisfactionly. The 5 men of Y Tp	

Wt.52938/1102 660M 2/44 W. H. & S. 51-9071

SHEET 5

Month and Year June 1944

Commanding Officer Lt. Col. J.L. MOULTON RM

Place	Date	Hour	Summary of Events and Information	References to Appendices
ASS Area ST AUBIN	6		present were joined with Z Tp (about 40) under comd Maj Freeman (alt from SAUDF) seconded RM). Maj de Stacpoole although wounded and exhausted by his swim, pressed for Employment but was ordered to remain in the Ass Area and being on the remnant S of Y Tp. The Co now issued a warning order for the advance and made his way to the prearranged RV with Lt. Col. Buell (Co N. Shere Regt). The latter informed him that the Rd on the inland side of ST. AUBIN was clear but that the strong point was still holding out against B Coy., N Shore Regt (it held out until nearly Dark). 'D' Coy. had reached the Rly Sta where it was in contact with Enemy dets. C Coy. was about to start for TRILLEVILLE.	
		1030	On returning to the assembly area, the CO ordered the Cdo to move off according to plan. B Tp was to move straight to the beach defenses immediately East of ST. AUBIN "Deaths head Sector" while the remainder with "A" Tp as advance guard moved on LANGRUNE. Supporting LCG's (331 Flot Lt Com York) were asked over the RT link to left fire from Deaths head sector at 1100 hrs. The advance was without incident; the vicinity of LANGRUNE church was	

SHEET 6

Month and Year June 1944

Commanding Officer Lt. Col. J.L. MOULTON RM

Place	Date	Hour	Summary of Events and Information	References to Appendices
LANGRUNE	6	1150	found unoccupied. X Tp was now detached to tackle the next sector of beach Defence (Dogfish One). 'A' and 'Z' Tps faced South to prevent an enemy counter attack. 'A' Tp sent a patrol to the Bridge at 037828 which was found unoccupied with orders to guard the bridge and make contact with 41(RM) Cdo. 41 Cdo, however, were badly held up at LION-SUR-MER and never reached this bridge.	
		1300	'B' Tp now reported 'Deaths head' clear; they had found it unoccupied and suffered only one casualty (Lt. Curtis) wounded by own naval supporting fire. 'B' Tp was ordered to report to Cdo HQ Established at 030836.	
		1327	A little later X Tp reported Dogfish One clear, and as Y Tp was absent, were ordered to continue clearing Dogfish Two, Here almost at once, they came under LMG fire from the area of the Cross Rds. The Tp comd was unable to make progress down the street and began to work round the right (inland flank). On reaching Rd 'A', he attempted to attack towards the sea but was unable to gain ground down this street Either and Eventually reported in person to Cdo HQ.	PLAN OF BEACH DEFENCES APPX 'B'

SHEET 7

Place	Date	Hour	Summary of Events and Information	References to Appendices
LANGRUNE	6	1430	On receiving this report, the Co decided to move towards the sea front on a Two Tp front, X Tp down Street 'A', and 'B' Tp Street 'B'. The Cross Rds AA. BB were the respective objectives of the Tps. 'A' Tp was	
		1445	held in reserve ready to exploit any success by B Tp. 'X'. Tp was moved back some 300 yds in land of the Rly and Naval support requested. The bombardment from the LCG's lifted at 1520 hrs and both Tps started to work down the street using the cover of houses and gardens. The line at the Rly was quickly gained by both Tps, but after that, both met LMG fire down the street, and sniping and mortar fire from the gardens.	
		1800	'B' Tp continued to make ground although progress was slow owing to the substantial and frequent walls and fences its required to be breached. However, about 1800 hrs the Co found Capt Perry (OC 'B' Tp) in the houses about 50 yds from the Cross rds 'BB'. From an attic light Capt. Perry could see the Germans and said that they appeared to be in a bad way and that he would be ready to assault shortly. The CO, who had been wounded earlier in the forearm did not climb up to the attic, but returned to move 'A' Tp down to exploit, 'B' Tp's Success.	

SHEET 8

Place	Date	Hour	Summary of Events and Information	References to Appendices
LANGRUNE	6	1815	Shortly after this, however, Capt. Perry was killed by a sniper and although the Tp continued slowly to make their way foward, no proper assault was made. Eventually 2/L+ Rubinstein (now OC 'B' Tp) reported that he was held up on the Edge of the cleared area some 20 yds short of the Cross Rds.	
		1823	On returning to Cdo HQ which had now been Established in a Farm at 033836, the Co found two CENTAUR tanks of the 2nd RMAS Regt which had been sent to assist. After some delay, one was sent down each Rd with improved means of comns with the infantry. The measure of these AFV's helped the infantry toward a little on 'B' Tps front and soon their Centaur reached the Cross Rds, BB, and was able to fire down the lateral street. The direction of the Centaurs fire was painfully slow for the crews were quite unaccustomed to cooperate with infantry, indeed to work as tanks - their role was that of St. Perry - However most of the houses around BB were soon knocked about, although the AE shell, which was all the tanks could fire, had no effect on the anti-tank wall and reinforced houses immediately East of it. 'B' Tp was now appeared to gain the houses around the Cross Rd, BB. 2/L+	

SHEET 9

Month and Year June 1944

Commanding Officer Lt. Col. J.L. MOULTON RM

Place	Date	Hour	Summary of Events and Information	References to Appendices
LANGRUNE	6	2030	Rubenstein led this assault and was able to gain the now badly damaged houses on the NW corner, but could not get into the reinforced houses on across the A TR wall. Over the top of this came a steady flow a stick greases which did surprisingly little harm. But 'B' Tp was unable to get beyond the first two houses in this sector and eventually with ? to the SW comms to ask to further assistance.	
			By this time 'B' Tp's Centaur had run out at Amo and was withdrawn. Another (two further Troops which had arrived) came up, but immediately set off a move which broke the track. This blocked the road. Meanwhile 'X' Tp had run into mines in street 'A' and lost a number of men from these and from LMG fire.	
		2100	At this time, Brig. B.W. Leicester (comd 4 SS Bde) called in at Cdo HQ. He said that that a counterattack might be expected at dawn and ordered the Cdo to consolidate LANGRUNE against attack. Light was now failing, and the CO decided that as the Cdo was much reduced in numbers, he would hold the ground gained with the smallest possible force and that the remainder around Cdo HQ to cover the approached from the South and East.	

Wt.52938/1102 660M. 2/44 W. H. & S. 51-9071

SHEET 10

Month and Year June 1944

Commanding Officer Lt. Col. J.L. MOULTON RM

Place	Date	Hour	Summary of Events and Information	References to Appendices
LANGRUNE	6/7	0830	The night passed quietly and the morning brought no signs of a counter attack. So the CO sent an LO to inform Bde that the Cdo was now too weak simultaneously to hold the Southern part of LANGRUNE and to attack the strongpoint. Meanwhile the one "3" mortar was brought into action to keep the enemy strongpoint occupied and harassed - It was later we learnt that it was most effective. From Bde, came the welcome reply that an enemy counter attack was no longer likely and that M 10 SP ATR guns would be sent to assist with the concrete.	
			As Road 'A' was mined and explosives owing to losses on the beach the previous day were short the co decided to attack own street B, using the M 10's to knock down the concrete wall and reinforced house. To do this it was necessary to clear a way though the minefield on which the centaur had been blown up. This was to be done by Bangalore Torpedoes of which just enough who available. 'A' Tp was to make the attack, while 'X' Tp were to contain the enemy down street 'B' with fire.	
		1130	The attack started at 1130; the Bangalore was laid and blown and the first M 10	

Wt.52938/1102 660M. 2/44 W. H.& S. 51-9071

ADM 202/306

Intelligence/war diary

2ND ROYAL MARINE ARMOURED SUPPORT
BATTERY HQ (3RD AND 4TH BATTERIES)

Month and Year June 1944   Commanding Officer Lt. Col. M. BRITTON JOHNSON RM.

Place	Date	Hour	Summary of Events and Information	References to Appendices
C. 9 Camp APO ENGLAND	1	–	Adv. HQ this Unit remained marshalled since 31 May 44. (Ref War Diary May 44)	
	2	1845	Adv. HQ embarked in LST 239. Move to docks a distance of 8 miles took 7 hours.	
			OC Craft load Major Ross, Cameron Highlanders of Ottowa. 47 RM Cdo were passed during move to docks. This Units 8 troops with Centaur Tanks moved today under MC orders to G.2 and 4 Hards at STOKES BAY, GOSPORT for embarkation in LCTs. This was partly witnessed by the Prime Minister and others visitors.	
	2	2130	LST at anchor off LEE ON SOLENT.	
LEE ON SOLENT	3	0830	CO and Capt Richardson disembarked from LST to an LCP and visited the 16 LCTs in which the Regiment are embarked. All Officers and ORs in good spirits and had no major problems. Amn was being loaded and waterproofed in Porpoises. There were however several craft overloaded in spite of the careful plan made by 3rd Cdn Inf Div.	
	4	2200	LST at anchor all day. Wind now force 4 (Beauforts). Weather has lead to a 24 hour postponement today.	
	5	1905	LST under way, weather slightly improved.	
	6	1030	French Coast sighted, weather improving after very rough passage.	
ENGLISH CHANNEL off COURSEULLES	6	1330	Orders received for no further disembarkation owing to lack of beach exits. Low ground in rear of MIKE SECTOR flooded.	
	6	1345	Information received that the objective in Phase I has been secured. At our present distance from the beach (1500 yds) it appears our Centaur Tanks have moved forward to plan :- Deploy on Beach at H. supporting Units as follows :- P & Q Tps. Royal Winnipeg Rifles S & T Tps. Regina Rifles. W & X Tps. Queens Own Rifles. Y & Z Tps. N Shore Regt. All of 3rd Cdn Inf Div. In addition Z Tp supports 48 RM Cdo.	
COURSEULLES	6	1710	Enemy Aircraft bombed MIKE & NAN Sectors, damage could not be observed.	
	6	2005	Disembarked from Ferry on MIKE RED Beach.	

Wt.47724/993 2,000,000 3/43 W. H. & S. 51/6375.

SHEET 2

               Commanding Officer Lt. Col. M. BRITTON JOHNSON RM.

Place	Date	Hour	Summary of Events and Information	References to Appendices
BANVILLE	6	2120	Visited P & Q Tps in Gun Positions.	
BERNIERAS-SUR-MER	6	2250	Arrived at 3rd Cdn Inf Div HQ. Beach area bombed during night.	
		0650	Visited W Troop in Gun Positions.	
BENY-SUR-MER	7	0840	Visited S & T Tps.	
REVIERS	(D+1) 7	1400	Div. HQ now moved to this location, received information that	
BENY-SUR-MER	7		X, Y & Z Troops are with RM Cdo. All remaining Troops with RCA Field Regts. Troops had not landed to plan, for details of actual employment refer to Report on Operation "OVERLORD" period D & D + 1.	
7	7	1430	Visited ST. AUBIN-SUR-MER and LANGRUNE-SUR-MER with Col. A.J. Harvey OBE RM and located X, Y & Z Tps. Brigadier LESTER RM reported that they had given valuable support in street fighting and gave his Cdo's added confidence. All Officers and ORS in high spirits. Total casualties to the Regt, Five ORs wounded.	See App. "A" Attached.
	8	1000	X, Y & Z Troops rejoined Regt. in this area.	
BENY-SUR-MER	(d+2) 9	1800	Day spent in rest and maintenance of Tanks and Equipment.	
	(D+3)	1800	Second ½ of W Troop were landed today and joined the Regt. Regt. now re-organised and distributed on 7th & 8th Bdes Fronts. S, T, X & Z Tps with 12th & 13th Regts at Camilly. P, Q & W Tps with 14th & 19th Regts at Basly. Remains of Y Tp owing to Tank Casualties to itself being used to reinforce the deficiences in other Troops. Troops with 12th &. 13th Regts. in support of 7th Cdn Inf Bde employed on Indirect Fire tasks, moved to forward area location BRAY and were later withdrawn to 12th, 13th Gun area owing to position forward being very fluid. P, Q & W Tps with 14th, 19th Regts in support of 8th & 9th Inf Bdes were kept back in Regtl Gun area at BASLY and were out of range most of the day. They could not be sent forward owing to the very fluid nature of the FDL's. Capt's L.L.A. McKay SAUDF and K R.M. Perrott RM however, moved forward independantly and found a N. NOVA BN. being counter attacked near ANISTY, they immediately produced supporting fire.	

Wt. 47724/993 2,000,000 3/43 W. H. & S. 51/6375.

DEFE 2/49
Intelligence/war diary
ROYAL MARINE COMMANDO ENGINEERS

Month and Year June 44   Commanding Officer Major E.T. GILBERT RM.

Place	Date	Hour	Summary of Events and Information	References to Appendices
STEYNING	3		Lieut. M.R. McLaren to Canadian Military HQ pm 3 Jun.	HB
	3		Pe/x 106504 Mre C.H. Atkins awarded 1st G.C.B. w.ef. 3 Jun.	HB
	5		Pe/x 106706 Mre L.W. Hunter awarded 1st GCB w.e.f. 5 Jun.	HB
			OPERATIONS IN FRANCE D-DAY	
	6		RM Engn Cdo Detachment HQ 1 SS Bde commanded by Lieut. Denis Nevile RM disembarked H + 75.(Detachment consisted of 1 Lieut. 1 Sgt. 5 Cpls & 32 marines)	HB
			RM L.C. O C U	
			Team 7 under command Capt. A.B. Jackson RM disembarked H + 20.	
			Team 8 under command Csm DJR Marss RM disembarked H + 20.	
			Team 9 under command Lieut. D.J. Cogger RM disembarked H.	
			Team 10 under command L/Sgt. P.H. Jones RM disembarked H.	
			Team 11 under command Lieut. D.J. Smith RM disembarked H +20	
			Team 12 under command L/Sgt. K.M. Briggs RM disembarked H + 20.	

M3524/1218 1200M 10/41 H.B. & Co. Ltd. 51-1541.

SHEET 2

Commanding Officer Major E.T. GILBERT RM.

Place	Date	Hour	Summary of Events and Information	References to Appendices
STEYNING	6		<u>Battle Casualties</u> The u/m ranks killed in action 6th June, 1944. Ch/x 104901 Mre HWG Rosson (RMLCOCU No 10). Ch/x 109879 (T) Mre A. Evans (RM Engn Cdo Detachment attached HQ 1 SS Bde). <u>Missing</u> The u/m rank 'MISSING' Delieved seriously wounded 6th June, 1944. Ex 4507(T) Cpl. (Ty) Robert Clark (RM Engn Cdo Detachment attached HQ 1 SS Bde). <u>Wounded</u> The u/m ranks wounded 6th June. 1944. Pe/x 102045 L/Cpl. F. P. Carolan (RM Engn Cdo Detachment attached HQ 1 SS Bde). Ch/x 105451 Mre Edward Darby (RMLCOCU No.10). Ch/x 103959 Mre K.W. Lewis (RM LCOCU No.9).	HB HB HB

M3524/1218 1200M 10/41 H.B. & Co. Ltd. **51-1541.**

SHEET 3

Commanding Officer Major E.T. GILBERT RM.

Place	Date	Hour	Summary of Events and Information	References to Appendices
Steyning	6 (contd)		Ch/x 109879 (T). Mre A. Evans & Ch/x 104901 Marine H.W.G. Rosson D.D to Chatham Division RM 6 Jun 44.	HB
	6		Ex 4507 (T) Cpl (Ty) Robert Clark discharged 'Missing' to RM Depot, Lympstone, 6 Jun 44.	HB
	6		Lieut. R. L. Nicholson from HMS Apple done pm 6 Jun 44.	HB

	8		Course. Results. The u/m obtained qualifications as
			stated in No.49 Bomb Disposal Course at SME Ripon.
			      Lieut. HAP. Milligan RM - Above average
			    Ch/x 1442 C/sgt. W.M. Clifford - Above average
			     Ch/x 105568 Sgt. Roy Break - Above average.
				HB

	10		The u/m rank wounded 10th June 1944. Ch/x 109901 Mre. D.M. Greer.	HB
	12		Lieut. S. Richardson R.E. from HMS Apple done 12 Jun 44 (tempy attached to this unit from H.O.C.)	HB
	13		Major E.T. Gilbert RM to Co HQ on duty pm 13 Jun 44 returning on completion.	HB

M3524/1218 1200M 10/41 H.B. & Co. Ltd. **51-1541.**

WO 171/919
Intelligence/war diary
62ND ANTI-TANK REGT RA.

Month and Year June 1944   Commanding Officer Lt. Col. R.B.W. BETHELL RA.

Place	Date	Hour	Summary of Events and Information	References to Appendices
SOUTHAMPTON	1st D-5	–	Lt. Col Bethell RA & Tac HQ Embarked at SOUTHAMPTON.	aw for compaction of parties see Appendix "A"
TILBURY	1st D-5	–	First party under and Major B. George RA embarked at TILBURY. -	aw ditto ditto
TILBURY	2nd D-4	16.00	2nd Party u/c Lt AW wright RA embarked at TILBURY - These parties anchored off SOUTHAMPTON and SOUTHEND until D-1.	aw
LST/1149	6th D	16.00	Tac H.Q. consisting Lt. Col. Bethill RA. Capt als. Dickson RA. Sql. Hughes driver & Signalman landed from LST/1149 on Mike Red Beach - COURSELLES in Support 7 Cdn Inf Bde. Half link in which above were traveling drove off LST & Struck patch of Soft Sand & "drowned"- in Spite of the fact that 4 Bdn Marsh (driver) kept engine running for over ½ hour. CO proceeded to Assembly Area (Elbow/Frankie) on M 10 belonging to 248 Bty remainder of HQ marched.	aw

Wt.47724/993 2,000,000 3/43 W.H. & S. **51**/6375.

SHEET 2

Month and Year June 1944   Commanding Officer Lt. Col. R.B.W. BETHELL RA.

Place	Date	Hour	Summary of Events and Information	References to Appendices
ELBOW/ FRANKIE	6th D Day	–	Lt. Col. Bethell RA Commandeered Carrier from Lt. Powell - & contacted Brigadier 7 Cdn. Inf. Bde. Tac HQ then moved from E/FRANKIE to PIERREPOWER	aw
	6th D Day		245 Bty - had landed in sp 3 Br Div.	aw See Separate War Diary
			247 Bty - in sp 9 Cdn Bde-3 Cdn Div.	aw " "
			246 Bry & 248 Bty in Sp 7 Cdn Bde 3 Cdn Div.	aw
PIERREPOWER	7th D + 1	12-00	Tac/HQ moved along Bde Centre fine reached BRETTEVILLE L' ORGUEILLEUSE (OAK OBJECTIVE) - CO made recce of Area selected pos. Final Allottment being 1 Tp in each fwd Bn. area - 1 Tp in each fwd Bn area - 1 Tp Area wood 909736 - RWR area S of RLY BRETTEVILLE - RRR area PUTOR - BESIN R.C.S.R. area SECQUEVILLE-EN-BESIN - 17 prs arrived varying times from 17.00 hrs onwards - (94 A/TK Bty 3 Cdn A/Tk regt were u/c 62 A/Tk - Regt.) 248 (M10) Bty placed in ashore area SECQUEVILLE-EN-BESIN after following infantry advance during day.	aw

Wt.47724/993 2,000,000 3/43 W. H. & S. **51**/6375.

WO 171/1121
Intelligence/war diary
73RD LIGHT ANTI-AIRCRAFT REGIMENT RA

Month and Year June 1944 — Commanding Officer Lt. Col. J.A. ARMSTRONG RA.

Place	Date	Hour	Summary of Events and Information	References to Appendices
	1-5		RHQ, 218, 220 322 Btys in concentration and marshalling areas prier to operation OVERLORD Sub-units split in a their assault groups.	ap
SLINFOLD	1-30		296 Bty, phased back, remains in the concentration area.	
	6		OC 218 with L Cp, A/218 has two guns, C/218 less two guns, landed on WHITE and RED beaches respectively as H+ 45, in	ap
LA BRECHE			time Beach under heavy fire 229673 Capt. T.E.DALE, OC ATP,	
HERMANVILLE			was wounded in the arm by mortar fire and was evacuated after	
CALVADOS			completing his recce. Bty Comd. also suffered minor wound in hand	
NORMANDY			from mortar splinter. Remaining guns of ATP landed at H + 240 & of CTP at H + 120. All guns in action by H + 300; BHQ established in first lateral by H + 360. CO work R Cp. landed at H + 240 & set up AARC as Beach Command Post	
HERMANVILLE		1630	2/1/C with R Cp landed at H + 530 (200 min late) & recce Reg which was established by 101 BSA by 1930 hrs.	ap

*6391. Wt.48123/1073. 319M. 2/43. Wy.L.P. Gp.656.

SHEET 2

Place	Date	Hour	Summary of Events and Information	References to Appendices
LA BRECHE	6		RMO landed at H + 60 (on time) He was early wounded in the back from mortar fragments, but set up a BDS in a German strongpoint. In view of RAME casualties, medical orderlies of A and C TPs 218 had to be called in The BDS continued to function here for the next two days until it was absorbed in to the FDS had moved inland.	ap
HERMANVILLE			OC 220 Bty & RCP landed at H + 530 (200 mins late) but recce of the area allotted was impossible as the ground was still in enemy hands. BHQ was eventually established with RHQ OC 6TP 322 Bty landed at H + 45 & carried out recce. First guns began to come a shore at H + 430 and were all in action by H+510. As recce parties of H/322 and I/322 had not landed OC 6TP recced their locations also located strong pts on the beach were shell holding and individual detachments were involved in mopping up ops.	ap

M3524/1218 1200M 10/41 H.B. & Co.Ltd. 51-1541.

SHEET 3

Place	Date	Hour	Summary of Events and Information	References to Appendices
	6		In the instance a Boters was need to neutralise a sniper's post.	ap
			SMOKE	
			As the main smoke parties of 112 Inr Smoke Coy. did not arrive at expected time an improvised organisation was formed out of Balloon crews & a parties from B/273/86 L A A Regt. They were not able & operate during the night of D + 1 - D + 2 owing & the fact that supplies of generators were not landed in time.	ap
			CASUALTIES	
			Total casualties for D-Day were 1 ofcr wounded, 1OR killed, 5ORs wounded and 1OR missing.	ap
HERMANVILLE	7		Regt. remained under comd HQRA 3 Brit Div. as Comns with 80 Bdn in MIKE Ndn sector was still impossible adgt. landed with padre at 1400 hrs, a head of A Cp.	
			Oc 220 Bty carried out recce for new gun position for his troops.	

M3524/1218 1200M 10/41 H.B. & Co.Ltd. 51-1541.

WO 171/1132
Intelligence/war diary
114TH LIGHT ANTI-AIRCRAFT REGIMENT RA.

Appx. "A".

DIARY OF EVENTS
114 LAA REGT. AND ATTD UNITS.

5 JUNE 44

D - 1 DAY   After a 24-hr postponement on the 4 June 44 the Assault Gps of the Regt sailed with 3 CDN DIV from SOUTHAMPTON and PORTSMOUTH at about midday. Recce parties, mostly in LSI 's, remainder in LSTs and LCTs.

     The voyage was uneventful except for a considerable swell which only diminished slightly on the morning of D-Day.

     The plan was that 372 'A' and 'B' Tps should land with Crusader mounted 40mm and a Mark I gun towed on MIKE Sector with D/321 Bty under command - equipped with triple Oerlikons mounted on Crusaders and each towing a triple equipment trailer.

     On Nan Sector 'G' and 'H' Tps 375 similarly equipped with E/321 Bty under command were to do likewise.

6 JUNE 44

D-DAY   For tactical reasons 375 Bty were to land on NAN earlier than the 372 landing on MIKE. The plan went fairly well to schedule on NAN but not on MIKE.

NAN Sector

Daylight   Between 0850 and 0920 AA Recce parties with 6 guns of G/375 and 2 guns 'H'/375 beaches on NAN WHITE: enemy opposition was encountered in the shape of SA fire and mortaring from BERNIERES: only one exit was usable at this time, and the beach was solid with vehicles. As ground was gained by 8 CDN BRIGADE temporary posns under the dunes, sea-wall, and inland.

     Final posns were occupied by 1700 hrs.

     'H' Tp Recce and 1 tractor of 'G' Tp landed on NAN RED at 0855 under heavy machine-gun fire and mortars. The tractor received a direct hit from a mortar and was burnt out.

     4 'H' Tp guns, due to land on Red Beach, were switched to NAN WHITE where they were joined by Tp Recce and deployed temporarily. At 14 hrs NAN RED Beach was closed.

     'E' Tp/321 (triple Oerlikons) landed on NAN GREEN at 17-hrs and were in action on the exit by 18.30 hrs. Less opposition was encountered on this beach.

     There was very little bombing despite the excellent targets offered all day.

     AA casualties were remarkably light during this landing, consisting of 2 men missing and 3 wounded. There were no Officer casualties.

     All guns came ashore successfully.

MIKE Sector

Daylight   The time-table on MIKE Sector did not work so well as on NAN; Delays were caused by enemy resistance on RED Beach and inland at VAUX - also by dense underwater obstacles, wrecking craft which, in turn, fouled the approaches. Bty HQs Recce landed at 1530 hrs – though scheduled to arrive at 1025 - and established the AARC; dispositions were made for siting of guns on arrival. 'B' Tp Recce, due in at 1130 hrs, actually landed at 15-hrs, and encountered sniping and mortaring on Red Beach. Enemy automatic fire also continued from houses in COURSEULLES until 2030 hrs; The guns of 'B' Tp landed at 1615 and went into action on the beach as all the dunes and approaches were heavily mined.

     'A' Tp Recce, due at 10.30 hrs, landed from LSI at 12 hrs; delay was due to enemy opposition and also to the heavy swell which made the loading of LCAs at sea difficult. The 'A' Tp guns with BHQ a Gp and RHQ Recce landed from LSTs at 19-hrs. Rhino ferries were most difficult in the heavy swell and stiff breeze; delay was caused in marrying them to the LST, and finally in unloading the ferries in 4-ft of water. The wind blew the rhinos sideways till they fouled each others - and also fouled wrecked craft.

     Many vehs were drowned, but only 2 belonging to the Regt.

     During this landing the craft were attacked by a JU 88, which was engaged by the guns actually landing. 'A' Tp guns were in action at 1910 hrs.

......./D/321 ...

SHEET 2

D/321 Bty Recce landed at 13.15 hrs (due at 10.35), and the guns at 19 hrs. The guns (triple Oerlikons) deployed round beach exits. During all the above operations no casualties were suffered by AA Units on MIKE Beach: all guns waded ashore successfully, though two tracks were broken in loose sand.

<u>D NIGHT</u>   Owing to the complete fighter cover few E/As had succeeded in penetrating to the beaches in the day; as soon as darkness fell, however, attacks started and continued for several hours.

Unfortunately on MIKE RED at 23 hrs a rhine ferry and LCP both struck underwater mines and went on fire, causing a large fire which illuminated the beach.

Dets 4 & 5 of 'B' Tp endeavoured by all means to warn the craft of the obstacles as they came in, but without success - subsequently an officer and 6 men from these dets went out to the burning craft and rescued 15 men; the Troop Comd on shore organized 1st Aid and artificial respiration – having summoned ambulances; 14 of the 15 rescued survived.

A further difficulty encountered was the absence of Radar owing to the late arrival of, and casualties - to, Heavy AA. : also the absence of S/Ls. It soon became apparent that uncontrolled Lt. AA barrages were the only remedy, and these were therefore permitted.

Craft to sea joined in, and a considerable - if inaccurate - barrage was put up.

E/A directed their main attention to shipping at sea, but also dropped a few bombs near the beaches (2 bombs on NAN, and 7 or 8 near MIKE).

No concentrated attack developed. E/A diving in singly. Average height appeared to be 2/4000-ft. Balloons were scarce on MIKE. The volume of fire directed against these attacks seems to have prevented any serious damage or accurate bombing.

1 man was wounded in 'B'/372 Bty.

Fighter cover was resumed at approx 05 hrs.

7 JUNE 44
D + 1 DAY

<u>Daylight</u>   At 0630 hrs Mike Green Beach was dive-bombed from low cloud by a ME109 - one bomb (anti-P) was dropped in a thickly-populated part of the Beach, causing casualties (20 +).

'A'/372 Tp suffered casualties - 3 men killed, 1 seriously wounded, and 2 wounded. 1 Gun (MK.I) was put out of action for 20-hrs. This plane was not engaged by 40-mm owing to the low cloud -, 20-mm of 'D'/321 engaged and claim hits.

During the day no further attacks developed, and guns were re-sited for Beach defence in areas now cleared of mines.

Det 6 of 'B'/372 Tp was re-sited in the dune, and found a German soldier in a deep dug-out - he was escorted to the POW cage.

In the German dug-out were found :- an American Red Cross parcel for POW (Capt. Hunter's report), some eye-shields, British type with instructions in Greek, several booby-trap mechanisms, NOT set.

Sniping continued during the day, especially from VAUX WOOD, and mines caused casualties.

Some Top Secret G documents, belonging to 51 DIV, were found washed up on the beach, and sent to Div. HQ.

At 19.30 hrs 'a' Gps of RHQ and BHQ 372 arrived intact - one vehicle drowned. Communications established with Tps and up to Bty. (372 had been linked to RHQ on D Day). Constant damage occurred to lines.

D + 1/D + 2

Darkness Raiding started at 2300 hrs – main target was shipping off-shore: few E/A actually attacked the beaches. A terrific barrage was put up by ships and shore guns.

At 2315 hrs a single JU88, flying level at 2000-ft, dropped a bomb on NAN Sector. This plane was engaged by 40 mm, but not hit.

...../Enemy

WO 171/1800
Intelligence/war diary
5TH ASSAULT REGIMENT RE HQ
(26TH AND 80TH ASSAULT SQUADRONS)

Month and Year June 44   Commanding Officer Lt. Col. A.A.B. Cocks.

Place	Date	Hour	Summary of Events and Information	References to Appendices
At sea	5	0830	Sailed from SOUTHAMPTON. Rough but uneventful, personnel very ill	CS
	6		D-Day. See Regt Records at Appx Bug. G.L WATKINSON Comd /aset Bdire comes with us.	CS
ST. AUBIN	7		Set HQ set up HQ. at 0186 supervision of Sqn rally. No contact possible with main RNQ. So unsuccessful in attack on RADAR sta at DOUURES	CS
	8		Establish comn with RHQ Capt P.J. DRAPER killed at 2100 hrs whilst attempting to neutralize German Reigel mine 43.	CS
	9		Visited by Adjt.	CS
	10		Regiment recced & est. HQ pened with main RHQ.	CS

22293 Wt. 33096/1140 1,000m 12/40—McC & Co Ltd—51-8212 Forms e2118/22.

WO 171/1610

Intelligence/war diary

262ND FIELD COMPANY RE

Appendix B to war diary June 44

262 Field Coy. R.E. 6-11 June 44

INTRODUCTION

For the Assault 26+2 Field Coy. R.E. were under comd. CRE 3 Cdn. Div.; our special task was the clearance of all obstacles on the beaches. For this purpose we were split on to three platoon fronts with a platoon from 19 Field Coy under my comd forming a fourth.

5 Cdn Field Coy. were to land at H hour from LCT, and, equipped with Bulldozers, attempt clearance mechanically; tide should be low and obstacles exposed. We were to land at H+20 from LCM, and assist, or alternatively destroy the obstacles by demolition method.

After clearance of obstacles our task was engineer assistance in the BMA.

EVENTS

<u>6 June</u>. The Company was initially under comd CRE 3 Cdn Div with the task of clearance of beach obstacles. One Pl from 119 Fd Coy (L.T. STORRY) was under my comd for the operation giving me four platoons in all.

The plan was to land from LCMs at H + 20, theoretically at fairly low water, deployed as follows:-

2 Pl. (plus 2 secs) Lt. OWENS on MIKE beach, ¾ mile west of COURSEULLES.
3 Pl. (less 2 secs) Lt. COLE on NAN GREEN at COURSEULLES.
Coy. HQ (O.C., R.O. 1 and 2 Sprs) with
1 PL. LT. GIBSON on NAN WHITE at BERNIERES.
4 Pl. (form 19 Coy) LT. STORRY on NAN RED at ST. AUBIN.

This frontage was approx 4 miles making communication in the early stages extremely difficult.

Support for the Assault landing was to be given by DD tanks, AVRE were to make initial exits from beach and Marine LCOCU were to assist in demolition of underwater obstacles. As can be seen by my operation Order 5 Cdn Fd Coy were to land ahead of us and attempt clearance by use of Mech Eqpt (Armoured Bulldozers).

Bad weather seemed to affect the timing and disposition of these units because in no case did all arrive at the right place and the right time. All my Pls did arrive at the right place but we must have been later as the tide was almost high.

The story of D-Day is best told by platoons for each worked entirely independently and under different conditions.

<u>No. 1 Platoon</u>
| 6 June 44 | Reveille on L.S.I. | 0330 hrs. |
| | Breakfast. | 0400 hrs. |

We were called to our stations at about 0625 hrs. The sea was very rough and there was difficulty in keeping the LCM alongside. After approx 15 mins the first man was able to slide down the canvas chute the whole party then taking 20 mins to embark. We cast off and moved toward the beach through heavy seas. We neared the beach just before 0800 hrs and found that practically all obstacles were covered and that DD tanks and Centaurs were only just getting ashore. We laid off for a few minutes and finally made a run in to the East of our centre line. We could not reach shore and had to scramble on to an LCT in about 5 ft of water and waded ashore. Time 0810 hrs Sgt. Dickinson organized the Pl. while Spr. Kane, L/Sgt. Thompsett and Lieut.Gibson attempted to remove shells from obstacles underwater. Immediate jobs on the beach were to help clear the exit, and to help sweep, an area behind the concrete wall. Mines lifted 1 S-mine and 2 French Light A. Tk Mines. Nos 3 and 4 sections moved off after about 1 hour and cleared tracks in the DUKW Park. As soon as the tide allowed Nos 1 & 2 Secs started clearing shells and mines off obstacles while Bulldozers and Churchills removed or crushed the obstacles. Finally the whole platoon were working on clearing the obstacles and continued working on the beaches until nightfall

TO SHEET TWO

SHEET 2

2 Platoon

?   On board MV LLANGIBBY CASTLE 0550 hrs at Assault Stations awaiting 2 LCMs for landing on MIKE RED-GREEN beach.

0800 hrs (approx) LCMs arrived, had been held up by heavy swell in Channel. Great difficulties experienced in boarding LCMs. Isacke fractured arm in doing so.

Beached on correct site at 0930 hrs approx. Water covered all obstacles, went successfully over the top. At this stage beach choc a bloc with vehicles of all types and no exits available from beach to first lateral,

1000 hrs 85 Coy. R.E. declared exit tracks on centre of beach O.K. Two Vehicles in going down track go up on mines.

262 asked to help.

2 mine parties put on centre track.

2 mine parties put on right hand track.

2 mine parties put on beach lateral.

Centre Track

Party under Cpl. Wiscombe set to widen track by 8 yds.

Party under L/Sgt. Todd set to bye pass vehicles which have blocked track. Duncan and Bridson badly injured due to truck trying to pass although it had been directed to stop and wait till a passage was swept for it.

L/Sjt. Todd's party find 20 French mines 11 'S' mines (6 rows French mines 2 rows 'S' mines 2 rows French mines) 85 Fd Coy. and Fd Coy. finally declare track open about 1030 hrs.

Right Hand Track

1 Party L/Sjt. Everson.

1 Party L/Sjt. Mackenzie.

Track under fire of snipers from pillbox 150 ^{X} to the right. Parties proceed to clear in spite of fire. Obtained 2 tanks from RAC to deal with pillbox. Tanks attack followed by L/Cpl. Field and another 3 Germans killed.

When half way along track parties under fire of enemy in wood ahead. Men return fire and German fire kept down. Progress ¾ length of track come to 2 vehicles blown up on mines. Gerry heavy fire. L/Sgt. Everson organises clearing of Gerry. 7 captured. Track eventually cleared almost whole length. Parties return to clear obstacles on beach. 85 Fd Coy. left to finish last bit of track. 3 French and 1 'S' mine lifted.

Laterals

1 Party Cpl. McManus.

1 Party Cpl. Atkins.

Track 8^X wide swept along entire front of MIKE Beach. No mines. 1300 hrs (approx) onwards tide falling quickly exposes obstacles. Due to nonarrival of Lt. Eddy 5th Cdn Corps Engrs with his party take under command 6 Bulldozers and one platoon (approx) C Engrs. Tellermines removed from obstacles and shells from timber piles. Bulldozer drill very efficient in clearing of obstacles. Beach cleared by approx 1530 hrs (in any case well before low tide).

1630 hrs. Commence clearing of WVTA Hand truck full of explosives on fire. Sjt. Dunn killed, Cpl. Greening, Spr. Faithfull injured when truck explodes. Dry in quiet night.

3 Platoon

Arrived off shore in LCM to find tide almost high and obstacles covered; craft manoevred between first rows but unfortunately hit fuzed shell on last row of "hedgehogs"; front of craft was blown off wounding 4 men; water poured in but moved men to back of craft and helped matters a little. Spr. CARE got ashore and despite tremendous difficulties in the rough sea, managed to get a line and all men including the wounded were dragged through over 6 ft of water to safety.

Some sniping at this stage; high tide, no detectors, no wireless, no explosives, men a little shaken. Exits were going ahead so contacted 5 Cdn Fd. Coy. dug in at top of beach, but impossible to get at obstacles. Tried to contact OC but enemy post half way.

Lateral road was important; O i/c Beach Gp R.E. had been killed, so took over his men and with Pioneers got organised on this. Later got back to obstacles and with aid of mech eqpt cleared the beach, and "deloused" all mines. Got back later to beach exits and had assistance from German POW. Improvised a ramp for stranded Rhino ferry and got vehicles and personnel ashore. Men feeling better, food position O.K. Contacted OC Four wounded men put aboard LCT for UK.

TO SHEET THREE

SHEET 3

<u>4 Platoon</u>

After embarking from L.S. I J.31 in LCM 1179 we picked up a position in convoy of LCTs etc heading in direction of shore; as we neared the beach I saw that our position was (a) too far down towards NAN WHITE beach and (b) we were going to land before AVRE, so I got the LCM to turn back out to sea and make fresh landing on our correct beach Nan Red and in the correct position.

Quite a bit of enemy fire was coming down, particularly mortar fire, trying to get the landing craft and numerous machine guns and snipers were firing.

We landed in about 5 ft of water amongst all the landing craft obstacles and I could see at a glance, that our job of removing the beach obstacles, was hindered by the tide being too far in.

The 5th Canadian Fd Coy RE Bulldozers were useless because of the depth of water so I attempted to blow a 200 yards gap in width and as deep as my men could go out to without drowning. This was quite successfully blown but the charges being under water were not very successful in some cases, about 80% being good.

All the time the men were working LMG and mortar fire was coming down and Sgt. Joffs and Cpls muddle and Waller showed an excellent example and disregard to danger and all the sappers worked well.

During this operation an LCI beached and hit a tellermine and was damaged, many of the men on it being hit by snipers and a number were drowning through the strong current running. Spr. Radcliffe had no hesitation in coming into the sea with me with to save as many as we could and between us got 7 men ashore, during this period I got hit by shrapnel but luckily on my respirator on my back and only sustained a bruise and a ruined respirator.

Having done all we could on the beach, we went on to mine clearing along the promenade and round the houses and across the 160 yard gap which was formed by a field running down to the shore from the first lateral road.

By now a tank had been hit and set on fire and was exploding every few minutes and the snipers were being a definite nuisance but a lull had come in the mortar fire and Sps. Ratcliffe Hunt set a grand example in carrying on mine clearing although so much trouble was about, and later when the mortars opened up again, they still kept on, ably led by Sjt. Jeffs who never hesitated to carry on at any time. During one bad spell of sniping Cpl. Muddle made good use of a Bren Gun in silencing a few snipers and enabling the work of clearing to carry on.

We continued mine clearing until about 1800 hrs when we were asked to report to NAN WHITE beach to give assistance there which we did.

During the afternoon 3 men were killed by a mortar bomb and Sgt. Jeffs wounded in the face and ear, but he kept on at his job after attendance by RAMC. Numerous tellermines and 'S' mines were lifted and no casualties from them to my platoon.

<u>Coy. H.Q</u>

We landed with 1 pl. and after doing all possible to remove obstacles, I connected up with 184 Coy. of the Beach Gp and started on beach exits and clearance of minefields inland.

We than tried to contact Pls to the right and left but at first could not get through owing to enemy positions holding out. Later I contacted both 3 Pl. and 4 Pl. and found all goingwell, but did not find 2 Pl. until next day.

Communication by wireless No. 46 set did not function owing to drowning of two sets but two other sets survived and were very useful later.

There was very heavy damage to mine detectors, chiefly owing to rough conditions in LCM and the fact that no man got ashore through less than 5 ft water.

Air activity was very slight by day, but small attacks were made on the beaches at night.

Casualties for the day were:

Sprs. Bridson and Duncan. Injured by Tellermine.

Sgt. Dunn Killed by explosion of Amn lorry.

Cpl. Greening and Spr. Faithfull. Injured by explosion of Amn lorry.

Sprs Lawton, Lewis, Holloway and Thompson. Wounded in Col's LCM when it hit a Shell.

Spr. Isacke. Broken arm getting into LCM.

Four men killed by mortar fire in STORRY'S Pl.

All evacuated to U.K.

TO SHEET FOUR

WO 179/3120
Intelligence/war diary
5TH FIELD COMPANY RCE

Place	Date	Hour	Summary of Events and Information 1 June 44 to 30 June 44	Remarks, references to Appendices and initials
TILLBURY (Anchorage Area)	5 June	44	Phase III personnel steamed out of Anchorage Area early Monday morning. All personnel were in high spirits anxious and ready to reach their ultimate destination. Morale was bolstered considerably at 1900 hrs. when all troops were given a goodly portion of ice cream. This was a perfect climax to all the other fine meals (Chicken, steak, turkey, etc) that had been tendered to the personnel on board this craft. In the afternoon initial briefing was passed to all troops and Capt. McMahon passed out a few pamphlets on France for the information of all ranks. These were read and digested as soon as possible.	
Southampton			Assault personnel on LCTs pulled out of SOUTHAMPTON docks at 0730 hrs, assembled in the Solent and proceeded on their course. Sea-sickness tablets were issued but were not wholly effective as sea was quite rough.	
Coast of FRANCE (MIKE-RED Sector)	6 June	44	Phase III arrived on the coast of France in the afternoon at approximately H plus 9 hrs and anchored opposite MIKE RED Beach. Final briefing and instructions were given by O.C. party. Some personnel were slightly sea-sick, but for the most part the excitement of the occasion gripped the men to such an extent that they forgot to get seasick.	
Coast of France (NAN Beach)			[Assaulting craft touched down at approx. 0745 hrs. All serials were surprised to find that the tide was considerably higher than they had been led to believe. It was impossible to do anything about clearance of obstacles as they were completely submerged in water. Most of the craft on NAN Beach beached in very deep water causing difficulty in getting off. Enemy fire opened on craft before disembarkation inflicting several casualties. All serials succeeded in getting Bulldozers and personnel who were not casualties off the craft and onto the beach.	
			Several more casualties occurred during this operation. Serials on NAN Beach subject to heavy mortar and machine gun fire. As tide receded Coy. was organized into 3 main obstacle clearing parties and work commenced immediately on clearing underwater obstacles and in removing mines and shells from the obstacles. Total clearance on NAN Beach by 2nd tide was approx. 1600 yds.]	App. 2 and 8

'GOLD' BEACH

'Overhead there was a continuous whiz of naval shells homing in on their targets to soften them up for us. We were soon within range of enemy mortars...and we could hear the sharp crackle of machine-gun fire. We had the word to get ready and tension was at its peak when the ramp went out. We were in the sea to the tops of our thighs, floundering ashore with other assault platoons to the left and right of us. Mortar bombs and shells were erupting in the sand and I could hear the burp of Spandau light machine-guns through the din. There were no shouts, only the occasional cry as men were hit and went down'.

PRIVATE HOOLEY, RADIO OPERATOR, A COMPANY, 1ST BATTALION THE HAMPSHIRE REGIMENT, 'JIG GREEN' SECTOR.[288]

'GOLD' BEACH

(From Port-en-Bessin in the West to La Rivière in the East)

German Defenders: 7th Army Commanded by Generaloberst Friedrich Dollmann

(Lower Normandy defended by LXXXIV Korps commanded by General der Artillerie Erich Marcks)

Coastal Defence: 716th Infantry Division commanded by Generalleutnant Wilhelm Richter

352nd Infantry Division commanded by Generalleutnant Dietrich Kraiss

Allied Attackers: British XXX Corps commanded by Lieutenant-General Gerard Bucknall

Assault Division: 50th (Northumberian) Infantry Division (Tyne & Tees) commanded by Major-General Douglas Graham

Naval Forces: Force 'G' commanded by Commodore C.E. Douglas-Pennant RN and Bombarding Forces 'E' and 'K'commanded by Rear-Admiral R.A. Dalrymple-Hamilton RN.

H-Hour: 07.25 hrs

Landing Sectors: 'HOW', 'ITEM', 'JIG' AND 'KING'[289]

D-Day Divisional Objectives: (i) Pierce and overwhelm shoreline defences. (ii) Capture the city of Bayeux. (iii) Establish a bridgehead across the N13 Bayeux to Caen road. (iv) Capture Arromanches and the German coastal battery at Longues-sur-Mer, (v) Capture the harbour at Port-en-Bessin and establish contact with the US V Corps on 'Omaha' beach (vi) To establish a link with the 3rd Canadian Infantry Division on 'Juno' beach.[290]

Casualties on D-Day (Beaches only): 413 (Killed, Wounded and Missing).[291]

NOTES

[288] Tim Saunders, *Gold Beach – JIG: JIG Sector and West - June 1944*, Battleground Europe series, (Barnsley, South Yorkshire: Pen & Sword, 2002), p. 64.

[289] Only 'JIG' and 'KING' sectors were used for the actual landings.

[290] Simon Trew, *Battle Zone Normandy: Gold Beach*, (Stroud, Gloucestershire: Sutton Publishing Ltd, 2004), pp. 34-38.

[291] *D-Day: Then and Now*, Volume 2, edited by Winston G. Ramsey, (London: Battle of Britain Prints International Ltd, 1995), p. 620.

69TH INFANTRY BRIGADE

WO 171/651
Intelligence/war diary
69TH INFANTRY BRIGADE HQ

Month and Year June 1944

Commanding Officer Brig. F.Y.C. KNOX, DSO.

Place	Date	Hour	Summary of Events and Information	References to Appendices
At sea	JUNE 5 (Cont'd)	1840	Personal messages from General Eisenhower, General Montgomery and General Graham were read to all tps. Sealed packets of maps were opened and marked up ready for the operation. When the convoy altered course to the SE round The Needles the ships began to roll and some of the smaller craft were seen to be having a severe tossing. The military personnal went to bed early to be ready for the early rise.	
"	6		D-Day. H-Hour 0725 hrs. The weather was cloudy with a choppy sea. Low cloud prevented the tps from seeing all of the enormous air sp provided by the RAF and USAAF. From the Frigate the landmarks picked out previously from air photographs could be clearly seen at first but as the supporting fire and aerial bombing increased in intensity the shore became blotted from view by great clouds of dust and smoke from the explosions. Owing to the choppy sea, DD tks could not be launched at sea as planned and had to be landed from their craft. Wireless comns were est as ordered and worked satisfactorily. The anticipated 'jamming' or interference did not occur. The bombardment increased in intensity towards H-hour as the leading LCA approached the shore. In the meantime the Frigate had closed to about two miles off shore. The Bde Comd and the SOAG were on the bridge watching the progress of the LCA. At 0745 hrs the report came through that two coys of the 5 E YORKS were ashore and in the right place, and a quarter of an hour later the report was received that two Coys. of 6 GREEN HOWARDS, the other assaulting Bn., were also ashore. At 0815 hrs the Bde Comd's party commenced the difficult and rather perilous business of embarking in an LCM from the HMS KINGSMILL. The LCM had a rough and wet passage. At this stage of the tide beach obstacles were almost covered and great difficulty was experienced in avoiding the beach obstacles which were mined.	

Wt.47724/993 2,000,000 3/43 W.H. & S. 51/6375.

SHEET 2

Commanding Officer Brig. F.Y.C. KNOX, DSO.

Place	Date	Hour	Summary of Events and Information	References to Appendices
At sea	JUNE 6 (cont'd)		The craft was skillfully handled by the Major of the RM in charge and the RM crew, and brought in between the obstacles within ten or fifteen yds of the shore when the Major RM jumped out and found the depth of water to be about four feet. Whilst the crew of the LCM assisted in keeping the craft clear of obstacles the Bde Comd's party disembarked. On landing, it was found that the party was about 300 yds WEST of the centre of the beaches. The Bde Comd's jeep stuck in soft and rather 'peaty' beach, was recovered by a nearby tk but suffered no ill-effects and once clear of the soft spot was driven off. Much of the grass of the sand dunes was burning and giving off clouds of smoke which obscured part of the shore.	
Foreshore		0930	Bde Comd's party arrived at the MBSS. By this time 7 GREEN HOWARDS (Res Bn) landed and were trying to find a suitable route inland.	
"		1000	In the meantime the BM's party with M14 control veh had failed to make the shore. The veh having been stranded in an underwater shell-hole. This was a minor tragedy as the carrier which disembarked from the LCM had shed a track on the beach when making for the MBSS. Thus both wireless vehs for Bde HQ were out of commission. 5 E YORKS reported that the MONT FLEURY Bty had been captured with 8 cas. The Bty Comd, committed suicide and 30 PW were taken. They also reported that enemy is still fighting in LA RIVIERE chiefly from the pillboxes and houses and that sniping in the town was particularly severe. Apparently the preliminary bombardment had not had as much effect as had been hoped and the gun casemate in the WEST end of the sea wall was still sheltering a group of enemy.	
"		1010	The Bde Comd whose jeep had been left on the beach on landing now left the MBSS with an LO and the IO in his jeep which had now arrived close to the MBSS on the Axis.	

Wt.47724/993 2,000,000 3/43 W. H. & S. **51**/6375.

3

SHEET 3

Commanding Officer Brig. F.Y.C. KNOX, DSO.

Place	Date	Hour	Summary of Events and Information	References to Appendices
Foreshore	JUNE 6	1030	Report was received from the 6 GREEN HOWARDS that they were on the first objective having captured enemy locality at 908869, gun posn 918861 and the MEUVAINES ridge which showed very good progress in the time.	
"		1120	Meanwhile 7 GREEN HOWARDS had advanced through 6 GREEN HOWARDS with the task of capturing gun posn 917844. On arrival the gun posn was found to be out of action, 40-50 PW were taken, and the advance continued.	
"		1130	Bde HQ moves fwd. As no wireless vehs were available it became necessary to use two handcart stations belonging to the MBSS which were taken fwd to the next posn of Bde HQ at VER-SUR-MER 914852. The party marched fwd up the dusty rd from the beach wheeling the handcarts, linking up with the BM's bedraggled party and attempting to follow the course of the battle which the Bde Comd was directing.	
"		1200	5 E YORKS report one Coy. in VER-SUR-MER and the Bn. ready to continue advance. Bde Comd ordered them to advance in accordance with the Op Order to ST. LEGER.	
VER-SUR-MER		1300	Bde HQ est in farm buildings off the main rd. News was received that 7 GREEN HOWARDS were in CREPON where NOT much resistance was met but a certain amount of sniping and an a tk gun firing into CREPON caused some cas but did NOT stop the advance.	
"		1500	7 GREEN HOWARDS report that they have captured the bridge at 906805 but that they were meeting opposition on bridge at 888797.	
"		1525	6 GREEN HOWARDS report two Coys. on report line YUKON (874833 - 921830).	

Wt.47724/993 2,000,000 3/43 W. H. & S. 51/6375   4

SHEET 4

Commanding Officer Brig. F.Y.C. KNOX, DSO.

Place	Date	Hour	Summary of Events and Information	References to Appendices
VER-SUR-MER	JUNE 6	1545	News received that fwd tps of 6 GREEN HOWARDS were 300 yds short of report line HUMBER (865805 - 915808).	
"		1645	Orders received from Bde Comd to move Bde HQ to VILLIERS-LE-SEC. The odd collection of handcarts, airborne MCs, bicycles and one staff car moved slowly fwd along the congested rd.	

893815		1800	BM saw Lt. Col. R.H.W.S. Hastings, MC, at his HQ est at 893815 and in order to keep clear of 6 GREEN HOWARDS est Bde HQ just behind Bn. HQ. At this time the posn of the three Bns. was:
			
			    7 GREEN HOWARDS held up SOUTH of CREULLY
			
			      5 E YORKS passing through 6 GREEN HOWARDS who were forming a firm base at VILLIERS-LE-SEC.
			
			Tps of 151 Bde were passing along our axis swinging right at VILLIERS-LE-SEC and moving in direction of LE MANIOR.	

"		1820	Tac/R reports 40 AFV moving NE from RUCQUEVILLE.	
"		1830	5 E YORKS had reached ST. GABRIEL where they were meeting some opposition. Bde Comd was with the CO Lt. Col. G.W. White, MBE, who shortly afterwards was wounded and evacuated. 7 GREEN HOWARDS report that they had overcome the resistance in CREULLY and leading tps are now 700 yds SOUTH of it. The Bde Comd directed 7 GREEN HOWARDS on COULAMBS (8876) 5 E YORKS on BRECY (8877).	
"		1930	5 E YORKS were held up 300 yds SW of ST. GABRIEL by heavy automatic fire from the woods NORTH of BRECY. The Bn. by this time was very tired and the Bde Comd decided to attack with the 6 GREEN HOWARDS on the right of 5 E YORKS. Objective - houses NW of Church. SL rd ST. GABRIEL – VAUSSIEUX. Time 2130 hrs.	

SHEET 5

Commanding Officer Brig. F.Y.C. KNOX, DSO.

Place	Date	Hour	Summary of Events and Information	References to Appendices
893815	JUNE 6 (Cont'd)	1930	The Bn. formed up quickly and the attack went in on time supported by 86 Fd and one pl B Coy. 2 CHESHIRE, and was successful. 5 E YORKS were then able to work their way fwd into BRECY itself and both Bns. consolidated for the night.	
"		1950	Capt W.E. Needler (Senior LO) arrived at Bde HQ with orders from the Bde Comd for Bde HQ to move fwd to 889796 where it would be est for the night.	
889796		2025	Bde HQ arrived at new location 889796 which was a large field beside a farmhouse possibly used by a German signal unit. Civs were already looting the German stores and it was impossible to tell which were German Army horses and which were farm horses. Bde Sigs, however, found a brand new four-wheeled trailer which could be towed by a jeep which had by this time arrived with Bde HQ.	
"		2230	Bns. were all est in their allotted posns: 5 E YORKS in BRECY, 6 GREEN HOWARDS 877785, 7 GREEN HOWARDS 887773.	
"	7		In accordance with Bde Comd's instrs issued during the night 7 GREEN HOWARDS moved fwd via COULOMBS to the farm and RDF station on the ST. LEGER feature at 876752 supported by 4/7 DG less one sqn. 6 GREEN HOWARDS moved fwd via RUCQUEVILLE 8777 to ST. LEGER 8675 with 5 E YORKS in res moving behind 6 GREEN HOWARDS were on the Bde axis.	
"		1015	6 GREEN HOWARDS reported approaching RUCQUEVILLE and 7 GREEN HOWARDS held up 1000 yds SOUTH of COULOMBS by outpost posns of the garrison of the fortified farm in 8775. A plan was quickly prepared for the capture of the farm and the attack was launched.	

Wt.47724/993 2,000,000 3/43 W. H. & S. 51/6375.

WO 171/1398

Intelligence/war diary

5TH BATTALION, THE EAST YORKSHIRE REGIMENT

Month and Year June 1944   Commanding Officer Lt. Col. R.B.Jame? D.S.O.

Place	Date	Hour	Summary of Events and Information	References to Appendices
France	6	1000 approx	Tpt landed. Bn. HQ carrier and jeep drowned with all docs and maps. C and D Coys. reorganise to form one coy under comd Capt. A. CONSITT. Bn. reorganise and moved off. From here until end of day snipers and small groups of enemy were encountered. Route through VER-SUR-MER – VILLIERS-LE-SEC – ST. GABRIEL – BRECY.	
		1500	CO Lt. Col. G.W. WHITE. MBE, wounded. MAJOR J.H.F. DIXON assumed cond. Bn. opposed by approx Coy. inf and two 75 mm SP guns NORTH of ST. GABRIEL.	
		1750	ST. GABRIEL occupied - POW taken were of FUS. Bn. 352 Inf Div and 915 Regt. MAJOR C.W.S. BELAS wounded.	
		1850	Strong enemy posts with MGs and two 88mm guns in wood 884787 held up advance from ST. GABRIEL. LT. F. LOWE (MC) wounded, later died of wounds, 2/LT. GRIEVE wounded.	
		2150	Bde attack, supported by 4/7 DG pushed enemy back through BRECY which was occupied by Bn. Approx 2300 hrs. Quiet night.	
	[7	0800	Bn moved in rear of 6 GREEN HOWARDS to occupy original Bde objectives. Bn switched to ST. LEGER feature 8675 occupied at 1000hrs. Enemy snipers and small parties of inf continue harrass Bn throughout day.] (Sketch map 1)	
	[8		Bn remained ST LEGER area.] a.m. 8 Armd Bde through Bn and reached area PT 103 8570 before dark.	
	[9		No change in location]. Maintainance of vehicles, weapons and equipment. C and D Coys reconstituted and reorganised. First packet of mail from England arrives. Lts. LEWISHON, EARLE-WELBY (both to LOB) and 50 ORs as reinforcements. Major H. C. COCKING from OC S Coy. to OC C Coy. (Appx'D')	
	10		No change. Lieut. HAMPSHIRE and 23 ORs rfts reported. (Appx'AI')	
	[11	1500	Bn. ordered to move to area PT 1038570 to relieve I DORSETS- as part of Bde plan to est. firm base as pivot for 7 Armd Div. Bn. moved off at 1500 hrs via AUDRIEU and HAUTES D'AUDRIEU	
		1800	overcoming slight opposition from MGs and snipers. A and B Coys. moving into posn SW of HAUTES-LES-VENTES became involved in armd counterattack by enemy directed on PT 103 Coys. not being dug in were ill-protected.	

Wt.47724/993 2,000,000 3/43 W. H. & S. 51/6375

SHEET 2

Commanding Officer Lt. Col. R.B.JA ?D.S.O.

Place	Date	Hour	Summary of Events and Information	References to Appendices
SOUTHAMPTON	1 2 3 4 5	 1830	Bn. embarks on LSIs G 67 and G 68 from embarkation camps CI4 and CI5 for operation OVERLORD. Vehicle serials embark on LCTs on June 2. Convoy collects in SOLENT. Convoy sails to join other naval forces engaged in operation.	R.R. James Lieut. Col. Commanding.
FRANCE	6	0725	Operation OVERLORD begins. 5 E Yorks intention to assault beach KING RED atb LA RIVIERE 9286 (ref map sheet France I/25000 37/I6) and reorganise on posn area LA PARO 8774. H hr 0725. Landing very wet-up to 4.' water.	
			Rt assault coy-A Coy.-landed against spasmodic opposition and went on to take coy objective, bty at MONT FLEURY with loss of 8 cas. A Coy. took 30 POW Comd of enemy bty committed suicide.	
			Lt assault coy-D Coy-met strong opposition from LA RIVIERE and were pinned on beach by MGs and one 88 mm firing from strong points to the EAST. D Coy suffered heavy cas.	
		0750B	B Coy-rt res coy-landed behind A almost unopposed and passed through A Coy. to VER-SUR-MER.	
			C Coy-lt res coy-landed behind D. Coy. together with Bn HQ. Opposition still almost intact. Tps wading ashore through deep water were picked off by small arms fire and were unable to reach shore. With AVREs and DD tks ins support C Coy moved intonleft flanking attack and neutralised enemy posts, inflicting heavy cas. 45 POW taken from LA RIVIERE locality all of 736 Regt of 716 Inf Div. Own cas on beaches killed and wounded Major K.C. HARRISON, Capt. W. SUGARMAN, Capt. J.H. WHITE (kia), Lieuts A. DAVIES (kia), W. McILROY, R. APPLETON and approx 85 ORs.	

WO 171/1302
Intelligence/war diary
6TH BATTALION THE GREEN HOWARDS

Month and Year June 1944   Commanding Officer Rheiham Lt-Col. R.H.W.S. Hastings MC.

Place	Date	Hour	Summary of Events and Information	References to Appendices
SOUTHAMPTON	1		A, B, C, and D Coys. safely aboard L.S.I's in SOUTHAMPTON WATER.	Rheiham Lt. Col.
	2		A/TK and Carrier Pls still in marshalling areas awaiting embarkation.	
	3	2300	A/TK and Carrier Pls moved to SOUTHAMPTON from Camp 13 arriving at dawn the following morning.	
	4	1000	Specialist Pls and Specialist personnel embarked on LCT's. The weather was not too good and the sea was 'choppy'.	
At Sea	5		Today should have been D-Day with 'H' Hour at 0635 hrs, but owing to adverse weather conditions, the Landing has been postponed for 24 hrs.	
		1815	LSI's with Coys aboard moved down the SOLENT towards the open sea.	
		1900	LCT's with Carriers, A/Tks and specialist pls aboard moved down the SOLENT towards the open sea in one huge array - flotilla following flotilla! Weather moderate to fair but the sea still rather 'choppy'.	
	6	0635	As the great armada of ships approach the French Coast in the dull mist of the dawn, many flashes can be seen from the coastline as Allied bombers and fighter-bombers fly in to engage enemy coastal batteries and targets that may hinder our landing.	
		0710	A, B, C, D Coys and BHQ safely aboard the LCA's made their hazardous dash for the mainland in a sea that did not favour a landing so important, whilst Allied cruisers and destroyers heavily engaged enemy shore batteries.	
Area Map Ref 9186 Ref Maps FRANCE Sheet 7/E/5 4/50,000.		0735		
		0737	'H' Hour.	
			A and D Coys. being the fwd Coys., assaulted the beach between Map Refs 910869 and 918 868. A Coy. attacked the highly fortified strongpoint at 908868 and D Coy. attacked the heavily concreted gun positions in area MONT FLEURY Map Ref 917863, The storming of both these enemy positions was highly successful and the Bn: suffered surprisingly low casualitites.	
			The reserve Coys. (C and B) followed the landing of A and D Coys.	
			B Coy. moved to area 908863 and attacked enemy posns, clearing a quarry en route occupied by the enemy.	
			C Coy. moved with little opposition to area of Pt 52 Map Ref 904850 the Bn. re-organising area.	

Wt 13474/1805 1,200,000 7/40 BPL 51-7171 Forms C2118/22

SHEET 2

Month and Year June 1944   Commanding Officer Rheiham Lt. Col. Hastings MC.

Place	Date	Hour	Summary of Events and Information	References to Appendices
Area Map Ref Ref Maps FRANCE Sheet 7E/5 1/50,000 SHEET 7F/1 1/50,000	6 (cont)	1000	By this time, the Coys BHQ and the majority of Support Coy. were firmly established ashore and proceeding as fast as possible to the Bn. re-organising area in the area of Pt 52. (Map Ref 904850). The enemy were falling back quickly, but many snipers were left behind hidden in the houses, woods and hedgerows to delay our advance. PW's were plentiful and these the Bn. sent straight back to the beach.	Rheiham Lt. Col.
		1200	By midday, the Bn. had reported to Bde the successful completion of Phase I and were fast pushing on to the area of CREPON. (Map Ref 900835)	
		1300	Although strong enemy resistance was reported West of CREPON, the Bn. Proceeded to advance along the Bn. axis and the CO fwd with the Coys, informed them that any resistance encountered was to be bypassed unless absolutely	
		1400	unavoidable. In a house near CREPON at 903845, a party of Germans were called upon by A Coy. to surrender. They refused, but when treated to a substantial dose of Bren and	
		1500	Sten fire, they came out under cover of a white flag. By this time, the Bn. were well South of CREPON and approaching VILLERS-LE-SEC (9980). BHQ passed through CREPON at 1530 hrs which had previously been reported clear of the enemy by 5EYR at 1510 hrs. The successful completion of	
		1700	Phase II was passed to Bde at 1520 hrs. Bde reported that Approx 100 enemy tanks and much MET were on the move West of CAEN. Meanwhile, the RAF continued to bomb and strafe the enemy on all sectors of the beachead. Although enemy tanks were reported advancing NE from RUCQUEVILLE, the Bn. continued its advance towards ST. GABRIEL which was	
		1800	being heavily shelled by the enemy. The enemy armour moving from RUCQUEVILLE was reported to have reached BRECY, and by 1900 hrs 86 Fd Regt RA reported much enemy movement in the area of ST. GABRIEL. At 1950 hrs the Brigadier ordered the Bn. to halt its advance towards ST. GABRIEL as the enemy inf and a:tk opposition in front was too much. At 2030 hrs the Bn continued its advance and at 2100 hrs proceeded to occupy an area West of ST. GABRIEL under cover of a heavy barrage laid down by 86 Fd Regt RA	

Wt.13474/1805 1,200,000 7/40 BPL 51-7171 Forms C2118/22

SHEET 3

Month and Year June 1944 Commanding Officer Rheiham Lt. Col. Hastings

Place	Date	Hour	Summary of Events and Information	References to Appendices
	6		and a heavy MMG concentration laid down by B Coy. 2 Ches.	
REF: MAPS FRANCE: SHEET 7E/5	(Cont).	2300	As last light failed, the Bn was holding an area West of St. GABRIEL (Map Ref 890795) with BHQ located at Map Ref 878785 A Coy. 875784 B Coy. 875782 C Coy. 878783 and D Coy. 874784.	
1/50,000.		2359	Enemy aircraft were not seen during the day, but by midnight many appeared over the beachead and many bombs were heard to fall.	
SHEET 7F/1 1/50,000	7	0430	The Bn. 'stood-to' for one hour. The night 6/7 passed quietly within the Bn area.	
		0815	CO held a conference with his Coy Comdrs and details were discussed for the immediate move forwardof the Bn. By 1000 hrs, th Bn had passed through RUCQUEVILLE and proceeded to advance on DUCY St. MARGUERITE.	
		1100	On reaching area 855734, the Bn. experienced difficulty in moving fwd owing to heavy enemy mortar fire and the activities of snipers. C Coy. ran into trouble with enemy tanks at 854733. Meanwhile the Brigadier had visited the CO and it was decided to withdraw the Bn 1000 yds North of DUCY St. MARGUERITE to area 8574. At 1330 hrs the Coys withdrew to the new positions. The Carriers were bombed and strafed by our own aircraft en route, and casualities were reported.	Rheiham Lt. Col.
		1500	Many conflicting reports were received of the situation in DUCY ST. M. Some reported tanks and inf, but the CO speaking to Bde at 1630 hrs said he thought the country side during the afternoon and at 1800 hrs approx 60 enemy Inf were seen moving through a cornfield near CANCAGNY heading SW for the woods and river as though they were trying to reach their own lines again.	
		1815	Bn. dispositions in front of DUCY ST. MARGUERITE were as follows:- BHQ located 857747 A Coy. 858743 B Coy. 855744 C Coy. 856747 D Coy. 859746	
		1930	All Coys. were warned to be on look-out for enemy paratroops. Reports stated that many had been dropped in the Canadians' area.	

Wt.47724/993 2,000,000 3/43 W.H. & S. 51/6375

WO 171/1303
Intelligence/war diary
7TH BATTALION THE GREEN HOWARDS

Month and Year June 1944   Commanding Officer Lt. Col. P.H. RICHARDSON.

Place	Date	Hour	Summary of Events and Information	References to Appendices
Out Sea	5 June	0800	LCT's moved out of SOLENT towards the NEEDLES 'D' day postponed 24hrs. c.o. visited other ships Top all preparing equipment for tomorrow. All LCA's loaded. Bng. united Bn HQ ship	
		1700	Final conference wih SNTO CO AH Lo and all officers of serials	
	6 June	0300	Reveille.	
		0400	Breakfast for tps.	
		0420	First LCA's commenced landing.	
		0520	Bn. HQ. on board LCM.	
		0530	C Coy. founded LCA's	
		0725	'H' Hr. leading two Bno approaching the beaches.	
		08	'B' & 'D' boys beached.	

Wt. 7724,993 2,000,000 3,43 W.H. & S. 51/6375.

SHEET 2

Month and Year June 1944   Commanding Officer Lt. Col. P.H. RICHARDSON.

Place	Date	Hour	Summary of Events and Information	References to Appendices
	6 June	08	'C' & 'A' Coys & Bn HQ. landed. Beach under slight mortar fire. Grass fires burning to the North of the Beach. Landing made at Rd leading south to VER-SUR-MER.	
			Bn. advanced upon one axis along North-South Rd through VER-SUR-MER, in the order B >, A C Coys. - TAC. Bn. HQ. VER-SUR-MER clear of enemy. MTO establishing Vehicle assembly area. B.D. A Coys. task WESTERN Road to CREPON halted at 912849 preparing to attack VER-SUR-MER gun Bty at 917843.	
			'C' Coy. proceded by Tac HQ travelled along Eastern Rd. VER-SUR-MER Bty appeared to be and of action movement seen. 40-50 prisoners were taken by 'C' Coy. from this locality.	

Wt. 47724/993 2,000,000 3/43 W. H & S. 51/6575.

SHEET 3

Commanding Officer Lt. Col. P.H. RICHARDSON.

Place	Date	Hour	Summary of Events and Information	References to Appendices
FRANCE	6 June		'C' Coy. continued on Eastern Rd Tac HQ switched to join other three Coys. who were meeting slight opposition from snipers and MGs 　　Five carriers, the Master Pl ad 6 A/th guns now joined the Bn. 　　Coys. continued the advance supported by 4/7 D.G. tks and 86 Fd Regt. arty. 　　'D' Coy. became involved in CREPON clearing up the Enemy 900835. 　　3 Remaining Coys. continued and 'C' Coy. leading met slight opposition at 903825. Bn. suffered first casualties which were slight. A further 40 prisoners were taken. 　　Mobile column under Major Bowly 2 i/c comprised of Sqn of Tks see of carriers and B Coy.	

Wt..1724/993 2,000,000 3,43 W.H. & S. 51/6375.

SHEET 4

Commanding Officer Lt. Col. P.H. RICHARDSON.

Place	Date	Hour	Summary of Events and Information	References to Appendices
	6		Bn contained the advance 'A' 'B' 'C' Coys. D Coy. were still detached and were advancing from CREPON towards ST. GABRIEL. 　　Bn. and Sqn. 4/7 DG's met enemy opposition MG's SP guns on the approaches to FRESNAY-LE-CROTTEUR. Four of our tps were hit. Naval Shelling hindered Bn. advance. 　　Bring united Bn. HQ. 　　Bn. Cor D Coy. continued advanced towards COULUMBS. 　　'C' Coy. leading. Village reported clear leading elements fired on from the fortified farm 878752 Bn. orders from Bde Bn. withdrew and consolidated for the night North of COULOMBS 887773. Patrols to the village and to the SOUTH met no opposition. Five prisoners were taken in the	

Wt. 47724,993 2,000,000 3,43 W.H. & S. 51/6375.

SHEET 5

Place	Date	Hour	Summary of Events and Information	References to Appendices
	6		moved off. Reached area of bridge 906805 knocked out an enemy staff car killing an officer. Encountered enemy A/Tk gun on far side of the Bridge. This was dealt with by the arty. 'C' Coy passed through to capture the bridge intact col continued through CREUILLY.	
			The Mobile Column switched to take the bridge at 889799. This proved to be only a footbridge. Bn. proceeded through CREUILLY met opposition in the way of MG fire on the SOUTH side. Civilians reported two of the guns in the locality. Mortars went into action.	
			Patrol from 'C' Coy. encountered enemy fire from the WEST. Reports of enemy armour to the SOUTH. approaching the Bn.	

Wt.47724,993 2,000,000. 3/43. W.H. & S. 51/6375.

SHEET 6

Place	Date	Hour	Summary of Events and Information	References to Appendices
	6		Bn. area. Bty bound and in support sniped returning from a conference.	
		1400 hrs	2nd Tide personnel arrived.	
			Bn. disposition A Coy. B Coy.	
			'C' Coy. BW HQ.	fax
	7	0100	'D' Coy. rejoined the Bn put in posn	
		0530	1 Pl. A Coy. on Right 1 Pl. C Coy. on left advanced towards the fortified form. A Coy. patrol got within 200 yds before being fired upon by M.G. The Bn. advanced through COULOMBS behind the two patrols C followed by D Coy. on the N.T Rd A Coy followed by B Coy. on the track to the West of the Road.	
			One Sqn. 4/7 DGs in support were on the	

WL. 7724,993 2,000,000 3,43 W. H &S. 51/6575.

151ST INFANTRY
BRIGADE

WO 171/670
Intelligence/war diary
151ST BRIGADE HQ

Month and Year June 1944   Commanding Officer Brig. D.S. GORDON, DSO.

Place	Date	Hour	Summary of Events and Information	References to Appendices
NIGHTINGALE CAMP, SOUTHAMPTON	1		Marshalling of troops into craft loads proceeded and loading of vehicles and stores continued.	
	2		Ditto	
	3	1800	Tac Bde HQ consisting of Bde IO, Bde Sigs Offr and Sigs personnel left marshalling area and later embarked on HMS ALBRIGHTON. Embarkation of battalions continued.	
	4	1200	Bde Comd, Brig R.H. SENIOR embarked on HMS ALBRIGHTON. Operation OVERLORD postponed 24 hours on account of weather.	
AT SEA	5			
	5/6	1930	Convoys formed up in SOUTHAMPTON water preparatory to sailing.	
	6		Voyage uneventful no interference from enemy attack. The weather which it was hoped would improve did not in fact do so and quite a strong wind caused a heavy swell.	
		0615	Anchorage positions reached off the coast of NORMANDY	
		0720	H hour for assault tps. By 0750 hrs news was received that the assaulting tps both 69 Bde and 231 Bde were ashore. 69 Bde going well. 231 Bde having	

Wt.47724 993 2,000,000 3/43 W. H. & S. **51**/6375.

SHEET 2

Month and Year June 1944   Commanding Officer Brig. D.S. GORDON, DSO.

Place	Date	Hour	Summary of Events and Information	References to Appendices
		0920	difficulty getting off the beach owing to enemy fire.	
			Reported that 6 GREEN HOWARDS had reached a position between MONT FLEURY and VER-SUR-MER with 7 GREEN HOWARDS in LARIVIERE. 5 EAST YORKS being passed through.	
		1015	News received that 1 HAMPS had not yet captured LE HAMEL but that both 1 DORSETS and 2 DEVONS had by-passed ASNELLES and were heading inland.	
		1030	Tac Bde HQ transferred from HMS ALERIGHTON to a LCM for the voyage to the beach and touched down on KING RED at approx 1200 hrs.	
		1245	Bde HQ established in assembly area 910854 where they were joined by the Brigade Majors' party and Staff Capts' party who had travelled on different craft.	
		1320	6 DLI ashore with HQ at 909854.	
		1330	8 DLI ashore with HQ at 918855.	
			9 DLI ashore in area MEUVAINE.	
		1345	Bde Comd visited HQ 69 Bde and discussed situation with Comd 69 Bde.	

Wt.47724 993 2,000,000 3/43 W. H. & S. 51/6375.

SHEET 3

Month and Year June 1944   Commanding Officer Brig. D.S. GORDON, DSO.

Place	Date	Hour	Summary of Events and Information	References to Appendices
		1530	Mobile columns of both 6 and 9 DLI started to advance according to plan.	
		1558	9 DLI SOUTH OF MEVVAINE.	
		1607	6 DLI approaching CREPON.	
		1630	9 DLI one and a half miles SOUTH OF MEVVAINE.	
		1700	9 DLI reported to have reached line X rds 863824 - rd June 885808.	
		1800	8 DLI following up behind 9 DLI reported on line X rds 863824 - rd June 885808.	
		1820	9 DLI reported that forward tps in SOMMERVIEU.	
		1830	9 DLI reported on line X rds 823811 - rd June 847791.	
		1910	9 DLI reported enemy opposition WEST of SOMMERVIEU.	
		1945	6 DLI reported on line rd june 839816 - rd June 885805.	
		1950	6 DLI Mobile Column reported on line of high ground from rd at 819808 - VAUX-SUR-SEULLES.	
		2000	9 DLI reported on line main rd BAYEUX - ST LEGER. Bde HQ moved to area 836822.	
		2100	Bde HQ moved to area 842819. Earlier in the afternoon at approx 1500 hrs,	

Wt.47724/993 2,000,000 3/43 W.H. & S. 51/6375

SHEET 4

Month and Year June 1944   Commanding Officer Brig. D.S. GORDON, DSO.

Place	Date	Hour	Summary of Events and Information	References to Appendices
			Bde Comd, Brig R.H. SENIOR, DSO, TD, accompanied by Liaison Offr, Capt. R.S. JACK left Bde HQ to visit Mob Colns of 6 and 9 DLI. No information was subsequently received this day as to their whereabouts and it was feared that they had been made PW. Accordingly Lt. Col. R.P. LIDWILL, DSO, CO 8 DLI assumed comd of the Bde. Div HQ was informed and GOC called at Bde HQ at 2200 hrs to discuss the situation. It was decided that no advance SOUTH of the main rd BAYEUX - ST. LEGER would be made that night but that the advance would be continued at first light next morning. Orders were given to Bns to this effect.	
			Situation at last light	
			9 DLI RIGHT dispositions. Bn. HQ 827798 A Coy. 828804 B Coy. 825796	
			C Coy. 835794	
			D Coy. 823809. LEFT 6 DLI Bn. HQ 852798 A Coy. 849791 B Coy. 857798 C Coy 851799	
			D Coy. area ESQUAY -sur-SEULLES. RESERVE 8 DLI Bn. HQ 837817 A Coy. 831814 B Coy. 835814 C Coy. 840814 D Coy. 842804.	
			The advance from the beaches only met slight opposition, the enemy appearing	

Wt.47724/933 2,000,000 3/43 W.H. & S. 51/6375

SHEET 5

Month and Year June 1944   Commanding Officer Brig. D.S. GORDON, DSO.

Place	Date	Hour	Summary of Events and Information	References to Appendices
			to be completely disorganised and not expecting a landing at that given point. A total of 44 PW were captured. Identifications confirmed the Intelligence prior to D-Day that 716 Coastal Div. was holding defensive posns in that particular sector.	
842819	7	0430	Situation at first light.	
			9 DLI reported that a patrol which had gone in the direction of BAYEUX had been told by civilians that the town was held by a force of about 200 GERMANS.	
		0530	The advance continued.	
		[0630	9 DLI reported on line of rly BAYEUX - CONDE - CONDE-SUR-SEULLES.]	
		0715	Mobile Coln 6 DLI reported approaching final objective.	
		[0755	6 DLI reported on final objective, X rds 7. 825739 875739 - CONDE-SUR-SEULLES.]	
		0800	Brig R.H. SENIOR being still missing it was decided to send out a recce patrol to search for him, the patrol to consist of one pl of inf supported by one sec of carriers supplied by 8 DLI. Their task was to search the area NORTH of BAZANVILLE between PIERRE ARTUS and CREPON over which none of our tps had	

Wt.47724/993 2,000,000 3/43 W.H. & S. 51/6375

WO 171/1290

Intelligence/war diary

6TH BATTALION THE DURHAM LIGHT INFANTRY

Month and Year June 1944   Commanding Officer Lt. Col. A.E. ??en.

Place	Date	Hour	Summary of Events and Information	References to Appendices
NIGHTINGALE WOOD, ROMSEY, HANTS.	1 2		Briefing continued during 1st and 2nd and some serials moved out from Camp C.17 to marshalling areas.	
(Camp C.17).	3	0900	Bn. Church Parade, (C of E) in NAAFI Tent.	
		1330	Main body of Bn. left Camp C.17 in Troop Carrying Vehicles and embarked in Landing Craft Infantry in SOUTHAMPTON WATER. The Prime Minister and Field Marshall Smuts were on the Pier during the embarktion. The Prime Minister shook hands with the Commanding Officer and wished "God Speed" to the Battalion. Landing Craft anchored for rest of day in SOUTHAMPTON WATER.	
SOUTHAMPTON WATER	4		Information was received during the day that D-Day had been put back for 24 hours. During the day, two craft loads in the morning and two in the afternoon, visited the Transit Camp set up Movement Control in the sheds on the quayside. Men had chance to have a good wash and were served with a hot meal. Camp provided writing facilities, entertainments, NAAFI and organised games and gave all ranks a chance to stretch their legs after the rather cramped conditions aboard the landing craft.	
	5		Craft still in SOUTHAMPTON WATER. Transit camp visited again during morning and afternoon. The Commanding Officer (Lieut. Colonel A.E. Green) was taken ill with Malaria and had to leave the Landing Craft for hospital. Major G.L. Wood (second-in-command) then took over command of the Battalion.	
			The Landing Craft sailed during the night 5/6 June.	
			In sight of the French Coast.	
Ref Map 1/50, 000 FRANCE. Sheet 7 F/1 - CAEN.	6	0900 1100	Battalion landed on the beaches. Sea was rough and most men of the Battalion were feeling ill effects of long sea journey. The waves made landing difficult and some serials were waist high in water as they went ashore.	

Wt. 47724/993 2,000,000 3/43 W.H. & S. 51/6375.

SHEET 2

Place	Date	Hour	Summary of Events and Information	References to Appendices
	6	1300	Battalion Assembly complete in Assembly Area near VER-SUR-MER 9085.	
		1500	Battalion left assembly area two hours late to move to final objective.	
			Advance of Mobile Column was slow and some opposition was encountered en route. Battalion reached its first objective, ESQUAY-SUR-SEULLES 8479 at 2030 hours and was ordered to stop. First Prisoners taken during the advance were Russians belonging to 642 Russian Battalion. They were of very poor fighting quality and quite willing to surrender.	
			Battalion dug in and patrolled immediate front.	
	7	[0500	Advance continued to second objective – area CONDE-SUR-SEULLES 8274.]	
		0730	Mobile Column reached final objective and was straffed by our Thunderbolts: two Carriers lost.	
		0900	Main body on final objective and to positions forecast in Operation Order.	
			Dug in immediately. Opposition on way down had been slight consisting chiefly of snipers. [Rear elements of mobile column met a convoy of German vehicles ar road junction 815763 and shot up three three-ton trucks without loss.]	
		[1100	Joint Post at CONDE 8373 occupied by Captain D.J. Fenner, but no forces from 69 Infantry Brigade turned up. Post was counter-attacked by enemy during the morning and our force driven out.] Captain Fenner and 15 Other Ranks were wounded. [4/7th Dragoon Guards in support beat off any threat to main Battalion positions and the post was reoccupied during the evening.] Anti-tank platoon claimed one lorry towing 37 mm A/A Gun at cross roads 815740.	
	8.		[Battalion Headquarters at 828747.]	
			"A" Company, established at cross roads 815740, provided the Battalion's offensive effort during the morning. Without loss they destroyed one amphibious car, one three-ton truck and captured a half tracked vehicle loaded with ammunition. All the men in these vehicles belonged to a new divison - 130 PZ LEHR Division which had only recently moved on to	

Wt. 47724/993 2,000,000 2/43 W.H. & S 51/6375.

WO 171/1289

Intelligence/war diary

8TH BATTALION, THE DURHAM LIGHT INFANTRY

Month and Year June 1944   Commanding Officer Lt. Col. R.P. LEDWILL DLO.

Place	Date	Hour	Summary of Events and Information	References to Appendices
			<u>Summary</u> The first three days of the invasion the Bn. met little opposition, what opposition was met was quickly brushed aside and the bn continued pushing in land. On the 9th JUNE the Bn. was under and 8 Armd Bde with the intention of capturing the TESSEL BRETTVILLE feature. Owing to strong enemy opposition with TKS and infantry we reached ST. PIERRE and remained there for three days. It was intended that this Salient would be broadened by 7 Armd Div moving on our right towards TILLY-SUR-SEULLES . This did not materialise owing to the enemy's strong A/TK defences. The Bn. returned under and 151 Quelan Duf Bde	

Wt.47724,993 2,000,000 3/43 W.H. & S 51/6375.

SHEET 2

Month and Year June 1944   Commanding Officer Lt. Col. R.P. LEDWILL DLO.

Place	Date	Hour	Summary of Events and Information	References to Appendices
			from then onwards through continually facing the enemy we were not engaged in any large scale operations. Offensive patrolling by day and night gave us considerable info about the enemy. Counter Bty and Counter mortar work reached a high standard. Supporting arms: The first few days the Bn. was supported by 90 Fd Regt. (S. P.). and later by 296 Bty. 74 Fd Regt. and 107 A/TK Bty. approx total of PWs taken and checks by this Bn. amounted to 96 all ranks. Same P.Ws. reported by car by our mortaring.	

Wt.47724/993 2,000,000 3/48 W.H. & S 51/6375.

SHEET 3

Place	Date	Hour	Summary of Events and Information	References to Appendices
CAMP. 17 foothill HANTS	3	1400	By 1400 hrs the Bn had moved in TCVs. by serials from C. 17 to SOUTHAMPTON DOCKS. As the troops were embarking the PM, General Sevets and Mr Ernest Bevin MP walked among the ranks.	Club
	4		During the day the Bn. was allowed ashore for recreational training and feeding at SOUTHAMTON REST CAMP.	Club
	5		Routine as for previous day.	
AT SEA		2030	Sailed out of SOUTHAMPTON Docks. as the LCIs sailed past the ISLE OF WIGHT. maps of FRANCE showing the invasion beaches were issued. down to PLN STTS. Hand books giving information of FRANCE were issued to troops.	Club
	6	0800	Coast of FRANCE sighted.	
		1000	The LCIs containing the B.n approaches the beaches	

Wt.47724/993 2,000,000 3/43/ W.H. & S 51/6375.

SHEET 4

Place	Date	Hour	Summary of Events and Information	References to Appendices
AT SEA. Ref map FRANCE 1/12 500 VER-SUR-MERE Sheet No 83	6		but orders we receive are to stand off for a short time.	
		1130	Bn. HQ ship beached on KING beach and moved along BLACK ROUTE (track 918868) to AA at 910855	
		1210	A Coy. beaches and arrived in AA. by 1305 hrs.	
		1330	C & D Coys. reported into AA.	
			CO meets Brigade Under at 911854	
		1335	MTO reports to Bn. HQ.	
		1350	LO from Bn. sent to Bde.	
		1355	Brigadien arrived at Bn. HQ.	
1/25000 Sheet 37/18SE. CREULLY		1400	B Coy. left Bn to cross track. HR. 862823. Capt. Woodneff OC barrier Phor reported to Bn. HQ with 6 barriers.	

Wt.47724/993 2,000,000 3/43/ W.H. & S 51/6375.

SHEET 5

Month and Year June 1944   Commanding Officer Lt. Col. R.P. LEDWILL DLO.

Place	Date	Hour	Summary of Events and Information	References to Appendices
"	6	1530	R.Ho wounded and evacuated.	
		1545	Bn. prepare to move in rear of 6& 9/D.WI.	
		1604	Bn. moved off in following order. 'A' Coy. 'C' Coy. Bn. HQ. as mobile Coln. consisting of A/TK guns Carriers and 'D' Coy. on bicycles.	
"		1620	Intercept report that 6/Out approaching CREPON.	
"		1700	Bn passed through MEUVAINES	
		1730	Intercept report 8/Out progressing well.	
"		1810	A Coy. passed first report line 865825.	
		1835	B Coy. rejoined Bn and fell in behind Bn. HQ as "A" "C" & Bintto passed	
"		1840	them.	
"		1853	Ho enemy AFVS reporter at 875773 approaching CRUELTY.	
"		1915	Bn. passed second report him at 840817.	
			Bn. Letter in fwd AA area 836815.	

Wt 47724/993 2,000,000 3/43 W.H. & S 51/6375.

SHEET 6

Month and Year June 1944   Commanding Officer Lt. Col. R.P. LEDWILL DLO.

Place	Date	Hour	Summary of Events and Information	References to Appendices
" 1/25000 Sheet 37/18 SW. RYES.	6	1945	Capt. H.E.CB Catford O'C' A/TK PLN reported to Bn. HQ.	
		2000	Coys in posn and digging in. A Coy. 831834?	
			B Coy. 835811 C Coy. 840813 D Coy. 842804	
"			Bn. HQ 835816.	
		2005	A Coy. send 3 PW to Bn. HQ.	
			CO & 1.0 80 to Bde HQ.	
		2020	CO & 1.0 return from Bde HQ called for 'O' groups and issues orders for defence of area held.	
		2230	Col. R.P. Seduire Dso take over send of Bde during the absence of Bring RH. senior Dso. reported missing.	
			Major A.H. Dunn assumed and of Bn.	
		2245	7. PW arrived from A Coy.	
	Night 6/7		2 Lt. J. Hannah M.M. made contact with 56 Bde.	
1/25000 Sheet CRUEULY. 37/18 S.E			It W. HW. galland patroller area PIERRE SOLLAINE where it was reported there was still odd enemy. No enemy found.	Club

Wt.47724/993 2,000,000 3/43 W.H. & S 51/6375.

WO 171/1291
Intelligence/war diary
9TH BATTALION, THE DURHAM LIGHT INFANTRY

Month and Year June 1944

Commanding Officer Lt. Col. H.WOODS DSO.

M.c.r Bar.

Place	Date	Hour	Summary of Events and Information	References to Appendices
ENGLAND SOUTHAMPTON	1/2		Brain Nightingale Wood Camp, SOUTHAMPTON	
	3	1000	Starting at 1000 hrs the Bn. moved to King George V Hock, SOUTHAMPTON	
		1600	and embarked on LCI(L)'s Embarkation completed by 1600 hrs	
	4/5		LCIs lying in clock, Parties allowed off to writing rooms to on quayside at 2000 hrs	
		2000	the LCIs moved down the Solent, reaching	
		2030	the open Na at 2030 hrs.	
KING BEACH, FRANCE	?	1020	The Bn. disembarked at KING BEACH. Owing to rough weather, it was necessary to wade through five feet of water carrying all kit. The troops moved direct to Assembly Area on the downs.	
		1605	W. of MONT FLEURY. By 1605 hrs word had come through that 69 Bde had fulfilled its task, and the mobcol. moved forward, leaving the main body	

Wt.47724,993 2,000,000 3/43 W. H. & S. **51/6375**

SHEET 2

Month and Year June 1944

Commanding Officer Lt. Col. H.WOODS DSO.

Place	Date	Hour	Summary of Events and Information	References to Appendices
KING BEACH, FRANCE SUMMERVEIN CAUGE FERME	6	1827	in rear. By 1827 hrs the column had reached SUMMERVEIN, and started to	
		1924	clear it of enemy, a task completed by 1924 hrs.	
			The main body then continued as far as CAUGE FERME, S. E. of SUMMERVEIN, and started to dig in for the night.	
	7	0300	Enemy patrol located in the area of Bn. HQ. On being engaged by HQ & B Coy., the patrol, numbering 15-20 men, withdrew S. They suffered two casualties, 1 dead, 1 wounded.	
Casby		0600	Bn. continued the advance towards CACHY. So far the casualties were 1 officer & 15 OR's missing, 1 dead, 1 wounded. Advance elements reached first objective, the high ground area CACHY, and were joined	
		0840	by main body and consolidated at 0840 hrs.	

Wt.47724,993 2,000,000 3/43 W. H. & S. 51/6375

231ST INFANTRY BRIGADE

Month and Year

Commanding Officer

Place	Date	Hour	Summary of Events and Information	References to Appendices
	5	0700	from S W. LGT sailed down the SOLENT passed the LSIs. At present operation is due to take place tomorrow. Zero hour will be 0725 hrs. Everybody on board in cheerful frame of mind with the news of the fall of Rome. SOAG, Bde Commander and Maj. Gen Chater visited the following ships in Force "G" to wish troops on board "God speed and Good Luck". The former two addressed personnel over the ships speaker on the following boats: HMS GLENROY, EMPIRE SPEARHEAD, EMPIRE CROSSBOW, EMPIRE ARQUEBUS, they then visited HMS BULLOLO to see Force "G" Commander and GOC 50 Div to receive any final instructions before sailing. The latest and up to date information concerning the defences on the Divisional sector were received. These consisted of the appearance of large anti-ank guns on the high ground between BAYEAUX and CAEN and heavy ack ack 88 mm around BAYEAUX. Some new field btys had also been located. All troops were in great heart and prepared for what may come.	
		1700	Capt. Farquar and Bde Commander addressed all personnel on board of the ship Lt. Comr D.G.Mansfield with the Bdes sincerest thanks. This has been erected in the wardroom.	
		1845	Air raid warning "Red" HMS NITH passed HAMPSTEAD boom near YARMOUTH.	
	6	0525	Arrived release position mid channel and dropped anchor LC. As lowered from LCIs and are making headway inshore. Bombing started at early hour on French coast and has been continuous throughout. HMS BELFAST opened fire on our sector. At present no enemy interference. Coast line quite	

Wt.47724/993 2,000,000 3/43 W. H. & S. **51**/6375.

SHEET 2

Place	Date	Hour	Summary of Events and Information	Remarks, references to Appendices and initials
			clear in the distance. Sea choppy and probably rather rough for the D DS but L.C.s seem to be making easy going.	
		0545	Most of the destroyers now firing.	
		0620	One of our planes has just been shot down near the coast line. Masses of heavy bombers and fighters flying overhead producing a tremendous amount of smoke along the coast. Heavy Ach ack can be seen inland probably BAYEAUX. 1st class destroyers are no closing inshore. First shell from the opposition has just landed about 500 yds short and to the east of this ship. Out landing beaches quite distinct and easy to pick out. The study of the oblique coastal photographs is a great success.	
		0640	The eight L.C.Ts carrying the D.D. Tanks having just returned through failure to float the tanks, is passing us going seawards. There is the sound of the most terrific fire which continues unceasingly.	
		0730	AVRES touch down.	
		0735	I Hamps touch down	
		0745	I Dorset touch down	
		0750	Tac Bde HQ left HQ ship HMS NITH in LCM. They were given a colossal farewell and cheers from the ships crew. Howard Marshall accompanied the craft inshore.	
	[	0905	After a hazardous journey during which the LCM received a direct hit from a shell and sunk under us we landed on the beach amidst complete chaos and disorder. Howard Marshall was wounded in the hand. Tac Bde HQ who were now without wirless comn proceeded to the MBSS.	
		0905	2 Devon landed.	
		0930	Situation at this time was very uncertain as heavy fire was observed in Le Hamel. I Dorset had now captured Les Roquettes and were trying to penetrate Buhot.	

Wt.47724/993   2,000,000   3/43   W.H.&S. 51/6975

SHEET 3

Place	Date	Hour	Summary of Events and Information	Remarks, references to Appendices and initials
	[	0930	2 Devon were on the back of the beach endeavouring to make an appreciation of the situation.	
		0950	47 R.M. Commando landed after having 3 craft sunk and with an estimated strength of 300. They then concentrated at the back of the beach during the clarification of events at the time.	
			Mortar fire and shelling of the beaches still continued. I Dorset having been held up at Le Hamel and Asnelles were trying to proceed via Les Roquettes and thence inland to enter Buhot from the rear.	
		1010	I Coy of 2 Devon committed in Le Hamel and another at Asnelles. The remainder of the Bn proceeded behind the Dorsets towards Ryes.	
		1100	I Dorset reported their fwd tps in Asnelle. 2 Devon in the same area.	
			In Le Hamel the situation was unchanged,	
		1130	I Dorset now East of Buhot and advancing towards it. 2 Devon less 2 coys in Le Hamel and Asnelle now advancing towards Ryes.	
			It is reported that I Hamps still engaged in severe street fighting in Le Hamel.	
		1245	I Hamps report HQ est 879859 with I coy working round Le Hamel onto high ground at Cabana.	
		1425	I Hamps still in Le Hamel clearing up enemy pockets. Sherwood Rangers at pt 54 at Buhot after very heavy fighting and casualties.	
		1700	2 Devon held up at Ryes.	
			2 Devon report capture of Ryes. I Dorset capture S.P. 856856.	
		1900	I Hamps capture S.P. and Radar Sta East of Arromanones.	
		1930	231 Bde HQ move to Meuvaines.	

Wt.47724/993   2,000,000   3/43   W.H.&S. 51/6975

Place	Date	Hour	Summary of Events and Information	Remarks, references to Appendices and initials
		2000	Siuation. 2 Devon holding Ryes. I Dorset pt 54. I Hamps have completed mopping up of Le Hamel and Asnelles and are est along to the coast and to incl Arromanches.	
		2100	Bde HQ moves to St Come de Fresne.	
	[			

Wt.47724/993   2,000,000   3/43 W.H.&S. 51/6975

WO 171/1278
Intelligence/war diary
2ND BATTALION THE DEVONSHIRE REGIMENT

Month and Year June 1944   Commanding Officer Lt. Col. C.A.R. NEVILL OBE.

Place	Date	Hour	Summary of Events and Information	References to Appendices
At Sea	5		Messages from General Eishenower, Supreme Allied Commander, General B.L. Montgomery, C-in-C, 21 Army Group, and Major General Graham, 50 (N) Div. Comd were read to all troops.	
	6	0515	HMS Glenroy containing Bn. Assault Group dropped anchor approx 10 miles NORTH of LE HAMEL, a village on the NORMANDY COAST.	Bn. was Res Bn. of 231 Bde Assault Group and timed to land at H + 40 min
		0705	Bn. Group in LCA's headed for the shore. Sea was extremely rough, and there were many cases of sea-sickness on the run in.	
FRANCE		0810	Fwd Coys. of the Bn. landed well to the the WEST of LE HAMEL. Landing was extremely difficult and hazardous due to the rough seas. It was during their landings that Major Howard MC, o/c, "B" Coy. was injured being run over by an LCA and his ribs crushed. The Landing was rendered more difficult by the presence of Enemy Beach Obstacles. Bn. HQ., followed by "C" & "D" Coys. landed.	See marked Map Sheet 7?/3 Creully 1/50,000
		0820	The beach was under fire from snipers and spasmodic gunfire and mortarfire. It was found that the Right Assault Bn, 1, Hamps, had failed to clean the	

1622/PMEA/1–500,000–9/41.

SHEET 2

Month and Year June 1944   Commanding Officer Lt. Col. C.A.R. NEVILL OBE.

Place	Date	Hour	Summary of Events and Information	References to Appendices
France	6	0820/Cont.	immediate beach defences and thus the Bn was held up on the Beach unable to go forward to the pre-arranged assembly area.	
		0915	By 0915 "C" & "D"Coys. had got clear of the beach, and were approaching Le HAMEL from the EAST.	
		0955	"A" & "B" Coys. started to move in land from the beach. During all this time communications with Coys. had been scant and the Commanding Officer had great difficulty in getting his orders for a change of plan to the Coys. concerned. The change of plan was necessitated since the pre-arranged Assembly Area was still in enemy hands. The new plan was that the Bn. should bypass the Assembly Area ASNELLES-SUR-MER and push on to the first objective, the Capture of RYES. By this time it was found that "C" Coy. had became Committed on the outskirts of LE HAMEL and could not dis-engage. However "D" Coy. was withdrawn	
		1120	from LE HAMEL and pushed in land from LES ROCQUETTES followed by "A" & "B" Coy.	

1622/PMEA/1–500,000–9/41.

SHEET 3

Place	Date	Hour	Summary of Events and Information	References to Appendices
FRANCE	6	1130	During the move inland the Coys. were harassed by mortarfire, and Major Parlby, OC. 'D" Coy. was wounded in the leg, together with some of his Coy. S.EAST of ASNELLES-SUR-MER, "A" Coy. took the lead and started to adv along the GRONDE RIVIERE towards RYES followed by "D" Coy. This was stage two of the original plan.	
		1202	"C" Coy. reported pinned down by enemy snipers on the outskirts of LE HAMEL.	
			Major Duke, MC., was killed here by a sniper; the Coy. suffered many other casualties.	
			Meanwhile "A" & "D" were pushing forward along the axis of the River but were held up by well concealed MG's & Snipers 1000 yds from RYES.	
			The country here was extremely close and it was quite impossible to locate the enemy MG's & Snipers though they held their fire to short ranges. In trying to adv in face of this opposition "A" & "D" Coys. suffered many casualties incl Capt Crawley, Lt. Bull, Lt. Morris, Lt. Foy, Wounded & Lt. Smith, Killed. Lt. Foy was later seem to be taken prisoner. Capt. DUPONT RA who was FOB att to the Bn. was also wounded. In view of the nature of the Country and since no support could be obtained from either our own mortars or Gunners Sp due to lack of Communications, the CO decided to leave "A" Coy. to contain the opposition and guard our laft flank whilst "B" & "D" Coys. bypassed the enemy and pushed into RYES.	
		1625	"B" Coy. reached RYES and occupied it with only slight opposition.	
		1630	The CO with 2 Sections of "D" Coy. pushed on to high ground N.WEST of RYES. which was found to be unoccupied. Later "C" Coy. and remainder of "D" Coy. moved up to this Area.	

1622/PMEA/1—500,000—9/41.

SHEET 4

Month and Year June 1944   Commanding Officer Lt. Col. C.A.R. NEVILL OBE.

Place	Date	Hour	Summary of Events and Information	References to Appendices
France	6	1630	"A" Coy. reported a counter attack which they held. Later they rejoined the Bn. N.WEST of RYES.	to fw
		1900	Bn was in position on high ground N.W. of RYES, with "B" Coy. in Ryes; and Bn. HQ., in a railway cutting. In view of the rather disorganised state of the Bn., the CO decided to hold his present position for the night and push on to the LONGUES Bty in the morning. Later it was decided to send "C" Coy. fwd to occupy MASSE-DE-CRADALLE that night. This "C" Coy were unable to do being held up at La ROSIERE a mile short of the objective.	
			At the end of the day it was found that the Bn. had sustained rather severe casualties.	
			Officers, Killed. 2. Wounded 6. this includes 3 Coy. Comds.	
			OR's. Killed. 20. Wounded 60.	
			During the landing much equipment had been lost, and most of what little tpt the Bn. was allowed to land on D-Day.	
			Many prisoners were taken by the Bn and valuable information was obtained	to fw

1622/PMEA/1—500,000—9/41.

SHEET 5

Month and Year June 1944   Commanding Officer Lt. Col. C.A.R. NEVILL OBE.

Place	Date	Hour	Summary of Events and Information	References to Appendices
FRANCE	6		by the Bn. from maps and POW's· the maps sent back were of great importance to Division and were the subject of a special para in the first Div Int Summary issued. The Bn. had been up against Elements of 716 Div and 352 Div.	FCrn

1622/PMEA/1-500,000—9/41.

WO 171/1305

Intelligence/war diary
1ST BATTALION THE HAMPSHIRE REGIMENT

Month and Year June, 1944   Commanding Officer Lt. Col. C.H.R. HOWIE

Place	Date	Hour	Summary of Events and Information	References to Appendices
BEAULIEU	1		Bn. briefed for the pending operations.	
SOUTHAMPTON	2		Bn. embarked as per operational orders.	
SOUTHAMPTON	3 – 5		Spent on the sea.	
LE HAMEL	6		Two assault Coys. and two reserve Coys. landed, as per operational orders, on the JIG GREEN Beach east of the village of LE HAMEL. The aerial bombardment did not seem to have been as effective as expected. Enemy machine-gun nests survived the aerial, naval and Arty bombardment and made the fullest use of their underground, well-concealed and well-built positions. The narrowness of the beach and the presence of mines added to the difficulties of Bn's task. In spite of heavy casualties, however, the Bn. drove the enemy from the beach and captured the villages of LE HAMEL and ASNELLES-SUR-MER, inflicting heavy casualties heavy casualties on the enemy. Lt. Col. H.D. NELSON - SMITH, M.C., O.C. Bn., became a casualty &	

Wt.47724/993 2,000,000 3/43 W. H. & S. 51/6375.

SHEET 2

Month and Year June, 1944   Commanding Officer Lt. Col. C.H.R. HOWIE

Place	Date	Hour	Summary of Events and Information	References to Appendices
LE HAMEL	6		was removed to the RAP. ARROMANCHES – LES-BAINS was then stormed. Enemy 88 mm guns and Spandan teams, which put up a determined resistance, were ultimately wiped out. Bn. reorganised and attacked TRACY-SUR-MER where enemy resistance was stubborn. The nature of the country, infested with woods orchards gave the enemy snipers good cover Bn. HQ was established at ST. COME DE FRESNE.	
ST. COME DE FRESNE	7		Lt. Col. C.H.R. HOWIE took over the command of the Bn. The enemy resistance at TRACY-SUR-MER was overcome and MANVIEUX was entered without opposition. After having cleared the LE HAMEL – ASNELLES SUR MER – ARRUMANCHES LES BAINS – TRACY SUR MER – MANVIEUX perimeter, the Bn. moved to RUBERSY and arrived there at about 1830 hrs. A number of snipers were reported to be in the area of the village of BUHOT. A patrol of 4 Jeeps was sent to winkle them out. Two	

Wt.47724/993 2,000,000 3/43 W. H. & S. 51/6375

WO 171/1284
Intelligence/war diary
1ST BATTALION THE DORSETSHIRE REGIMENT

Place	Date	Hour	Summary of Events and Information	Remarks and references to Appendices
SOUTHAMPTON A?	June 1–5		Bn was on board LSI 62 "Empire Spearhead" with exception of C. Coy. on LSI. G64. "EMPIRE CROSSBOW" and Sp. Coy. on LCT's and LST's 2 l/c was in L.C.H. 317, with D.S.OA.G.	
	4		Final briefing for landing due to take place first light 5 June. This, however, was postponed for 24 hours due to inclement weather.	
	5	1900	Convoy weighed anchor and left the SOLVENT and passed W. of ISLE of WIGHT.	
In the field	6	0545	Sea rough as convoy cause in to the CHANNEL. First flight of assault Coys. - A. and B. - were lowered in their LCAG. Sea still immediately rough. (force of wind 4-5 - SICILY was 6-7). Sp. was given by naval and R.A. guns. LCG, IL LCT. (R), LLA (HRound) and LCS during was in according to programme. Heavy and medium bombers of RAF also gave support.	APPENDIX A includes detailed account of landing operations, Bu.o.o. for assault and not covering area of op, and air photes
LES ROCQUETTES		0725	A and B Coys. touched down on beach, A Coy. right, B. Coy. left Both Coys. landed approx. 600 yards E. of correct posn. A Coy pushed fwd. to leave off road running E. from LE. HAMEL without difficulty Coy. Comd., Major R.A.E. JONES, LL. ELLIS. And C.S.M. HOWELL, were all wounded soon after landing by shell and mortar fire, and Capt. ROYLE took over comd. 1/Hamps were landed opposite A. Coy's objective - the strong point at 886866 - which they captured and mopped up without difficulty. B. Coy. on left suffered considerable casualties from shell, mortar and MG fire on the	

D & L., London. E.C.

(A10266) wt W5300/P713 750,000 2/18 Sch. 52. Forms/C2118/16.

SHEET 2

Place	Date	Hour	Summary of Events and Information	Remarks and references to Appendices
LES ROCQUETTES	June 6	0725(cont)	beach, pushed inland through several minefields and securing their objective LES ROQUETTES, where they found C Coy., part of whom had landed opposite LES ROQUETTES, already established.	
		0915	B Coy. established themselves as firm base at LES ROQUETTES according to plan.	
		0745	The reserve Coys., C and D, landed, C right, D. left. A proportion of C. Coy landed opposite A. Coy's objective at 886866. They found this already liquidated by 1/Hamps. They therefore pushed inland to LES ROQUETTES without difficulty, but C.S.M. ROBINS was wounded during this short advance. C. Coy remained here until relieved by B Coy.	
		0750	D. Coy ashore 600 yds to east of correct posn. having suffered cas. from mines and mortar fire. D Coy. then followed B Coy. to LES ROQUETTES.	
		0750	Bn. Toc H.Q. also ashore, having landed with D Coy.	
		0915	C Coy. in co-operation with A Coy. of 1/Hamps, - who were to capture the village of ASNELLES - continued the advance towards BUHOT. Considerable opposition was met during advance, chiefly from houses at southern end of ASNELLES, where a party of 6 Germans were killed and 10 captured.	
		0930	D Coy. following up C Coy.	
		1130	C and D Coys. continue advance towards BUHOT.	
		1330	BUHOT reached by both Coys.	
		1400	C Coy. in possesion of ph.54, after meeting stronger opposition than anticipated 7. Germans were killed. and 2 officers, and 15 OR were taken prisoner.	

D D & L., London, E.C.

(A10266) Wt W5300/P713 750,000 2/18 Sch. 52 Forms/C21I8/16.

SHEET 3

Place	Date	Hour	Summary of Events and Information	Remarks and references to Appendices
BUHOT	June 6	1400	C Coy. took up posn. to support D Coy's attack as PUITS D'HERODE	
		1400	D Coy. pushing south through BUHOT suspursed and captured a coy. of german pioneers with their transport.	
		1500	D Coy. and C. Sqn of Sherwood Rangers, put in attack on PUITS D'HERODE. Supported by C Coy. from pt.54. Owing to cas occurred by D Coy. already, they were unable to capture this posn., and the CO therefore ordered A Coy. supported by C.Sq. Sherwood Rangers to attack and capture the posn. from the Southwest.	
		1700	A Coy. attack successful, a number of Germans being killed and 40 POW taken.	
		1700	During A Coy's attack, a party of enemy put in an attack on C Coy's flank, who were at about 853848. This was repulsed, six Germans being killed, and 4 captured.	
		1830	The attack on the BU's final objective, the Bty. posn at 848852 was carried out by A and C Coy's with support of C Sqn Sherwood Rangers and duty. support from 90 Fal Regt. D Coy. remaining in posn, at 852848 as file Coy. The Bty posn. was found to have been abandoned 4×105 mm. guns and a large quantity of equipment being left.	
		1700	B Coy. ordered to move from LES ROQUETTES and take over RYES firm 2/Devons.	
		2000	B Coy. arrives in RYES.	
		2100	BU. HQ. organises and is in posn as follows:- A Coy. 848843 C Coy. 852843 Bn. HQ B Coy. RYES D Coy. 853842 851841	

D. D. & L., London, E.C.

(A10266) Wt W5300/P713 750,000 2/18 Sch. 52 Forms/C2118/16.

SHEET 4

Place	Date	Hour	Summary of Events and Information	Remarks and references to Appendices

RYES	June 6/7		Patrolling during night to link up with 2/Devon to the west and along line of LA GRANDE RIVIERE, E. of RYES.
			Enemy a/c active over beach head during night.
			Casualties suffered by Bn. during the day was: Killed 4 Officers and 17 ORs
			<div align="right">Wounded 10 Officers and 88 ORs</div><div align="right">Missing 9 ORs</div>Officer cas Killed list:
			            LANCASTER T.G.
			            BRADBURY. C.
			            WHITERBOOK. J.
			            YOUNGS. J.P.
			Wounded: Major JONES A.A.E. (injured A. Coy. following)
			            Capt. WHITTINGTON C.R.
			            Capt. A.L. HARRIS (carried on his duties)
			            Lts. ELLIS R.J.
			            HAMILTON J.
			            JONES R.E.
			             ROBJOHN P.J.
			            STARATTON J.P.
			            THOMAS, J.A.
			            WEBB. H.J.	

D. D. & L., London, E.C.

(A10266) Wt W5300/ P713 750,000 2/18 Sch.52 Forms/C2118/16.

DIVISIONAL
TROOPS

WO 171/513
Intelligence/war diary
50TH INFANTRY (NORTHUMBRIAN) DIVISION HQ

Month and Year June 1944   Commanding Officer Maj. Ge?

Place	Date	Hour	Summary of Events and Information	References to Appendices
	1	1100	GOC and HQ 50 (Northumbrian) Division embarked HMS BULOLO at SOUTHAMPTON.	
	3	1430	The Rt. Hon. Winston S. Churchill PC Prime Minister, Field Marshall J. Smuts Prime Minister of the Union of South Africa attended by Mr Ernest Bevin Minister of Labour, Mr Duncan Sandys Financial adviser to the War Cabinet, Admiral Tovey, General Ismay Military adviser to the Prime Minister, visited HMS BULOLO. The Prime Minister addressed all ranks.	
		1700	HMS BULOLO slipped and anchored in the Solent at the head of Naval Force G.	
	4	1200	Operation "Overlord" postponed 24 hrs owing to unfavourable weather.	
	5	1830	Force G sailed down Solent and SOUTH into channel.	

Wt.47724/993 2,000,000 3/43 W. H. & S. **51**/6375

SHEET 2

Month and Year June 1944   Commanding Officer Major General D.A.H. GRAHAM, CBE, DSO, MC.

Place	Date	Hour	Summary of Events and Information	References to Appendices
	6		General. D-DAY.	
			Day dawned fairly clear but with some mist and a choppy sea. Naval bombardment most heartening.	
		0725	H HOUR	
		0735	1 Hamps touched down.	
		0745	2 Coys. 5 E YORKS ashore.	
			2 Coys. 6 GREEN HOWARDS a shore	
			1 DORSET ashore.	
		0845	Comd 69 Bde reported ashore with Tac Bde set up at MBSS.	
		0905	Comd 231 Bde ashore having lost wireless sets on way in.	
			Bde HQ set up at MBSS.	
			2 DEVON landed.	
		930	1 DORSET captured ROCQUETTES and pushing on to BUHOT 8655.	
		0950	47 RM COMMANDO landed.	

Wt. 47724/993 2,000,000 3/48 W, H. & S. **51**/6375.

SHEET 3

Commanding Officer Major General D.A.H. GRAHAM, CBE, DSO, MC.

Place	Date	Hour	Summary of Events and Information	References to Appendices
	6		1 DORSET having bypassed LE HAMEL 8786 and ASNELLES 8785 attempting to take BUHOT from SOUTH.	
		1010	2 DEVONS less two Coys. moving toward RYES 8483.	
		1030	6 GREEN HOWARDS reported on 1st objective.	
		1100	Tps of 1 DORSET mopping up ASNELLES.	
		1120	7 GREEN HOWARDS on 1st objective.	
		1130	Two Coys. 2 DEVONS and one Coy. 1 HAMPS street fighting in LE HAMEL.	
		1200	Tac HQ 151 Bde reported ashore.	
		1215	56 Bde HQ ashore.	
		1245	151 Bde HQ established in assembly area 910854.	
		1300	69 Bde HQ established at VER-SUR-MER 914852.	
			7 GREEN HOWARDS in CREPON 9083.	
		1320	6 DLI ashore in assembly area at 909854.	
		1330	8 DLI ashore established in assembly area at 918855.	

Wt.47724/993 2,000,000 3/48 W.H. & S. 51/6375.

SHEET 4

Commanding Officer Major General D.A.H. GRAHAM, CBE, DSO, MC.

Place	Date	Hour	Summary of Events and Information	References to Appendices
		1300	9 DLI ashore established at MEUVAINES 8884.	
		1400	Tac HQ 50 (NOrthumbrian) Division established MEUVAINES 893844.	
		1425	1 DORSET leading elements at Pt. 54 869851.	
		1500	7 GREEN HOWARDS mob colns report br 909805 captured.	
		1530	Mob colns 6 DLI and 9 DLI started advance.	
		1655	9 DLI reported 2,000 yds SOUTH of MEUVAINES.	
		1745	56 Bde report assembly complete in area 8584.	
		1800	69 Bde reports Bde HQ at 893815. 5 E YORKS NORTH of VILLIERS-LE-SEC 8880 and advancing. 6 GREEN HOWARDS NORTH of VILLIERS-LE-SEC. 7 GREEN HOWARDS held up SOUTH OF CRUELLY 9080.	
		1820	Fwd tps 9 DLI in SOMMERVIEU 9281.	
			69 Bde reports 40 tks moving NE from RUCQUEVILLE 8777.	
		1830	5 E YORKS reported in ST. GABRIEL 8879 meeting fairly stiff opposition.	

Wt.47724/993 2,000,000 3/48 W.H. & S. 51/6375.

SHEET 5

Commanding Officer Major General D.A.H. GRAHAM, CBE, DSO, MC.

Place	Date	Hour	Summary of Events and Information	References to Appendices
	6	1930	56 Bde report line of fwd tps RYES - LA ROSIERE 8284.	
			HQ 231 Bde established at MEUVAINES.	
		1950	6 DLI mob coln on line high ground from 819808 to VAUX-SUR-SEULLES 8477.	
		2000	9 DLI on line main rd BAYEUX 7879 - St LEGER 8675.	
			HQ 151 Bde established 836822.	
			Situation 231 Bde, 2 DEVONS in RYES. 1 DORSET Pt. 54.	
			1 HAMPS mopped up LE HAMEL and ASNELLES and established ARRUMANCHES 8586 to coast.	
		2100	2 ESSEX in contact at St SULPICE 8181. 2 SWB in contact at RDF station 8183.	
			HQ 151 Bde established area 842819.	
			HQ 231 Bde established St COME de FRESNE 8686.	
		2200	G.O.C. visited HQ 151 Bde and ordered no advance from rd BAYEUX to ST. LEGER until first light 7 Jun.	

SHEET 6

Commanding Officer Major General D.A.H. GRAHAM, CBE, DSO, MC.

Place	Date	Hour	Summary of Events and Information	References to Appendices
	6	2230	69 Bde HQ established 889796.	
		2345	HQ 56 Bde and 2 GLOSTERS moved to area MAGNY 8182.	
			Last light line of FDLs ARROMANCHES – LA ROSIERE – VAUX-SUR-AURE - ST. SULPICE – excl ST. MARTIN LES ENTREES 8178 – VAUX SUR SEULLES excl main rd to ST. GABRIEL – CREULLY.	
			During afternoon Brigadier R.H. SENIOR, DSO, TD left with LO to visit mob colns and failed to return. Lieut. Colonel R.P. LIDWELL, DSO assumed comd 151 Bde.	
			PW during day identify 716 Coastal Div and 1 Bn 916 Regt of 352 Inf Div.	
	7		Quiet night on Div. front with only mopping up of isolated parties of enemy. Some sniping.	
		0530	151 Bde advance continuing.	
		0730	GOC visited HQ 231 Bde.	
		0800	6 DLI reported on final objective cross rd 875739 – CONDE SUR SEULLES 9373.	

WO 171/982
Intelligence/war diary
90TH FIELD REGIMENT, RA

Month and Year June 1944   Commanding Officer Lt. Col. I.G.G.S. HARDIE, RA.

Place	Date	Hour	Summary of Events and Information	References to Appendices
B & C Marshalling areas at sea.	1		Personnel and vehs of the Regt. marshalled in craft loads in various marshalling camps in B and C Marshalling areas. Embarkation commenced.	
	2		Embarkation of guns and vehs on to LCTs.	
	3		Majority of Regt. loaded on craft. LCTs moved to buoys in the SOLENT.	
	4			
	5	0710	LCTs slipped and proceeded towards the NEEDLES. Later returned and tied up again.	
	6		Various Craft sailed on operation known as OVERLORD.	
			D Day for operation. Regt landed on coast of NORMANDY.	
		0650	Run in shoot by Regt, controlled by Maj. WELLS and Maj. GIRLING in LCSMs and by Capt. MORRIS in ML. Ops deployed as follows:- Maj. COMYNS with 2 DEVONS. Capt. BISHOP with 1 DORSET. Capt. JOHNSEN with 56 Bde. Capt. BLAND in LCH as adviser to D/SOAG. Capt. SMEDLEY with CO.	
			Capt. VINE with 1 HAMPS. Capt. COOK with 1 DORSET. Lt. CANDLISH and Lt. PERKS should have landed with RMA Sp. Regt, but their LCTAs did not reach the beach; one returned to UK the other beached days later.	
		0725	H-hour. Gnr MAJOR (Surveyor) landed.	
		0745	CO with HQ 1 DORSET, Capt COOK Sp C Coy., Capt BISHOP Sp D Coy. land JIG GREEN.	
			Spasmodic DF on beaches from 75 mms, 88 mms, 105 mms, 150 mms.	
		0825 (approx)	A, C, E Tps and LCTs containing some RHQ vehs beached. Difficulties experienced; underwater obstacles (mainly mines and devices on stakes), heavy swell, congestion on narrow beach. Some vehs "drowned" particularly M14s and Jeeps.	
T900871			A, C, E Tps went into action A 910870, c 909870, E 0845 hrs 909820. RHQ functioned in two M14s, both "drowned" on the beach approx 900871, one recovered soon after. No guns nor OP, &c, Tks drowned.	
		0925 (approx	B, D, F Tps landed and went into action B 897802, D 888865, F 0945 hrs 904863.	

(3062) Wt 36171/LS? 500M 11/39 BPL 51/5436 Forms C2118/22..

SHEET 2

Commanding Officer Lt. Col. I.G.G.S. HARDIE, RA.

Place	Date	Hour	Summary of Events and Information	References to Appendices
	6	1100	Lt. CALKIN killed by a sniper in LE HAMEL 8786 whilst bringing CO's tank to CO.	
		0900	Two 88mms in action approx 890843; 1030 hrs the two signalers of Capt. BISHOP'S Op party (L/Bdr BLANCHARD and Gnr LEOPOLD) were killed by these guns, which also caused many inf cas. Capt. BISHOP'S wirelesses were both put out of action - he was lent one of the CO's R Signals operators and one of the CO's 68 sets. 68 sets did not react well to the rough handling some received.	
		1200	Capt. BISHOP'S OP 860852.	
		1345	D Coy. 1 DORSET with tk sp take coy posn 856855.	
		1500 (approx)	Fire brought down on enemy bty 852855, in sp of DORSET'S attack - attack successful.	
		1500	Regt. in Sp 151 Bde for Phases III and IV. Co goes to 151 Bde HQ (897863) and moves with them. 357 in sp 6 DLI, 358 8 DLI, 465 9 DLI.	
			Regt. changed to normal 4-frequency wireless layout from 2 frequencies.	
T884851 1400	6	1600 1400	Regt. in action area MEUVAINES 8885. Some shelling by 88 mms. Bdr Prince (465 Bty) killed. L/Sgt WILD (465 Bty) wounded. Posns 357 A 878857 (moved to 876850 after shelling) B approx 876850, 358 area 878852; D tp moving to 888849 (approx) after shelling - two killed (Gnr WYATT and L/Bdr GATES) and two wounded (Sgt GRIFFITHS and L/Bdr CHURCH), 465 E Tp 882851, F Tp 878849.	
		1800	CO2 orders recce of posns in intermediate area (as per OP Order). 1900 hrs recce complete.	
T859819		2030	Regt. in action; 357 area 855821, 358 area 852820, E 862823, F 861822.	
		2100	Phase III of attack complete. CO with 151 Bde HQ 836818.	
T843788	7	0730	CO2 orders recce of new posn in sq 8478. Posns A 844784, B 843787, 358 area 843790, E 847781, F 846780. 465 on Regt grid by 1000 hrs. 357 moved later to this posn.	WM
		1130	Phase IV of attack complete.	

(3062) Wt36171/1838 500M 11/39 BPL 51/5436 Forms C2118/22.

WO 171/929
Intelligence/war diary
102ND ANTI-TANK REGIMENT
(NORTHUMBERLAND HUSSARS) RA

Month and Year June 1944				Commanding Officer Lt. Col. A.K. MATTHEWS, R.A.

Place	Date	Hour	Summary of Events and Information	References to Appendices
FIELD	1		CO and IO in Camp B 8. Nothing to report, not yet loading. Due to leave for embarkation at 1500 hrs but postponed for 24 hrs at 0930.	
	2	1600	Loading commences. Vehicles of the Tac HQ Party line up. Do not move past SP until 1730. Arrive at dock 1920 hrs and eventually commence loading at 0215 hrs 3rd Jun. CO watches local cricket match. Ship with Tac HQ on board moves out to new docks assembly point.	
	3		A cold and dull day with promises of visits to NAAFI and baths ashore. Move off 1930 and arrive 2130 South of CALSHOT. Many craft of all sorts in all	
	4		directions.	
			Sea very rough. Ships do not move. A Service is held in CO's ship by Ship's Captain, and General EISENHOWER's message read out. Possible move at 1245	
	5		cancelled as D-Day has been postponed 24 hrs.	
		1315	Ships sail from SOUTHAMPTON although sea still rough. ROME has been captured by FIFTH and EIGHTH Armies. 50 percent of the troops are seasick.	
	6		<u>D-DAY</u>.	
		0600	Land in sight. A mass of gunfire from our supporting craft. Very little from the shore.	
		0800	Tac HQ ship hits a mine. The ship pulls out and it is decided to try again. On the second attempt another mine blows out the engines. The OC Troops decides to send off a Jeep which goes out of sight under the water. Many vehicles are drowned through foolishness.	
		1130	CO's craft unloads at low tide. Almost dry landings.	
		1200	CO meets Brigadier R.H. SENIOR, DSO, TD, (Commanding 151 Infantry Bde) and GOC 50th (Northumbrian) Infantry Division (Major General D.A.H. GRAHAM, CBE, DSO, MC,) at 895859.	
		1230	CO goes to HQ 69 Bde (920859) to contact the Brigadier and Major G.W. DUNKERLEY, MC., (OC 99 A/Tk Bty RA). IO goes to Tac HQ 50 (Northumbrian) Division at MEUVAINES (890850).	
		1500	IO meets Major G.R. BALFOUR, M.C. (OC 288 A/Tk Bty RA) who gives information that he has 4 × 15cwts, 1 × M.14, and 1 × Jeep drowned and 1 × M.10 with track blown off by a mine.	

SHEET 2

Month and Year June 1944   Commanding Officer Lt. Col. A.K. MATTHEWS, R.A.

Place	Date	Hour	Summary of Events and Information	References to Appendices
FIELD.	6	1800	CO returns to Tac RHQ at MEUVAINES where RHQ M.14 and Signal Section Jeep and trailer join up.	
A + G		2200	Signal Section Humber netted on CRA's Link arrives. Lieutenants TONGUE and VAN BERGEN are wounded.	
	7	0040	CO2 73 A/Tk Regiment RA (Major R. HEMELRYKE, R.A.) reported to Tac RHQ to visit CO.	
		0045	Regiment informed by HQ, RA, that D-Day phases will be completed and exploited during the day.	
		0900	All objectives taken but those of 231 Inf Bde.	
		1045	Lt. G.I.R. MILLIKEN reports to RHQ with Troops. M10 3". He has left 2 Porpoise with 120 rds 3" M 10 amn at 878852.	
		1130	Mopping up in progress at BAYEUX.	
		1215	Infantry being pushed back at 7782.	
		1220	Enemy tanks reported on road ST. LO - BAYEUX.	
		1225	Enemy attack developing on SULLY (7682)	
		1310	Fd Arty engage enemy tanks at SULLY.	
		1325	Infantry hold on at SULLY.	
		1400	"VOLGA". HQ RA move to 830813. Tac RHQ moves with them. CO 73rd A/Tk Regiment RA visits CO.	
		1700	Fighting in PORT EN BESSIN (7587).	
		1705	Tac RHQ arrives at new location.	
		1845	Major R.A. BARNETT, (OC 107 A/Tk Bty RA) and Captain C.R. PAINE, R.A. report to Tac RHQ with 4 × 6 pdrs.	
		2015	Lieutenants P.G. O'NEILL and C. PACKHAM report to Tac HQ with 2 × 6 pdr Troops. They are moving to CREPON (9083) to join 107 Bty.	
		2115	107 Bty move up to relieve 288 Bty in 151 Bde area.	
		2330	Capt. J. LESLIE (Technical Adjutant) reports to Tac HQ.	
	8	0710	288 Bty move off with 8 Armoured Bde.	
		1050	Tank threat from NORTH WEST. 289 Bty move into position WEST of BAYEUX to meet it.	
		1100	Lt. P.G. O'NEILL posted from 289 Bty to 99 Bty.	

Wt.47724/993 2,000,000 3/43 W. H. & S. 51/6375.   To Sheet Number Three......../

WO 171/1596
Intelligence/war diary
233RD FIELD COMPANY RE

Month and Year June 1944   Commanding Officer Major J.R. CAVE BROWNE, R.E.

Place	Date	Hour	Summary of Events and Information	References to Appendices
	1 - 4		Company assembling, marsalling and loading in SOUTHERN ENGLAND prior to Operation "OVERLORD"	
	5th		Operation postponed 24 hours.	
	6th		D Operation "OVERLORD"	
			Zero hour 0725. Weather: Overcast and Cloudy; Sea: Rough.	
			The Company was in the initial stages split up under comd of the Assault and Reserve waves of infantry and accordingly mention is made of individual Platoon achievements. No. 3 Platoon 1 & 4 sections with pl comd and wireless operator landed at H + 5 on KING GREEN beach with the assault wave. They were landed well out to sea below the obstacles and waded ashore. As the last men were leaving the water mortar bombs began to fall on the beach causing casualties. Although the grass in the minefields covering the beach had caught fire and was giving off considerable smoke, the assaulting infantry were taken through the minefields by the 'thug' parties. Casualties sustained during the initial stage made further gapping impossible until	

Wt.47724/993 2,000,000 3/43 W. H. & S. 51/6375

SHEET 2

Month and Year June 1944   Commanding Officer Major J.R. CAVE BROWNE, R.E.

Place	Date	Hour	Summary of Events and Information	References to Appendices
			all sections were collected together - when a further personnel gap was made to the left of the central road: here a shoe mine and 2 French A/Tk mines were lifted.	
			At H + 25 approx, Nos. 2 & 3 sections landed in similar conditions with Pl Sgt. and recce L/Sgt. in comd. The latter was wounded and unable to carry out his task; 3 men in the same LCA were also reported missing - all four have since be recorded as killed in action. The LCA carrying the Pl Sgt and 4 men broke down and was very late in landing. These two reserve sections were grouped together and proceeded up the coastal road which had been flailed. A large crater was near O.P. house had been bridged by ARE, but a further diversion was cleared by these two sections through the flanking minefield. A gap was then made from VER-SUR-MER on the central road through the 88 mm gun position in front of the wood to the open ground on the right.	
			The remaining men of the assault sections were collected on the beach and moved up into VER-SUR-MER to assist in gapping, while a Bulldozer was	
			/called	

Wt.47724/993 2,000,000 3/43 W. H. & S. 51/6375.

SHEET 3

Month and Year June 1944   Commanding Officer Major J.R. CAVE BROWNE, R.E.

Place	Date	Hour	Summary of Events and Information	References to Appendices
			called up to improve the diversion around the crater. In the afternoon the platoon assembled with the remainder of the Coy. which had moved forward to CREPON. Early in the evening 2 & 3 sections went forward to CREUILLY to improve the approaches to an important bridge. Total casualties for the day were: 6 killed, 6 wounded 1 missing. 2 Platoon was divided in the initial phase as follows:- (i) 2 thug parties one with each of the Assaulting Companies of the 5 EY. (ii) 2 assault sections and a reserve section. One of the thug parties had 2 casualties 1 killed 1 wounded. The assault section on the left beach was pinned to the beach by accurate SA fire, while the other succeeded in clearing 2 personnel exits from the beach - casualties: 2 wounded. One track exit was developed left of the NS minefield as far as the coast road, but it was not until 1100 hrs that it was declared open to vehicles. Following the initial assault the platoon proceeded inland clearing debris and creating diversions along route La Riviere - Mont Fleury - Ver-Sur-Mer. It then harboured with remainder of Coy. at	

Wt.47724/993 2,000,000 3/43 W. H. & S. 51/6375.   /CREPON

SHEET 4

Month and Year June 1944   Commanding Officer Major J.R. CAVE BROWNE, R.E.

Place	Date	Hour	Summary of Events and Information	References to Appendices
	7th		CREPON. A recce was completed in the evening for Bde Water point. 1 Platoon landed with the reserve Infantry Coy. and beached 800x to West of expected position at 0810 hours approx. 3 sections of Pl assembled and a gap was made through 80x minefield from beach lateral road to start of inland road to VER-SUR-MER, the 4th section made up "recce party" working inland with the Infantry. Two "Recce" officers and parties landed at H + 5 and H + 45 with tasks of finding a suitable route through the minefield, and securing the bridge at CREUILLY against demolition. Later in the afternoon the forward recce party and two compressors started to demolish a dam which was holding back flood water at the bridge at CREUILLY. Lieut. TURNBULL was wounded on the beach. D + 1 No 4 section 2 PL left at first light to set up water point at CREUILLY and remainder of platoon mobilised to complete task. Water available at 1800 hrs. At 1700 hrs approx the water point was engaged by enemy patrol moving W to E on N side of River SEULLES: pl accounted for 1 Officer and / 1 OR	

Wt.47724/993 2,000,000 3/43 W. H. & S. 51/6375.

WO 171/1625
Intelligence/war diary
295TH FIELD COMPANY RE

Month and Year June 1944   Commanding Officer Major C.W. WOODS RE.

Place	Date	Hour	Summary of Events and Information	References to Appendices
FAWLEY HANTS	MAY 29	–	No. 3 Platoon Briefed. Final packing up preparatory to MiCL.	
	30	–	All troops were marshalled into craft loads, and the company was split between pennerley and Cadlands camps.	
	31	–	All 1st tide troops in LSI embarked.	
	June			
	1-3	–	Embarkation of vehicles.	
	4	–	All troops are on board craft now awaiting the big event, which is scheduled to take place tomorrow, but we hear at 1000 hrs that D-Day is postponed 24 hours owing to bad weather.	
	5	–	We are told after breakfast that D-Day will be tomorrow, there is still a very strong wind and an overcast sky and everyone is most anxious about the weather, but it is too late for any cancellations now.	
	6		The night was quiet and all craft in the convoy passed through the minefield without damage. We arrived at the lowering position at 0430 hrs. The coast of NORMANDY was visible faintly, there	

3043-PMED-500.000-4.42.   /was very

SHEET 2

Month and Year June 1944   Commanding Officer MAJOR C.W. WOODS RE.

Place	Date	Hour	Summary of Events and Information	References to Appendices
AT SEA	6	–	was very spasmodic bombing from shore batteries. Breakfast was given to troops on board LSI before lowering. There was a fresh wind and the sea was choppy.	
		0725	H-Hour was at 0725. The air and other types of support which should have been put on the defences at LE HAMEL failed completely with the result that heavy opposition was met from strong points on the sea wall, which fired LMGs along the beach. These were not finally cleared until after H + 6 hours. Snipers were very troublesome, both on the beach and inland. Very few under-water obstacles were cleared with the result that many landing craft were damaged and beached far out, causing heavy losses in vehicles. The assault platoons managed to open exits from the beach by about H + 2 hours. Movement inland was very slow as the enemy opposition was stiff and continued to a depth of some miles. By the evening most of the company had reached the assembly area	

3043 - PMED - 500.000 - 4.42.   / in ASNELLES

SHEET 3

Commanding Officer MAJOR C.W. WOODS RE.

Place	Date	Hour	Summary of Events and Information	References to Appendices
Le Hamel	6		in ASNELLES. A recce party under Lt. Austin were with the forward troops on the main Bde axis. Two craters, caused by	
RYES	6	2030	RAF bombs were located in the road at RYES and were filled in by bulldozer. The Coy. moved to a harbour area just N of RYES for the night. Casualties during the day were 5 killed and 10 wounded. These were lighter than might have been expected. Vehicle casualties were heavy, and consisted of 3 Half-track M.14s drowned. 3 Compressors drowned 1 Winch 3 ton lorry drowned. 1 jeep drowned. 1 Stella Water trailer drowned several m/c's drowned. The greatest loss on these vehicles was 4 No. 19 and 1 No 22 radio set, comprising almost the entire communications of the Coy.	
RYES	7		No.1 pl swept a 'belly' landing strip clear of mines. Lieut. Meigh recconoitred BAYEUX and discovered a bridge demolition /on the ST. LO road	

3043 - PMED - 500.000 - 4.42.

WO 171/1629
Intelligence/war diary
505TH FIELD COMPANY RE

Month and Year June 1944   Commanding Officer Major C.A. O'B ?pton, MC, RE.

Place	Date	Hour	Summary of Events and Information	References to Appendices
SOUTHAMPTON	1-5		Unit serials load under command DRAFT SERIAL COMMANDERS. Sail at approx 1900 hrs 5 June 44.	WL Kent Capt. R E.
	6		Arrive off beaches at approx 1300 hrs. Nothing unloaded except 2 Recce Parties. 2L/t Round and 11 ORs land at KING RED at 1500 hrs. Lt. Landreth and 9 ORs land at JIG RED at 1530 hrs. Both parties proceed to Assembley Area.	
BEACHES OF FRANCE.		1700	2/Lt. Round and party contact HQ 151 Durham Inf Bde. and send L/Sgt. and 3 ORs with a column of DLI. L/Cpl Duck and 2 OR's sent back to beach to contact Stella water trailers and Bull dozers.	
		1700	LT. Landreth and party locate HQ 50 Div at MEAUVAINS. Recce for Coy. Area near CREPON. L/Cpl. Bird and 1 OR to beach to locate Coy. as it landed and guide into Unit Assembley Area.	
		2100	Both parties locate Coy. Assembley Area CREPON. Bulldozer	

Wt.47724/993 2,000,000 3/43 W. H. & S. 51/6375

SHEET 2

Month and Year June 1944   Commanding Officer Major C.A. O'B C?pton, MC, RE.

Place	Date	Hour	Summary of Events and Information	References to Appendices
BEACHES OF FRANCE.	6	2100	harboured just off Axis Area CREPON.	WL Kent Capt. RE.
		2330	No. 2 Pln. and Lt. Stern, RE landed on KING RED, proceeded to JIG GREEN. Bedded down.	
	7	0600	No. 2 Pln proceeded to MEAUVAINS. O i/c Pln and 6 men recce beaches for Pl Tpt, and Pl Sgt with remainder of Pl and Tpt.	
		1100	Coy Tac HQ and No 1 Pl land on JIG GREEN and proceeded to ARROMANCHE.	
		1900	No. 3 Pl landed on JIG GREEN, and proceeded to Coy. Area at SOMMERVIEU. No. 2 Pl receives orders to move to Coy. Assembly Area at CREPON.	
		1930	Coy Tac HQ and No. 1 Pl arrive Coy. Assembly Area at CREPON and transport joined marching party.	
		2100	2L/t Round reported to CRE at MEUVAINS and received order to establish Coy. area at CREPON and recce Coy. Area at SOMMERVIEU	
		2200	No. 2 Pl received orders to move to SOMMERVIEU.	

Wt.47724/993 2,000,000 3/43 W. H. & S. 51/6375

WO 171/1598
Intelligence/war diary
235TH FIELD PARK COMPANY RE

Month and Year June 1944   Commanding Officer Major I.L. Smith R.E.

Place	Date	Hour	Summary of Events and Information	References to Appendices
BECKTON	1.		NTR.	
	2.	1230.	Embarked on HMT Neuralia at King George V Docks.	
	3-11	-	On board. NTR.	
FRANCE.	6.		Mechanical Equipment consisting of 2 D4, 1 TD9, 1 D6, 1TD 18, and 4 armd. D7 landed on King and Green beaches, between LE HAMEL 8786 and LA RIVIERE 9286, between H-hour and H + 90 Minutes. One armd. D7 and one TD9 drowned. One operator No. 4207363 Spt. Catherine missing, presumed drowned.	REF: MAPS. FRANCE 1/50000 SHEET 7E/5 SHEET 7F/1
			Clearing obstacles on beaches and filling craters on road LE HAMEL - LA RIVIERE. Creating gaps in sea wall for heavy trucks, area 8880.	
		2100	D4 and D7 with 295 Field Company to RYES 8483. Remainder with 233 Field Company to CREPON 9083.	
		1200.	D7 to 295 Field Company.	
	8.	1700.	2 armd. D7 with 295 Field Company to BAYEUX for work on diversion at 782788.	
		1100.	Remainder less D4 to SOMMERVIEU where TD 18 and D6 joined 505 Field Company.	
			2 armd. D7 with operator posted to C.R.E. 104 Sub Beach Area.	
	10.		2 armd. D7 and D4 with operators posted to 51 Mech. Eqpt. Section RE.	
	11.	1200.	(Main Body) Disembarked by LCI at 919868. Marched to Assembly Area at 9082. OC proceeded to Unit concentration area near SOMMERVIEU 838819 where contact was made with Mech. Eqpt. Section under Lieut. J. Christy RE and 15 Bridging Platoon under Lieut. G. Summer RE.	
	12.			
		1400.	Company picked up by transport sent from concentration area.	
		1500.	Arrived at concentration area. Bivouac area organised and workshops set up.	

Wt.47724,993 2,000,000 3/43 W. H. & S. 51/6375.

WO 171/521
Intelligence/war diary
50TH (NORTHUMBRIAN) DIVISIONAL SIGNALS

Month and Year June 1944　　　　　　　　　　　　Commanding Officer Lt. Col. G.B. STEVENSON, R. SIGNALS.

Place	Date	Hour	Summary of Events and Information	References to Appendices
AT SEA	4		for 24 hours. Force remains anchored in SOLENT.	
	5	0700	In spite of continued bad weather, force begins to sail, slowest craft going first. Later in the day there is a slight improvement in weather.	
		1845	HQ Ship sails via NEEDLES channel. At last light the ISLE OF WIGHT is still just visible astern. All wireless silent but listening watch is kept from time of sailing on the lateral link to Force U, 5 US Corps.	
	6	0500	As we approach the French coast, it is possible to see the flashes and explosions of the preliminary air bombardment.	
		0600	Arty bombardment starts from warships and SP arty in LCT.	
			Weather is still far from good as, though the wind has dropped, there is quite a considerable swell.	
			Most of the coast defence batteries have been silenced on our sector but there is one gun still firing which might be a nuisance, and has in fact got a bracket on the HQ ship. No sign of enemy air activity.	

SHEET 2

Month and Year June 1944　　　　　　　　　　　　Commanding Officer Lt. Col. G.B. STEVENSON, R. SIGNALS.

Place	Date	Hour	Summary of Events and Information	References to Appendices
AT SEA	6	0710	H - 15 minutes - Wireless silence broken on all nets; communication established all round very quickly with very little interference.	
			The ships signal sections work extremely well and are largely responsible for the efficient working.	
			Details of communications at H-hour and subsequently are given in the OVERLORD Signal Instruction.	
		0720	W/T Dets 5 E Yorks and 6 G Howards (2 assault bns 69 Bde) have rough landings with heavy seas and enemy action with snipers and mortar bombs. 5 E Yorks Det pinned down with infantry for over an hour against shelter of sea wall.	
		0750	Tac 231 Bde leave HMS NITH in LCM with Bde comds Recce in a jeep.	
		0830	1 Hants fail to answer on 231 Bde A as handcart, station and operators landed in deep water and had to swim ashore.	
		0905	231 Bde LCM hit by shell and sinks. Bde Comds Recce jeep and set lost but Cpl. Divison manages to get the carrier ashore with all personnel	

SHEET 3

Month and Year June 1944   Commanding Officer Lt. Col. G.B. STEVENSON, R. SIGNALS.

Place	Date	Hour	Summary of Events and Information	References to Appendices
AT SEA	6	0905	by skilful driving.	
			Tac 231 Bde HQ proceed to M.B.S.S. as all W/T sets are drowned, where HQ set up and full use made of Beach Signal communications.	
			69 Bde Sigs lose their M.14, this dropping into deep water, then jugging along and eventually disappearing from view in the wake of the line jeep into a deep water-filled bomb crater. BM 69 Bde party incl Lt. A.G. Conroy, R.Signals have to swim for it.	
		1000	Replacement set for 47 RM Commando found by 231 Bde.	
			Tac Div HQ reports it is ashore but unable to get off the beach.	
			Assault Bdes (69 & 231) progressing inland slowly.	
			Bde HQs W/T has taken over from Beach Signals. In the case of 69 Bde they have had to keep two wireless sets complete from Beach Signals with some charging sets.	
			Tac 151 Bde HQ transferred to LCM containing carrier and jeep.	
			Heavy swell running and much seasickness amongst personnel.	

1622/PMEA/1-500.000-9/41.   Page 5

SHEET 4

Month and Year June 1944   Commanding Officer Lt. Col. G.B. STEVENSON, R. SIGNALS.

Place	Date	Hour	Summary of Events and Information	References to Appendices
AT SEA	6	1100	GOC leaves HQ ship to join Tac Div ashore.	
		1130	151 Tac Bde touch down on beach and land successfully. Marching personnel in LCI's have water 'breast high' on landing.	
			Handcart W/T sets float ashore alright.	
		1245	151 Bde HQ are reorganised at VER-SUR-MER.	
MEUVAINES		1300	GOCs party just joined Tac Div in MEUVAINES. Tac party landed without casualties but one jeep with 19 set drowned which was later recovered.	
		1330	Tac Div. HQ takes over control on Div. A and CRA waves from HQ ships.	
		1400	Duplicate 231 Bde HQ joins Tac HQ at MBSS 22 set handcart stations at 1 Hants and 1 Dorsets replaced by M. 14's with 19 sets. The M.14 attached 2 Devons had been drowned on landing.	
			1 Hants clearing pockets of enemy resistance in LE HAMEL.	
		1500	Mobile column of 6 and 9 DLI (151 Bde) push forward to first objective which is high ground E. of BAYEUX.	

1622/PMEA/1-500.000-9/41.   Page 6

SHEET 5

Commanding Officer Lt. Col. G.B. STEVENSON, R. SIGNALS.

Place	Date	Hour	Summary of Events and Information	References to Appendices
MEUVAINES	6	1600	Marching parties arrive at Div. HQ with additional wireless sets and signal office equipment.	
		1645	Brig. Senior, Comd 151 Bde, with L/Cpl Horton, MM reported missing, believed captured, holding all Div. code signs and codes for next 14 days. Impossible to take any action.	Why?
		1800	More vehicles of line section and two CVs HP arrive together with Corps Comds CV to work to Army Comd.	
		2359	All communications established and working except AIMBW for which Beach signals have no sets.	
			Disembarking is many hours behind schedule.	
			Casualties in the unit are as shown :-	
			14328060 Sigmn HARRIS J. (20 Beach Sig Sec) ⎫ ⎬ Killed in action 2385859 Sigmn VANE J. (69 Bde Sigs) ⎭	
			14381374 Sigmn CAIRNS A.C. (69 Bde Sigs) ⎫ ⎬ Wounded in action 3718547 Corpl KELLETT T.C. (69 Bde Sigs) ⎭	

SHEET 6

Commanding Officer Lt. Col. G.B. STEVENSON, R. SIGNALS.

Place	Date	Hour	Summary of Events and Information	References to Appendices
MEUVAINES	6		2362602 Sigmn HODGES W.F. (69 Bde Sigs) ⎫ ⎬ Wounded in action 2381804 L/Cpl DEWHIRST J. (231 Bde Sigs) ⎭	
			2584843 L/Cpl HORTON P.J. MM (151 Bde Sigs) Missing believed captured	
	7	0300	Further parties of D-Day personnel land.	
		0700	K Sec (231 Bde) still unable to get in W/T touch with 47 RM Commando and 16 RCT.	
			Swarms of British fighters overhead.	
			Pte Abbott, cook in L Sec, reports with 16 German prisoners from ST. GABRIELE.	
			Transport in Bde sections was mainly 'Shanks Pony' or bicycles.	
			Recce party goes forward to select new location for Div HQ in area SOMMERVIEU.	
		0900	OC 3 Coy. reports Sigmn Vane J. (L Sec) previously reported killed, now reported wounded in action and evacuated.	
		1000	Bdes pushing forward to objectives and encountering stubborn resistance.	

WO 177/735

Intelligence/war diary
149TH FIELD AMBULANCE RAMC

Month and Year June 44   Commanding Officer Lt. Col. S.R. TRULLY

Place	Date	Hour	Summary of Events and Information	References to Appendices
ROMSEY	1	1800	Fine & Warm. Sub. units commenced moving to embarkation points SRT.	
HANTS AT SEA	2	1800	Fine & Warm. Embarkation in progress. Craft moved into SOUTHAMPTON Water as loaded S.R.T.	
	3	1800	Cooler. Dry. Embarkation continued. D-Day parties at Sea. Reembarked ashore SRT.	
	4	1800	Cool, dull, patches high wind. Situation unchanged.	
	5	1800	Weather improved. D day Convoy sailed during afternoon & evening.	
THE BAYEUX REMAINDER, FRANCE	6	1800	Fine & Warm. Assault Sections landed with Bus of DLI. 151 (Durham) mt Bale on FRENCH COAST just west of the Hanne U 8786 approximated 1000 hrs. B.u. H+2½. Moved with Bus. K continues objectives during day. One Casualty in Coy. Most D-Day tps unloaded during day, but some of it delayed owing to difficulty in offloading LSFs on to rhino. ferries Sut.	
	7	1800	Fine & Warm Remainder of D-Day tps landed also D&I Marching party of 298 & 330. Ro B Coy. m section moved up to final Bdm objectives during morning. During Afternoon Sections Coalesced to form ADS at u 822763. HQ Marching party Concentrated at 885835. Brigade casualties light SRT.	
	8	1800	Dull. little rain. D + 1 day tps landed (24 hrs late) moved up to form HQ at 885835.	

Wt.13161/317 200/000 5/39 H.E.J.Ltd. 51-3911 Forms C2118/21

WO 177/785
Intelligence/war diary
186TH FIELD AMBULANCE RAMC

Month and Year June 1944   Commanding Officer Lt. Col. C.W. ARNOT, OBE, MC, RAMC.

Place	Date	Hour	Summary of Events and Information	References to Appendices
SOUTHAMPTON AREA.	1		Unit marshalled by Serial Nos. and Craft loads, in sealed camps preparatory to embarkation for Operation Overlord.	CWA
-do-	2	0800	Routine. One OR, RASC sick, evacuated to hospital. 2/Lt. J.E. Young, RAMC, posted to No. 1 Depot and T.E. Aldershot.	CWA
	3		Embarkation for D-Day personnel proceeds.	
AT SEA	4		Nil to report.	CWA
-do-	5		D-Day postponed for 24 hours owing to bad weather.	CWA
-do-	6	0720	H-Hour.	
-do- MR 914866 Sheet 7E5 CREULLY		0815	OC lands on KING RED Beach and contacts on the beaches sections of "B" Company who are to accompany the assault Battalions, 5 East Yorks and 6 Green Howards in a mobile role. Sections despatched to their respective Bns. Casualties treated and nested on the beaches en route. OC recces unit assembly area which had also been previously earmarked from the map as the site for the Beach FDS. The site was considered unsuitable for the FDS which was established in the school at VER-SUR-MER. Pending their establishment in the school an Aid Post was established by A Section from H.Q. Coy. (Capt. D. Joy) at the original site. This section lands at 1200 hours. Four Jeep Amb Cars (and four Motor Cycles land at H + 45 mins. Used for evacuation of casualties, at first to Beach Dressing	CW. Arnot Appx. A, B, C

Wt. 52938/1102 660M. 2/44 W. H. & S. 51-9071.

SHEET 2

Commanding Officer Lt. Col. C.W. ARNOT, OBE, MC, RAMC.

Place	Date	Hour	Summary of Events and Information	References to Appendices
MR 914866	6 cont.		Station and later to Beach FDS.	
			OC during the course of the morning contacts HQ 69 Bde., RM Os. of 69 Bde and constant liaison maintained with these and with sections of B Coy. attached to the battalions. Contact also maintained with sections of B Coy., 149 Fd. Amb. and RMOs. Of 151 Bde.	
		0900	Four Motor Cycles land.	
		1600	OC recces Bazenville district for suitable ADS. site, but finds it still occupied by the enemy who are holding isolated strong points. Site for ADS chosen at MR 885833. One 3 ton-lorry and one 4-str. Ambulance Car land.	
		1700	Major W.S. Gale, RAMC and 39 ORs land.	
			6 2-str. Ambulance cars, 3 15-cwt trucks, 1 3-tonlorry, 1 4-str. Ambulance car, and 4 Motor Cycles land.	
		1800	Personnel and Vehicle Assembly Area established at VER-SUR-MER.	
		2130	DS opened at MR 885833 by H: Q. and "A" Coy.	
		2200	DMS 50 (Northumbrian) Division (Col. J. Melvin) visits unit. Lt. Col. White, MBE., OC, 5 East Yorks evacuated wounded.	
MR 885833 Sheet 7E5 CREULLY	7	0930	Capt. I. M. Kerr RAMC and 27 ORs land.	CWA
			Landing delayed 12 hours owing to rough weather.	
			DS receiving casualties from 69 and 151 Bdes and 8 Armd. Bde.	
		1045	Message received from B Coy., 149 Fd. Amb notifying establishment of Light ADS at MR 817762.	
		1100	OC contacts HQ and RMOs. 69 Bde., Sections of B Coy.,	

Wt.52938/1102 660M. 2/44 W. H. & S. 51-9071.

WO 177/799
Intelligence/war diary
200TH FIELD AMBULANCE RAMC

Month and Year June 1944   Commanding Officer Lt. Col. W.A. ROBINSON OBE

Place	Date	Hour	Summary of Events and Information	References to Appendices
	1	0630	Embarkation of some serials of unit commenced	WAR
Marshalls one as	2		" " " continued	WAR
Marshalls one as	3		" all " completed.	WAR
AT SEA	4		On board LSI, LST, + LCT in SOUTHAMPTON water	WAR
AT SEA	5	0730	Force "G" (Carrying 231 Bde) sailed for French coast	WAR
			Voyage uneventful - no enemy interference	WAR
LA HAMEL	6	0740	H-hour of D-Day.	WAR
		0800	Assault secus: land E (Resume Coss of	WAR
		0815	Assault Bur. Late in landings; Sea cough. Wrong Beach enemy strongpoints not neutralized by Air and sea bombardment. ULO party landed late.	WAR
		0900	CO landed. Casualties town personnel – Lt. W.L. Pain missing believed drowned, Pte. Bower. ditto Pte. Armstrong killed; these occurred while landing.	WAR WAR WAR

Wt.47724/993 2,000,000 3/43 W. H. & S. **51**/6375.

SHEET 2

Month and Year June 1944   Commanding Officer Lt. Col. W.A. ROBINSON OBE

Place	Date	Hour	Summary of Events and Information	References to Appendices
FRANCE	6	0900	Casualties of Bus: collected into nests. One orderly left with each nest. There were later picked up by Fd-Amb SBS: and taken DBDS which was very late in landing (all times landing were delayed)	WAR
	"	1500	Main First Tide party Q HQ landed (three hours late). ADS at: MR. 882862 (Sheet 7E/5 France 1,50,000) raking over from RAP 1)Dorsets all car	
		1600	evacuated DBDS 31 FDS (Beach Group) arrived and look over site prior to moving to a second file)	
	6 to 7	1700	HQ ADS moved to BUHOT 8 MR. 862855 (same sheet) and were receiving casualties from Lt. Sees, and, later, 203 Fd. Amb.	
		0630	Div. Cdr. visited HQ ADS.	
		0800	CO visited sects and FDS.	WAR

Wt. 47724/998 2,000,000 3/43 W. H. & S. **51**/6575.

WO 171/525
Intelligence/war diary
50TH (NORTHUMBRIAN)
DIVISIONAL PROVOST COMPANY

Month & Year. June 1944   Commanding Officer – Capt. W.R. HUNTER, Camero?.

Place	Date June	Hour	Summary of Events and Information	Remarks and references to Appendices
On board HMT "GLENROY"	1 to 4		Nil.	
"	4		Sgt. i/c 151 Bde. Sect. to Hospital ex Ship. RSM with 151 Bde. Sect.	WRH
"	5	17.00	Sailed for FRANCE.	
"	6	06.00	Bde. Sections & Officers landed in LCAs. Sea rough – wet landing.	WRH
FRANCE			5 Casualties. Beach exits & routes to assembly areas & Div. area marked.	
"	6	15.00	Coy. HQ disembarked. Location MEAUVAINES MR 893850. 56 Bde Sect. MR 910854 (Ver-sur-Mer), MR 863822, MR 842819 (SOMMERVIEU). Sheet 37/18 SE. 8 ORs. PW received.	WRH
"	7		Location same. 1 Casualty. 1 Officer & 19 ORs PW received.	
"	7	14.00	Coy. HQ move to MR 824807. 56 Bde Sect. to MR 831829. 151 Bde Sect. to MR 818758 (Damigny) & 817763. 69 Bde Sect. to VER-SUR-MER, VILLIERS BLE Sec & St. Gabriel. 231 Bde Sect. to ST. COME-DE-FREUL & MEAUVAINES 1:1,000,000 Sheet 7F. Lt. McCall to Coy. HQ. from 69th Bde Sect. 4 ORs PW received.	WRH
"	8		Lt.1\2 McCall to Main Div. HQ. 69th. Bde Sect to St Leger, 231 Bde Sect to SOMMERVIEU & 56 Bde Sect to BAYEUX 1 Officer & 39 ORs PW received.	WRH
"	9	15.00	Coy. HQ to MR 825810. PW Cage established 117 ORs PW received. RSM Beer i/c 151 Bde Sect.	WRH
"	10		RSM Beer in to Coy. HQ. from 151 Bde Sect. Sgt & ½ Sect to BAYEUX. 231 relieve 56 Bde outside BAYEUX. 56 Bde Sect return to Coy. HQ. 2 Officers & 77 ORs PW received.	WRH
"	11		68 ORs PW received. 69 Bde Sect to DUOY ST. MARGUERITE. Sgt. to 151 Bde Sect.	WRH
"	12		21 ORs PW received. Coy. HQ to MR 814767. PW Cage opened.	WRH
"	13		Main Div Sect to South of BLARY. 69 Bde resting. 231 Bde Sect to MR 783735 (ST. AMATOR) 3 L/Cpls Reinforcements arrive. 5 ORs PW received.	WRH
"	14		231 Bde Sect to MR 774718 (Tringy). ½ Sect withdrawn from BAYEUX. Sect to 56 Bde at MR 805732. & 151 Bde Sect to MR 818725 (Jerusalem) 6 ORs in PW Cage.	WRH

1623/PME/2 – 150000 – 9/41.

UNITS
ATTACHED TO
BRITISH
50TH INFANTRY
DIVISION FOR
THE ASSAULT

WO 171/613

Intelligence/war diary

8TH ARMOURED BRIGADE HQ

<u>SERIAL No. 52. JUNE 1944</u>

Place	Date	Hour	Summary of Events and Information 1	Remarks and references to Appendices
	1 to 4		Personnel to be landed on D-Day in forthcoming operations were marshalled from sealed camps in area ROMSEY - WINCHESTER BY ship loads to craft at SOUTHAMPTON and loaded.	See sheet 11 for list of Appendices
	5		D-Day postponed 24 hrs owing to rough weather.	
	6		D-DAY. H Hour was 0640. There was a very heavy swell and the sky was heavily overcast. The DD S qns of 4/7 D.G. and SRY were not launched as planned and except for a few tanks which made a swim of up to 50 yds all DD tanks were landed from their LCTs.	
			Opposition on the beaches was only light except for two 88 mm guns on the high ground Pt 22 MR 8885 which brewed up 4 SRY tanks on the beach. There was little or no observed arty fire on to the beaches. The main trouble was from congestion. The beach at high water was extremely narrow and the exits inadequate.	
			On the right 231 Bde with SRY met very strong opposition in LE HAMEL 8786. Lt. Col. J. D'Anderson SRY was wounded by a sniper and Major Laycock assumed command SRY.	Appx "A"
			By midday little progress had been made to BUHOT 8684. On the left 4/7 D.G. by D + 100 got one Sqn. up on to MONT FLEUAY 9185. With two Sqns. and Flails from W. Dgns they supported the attack of 69 Bde from the West into LA RIVERE 9286.	
			By noon LA RIVERE, MONT FLEUAY and VER-SUR-MER 9184 had been cleared.	
			Bde Tac HQ landed about H + 70 and moved after an hour to 898849, moving later to its final location for the day at 896847.	
			The build up of the follow up Bde was delayed by the weather and the congestion on the beach exits. During the afternoon 4/7 DG pushed on South supporting 69 Bde with two Sqns and 151 Bde with one Sqn. Resistance came from small pockets of enemy Infantry. One of these held the Bde concentration area BAZENVILLE 8182 until the evening.	
			By 1800 hrs 4/7 DG reported CREULLY 9080 lightly held and the bridge unblown. One Sqn 4/7 DG with 151 Bde reached the river bend 8579. Before last NIGHT 4/7 DG were reporting little resistance for 3000 yds South of the River towards ST. LEGER.	
			SRY during the afternoon were heavily involved with 231 Bde in street fighting in LE HAMEL where enemy opposition was most fierce. BUHOT was taken during the afternoon and progress made to the high ground to the West.	
			In the early evening one Sqn SRY came in support 56 Bde which began to advance on BAYEUX. By last light SRY had reported good progress. BAYEUX did not appear to be held in strength, if at all, and SRY reached ST. VIGO? 7980.	

Place	Date	Hour	Summary of Events and Information 2	Remarks and references to Appendices
	6 (Cont)		By last light practically none of the forces for the proposed mobile column (see O.O. No. 25) had been landed. No tanks of 24 L due on the second tide came in. The Brigade at last light on D-Day had two Regts committed and no reserve force landed.	Appx 'B'
	7		At first light the advance continued on right and left. [By midday SRY had reported BAYEUX clear and sent patrols down the roads running SE, S and SW from the town. Progress during the afternoon was steady towards the Phase IV objectives which were taken and secured by 1800 hrs.	
			4/7 DG with 151 and 69 Bdes advanced to the ST. LEGER feature and the line of the railway West of NONANT 8275 and these Phase IV positions were consolidated.]	
			Tanks of 24 L began to land during the day and by the evening two S qns less R.H.Q. had landed and assembled in the area 8984. Lt. Col. WAC Anderson Comd 24 L reported during the afternoon that in general the LST's would not close the beach and the sea was too heavy for tanks to land from RHINO FERRIES.	
			At 1500 hrs Tac HQ moved to 878773 and at 1800 hrs the first increment of Main Bde HQ arrived. The area South of the road 881776 was allotted as B Ech area and Regtl B Ech vehicles began assembling there during the evening.	
			[At 2200 hrs Bde Comd received codeword YAR, the order to form the mobile column (see OO No. 25) on the morning of June 8.] Warning order was sent to all comds concerned.	Appx 'B'
			[24 L were unloaded during the late afternoon and the Regt. was ready for action by midnight.]	

WO 171/861
Intelligence/war diary
THE NOTTINGHAMSHIRE YEOMANRY
(THE SHERWOOD RANGERS)

Month and Year June 1944   Commanding Officer Lt. Col. J.D.A. ANDERSON DSO.

Place	Date	Hour	Summary of Events and Information	References to Appendices
S. ENGLAND	1		Lt. Col. Anderson visited various camps. The weather is still cold and there is a possibility that the forthcoming exercise may be postponed. Feeding arrangements and the quality of the food differed considerably in each of the staging camps. Camp C.10. appears to be quite the best organised.	
	2		The Regiment left from the various camps for loading from the various Lands at SOUTHAMPTON Docks .The organisation for this complicated move was remarkable both as regards movement itself, replenishment rations etc. most of the Regiments, including DD Squadrons embarked on the tank landing craft, which was completed by early evening.	
	3		The Regiment has been embarked on craft belonging to 15 and 43. LCT Flotilla	

3043 - PMED - 500,000 - 4,42.

SHEET 2

Month and Year June 1944   Commanding Officer Lt. Col. J.D.A. ANDERSON DSO.

Place	Date	Hour	Summary of Events and Information	References to Appendices
At Sea	3		The weather is still unpleasant.	
			All the craft moved off from the quayside and anchored out of SOUTHAMPTON water. Most of the craft are crammed with vehs and tps have difficulty in moving and finding sufficient space to sleep at nights. Owing to bad weather the exercise was postponed 24 hrs. The Padre managed to conduct services in two of the craft which were drawn up alongside each other.	
	5		The Invasion Fleet sailed at 1230. The weather was windy and cold. We all expected some kind of enemy interference, but we experienced no trouble at all.	
	6		D-Day. H-Hr 0725. Regt in sp of 231 Bde. who were assaulting beaches between LE HAMEL on WEST and LA RIVIERS on EAST. B Sqn. (DD) were supporting	

3043 - PMED - 500,000 - 4.42.

SHEET 3

Month and Year June 1944   Commanding Officer Lt. Col. J.D.A. ANDERSON DSO.

Place	Date	Hour	Summary of Events and Information	References to Appendices
	6th		1 HAMPS on night and b Sqn (DD) were 1 DORSETS on left. The two DD Sqns. were due to touch down at H-5 after a tremendous bombardment from air and sea along the whole length of beach, and on all known enemy posns. "A" Sqn. was to arrive at H + 90 in sp of DEVONS. Owing to bad weather the DD Sqns did not swim in, but were landed on the beach, and as a result of this, the plan became rather disorganised. Owing to bad weather "B" Sqn had 5 tanks drowned and "B" Sqn. 3 tanks drowned, but most of the crews were rescued. A Sqn landed at H + 90, and by that time the beaches were incredibly congested, and at one period the situation appeared rather difficult. However, vehs gradually made progress and the Regt eventually assembled in the neighbourhood of BHOT according to plan, where it passed into sp of 59 Bde. 56? 69?	

3043 - PMED - 500,000 - 4.42.

SHEET 4

Place	Date	Hour	Summary of Events and Information	References to Appendices
	6th		Lt. Col. Anderson was wounded when endeavouring to find a way to the village of LE HAMEL which continued to hold out in spite of terrific bombardment.	
			Lt. Horley was killed as he was bringing his tank on to the beach.	
			Capt. Enderby was wounded when his landing craft received a direct hit from an 88 mm.	
			"A" Sqn, having arrived at BUHOT after completing a circular route through MEUVAINES, from there moved on to RHEYS in sp of DEVONS. from there they had to move back to sp the ESSEX.	
			That evening B&C Sqns. leaguered together in the neighbourhood of BUHOT and "a" sqn leaguered with the ESSEX just short of BAYEUX.	
			Having got clear of the beaches	

3043 . PMED . 500,000 . 4.42.

SHEET 5

Place	Date	Hour	Summary of Events and Information	References to Appendices
	6th		we have not met a great deal of opposition except from enemy snipers, and Lt. Holman met one at 20 yds, who had fired at him with a rifle, and in return he fired back with his 75 mm, and completely knocked his head off.	
	[7th		L "A" Sqn, with the ESSEX, attacked BAVEUX, "B" Sqn. With (DSWB) came in from the NORTH. "C" Sqn. remained in reserve with RHQ in ST. SULPICE.	
	[8th		8 Armd Bde Gp with various sp. arms is formed up into a mobile coln to move South. This Regt. is given the task of a minor night look in order to capture some high ground known as Pt. 103. The Regt. moved with remarkable speed and in spite of minor enemy opposition from A'Tk guns positioned itself on Pt 103 at approx 1600 hrs. Pt. 103 held.	

3043 . PMED . 500,000 . 4.42.

WO 171/838
Intelligence/war diary
4TH/7TH ROYAL DRAGOON GUARDS

Month and Year June, 1944   Commanding Officer Lt. Col. R.G. BYRON.

Place	Date	Hour	Summary of Events and Information	References to Appendices
SOUTHAMPTON	5		Sherman Mk V specially equipped for swimming with twin propellors and collapsible canvas sides (to give freeboard when afloat and prevent water coming actually on to the top of the tank) set sail in the morning and 51 Flotilla carrying "A" & RHQ tanks set sail at 1230 hrs. D-Day is to-morrow. H-Hours (i.e. time of A.V.R.E. touching down) is 0725 hrs. Maps were distributed on the craft and all informed of actual place of landing. As practised on all recent exercises "B" Sqn were to come in on the right and support 6 Green Howards in the assault and "C" Sqn on the left supporting the 5 E Yorks: "A" Sqn coming in with RHQ at H 60 to support the 7 Green Howards. The sea was moderate to rough and all the craft were tossed about quite a bit.	
LA RIVIERE	6	0720	"B" & "C" landed (being put right in by the LCTs as the sea was too rough for DD) on the FRENCH coast on the beach running west from LA RIVIERE (on the coastline between CAEN & BAYEUX):	

Wt.47724/993 2,000,000 3/43 W. H. & S. 51/6375.

SHEET 2

Month and Year June, 1944   Commanding Officer Lt. Col. R.G. BYRON.

Place	Date	Hour	Summary of Events and Information	References to Appendices
LA RIVIERE	6	0720	this is the spearhead of the 30 Corps assault with the Canadians on our left and Americans on our right. The assault went well and after some trouble in getting off the beach "B" & "C" pushed on with their infantry inland. Lieut. D. Mann and Lieut.W.M.A.Lewis were rounded by snipers in LA RIVIERE and Sgt. Vaughan of "C" Sqn was killed while commanding his tank.	
		0850	"A" & RHQ were all successfully brought in but two tanks of "A" Sqn. failed to get off the shore, one going into a large shell hole on the shore. The beach now was very crowded and narrow as the tide was rising but as yet we were not under fire, the enemy seeming to have been taken completely by surprise.
			Opposition met was from isolated pockets, platoon localities and snipers: the infantry worked closely with the tanks.
	7		Early stand to a 0430 hrs. [Move further South through CREULLY on to BRECY with "A" Sqn. leading.] 69 Inf Bde were in front and

Wt.47724/993 2,000,000 3/43 W. H. & S. 51/6375.

WO 171/849
Intelligence/war diary
24TH LANCERS

Month and Year June 1944   Commanding Officer Lt. Col. D.A.L. ANDERSON

Place	Date	Hour	Summary of Events and Information	References to Appendices
SOUTHAMPTON WATER	1-3		The Regiment remained in LSTs	P.I
	4		Information was received that D-Day was postponed for 24 hours.	AG
	5		Information was received that the operation moved begin on 6 June	
		1800	The convoy left SOUTHAMPTON Water and crossed the channel during the night. There was no enemy interference with the crossing and all the LSTs which carried the Regiment arrived safely.	AG
ASNELLES	6		The Regiment was lying up in LSTs off ASNELLES in the late morning. During the evening most of "B" sgns tanks disembarked also some tanks and other vehicles from "A" and "C" sgns. Few enemy aircraft were observed during the day. and the AA opposition put up by the numerous small craft off the FRENCH COAST was very considerable.	AG

Wt.34859/1676 800,000 11/43 W. H. & S. 51-7676.

SHEET 2

Month and Year June 1944   Commanding Officer Lt. Col. D.A.L. ANDERSON

Place	Date	Hour	Summary of Events and Information	References to Appendices
			The Regiment suffered the following casualties during the month of June.	

Officers: 4 killed, 23 wounded.

ORs: 20 killed, 95 wounded, 4 missing believed killed.

The Regiment lost 28 tanks destroyed and 10 damaged.

The Regiment inflected the following casualties in vehicles an the enemy during the same period.

Tanks destroyed	19
ATM guns	2
SP guns	3
½ tracked vehicles	5
Armoured cars	5.

Wt.47724/993 2,000,000 3/43 W. H. & S. 51/6375.

WO 171/995

Intelligence/war diary
147TH ESSEX YEOMANRY FIELD REGIMENT RA

Month and Year June 1944

Place	Date	Hour	Summary of Events and Information	References to Appendices
FAWLEY	1	RFW	RHQ established at Camp B2, FAWLEY.	
SOUTHAMPTON	3	RFW	RHQ afloat.	
	4	RFW	Attempt to set sail for OVERLORD. OVERLORD postponed 24 hours owing to adverse weather conditions.	
	5	RFW	OVERLORD expedition sails.	
FRANCE	6	RFW	D-Day OVERLORD. H-Hour - 0730 hours.	
			RHQ lands 0930 hours on Jig Red Beach.	
			Major R.B. Gosling, Battery Commander, 431 Battery, wounded - Capt. M.G. Beale assumes command.	
			SP 25-pr, 511 Battery, knocked out two A/Tk guns at LE HAMEL with open sight shooting.	
			RHQ established by 1200 hours 908863.	
		1430	FOOs with I Hamps reported still mopping up in LE HAMEL.	
			RHQ established night 6/7 June 836828.]	
			431 Battery supported Royal Marine Commando attack on PORT EN BESSIN.	
	7	RFW	Remainder of Regiment in support 56 Inf Bde.	
			BAYEUX reported captured by 1530 hours.	
			Location RHQ 1745 hours - 830757.	
			RHQ moved 0830 hours to RUCQUEVILLE 874774.	
	8	RFW	One troop continued to support Royal Marine Commando. Reminder of Regiment under command 8 Armd Bde.	
			Regiment in conjunction with 86 Fd Regt supported 8 Armd Bde attack - areas BRONAY, PUTOT EN BESSIN. Attack meets stiff opposition.	
			RHQ spends night same position.]	
			Major C.J. Sidgwick, Battery commander, 413 Battery, wounded - Capt E.C.B. Edwards assumes command.	
			Several 'Y' targets engaged.	
	[9	RFW	8 Armd Bde advance form RUCQUEVILLE area to Point 103 Square 8570.	
			RHQ established at 854707 - all vehicles arrived safely.	
			Regiment 8 Armd Bde now two miles further into FRANCE than any other Allied Unit.]	
			[Sunday 'M' targets shot - fire support given by 86 Fd Regt in addition.	
			FOOs with I Dorsets reported heavy and bitter fighting at ST. PIERRE.	
			ST. PIERRE held by us at last light. Enemy holding TILLY-SUR-SEULLES. Dividing line between troops being RIVER SEULLES.]	

(3110) Wt. 35842/1764 1000M 12/39 BPL. 51/5684 Forms C2118/22.

WO 171/1801

Intelligence/war diary
6TH ASSAULT REGIMENT RE HQ

Month and Year June 44   Commanding Officer Lt. Col. R.P.G. ANDERSON. RE.

Place	Date	Hour	Summary of Events and Information	References to Appendices
STANSWOOD, HANTS	1	2000hrs	Moved to Marshalling Camp C21 and C13.	
SOUTHAMPTON	2	1600"	Loaded onto LST. CRE, RSO and 3 men onto LST 2816; Adjt, T.O. and 2 men onto LST 2815. Craft moved into Solent to anchor.	
AT SEA	5		Craft moved into ENGLISH CHANNEL to cross to FRANCE.	
FRANCE (NORMANDY)	6		Lay off beaches on "KING" sector.	
		2230	Adjt & pty off loaded onto Rhino ferry for landing.	
	7	0030	Landed opposite LA RIVIERE nr VER-SUR-MER. Moved to harbor with 81 Assault	
			Sqn. RE near CREPON. CRE & pty landed 1700 hrs and joined Adjt. at TAC 50 Div.	
MEUVAINES	8	0900	Joined Tac HQ 50 (N) Div at MEUVAINES 8985.	
SOMMERVIEU		1600	Moved to new locn tac HQ 50 Div nr SOMMERVIEU 8181.	
ST. SULPICE	9	1500	RHQ moved to st SULPICE 8181.	
	9	1500	Office truck with 10 ORs and 2 trucks LAD with EME and 9 ORs landed and joined RHQ at St SULPICE 8181.	
	10		6 ARRE placed under comd 30 Corps	
LE MONNERIE	13	1100	Moved to LE MONNERIE 790766	
NONANT	13	1700	Moved to NONANT 832757	
	15	1800	Placed under comd 30 Corps for adm.	
	16	0930	D + 5 lorry and two R. Sigs trucks reported to RHQ. I.O. & 130Rs.	
	18	0600	6 ARRE placed under comd 50 (N) Div. ½Tp 149 Assault PK Sqn. reported RHQ.	
	20		6 ARRE less 82 Sqn reverted to 30 Corps comd.	
	21		82 Sqn. revert to comd 6 ARRE (under 30 Corps)	
	22	0900	81 Sqn. go under comd 8 Corps & move to ST. GABRIEL mr 8979	
	23		82 Sqn. go under comd 49 Div. D + 11 Residents reported to RHQ.	
	1			
	30		Halting & Report.	
			Lt. Col. R.E. Comd. 6 Assault Regt. R.E.	

22293 Wt. 33096/1140 1,000m 12/4c-McC & Co Ltd-51-8212 Forms C2118/22.

WO 171/1809
Intelligence/war diary
81ST ASSAULT SQUADRON. RE

Month and Year June 44   Commanding Officer Major R.E. THOMPSTONE, RE.

Place	Date	Hour	Summary of Events and Information	References to Appendices
SOLENT	4	0730	D-Day postponed one day to 6 June. Remained on LCT in SOLENT (.) Very rough (.) Too many on each craft, average of 34 men of the assault teams, and 25 men of 280 Fd. Coy. RE on each craft (.) Tank decks wet and no where for men to go to keep dry and sleep properly.	R.E.T
AT SEA	5	0730	All craft sailed (.) still rough and big swell when past The NEEDLES (.) Most men feeling slightly sea sick in spite of tablets (.) This has rather damped the excellent heart of all men.	R.E.T
[VER-SUR-MER Sheet No 37/18 S.E. FRANCE 1/25000 Ref. 9185	6	0645 0700	Sighted French coast (.) Could pick out landmarks easily on west especially sea wall, at LARIVIERE Ref. 9286 and Lighthouse MOUNT FLEURY 9286](.)	

Wt.41030/1900 600,000 12/41 W.H. & S 51-4070.

SHEET 2

Month and Year June 44   Commanding Officer Major R.E. THOMPSTONE, RE.

Place	Date	Hour	Summary of Events and Information	References to Appendices
		[0725	All L.C.T. touched down at correct positions (.) 2424 had difficulty with steering and touched down 5 minutes late (.) Water rough (.) All Roly Poly when pushed off were carried east by the tide and the stoms of all LCT were also carried east, leaving them at angle of 450 to coast line (.) Consequently no Roly Polys were pushed satisfactorily but were abandored (.) One AVRE found one LCT 2414 wounded on run in and left one craft. (.) L/gel. took over this AVRE. (.) This AVRE was run over by an LCT the fascine knocked off by the LCT door and the AVRE drowned. (.) crew last seen climbing out all other AVRE and reached waters edge satisfactorily (.) Boffin AVRE lane 4 R.E T had waterproofing shutes damage by fire and subsequently drowned (.) Lanes 1, 2 & 3, the 3 Roly	

Wt.47724/998 2,000,000 3/48 W.H. & S. 51/6375.

SHEET 3

Commanding Officer Major R.E. THOMPSTONE, RE.

Place	Date	Hour	Summary of Events and Information	References to Appendices
			Poly [AVRE commanded by capt. King broke off to the right and supported 6 Green Howards into HABLE DE HEURTOT Ref.9086] [(.) They silenced 4 pillboxes including a 50 m.m. gun position in the sea wall, surmounted sea wall and attacked defended position in village (.) They rejoined soon at Rally Position at 1500 hrs.] (.) Three Boffin AVRE of lane 1,2,&3 arrived at HWM having laid their Boffin shuttering. and returned to tow away beach obstacles. (.) Rejoined unit at 1600 hrs at RALLY (.) Three fascine AVRE and bridge carrying AVRE used by Major Sutton to complete two lanes up road due south to MOUNT FLEURY (.) Bridge used over 25' drain. bomb crater at about ref. 918863(.) Lane also made west along rd. under construction by crabs to open country on rt. of 69 Bde. Sector(.) There AVRE rejoined unit at RALLY at about 1500 hrs(.)	

SHEET 4

Commanding Officer Major R.E. THOMPSTONE, RE.

Place	Date	Hour	Summary of Events and Information	References to Appendices
			[Lane 4. RET Roly Poly AVRE hit by 88 mm in end of wall at LA RIVIERE and blew up (.) One survivor, badly burned] (.) 2 Crabs Commenced flailing into lateral minefield, reached lateral rd and became bogged (.) Bobbin AVRE had waterproofing shutes damaged and drowned eventually(.) Fascine AVRE followed flails and attempted to pull then out of bog. (.) Rejoined unit about 1300 hrs. (.) [Lane 5. Roly Poly AVRE Lt. Croxall proceeded up path flailed by 6 team and left on lateral road into LA RIVIERE in support 5 East Yorks.(.) joined by 5 East Yorks in village at 0820 hrs having arrived at about 0745 hrs. in village. Bobbin AVRE hit by 88m.m. and exploded at H.W.M.(.) Five crew escaped,one badly burned, Crew Comd injured and one of the five killed by some means on beach after leaving AVRE.] (.) Crabs commenced flailing lateral minefield and	

Wt.47724/998 2,000,000 3/43 W. H. & S. 51/6375.

SHEET 5

Month and Year June 44 · Commanding Officer Major R.E. THOMPSTONE, RE.

Place	Date	Hour	Summary of Events and Information	References to Appendices
			bogged a few yards into field(.) fascine AVRE proceeded to try to pull these out (.) Rejoined unit at Raally about 1100 hrs. (.) Lane 6. Roly Poly AVRE stuck on beach with brake and mechanical trouble but cleared itself about 1000 hrs and reach RALLY about 1100 hrs.(.) This one was intended to assist in clearance of LA RIVIERE (.) 2 Crabs fired on orders at 88 mm and finally silenced this weapon (.) Both flailed through lateral minefield to road, turned right as planned to got through north south minefield leading up to MOUNT FLEURY but became bogged.(.) Fascine AVRE followed crabs and broke up fascine, laid carpet and dragged out crabs (.) By this time, all AVRE and crabs in lane 4, 5 & 6 were either out of action, bogged, or employed in trying recover bogged	

Wt.47724/993 2,000,000 3/43 W. H. & S. 51/6375.

SHEET 6

Month and Year June 44 Commanding Officer Major R.E. THOMPSTONE, RE.

Place	Date	Hour	Summary of Events and Information	References to Appendices
			Crabs which it was anticipated might be badly required to push in one lane somewhere (.) [Major Thompstone contacted Officer i/c 280 Fd. Coy. RE and discovered he was incapable of using AVRE for towing beach obstacles as planned and therefore decided to use the one remaining bobbin AVRE detailed originally for this job to push a lane through in conjunction with his own vehicle] (.) [These two vehicles went through to lateral road followed by Sqn. of DD Tanks, turned left on lateral road, and right in LA RIVIERE up to MOUNT FLEURY and eventually through VER-SUR-MER to open country. (.) On the way both vehicles aided 5 East Yorks to mop up resistance in certain houses by using Petard (.) This was found to be very effective with fuges 291 although fuges 289 were very poor] (.)	

Wt.41030/1900 600,000 12/41 W. H. & S. 51-4070.

SHEET 7

Commanding Officer Major R.E. THOMPSTONE, RE.

Place	Date	Hour	Summary of Events and Information	References to Appendices
VER-SUR-MER 9184	7]	1800	The Sqn. RALLY POINT was in the orchard south end of VER-SUR-MER village. (.) 'C' Sqn. Westminster Dgns. our team partners rallied in next orchard. (.) [At 1600 hrs. sixteen out of twenty AVRE had rallied. (.) Casualties were 11 RFT missing, one killed, RFT four wounded who were returned to England (.) No officer casualties.]	
		1800	Sqn. harbour was made in the RALLY POSITION us 69 Bde, required us no were and we had returned to Command of 50 Div. (.) Two groups landed and joined Sqn.	
		0645	One three ton 4x4 vehicles landed D-Day on our RET beach and ARV landed on our beach found and joined Sqn. (.) One still outstanding, should have landed by now(!)	R.E.T.
		0800	Two AVRE sent to beach where they spent the day helping clear beaches of vehicles and obstacles	R.E.T.

Wt 43350/1614 560M 3/41 BPL. 51/3792.

WO 171/1810
Intelligence/war diary
82ND ASSAULT SQUADRON RE

Month and Year June 1944   Commanding Officer Major H.G.A. ELPHINSTONE, RE.

Place	Date	Hour	Summary of Events and Information	References to Appendices
FAWLEY - UK	1st		Preparations for Exercise "NEPTUNE" completed	
"	2nd	1800	Moved to area of Q2 Hard T bivouac for the night	
"	3rd	0200	Commenced embarkation at Q2 Hard, Squadron being disposed in 6 LCT IV of Flotilla D28 - 20 AVRE, 8 Officers & 112 ORs Lay off in the SOLENT for remainder of day.	
	4th		Loading	Appendix 'A'
	5th	0730	Sailing Orders cancelled owing to rough seas.	
			Flotilla slipped anchor & Proceeded on Operation "NEPTUNE" - Crews finally briefed. Sea rough, conditions on craft extremely bad :- 6" - 12" of water in the hold of craft - no sleeping space for men	
NORMANDY	6th	0720	[Craft beached at following points approximately LCT Serial No. 2025 – 878867 LCT Serial No. 2027 – 883868 LCT Serial No. 2026 – 884868]	

Wt.47724/923 2,000,000 3/48 W. H. & S. 51/6375.

SHEET 2

Month and Year June 1944   Commanding Officer Major H.G.A. ELPHINSTONE, RE.

Place	Date	Hour	Summary of Events and Information	References to Appendices
			[LCT Serial No 2028 – 894871 LCT Serial No 2029 – 895871 LCT Serial No 2030 – 901871.]	
			[The landing points differed considerably from the original intention with the nett result that the breaching teams were dispersed on too great a length of beach & disposed to far to the EAST.	
			[LCT Serial No. 2025 landed at the correct point, but was immediately hit in several places by a field gun sited in large concrete pillbox at LE HAMEL approx. 878867.] No vehicles or personnel disembarked from the craft until it dried out at approx 1330 hrs. The leading AVRE carrying a Roly Poly endeavoured to do so, but the Roly Poly fouled an obstacle which jammed it, & the AVRR, in the exit from the craft.	
			LCT Serial No. 2026 – all vehicles & personnel disembarked, the Roly Poly failed in its intention, but the AVRR succeeded	?

Wt.47724/993 2,000,000 3/43 W. H. & S. 51/6375.

SHEET 3

Place	Date	Hour	Summary of Events and Information	References to Appendices
			in passing the Bobbin AVRE which followed failed to lay its carpet owing to the failure of the puff charges to blow out the quick release pins - the frame having become twisted. The following Cond. AVRR - MAJOR H.G.A. ELPHINSTONE i/c reached the shore and engaged pillboxes with Turret T Hill Besas. Fascine AVRE beached & made for LANE 1, but as this had not been started returned to lane 3. Gears jammed in reverse - efforts were made to remedy the defect both from inside & outside AVRE these failed & the AVRE was abandoned. The Fascine was jettisoned on the Beach under orders of the Beach comd - the release mechanism having been damaged by fire & rendered unavailable This lane whilst opened eventually failed owing to the Shennan Crabs becoming bogged in the marshy minefield between the beach & the lateral road.	

Wt.47724/993 2,000,000 3/43 W. H & S. 51/6375.

SHEET 4

Place	Date	Hour	Summary of Events and Information	References to Appendices
			<u>LCT Serial No. 2027</u> Roly Poly again failed, but all vehicles successfully disembarked. The sand on this portion of the beach was firm & the Bobbin was not laid on the Lane, but was later used under orders of the Beach RE. By this time the Roly Poly AVRE had been hit on the RH splined spigot, but was not immobilized. The Fascine AVRE arrived at the bottom of Lane 3 – a direct hit on the vision port killed comd. of AVRE & injured the driver. The blow plates were damaged by shell-fire & the fascine dropped, the AVRE then over-ran the fascine & turned over on its side. This lane was cleaned by one Crab, but was temporarily blocked by the following Roly Poly AVRE which struck a mine. This lane did not appear to be used to any extent initially. <u>LCT Serial No. 2028</u> Roly Poly again failed, but all vehicles	?

Wt.47724/993 2,000,000 3/43 W. H. & S. 51/6375.

SHEET 5

Commanding Officer Major H.G.A. ELPHINSTONE, RE.

Place	Date	Hour	Summary of Events and Information	References to Appendices
			disembarked successfully. The Bobbin AVRR did not lay it matting as the first two AVRES had no difficulty in crossing the beach. One of the two following Crabs immediately became bogged, whilst the second crab endeavoured to find the entrance to LE ROCQUETTE. The two Fascine AVRE took up a hull down position at the head of the beach-the lane having failed. The Roly-Poly AVRE then proceeded via Lane 5 to the lateral road & turned west towards LE HAMEL until stopped by a large crater at 893865. (50' diameters & 9'-10' deep). Lieut. G.R. ELLIS RE – the Roly Poly AVRE from LCT Serial No 2029 had already reached this crater & instructed his Fascine AVRE to drop the Fascine in this crater - owing to the marshy nature of the crater, the road remained impassable to all vehicles. The two fascine AVRE from Lane 4 were then called up & the fascines laid The main bulk of armour held up by this crater was then	?

SHEET 6

Commanding Officer Major H.G.A. ELPHINSTONE, RE.

Place	Date	Hour	Summary of Events and Information	References to Appendices
			able to proceed. <u>LCT Serial No. 2029</u> The Roly Poly in this case was laid successfully and all vehicles disembarked. The Bobbin AVRE did not lay its carpet owing to the firmness of the beach The Fascine AVRE proceeded to the lateral road via the lane cleared by the crabs & laid its fascine in the crater at 893868. This lane was successful. <u>LCT Serial No. 2030</u> Roly Poly was not successfull - matting was laid successfully from the Bobbin AVRE, Fascine AVRE jolted on leaving LCT & shear pins of blow plates broke. This AVRE made for Lane 5, fascine holes cover at the entrance to the Lane. This fascine was then spread to improve the lane. Lane 6 was also successful.	?

SHEET 7

Month and Year June 1944   Commanding Officer Major H.G.A. ELPHINSTONE, RE.

Place	Date	Hour	Summary of Events and Information	References to Appendices
			[Having assisted the passage of the armour through the lateral road, the remaining AVRE less those detailed for beach clearance, rallied at LES ROCQUETTES, owing to the flow of traffic. ½ Tp AVRE u/c Lieut. ELLIS proceeded towards ASNELLE to assist the infantry. On arrival it was discovered that one AVRE from Lane 2 u/c L/sqt Scaife HM No. 2118916 had left the beach via Lane 3 & proceeded to LE HAMEL in company with some DD tanks, and contracted a party of 1 HAMPS in ESNELLES & assisted in house clearance. This AVRE remained with the party & attacked the LE HAMEL Sanatorium from the land ward side, using the petard & also cleared a large concrete gun emplacement to East of sanatorium by placing a round through the rear-opening. The inferior of this emplacement was completely shattered by one petard round, & as a result]	?

Wt.47724/993 2,000,000 3/43 W. H. & S. **51**/6375.

SHEET 8

Month and Year June 1944   Commanding Officer Major H.G.A. ELPHINSTONE, RE.

Place	Date	Hour	Summary of Events and Information	References to Appendices
[BUHOT	7th	0400	[many prisoners were taken. 　　All AVREs then proceeded to CABAN & then to ARROMANCHE - further assistance was not required by the infantry. The Squadron less AVRE u/c Capt. Somerset then rallied & harboured for the night at BUHOT.] Casualties – Major H.G.A. Elphinstone & 1 OR killed 　　　　Capt Wilford, Lieut Greene & 3 ORs wounded. 　　　　AVRE, - bogged on beach & drowned by tide. 　　　　　1 hit on R.H. splined spigot but not immobilized 　　　　　1 direct hit on vision port & later overturned. Squadron placed u/c 56 Bde - 2 Troop u/c 2 Essex Regt. 　　　　　　1 Troop u/c 2 Glosters assisted in advance on BAYEUX Rallied for the night at St Sulpice] Capt. J.M. Leytham assumes command.	

Wt.47724/993 2,000,000 3/43 W. H. & S. **51**/6375.

WO 171/1530
Intelligence/war diary
73RD FIELD COMPANY RE.

Month and Year June 1944   Commanding Officer Major L.E. WY?T RE.

Place	Date	Hour	Summary of Events and Information	References to Appendices
	3 contd.		Embarkation went without a hitch and craft moored alongside LSTs in the SOLENT. Stores carried included 8000 lbs PHE with 1500 igniter sets for demolition of beach obstacles.	RW
GOSPORT	4	1400	D-Day tpt embarked GOSPORT on LST.	
BOTLEY			D + 2 day party moved to Camp A 14.	
SOUTHHMPTON			D + 3 day party moved to Camp C 2.	
SOLENT			D day marching party sailed round the SOLENT & back to anchor.	RW
SOUTHAMPTON	5		D + 3 day party moved to Camp C 19.	
SOLENT	5	0735	Weather: bright, windy with high seas. After rounding NEEDLES large percentage of men overcome with seasickness.	
CHANNEL		2100	Lot of rum issued to all ranks.	RW
FRANCE	6	0530	Sighted French coast.	Report on D-Day. refer to Appx A. RW
		0725	All craft beached.	

22293 Wt. 33096/1140 1,000m 12/40—McC & Co Ltd–**51-8212** Forms C2118/22

SHEET 2

Month and Year June 1944   Commanding Officer Majr L.E. WYAT? RE

Place	Date	Hour	Summary of Events and Information	References to Appendices
FRANCE	6	1500	Half tracked M 14 landed with 5 ORs & reported to Coy. HQ on the beach.	RW
LE HAMEL	7		Casualties at end of D-Day were: Killed Capt. P.W. Smith and 3 ORs. Wounded Lt. L.P. Brownrigg and 9 ORs. Missing believed killed 1 OR. Missing believed returned to England 11 ORs.	
			Party continued clearance of obstacles on JIG and ITEM beaches until about 2500 yds had been cleared.	
LES ROQUETTES		1200	Party moved to LES ROQUETTES en route for PORT EN BESSIN	
ST CÔME DE FRESNES		1530	Party moved to ST CÔME DE FRESNES. Came under desultory fire from snipers left in strong point above village. Two prisoners taken.	
"		1900	D-Day tpt disembarked on KING GREEN beach and Lt. Sprague contacted the Coy. HQ 2230 hrs.	
GOSPORT		1900	D + 2 day party embarked on LCT Mk IV	RW

Wt 13474/1805 1,200,000 7/40 BPL 51-7171 Forms C2118/22

WO 171/1619
Intelligence/war diary
280TH FIELD COMPANY RE.

Month and Year June 1944   Commanding Officer Major L.S. CLAYTON, RE.

Place	Date	Hour	Summary of Events and Information	References to Appendices
			a strong S.W. wind made conditions very unpleasant. Most of men affected by sea sickness. Convoy proceeded through out the day in bad weather. No enemy interference from air or ships.	
ENGLISH	6th	0600	D-Day. Sighted enemy coast – still no enemy interference.	See Appx B.
CHANNEL	6	0630	Naval bombardment of coastal defenses started. L.C.O.C.U's	69 Bde Gp 0.0.
- do -			3 and 4 under commd for the operation came into	No 3.
- do -			station in LCA's astern of my LCT.	Appx C. Map
- do -	6	0700	All assault craft "hove to" about three while out waiting	
- do -			for air force 15 carry out their bombing task. Convoy	
- do -			being shelled by enemy guns from the shore.	
- do -	6	0730	All LCT's laid down and AVRE taken proceed ashore	
LA RIVIÈRE			L.C.O.C.U beach and commence demolishing obstacles. Folding back in while supports were being taken ashore by AVRE's prove too flimsy for the heavy seas	

22293 Wt. 33096/1140 1,000m 12/40—McC & Co Ltd–51-8212 Forms C2118/22.

SHEET 2

Month and Year June 1944   Commanding Officer Major L.S. CLAYTON, RE.

Place	Date	Hour	Summary of Events and Information	References to Appendices
LA RIVIERE	6 "D day"	4. 0730.	and most of them capsize. Men swim and wade ashore. Heavy enemy opposition encountered from MGs Mortars and 88 mm 9 m. No flank protection from DD tanks owing to heavy seas. In spite of this all ranks carried on with the job and two 200 9 yrds were cleared for craft in the under water obstacle before the advancing tide made further work imposible. The enemy were still very active and several men fell about this time, most of them as a result of hand grenade lobbed over the sea wall. After about half an hour, however, an assault party succeeded in disposing of all the enemy with the exception of a few snipers operating from inland. The beaches dealt with were KING RED and KING GREEN situated at LA RIVIERE FRANCE.	

22293 Wt. 33096/1140 1,000m 12/40—McC & Co Ltd–51-8212 Forms C2118/22

SHEET 3

Commanding Officer Major L.S. CLAYTON, RE.

Place	Date	Hour	Summary of Events and Information	References to Appendices
LA RIVIÈRE	6	0830	Further work being impossible for the time being owing to the tide, the roll was called and it was found that eight men were killed and twenty six wounded. One officer Lieut. C.R. Peard RE was seriously wounded and was later evacuated to U.K together with eighteen seriously wounded ORs. One naval rating was killed and five wounded form L.C.O.C.U's under command.	
LA RIVIÈRE	6	1300.	The tide having receded work was again commenced on the demolition and removal of obstacles, and by 2030 hrs when the tide again made further work impossible, 1200 yds of beach had been completely cleared of enemy obstacles. All ranks, both in the company and the L.C.O.C.U's under command did marvelous work from the time	

22293 Wt. 33096/1140 1,000m 12/40—McC & Co Ltd–51-8212 Forms C2118/22

SHEET 4

Commanding Officer Major L.S. CLAYTON, RE.

Place	Date	Hour	Summary of Events and Information	References to Appendices
			of landing and showed great courage and determination in the face of heavy enemy opposition.	
			Types of obstacle dealt with :- 1 HEDGEHOGS. each with either a teller mine as a shell attached. (both fited with a DZ35 ignited) 2 WOODEN RAMPS approx 10' high fited with AA shells) 3 WOODEN STAKES approx 10' high fited with shells & tiller mines 4 concorde TETRA HEDRA See Appx A.	
LA RIVIÈRE	7. D+1.	0300.	Work again commenced on clearance of obstacles. By the end of D+1 nearly two miles of beach had been cleared, involving the destruction of approx 2000 obstacles.	
		1230.	In a recce of the EASTERN end of the sea wall. OC realized possibilities of constructing hard for beaching LCT's during the high water stand of two and half hours.	
			Permission received from CRE 104 Beach sub area to commence	

22293 Wt. 33096/1140 1,000m 12/40—McC & Co Ltd–51-8212 Forms C2118/22

WO 171/864
Intelligence/war diary
THE WESTMINSTER DRAGOONS
(ROYAL ARMOURED CORPS)

Month and Year June 44

Commanding Officer Lt. Col. W.Y.K. BLAIR-OLIPHANT, MC.

Place	Date	Hour	Summary of Events and Information	References to Appendices
ENGLAND	1 June		Marshalling into craft loads began. Weather which was hitherto very hot with no wind appeared to be breaking.	
	2		Marshalling continued. Weather hot but some wind. Considerable quantities of stores and equipment were still arriving, causing considerable difficulties in the dispersed state of the Regt.	
	3		Embarkation began. Weather fine with strong wind. Many of the barrage balloons carried by landing craft were carried away.	Appx E
	4	0730	D-Day announced as 5 Jun, but sailing postponed immediately by rough weather.	
	5		Craft moved off. Hyoscine Bromide anti sea-sickness tablets were issued with varying results. 10 or 15% were extremely sick.	
	6		D-Day. H-hr was 0715 B, and at this time craft carrying 13 CRABS of B Sqn. under comd 231 Inf Bde, and 13 CRABS of C Sqn. under comd 69 Inf Bde were due to touch down.	WBO

22293 Wt. 33096/1140 1,000m 12/40—McC & Co Ltd-51-8212 Forms c2118/22.

SHEET 2

Commanding Officer Lt. Col. W.Y.K. BLAIR-OLIPHANT, MC.

Place	Date	Hour	Summary of Events and Information	References to Appendices
FIELD	6		Accounts of D-Day action are appended, by Sqns. Lt. Col. WYK Blair-Oliphant landed at H + 60 m (SQN ARV as ms rank was not due until H + 18 hrs. By night B Sqn. ARV. (Sqn. m14 and 4 amn and pet lorries were ashore.	Appx A
	7	1500	Lt. M.J. Eedy with COs rank, RQMS Evans, and two lorries due in at 0100 hrs, landed and joined CO and B Sqn. at BRECYT8978 C Sqn. arrived in harbour area.	Appx A.
BRÉCY	8	0900	CRAB state was then as follows:- B C Fit 3 6 Ready in 24 hrs 3 - Reparable when spares arrive 2 5 Beyond repair 5 2 Total 13 13	
		1300	Harbour area was not mopped up and two POW taken	
		1500	One tp 141 RAC (CHURCHILL CROCODILES) arrived for a task which did not materialize.	
		1800	Regt refilled with POL, amn and sup 5 from, 50 Div. points. All transport was continually run regimentally under RQMS.	

22293 Wt. 33096/1140 1,000m 12/40—McC & Co Ltd-51-8212 Forms C2118/22.

APPENDIX "A"

1. At approx 0725 hrs 6 Jun 44 the six LCT Mk III containing 13 Crabs of C Sqn. Westminster Dragoons touched down at their appointed places on the beach West of LA RIVIERE.

2. The three right hand craft contained "X Breaching Sqn" consisting of 7 Crabs and 10 AVRE's, commanded by Major S.P.M. Sutton. The 7 Crabs consisted of HQ Crab, 5 3 Tp Crabs and 1 4 Tp Crabs attached to 3 Tp.

"X Breaching Sqn. consisted of 3 times. Each team will be considered separately as follows:-

No. 1 Team

Task - To breach the minefield up to the lateral road, turn left on the lateral road and remain in reserve. While in reserve to give fire support and on orders from Sqn. Comd to make a lane from the O.P. House to the Quarry.

Actual Course of Events

Came off the craft into 4' 6" of water and did a wade of about 100 yds. Both tanks got through the beach obstacles but the rear tank stuck in the claybog on the beach. The remaining tank which was commanded by Lt. Pear proceeded up the beach, flailed a lane up to the lateral road, and turned left as planned.

On arriving that No. 3 Lane and failed the Sqn Comd ordered Lt. Pear to proceed up to the X rds, turn right and go up the hill to the OP house. Lt. Pear found first that the small bridge over the stream had not been blown and an even greater surprise was that the road over the A tk ditch was also not blown. He proceeded about another 25 yards up the road and found a crater on the road opposite the OP house about 25 ft wide probably caused by one of our own shells. The Sqn. Comd ordered the bridge which had been brought up for putting across the A tk ditch to be dropped across this crater, this was done very quickly and accurately by Capt. Davis RE. Lt. Pear then crossed the bridge and continued with his final task as stated above. He completed this task by himself, the lane later being widened by the Sqn. Comd. This final lane from the OP house to the Quarry was for the DD tanks to get out to the open country. The information was passed over the wireless to the DD Sqn Ldr personally and the DD Sqn. arrived on the heels of the flails just as the lane was completed.

No. 2 Team

Task - To breach the minefield up to the lateral road, turn left advance up the lateral road passed the X rds, turn right into the so called marsh where the ground looked suitable and make a lane to the outskirts of VER-SUR-MER.

Course of Events

After a wade of 5 ft for 150 yds both flails successfully crossed the beach and made a lane up to the lateral road. They turned left, passed the X rds and the leading Crab commanded by Cpl. Walker turned right off the road as planned. He felt himself sinking into a bog and at once reversed back on to the road. He then proceeded further along the road looking for less marshy ground. He found the road barred by deep craters from our own bombs, both Crabs made a sporting effort to get past them but the leading tank got bogged in the crater and the second one in the marshy ground to the left of the road.

No. 3 Team

Task - Breach the beach minefield at as near the X rds and open up the road as far as the C.P. House.

Course of Events

Came off craft into 4' 6" of water and did a wade of 100 yards. Both flails crossed the beach successfully but were both hit in the rotor by the 88 mm at La Riviere as they were about to enter the beach minefield. The bridge which was in this team was directed by the Sqn. Comd through No. 2 Teams lane through the beach minefield and so to the crater as already explained.

SHEET 4

3. "The three left hand craft contained "Z" Breaching Sqn", consisting of 6 Crabs and 10 AVREs, commanded by Major Thompstone RE. The 6 Crabs consisted of 1 HQ and 5 1 Tp.

"Z" Breaching Sqn considered of 3 teams each team being considered separately as follows:-

No. 4 Team

Task - To breach the beach minefield up to the lateral road, proceed straight across and take up, position behind hedgerow 50 yds beyond the road and remain there in reserve.

Course of Events

Came off the craft into 4' 6" of water and waded for 100 yards Both tanks got through the beach obstacles and started to flail up to the lateral road; however, both tanks got bogged before reaching the road.

No. 5 Team

Task To breach the beach minefield up to the lateral road, to the North - South minefield, turn left handed 50 yards across the road the breach the N/S minefield. To turn right at the end of the minefield and make a lane up to the lighthouses position.

Course of Events

Came off craft into 4' 6" of water and waded for 100 yards. Both tanks got through the beach obstacles and started to flail up to the road but both tanks get bogged before reaching the. From there they gave cover to No.6 Team and also supported the infantry attack on LA RIVIERE by HE and smoke.

No. 6 Team

Task - To breach the beach minefield up to the lateral road left of the N/S minefield, turn right handed immediately after crossing the road, breach the N/S minefield and take up a position - behind the hedgerow. From there on orders from the Sqn. cond to make a lane up to the road just to the right of the right of the lighthouse position.

Course of Events

Owing to a wire in the starter scienoid burning out on Capt. Bell's tank whilst on the craft it was necessary for him to be towed to start by the Bobbin thus changing the order of the Flairs, leaving the craft. This led to Capt. Bell's tank couching one of the assault boats without him knowing it, as a result all remaining vehicles were delayed coming off the LCT.

Capt. Bell saw an AVRE hit by what he assumed to be the 88 mm on the end of the LA RIVIERE sea wall, he advanced to a position from where he could engage the gun and silenced it.

He then proceeded to make a lane through the minefield and became bogged just as he reached the road. Cpl. Thorpe followed up, made a lane beside his tank, crossed the road but had his track blown by a mine immediately across the road.

The lane was made usable by towing Capt. Bell's tank onto the road with the fascine AVRE and dropping the fascine into the boggy patch just before the road where it was used by the Fo Coy. RE to cover up the boggy patches.

As the ground beyond the lateral road was sheer bog, Capt. Bell was ordered to proceed up the road to VER-SUR-MER and ensure it was open.

4. GENERAL REMARKS

(a) The area which contained the 88 mm gun on the end of the sea wall at LA RIVIERE was dealt with in the fire plan by 6 Sqns. of Fortresses (88 mm was aiming pt), 4 Destroyers, 86 Fd Regt., 2 LCT (R) and sundry smaller supporting craft.

How much of this fire support actually took place is not known, in any case the primary target the 88 mm gun was active when we touched down on the beach. It was silenced by a tank of C Sqn. namely that commanded by Capt. Bell.

(b) Information regarding minefields was inaccurate, there were far more minefields than we had been told about, they were, however, well marked by signs.

(c) Information about the marsh was even more inaccurate; the only ways off the beach on the front in which we were put down, were along the roads.

"B" SQN WESTMINSTER DRAGOONS WAR DIARY

June 6th 1944

1. At 0730 hrs on the morning of the 6th June 1944 five out of six LCT IVs carrying breaching teams comprising AVRE, Flails and Bulldozers touched down on German occupied France East of LE HAMES.

The sixth LCT IV was unable to discharge its lane team owing to heavy seas and enemy shellfire putting the craft out of commission.

2. Craft touched down at approx half tide in heavy seas.

3. Beach obstacles compresed:-

> Element 'C'
> Tetrahedra
> Ramp type Obstacles
> Hedgehogs.

with Teller mines and shell heads attached.

Minefields and wire were encountered on the mainland.

In no cases, with the exception of the bad clay were beach obstacles troublesome and it was possible for all troops to bypass the artificial obstacles.

4. The beach was fairly flat leading up to small sand dunes 3 to 6' high. Clay patches were present on the beach in varying depth and were another obstacle to tanks.

5. The craft did not touch down exactly at the places as planned. This was due to a slight sea mist rising when the LCTs were some 1000 - 2000 yards out from the shore making recognition of landmarks difficult. As a result all lane teams were landed to the EAST of the selected points by some 400 yds and the position of the teams detailed for lanes 2 and 3 were reversed.

6. Lane 1 Team did not land as LCT IV was hit before it could touch down. Tank Comd - E/Sgt Byrne and Cpl. Middleton.

7. Lane 2 was unfortunately set down in Lane 3. Leading AVRE rolled out its matting and the Bobbin AVRE was not required to cover the bad ground.

The leading flail (Lt. Townsend-Green) began flailing at HWM, flailed some 20 yds inland and was bogged in the very marshy ground. The second flail (Cpl. Barton) was not committed to the lane owing to the bad going and the troop leader (Lt. Townsend-Green) from the bogged tank took over command of this vehicle. As orders had been given that the ramp exit at the EASTERN end of LE HAMEL was vital, this tank then proceeded across the beach towards this exit but unfortunately was bogged in the clay. This tank was subsequently hit three times by an 80 mm Fd gun sited at the EASTERN end of LE HAMEL to filade the beach.

The fascine AVRE on this lane reached HWM and as it jettisoned its fascine a burst of MG fire killed the driver. The tank being gear slowly climbed the fascine and turned over on its side.

8. Lane 3. The team of this lane touched down roughly in its correct position and was thus on the wrong side of Lane 2. The Roly Poly laid its matting. The Bobbin AVRE was not required as the condition of the beach was good. The leading flail (Sjt Lindsay) began flailing at HWM and flailed a path through the minefield on the minefield. On reaching the lateral road into LE HAMEL the flail turned right to carry out the task ordered in the support of the 1 HANTS. Unfortunately, the attack on LE HAMEL did not go according to, plan and this flail was destroyed in the town by A/tk gun fire. Details cannot be ascertained as crew were wounded and returned to UK.

The second (Capt B. Taylor) flail echeloned right of the leading flail passed almost through the minefield and was blown up by what was thought to be two mines connected on the same fuse.

Number of mines destroyed on this lane were eight. The fascine AVRE was not required in the breaching of this lane. Although the second flail was blown up on the lane it was possible for track vehicles to use it. It was subsequently used as heavy track exit.

9. Lane 4. The team on this lane was put down Some 400 - 500 yards EAST of its prearranged objective. The leading AVRE rolled out the Bobbin AVRE was able to cross the bad ground without laying its matting and the AVRE tank comd did not therefore lay the matting.

SHEET 6

The first flail followed immediaetly behind the Bobbin was sole to get across the clay but the second flail became bogged.

The leading flail (Cpl. Adams) having crossed the bad ground tried to find his objective but was unable to discover the correct place. He eventually made a gap through the minefield but became bogged in the marshy ground on the mainland.

The fascine AVREs were not required to,lay their fascines on the initial breaching.

10. Lane 5. The Roly, Poly AVRE laid its matting on leaving the LCT. It was then followed by the Bobbin AVRE which was not required to lay its matting as the clay patches were small and easily distinguishable.

The two flails (L/Sjt Poole and Cpl Roberts G.) then started flailing at HWM and flailed a path through the minefield on to the lateral road and went towards the X rds at LES ROQUETTES. Some 200 yds from the cross roads shell fell on to the road making a crater which proved to be a tank obstacle. The leading flail then called up the fascine AVRE which had followed the flail off the LCT continued up to the X rds turned left and flailed a 16 ft gar the infantry through the minefield on the SOUTHERN side of the road in order that the infantry could get through their carriers and wheels. Subsequently a gap the AA gunners.

The final flail off this LCT carrying the Breach Comd (Capt. H.P. Stanyon) was struck on the petrol tank by a heavy mortar or gun shell which pierced the petrol tank.

The tank immediately went up in flames. The lane to the lateral road was completed at approx H plus 15.

11. Lane 6. The Roly Poly AVRE laid its matting and was followed by the Bobbin which laid its matting over a bad patch of clay. The two flails then crossed the matting and started flailing at H.W.M.

The two flails (Sgt Marsh and Cpl Roberts A) were successful in breaching the minefield up to the lateral road and the lane was open at approx H plus 22. The fascine AVRE was used to place its fascine in the crater mentioned in para 10 to make a more effective bridge. The leading flail having breached the minefield was then ordered to rally and come to 231 Inf Bde res.

12. Subsequently the Sqn. reverted to Comd of 231 Inf Bde and came under control of Regt. HQ. The Sqn. harboured for the night DD plus 1 on the outskirts of MEUVAINE.

13. On D plus 1 work went on preparing the tanks for further action and recovering the bogged tanks. At 1200 hrs on this day the Regt. was ordered to a fwd rally at BRECY where it remained for the night D plus 1/D plus 2.

14. Throughout the whole of the action on D-Day casualties were as follows:-

Vehicles

    (a) By enemy action   3

    (b) Stuck in mud and subsequently
        inundated by the Sea owing to failure of Beach Rec.   2

Personnel

  Killed

	Officers -	NIL.
	ORs -	NIL.

  Wounded

	Officers -	NIL.
	ORs -	Sgt Lindsay.
		L/Sgt Butcher
		Tpr cooper
		Tpr Shaw.

  Missing believed wounded

        Tpr Field.

        Tpr Gray.

"C" SQN WESTMINSTER DRAGOONS

D-Day Continued

On completion of the initial assault operation the Sqn rallied in an orchard on the Southern outskirts of VER-SUR-MER. Five Crabs had reached the rally by 1400 hrs when the Sqn was ordered forward to VILLERS 1e SEC..

Before reaching there the four Crabs commanded by Major Sutton with the comds Lt. Hoban, Lt. Pear, Cpl. McCall were ordered SOUTH of CREULLY. On passing through CREULLY information came over the air that 30 - 40 German tanks were moving NE from RUCQUEVILLE 3 miles away.

The four Crabs took up position on the high ground on the Southern outskirts of CREULLY where they were joined ½ hr later by 7 more Crabs of the Sqn. which had been recovered from the beaches. However, the enemy tanks did not come within range and the battle passed a mile to the SOUTH.

At midnight the Sqn moved back just South of CREPON where it leagured for the night.

D plus 1

At 0545 hrs the Sqn moved alongside a hedge on the immediate South outskirts of CREPON. At approx 0610 hrs a shell exploded in the trees above the Sqn followed by SAA fire. A second shell fell shortly after by the Sqn. Ldr's tank killing Tpr Birch and wounding Cpl. Adcock. A third fell wounding the Sqn. Ldr, Cpl. Gillespie and L/Cpl. Lennon. The Sqn. Ldr spotted the gun a 10 cm Fd gun about 150 yards away, and jumped on to Lt. Hoban's tank which put the gun out of action with one shot, killing one member of the crew and wounding the rest. Cpl. Baldwin carried out First Aid most efficiently and coolly under fire.

The Sqn. then moved back 400 yards taking the wounded to 86 Fd Regt RAP. As a pillbox had been seen left of the gun position a composite force was formed consisting of 1 Tp C Sqn. 2 Crocodiles 141 RAC and 10 men from 86 Fd Regt. as infantry to mop up.

1 Tp commanded by Lt. Hoban covered the Crocodiles which moved within 30 yards of the pill box before squirting. There proved to be no one in the pillbox but the 86 Fd Regt. party on reaching it saw Germans in dug outs 50 yards to the rear covered by wire and mines. These were engaged by 1 Tp with Browning and HE, whereupon 100 Germans surrendered with one 88 mm and four 75 mm guns intact except for one of which the breach block was missing. This was destroyed by 75 mm HE.

During this action 4 Germans surrendered to a Crab crossing the oatfield to which the rest of the Sqn. had moved.

At 1200 hrs, 3 Tp were sent off to recover an RAF I truck which had been shot up at BAZENVILLE; however, there was no sign of the truck and so after shelling one or two houses known to contain enemy 3 Tp returned.

The afternoon's maintenance was considerably interrupted by snipers from CREPON and at 2015 hrs Sgt. Birch reported a party of 30 Germans 1,500 yards away moving across our front from the direction of BAZENVILLE. 3 Tp were despatched to deal with them capturing 1 Officer and 6 ORs and certainly killing and wounding more. The exact number was impossible to discover as the party was engaged in a field of oats; blood trails showed that some got away.

C Sqn. leagured for the night in the same location.

D plus 2

The Sqn. remained just South of CREOON all day, petrol being fetched from the Beach Group. In the evening out D-Day 2 lorries arrived. Orders were received in the afternoon to join RHQ and B Sqn at BRECY the following morning.

"A" SQN WESTMINSTER DRAGOONS
INTRODUCTION

On May 44 A Squadron were ordered to provide 22 Flails for 1 Corps which were to be allocated as follows:-

12 to 27 Armoured Bridgade to come under command of Major Clifford of 22 Dragoons and for the initial landing to be divided into two parties, one of eight flails under Major Wallace and the other of four under Capt. Beaumont.

5 to 266 Forward Delivery Squadron. This in fact was 1 Tp under Lt. Ingram.

5 to 'C' Sqn. Canadian Armoured Delivery Regiment. This was 3 Tp under Lt. D.S. Squirrell and subsequently Lt. A.K. Dick.

The above parties waterproofed their vehicles at Thorpeness Suffolk and proceeded from there by Transporter to Concentration Areas as follows:-

> Major Wallace's party to BOLNEY, SUSSEX with Staffordshire Yeomanry.
>
> Capt Beaumont's party and 1 Tp to PERWORTH, SUSSEX.
>
> 3 Tp to GOSPORT, HANTS.

The remainder of A Squadron under Capt. P.J.S. Squirrell and consisting of one crew of Sqn. HQ, 5 Tp (Rollers) and all administrative personnel and vehicles less Sqn Ldr's Jep with driver and three fitters remained behind in THORPENESS.

After about a week in Concentration Areas parties moved to Marshalling Areas and on 3rd June Major Wallace's party left their Marshalling Area at STANMER PARK and emarked in LCT's at NEWHAVEN Two flails were allotted to each LCT and loading went very well, particularly in view of the fact that crews had not done it before, and was completed by 2000 hrs.

4th June The convoy of LCT's was to have sailed at 0800 hrs but this was cancelled, probably due to bad weather in the CHANNEL. In the late afternoon crews were ferried back to the Marshalling Area Camps for a wash and hot meal, returning on board about 2100 hrs.

5th June Convoy put out from NEWHAVEN starting at 0800 hrs and anchored outside for an hour or two. Convoy then sailed and was under way for the rest of the time. The sea was rather choppy and most of the men (and officers) felt seasick. Maps were issued during the evening when it was known that the operation was definitely on.

6th June (D day). Sea was still rather rough and personnel not in very good form for the coming operation. H hour was 0725 and 8 Flails of Major Wallace's party landed at H plus 3 hours 5 minutes on QUEEN WHITE Beach at HERMANVILLE-SUR-MER. LCTs were shelled while coming ashore and at least one destroyed. On landing there was considerable congestion at the beach exits which were under mortar and possibly field gun fire. However, all flails eventually reached Assembly Area with Staffs Yeomanry just S of HERMANVILLE. On moving forward two flails commanded by Cpl. Coop and L/Cpl. Daves were knocked out by 88mm fire from the West. Cpl Coop's tank went on fire and two members of the crew, Tpr Woodhouse and Tpr Kelly, wounded, the former seriously. Lt. Bullock's tank was also hit and the jib and 75 mm gun damaged but was able to proceed. The advance continued as far South as BIEVILLE where the Staffs Yeomanry took up battle positions and engaged about ten enemy tanks reported to be Tigers but later turning out to be Mark IV's disguised as Tigers; about six of them were knocked out. The flails were given the task of covering the left flank and did not actually engage the enemy. The positions occupied were shelled intermittently and had to be changed from time to time. During the previous advance to BIEVILLE Cpl. LoveDay's tank was fired on and intaking avoiding action went over a sharp drop and damaged the rotor and jib and Cpl. Loveday himself became a casualty owing to the turret flap crashing onto his hand and breaking three fingers. A large force of British gliders were seen to land to the East during the late afternoon. About midnight flails went into close harbour with Staffs Yeo and refuelled about 0200 hrs. Of the eight flails of Major Wallace's party five were now left and these had been joined by two of the 22 Dragoons which had taken part in the initial assault at H hour, bringing the total up to seven. Major Clifford was travelling in an ordinary Sherman V.

SHEET 9

It was a long and exciting day, which one felt to be something historic on which one could look back in due course and from the comfort of an armchair feel glad that one had been there.

Capt. Beaumont with four flails landed at H plus 5 1/2 hrs with the East Riding Yeomanry and received a slight shrapnel wound on one hand on the beach. Apart from this, this party suffered no casualties and harboured the night at COLLEVILLE-SUR-ORNE.

June 7th All flails of Major Wallace's party were withdrawn into Brigade reserve at HERMANVILLE-SUR-MER where they joined up with a number of flails from 22 dragoons who had taken part in assault on the beach. Snipers were still active in the town, which was bombed during the night.

June 8th Major Wallace and Lt. Hall with four flails took part in mopping up an enemy strongpoint at LION-SUR-MER, which was giving trouble to our forces. The defences included at least one 88 mm which had accounted for two AVRE's and a number of flame throwers. Two platoons of Infantry from B Coy. South Lancs Regt and two SP artillery bombardment which probably destroyed the 88 mm before the attack was launched. The job given to the flails was to clear a path through a minefield just South of the gas works in order that the SP guns could advance and engage the enemy positions. In fact the minefield consisting of light French mines was only 200 yards in depth and the SP guns could easily have engaged the targets without entering the lane. Flails and SP guns engaged enemy in houses and in the open with HE and Browning and parties of the enemy started surrendering. The minefeld proved not great obstacle and one tank flailed through a thick belt of wire at the end of it. Prisoners totalled about 80 including three officers from 736 Infantry Regiment. Two men from one of our own Commandos captured on D-Day were released. All prisoners were handed over to B Coy. South Lancs for disposal. The number of enemy dead and infantry losses were light.

9th June Major Wallace and Lt Hall with four flails proceeded to CAZELLE and came under command of East Riding Yeomanry for an attack being launched from ANISY on CAMBES GALMANCH and ST. CERTEST. Contact was reestablished with Capt. Beaumont's party which was still attached to the East Riding Yeo. Attack secured first objective but no minefields were encountered and flails were kept in reserve. Sgt. Wilson, however, did a useful job of work with his tank in recovering the crew from a tank of the East Riding Yeo which had been hit and set on fire.

10th and 11th June All flails of Major Wallace's and Capt. Beaumont's parties were withdrawn and concentrated in Brigade reserve SW of HERMANVILLE-SUR-MER in an area literally scattered by the Germans with Butterfly Bombs. Attempts were made to flail these but only two were exploded on landing. Sqn remained in this location until 15th June during this time area was heavily bombed at night and troops learned to dig themselves in well. On 13th June flails were asked to clear an enemy minefield surrounding a strongpoint now in our hands SOUTH of Ouistieham. This would have envolved flailing an area containing 400 lorry loads of mines and was not considered a worth while task in view of the casualties which would have certainly occurred to the jibs and cotors and tanks themselves. In the end, two lanes of one tank width each were made into the strongpoint and the RE were very satisfied. Teller, Belgisn, anti tank and 'S' mines were all encountered but no major damage was done to the flails.

15th June A Sqn. rejoined remainder of regiment in harbour at JUAY Monday with 19 Flails including five from 3 Tp and two from 1 Tp which were picked up with their crews from Forward Delivery Sqn. on the way over. Two flails were left in 27 Armoured Brigade Workshops awaiting repairs with two men per crew.

WO 171/877

Intelligence/war diary

C SQUADRON 141ST REGIMENT RAC

Month and Year June 1944   Commanding Officer Lt. Col. H. Bailey

Place	Date	Hour	Summary of Events and Information	References to Appendices
Blackdown, HANTS	12	(1)	Movement to Marshalling Area. HB	
		(2)	Report received (att as appx) of Tps 13 and 15 under Lieut. J.W.G. Shearman and Lieut. E.M. Davies in action since D-Day. Summary of their actions is as follows :-	
			(a) <u>June 2nd 1944</u>: Lieut. JWG. Shearman in sp 69 Inf Bde Gp and Lieut. EM. Davies in sp 231 Inf Bde - 50 (W) Div - embarked SOUTHAMPTON.	
			<u>June 3rd 1944</u>: Skeleton HQ and Echelon under Capt. H.C.D. Barber embarked SOUTHAMPTON.	
			[(b) <u>6th June 44</u>: FRANCE - D-DAY : 15 TP landed H + 35 and lost all three Crocodiles on the beaches - one man drowned and one man missing, one Crocodile subsequently receovered.	
			13 Tp underLt. Shearman landed H + 45 hrs. One tk was lost on the beaches - drowned - remaining two advanced in sp of 7 Green Howards to attack gun posn at pt 44 (918844). Enemy surrendered after 2 rds of 75 mm. Remainder of th day sp inf along axis CREPON - VILLIERS-LE-SEC – CREULLY and assisted in taking several hundred PW by use of the 75 mm and Besa only. Night 6/7 harboured at CREPON.	
			(c) <u>7th June 44</u>: 13 Tp shelled at first light by close range enemy byt. Assisted by RA signallers armed with grenades and the Westminster Dgns flails the two tks assaulted the posn and after 8 shots of flame 150 PW surrendered. Tk recovered from 15 Tp joined 13 Tp.	
			(d) <u>8th June 44</u>: The 3 tks moved to BRECY and the skeleton echelon to SOMMERVIEU.	
			(e) <u>11th June 44</u>: Two tks sp HAMPS from ST. ANDRE to main rd S of ST. PAULS DU VERNAY. No opposition. Tks returned to 231 Bde HQ at ST. ANDRE. During the evening jettisoned trailers and participated in counterattack on LA BELLE EPINE firing 75 mm and Besa into the houses.	
			(f) <u>12th June 44</u>: Tks harboured at JUAY MONDAY and 15 TP crews took over.]	
			(g) <u>14th June 44</u> :15 Tp attacked. LA SENAUDIERE 782689 alone. KO'd one Pz Kwepf Mk III and one Panther. Casualties - one Crocodile, one killed, two wounded, two missing. Remaining 2tks returned to SOMMERVIEU.	
		(3)	<u>Main Lessons</u>:	
			(a) Mk VII Crocodile must be used primarily as flame NOT as A/tk gun. In the early days of the invasion, however, general principles had to go by the board in emergencies.	
			(b) The few shots of flame actually fired did prove a success and whilst disappointed at the wastage (4 out of 6 drowned and one knocked out whilst moving in a recce.	

Wt.47724 993 2,000,000 3/43 W. H. & S. 51/6375.

WO 171/650

Intelligence/war diary

56TH INFANTRY BRIGADE HQ

Month and Year June 1944   Commanding Officer Brig. E.C. PEPPER, CBE.

Place	Date	Hour	Summary of Events and Information	References to Appendices
	1/2		This period was spent in recreation and general relaxation prior to Operation OVERLORD.	
	3	2200	Bde Comd and Staff embarked LYMINGTON to await D-Day.	
	5	1920	Sailed for FRANCE, Operation OVERLORD having been postponed for 24hrs.	
East of LE HAMEL	6	1215	HQ beached and proceeded via MEUVAINES - BUHOT to assembly area856845	
		1745	Bde Gp concentrated. Bde Comd ordered that Bns. move as for prearranged plan. 2 ESSEX ordered to move along rd RHYS – BAYEUX 2 SWB to proceed via LA ROSIERE – VAUX-SUR-AURE. Sqn tks (SHERWOOD RANGERS) placed under Comd 2 ESSEX.	
		1930	Line RHYES – LA ROSIERE reached by fwd bns. PW RYES area identified as I Bn. 916 Gr Regt 352 Inf Div.	
		2100	2 ESSEX adv to came into contact with lt enemy forces at ST SULPICE. 2 SWB contacted enemy at RDF sta 8183. Bde Comd ordered 2 ESSEX to stay on ST. SULPICE feature for night 6/7 JUNE and to patrol towards BAYEUX and 2 SWB to take br at VAUX-SUR-AURE 791826.	
		2345	2 GLOSTERS and Bde HQ moved up to area MAGNY 8182.	
	7	1000	Sit - no news of US progress. 50 Div, 56 Inf Bde with 2 SWB on ridge NW BAYEUX, 2 ESSEX ST. SULPICE feature patrolling A/Tk ditch NW of BAYEUX, 2 GLOSTERS in res. 151 Inf Bde on line of BAYEUX – CAEN rd. 69 INF BDE still SOUTH ST LEGER feature. 3 Cdn Div. with D-Day programme complete and 3(Br) Div. in CAEN.	
		1100	Bde Comd ordered 2 ESSEX supported by Sqn. tks to make attack on MONUNIRE feature skirting BAYEUX, ST CRIOX and main ry sta, and 2 GLOSTERS to clear centre of town with assistance of Sqn. tks and AVRES.	

Wt.47724 993 2,000,000 3/43 W.H. & S. **51/6375**

WO 171/1380
Intelligence/war diary
2ND BATTALION THE SOUTH WALES BORDERERS

Month and Year June 1944   Commanding Officer Mac?

Place	Date	Hour	Summary of Events and Information	References to Appendices
APO	1	1600	Trg under coy arrangements	WS.
	2	1400	ULO party left the Bn.	WS Appx "A":-
	2	1600	Trg under Coy. arrangements.	WS AFs W 3008-9E.
	3	1430	Bn. left Marshalling Area to embark.	WS
	3	1730	Bn. embarked on 3 US Navy LCI (L)s at LYMINGYTON.	WS Appx "B":-
	3	1900	Bn. arrived SOUTHAMPTON water	WS Bn. Orders.
	4		Bn. spent the day on the docks where recreation was laid on for them.	WS
	5	2030	Bn. sailed for FRANCE.	WS
	6	1200	D-Day. Bn landed in FRANCE on the coast of NORMANDY one mile EAST of ARRAMANCHES.	WS WS
	6	1700	Bn. arrived in Assembly Area. Fwd Body commanded by Major F.F.S. Barlow with "D" Coy. under comd cleared RDF Station at map ref 814837.	WS WS
	6	2350	Fwd Body captured bridge at VAUX-SUR-AURE and held it till the main body arrived. Bn established defensive locality VAUX-SUR-AURE. Active patrolling by enemy during the night twelve prisoners taken.	WS WS WS

M3524/1218 1200M 10/41 H.B. & Co.Ltd. 51-1541)

WO 171/1298
Intelligence/war diary
2ND BATTALION,
THE GLOUCESTERSHIRE REGIMENT

Month and Year   Commanding Officer

Place	Date	Hour	Summary of Events and Information	References to Appendices
	5 6 D DAY	1930	LCI's sailed from SOTON DOCKS to join convoy to FRANCE without incident. Crossing to the FRANCE COAST went well in a rather rough sea. Some ranks were sea sick but this passed off before the time for landing. All ranks have shown great interest the assaulting Bdes (231 Bde Right - 69 Bde left) going in; also the naval bombardment on 50 (N) Div. beachhead, and everyone was in good spirits and keen to get on with the job. 2 Glosters were reserve Bn. of 56 Inf Bde Gp acting as reserve Bde to 50 Div.	
		1158	Three LCI's touched down on the NORMANY COAST at area HABLE DE HEURTOT 9807 map sheet 7 E/5. Each Gp quickly cleared KING RED Beach area and began to advance along coast rd towards Bn. conc area at BUHOT. Some mortar fire was encountered along this rd and pockets of enemy resistance were still holding out in area BUHOT and high ground to SW of this village. BUHOT was finally cleared by marine Commandos and the Bn. arrived at conc area as arranged.	
		1607	Bn. HQ arrived conc area and Rifle Coys. arrived complete except for two cas.	
		1735	RYES was reported clear of enemy by Right assault Bde (231 Bde)	
BUHOT		1900	2 Glosters conc was completed.	
		1940	Bde decided firm base for the night, 2 Glosters were still res Bn. and advanced Southwards as follows :- B Coy. Gp. A Coy. Bn. HQ. D and C Coys.	

22293 Wt. 33096/1140 1,000m 12/40—McC & Co Ltd—51-8212 Forms C2118/22

WO 171/1295

Intelligence/war diary

2ND BATTALION THE ESSEX REGIMENT

Month and Year June 1944				Commanding Officer LT. Col. J.F. Higson, C.

Place	Date	Hour	Summary of Events and Information	Remarks and references to Appendices
BEAULIEU	1 2		During the last few days all ranks of the Bn., have been briefed most thoroughly for the forth coming invasion of NORMANDY. A briefing tent, complete with large-scale models, air photographs, maps and a complete picture of the enemy order of battle, has been placed at the disposal of coys. To date only Coy. Comds know the exact area of operations; maps with code names have been used to brief all other officers and men.	
			Essex Operation Order No: 1 has now been issued to Coy. Comds.	Fwd under separate cover
	1 - 2		Coys have given final attention to administrative problems and every effort has been made to ensure that all ranks are fighting fit and fit to fight. Early morning PT and route marches have been included in the keep fit programme.	
	3	1700	Battalion left Pennerley Camp, B 3, in TCVs for LYMINGTON where it embarked in LCIs (L) for SOUTHAMPTON. The incredible number of craft of all sorts and sizes seen in the SOUTHAMPTON water, together with the large flights of aircraft, was a most inspiring spectacle.	
	4	1700	The day was spent in the Docks, the operation having been delayed 24 hrs. There were recreational facilities on the quay side, and an aerial circus of English and German machines likely to be seen in operations, flew overhead during the afternoon.	
	5	1900	Bn. sailed from SOUTHAMPTON for operations in NORMANDY. The evening was dull and overcast and a heavy swell was running. It was to be a quiet crossing. (8786)	
FRANCE	6	1230 1800	D-DAY. The Bn. landed without any casualties EAST of LE HAMEL which was still in enemy hands. During the approach march to the assembly area at BU HOT 8584 by the "Yellow" route the Bn. came under mortar fire. Information was received that RYES (8483) was still held by the enemy. The forward body moved off to secure Bn. objective at X Rds ST. SULPICE (8181) and at 2130 hrs the Bn. had occupied this area. Civilian sources said that the enemy had left several hours earlier and had also probably left BAYEUX. (7878) hrs ORs wounded.	
	7	1030 1300	After a quiet night during which our patrols left towards BAYEUX and the A/Tk ditch to N W, the forward body supported by tanks of the "Sherwood Rangers," and the Bn. moved on the BAYEUX from the SE. At 1300 hrs we had entered the town without opposition. The local inhabitants showered flowers on our troops and many bottles of wine were brought out.	
			The Tricolour was soon to be seen flying from many houses. The town was quickly searched, and the Railway Station and the German Garrison was secured intact. The Bn. moved on.	

????

WO 171/981
Intelligence/war diary
86TH (HERTFORDSHIRE YEOMANRY)
FIELD RGT. RA.

Month and Year June 1944   Commanding Officer Lt. Colonel. G. ??shane OBE. RA.

Place	Date	Hour	Summary of Events and Information	References to Appendices
ROMSEY SOUTHAMPTON	June 1-2		86 Field Regiment in Marshalling Camps : OP Parties loaded in LST, and second tide vehicles loaded on LST.	
SOUTHAMPTON	June 3		Assault Scale and attached Troops of 1 Royal Marine Armoured support Regiment Pouched in LCT and LCT (A) of Force 'G' at hards in Southampton. Craft then proceeded to moorings in SOUTHAMPTON water.	
SOUTHAMPTON WATER	June 4	0800	Leading Hotillas of Force G slipped and proceeded down SOUTHAMPTON water on operation "Overlord".	
	"	0900	Operation "Overlord" Postponed one day for bad weather.	
SOUTHAMPTON WATER ENGLISH CHANNEL	June 5 Night 5-6 June	0830	Leading Hotillas of Force 'G' Sailed On Operation "Overlord" LCT (A) with one section 1 Royal Marine Armoured Support Regiment and carrying 2/Lieut. Rentis J. Regimental Liais on Officer capsized in mid-channel : two other LCT(A) each carrying section of 1 Royal Marine Armoured Support Regiment forced back to SOUTHAMPTON Water by half gale. 2/Lieut. Prentis Subsequently reported missing.	

Wt.47724,993 2,000,000 3/43 W.H. & S. **51**/6375

SHEET 2

Commanding Officer Lt. Col. G.D. OBE, RA.

Place	Date	Hour	Summary of Events and Information	References to Appendices
NORMANDY	6 Jun	06.45	86 Field Regiment commenced run and shoot on enemy battery and company localities in area LA RIVIERE – MONT FLEURY.	?
"	"	0825	First half of Regiment (EAC Troops) landed half an hour early to support infant, as all but three sections of 1 Royal Marine Corppal Regiment had failed to reach gun area 918868.	?
"	"		OR parties of 462 battery landing with 5 East yorks. In front of LA RIVIERE badly shot up. Captain Platt. FOB attacked from No 1. Bombardment Group and two of his party killed.	
"	"	10 00	Second half of regiment (BDF Troops) land and come up to Regimental gun area 917864, near VER-SUR-MER.	?
"	"	14.55	Half of Regiment moves into gun area at CRÉPON -898827- joined by Det at 15.30. Gun position met from snipers in village from nearby wood - slight enemy mortaring - which continues till night fall.	?

Wt.47724 993 2,000,000 3/43 W.H. & S. **51**/6375

SHEET 3

Commanding Officer Lt. Col. G.D. F? BE, RA.

Place	Date	Hour	Summary of Events and Information	References to Appendices
NORMANDY	6 Jun		Major G.A. Loveday RA, BE. 341 Battery, seriously wounded by sniper returning to his OP by Cycle - hour R.H.Q. Shot through the lung he managed to reach a track by infantry, and was picked up.	?
CRÈPON	[7 Jun		86 Field Regt. still in support 68 Brigade. 50 (N) Division.	?
"	"	0535	AVREs of 8 Armoured Brigade coming into harbour by 462 Battery gun position are fired at by infantry gun positioned in wood on edge of battery area. AVREs withdraw.	?
"	"	0930	2 Shermans. 1 Flame Thrower Churchill and 12 men from 462 Battery led by J. A. Carpenter enter wood to clermont surpierl - they discover wood is held in force. The enemy surrendered and 1 officer and 56 other troops together with 4,75 mm and 1,88 mm were captured. Four wounded officers were also taken.	(see Appendix A). ?
"	"	1220	Request move into gun area at 867793 462 Battery moved to Martragny 862762 to support Armoured Reconnaissance by 4/7 Dragoons South from ST. LEGER Feature.	?

Wt. 47724, 998 2,000,000 3/43 W.H. & S. **51**/6375

WO 171/1135

Intelligence/war diary
120TH LIGHT ANTI-AIRCRAFT REGIMENT RA

Month and Year June 1944   Commanding Officer Lt. Col. J.B. All, RA.

Place	Date	Hour	Summary of Events and Information	References to Appendices
FIELD	1		Regiment split into groups in Marshalling Areas – for Exercise OVERLORD. al	
	6		D-Day for OVERLORD. Weather not ideal. Heavy cloud and strong breeze. al	
			Sea fairly choppy. R.H.Q. Command Group, consisting of CO, MO, OO, and Driver Operator landed at approx. 0930 hrs two hours after H hour. Spent night in shell crater, about ½ mile inland from KING Beach, Slight enemy air activity over Beach area.	
	7		RHQ occupied in VER-SER-MER. House had been German Infantry Company HQ. All signs of enemy having left in a hurry. RHQ 'Recce' and 'A' Groups arrived. Slight activity by night on the part of E/A. No RHQ vehicles drowned.	
			Copy of personal experiences of Regtl. Officers on landing collected and sent to Bde. HQ Copy enclosed.	Appendix 'A'
	10		Field return of OR's.	Appendix 'B'
	14		Capt. Handley and part of REME Workshop arrived.	
	16		RHQ 'Y' Group arrived.	

Wt.47724/993 2,000,000 3/43 W.H. & S. 51/6375.

WO 171/1158
Intelligence/war diary
113TH HEAVY ANTI-AIRCRAFT REGIMENT RA

Month and Year June 1944   Commanding Officer Lt. Col. F.R. GIL?T TD, RA.

Place	Date	Hour	Summary of Events and Information	References to Appendices
IPSWICH	1	0130	"R", "A" groups proceeded to embarkation land at FELIXSTOWE and SOUTHAMPTON.	KRS
		0930	"R", "A" groups loaded into craft.	KRS
	5		"A" set sail from Felixstowe and "R" groups sail from SOUTHAMPTON	KRS
FRANCE	6	1500	"R" group disembarked at LE HAMEL	lhs.
MEUVAINES	7		"A" group disembarked during day at Le HAMEL RHQ estab at 892852	lhs.
	8		All troops in action on the following posns for defense of BMA:-	lhs.
			362 Bty on posns 907863 & 888862	
			366 " " " 842860 & 858830	
			391 " " " 872858 & 892852.	lhs.
	9		During night 7/8 June A Ip., B Ip & E Ip engaged E/A firing over 100 rds.	
			During night 8/9 June E. Ip fired 226 rds, F Ip 31 rds A Ip 2 rds, B Ip 96 rds C Ip. 35 rds. Raiders were	

M3524/1218 1200M 10/41 H.B. & Co.Ltd. 51-1541)

WO 177/803
Intelligence/war diary
203RD FIELD AMBULANCE RAMC

Month and Year June 1944   Commanding Officer Lt. Col. J.J. MYLES, RAMC.

Place	Date	Hour	Summary of Events and Information	References to Appendices
	1		Personnel landing on D-Day embarked on crafts. Capt. Da Fane RAMC, 160 Fd Amb, temporarily attached to D + 1 Marching Party at Ipswich.	
	3		Personnel of Marching Party and Vehicle Party D + 1 embarked. Notified D-Day was 5 Jun.	
	4	1630	Notified that D-Day postponed 24 hrs owing to weather conditions.	
	5		D-Day personnel sailed from the Solent.	
MR.858845 (Sheet CREULLY)	6		Sections of 'A' Coy. landed with battalions at H + 2½ at LE HAMEL, N. FRANCE. CO landed later with the Transport. Light ADS established at 1800 hrs by 2 sections at MR 858845 (1:50,000, Sheet CREULLY) which is on the road between Buhot and Ryes, one section remaining with SWB as they were actively engaging the enemy and expecting casualties. Admission of casualties to light ADS were few.	
	7		56 Inf Bde captured town of BAYEUX at 1500 hrs. Recce made of town later in afternoon and a building selected for light ADS. Two sections now located at BAYEUX. D + 1 Marching Party landed.	
	8		D + 1 Vehicle Party landed. Third section joined light ADS at BAYEUX leaving the main ADS at MR 858845, line of evacuation being to light ADS at BAYEUX, to the main ADS, and then to 200 Fd Amb who were located at MR 863855 (Sheet CREULLY), then to BDS where casualties were evacuated by LST. Severe fighting in progress west of BAYEUX and large number of casualties admitted to ADS.	
	9		Evacuation now switched to 3 CCS located at MR 862826 (Sheet CREULLY). CO visited Bde and Div and RMOs. Notification received at 1800 hrs that 56 Bde comes under command 7 Armoured Div at 0800 hrs 10 Jun and proceeds south of BAYEUX in support of the armour.	
BAYEUX	10		CO visited 7 Armoured Div HQ at MR 841836 and saw DADMS – ADMS not yet arrived. Main ADS moved into BAYEUX at first light. 'A' Coy. packed equipment ready to move forward if necessary. CO accompanied by DADMS 7 Armoured Div visited 56 Bde HQ and 27 Armoured Bde HQ. Two ambulance cars attached to each battalion of 56 Bde for this operation. Visited by DDMS 30 Corps and ADMS 50 Div. On order from ADMS 50 Div. Capt. Scott and Capt. Da Fane ceased to be attached to this unit.	
	11		CO contacted 56 Bde HQ who are now situated at 805730; saw Brigadier and DAAQMG and was given details of the tactical situation. Later he visited RMOs. In the early afternoon two sections of 'A' Coy. moved forward and established light ADS at 807753 (1:50,000 Sheet CAEN). Visited by ADMS 50 Div and later by ADMS 7 Armoured Div under whose command the unit now falls. D + 3 personnel arrived. Large number of casualties admitted during late evening, personnel being kept busy the whole night. RMO of 2 SWB admitted to Main ADS sick and it is hoped to retain him. Capt. Hearne attached to the battalion for temporary duty. CO visited DDMS 30 Corps.	

M3524/1218 1200M 10/41 H.B. & Co.Ltd. 51-1541)

WO 171/881
Intelligence/war diary
168TH (CITY OF LONDON)
LIGHT FIELD AMBULANCE RAMC

Month and Year May and June 1944

Commanding Officer Lieut. Colonel T.M. ROBB, RAMC.

Place	Date	Hour	Summary of Events and Information	References to Appendices
	June 5	1500	Message broadcast that L. S. T. 280 would get under way at 1830 hours.	
		1630	Sections A, B, and C got under way and left SOLENT en route for coast of FRANCE.	
			PLAN. 50 Division would land on beaches between LE HAMEL M.R. 876866 and LA RIVIERE. 927867	
			151 and 69 Inf. Bdes. supported by the Sherwood Rangers Yeomanry and 4/7 Dragoons in DD Tanks would assault the beaches 151 on Rt, 69 on Lt.	
			1 Section of 168 Lt. Fd, Amb. would land in rear of each of the armoured regiments, 1st tide or 2nd tide. C Section would land with 24 Lances at approximately D + 6.	
			The Canadians were attacking and landing on the left. The United States Forces on the right.	IMR
			Landings made.	
			'A' Section landed at 1320 hours.	
	6		'B' Section landed at 1630 hours.	
			'B' Section lorry broke Stub Axle on leaving the LST but managed to proceed under its own power.	
			Operations proceeded, though not as fast as anticipated. DD Tanks of 4/7 Dragoons swam a shore, but those of Sherwood Rangers Yeomanry were landed from LCTs as sea was too rough.	
			'C' Section on LST 280 arrived off shore but did not land.	

Wt. 47724, 993 2,000,000 3/43 W. H. & S. 51/6375

ADM 202/305
Intelligence/war diary
1ST ROYAL MARINE ARMOURED SUPPORT REGIMENT

Month and Year June 1944   Commanding Officer Lt. Col. S.V. PESKETT, RM

Place	Date	Hour	Summary of Events and Information	References to Appendices
KNIGHTS COPSE	2	0350	Lt. Col. S.V. Peskett, RM, Major B.J. Mabbott RM and 1 Sgt. (comprising CO's party) left Camp B6 veh park in Jeep for embarkation point for Operation "OVERLORD"	
SOUTHAMPTON		0730	CO's party embarked in LCT(4) No. 1073 (Serial No.2140). Proceeded to New Docks, S'TON.	
			Loading and embarkation of Tps in LCT(A) continued at Hards S3 and S4.	
	3	1830	Slipped and proceeded to SOLENT anchorage.	
	4	0700	Slipped and proceeded with Force G but turned back at the boom on orders to return.	
	5	0730	Slipped and proceeded. D-Day for the Op is fixed for 6 Jun with H-Hr at 0730 hrs.	
LE HAMEL	6	0730	1 Sherman and 4 Centaurs landed on the 231 Inf Bde Sector (JIG), having engaged no tgts by direct fire during the run-in. The Sherman was hit twice by enemy arty - possibly 88 mm - and all members of the crew wounded or injured by burns. One Centaur had its tracks blown off, another was hit without casualty and a third had its tracks blown off.	
		0830	CO's party landed, after the Jeep had been drowned and all stores and kit lost in the heavy sea. The party had transferred to a LCM for the final 150 yds to the shore, and Major B.J. Mabbott, RM was wounded in the left hand when a near miss on the craft was scored by enemy arty. He was later evacuated in a LCT.	
		0850	2 Centaurs of C Tp landed on King sector	
		0930	1 Sherman and 2 Centaurs of D Tp landed on King sector. Sherman of F Tp landed on Jig sector and was ordered by CO to contact its 2 Centaurs and deploy under orders of 147 Fd Regt RA	
		0950	1 Sherman and 2 Centaurs of G Tp landed on King sector.	
		1020	CO contacted M14 of HQRA 50(N) Div at 897869 and proceeded with it to MEUVAINES	
MEUVAINES		1200	1 Sherman and 1 Centaur of F Tp moved off the beach to 147 Fd Regt. area	
		1330	Tac HQRA est at 892850. Lt-Col Peskett reported situation regarding the Regt. to CRA (Brig. C.H. Norton).	
CRÉPON			A composite Section and a composite Troop in action at 900827, under Capt. S.T. Wigmore, RM and Capt. D.C. Thomas, RM respectively, and under comd 86 Fd Regt. RA and in their area.	
BUHOT		1630	A composite Tp under Capt. C.C.W. Swift, RM in action at 865847 in area of and under comd 147 Fd Regt. RA. First call for fire received at 1730 hrs and programme of	

*5973. Wt.22661/1499. 300M. 8/42. Wy.L.P. Gp. 656.

SHEET 2

Place	Date	Hour	Summary of Events and Information	References to Appendices
			21 rpg was fired in support of the right flanking movement of 231 Inf Bde towards LA ROSIERE and LONGUES.	
LA ROSIÈRE	7	2000	Tp ordered by 147 Fd Regt to move to LA ROSIERE 8284 but ordered them to return as soon as they moved off as enemy resistance was suspected NW of RYES 8483.	
		1000	Tp under comd 147 Fd Regt moved and deployed in the area LA ROSIERE in advance of 431 Fd Bty RA.	
VIENNE-EN-BESSIN SOMMERVIEU		1200	Tp ordered to protect left flank of advance from present posn by direct fire against tk and inf threat from direction of BAYEUX.	
		1200	Sec and Tp under comd 86 Fd Regt RA moved to Regtl RV at 868792 but did not deploy.	
–		1430	HQRA moved from MEUVAINES.	
		1600	HQRA and Lt. Col. Peskett's HQ est at 825808.	
		1600	Tp u/c 147 Fd Regt moved to Regtl area at 828795 end deployed at 2000 hrs. 1 Centaur broken down with mechanical trouble at 830047.	
MARTRAGNY		1845	Lt-Col Peskett left to visit Tps.	
	8	1915	2 Centaurs of A Tp which had landed on NAN RED beach at 0900 hrs today arrived in 86 Fd Regt area and joined up with Capt. Wigmore's Section to form a Troop Both Tps u/c 86 Fd Regt moved and deployed 2000 yds in front of Regtl area at 864762 and later fired a Regtl fire plan of 40 rpg.	
–		1000	Lt. Col. Peskett left to visit Tps. Found that Capt. Swift and his 2 Centaurs had been left at 828795 with no orders. At 0125 hrs HQRA had transferred this Tp to u/c 90 Fd Regt RA, to whose area at 843786 they were now led by CO.	
MARTRAGNY SOMMERVIEU		1205	Lt. Col. Peskett contacted Col. A.J. Harvey OBE at MARTRAGNY and reported present situation.	
		1540	Lt. B.N. Coles, RM reported to CO at HQ RA that he had landed with 2 Centaurs of H Tp on the evening of 7 Jun and had spent the night in the square at BAYEUX in default of any infm regarding own or enemy dispositions. 1 Centaur now requires REME assistance at 895846, which was arranged. He was ordered to join Capt Swift's Tp	A.1
DA?NY	9	0800	Capt. Swift and Section of 2 Centaurs moved to new posn at 815766 still u/c 90 Fd Regt.	
		1330	Lt. Col. Peskett visited Tps.	
		1600	Lt. Col. Peskett met Lt. Casper, RM who had landed with 2 Centaurs of E Tp am today. 1 Centaur needs REME attention. He was ordered to join Capt. Swift's Tp.	

*5973. Wt.22661/1499. 300M. 8/42. Wy.L.P. Gp. 656.

APPENDICES

APPENDIX 1

50th (Northumberian) Infantry Division (Tyne & Tees)

Sub-Area Units under command for Assault Phase (104 Beach Sub-Area HQ & Signals Section – 9 &10 Beach Groups)[292]

Royal Engineers
69 Field Company
89 Field Company
90 Field Company
21 Stores Section
23 Stores Section
51 Mechanical Equipment Section
74 Mechanical Equipment Section
1043 Port Operating Company
953 Inland Water Transport Operating Company
961 Inland Water Transport Operating Company

Medical
3 & 10 Casualty Clearing Station
3 Field Dressing Station
25 Field Dressing Station
31 Field Dressing Station
32 Field Dressing Station
Field Surgical Units Nos 41, 42, 47, 48
Field Transfusion Units Nos 24, 30
22 Port Detachment
23 Port Detachment

Infantry
2nd Battalion Hertfordshire Regiment
6th Battalion The Border Regiment

Stores (Royal Army Service Corps)
305 General Transport Company RASC
536 General Transport Company RASC
705 General Transport Company RASC
2 Detail Issue Depot
5 Detail Issue Depot
244 Petrol Depot

Ordnance
7, 10 & 36 Ordnance Beach Detachments

Royal Electrical Mechanical Engineers
24 & 25 Beach Recovery Sections
XXX Corps Workshop

Provost
240 & 243 Provost Companies

Labour (Pioneer Corps)
75, 173, 209 & 280 Pioneer Companies

APPENDIX 2

3rd Canadian Infantry Division

**Sub-Area Units under command for Assault Phase (102 Beach Sub-Area HQ &
Signals Section – 7 & 8 Beach Groups)**[293]

Royal Engineers
HQ 7 GHQ Troops Engineers
72 Field Company
85 Field Company
184 Field Company
240 Field Company
19 Stores Section
20 Stores Section
59 Mechanical Equipment Section
11 Port Operating Group
1034 Port Operating Company
966 Inland Water Transport Company

Medical
32 Casualty Clearing Station
1 Field Dressing Station
2 Field Dressing Station
33 Field Dressing Station
34 Field Dressing Station
Field Surgical Units Nos 33, 34, 45, 46, 56
Field Transfusion Units Nos 13, 14, 36
3 Field Sanitary Section
4 Field Sanitary Section
21 Port Detachment

Infantry
8th Battalion The Kings Regiment
5th Battalion The Royal Berkshire Regiment

Stores (Royal Army Service Corps)
HQ 30 Transport Colonel RASC
199 General Transport Company RASC
282 General Transport Company RASC
139 Detail Issue Depot
140 Detail Issue Depot
240 Petrol Depot
242 Petrol Depot

Ordnance
15 Ordnance Beach Detachment
45 Ordnance Ammunition Company

Royal Electrical Mechanical Engineers
22 & 23 Beach Recovery Sections
Provost
242 & 244 Provost Companies
Labour (Pioneer Corps)
58, 115, 144, 170,190, 225, 243 & 293
Pioneer Companies

APPENDIX 3

3rd British Infantry Division

**Sub-Area Units under command for Assault Phase (101 Beach Sub-Area HQ &
Signals Section – 5 & 6 Beach Groups)**[294]

Royal Engineers

HQ 18 GHQ Troops Engineers
84 Field Company
91 Field Company
8 Stores Section
9 Stores Section
50 Mechanical Equipment Section
9 Port Operating Group
999 Port Operating Company
1028 Port Operating Company
940 Inland Water Transport Company

Medical

16 Casualty Clearing Station
9 Field Dressing Station
12 Field Dressing Station
20 Field Dressing Station
21 Field Dressing Station
30 Field Dressing Station
Field Surgical Units Nos 37, 38, 39, 40, 55
Field Transfusion Units Nos 21, 22, 29
1 Field Sanitary Section
2 Field Sanitary Section
20 Port Detachment

Infantry

5th Battalion The King's Regiment
1st Battalion The Buckinghamshire Regiment

Stores (Royal Army Service Corps)

HQ 21 Transport Colonel RASC
39 General Transport Company
101 General Transport Company
299 General Transport Company
633 General Transport Company
96 Detail Issue Depot
138 Detail Issue Depot
237 Petrol Depot
238 Petrol Depot

Ordnance

11 & 12 Ordnance Beach Detachments
44 Ordnance Ammunition Company

Royal Mechanical Electrical Engineers

20 & 21 Beach Recovery Sections

Provost

241 & 245 Provost Companies

51st Highland Infantry Division
5th Battalion The Black Watch
1st Battalion The Gordon Highlanders
5th/7th Battalions The Gordon Highlanders

GHQ Liaison Regiment (Phantom)

Labour (Pioneer Corps)
53, 85, 102, 129, 149, 267, 292 & 303
Pioneer Companies

APPENDIX 4

Royal Naval Units which landed during the Assault Phase[295]

XXX Corps Sector – 50th (Northumbrian) Division – 'JIG' and 'King' Beaches 'Gold' Area:
Naval Beach Commando 'J'
Naval Beach Commando 'Q'
Naval Beach Commando 'T'

1st Corps Sector – 3rd Canadian Division Front – 'Mike' and 'Nan' Beaches 'Juno' Area:
Naval Beach Commando 'L'
Naval Beach Commando 'P'
Naval Beach Commando 'S'

1st Corps Sector – 3rd British Division Front – 'Queen' and 'Roger' Beaches 'Sword' Area:
Naval Beach Commando 'F'
Naval Beach Commando 'R'

APPENDIX 5

Royal Marine Units which landed during the Assault Phase[296]

Landing Craft:

'E' Squadron	605 Flotilla
	606 Flotilla
	607 Flotilla
	654 Flotilla
	698 Flotilla
'B' Squadron	805 Flotilla
	806 Flotilla
	807 Flotilla
	808 Flotilla
	809 Flotilla
Independent	700 Flotilla
	706 Flotilla
	557 Flotilla

Landing Craft Obstacle Clearance Units:

Nos 7, 8, 9, 10, 11, 12 formed from Royal Marine Engineer Commandos

APPENDIX 6

RAF Ground Crew Units which landed during the Assault Phase[297]

1304 Mobile Wing HQ RAF Regiment
1305 Mobile Wing HQ RAF Regiment
104 Beach Section
107 Beach Section
15082 Ground Controlled Interception Unit
15083 Ground Controlled Interception Unit
21 Base Defence Sector
24 Base Defence Sector
51 Beach Balloon Flight
Provost and Security Unit
Emergency Landing Strip Echelon
11 Air Formation Signals
16 Air Formation Signals
Mobile Signals Units:
Nos 543, 554, 582, 585, 5006, 5030, 5132, 5141, 5153, 5160 & 5276

BRITISH 6TH AIRBORNE DIVISION ORDER OF BATTLE FOR D-DAY

General Officer Commanding: Major-General R. N. Gale

3rd Parachute Brigade
8th Battalion, The Parachute Regiment
9th Battalion, The Parachute Regiment
1st Canadian Parachute Battalion

5th Parachute Brigade
7th Battalion, The Parachute Regiment
12th Battalion, The Parachute Regiment
13th Battalion, The Parachute Regiment

6th Airlanding Brigade
12th Battalion, The Devonshire Regiment
2nd Battalion, The Ox & Bucks Light Infantry
1st Battalion, Royal Ulster Rifles

DIVISIONAL TROOPS
HQ 6th Airborne Division
22nd Independent Parachute Company
6th Airborne Armoured Reconnaissance Regiment

Royal Artillery
211 Battery 53 Airlanding Light Battery RA
3 Airlanding Anti-Tank Battery RA
4 Airlanding Anti-Tank Battery RA

Royal Engineers
3 Parachute Squadron RE
591 Parachute Squadron RE
249 Field Company (Airborne) RE

6th Airborne Division Signals

Army Air Corps – Nos. 1 & 2 Wings Glider Pilot Regiment

Royal Army Service Corps

716 Light Composite Company RASC

398 Composite Company RASC

Royal Army Medical Corps

224 Parachute Field Ambulance RAMC

225 Parachute Field Ambulance RAMC

195 Airlanding Field Ambulance RAMC

Royal Electrical and Mechanical Engineers

6th Airborne Divisional Workshop REME[298]

BRITISH 3RD INFANTRY DIVISION ORDER OF BATTLE FOR D-DAY

General Officer Commanding – Major-General T.G. Rennie

8th Infantry Brigade
1st Battalion, The Suffolk Regiment
2nd Battalion, The East Yorkshire Regiment
1st Battalion, The South Lancashire Regiment

9th Infantry Brigade
2nd Battalion, The Lincolnshire Regiment
1st Battalion, The King's Own Scottish Borderers
2nd Battalion, The Royal Ulster Rifles

185th Infantry Brigade
2nd Battalion, The Royal Warwickshire Regiment
1st Battalion, The Royal Norfolk Regiment
2nd Battalion, The King's Shropshire Light Infantry

DIVISIONAL TROOPS
HQ 3rd Division
Royal Artillery
7th Field Regiment RA
33rd Field Regiment RA
76th Field Regiment RA
20th Anti-Tank Regiment RA

Royal Engineers
17th Field Company RE
246th Field Company RE
253rd Field Company RE

3rd Division Signals

2nd Battalion The Middlesex Regiment (Machine Guns)

Royal Army Medical Corps
8th Field Ambulance RAMC
9th Field Ambulance RAMC
223rd Field Ambulance RAMC

3rd Division Provost Company

UNITS ATTACHED TO BRITISH 3RD INFANTRY DIVISION FOR THE ASSAULT

27th Armoured Brigade
13th/18th Royal Hussars
1st East Riding Yeomanry
The Staffordshire Yeomanry

1st Special Service Brigade
No. 3 Commando
No. 4 Commando
No. 6 Commando
45 Royal Marine Commando
2 Troops 10 (Inter-Allied) Commando
1 Troop Royal Marine Engineers Commando

4th Special Service Brigade
41 Royal Marine Commando

Royal Marines
5th Independent Armoured Support Battery

Royal Armoured Corps
A Squadron 22nd Dragoons

Royal Artillery
HQ 53rd Medium Regiment RA
HQ 73rd Light Anti-Aircraft Regiment RA
92nd Light Anti-Aircraft Regiment RA
93rd Light Anti-Aircraft Regiment RA
9th Survey Regiment RA
'B' Flight 652 Air Observation Point Squadron

Royal Engineers
HQ 5th Assault Regiment RE
77 Assault Squadron RE
79 Assault Squadron RE
71 Field Company RE
263 Field Company RE
629 Field Squadron RE

Royal Army Service Corps
106th Brigade Company RASC
90th Armoured Brigade Company RASC[299]

CANADIAN 3RD INFANTRY DIVISION ORDER OF BATTLE FOR D-DAY

General Officer Commanding – Major-General R.F.L. Keller

7th Canadian Infantry Brigade
The Royal Winnipeg Rifles
The Regina Rifles Regiment
1st Battalion The Canadian Scottish Regiment

8th Canadian Infantry Brigade
The Queen's Own Rifles of Canada
Le Régiment de la Chaudière
The North Shore (New Brunswick) Regiment

9th Canadian Infantry Brigade
The Highland Light Infantry of Canada
The Stormont, Dundas & Glengarry Highlanders
The North Nova Scotia Highlanders

DIVISIONAL TROOPS
HQ 3rd Canadian Division
7th Reconnaissance Regiment (17th Duke of York's Royal Canadian Hussars)
The Cameron Highlanders of Ottawa (Machine Gun and Heavy Mortar Battalion)

Royal Canadian Artillery
12th Canadian Field Regiment RCA
13th Canadian Field Regiment RCA
14th Canadian Field Regiment RCA
4th Canadian Light Anti-Aircraft Regiment RCA

Royal Canadian Engineers
6th Canadian Field Company RCE
16th Canadian Field Company RCE
18th Canadian Field Company RCE

3rd Canadian Division Signals

Royal Canadian Army Medical Corps
14th Canadian Field Ambulance
22nd Canadian Field Ambulance
23rd Canadian Field Ambulance

UNITS ATTACHED TO CANADIAN 3RD INFANTRY DIVISION FOR THE ASSAULT

2nd Canadian Armoured Brigade
6th Canadian Armoured Regiment (1st Hussars)
10th Canadian Armoured Regiment (Fort Garry Horse)
27th Canadian Armoured Regiment (Sherbrooke Fusiliers)

4th Special Service Brigade
48 Royal Marine Commando
1 Section Royal Marines Engineer Commando

Royal Marines
2nd Royal Marines Armoured Support Regiment HQ – 3rd and 4th Armoured Batteries

Royal Armoured Corps
C Squadron, The Inns of Court Regiment

Engineers (RE and RCE)
26th Assault Squadron RE
80th Assault Squadron RE
71st Field Company RE
262nd Field Company RE
5th Canadian Field Company RCE

Artillery (RA and RCA)
19th Canadian Field Regiment RCA
62nd Anti-Tank Regiment RA
73rd Light Anti-Aircraft Regiment RA
TAC HQ 80th Anti-Aircraft Brigade RA
93rd Light Anti-Aircraft Regiment RA
114th Light Anti-Aircraft Regiment RA[300]

BRITISH 50TH INFANTRY DIVISION ORDER OF BATTLE FOR D-DAY

General Officer Commanding – Major-General D.A.H. Graham

69th Infantry Brigade
5th Battalion, The East Yorkshire Regiment
6th Battalion, The Green Howards
7th Battalion, The Green Howards

151st Infantry Brigade
6th Battalion Durham Light Infantry
8th Battalion Durham Light Infantry
9th Battalion Durham Light Infantry

231st Infantry Brigade
1st Battalion Hampshire Regiment
1st Battalion, The Dorsetshire Regiment
2nd Battalion, The Devonshire Regiment

DIVISIONAL TROOPS
HQ 50th Division

Royal Armoured Corps
2 Squadrons from 61st Reconnaissance Regiment
2nd Battalion The Cheshire Regiment (Machine Gun and Heavy Mortar Battalion)

Royal Artillery
90th Field Regiment RA
102nd Anti-Tank Regiment (Northumberland Hussars) RA
25th Light Anti-Aircraft Regiment RA

Royal Engineers
233 Field Company RE
295 Field Company RE
505 Field Company RE
235 Field Park Company RE

50th Division Signals

50th Division Provost Company
Royal Army Medical Corps
149th Field Ambulance RAMC
186th Field Ambulance RAMC
200th Field Ambulance RAMC

UNITS ATTACHED TO BRITISH 50TH INFANTRY DIVISION FOR THE ASSAULT

56th Infantry Brigade
2nd Battalion Essex Regiment
2nd Battalion Gloucestershire Regiment
2nd Battalion, The South Wales Borderers

8th Armoured Brigade
4th/7th Royal Dragoon Guards
Nottinghamshire (Sherwood Rangers) Yeomanry

Royal Armoured Corps
B&C Squadrons, Westminster Dragoons
13th and 15th Troops, C Squadron 141st RAC

Royal Artillery
86th Field Regiment RA
147th Field Regiment RA
73rd Anti-Tank Regiment RA
93rd Light Anti-Aircraft Regiment RA
120th Light Anti-Aircraft Regiment RA
113th Heavy Anti-Aircraft Regiment RA
152nd Anti-Aircraft Ops Room
356th Searchlight Battery
662nd Air Observation Point Squadron

Royal Engineers
HQ 6th Assault Regiment RE
81st Assault Squadron RE
82nd Assault Squadron RE
73rd Field Company RE
280th Field Company RE

Royal Army Medical Corps
203rd Field Ambulance RAMC
168th Light Field Ambulance RAMC

Royal Marines
47 Royal Marine Commando
1st Royal Marine Armoured Support Regiment[301]

NOTES

[292] Lieutenant-Colonel H.F. Joslen, *Orders of Battle of the Second World War, 1939-1945: United Kingdom and Colonial Formations and Units*, Volume II, (London: HMSO, 1960), p. 582.

[293] Ibid.

[294] Ibid.

[295] Ibid.

[296] Ibid.

[297] Ibid.

[298] The British 6th Airborne Division's Order of Battle for D-Day is drawn from Lieutenant-Colonel H.F. Joslen, *Orders of Battle: United Kingdom and Colonial Formations and Units in the Second World War 1939-1945*, Volume II, (London: HMSO, 1960), p. 586 and Lloyd Clark, *Battle Zone Normandy: Orne Bridgehead*, (Stroud, Gloucestershire: Sutton Publishing Ltd, 2004), pp. 22-23.

[299] N.B. War Diary entries for 9th Survey Regiment, 'B' Flight Air Observation Point Squadron, 106th Brigade Company and 90th Armoured Brigade Company are not included in this volume. British 3rd Infantry Division's Order of Battle for D-Day is drawn from Lieutenant-Colonel H.F. Joslen, *Orders of Battle: United Kingdom and Colonial Formations and Units in the Second World War 1939-1945*, Volume II, (London: HMSO, 1960), pp. 584-585 and Ken Ford, *Battle Zone Normandy: Sword Beach*, (Stroud, Gloucestershire: Sutton Publishing Ltd, 2004), pp. 28-29.

[300] N.B. War Diary entries for TAC HQ 80th AA Brigade RA, 474th Searchlight Battery RA, 'A' Flight 652nd Air Observation Point Squadron, 155 AA Ops Room and 160 AA Ops Room are not included this volume. Canadian 3rd Infantry Division's Order of Battle for D-Day is drawn from Lieutenant-Colonel H.F. Joslen, *Orders of Battle: United Kingdom and Colonial Formations and Units in the Second World War 1939-1945*, Volume II, (London: HMSO, 1960), p. 583 and Ken Ford, *Battle Zone Normandy: Juno Beach*, (Stroud, Gloucestershire: Sutton Publishing Ltd, 2004), pp. 24-25.

[301] N.B. War Diary entries for 22nd Field Hygiene Section RAMC, 152nd Anti-Aircraft Ops Room, 356th Searchlight Battery RA and 662nd Air Observation Point Squadron are not included in this volume. The British 50th (Northumbrian) Division's Order of Battle for D-Day is drawn from Lieutenant-Colonel H.F. Joslen, *Orders of Battle: United Kingdom and Colonial Formations and Units in the Second World War 1939-1945*, Volume II, (London: HMSO, 1960), p. 581 and Simon Trew, *Battle Zone Normandy: Gold Beach*,(Stroud, Gloucestershire: Sutton Publishing Ltd, 2004), pp. 36-37.

INDEX

INDEX